Networking Bible

Barrie Sosinsky

Wiley Publishing, Inc.

Networking Bible

Published by
Wiley Publishing, Inc.
10475 Crosspoint Boulevard
Indianapolis, IN 46256
www.wiley.com

Copyright © 2009 by Wiley Publishing, Inc., Indianapolis, Indiana

Published by Wiley Publishing, Inc., Indianapolis, Indiana

Published simultaneously in Canada

ISBN: 978-0-470-43131-3

Manufactured in the United States of America

10 9 8 7 6 5 4 3 2 1

For general information on our other products and services or to obtain technical support, please contact our Customer Care Department within the U.S. at (877) 762-2974, outside the U.S. at (317) 572-3993 or fax (317) 572-4002.

Library of Congress Control Number: 2009932713

This book is dedicated to my wife Carol Westheimer, with all my love.

About the Author

Barrie Sosinsky has written about computers and technology for over 25 years beginning with writing about personal computers for the Boston Computer Society in the early 1980s. He has published books on operating systems, applications, databases, desktop publishing, and networking for publishers such as Que, Sybex, Ventana, IDG, Wiley, and others and seen the industry change and reinvent itself several times.

At heart Barrie is a PC enthusiast. He loves building computers, finding and learning about new applications that allow him to do new things, and keeping up with the latest advances in the field of computer technology, which he believes is just in its infancy. Having lived long enough to see the Boston Red Sox win not one but two World Series, he remains committed to living long enough to see grandchildren and to someone clone a wooly mammoth. To this list (replacing the Red Sox) he adds the new milestone of holding a universal translator in his hands; a device he believes will appear within this next decade.

The author lives in Medfield Massachusetts about 25 miles southwest of Boston with his six cats Stormy, Shadow, Smokey, Scamper, Slate, and Spat; his son Joseph, his daughter Allie, his wife Carol; and Brittany the turtle surrounded by pine trees, marauding deer, and wild turkeys.

You can reach Barrie at bsosinsky@mindspring.com, where he welcomes your comments and suggestions.

Credits

Acquisitions Editor
Courtney Allen

Project Editor
Sarah Cisco

Technical Editor
Steve Wright

Copy Editor
Marylouise Wiack

Editorial Director
Robyn Siesky

Editorial Manager
Cricket Krengel

Business Manager
Amy Knies

Senior Marketing Manager
Sandy Smith

Vice President and Executive Group Publisher
Richard Swadley

Vice President and Executive Publisher
Barry Pruett

Project Coordinator
Kristie Rees

Graphics and Production Specialists
Carrie Cesavice
Andrea Hornberger
Jennifer Mayberry
Mark Pinto

Quality Control Technicians
Melissa Cossell
John Greenough

Proofreading and Indexing
Broccoli Information Management
Christine Sabooni

Contents

Table of Contents

Contents

Contents

Part III: Network Types   233

Chapter 10: Home Networks 235

Chapter 11: Peer-to-Peer Networks and Personal LANs 255

Contents

Contents

Contents

Contents

Contents

Contents

Acknowledgments

This book is the culmination of many months of really hard work during which my family and publisher were very supportive. For many years now I've watched and read numerous books on network technology that have appeared — some highly technical, others specific to a particular platform — and all written to various levels of expertise. This book aims to be a general introduction that will take a knowledgeable computer user from the basics to a much higher level of expertise in computer networking. As much as possible I have tried to not only include multiple platforms, but include developments that are on the cusp of their introduction.

I would like to thank my literary agent Matt Wagner at Fresh Books for recommending me for this title. His support and friendship over the years has been very gratifying to me.

The chance to write the Networking Bible for Wiley was something I really enjoyed doing. The Bible Series was created by IDG Books, acquired by Wiley, and has nurtured many high quality books that have helped people learn about different fields of technology for many years. I very well remember the people who started IDG, and although most of them are not now associated with these books their contribution to the field of computer publishing continues on.

I also would like to acknowledge the support of the staff at Wiley for their support in this project. They have been very professional and easy to work with. In particular I would like to thank the three people most associated with this project: Courtney Allen, who was the Acquisition Editor; Sarah Cisco who was the Project Editor; and Steve Wright, who was the Technical Editor. Steve did a terrific job with his technical oversight, as did Sarah and the others involved in the editing project. My special thanks to them all.

All book projects involve a considerable investment by both the author and the publisher. Shared risk. This book also required sacrifice by my family, who put up with my disappearance for many days at a time. During the course of writing this book, over many days and late nights I was constantly visited by a large number of small grey creatures who were my companions. With this book completed, I look forward to spending more time with them.

Introduction

Networking is a vast subject that touches all aspects of computer technology. Indeed, some will argue that a computer that isn't networked isn't really a computer at all. It may be hyperbole to suggest that "The network IS the computer" as Sun did some years ago, but every important computer technology has incorporated some method for sending and receiving data to and from other computers. If you go as far back as you care to, the very first commercial computers were built to amortize their costs by allowing users to time share. Computer reservation systems such as SABRE linked to terminals worldwide, and when the personal computer became nearly as cheap as a dumb terminal, those PCs became the distributed nodes.

The rise of the personal computer in the early 1980s and 1990s helped to spawn networking technologies that made connectivity easier to achieve, cheaper, and most importantly more standardized. A whole host of different proprietary networking technologies have given way to the networking technologies of the Internet, TCP/IP networking. Although this book discusses some of the older technologies, the focus of this book is on the current state of computer networking and, therefore, much of the book explains internetworking standards based on TCP/IP. In ultrafast, high-bandwidth, and highly reliable networks, other technologies are used.

A number of these alternative technologies are presented in the context of the different capabilities that they provide. So while you will learn about local area networks of various types, a number of chapters in this book describe important technologies in the field of wide area networks, fiber optics, storage area networks, grid and cloud computing, and other advanced technologies. Sprinkled in the book are descriptions of new products such as the X0-1 laptop created by the One Laptop Per Child organization, SETI @ Home grid system, SONET networking, optical solitons, and many other things that you may not have heard about but that make the experience of reading this book I hope richer for you.

This book was written to be a general networking book and not to favor one computer platform over another. By nature I'm not a computer platform zealot. My first computer was a Macintosh, and over the years I've switched to Windows systems. Recently I've been working on a Ubuntu system, and at various times I've worked on different Linux as well as Solaris systems. I work on a small network, but over the years I've worked on both large and small, homo- and heterogeneous networks. Each network operating system has its plusses and minuses, but I've found that it is rare that I couldn't perform some essential function on all of these operating systems.

This book presents examples of networking technology using a number of different platforms. Unfortunately (from my way of thinking) there are more examples drawn from Windows that I would have liked. Please take this as being largely the result of the time I had and the convenience these examples offered, more than a statement of their being particularly special.

Introduction

I've tried to walk the fine line between being theoretical enough to give you a solid foundation in computer networking, while being practical enough for you to find and use new technologies and products in your everyday work. There is a considerable amount of product information in this book, and I've tried very hard to make this information both accurate and up to date. Unfortunately, product information ages faster than any one of use would like, and many times in the course of writing this book, I've encountered products and companies I've known that are no longer with us. Many of these products were associated with people I've either met, known, or had some acquaintance with, so the passing of these products forces me to reminisce about times gone by.

This book is organized into seven parts:

- Part 1. The first part of this book presents general theory and networking principles. I've presented much of the material in the context of different networking models that have been widely used in the industry.

- Part 2. The second part of this book looks at various network hardware components, which includes systems, network interfaces, various physical media, and methods for creating and maintaining circuits with particular emphasis on routing.

- Part 3. The third part of this book focuses on different network types, small and home networks, peer to peer technology, LANs and WANs, storage networks (SANs), as well as various high speed and high performance networks.

- Part 4. The fourth part of this book describes the various parts of the TCP/IP networking suite. This includes not only how TCP/IP is used, but details on addressing, name resolution, and other features that both bedevil and occupy modern network administrators.

- Part 5. The fifth part of this book describes different applications and services that run on computer networks. Various network operating systems are discussed from a general principles viewpoint, and network services such as directory services, file services, mail, streaming media, and voice over IP round out this part of the book.

- Part 6. The three chapters in Part 6 focus on computer network security. In these chapters, you learn about: security protocols and services; firewalls, gateways, proxy servers, and other isolation technologies: and virtual private networks.

- Part 7. In the final part of this book, different network management and diagnostic technologies are discussed. This includes classes of network management applications, some of which are large management frameworks that you might be unfamiliar with. Two chapters on network diagnostics and remote access technologies round out this book.

I hope that you enjoy reading this book as much as I have enjoyed writing it.

Barrie Sosinsky

Medfield, Massachusetts

March 18, 2009

Part I

Network Basics

Networking Introduction

A computer network is a connection or set of connections made between two or more computers for the purpose of exchanging data. Networks are built from a variety of building blocks: computers, switches, cables, and so forth. In order to classify networks into different types, you need to consider factors such as the number of elements, distribution of objects, and connection methods. In this chapter, different types of networks are described, as well as how the different network types impact their design.

The smallest network is a direct attachment between two computers with a cable. Peer-to-peer systems are used in computer workgroups where there are a small number of systems that don't require a central service. Some computer buses are configurable and thus are considered small networks. These are called personal LANs, or pLANs, and Bluetooth is an example of this type of network. USB is not configurable and is therefore not a network.

A network that spans an office, floor, or building is called a local area network, or LAN. LANs can support multiple protocols, and connect different types of clients. A LAN that is separated by a bridging element would be considered a separate LAN. When the bridge separates multiple LANs that are geographically dispersed, it is considered a wide area network, or WAN.

You can analyze and categorize network topologies in terms of graph theory. Networks can be formed in a variety of ways that involve forming lines or chains, stars or hubs, rings, or mesh topologies. Different topologies offer different capabilities and have different requirements. The processes of mapping a network's topology can be done for physical or logical network elements, or based on how signals propagate through the network.

Defining Computer Networking

To be considered a network, a collection of elements needs to have the following: connection software, systems, and network elements (such as switches, physical transmission media, and an addressing system). Any computer network has the following essential components:

- The connected systems
- Connection software
- Networking hardware
- Physical transmission media
- An addressing system for each of the aforementioned components

This definition is sufficiently broad to allow us to discuss not only systems composed of computers, but also cell phones and other aspects of telephony, storage devices, Wi-Fi, streaming, broadband connections, and a wide range of disparate systems that you are likely to want to network together in some way.

Connection software is ubiquitous in all systems that must be networked together. You will find network software inside your computers' operating systems, inside your networking hardware (routers or firewalls), in custom ASICs (Application Specific Integrated Circuit) or flash memory in network cards or hubs, and even inside the physical transmission medium if the medium is intelligently switched or amplified.

The physical transmission medium refers to any medium that can transmit an electromagnetic signal. A signal is a time varying pattern in signal amplitude, voltage, or frequency that represents information in the form of data that can be propagated some distance and recognized by a receiver. Signals can be continuously variable (analog), or they can be discrete and limited to specific states (digital). Although analog computers exist, in nearly all circumstances the systems in use are digital, and more specifically binary. Binary systems transmit information in one of two states: ON or OFF, 1 or 0, YES or NO, or voltage 1 or voltage 2. Digital computers use binary signals and Boolean logic because signaling is relatively simple and fast, and because binary signals can be made to represent any character or solve nearly any mathematical equation.

The transmission of binary signals for the data stream between two systems in a network means not only that the physical media can be wires and cables, but also that any part of the electromagnetic spectrum can theoretically be used to transmit data. When you open a browser on a cell phone, you are connecting to a network with a radio frequency connection. When a cellular network wants to transmit data across a long distance, it does so by using microwave transmitters. The 802.11 Wi-Fi standards are radio frequency transmissions. You can get interference from a 900 MHz wireless telephone that overlaps with the 802.11b standard, or from a microwave oven that operates at 2.4 GHz and interferes with the 802.11g Wi-Fi standard. Most of the networks described in this book use fixed wires to connect computer systems. However, radio frequency connections have no physical transmission medium.

Cross-Ref

Radio frequency connections are covered in Chapters 5, 8, and 14.

Any operations where data isn't transmitted automatically aren't part of our network definition. For example, if you copy data on one computer to a USB key and walk that USB key over to another computer, that wouldn't be considered a computer network. The term we use to describe manual data transfer is *sneakernet*; this is not a network because it doesn't conform to the principle that networks allow data to be sent to a system based on an address or identification scheme — the data in the USB key isn't being sent to any address.

It's best not to be too doctrinaire when using the addressing requirement, however. Broadcast communications would be considered network communications, although there is no specific address to a receiving system. Any system that fits the definition of a receiver can accept broadcast communications. Indeed, broadcast communications are essential in most network technologies. Systems send out broadcasts to indicate that they are available to perform a service, or that they exist and can service a request. Broadcast communications are used to identify a system or to browse the network. Implicit in the definition of a broadcast is that any system that conforms to the requirement meets one of the following conditions:

- It is on the same network, or runs the same identification protocol, such as Windows NetBEUI or WINS; or
- It has the software installed to accept and manage a data stream and can participate in broadcast communications.

In this book, I define a computer network as simply a connection or set of connections made between two or more computers for the purpose of exchanging data. Using this as a guiding principle, I cover the most common problems encountered by network administrators in business networks; by average users connecting to various important services (such as e-mail); or by people who require fundamental networking skills to manage the collection of devices that are typically found in a connected household. This book teaches you the basic principles of computer networking, which can help you solve some of the problems you might encounter in your daily work or play.

Network Type Overview

Networks are categorized by distribution, size, and architecture. A network can be as simple as a single serial, parallel, or USB cable joining two computers in a peer-to-peer relationship. When you connect a cable between two computers for the purpose of moving your installed software, you are creating a peer-to-peer network. These relationships can be *ad hoc*, meaning that the network is configured as needed when it is needed. Most people wouldn't consider two systems connected in this manner to be a network. However, if you had several systems joined in a workgroup and connected though a hub, then this would fit the definition of a peer-to-peer network. A *workgroup* is a collection of computers that do not share a common security database, and where network services can be provided by any member of the workgroup as required.

The smallest networks from a distribution standpoint are personal area networks, which have come to be called pLANs (alternatively abbreviated as PANs). A pLAN is usually applied to a set of peripheral devices that connect to a single computer system. Bluetooth is a good example of a pLAN. Bluetooth devices are radio frequency connections that use frequency hopping spread spectrum technology (the communication channel constantly changes) that segments the data stream and transmits it over 75 different frequencies with approximately a 30-foot (10-meter) range. Although this kind of network is small in size, pLANs can be quite sophisticated in terms of their technology. Bluetooth has the ability to self-configure, be secured, and advertise each device's available abilities and services. Some phones, headsets, mice, keyboards, printers, GPS devices, game consoles, and PDAs use Bluetooth technology and are common examples of Bluetooth devices.

Bluetooth certainly fits this book's definition of a network because it has all of the necessary components of a network. Bluetooth is discussed in this book because it is something that you have to configure. On the other hand, Universal Serial Bus (USB) can connect up to 127 devices per host controller, but it is self-configuring and is therefore considered a computer bus. All of the aforementioned Bluetooth devices can be connected to a computer using a USB connection. So while they are devices on a Bluetooth pLAN, they are more correctly described as peripheral devices. While USB is very capable of transferring data, it is only described as needed in this book.

Cross-Ref

For more on USB, see Chapter 11.

A large portion of this book is dedicated to the subject of local area networks, or LANs. The term *local* is subjective. A LAN is a connected set of systems that spans a single room, floor, or building, and can be as small as a couple of systems connected through a hub. LANs are differentiated by their addressing scheme, as well as by the set of rules or protocols that they use to communicate. Therefore, an AppleTalk and a Netware network are considered to be separate LANs. Heterogeneous networks are common, and so you may find that a LAN has a Windows network with a domain server that contains Macintosh clients and Netware servers. Those Macintosh and Netware systems can still participate on an AppleTalk or Netware network, but the software and addressing used are separate for each particular LAN.

A LAN ceases to be a LAN when the addressing changes in some meaningful way, or when there is a bridging function that links two or more networks. For example, if you had a network of computers and chose to give one group of computers one set of related addresses and another group of computers a different set of addresses, then that arrangement would still be considered a LAN. You can do this with Internet Protocol (IP) networking by using a different IP range (192.168.1.x versus 192.168.3.x), or by defining a part of any range as two or more subnets (192.168.1 through 192.168.1.99 and 192.168.1.100 through 192.168.1.199). In either case, this would still be considered a LAN. If you put a couple of routers or bridges, which are intelligent switches, in between the two network types, you would now have a set of distinct networks. The case is even more compelling when the connection between the two switches is long or when there are additional switches in between the two that provide entry to the different networks.

A variety of terms are used to describe long-distance networks or multinetwork scenarios. The most common term is the wide area network, or WAN, which is applied to any network of networks. The Internet is the most common example of a WAN, and the term *internetworking* is occasionally used to describe this scenario. Other terms in use are campus area networks, or CANs (uncommon), and metropolitan area networks, or MANs. CANs span a set of buildings, while MANs span a city.

Large, geographically dispersed networks typically use a high-capacity interconnect such as fiber optic cable with signal repeaters to span the distance. A high-capacity line is referred to as a *backbone*. For example, if a bank on Wall Street in New York City were to back up or mirror their data over a fiber optic line under the Hudson River to a data center in New Jersey, then that would be considered a MAN.

Transmission Types

Networks use two different types of data transmission: Point-to-point communication and broadcast communication.

Point-to-point communication

Point-to-point network communication creates named connections between two systems in the network: the sending and receiving systems. In point-to-point communication, there may be one or more intermediate systems that process the data stream along its intended route. Many point-to-point networks have redundant paths through the network, often of differing length. Therefore, the role of routers in a point-to-point network is a key factor in determining network performance.

Various technologies are applied in point-to-point networks to ensure that the connection is made correctly, particularly when the connection spans multiple subnets, as it would in a WAN, as shown in Figure 1.1. The WAN in Figure 1.1 has three subnets — a ring network, a bus, and a wireless LAN. One technique of data transfer, called store-and-forward, takes an incoming packet sent by one router, and at a second router stores those packets until the desired point-to-point connection or connections become available. Once the connection is free, the packet is sent onto its destination. This mechanism is sometimes referred to as *packet switching*. A packet-switched network composed of small, equally sized packets referred to as *cells* is important in the area of wireless telephony, and is the basis for the cellular networks in common use today.

Broadcast communication

Broadcast communication networks take a message from the sending system and then transmit that message to all systems on the network. A satellite network is an example of a broadcast network. When a broadcast network is configured to send a message from one system to a subset of the available nodes (communication endpoints), that process is called *multicasting*. Multicasting is common for systems that stream media, as the same data stream can be targeted to multiple systems.

FIGURE 1.1

A packet-switched WAN

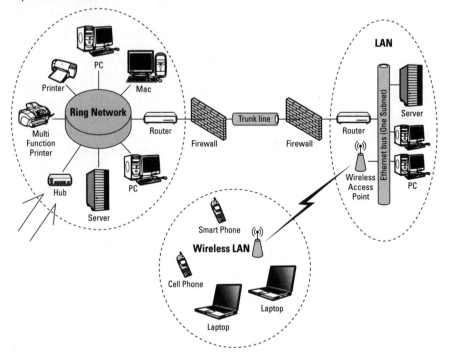

Broadcast packets contain addressing that specifies which system is to be the receiving system or systems. The receiving system can be a single computer or multiple systems, but every node on a broadcast network gets to examine the packet. When the broadcast packet arrives at a node on the network, the address is examined and if the address matches, it is processed. When the address doesn't match, the system ignores the packet.

Tip
As a general rule, the larger a network is in terms of geographical distribution, the more likely it is to be a point-to-point network. A smaller network can more efficiently utilize broadcast technologies.

Topologies

Another classification for computer networks is the topology that they use. A topology is the distribution or arrangement of network elements, usually both devices as well as connections. Because anything that can get an address is considered a network element, you can define a logical or virtual network element in software, and these two must be accommodated in any topological description.

A network may be described in terms of a physical topology, which describes the relationship between devices or elements; a logical topology, which describes a relationship or hierarchy between entities on the network; or a hybrid topology, which is a combination of the two into a single topological design. In very rare circumstances, a network may be described in terms of a signal topology. A logical topology might be mapped to indicate how the nodes of a network are arranged and communicate with each other. Physical topology would define the network in terms of the physical connections and the physical structure of the network. A signal topology might be constructed to show how specific types of signals move about the network. The physical and logical topologies may be identical, but they often are entirely different.

The mathematical study of linked systems is part of graph theory, and this discipline can make predictions as to the number of nodes required for different topologies, the number of links or fanouts, and so forth. The specific topology used by any network can be the same, regardless of the speed of the network, the protocols used to communicate, the network node, or the connection types. Topology only refers to the relative arrangement of the elements.

Physical topologies

A physical topology describes the arrangement of devices used to implement the network. Topological devices can be either nodes or endpoints, or they can be connections or links. A physical topology can take many forms:

- **Buses.** Where nodes attach to a linear trunk line
- **Stars.** Where multiple nodes connect through a single node to one another
- **Rings.** Where nodes are connected to a cyclical trunk line
- **Meshes.** Where nodes are connected to other nodes directly (a web)
- **Trees.** Where the nodes in a network radiate outward like the branches of a tree

Many networks are combinations of these types.

It is possible to calculate the required number of connections that a theoretical mesh network would have when each node is connected to every other node. With a single-link, a permanent point-to-point mesh topology between nodes is both the simplest arrangement that exists and the most impractical. To service n endpoints would require $2(n + 1)$ connections, which for any large network would require an unsupportable infrastructure of permanent connections. Most point-to-point networks, like the telephone networks, are switched, eliminating the need to have point-to-point connections between every node. Switching can be done either in hardware through *circuit switching* or by altering the addressing within the data stream, which is referred to as *packet switching*.

Robert Metcalfe, who was one of the main developers of Ethernet technology, described the value of switched networks in terms of the number of users. Metcalfe's law states that the value of a telecommunication network is proportional to the square of the number of users in the network. The number of unique connections N in a point-to-point system is equal to

```
N = n(n-1)/2
```

where n is the number of nodes. As the number of nodes grows, it becomes asymptotically proportional to the curve for $n2$. An asymptote is an equation that approaches some function or value as one of its variables gets larger. In the example above when n becomes large the equation $(n2-n)/2$ would be dominated by $n2$ and that curve would be 1/2 the size of $n2$.

Bus systems

A bus is a common transmission medium that connects to two or more network nodes called *endpoints*. An endpoint is equivalent to a node, and on a network it has the fundamental property that it is addressable; that is, it is assigned an address. A computer NIC can be a node or endpoint and so can a router. From a fundamental perspective, a port on a switch or router can also be an endpoint or node.

A backbone or trunk line is an example of a linear bus (see Figure 1.2) because all data travels from one endpoint to another over the bus line. In Figure 1.2 the bus is defined as the collection of connections or links, and each circle is a network node or endpoint. Data traveling from one node on a bus to another starts off by traveling down the bus to the next node, where it announces its intended recipient. If that node isn't the recipient, then the signal continues down the bus until the intended recipient is reached. This behavior introduces a propagation delay, but in modern networks, these delays are small.

FIGURE 1.2

A linear bus system

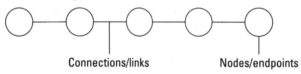

Connections/links   Nodes/endpoints

All endpoints in a bus system (see Figure 1.2) require that they be logically differentiated from one another, and come with devices that perform this function, which are called *terminators*. Termination takes the signal and absorbs it so that it prevents data from continuing on down the bus. Termination is designed to match the impedance of the transmission line and is often a simple resistor. Some terminators are active devices that have an electrical circuit that eliminates the signal reflection.

A linear bus system that uses a backbone or trunk transmission line is an efficient technology, but is not very flexible. By flexible I mean that it's difficult to adapt a linear bus system to changes in the number of hosts, locations of hosts, and other changes that might take place. To improve the adaptability of a bus network, it is common to use a distributed bus technology. A distributed bus adds more branches to the transmission line so that it connects additional nodes. In nearly all respects, a distributed bus is similar in function to a linear bus. Nodes still require termination. A distributed bus is often confused with a tree topology, which is the kind of topology that a file system uses. However, in a distributed bus, there is no central node that connects to all the other nodes, and there is no hierarchy defined. Figure 1.3 shows a distributed bus structure.

FIGURE 1.3

A distributed bus structure

Star networks

The star network is a very common network topology. In a star network, point-to-point connections radiate out from a central node, in an arrangement that is also called a hub and spoke, as shown in Figure 1.4. In a star network, all data traveling over the network must flow through the central node. The simplest star network is constructed using a single connection point such as a punch down block, or it can be an active connection that retransmits data, performing error correction first and then signal amplification. A punch down block, or more simply a punch block, is an electrical connection matrix with open ends on both sides that allow you to connect wires together by punching the wire into the holes in the matrix.

Star networks can be constructed so that the hub connects two or more star networks together, as is the case for both extended star and distributed star topologies. An extended star uses one or more repeaters in-line to extend the distance that the signal can be propagated from the hub to a spoke. When you replace a repeater in an extended star with a switch, you create a hybrid topology that is sometimes called a physical star topology. Figures 1.5 and 1.6 show examples of an extended star and a distributed star topology, respectively.

FIGURE 1.4

A star or hub-and-spoke network

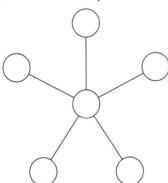

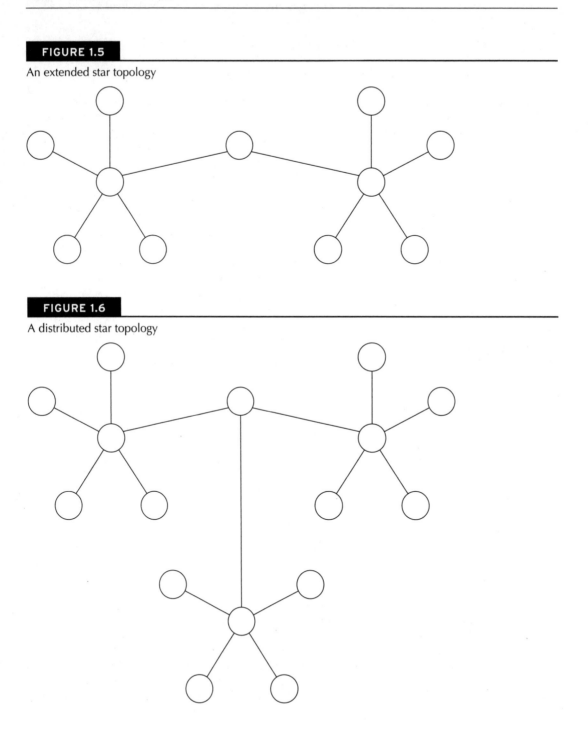

A distributed star topology connects multiple star networks with a daisy chain in a linear fashion. The distributed star has no hierarchy and no central or primary connection from which a set of stacked hubs emerge. All of the star networks in a distributed star network are peers.

When star networks use a broadcast, they are referred to as *broadcast multi-access* networks, and the signal is sent to all of the spokes on the network. Some star networks use addressing to send signals from one node to another through the hub, and they are called *non-broadcast multi-access* (NBMA) networks.

Rings

A ring network, shown in Figure 1.7, is a closed loop topology where each node in the network is both the beginning and endpoint of any data transmission. In a ring network, data travels in one direction around the ring from node to node until the receiving system accepts the data. The reason that data travels in one direction is to prevent signal contention and interference. Such interference leads to signaling errors. A dual ring topology provides the potential to transmit traffic in two directions (one on each ring), or to use the second ring as either a control circuit or a failover circuit for improved fault tolerance. A failover is the process that replaces a faulty component with another component.

FIGURE 1.7

A ring network

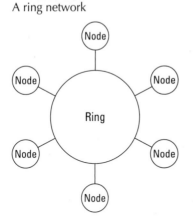

The most famous examples of a ring topology are token ring (IBM), ARCNET, token bus, and fiber distributed data interface (FDDI) networks. In a token ring, an identifier called a token is passed around the ring's nodes in sequence until the correct node has the token. The node with the token is the system that can actively work with the data that is circulating on the ring. Token ring networks are wired using a star or hub-and-spoke system, but each spoke has two connections to the hub that creates the ring. In an 802.5 Token Ring network, the central node or hub is referred to as a *multistation access unit*.

Mesh networks

A mesh network is one in which each node in the network can be connected through a point-to-point connection to another node, as shown in Figure 1.8. In this regard, mesh networks are an extension of the bus system described earlier. Mesh networks are described by Reed's law as having a value that is proportional to the exponent of the number of nodes,

$$2n-n-1$$

where *n* is the number of nodes. As a consequence, mesh networks exhibit what is called high fan-out. Their value grows exponentially greater than either the number of nodes, *n*, or the number of pair connections, $n(n-1)/2$, which was derived as Metcalfe's law.

FIGURE 1.8

A partially connected mesh network

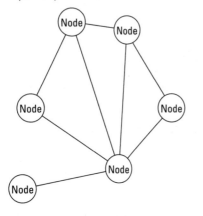

A mesh network can be either partially connected (as shown in Figure 1.8) or fully connected (as shown in Figure 1.9), depending on whether each node in the network is connected to each other node with a point-to-point link. You almost never find a fully connected mesh network except in small networking, because the number of links required to complete a mesh network tends to make them too costly to construct. In a partially connected mesh network, some nodes, and often most nodes, are connected to more than one node with a point-to-point link. The lack of unique connections introduces some latency into mesh networks, but this is something that can be managed through the use of intelligent routing, so that when the direct path isn't available, another route is chosen. An example of a partially connected mesh network is the Internet.

FIGURE 1.9

A fully connected mesh network

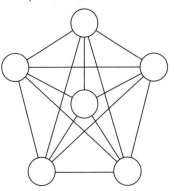

Trees or hierarchical networks

A tree network starts out with a highest level or root level, where a single node is connected to nodes in a second level of the hierarchy. Second-level nodes each connect to one or more nodes in the third level, and each level fans out further. There must be at least three levels in a hierarchy, as two levels define a star topology.

The number of connections in a tree topology may be calculated using the formula

    L = n - 1

where *L* is the number of point-to-point links and *n* is the number of nodes.

The number of nodes attached to a parent is referred to as the *fan-out* or *branching factor*. Some networks impose symmetric branching, and if so, the branching factor (*f*) must be 2 or more, as a factor of 1 only defines a linear topology. Although this is called a tree network, its shape is usually drawn with the root at the top of the diagram, which means that the tree is upside down, as you can see in Figure 1.10.

Most file systems, databases, and directory systems adopt a hierarchical topology. This is because search algorithms are much more efficient in a hierarchy than in linear or mesh type topologies. This is especially the case when the values stored at any node are indexed. As a search algorithm descends the tree, moving to the next level below eliminates 1/*f* of the tree's population.

One disadvantage that is noted for hierarchical topologies is that any overhead associated with data transmission between levels is amplified as you move up the hierarchy. The nodes in each level above add to the overhead needed to process data communication.

FIGURE 1.10

A tree network

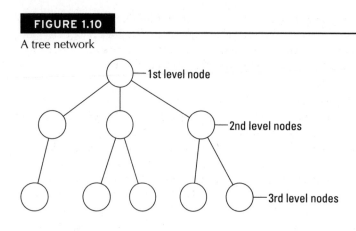

Hybrid topologies

All of the aforementioned topologies may be combined with one another to form hybrid topologies, which provide more complexity, as well as more flexibility, into a single topological design. You can create the following topologies:

- **Star-bus**. A star-bus network connects two or more physical star networks along a single common network bus. In practice, this requires that a network line be terminated by two or more hubs, with each hub's uplink port connected to another hub that fans out to create the physical star. From the standpoint of the network, each of the uplink ports is connected to the star hub through the use of drop cables. As you learn in Chapter 9, an uplink port is a port on a switch that can be set so that two connected switches behave as one.

- **Hierarchical star**. In a hierarchical star network, each node of the tree hierarchy is a hub from which spokes radiate. Each subsequent level in the hierarchy is a hub with spokes radiating out. There is no common bus that connects the different stars, with only point-to-point connections existing in this topology. Sometimes the root node is connected to a high-speed interconnect backbone or trunk line, which further hybridizes this technology.

- **Star-ring**. The star-ring hybrid consists of a central hub where the signals are routed sequentially between all available spokes attached to the hub to simulate the ring portion of the network. The spokes from the central hub are point-to-point connections to individual nodes.

- **Hybrid mesh.** A hybrid mesh combines a mesh topology, with one or more nodes of the mesh being connected to different network topologies. A hybrid mesh technology is highly redundant and fault tolerant, and so it finds widespread use. The Internet uses a partially connected hybrid mesh topology.

Logical topologies

Logical topologies map out the path that data takes as it travels from node to node. A logical topology requires that a node be available on the network by the protocol used for data communications. To be available, a device has to have a unique identification number, referred to as a *MAC address*, which refers to Media Access Control, a method for determining that node on a network.

Virtual network interfaces can be created, and they can also be assigned MAC addresses. When you use intelligent routers and switches on a network, the configuration of the logical topology can be dynamically changed, depending upon conditions. Logical daisy chain, logical star, and logical mesh are all types of logical topologies, and are described in the following sections.

Logical daisy chain topology

A daisy chain network is a logical topology that can be implemented as either a linear or a ring topology, as shown in Figures 1.11 and 1.12, respectively. As you add systems to a linear daisy chain, you add a two-way connection between the new system and its neighbor or neighbors. A system in the middle of the chain must have one transmitter and one receiver for each of the connections to adjacent systems. The terminus system in the chain requires only one receiver and transmitter. In a daisy chain configured in a ring topology, the data travels around the ring in one direction, and so each node requires only a single receiver and transmitter. Ring topologies have greater latency because the data can take up to twice as long to get to its destination compared to a linear topology, but this makes them much cheaper to implement.

FIGURE 1.11

Linear daisy chain network

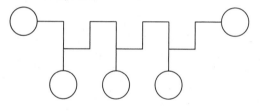

FIGURE 1.12

A ring daisy chain network. Data can flow either clockwise or counterclockwise, and links can be either half duplex (one direction) or full duplex (both directions).

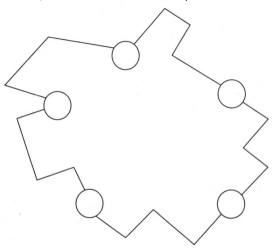

Logical star topology

Star networks exist as both physical and logical topologies. In a logical star Ethernet network, the central node broadcasts a signal from any node to all of the other nodes attached to the network. When the signal is acknowledged by the proper system, the data is transmitted. Logical star networks can fail spectacularly when the central node fails, but the failure of any point-to-point connection only affects the function of the node attached to that spoke.

Star networks can be categorized as either passive or active. In a passive star network, the sending node must be able to recognize its own signal echo returned to it from the central node. An active star network has circuitry in the central node to prevent a signal being echoed back to its originating system. Network switches are used in the various star topologies that build lookup tables of data transmission types, and the destinations and ports that were used to process them. As the lookup table becomes populated, the data that corresponds to the parameters stored in the lookup table serves as the routing table, and the data is sent to the stored destination directly.

If you create a set of logical star networks and connect them in a hierarchy, you create a tree topology. Hubs in a logical star network typically either repeat or regenerate data as it moves through the network, although networks of this design usually distribute the workload between the different hubs. Each node in the star has one point-to-point connection. So the logical star network has the entire leaf of the tree fail when a hub fails, but only the single node fails when the point-to-point connection is broken.

Logical star networks can also be configured in hybrid network forms. Two common hybrids are the star ring and the star bus network.

Logical mesh topology

A logical mesh topology is one where there are additional paths between network node pairs. Figure 1.13 shows an example of this kind of topology. There are several logical mesh designs. Highly distributed mesh networks built using a linear or ring topology are referred to as a *grid network*. Mesh networks can also be constructed using a toroidal or multi-ring topology, or using hypercubes.

As with physical mesh topologies, logical mesh topologies can be either fully connected or partially connected. Partially connected mesh networks are much more common than fully connected mesh networks due to the expense involved in creating the complete set of connections. Some fully connected mesh networks exist where highly redundant connections are required, typically in mission-critical applications. However, one fully connected *ad hoc* network that you might encounter is that used by the BitTorrent file sharing system. When a user initiates a torrent to perform a file transfer, pieces of the file are found on multiple systems. Those systems are temporarily connected while their pieces of the file are transmitted, and then the connection is broken.

FIGURE 1.13

A grid network is an example of a logical mesh topology.

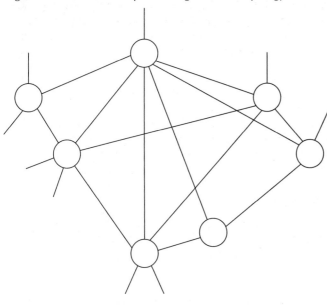

Summary

In this chapter, you learned the different types of networks and how to classify them. Networks can be differentiated based on their geographical distribution as personal, local, wide, campus, or metropolitan local area networks. Each network type generally uses its own specially designed industry-standard protocol that is meant to optimize the network for the types of devices that are in use.

You can also characterize networks based on their shape or topology. Common topologies are buses or chains; stars or hub; and spokes, rings, and meshes. Various hybrid topologies exist that mix and match these topologies with one another. When you map a network, you can form the topology based on the arrangements of physical elements, or using logical elements, as well as by observing the paths that signals use to traverse the network.

The Network Stack

The network stack refers to an architectural model that is used to describe network transactions starting at one computer system and ending at another system. Models were developed to standardize devices and services, and to allow industry standards to evolve that allowed communications from one level of the network to another.

This chapter discusses the two most important network models in use today: the ISO's Open Systems Interconnection model and the Internet or TCP/IP model. Each model subdivides the different types of network devices, services, and software into a set of architectural layers, the definitions and relationships of which provide a means to categorize and discuss modern network technology. The vocabulary described in this chapter provides a means of framing the discussions in the remaining chapters in this book.

Standard Development Organizations

As networking standards developed in the 1970s and 1980s, the computer industry was faced with the common problem of making vendors' products interoperate with each other. Operating systems vendors such as Microsoft were able to create a de facto standard like Windows; but computer network hardware and software had no such dominant vendor. Standards could only emerge by consensus from the joint work of industry and academic standards organizations. When a new technology such as Ethernet arrived, the packet-based network protocols that communicated over this new medium arose as a set of standards from groups of vendors.

Standards committees are typically formed by standards organizations that manage many groups of standards, or they can be created by an industry group that is organized for the sole purpose of standardizing one technology or a related set of technologies. An example of a standards organization is the American National Standards Institute, or ANSI.

In either case, the development of any standard requires a process, and the more open, the better. As a result, you will find that the standards process is organized around a set of stages, which include any of the following:

1. **Formation** of a group that represents the industry.

2. **Request for a proposal** (RFP) of a standard, draft of a proposed standard, or the receipt of a proposed standard for review.

3. **Request for comments** (RFC) on the proposed standard or standards from the community.

4. **Testing and modification** of the proposed standard. Plugfests are often organized to test interoperability. A plugfest is an industry meeting where product vendors test their hardware and software with other vendors' products in order to ensure compatibility and to establish new standards.

5. **Draft standards**, which are the proposed standards that have not yet been fully codified.

6. **Accepted standard**, which is the final version of a particular standard. A standard can develop over time through iteration, such as the 802.11x Wi-Fi standards, which include a, b, g, and n.

Considering the time and effort involved in creating standards, as well as the stakes involved in their commercialization, standards are prone to considerable controversy. Not all standards survive far beyond their introduction. Consider the effort that went into creating both the Betamax and VHS videotape standards, or more recently, HD DVD and Blu-ray, where the latter standard of each pair is the one that survived. The clout of the organization is important and can often override a superior technology.

In the networking industry, the following standards organizations are important:

- **American National Standards Institute (ANSI; www.ansi.org)**. ANSI is a non-profit organization that creates standards for products and services.

- **International Organization for Standardization (ISO; www.iso.org)**. ISO standards are found in various data communications fields, including the standards and model described in this chapter.

- **International Telecommunications Union-Telecommunications Group (ITU-T; www.itu.int); Radiocommunications Group (ITU-R); and Telecom Development (ITU-T)**. ISO is a member of the ITU. Each group develops communication standards.

- **Internet Engineering Task Force (IETF; www.ietf.org)**. IETF creates Internet standards and is part of a group of bodies that define the TCP/IP and Internet protocols.

- **Institute of Electrical and Electronics Engineers (IEEE; www.ieee.org)**. IEEE ("I triple E") is the main standards body for wire and radio communications.

- **Storage Networking Industry Association (SNIA; www.snia.org).** SNIA defines storage network standards for fiber channel, high-speed Ethernet, iSCSI, and others.
- **World Wide Web Consortium (W3C; www.w3.org).** W3C is the central standards body for the World Wide Web, and defines HTML and related standards, as well as protocols used by Web servers.

Note
You can find an explanation of how standards organizations work, as well as a longer list of standards development organizations, or SDOs, at `http://en.wikipedia.org/wiki/Standards_organizations`.

The OSI Reference Model

The most important networking model in use today is the ISO's Open Systems Interconnection (OSI) Reference model. This model divides network communications into seven different layers and highlights how each layer is used in the communication process. Each layer adds more information to data during the sending process, while using and removing that information during the receiving process. Documentation for the OSI model can be downloaded from the ITU-T under their X.200 series, from their Web site at `www.itu.int/rec/T-REC-X/en`.

The OSI model defines seven layers, using the numbers 1 to 7, in the following order: the Physical, Data Link, Network, Transport, Session, Presentation, and Application layers. The first four layers are hardware related, while the last three layers are essentially software.

The OSI model defines the following seven layers, as shown in Table 2.1.

TABLE 2.1

The OSI Model Layers

Layers	Traffic Type Supported	Function
Application	Data	The Application layer manages the network connection between an application and the network.
Presentation	Data	In the Presentation layer, data is formatted into a form that can be processed at the receiving system.
Session	Data	The Session layer creates the unique connection between sending and receiving systems and ensures that the data was transferred correctly.
Transport	Segments or Datagrams	The Transport layer manages aspects of data transmission and reception.
Network	Packets	The Network layer controls the addressing used for data transmission.

continued

TABLE 2.1	(continued)	
Layers	**Traffic Type Supported**	**Function**
Data Link	Frames	The Data Link layer manages hardware addresses.
Physical	Bits	The Physical layer defines the transmission medium, such as wire, radio, light beam, or some other transmission method.

Tip
Some common mnemonic devices are often used to remember the OSI model and the order of each layer. They are: All People Seem To Need Data Processing, or Please Do Not Take Sales-People's Advice.

It is very rare to find a network that uses these seven layers as the basis for its architecture. However, this is the most widely used model to describe different network devices and technologies.

An alternative model based on TCP/IP networking was developed that uses five different layers to describe packet switching networks (the TCP/IP Reference model). Most modern networks now use devices based on the TCP/IP Reference model, but it isn't as flexible in describing other network types. The TCP/IP Reference model is discussed later in this chapter.

How Layers Communicate

All communication between two systems requires that the data being transferred travel down though the sending system's network stack, across the Physical layer, and then up through the receiving system's network stack. While the protocols used within a layer must be identical for peer devices, the protocols used at layer interfaces are undefined and can be changed.

Communication begins at the Application layer on the sending system with a command or perhaps some other kind of event. That event is interpreted into an Input/Output, or I/O, request (that either sends or seeks information from a device), and translated to data that is transmitted down through the different layers of the network stack to the Physical layer for transport. Data travels over the link at the Physical layer using the specific connection that leads back up the intended system's network stack. The data then ascends the different layers of the target system's network stack to arrive at the receiver's Application layer where the data is used in some way.

In order for data to be sent to the correct system or systems, additional information must be added to the data that describes the content and how to use it. That kind of information is commonly referred to as *metadata*, which is literally "data about data." The process by which metadata is added is referred to as *encapsulation*; when the metadata is removed, the process is referred to as *decapsulation*. As data passes down through the network stack, metadata is added; as that data ascends, the network stack metadata is removed.

Referring to Figure 2.1, you can see that the encapsulation process begins by formatting and segmenting data so that it is the optimum size for transmission. Each layer of the OSI model adds a layer header to the data containing the information necessary to support the functionality of that particular layer's protocols. Application (L7H), Presentation (L6H), Session (L5H), Transport (L4H), Network (L3H), and Data Link layer (L2H) headers are successively added. Each header contains addressing information, parameters, and the instructions on how the different layers use the information encapsulated within. A trailing section is added to the packet at the Data Link layer, which identifies the end of the packet. This trailing section also includes a data check so that the transport of the packet over the physical layer can be verified as being correct. At the receiving system, the packet is read and each OSI layer of the receiving system strips away its particular header exposing the information contained within successively.

An algorithm such as a Cyclic Redundancy Check, or CRC, is applied to the data. This algorithm is run when a packet arrives at a destination (even an intermediate destination) to determine that the packet was correctly transmitted. If the calculated CRC value of the packet matches the value in the CRC data field, then the packet is assumed to be correctly received. A data check is done in the Data Link layer, but other layers may also include data check fields. The CRC is a hash function, and an algorithm is applied to the data contained in the communication to create an output value that is essentially unique, typically in the form of a 32-bit integer. The CRC is then used as a checksum to validate that the data sent matches the checksum contained within the data itself. The change of even a single digit in the data is enough to affect the value of the checksum and to require a retransmission of the data. Because data is binary, the CRC algorithm is very fast and efficient and doesn't add much overhead to the data transmission process. CRC-32 is now an Ethernet standard, and without this type of technology, network communications would be unreliable.

FIGURE 2.1

OSI data encapsulation and transport

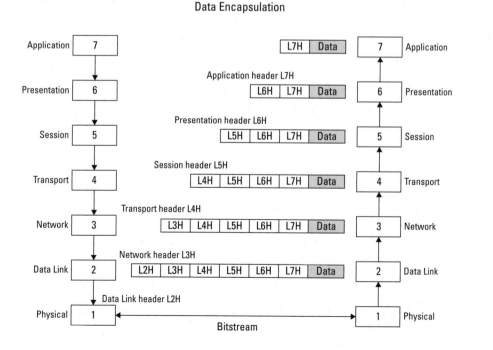

Data Encapsulation

Seven layers are defined in the OSI model, each with its specific purpose representing a different area of networking technology. If only life were so simple. It is unlikely that you will ever work with a network comprised of seven different layers that correspond to each of these different areas; although rare, they do exist. However, economies of scale, as well as convenience provided by different packaging, costs, and other factors, lead to devices that might span two or more layers, and you should be aware that there are several other networking models that use fewer layers to define the network stack. Five layers is a common alternative.

Tip

To get an idea how people subdivide the network stack, refer to the layer names table found at `http://en.wikipedia.org/wiki/Internet_Protocol_Suite.`

In practice, network devices and protocols will work at multiple layers in any networking model. The Cisco router is a good example of an appliance spanning multiple layers of the OSI model. Although the first routers were software that was built into operating systems such as UNIX or Solaris, Cisco achieved dominance in this area of technology by turning routing into an appliance, and by optimizing its performance. Cisco routers span both the Transport and the Network layers. However, the model still serves as the means for describing network communication and identifying devices, and it is the basis for a number of other models used to define Internet traffic, storage area networks (SANs), and more.

It's best not to take the OSI model too literally. However, it provides the vocabulary needed to frame different vendors' products, which is why it is so useful. The real value of the OSI model is that it provides you with an understanding of how components communicate with one another. Each layer in the model describes a protocol or set of protocols, and so the model is sometimes referred to as a *protocol hierarchy*. Each boundary between two levels represents a vertical relationship and requires that an application programming interface, or API, be used in order to communicate with the levels above and below it. A vertical relationship between layers 4 and 5 would be referred to as the Layer 4/5 interface. Implicit in the use of the word *interface* is the need for a communication mechanism based on an API.

Horizontal relationships, referred to as *Layer* n *protocols*, are considered to be peer layer communication, and often don't impose an API requirement. Horizontal relationships are only truly peers when two different entities on the same computer system use that same level: two mail applications, for example. When the same protocol layer is used by devices or entities on different computer systems, their relationship may be termed a peer relationship, but any communication between the two requires that both network stacks be traversed.

As data travels through the network stack, it does so across the boundaries in a set of named connections or channels. Some technologies use a single pipe, similar to a one-lane road, through which data travels in one direction only; this is *simplex* communication. You can also use a single connection to send traffic first in one direction and then in the reverse direction; this is referred to as *half-duplex* communication. When communications travel in both directions at the same time, this is referred to as *full duplex*. Full duplex can be achieved by having a channel that is wide enough to dedicate to each direction or by having multiple channels. The type of communication used is determined by the hardware and software involved and is not specified as part of the OSI model.

Each layer in the OSI model has one or more active elements that are sometimes referred to as an *entity*. An entity can be a software module or it can be dedicated logic on a chip that is part of a network function. An entity or set of entities in a layer that communicates to the layer above is referred to as a *service provider*, and the entity that uses the service in the layer above is the *service user*. The address that is used to access a service provider defines a Service Access Point, or SAP. Once two entities establish communications through an interface using an SAP, they pass what is called an interface data unit (IDU) through the SAP. Contained within the IDU is a service data unit (SDU), control information, and the data that is communicated.

Some layers require that the data be segmented in order to be processed. When that happens, each piece of data gets a header and is transmitted as a distinct unit of data called a protocol data unit (PDU). An example of PDUs is the packetization of data for transmission, and the reassembly of those packets once they are received, verified, and sequenced.

Services are the mechanism used to communicate between different layers in the OSI model. Services have a certain functionality and often can be accessed using an API. Services can operate between layers in either a connection or connectionless model. A connection model specifies that once your connection is established, that connection is dedicated to the service being provided. The best example of a connection-oriented service is the telephone network. The service establishes a connection by dedicating a circuit to the communications. When the call ends, the circuit is broken and released for use. A connection model offers some advantages in terms of reliability and in providing quality of service. However, once the connection is broken, the communication ends, which demonstrates the weakness of this approach: it is not fault tolerant or redundant.

The alternate model of a connectionless service is adopted by the Internet at the Physical layer and is accounted for by the TCP/IP or Internet model. The communication carries its own addressing, and the route taken to reach its destination is unspecified and can be different, depending upon conditions. Connectionless services are characterized by high fault tolerance, but with slower performance and some additional overhead as compared to a connection-oriented service model.

All data communication is characterized by the use of basic commands to initiate and control the connection. Connection-oriented services begin with a process called *negotiation*, where the characteristics of the connection are established. The squelches your modem makes with dial-up connections when it connects are its advertisement of its connection capabilities. Basic control commands or service primitives that play a role in the negotiation process take the following forms:

- **Initiation or connect request.** This is the advertisement for a service to perform an action.
- **Status or indication.** This is an informational event that provides information about the state of the software module or active element (entity) involved in providing the service.
- **Response.** The provider sends a message that it can respond to a request.
- **Confirmation.** The result of the communication is sent back to the initiating entity. Not all services use a confirmation as part of their service.

Keep in mind that the negotiation process takes place on two different systems. Therefore, although the negotiation involves the interface between two different layers in the network model, each control command travels either up or down between the two layers on one system and is then responded to in those same two layers on the second system. A service is defined by the set of operations or command primitives, as well as the two layers that are interfaced by it.

Services do not specify how the operations are implemented in practice. Implementation using services is left to specific protocols. A protocol is an agreed-upon set of rules for data format that can be used by peer entities within a layer to provide a service. By isolating the command set from the implementation, a network is able to switch protocols to accommodate different vendors' products, different network types, and other variables that affect performance.

The Physical Layer

The Physical layer is the lowest level of the OSI model and in other related architectural models, and is the layer responsible for moving bits of data from one location to another. In defining the parameters of Physical layer devices, it is necessary to set the standards for what represents a Boolean value of 1 and 0, the voltage difference, and how long the bit should last before a new bit begins. Physical layer devices must include the electrical connections that are made, how different devices connect to one another, and other electrical and mechanical aspects.

The most commonly used media for the Physical layers are:

- Copper cabling or wires, which include different categories of Ethernet cable (designated by specifications such as CAT5 or CAT6), twisted pair wiring like the ones used in your phone lines or that were used for smaller peer networks such as AppleTalk from Apple, and others.
- Fiber lines where light travels through doped glass strands.
- Radio communications using the different Wi-Fi 802.11 standards, microwave, and other parts of the electromagnetic spectrum in the radio range.

The Physical layer also includes the devices that provide the connections between media, and includes computer network interface cards (NICs), modems, hubs, and other devices.

The Data Link Layer

The Data Link layer connects the data in bits flowing through the media of the Physical layer with the connection that is the network path either to the receiving system or from the sending system. It provides the control mechanism that determines which path the data takes. As is the case with the Physical layer, the Data Link layer appears not only in the OSI networking model but also in other related models such as the model used to describe Internet traffic.

The control over the data link requires that this conceptual layer of the networking model format messages to mark the beginning and end of a message. It does so by breaking the data into data frames, or more simply, frames. A frame takes a large message and segments it into pieces that are between several hundred and several thousand bytes in size. The size of the frame depends upon the technology being used and can be adjusted somewhat by the user to improve performance and reliability. You might want to have a larger frame size when you are transmitting your data over a high-speed connection, or perhaps drop down to a small frame size when a low-speed or unreliable connection is in use.

The segmentation process for frames imposes a sequence on the transmission, and the Data Link layer must provide the necessary means to recombine the frames into data at its destination. Because data can be damaged by noise, and because multiple frames may arrive that duplicate each other, it is up to this layer of the model to resolve these problems. The Data Link layer does so by returning Acknowledgment frames to the sender to indicate which frames were received. The mechanism by which errors can be detected and corrected is part of the Data Link layer's action. Data can be corrupted for many different reasons, including noise in the physical media, and mistakes in transmission or dropped data. When an error is detected at the Data Link layer, a message is sent to the sender that the data needs to be retransmitted.

Part of the Data Link layer's function is to manage the speed of data transmission: too fast and data is lost, which requires that data be retransmitted; too slow and the communication wastes valuable bandwidth and isn't well optimized. The system by which the Data Link layer regulates the data transmission speed involves the use of frame buffers to store data as it is received. A frame buffer is a portion of memory set aside to contain frames that have been received recently. Data flowing into and out of the frame buffers requires flow regulation and error correction in order to be both efficient and well formed. Therefore, the Acknowledgment frames must contain current information about the state of the frame buffer. Because Acknowledgment frames travel over the same physical path as Data frames, one optimization that the Data Link layer uses is a piggyback scheme to send control data back to the sending system. In any broadcasting network communications, such as TCP/IP traffic flowing over Ethernet, the Data Link layer provides a control function in the medium access sublayer of the Data Link layer that determines which frames have access to shared data channels. A shared data channel is a network path that is used by two or more sending and receiving systems.

The Network Layer

The Network layer provides a routing and control function that determines which path data packets use to travel from one network to another, and provides the flow control needed to ensure that a subnet isn't flooded with too many packets at any one time. The concept used to define Network layer communication is called the *session*, and the logic used to manage sessions relies on specific routes determined by the routing function.

Routing plays a fundamental role in switched networks because it provides the means by which traffic can adjust to dynamic changes in the network. When a router fails an acknowledgment request from a sending router, the router can fall back to the next best path. Routers store connections and routes in a routing table, which can either be statically or dynamically created. For small networks where the addresses rarely change, or for large networks where high-speed connections at well-known addresses exist, static routing tables make the most sense. For large networks, dynamic routing provides a better solution than static routing.

Different networks or subnets can require data to be formatted in different ways. This commonly occurs when data travels across international boundaries. Addresses can change across a boundary, and so too can the data rate or the protocol used for the transmission. Some subnets require packets to arrive with information that supports an accounting function to keep track of frames forwarded by subnet intermediate systems, to produce billing information. The network layer provides the necessary means to solve these incompatibilities.

Both the OSI model and the Internet model contain a Network layer. However, when network traffic is broadcast, it is sent out to any network system that requests the data. Broadcast data doesn't require most of the functions provided by the Network layer. Therefore, for broadcasting systems, the Network layer can be either minimal or completely missing.

The Transport Layer

The Transport layer connects the Network layer above it and the Session layer below. The purpose of the Transport layer is to segment the data from a session and pass appropriately sized and formatted data to the Network layer. When data is received from the Network layer, the Transport layer is responsible for ensuring that all the packets have arrived correctly, reforming the session data, and acknowledging (an ACK command) the receipt of the transmission. The Transport layer can support either connection or connectionless data transmission.

The Transport layer manages the connection between its two adjacent layers — the Session layer and the Network layer — and when appropriate, it can create and manage multiple network connections for each Transport connection. Because the Transport layer is responsible for maintaining and managing the connection between the Session and the Network layers, it abstracts the upper layers of the network stack, which are software-based, from the hardware layers below it. As data is exchanged, the Transport layer is responsible for managing the multiplexed streams, and opening and closing connections as required. This management function is a form of flow control.

Transport layer connections provide the only direct link that exists between the two network stacks during any communication. Whereas all other layers of the network stack work independently of their counterparts in the other network stack, the Transport layers of the sending and receiving systems talk directly to one another through the use of their message headers and control messages. A message header is a special field within a packet that contains message information, while a control message is an entire packet (usually a very short one) that is a message. Indeed, the hardware layers can only establish a connection between adjacent layers because the systems involved in the connections between the Network, Data Link, and Physical layers are indeterminate. Depending upon network conditions, routing may employ any number of systems to make the connections required by hardware. The higher layers in the network stack — the Application, Presentation, and Session layers — are all single-channel, end-to-end communications.

The Session Layer

The Session layer provides the means for creating and managing sessions, as well as providing the services needed to initiate those sessions. Security mechanisms, such as logons and other forms of dialog control, are a fundamental part of the Session layer.

Traffic can flow through the Session layer in one direction at a time, or in both directions: either using a half-duplex or full-duplex mode. When a single direction is used (half duplex), the Session layer passes an identifier called a token to the traffic in one direction when its turn comes to use the channel, and then when the token is released, it is passed to the communication going in the opposite direction.

As data flows through the Session layer, checkpoints or separation markers are inserted into the packet data so that if the transfer is interrupted, it can be reestablished without having to resend all of the session data. By synchronizing the data transfer, the Session layer ensures not only that the session is reliably transmitted but also that the transfer is efficient.

The Presentation Layer

The Presentation layer formats Application layer data and can compress and encrypt data before handing the data off to the Session layer. When data from the Session layer appears at the Presentation layer, it is decrypted and decompressed if necessary, so that the data can be sent to the Application layer in a form that the Application layer can accept.

Presentation layer software takes the data objects that applications create in the different data types, such as character, integer, or binary, and converts that data into a form that can be passed along to a different system in a standard encoding format. Wire protocols bridge operating system and application differences so that a computer with one character code, such as ASCII, can communicate with another computer that has a different ASCII character set, or that is using Unicode as its character set.

The Application Layer

The Application layer contains the software that a user interacts with. Application layer programs include Web browsers, e-mail clients, command shells (the Command Line Interface), and office applications to name but a few. The network operating system also contains a number of Application layer programs. Not all software is Application layer software. Microsoft Word, for example, is not exclusively an Application layer application; it contains many modules that work at different layers of the network model and many modules that aren't network related. However, when you initiate a command to perform network printing, the print subsystem used to communicate this action to the network is an Application layer application.

Application layer software is often described in terms of terminal session. A terminal session is an application that provides system status information, allows for system commands, and serves as an interface for user interaction to a system. When you open a terminal session and log into a remote system, you are using an Application layer program. In order for a terminal session to interact with a wide variety of programs, there must be a uniform way for those programs to communicate with the terminal session. Many terminal session programs use a network virtual terminal to standardize the interaction between applications such as text editors with all of the different terminals that exist so that variables such as screen resolution and keyboard equivalents are standardized.

The Application layer hosts a very rich range of services, and the particular services are highly variable from system to system. Applications are responsible for many application service functions, including the following:

- Display characteristics
- Initiating and managing I/O (Input/Output)
- File transfers
- E-mail
- Network printing
- Information lookups in directory services

The Application layer uses the largest set of network protocols. The Hypertext Transfer Protocol (HTTP) used by Web servers and browsers, File Transfer Protocol (FTP) used in uploads and downloads, Simple Mail Transfer Protocol (SMTP), and the Post Office Protocol (POP) used for e-mail transfers are all Application layer protocols.

The TCP/IP Reference Model

Although the OSI Reference model is the best known, it is not the only layered network stack model in use. The best-known alternative model is called the TCP/IP model.

Cross-Ref
The TCP/IP model is discussed in more detail in Chapter 18.

The TCP/IP model uses three different protocols for transport and data format. The Transmission Control Protocol (TCP) describes how to make connections between systems on the Internet, while the User Datagram Protocol (UDP) describes how to work with connectionless data communication. The third protocol, the Internet Protocol (IP), describes how to format packets for transmission. TCP and UDP are Transport layer protocols, while IP is a Network/Interface layer protocol.

The TCP/IP Reference model uses four different layers in its communication model. Layers 1 and 2 in the OSI model (Physical and Data Link) correspond roughly to the Host-to-Network layer in the TCP/IP model. Layer 3, the Network layer in the OSI model, corresponds directly to the Internet layer in the TCP/IP model; Layer 4, the Transport layer, exists at the same level in both. The TCP/IP model does away with Layers 5 and 6 (Session and Presentation). Finally, both models have a top-level Application layer, which was Layer 7 in the OSI model. Figure 2.2 shows the OSI and TCP/IP models side by side.

FIGURE 2.2

Comparing the OSI and TCP/IP network models

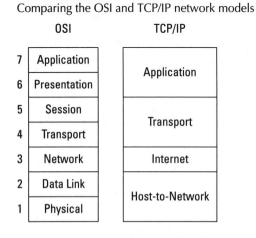

Comparing the OSI and TCP/IP Reference Models

Over the years, both the OSI and TCP/IP Reference models have shaped the vocabulary of the networking industry. However, they both contain flaws in their application to real-world networks that are important to understand. Whereas the TCP/IP model has expression in real products and technologies, based on a set of protocols that have become dominant standards, the OSI model is not supported by products to any significant extent. As a result, the OSI model is essentially an abstraction that is used to understand network communications.

Even in networks that adopt the OSI 7-layered model, some of the layers, particularly the Session and Presentation layers, are thinly populated, if at all. At the same time, the hardware layers, such as the Data Link and Network layers, have so many functions and services that any serious analysis of them would tend to segment those layers into several sublayers.

Part of the complexity of the OSI model is that it doesn't implement key technology in a single layer, but distributes command and control features such as flow control in each of the different layers. This redundancy makes the OSI Reference model more complex than it should be. In the real world, devices get around these issues by spanning several layers of the OSI model within the same device.

The main reason that the OSI model seems to have been adopted with seven layers is that the Systems Network Architecture (SNA) from IBM was a seven-layer architecture. In the 1970s, it was supposed that IBM could control the networking industry, and so the OSI model was constructed in a way that it could be applied to SNA technology without too many modifications.

While the TCP/IP Reference model is supported by a large number of products in the marketplace, it has been criticized for not being general enough to be applied to networks using other protocols. The delineation of interfaces, services, and how protocols are integrated into the model isn't clearly defined. For example, the Host-to-Network layer doesn't really implement separate protocols, and is more properly defined as an interface; there is also no formal Presentation or Session layer. This has generally been expressed in practice by the development of ad hoc protocol standards.

It's best not to take these network models too seriously. While OSI provides a highly flexible model that is widely used in theoretical discussion, and the TCP/IP model finds expression in products, neither model can be directly applied to real-world networks.

Note
Perhaps the best compromise is one of the alternative formulations considered but not adopted when the OSI model was being developed that uses a five-layer system. These unnamed models eliminate the Session and Presentation layers in the OSI Reference model and blend their functions into the Application and Transport layers. Hybrid models left the Network, Data Link, and Physical layers intact.

Summary

In this chapter, the OSI Reference model was presented as an architectural framework that can be used to describe computer networks and devices. This seven-layer protocol conceptualizes a network stack, beginning with applications and software at the top, formatting and data-handling layers in the middle, and hardware layers at the bottom. To communicate, data must travel from the sending system's network stack to the receiving system's network stack.

The boundary between each layer of a network model defines an interface that requires an API be used to create a service that connects the two layers. The OSI Reference model doesn't specify the interface or the service, but highlights its need and use.

Other architectures exist, including one based on the TCP/IP protocols. Whereas the TCP/IP model is expressed by more networks and devices, the OSI Reference model is more flexible and is more commonly used to describe aspects of computer networking. Hybrid models exist that use fewer layers than the OSI Reference model and reduce the OSI Reference model's complexity somewhat.

Architecture and Design

I n this chapter, you learn about different aspects of network design and
architecture. Designs can be based on different connection types and
topologies; architectures are network systems based on a common protocol. In determining whether you are considering an architecture or topology, an argument based on the highest-level protocol used is presented.
Topologies are based on physical transport, while architectures use higher-
level protocols.

Different point-to-point connections are considered. Four different types of connections between endpoints can be specified: physical connections, virtual connections, transient connections, and links where there is no defined (unique)
connection. These different types are the basis for all modern networks.

A collection of nodes sharing a common physical medium is called a *segment*.
Segments are the basic unit of networks; they do not have to have their traffic mediated, and nodes share a common logical address as opposed to a
node's physical (e.g., Media Access Control or MAC) address. Segments also
define collision domains.

To separate segments, you add connection points such as switches or routers.
Networks with multiple segments must have traffic travel over defined routes.
These routes may have any of the four kinds of connections. Routing can be
1:1 or *unicast*, 1:many or *multicast*, 1:all or *broadcast*, and 1:any or *anycast*. The
effect of switched and packet transfer on networks will be considered.

Several different network architectures will be briefly considered from an overall network design viewpoint. They include peer-to-peer (P2P), client-server,
multi-tier, and thin client/server architectures. These different network types

IN THIS CHAPTER

Different network topologies

**How network connections
influence network types**

Segments and routing

**Different network
architectures**

determine how network resources must be deployed, where systems can be located, and which of the many different network protocols they may use.

Network Architecture and Topology

The methods used by systems to communicate on a network are referred to as the *network architecture*. The manner in which the physical infrastructure is deployed to connect a network is referred to as the *network topology*. A topology describes the physical means for transporting data; an architecture describes the technology used to manage and manipulate data.

In some instances, a particular architecture will dictate that a particular topology be used, and in other instances a particular topology will only be suitable for a particular architecture. However, it isn't always the case that an architecture and a topology are so tightly bound.

Most of the time, an architecture is selected to support a particular geographic distribution, organizational structure, user or system load, performance requirements, and the staff available to manage the infrastructure.

The most common architectures in use are described as:

- Peer-to-peer networks
- Client/server (two-tier) networks
- Multi-tier networks
- Directory service or federated networks
- Grid or distributed networks
- Hybrid combinations of the above

Cross-ref
Directory services are covered in Chapter 21.

Note
Hybrid networks are just two or more of the aforementioned architectures.

You can determine whether a description of a technology represents a network architecture or a network topology by the highest layer of the OSI model that the technology requires. A topology describes technology that operates at the Physical and perhaps the Data Link layer. An architecture describes technology that operates at the Network level and above.

The difference between topology and architecture can be illustrated by some examples. Ethernet describes a technology that involves frame-based communication over media. While there are variants of Ethernet that run over twisted-pair copper, there are also versions that run over fiber optic cable. The highest layer that the Ethernet standard operates at is the Data Link layer, where a common addressing format based on Media Access Control (MAC) addressing is defined. Ethernet is a network topology. There are many different ways in which Ethernet networks may be constructed — linear buses, hierarchical trees, rings, and so forth — but all of them still are limited to MAC addressing as the single highest protocol that Ethernet supports.

Cross-Ref

For more discussion on Ethernet network construction, including linear buses, hierarchical trees, and rings, see Chapter 1.

The Internet is governed by a number of protocols or standardized agreements on how data should be composed and managed. As a group, those protocols are referred to as the *Internet Protocol suite*. Much of this book is concerned with explaining Internet Protocols, because this form of networking is so overwhelmingly prevalent today, and indeed you are likely very familiar with them.

The Transport Control Protocol and Internet Protocol (TCP/IP) are the two core protocols that give the Internet much of its flavor. Transport Control Protocol (TCP) is a Transport layer protocol, and the Internet Protocol (IP) is a Network layer protocol in the OSI model. Actually, IP is more often described in terms of a different networking model, the TCP/IP networking model, where IP is part of the Internet layer. The TCP/IP Internet layer overlaps with the Network layer in the OSI model, but the OSI model includes certain technologies that involve address resolution in the Network layer that would be better placed into the Link layer of the TCP/IP model. The Address Resolution Protocol (ARP) is the one example that is commonly mentioned. The main reason that these two models diverge is that OSI makes no distinction between communication that is connection oriented and communication that has no defined connection. Be that as it may, if you were to examine the different layers of the TCP/IP model, you would find that nearly all of them are above what would be the Data Link layer of the OSI model; also, many of them, particularly routing protocols, are Application layer protocols. The higher-level protocols make the Internet Protocol an architecture.

Figure 3.1 compares the two different network models: OSI to the TCP/IP architecture. The TCP/IP architectural model is described in the IETF's RFC 1122 (`http://tools.ietf.org/html/rfc1122`). You will find a considerable amount of variation in the literature describing how these two models relate to one another, or indeed how the TCP/IP model is structured and named. As a result you should take Figure 3.1 lightly. Some authors break the TCP/IP model into four or five different layers and refer to the different layers with different names. In some discussions, the Network Interface layer is referred to as the Link or Host to Network layer. In other discussions, the Network Interface is broken up into a Network Access/Physical, Data Link/Hardware, or Data Link/Physical coupling. The reason that the Application layer in the TCP/IP networking models consolidate the Application, Presentation, and Session layers into a single Application layer is because the upper layer IP protocols span the different layers.

FIGURE 3.1

Comparing the OSI model to the TCP/IP architecture

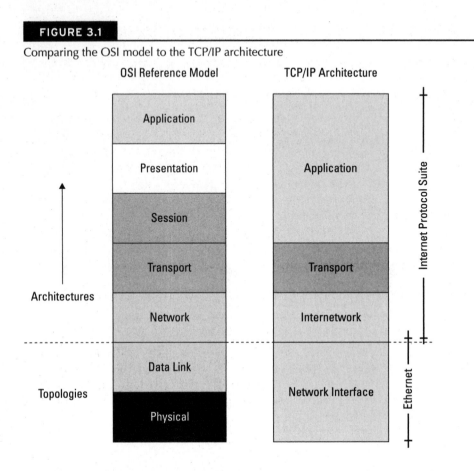

Point-to-point

A point-to-point connection is the simplest network connection that can be defined for any two systems. Simple, that is, before you stop to think about how even just a few elements can be manipulated to radically change topology and architecture. There are three components to any connection: two endpoints and the path or connection between them. The variation in the condition of these elements defines the type of connection, and each connection type has a defined state that determines the properties of the connection. The state of a connection may be characterized by:

- **Physical.** The component (endpoint or connection) can be physical or virtual.
- **Logical.** The logical state is the name or identifier that is assigned to the endpoint or connection. That name can be an IP address or an actual pathway through a network (the wired and switched connection), or the address and path can be virtual or transient.

- **Signal.** Different types of connections can support one or more session, data sent as an entire message or packetized, and so forth.
- **Performance.** Based on the physical, logical, and signal types, different types of connections can support different levels of performance, and the component that is the rate limiting component varies.

The following sections discuss the four connection types. You can use the accompanying figure for each connection type to compare the connection types, the manner in which they may be physically or logically defined, and the implications that the connection type has on both the signal types that can travel over the connection and the performance characteristics and limitations. The chart next to each connection type in the figures is meant to summarize this.

Physical point-to-point connections

The most straightforward connection is a point-to-point connection. Figure 3.2 shows a physical connection with physical endpoints. Sp1 on the left is the sending system, and Sp2 on the right is the receiving system. The connection is made through a permanent medium, most often a wire or fiber, and most higher-level protocols dictate that a negotiation establish the session parameters. Depending upon the power and efficiency of the two network interfaces, as well as their sensed ability to transmit data over the connection, a speed is determined and data flows from left to right during a half-duplex session. If the session is full duplex, then traffic flows in both directions.

The table to the right of each connection type lists the various characteristics of the two endpoints (Sp1 and Sp2) and the Connection (Cp1). For the point-to-point connection type, the endpoints are physical network interfaces (NICs) and the connection is a physical wire. To describe this type of connection you would need to have an address that corresponds to each of the two endpoints, and you would be able to differentiate the circuit or exact path that a signal takes traveling from one endpoint to the other. That path's physical and logical definition wouldn't change for the time that the point-to-point connection was in force.

The advantage of a point-to-point connection is that it is capable of supporting multiple signals because the circuit includes a dedicated connection. The limiting factors of performance are the limiting factors of the physical elements involved. That is, the speed will be determined by the slowest of the following three factors: the signal rate that the sending endpoint Sp1 can send signals, the bandwidth of the network connection Cp1, or the speed at which the receiving endpoint Sp2 can accept incoming signals.

The speed of transmission is determined by a gating factor:

- The media's bandwidth
- The slower of the two endpoints
- The ability of the particular higher-level protocols to process the data

FIGURE 3.2

A point-to-point connection and its connection state table

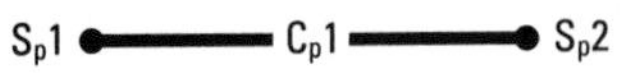

$S_p1 \bullet\!\!-\!\!-\!\!-\!\! C_p1 \!-\!\!-\!\!-\!\!\bullet S_p2$

STATES	S_p1	C_p1	S_p2
Physical	Physical Network Interface	Physical Connection	Physical Network Interface
Logical	Address	Defined Circuit	Address
Signal	Sent Single or Multisession	Physical (Dedicated)	Received Single or Multisession
Performance	Signal Rate	Full Bandwidth	Signal Rate

If data is sent compressed and/or encrypted, the gating for performance is measured in terms of throughput (bits per second, for example) and may be determined by the ability of the endpoint system to transform the data into clear text — or whatever form is required. To some extent, content buffering can aid in intermittent data transfer, but if you have a connection operating at full speed for a length of time, buffering will only be effective so long as incoming data doesn't overrun the buffer.

A purely physical point-to-point connection is common in small networks and prevalent in peer-to-peer networking. Whereas a point-to-point connection is a topology, peer-to-peer is a network architecture. Picture, if you will, a network of many point-to-point connections forming a web, mesh, or grid of terrifying power (á la Twilight Zone); is that a topology or an architecture? These three different descriptions with a high order of connectivity to other network endpoints are described as a mesh or a grid architecture. If the mesh network exists simply to pass traffic around, then it is a topology; however, if the network distributes processing tasks, as is the case with distributed applications, then the grid is an architecture according to the rule that's been posited in this chapter.

Cross-Ref

Peer-to-peer networking is discussed at length in Chapter 11, and large mesh or grid networks are described in Chapter 17 where high-performance networks are discussed.

Virtual point-to-point connections

In the second example of a point-to-point connection, shown in Figure 3.3, all three components of the connection are virtualized. The endpoints Sv1 and Sv2 are virtual network interfaces, and the connection Cv1 is a virtual circuit. A virtual network interface is a simulation in software of a physical network interface. In order to have one or more virtual network interfaces on a system, you must have a physical network interface that network traffic flows through, but any number of virtual interfaces may be defined and given logical addresses that use a physical interface. Network interfaces (including virtual ones) are described in Chapter 7.

FIGURE 3.3

A virtual point-to-point connection and its connection state table

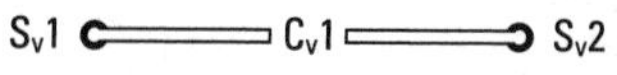

$S_v1 \;\rule[0.5ex]{2em}{0.4pt}\; C_v1 \;\rule[0.5ex]{2em}{0.4pt}\; S_v2$

STATES	S_v1	C_v1	S_v2
Physical	Virtual Network Interface	Virtual Connection	Virtual Network Interface
Logical	Address	Defined Circuit	Address
Signal	Sent Single or Multisession	Temporary (Dedicated)	Received Single or Multisession
Performance	Signal Rate	Allotted Bandwidth	Signal Rate

The state table for a virtual point-to-point connection is shown in Figure 3.3. To describe this type of connection, you would need to have an address that corresponds to each of the two endpoints, but those addresses aren't unique to the physical interface that either Sv1 or Sv2 uses.

The path or connection is a virtual circuit, Cv1. This means the circuit is built at the start of a session and discarded or torn down when a session is complete. You would not be able to differentiate the circuit or exact path that a signal takes traveling from one endpoint to the other after a session ends because that path changes on a session-by-session basis. However, during a session, the virtual circuit is defined. The process of buildup and tear down of virtual circuits introduces latency into virtual point-to-point circuits that don't exist in a physical point-to-point circuit.

The advantage of a virtual point-to-point connection is that it is capable of utilizing all physical network interfaces and physical circuits because virtualizing all components allows this type of connection to use whatever is available. A virtual circuit is assigned to a session, and therefore, although endpoints can send single or multiple sessions over a virtual point-to-point connection, the circuit is still dedicated to the two endpoints involved, Sv1 and Sv2. Performance over a virtual point-to-point circuit is limited by the endpoint's signal rate or by the bandwidth that is allotted to the Cv1 connection.

A virtual point-to-point connection has properties of a physical connection. Once the session is established, the signals travel over a circuit that is a dedicated connection. The limiting factors of performance are the limiting factors of the physical elements involved. That is, the speed will be determined by the slowest of the following three factors: the signal rate that the sending endpoint Sp1 can send signals, the bandwidth of the network connection Cp1, or the speed at which the receiving endpoint Sp2 can accept incoming signals.

A virtual connection is a circuit that is built for a particular session and exists for that session. When the session is over, the virtual circuit is released. Most LAN topologies build virtual circuits by providing the appropriate connections at a router or switch, because it is impractical to maintain a full set of physical circuits. In order to build a virtual circuit, the switching devices have to have knowledge of their neighbors and a method for optimizing routes, and there is a certain amount of system overhead involved in "building the virtual circuit" and "tearing the circuit down." That overhead can range from being very resource-intensive to insignificant, depending upon the technologies used. From the standpoint of desirability, once the circuit is built, there is no disadvantage to sending traffic over a virtual circuit versus a physical circuit because a virtual circuit uses a combination of physical connections as its route. Virtual circuits are the central construct necessary to create virtual private networks, which are the topic of Chapter 29.

Virtualization is one of the great unifying concepts in computer science, one that becomes increasingly important as the industry attempts to optimize system performance. Virtual machine technology is becoming a standard method for all servers and will eventually migrate to the desktop. It is possible to virtualize anything in computer science, provided that you have at least one physical system to provide the needed hardware to perform the heavy lifting. In a sense, virtualization is a form of redirection and partitioning.

Packet switched or transient connections

Figure 3.4 represents a completely different model for a point-to-point connection — packet-switched or transient connections — where no connection is defined. The connectionless or stateless model is the one that the Internet uses. The lack of a defined circuit completely changes the mechanism by which data is sent and received over the network.

FIGURE 3.4

A packet switched or transient connection and its connection state table

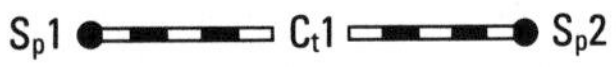

STATES	S_p1	C_i1	S_p2
Physical	Physical Network Interface	Packed Switched or Transient	Physical Network Interface
Logical	Address	No Circuit Defined	Address
Signal	Sent Fragmented	Multipathed	Received and resequenced
Performance	Variable Signal Rate	Variable Bandwidth	Variable Signal Rate

Referring to Figure 3.4, this type of connection uses what is essentially a connectionless model. The sending and receiving systems are shown as Sp1 and Sp2 as two physical endpoints, but they could just as well have been virtual endpoints Sv1 and Sv2, or any mixture of virtual and physical such as Sp1 and Sv2. I've just shown one case for simplicity. The nature of the endpoints is not the important differentiating factor here. The key differentiator is the lack of a defined path, which is shown as the dotted line Ct1 in the figure. No defined "circuit" means that the path varies and that traffic travels over whatever route is the best available route at the time. The best way to think about circuitless or stateless connections is that transmission proceeds on a "best efforts" basis.

This is the first of the point-to-point connections that is stateless; both A and B were stateful. There are some very important conclusions that you can draw from this difference. In a stateful connection, the circuit is defined, whereas in a stateless connection there is no path defined.

Stateful connections can be permanent, which supports sending traffic in a complete stream as a series of bits, bytes, and characters. Traffic sent this way arrives sequenced (in order) and doesn't require reassembly. Indeed, traffic might not even need to be fragmented at all, depending upon the size of the data being sent. In studies of corporate e-mail that I have been involved with, some fraction over 90 percent of the messages are quite small, 3KB or less, but the remaining 10 percent make up 90 percent of the data. With different applications, your mileage will vary, but the implication is that most data is fragmented because most protocols impose a limit on size in order to make their error correction mechanisms tractable.

By contrast a stateless connection uses whatever physical path is available or whichever is the solution of some optimization or routing algorithm. Data as it arrives at an endpoint can travel the same path or any other path. That means that packet-switched networks are able to more fully utilize the physical network than any other type of connection can. For this reason nearly all commercial network connections are based on a switching technology. Only high speed backbone connections tend to deviate from this route. As shown in the associated state table, circuit switched networks tend to send data in a fragmented form and use multiple paths. Performance is something that can be throttled allowing endpoints to vary the sending/receiving rate and modifying the amount of bandwidth allotted to the connection dynamically.

A point-to-point connection can also be defined, but can be intermittent or transient, as is the case in Figure 3.3. This is the case for token ring networks; hosts on the network get full use of the token ring but only on a prioritized basis and only for a session. It is also the case for Virtual Private Networks (VPNs) where the circuit is defined for the session.

To make a connection work when there is not a defined circuit, the sending system always chops data up into chunks, called packets, frames, or datagrams. Each chunk is prepared in sequence, encrypted if needed, tagged with a sequence number, made verifiable with an error correction mechanism (usually a checksum), almost always encapsulated, and sent on its way. As each chunk goes out, it is sent to a branch point in the network and routed by the best available path on a hop-by-hop basis.

If a link goes down, no problem — the chunks of data are sent by other routes. Stateless connections are highly fault tolerant; they will survive even limited nuclear war. Not only that, but because chunks may be routed over the best available path, the entire network can be utilized and bandwidth may be fully exploited. This is not the case with stateful connections. It is for these reasons that packet switched or transient circuit point-to-point connection technology dominates the networking industry.

Notice that I called packet switched circuits an architecture and not a topology. While endpoint addresses are known, the state of the connection cannot be defined. That means that higher-level protocols must always be employed to make sure that data arrives where it is intended to, above and beyond the Physical or Data Link layers.

Along the different routes, some packets will arrive faster than others and be out of sequence, other packets will hit dead ends and need to be resent from the source, and some may arrive corrupted. It is up to the destination endpoint to error check, resequence, and unencrypt the data. Stateless connections require that each node in the network, as well as the destination endpoint, be able to participate in messaging that makes requests for data and acknowledges receipt. Messaging is an additional overhead that stateless connections impose. In some cases, especially when there is a high error rate, overhead can be a very significant burden. When applying Quality of Service (QoS) protocols, it is always easier to manage QoS in a stateful connection and to guarantee a level of service than it is in a stateless technology.

Switched connections

Figure 3.5 represents a switched point-to-point connection. When a circuit is available on a time-varying basis, there are two different methods that can be used to provide access to the circuit: *time slicing* and *negotiated access*. The public switched telephone network (PSTN) is the classic example of this connection type.

FIGURE 3.5

A switched connection and its connection state table

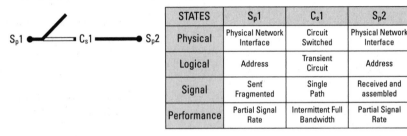

STATES	S$_p$1	C$_s$1	S$_p$2
Physical	Physical Network Interface	Circuit Switched	Physical Network Interface
Logical	Address	Transient Circuit	Address
Signal	Sent Fragmented	Single Path	Received and assembled
Performance	Partial Signal Rate	Intermittent Full Bandwidth	Partial Signal Rate

With time slicing, a node has access to the circuit at regular intervals. Time slicing is common in microprocessors, but extremely rare in network technology. When you time slice access to a CPU, there is nearly no latency involved in fetching information from a primary cache. On the other hand, time slicing access to a connection requires circuit buildup and teardown, and that introduces unacceptable latency into a network. That latency results in a very poor use of a network's bandwidth.

In Figure 3.5 the endpoints shown are physical endpoints Sp1 and Sp2. This is more commonly the case for switched networks because it is the lack of physical connections and many physical endpoints that typically drive the development of this network type. As with the packet-switched network described in the previous section, the circuit switched connection Cs1 is defined at the time the session is initiated. However, unlike packet switching, a circuit switched network's connection is complete during the entire session. The data sent over the connection may be fragmented, but it travels the same defined transient path. The advantage of a circuit switched technology is that it can support data streams, allows for the physical path to be divided into channels, and by allowing the signal quality to drop can support a bursty operation.

The predominant method used for a switched connection is a negotiated access to the network. Any network technology that uses a token passing system for network access simulates a switched network connection. Token passing is done on regular intervals so that even a node with a high priority can't entirely command a network's bandwidth indefinitely. From the standpoint of other users, a network that is controlled by a single node seems to be frozen and crashed.

Most network connections are switched to guarantee that a path exists between two endpoints. Some network connections, such as bridging links, backbones, and others, are dedicated connections, but they usually represent only a small fraction of the connections on most networks.

Cross-Ref

For more discussion on routers, bridges, and switches, see Chapter 10. For more details on WANs and backbones, see Chapter 13.

Switched and Packet Networks

There's a lot of confusion regarding the terms *packets*, *frames*, and *datagrams* because their meanings are rather similar and depend upon the particular technology in use. A packet is a formatted data chunk that is sent over a packet switched network. Packet switching is a stateless technology that routes traffic on a packet-by-packet basis.

Packet switching was illustrated in Figure 3.5. On a packet switched network, the data is always sent as chunks that are encapsulated with addressing, and there is no circuit defined. The switching is done at a computer, switch, router, or some other device, and the only role that the packet plays in determining the route that it travels is to present its addressing, and perhaps other data such as priority to the routing device.

The term *circuit switching* is applied to a network that builds a stateful connection between two endpoints over which network traffic flows. The classic example of a circuit switched network is the plain old telephone system, or POTS. As you can see in Figures 3.2 and 3.3, circuits can be permanent or virtual. A circuit switched network can support the widest range of transport protocols because data can be sent as a continuous stream, in whole, intermittently, or in chunks such as packets. Because the endpoints "own" the circuit, at least for the session, the data can be sent in any way that can be successfully negotiated between those endpoints.

In order for packets to be sent and received correctly, the packet data or payload is encapsulated with supporting data such as addressing, checksums, and sequencing. This process is referred to as *framing* or *packet framing*, and the data that is sent is referred to as *frames*. So packetization is the process of chunking the data, and framing is a data format. This is entirely analogous to sending a letter to someone composed of text and then formatting the data inside a word processor document. The text is the letter and the formatting is the envelope.

Remember that packet switching also requires a messaging component. Messages are packetized, but because they may only require a command and no data, what's important for message frames is the data contained in the envelope.

The term *packet* can be applied to connections that are both stateful and stateless, as it refers to the chunking process and nothing else. The term *datagram* is used when the technology employed is over a stateless technology and uses what is considered to be an unreliable service. From the standpoint of this discussion, an unreliable service is one that requires that each step in the process of communication be matched by a messaging infrastructure.

Cross-Ref

Chapter 17 describes the Transmission Control Protocol and the User Datagram Protocol. Chapter 18 describes the Internet Protocol. A more complete discussion of stateful and stateless communication and the mechanisms used for each is contained in these chapters.

A reliable service that uses packets may or may not send a message back to the sending system that the data was received correctly, but an unreliable service always sends a message back to the sending system. Not only that, but an unreliable service may also send a message back at each individual node that a packet or frame reaches. The Transmission Control Protocol (TCP), when combined with the Internet Protocol (IP), constitutes what may be considered a reliable service, TCP/IP. TCP/IP was constructed to ensure that the data sent is the data that is reconstructed exactly at the receiving endpoint. As a rule, TCP/IP is slower than methods that don't enforce reliable delivery or impose a quality of service.

In the Internet Protocol suite, you can see the impact of messaging on a hop-by-hop basis when you issue a TRACERT command. That command builds a table from returned ICMP messages at each step along the path that the PING packets take to their destination.

By contrast, the User Datagram Protocol (UDP) over an IP network represents an unreliable service. UDP sends data in framed packets, but doesn't require that the data be faithfully reproduced at the receiving endpoint. UDP is used for streaming media and other applications where large amounts of data are being transferred and where the loss of some data isn't important. In a movie passing by at more than 30 frames per second, your mind can't perceive a frame that is missing or out of place. It's easy to remember what a datagram is if you remember that the *D* in UDP stands for *datagram* and that this is the technology used for streaming music and video. So for anything sent as a stream, the use of the term *datagram* is the correct one, although few people would ever correct you if you used the term *frame* or even *packet*, instead. It's a subtlety, but it's worth keeping in mind.

Bus Architectures

The logical extension of a point-to-point connection is a set of point-to-point connections forming a bus structure, with many nodes sharing a common medium in a daisy chain topology (described in Chapter 1). Early Ethernet versions, such as 10BASE5 (which used vampire taps) and 10BASE2 with coaxial cable mated with BNC connectors, have this type of topology.

In a bus architecture, the network bus defines a network segment that is a logical subgroup of network nodes. Network segments not only have the property of common addressing but they also serve as the boundaries for broadcast messages and represent the portion of the network over which network collisions occur. Signals traveling on a network segment require that the signal not be endlessly reflected back and forth on a network segment in order to limit collisions and lower network traffic, which is accomplished by a mechanism called termination. A description of network segments, collision domains, and how termination works is described in the sections that follow.

Network segments

A bus may be viewed as a set of one or more network segments that share common network characteristics and can communicate with one another with the least possible overhead. Every type of network has at least one network segment. At a minimum a network segment consists of two or more computers that share the same physical medium. Because a network segment represents a fundamental unit in networking technology, let's consider exactly how a network segment is defined and what characteristics it might have.

In some instances, a network segment is a single point-to-point connection, but more often, it is a collection of point-to-point connections. Some network devices, such as couplers, hubs, and repeaters, extend a network segment across both connections. On a token bus network, a network segment is defined as the physical layer between two different Media Access Units. Because a token bus network works by passing a token along the bus from beginning to end, token bus networks are considered a single network segment.

The definition of a network segment as one where systems share a physical network isn't universally applied. Many times, network segments are defined as that part of a network where systems can communicate with one another at the Data Link layer. That is, one system can communicate to another system based on the system's MAC addresses. Another way to look at this definition of a network segment is that it represents a collection of systems where messages can be broadcast to one another, or where all systems are on the same subnet.

Because a subnet is defined as all systems sharing a common IP routing prefix, by definition, all systems in a subnet are in the same broadcast domain. A system on a subnet should be able to browse or PING another system on that subnet. A router, by definition, separates two connections into individual network segments. A broadcast domain is bounded by any Network layer (Level 3) device such as a router or switch.

Tip
A collision domain may be bounded by any Data Link layer (Level 2) device, such as a switch. A broadcast domain may be bounded by any Network level (Layer 3) device, such as a router. Chapter 2 describes the OSI data model in detail.

Because a subnet is based on a routing prefix, in theory, each connection on the router should be an individual route. At the Physical layer, this is true, but a subnet is defined at a higher protocol level: at the Network layer in the OSI model, or for TCP/IP, at the Internet layer of the TCP/IP model. There is nothing that prevents having systems with the same subnet on both sides of a router, provided that the addresses of the systems are unique. So while in most cases, networks choose to isolate subnets on one connected link of a router for performance reasons, it isn't always the case. It's a subtle point, but one you should be aware of.

If you separate parts of a subnet across a router, you are separating those fragments into different broadcast domains. Therefore this book uses the term *broadcast domain* to represent any system in a group that can receive a broadcast from another system, which is not necessarily the same thing as a subnet.

Collision domains

It is important to be able to recognize the boundaries of a network segment in Ethernet networks in particular, because they define what is known as a *collision domain*. A collision domain represents the physical layer over which collisions are possible. A collision domain is bounded by any Data Link layer (Level 2) device such as a switch. In designing networks, an important consideration is to limit the size of any one network segment in order to minimize the number of collisions that packets have. In a token ring or token bus network, only one node can communicate over the network at any one time, collisions are largely avoided, and the idea of a collision domain does not apply. As a general rule, collision domains are smaller than and contained inside broadcast domains.

Figure 3.6 shows a representation of collision domains and broadcast domains. The collision domains are indicated by the circles in the diagram, while the broadcast domains are bounded by the rectangles. On the left-hand side of the figure the two collision domains labeled PCs on Segment_1 and PCs on Segment_2 are two different subnets each separated by a switch. Each of those subnets has their own logical address (subnet) and is bounded by a Data Link layer (Level 2) switch which defines the collision domain. The collision domain indicated by PCs on Segment_3 includes Hub_2 since a hub is a logical Physical level (Layer 1) device. The broadcast domains include the switches that the subnets are connected to, but end at the routers, which are Network layer (Level 3) devices.

Collisions occur on networks that use a shared transmission medium. By the term *shared*, I mean that the wires are shared, as is the bandwidth of the connection. As mentioned previously, you can use different token passing techniques to restrict network access. Systems of this type typically have a node send data as a complete stream from the source to the destination. That means that for the time that the entitled system has network access, it is in possession of a "dedicated circuit," and the throughput of that particular transaction is high. A dedicated circuit is one that can only accept traffic from a single endpoint or network node. Data arrives at its destination in sequence and generally requires less error checking. However, not all networks operate in this way, nor is it desirable for them to do so.

FIGURE 3.6

This idealized network shows different collision and broadcast domains.

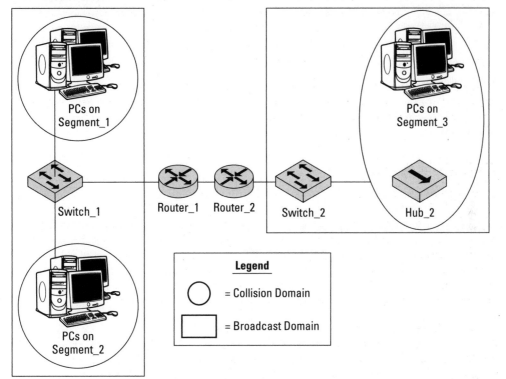

A network collision occurs when an endpoint or node starts to read the signals coming from one source, and before that data is completely received, it detects signals coming from another source and either appends the signals or intersperses them with the first source's data. Every type of network connection has a certain error rate due to collisions, and every network transport method employs a means for validating the integrity of the data it receives. The exception to this rule is a full-duplex circuit where traffic flows in both directions and each direction is separated from the other. As traffic on a network increases, the percentage of traffic suffering collisions rises, eventually becoming a significant burden.

To prevent network collisions, nearly all networking protocols include a messaging component that acknowledges successful receipt or requests retransmission of any suspect communication. There are different technologies employed to detect collisions. The two most common are:

- **Carrier Sense Multiple Access with Collision Detection (CSMA/CD).** This is the protocol that many wired networks, such as IEEE 802.3 Ethernet, use. This method has network nodes listen (carrier sense) to the channel they are on for quiet periods before they transmit new data.

- **Carrier Sense Multiple Access with Collision Avoidance (CSMA/CA).** With this protocol, nodes actively signal to the network that they are about to transmit before doing so. Collision avoidance is slower than collision detection because it adds additional steps to each data transfer.

Note

The two CSMA protocols are discussed in detail in Chapter 12 (for Ethernet CSMA/CD) and in Chapter 14 (for Wi-Fi CSMA/CA).

Signal termination

It is possible to have high collision rates, even on networks with low traffic, if the connections you use aren't properly configured. Many network technologies, just like system buses, require that segments be properly terminated at their endpoints. Failure to do so results in reflection of the signal and collisions. Termination is meant to reduce signal strength to a point where any reflected signal's amplitude falls below the threshold of a recognized signal and is ignored.

A dedicated circuit means that during the periods when that circuit is not in use, the bandwidth that the circuit represents is wasted. A dedicated circuit also means that the network must ensure that the circuit is always available in order to provide a certain level of QoS. When you want to maximize a network's bandwidth or you are sending data over links that may be transient or of varying quality, a different method must be used. That is the situation that the creators of the Internet faced, and the purpose that TCP/IP was designed for. In TCP/IP, data is sent in pieces over the best available route, and retransmitted when necessary. Packets arriving at their destination are resequenced and validated. This allows for maximum use of bandwidth and fault tolerance at the expense of additional overhead.

There are examples of network technologies that use neither a broadcast domain nor a collision domain. They are categorized by the creation of a single dedicated link, usually established at the Data Link layer (Level 2). Examples of these kinds of technologies are VPN and the Point-to-Point (PPP) protocol. PPP links are authenticated, and data sent over the link is both compressed and encrypted. PPP is used on many different types of Physical layer connections, from Unshielded Twisted Pair such as phone lines, serial cables, cell phone links, and even fiber optic connections, to Synchronous Optical Networking (SONET) networks. There is no broadcast domain because the endpoint of the communication is the endpoint of the PPP link. There is no collision domain because the link is dedicated and the PPP protocol does not support broadcast. However, the encrypted data within a PPP frame can include a broadcast, but that is handled by the system to which the data is forwarded.

Connection Points

Few networking technologies use a bus topology anymore; the increasingly low cost of switches and routers have seen to that. Switches and routers serve as a locus at which a collection of endpoints may be connected. The problem is that a bus offers only limited upgrade capabilities and hardly any flexibility for moving things around. Most networks use connection devices of various types: hubs, repeaters, switches, routers, and gateways. Chapter 9 describes these devices and how they operate in detail, but for the purposes of this chapter it is worth taking a moment to discuss why they are used and what complexity they offer in network design and architecture.

Cross-Ref

Chapter 9 describes hubs, repeaters, switches, routers, and gateways. Token rings are described in Chapter 12.

Hubs are the simplest devices; they are simply ways of extending a network segment. All devices connected to a hub are on the same network segment, and the hub is simply a Physical layer device that is almost like an extension of the wire. Signals travel through the low-resistance connections of a hub unimpeded. From the standpoint of network topology, hubs create star shapes or can be linked to create a hierarchical tree structure. A repeater is a hub that provides signal amplification. In a network segment that contains a hub, all of the previous discussion on a collision domain and network segment applies.

Switches can be Network layer (Level 3) or Data Link layer (Level 2) devices, and they introduce a physical separation between network segments. Routers are switches that are endowed with the ability to route data intelligently using protocols that they understand and algorithms that run on them, and by creating and exchanging stored routing data in memory or permanent storage. The concept that these devices introduce is the route. A route is a defined path through a network from the source to the destination. At a switch or router, the route would be defined as the path through a network from that connection point to the endpoint. A route is composed of the different hops taken through the network, which represents individual network segments.

Switches and routers are widely used on most networks today. They introduce great flexibility into a network, provide node fan-out, fault tolerance due to route switching based on conditions, and for routers, the ability to adapt and optimize the route that data takes. In networks with only switches, routing may be done at a host, but in networks with routers, the router is responsible for routing traffic.

Route optimization is necessary because there may be many paths from one endpoint to another and some may be very slow or even intermittent. There are different types of routing optimizations possible that algorithms try to calculate, one based on the time it takes for travel, one based on calculating the smallest number of network segments that must be traveled, and another based on maximizing throughput. In most instances, optimization is done by providing the fastest route or the route that offers the most throughput. It is possible to manually create and modify static routing tables.

Cross-Ref

Static routing tables are covered in Chapter 9.

There are four common routing topologies and include the following:

- **Unicast (1:1).** Communications that are sent from one endpoint to another endpoint are referred to as *unicast*, and the process of sending this kind of message is called *unicasting*. Unicasting represents a single destination system by whatever route or routes are used. Many streaming services, such as Real Audio, use unicast technology.

- **Broadcast (1:all).** A broadcast is sent to any system on a network (usually a network segment) that can hear the message. Broadcasts are generally confined to a single network segment because they are very bandwidth intensive.

- **Multicast (1:many).** Multicasting is a message delivered to a group of nodes, usually through a subscription or opt-in mechanism.

- **Anycast (1:any).** Anycasting is a message sent to the nearest or best destination, where it is responded to by a single system.

Figure 3.7 shows these different routing topologies.

FIGURE 3.7

The four common routing topologies

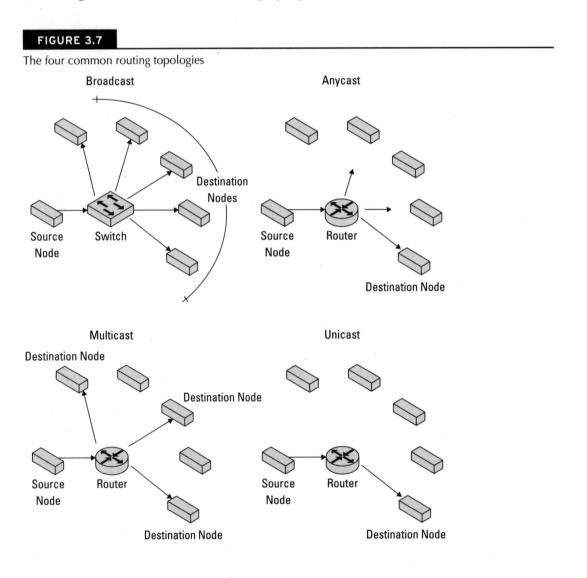

Gateways are Application layer (Level 7) devices. They are used to connect two different network types together at any level of the network model. You might use this type of device to connect an AppleTalk or IPX network to a TCP/IP network, although these days, most networks with Apple Macintoshes and Novell Netware use TCP/IP as the preferred protocol. Gateways can also work with applications, providing translations from an application such as a Web server to an e-Commerce server.

Bus networks are open networks where there are no close paths; but many networks are built using a ring topology. The most common examples of ring networks are the IBM Token Ring and Fiber Distributed Data Interface (FDDI) networks. Were it not for marketing, we might all be using Token Rings today instead of Ethernet, but that is another story. Rings are created in many ways. In Token Rings, they are often wired together using a star topology where hubs connect to nodes called stations, and one wire leads into the loop and another wire leads out. A ring topology has a single collision domain and theoretically is a single network segment.

On a ring network, if a connection fails, the segment would be broken and the ring destroyed. To alleviate this problem, ring networks use failover rings and MAUs. Many ring networks are built using two rings, and can either use the second ring as an additional data path or keep it in a hot backup capacity. The second technology uses devices that IBM calls Multistation Access Units, or MAUs. A MAU works at the Data Link layer (Level 2) to create a logical ring structure from a network comprised of star units.

To avoid collisions on a ring network, a method of network access called *token passing* is often used. A token is sent around the network, and each node that receives the token compares their priority to the one contained in the token. As data from one node is delivered, the arrival of a token then allows another node to begin communication. With a token passing scheme, only one node at a time has access to the network, but when that node is communicating, it is able to do so at the full network speed using the entire network bandwidth.

Peer-to-Peer Networks

Peer-to-peer (P2P) networks are the first of a set of network architectures that will now be considered from a design standpoint. The previous networks described were bus networks that could be considered as simply a collection of unrelated connections. P2P networks are created as a logical extension of a collection of point-to-point links. P2P networks can use any one of a number of technologies, and even be composed on the fly, creating a network composed of ad hoc connections. The key differentiating factor that determines whether a network is P2P or some other architecture is whether each node participates in the network interaction as a nearly equal partner in processing data. Chapter 11 covers the topic of P2P networks in detail, but it is valuable here to say a few words about P2P networks as context for other architectures such as client-server, X-architecture, and multi-tiered networks that follow.

Cross-Ref
Chapter 1 covers the various network topologies that the different architectures can use, including bus, ring, mesh, and hybrid networks.

A peer-to-peer network has a different meaning, depending upon the context in which the term is used. Microsoft uses the term *workgroup* for a peer-to-peer network on their operating system. The services participating in a peer-to-peer relationship are the security service, file and print service, and a shared Internet connection. In a Windows workgroup, only those workgroup members that are on the same network segment using the TCP/IP protocol may share network resources of the workgroup of which they are members. Microsoft differentiates their workgroup from a domain network, which uses a directory service.

If you examine the situation more closely, you will find that Windows workgroups distribute the server functions on whichever member of the workgroup is either attached to and sharing the resource, such as a file or printer share, or attached to the first system on the workgroup to recognize that a particular network service such as a browser is required. Microsoft imposes connection limits on their workgroup members so that a personal Web server can only serve up to ten connections on a network. Microsoft Windows desktop operating systems are detuned versions of the core server operating system with restrictions placed in the code in several other important areas.

Microsoft packages different sets of modules and extensions that seem to differentiate these OS versions more substantially than they are in fact differentiated. If you are willing to spend a little time installing interface components, adding some additional features, and changing some of the runtime behavior of services, you can make a Windows Server appear to an outsider to be nearly identical to a Windows desktop. So even though it appears that workgroups are P2P, they are actually a fully distributed client-server system. A true P2P application, to my mind, uses other systems for data sources and processes each application locally. This is a fine point, but it is worth keeping in mind.

Many people skirt this definition and only say that on a P2P network, nodes are equal in terms of functioning as both a client and a server on the network. When you examine P2P applications such as BitTorrent, Kazaa, and other applications that use this architecture, they tend to use a pure P2P model for some functions and an ad hoc client-server model for other functions. You will find some P2P networks use centralized (server directed), decentralized, structured, and unstructured models, as well as hybrids of these types.

Cross-Ref

Chapter 11 goes into detail on the architecture of some of the better-known P2P applications, such as BitTorrent and Kazaa.

Client-Server Networks

A client-server network is a two-tiered software architecture where a server system performs processing that is used by a client system or systems. Client-server systems are currently the most commonly deployed form of distributed network computing and are often used in network applications such as databases, e-mail, browsers/Web servers, and other technologies that you are familiar with. Client-server technology requires that the server run server software and the client run client software; it also requires that these two pieces of software be either different or the same but serve different functions.

There is no restriction other than the ability to communicate with one another using the required protocols where the server and clients are located. In most instances, clients and servers are on different systems. In some instances, the server and the client are on the same system; this is called a single seat system.

In order to make a client-server application work properly, there must be a protocol that is used to request services from the server and a protocol that allows the server to provide data and/or transfer necessary data for processing from client to server. Often these protocols are part of a unified protocol. Commonly used network data transfer protocols include HTTP (Hypertext Transfer Protocol), SNMP (Sip), Java RMI, .NET remoting, TCP (Transmission Control Protocol), UDP, (User Datagram Protocol), Sockets, Windows Communication Foundation (WCF), CORBA, (Common Object Requesting Broker Architecture) and others.

The literature describes client-server interactions in terms of sequence diagrams — which are flow charts that illustrate how messages are related and sequenced — and store these diagrams in files formatted in a standard interchange file format. You may encounter the terms *timing diagram*, *event scenarios*, or even *event tracing diagrams* in place of the term sequence diagram. These days, sequence diagrams are stored most often in Unified Modeling Language (UML) files. Figure 3.8 shows a sequence diagram in Effexis Software's Sequence Diagram Editor utility (www.sequence diagrameditor.com). This utility and others in its class allow you to design a sequence graphically and then save it out to a UML file.

FIGURE 3.8

Effexis Software's Sequence Diagram Editor utility

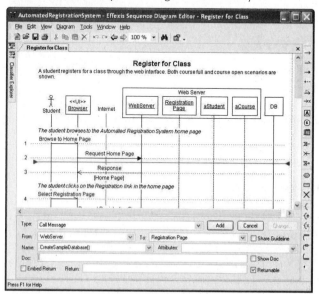

In a classic client-server architecture, there is a clear differentiation between the actions of a client and a server. A client can initiate a request and processes the response when the reply is received. An application on the client that has made a request is dedicated to that request and waits for the server's reply. Clients can be connected to one or more servers concurrently, but most often there are a limited number of connections in order to preserve client performance. For example, Microsoft Internet Explorer can create and manage four connections, and Apple iTunes can manage three connections. Because actions at clients usually involve user interaction of some sort, clients often provide a graphical user interface, or GUI, application.

The term server can be applied to a specific application, program, or software module that can perform computing upon request. A server can also refer to a hardware platform or appliance that runs any of these categories of software. Servers can advertise the availability of their service, but do not send data to clients without a request. Servers can be configured using a configuration utility; sometimes they are GUI applications, and many times they are Command Line Interface (CLI) utilities. When a server is running, it creates a process called a service. Services related to operating system functions are often managed within the Services utility provided by the server's operating system.

Windows Server's services, for example, can be managed within a Microsoft Management Console (Services in Administrative Tools) for later versions of the operating system, or within a Control Panel for earlier versions. Services also appear in the Manage Your Server utility for Windows Server 2008. When a service is part of an application such as an enterprise database, it is common for the vendor to include a management utility or console in which services are configured and turned on and off. Services can be disabled, turned on automatically at startup or after a delay (Windows Server 2008), or set to be turned on manually.

Multi-Tiered Networks

Multi-tiered architecture, sometimes referred to as *n-tiered* or n-layer architecture, is a form of client-server architecture where a middleware service negotiates transactions between client and server. In this architecture, the client talks to the middleware server, the middleware server talks to the server, and in return the server talks to the client through the middleware layer. Examples of middleware applications are the various transaction servers and Java 2 Enterprise Edition.

Figure 3.9 shows a two-tier or client/server versus a three-tier architecture. In nearly all deployed n-tier applications, a three-tier architecture is used. A client/server has two different layers only, the client and the server. The different layers in a three-tier architecture provide separation between different fundamental network functions as follows:

- The client layer or presentation tier provides user interaction and system management tools.
- The middleware layer or logic tier enforces the logical rules of the system and manages interactions in the form of discrete transactions.
- The server layer or data tier consists of server applications and services, which provide access to stored information.

FIGURE 3.9

Two-tier versus three-tier architectures

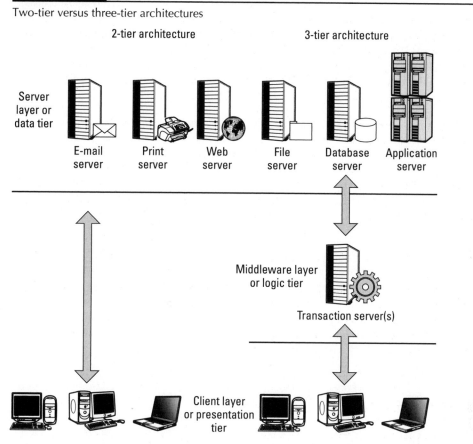

Adding a third tier to a client-server architecture provides a number of very specific benefits. By decoupling client from server, you can use the middleware server as a translation service, talking to each with a different protocol. The middleware layer abstracts both the client and the server, making both locations transparent to the other, and allowing any transaction that reaches the middleware server intact to survive a loss of the client or server's connections or the loss of either system for any reason. Transactions provide the ability for exchanges to be message-based and to comply with the ACID (Atomicity, Consistency, Isolation, Durability) model. When there is a transaction failure on an n-tiered network, those transactions can be rolled back. The ACID model describes the properties that a database transaction must maintain in order to be reliably processed as a well-defined single logical operation.

Three-tier systems are much easier to scale and provide much greater range for modular design and non-disruptive upgrades. The reason that this is true is that the middleware layer essentially decouples the client layer from the server layer. Should you require a major upgrade or change to the middleware layer, you can create this new system and change the references in the client and server software to point to the new middleware systems. Often it is possible and desirable to deploy multi-tier systems with different operating system platforms.

Thin Client/Server

The last of the network architectures that you will consider are client-server and server-client architectures based on *thin clients*. A thin client can be a terminal with networking and display subsystems but with little processing power. Thin clients can also be computers or portable devices running a lighter-weight operating system such as a stripped-down form of Linux, an embedded Real-Time Operating System (RTOS), or Windows CE. They can also be fully enabled computers running client software. Thin clients are thin because most of the processing is being done on a "server"; the thin client serves to provide input and display.

I've placed the term "server" in quotes because there are two different types of client-server networks in use; they both do more or less the same thing. X-windows calls the application running on the client the server and refers to the server or provider of the data as the client. X-windows runs graphical applications on workstations with the workstation being responsible for display and the server being responsible for processing everything else.

The second type of thin client/server is essentially the same thing, but reverses the naming convention. In Windows Terminal Server, for example, the thin client is the workstation that displays the application on its monitor, and the server is the system that does all of the processing. A Windows terminal is taking graphics information that was processed on the server and rendering that information. The key point is that a thin client/server has the workstation as the client, whereas in X-windows, the workstation is considered to be the server because that is the system that is initiating the commands (as is also the case for the client in a thin client/server system).

Terminal servers

A terminal server is an example of a thin client network where the server runs processes for multiple connected clients. The best-known examples of this centralized computing model are Windows Terminal Server (a service of Windows Server 2008/3) and Citrix XenApp (formerly Citrix MetaFrame (www.citrix.com/English/ps2/products/product.asp?contentID=186). In these network systems, the server's memory is partitioned and instances of the unique portions of the desktop operating system are run on the server inside each partition. The parts of the operating system that are common to all running instances are runs in a shared memory space, which is why a server can run many terminal sessions at the same time.

When a thin client logs into the server using a special display transfer protocol such as Microsoft's Remote Desktop Protocol (RDP) or Citrix's Independent Computing Architecture (ICA), in both cases the display of the desktop running on the server is sent over the wire in compressed form to the thin client. Applications and services can be run in the client instances on the server, and the results appear as they are calculated and transferred with little data actually being exchanged.

The nature of terminal server technology means that a powerful server with enough memory can run many desktops on a single system, or that a server farm can be employed to distribute the processing load as needed. Because the server is under administrative control and the desktops closely constrained by system policy, the user has little opportunity to modify the software or alter the hardware in ways that would be problematical. Indeed, many thin clients are sold as diskless systems.

X Window networks

The second type of thin client solution is the X Window System, which is based on the X11 network protocol. In an X Window system, the server is the application on the thin client (X terminal) that provides access to the system on which processing is occurring using the X display protocol. X Window calls the processing system the *client*. The oldest versions of X Window ran on UNIX and DEC OpenVMS, but modern versions of X Window can be downloaded for any desktop operating system you can name.

Note

For information on X Window products go to: www.x.org, http://xwinman.org/, and http://en.wikipedia.org/wiki/X-windows.

The X Window System server opens a graphic user interface such as GNOME or KDE on Linux in the window. X Window is particularly useful when you want to run a process on a computer with a different operating system from another system on the network. X Window's applications are transparent over the network; what you see on the desktop (the display server) is running as an application on the client. X Window is a client-server technology, just as terminal servers are. However, here the server is the system giving the orders (user commands) and the client is the application. X Window considers that it is the application that is using the display services of the thin client as its server. Although the names applied are direct opposites, the underlying network architecture is the same.

X Window has a long history behind it and many unique features. If you are working on a heterogeneous network, it might be a technology you want to look at.

Summary

This chapter presented a number of general network design principles imposed by different network devices. Among the topics described was how topology can relate to the type of network architecture. The difference between a topology and an architecture was considered.

Point-to-point connections are considered physical connections, virtual connections, transient connections, and links where there is no defined (unique) connection. When nodes share a physical medium, they are a segment. Segments define collision domains. Collections of segments are separated by connection points such as switches or routers. Different routing types, as well as switched and packet networks, were discussed.

In this chapter, you learned about peer-to-peer, client-server, multi-tier, and thin/client server architectures.

In the next chapter, you will learn about different methods for network discovery and how you can use them to map out a network and the resources that it contains.

Network Discovery and Mapping

N etwork discovery is the way systems and devices are located on a network. There are various mechanisms that are used to enumerate devices, including node advertisement or broadcasting, browse lists, polling, and direct connections. Many times, combinations of these approaches are used. These different approaches are protocol independent, although many protocols are developed with a particular method of discovery in mind.

Network discovery uses a separate set of processes and protocols from name resolution. In order to be useful, both must work properly on a network. The methods used to look up names on a network are described. They include checking the HOSTS file; doing a DNS lookup; checking the NetBIOS name cache, WINS servers, and ARP broadcasts; and checking the LMHOSTS file.

A network connection is a defined path with two endpoints. Different types of network connections can be defined. Paths (or circuits) and endpoints can be either physical or virtual devices. A private circuit or channel can also be defined that is the basis for virtual private networks. Connections can be either stateful or stateless. A *stateful* connection retains the definition of a connection during and sometimes between sessions. *Stateless* connections are used when the path isn't defined.

Simple Network Management Protocol, or SNMP, is the Internet Protocol used to provide rich information about managed network devices. It works with local agents on managed nodes and stores data in a database with a standard structure. SNMP can be used to map networks and to send commands to and change the configuration of systems and devices.

Mapping is a process by which discovered network elements are graphically displayed in relationship to one another. Discovery creates a populated database of network objects: devices that are endpoints, wires that are network paths, and other elements. Discovery then establishes how different objects are connected. Mapping relies on the discovery process to establish the current condition of the network. Because networks change and different objects may appear or disappear over time, the state of any network map is often necessarily incomplete.

Network Discovery

Network discovery is a set of processes by which one system or device finds other network systems and devices. Discovery can take the form of advertising network elements using a broadcast message, by collecting and distributing a list of network elements through browsing, by polling which uses a broadcast request/response mechanism, and also by directly communicating between different nodes or systems. All of these mechanisms are used, and each mechanism has different characteristics that make it useful in different circumstances.

Network devices advertise themselves as being attached to the network, or when asked by another device to respond to a discovery request, as shown in Figure 4.1.

The simplest form of network discovery is through a broadcast message that advertises the availability of a network element. In this scenario shown in Figure 4.1, node A initiates a broadcast after initializing its network interface. The workstation labeled A in the figure appears on the network and sends out a short message indicating that the system is now up and giving the system's interface address. Systems that receive the broadcast from node A add that node to their network list.

An example of a protocol that uses network advertisement would be the Bootstrap Protocol (BOOTP), where an advertisement is sent to obtain a dynamic IP address. In a broadcast advertisement system, the message indicating the system's availability is added to routing tables on a router, and to individual systems. Broadcast advertisement is a reasonable mechanism for obtaining information from a single system, such as a DHCP server, on small networks and for workgroups; but on medium and large networks, a broadcast mechanism is a very inefficient method for network discovery.

Because assigned friendly names change over time, broadcasts do not usually provide a system's friendly name. Networks rely on name resolution services to translate a network address into a friendly name. Examples of name resolution services are the Domain Naming Service (DNS), NetBEUI, NFS, and others.

Network discovery is most often the result of an Application layer event, such as opening a Network folder or a Get (Open) or Put (Save) dialog box that requires the network be displayed. What happens next is a function of the particular applications, the protocols in use, and the operating system.

FIGURE 4.1

Network discovery using a broadcast advertisement mechanism

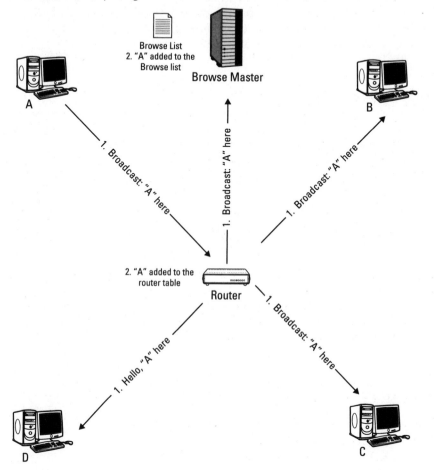

A more efficient mechanism is to create a list of network elements that is dynamically updated. That list is often called a *Browse list* because when a system initiates a network discovery, the list is used to populate the network in the application. The system that manages the Browse list is called the *Browse Master*, and different NOSs and protocols handle this process in different ways. In workgroups, the Browse master is based on an election; in domains, the Browse master may be a domain server. In any event, a browse operation finds the Browse Master and requests the Browse list in order to store a local copy. Browse lists usually have an expiration period after which a system will attempt to refresh its local copy. A browse mechanism will sometimes be missing systems that have appeared on the network recently or show systems that are unavailable, but the mechanism has the advantage of greatly reducing network traffic compared to a broadcast mechanism and is a fast process.

Figure 4.2 shows a browse operation. A network window is opened on B which causes a browse request to be issued. That request finds the Browse Master, which returns the current Browse list. The Browse list is then used to populate the network window. Notice that nodes A, C, and D do not need to be involved in a Browse operation.

FIGURE 4.2

Network discovery using a browse mechanism

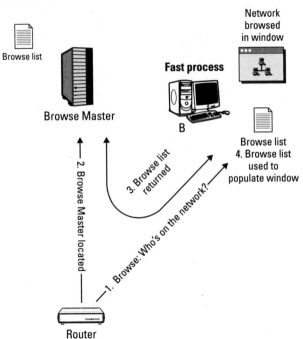

Another broadcast mechanism is called *polling*. In polling, as shown in Figure 4.3, a node broadcasts a message requesting that other network elements respond and make themselves known. As responses come back, the responses of the network elements are used to populate the network list. A common use of a polling mechanism is in the area of router discovery where a router builds it routing table or Routing Information Base (RIB) through this mechanism. Polling has all of the disadvantages of any broadcast mechanism and is a slow process.

FIGURE 4.3

Network discovery using polling or direct communication mechanisms

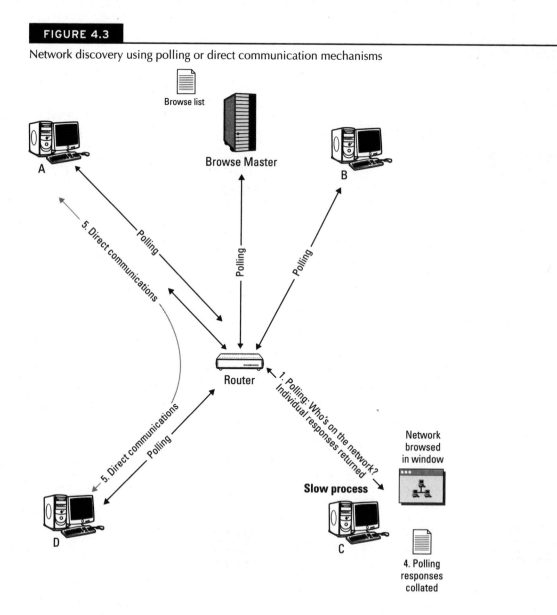

The last of the discovery mechanism involves enumeration of network elements through direct communication. If a node maintains a list of network elements, it can use a direct communication to talk with nodes that it knows about and get those nodes to tell it about nodes that they know about, and so on. A direct communication method coupled with polling is the preferred method for discovery in routers today.

Network discovery is ubiquitous, and it's built into all networked devices at a fundamental level. Network Interface Cards (Network Adapters or NICs), routers, switches, and even printers all store what is called a Media Access Control (MAC) address in their firmware. A MAC address is unique and is assigned by the manufacturer during the manufacturing process. Two identical MAC addresses represent a fundamental network error.

Caution

Although MAC addresses are unique, they can be spoofed. Spoofing incorrectly identifies the MAC address in communicated data and is an attempt to disguise the true origin of the sender. MAC addresses can sometimes be changed in software.

Notice that so far, I've made no mention of any particular technology used to implement the processes described in this list. Most books tell you that some networks use the Small Message Block, or SMB, protocol for browsing, or that they use NetBIOS over TCP/IP (NBT) for name resolution, or that they use the Address Resolution Protocol (ARP) to broadcast over IP networks; and, indeed, later chapters in this book will say the same thing. You might not remember those TLAs (three-letter acronyms), but chances are you can remember the general principles in this chapter. As a group, discovery technologies tend to be treated in a fragmented manner by many networking books, often as almost an afterthought. However, network discovery is fundamental to every modern network's function and needs to be grasped on a conceptual level.

It's important to understand that while there are many different network protocols in use for the network discovery functions just described, it is the functionality that drives the protocols and not the other way around. All modern network operating software, management software, and just about any application or utility you use relies on discovery to perform the services and functions that the software provides. You can't open a GET (Open command) or a PUT (Save or Save As command) operating system dialog box that involves an external device without initiating a discovery operation.

Some discovery services can be very rich, indeed. A rich discovery service not only advertises the existence of devices, but it also passes a set of attributes from the responding device. Rich discovery services give, at a minimum, the device status and may contain a listing of hundreds of attributes that you can query, or these services may provide a command and control function that can reconfigure devices. Some discovery services can automatically map networks — even complex networks with tens of thousands of network nodes — which is an amazing process to behold. Mapping is used for asset management, network optimization, and a truly varied range of capabilities that make modern networks practicable.

The most widely used rich discovery method is the Simple Network Management Protocol (SNMP), which is described in more detail later in this chapter. The Windows Management

Interface (WMI) is another technology that extends the Windows driver model to provide device characteristics on Windows networks. Both store device information in a database format: a Management Information Base (MIB) file for SNMP devices, and a Common Information Model (CIM) repository. A technology called Web-Based Enterprise Management (WBEM), and pronounced "Web-em," is related to CIM and is yet another systems management function that is briefly mentioned later in this chapter. All these technologies are based on the Common Information Model.

Network management systems rely on these technologies for their operation. Any device that can be managed in network software is discoverable; the denial of discovery is the basis for many security devices such as firewalls. Network management tools can make difficult tasks easy, such as automatically deploying an operating system to many systems on a network, or complying with Byzantine licensing regulations scattered over a diverse collection of hardware.

Node advertisement

In node advertisement, a system or device wants to establish that it is available to provide a service, and so it broadcasts its availability, as shown in Figure 4.1. Some broadcast methods request a response when they reach their target system, or when the first located system that meets the criteria of the broadcast replies. In this section, you learn about some of these broadcast discovery protocols.

There are four common broadcast services that use this type of approach on current networks:

- Dynamic Host Configuration Protocol (DHCP)
- Bootstrap Protocol (BOOTP)
- Routing table updates
- Simple Network Management Protocol (SNMP)

Cross-Ref
Routing is described in Chapter 10, and ARP is cov ered in Chapter 19.

DHCP is the method used for dynamic IP assignments on networks. DHCP is a required broadcast service because it needs to be found by any system that requires a dynamic address assignment, when that system requests a dynamic address. Similarly, the BOOTP protocol is used to advertise for systems that haven't yet loaded their operating systems and need to obtain an IP address from a pool that the BOOTP server maintains. The BOOTP protocol is used to push an operating system image down to a bare metal computer (one that has no software), or to boot a thin client that has no hard drive and runs its software on a terminal server.

All of the common routing protocols use a broadcast technology to update their routing tables on the network. These protocols include the following: the Routing Information Protocol (RIP), which is used in UNIX systems such as BSD (Berkeley Software Distribution) in the routed daemon; Open Shortest Path First (OSPF); the External Gateway Protocol (EGP); and the Border Gateway Protocol

(BGP). RIP is referred to as an Interior Gateway Protocol (IGP) and uses a distance vector routing algorithm for updates that time out after a certain number of seconds. OSPF is the most commonly used IGP on large networks. Of the two Exterior Gateway Protocols (EGP) used today on the Internet, the most commonly used is BGP, which uses a broadcast discovery technology.

Cross Ref

Routers are described more fully in Chapter 9.

SNMP is covered later in this chapter.

Browsing

When you open a Network folder to view connected systems, you are performing a browse operation. The fact that the result is so simple — items show up in the window — is the result of many different processes that are going on. It includes actions that have previously occurred, and actions that your system and the network take, based on your browse request. Figure 4.4 shows a browse sequence. The sequence for actions would start with the opening of a network window on system B. If a current Browse list is cached locally, then that is used to populate the Network window. If not, a Browser request may be made using a protocol such as NetBEUI to the Browse Master and the Browse list is obtained from that system.

FIGURE 4.4

A browse operation

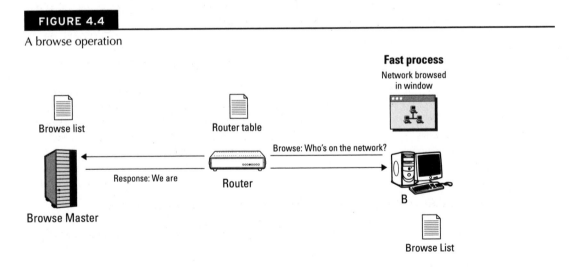

A network browse command can rely on the following preexisting network characteristics:

- Systems and devices that have already registered themselves on the network, are on the Browse list found on the Browse Master.
- The router maintains a router table containing other routers and known addresses.

- Systems and devices have announced their presence on the network to the Browse Master when they are polled, updating the lists.
- Clients that have previously queried the Browse Master may cache the list of machine names for later use.

Depending upon the system used, a browse list can take a long time to populate. The refresh interval is something that can often be modified, either as a Registry entry in Windows or as a preference in the Browse Master software, such as nmdb on a Samba server. A Browse Master is a network service running on a system that maintains a master list of network elements.

Different operating systems and software can replicate the Browse Master across a set of systems to improve performance, add fault tolerance, and work with different protocols. You may find that a browse system contains not only a Browse Master but also a Domain Master, Local Master, Preferred Master, or some other type of system list management server. The Browse Master does not need to be a domain server. In a workgroup, it can be any system. Some applications also have this capability; on a Samba file server, for example, you can elect to have that system be the Browse Master. A domain server is a system that maintains the security database for member systems of a network domain.

The browse command can initiate the following actions:

- Go to the local name cache to start the browse process, and partially populate the browse operation if the system has been started and is running for a while. Keep in mind that the browse list can take up to an hour to populate accurately.
- Go out to the Browse Master and obtain the browse list stored on that system.
- Send out a request for available systems (polling is discussed in the following section).

The discovery of network systems and devices is only half of the problem; many services and protocols must match a network address to an assigned or friendly name. When a system wants to communicate with another system or device, it requires a network address; only a few services can work with machine names directly. That address is determined as a lookup operation in a table maintained by a service that is queried as part of the name resolution process.

Cross-Ref

Chapter 19 covers the different technologies used to determine addresses on TCP/IP networks.

A lookup operation may include any of the following steps and is performed in the order listed below:

1. Look up the system name in the HOSTS file.
2. Perform a DNS lookup.
3. Check the NetBIOS name cache (on Windows). Note that NetBIOS over TCP/IP is being deprecated in favor of DNS.
4. Query the WINS server (on Windows), if one exists.

5. Perform an ARP broadcast name lookup over UDP.

6. Check the entries in the LMHOSTS (on Windows) file. LMHOSTS stands for the LAN Manager HOSTS file, and is the Windows version of the HOSTS file.

Polling

Polling is a much slower process than finding a list cached somewhere on the network and returning the list to build a network list. Polling is a slow process that requires clients' responses to build a browse list. Figure 4.3 shows an example of polling. Because of the overhead involved in polling, only the Address Resolution Protocol (ARP) is in common use. ARP provides a fallback protocol for name resolution when other methods fail. ARP is used on all types of networks, not just TCP/IP networks. You can use ARP on any LAN network — Token Ring, 802.11x wireless, or IP over ATM — to resolve IP addresses. ARP's major disadvantage is that it is a non-routable protocol. As a Link Layer protocol, ARP cannot be broadcast across a router; it applies to a single subnet.

Cross-Ref
DHCP is discussed in Chapter 18.

Connections

A network connection or *circuit* is a communication path between two endpoints. Network connections can have a variety of characteristics, some of which are universal and others which are dependent on the type of network in use.

An endpoint is an addressable entity that can send and receive network traffic. Endpoints are the network interface and not the systems or devices that the network interface resides in. To be even more specific, a NIC is simply an add-in card and a packaging device for an application-specific integrated circuit (ASIC), which is the integrated circuit that is part of the Physical and Data Link layers in the OSI model. To be precise, the endpoint of a network connection is defined by a set of software routines that can send and receive network traffic over the wire, with some portion of the interface defined by the physical implementation of digital signal processing required to turn data into signals that are transmitted.

The concept that an endpoint can be captured in software leads you naturally to a central concept in computer science, that of virtualization. Virtualization is where a system or device is emulated in software. It is possible to create a virtual endpoint or virtual interface in software whenever you need it. If you work in a virtual machine environment, and many systems create these types of emulated machines, then not only is the computer's operating system virtualized, but devices such as network interfaces are also virtual. Virtualization abstracts function from implementation, and appears in systems where emulation is required, in products like Virtual Server and VMWare, and in many other applications besides.

A path or circuit is the second part of a connection's definition. A path can be a dedicated physical circuit that can be traced from one endpoint to another over a wire that can be identified and is unchanging. Some networks work in this manner, mostly smaller networks where the number of connections is manageable. However, because network fan-out creates an exponential number of possible connections, most networks do not define persistent physical circuits because that would be prohibitively expensive. Instead, networks use a switching technology to create a transient circuit, depending upon network conditions. Transient circuits are created and then released after their use. They are contrasted to permanent circuits where the same path is used for an entire session, and not just for a data transfer. Network traffic is routed over a transient circuit, based on sophisticated routing algorithms that determine the shortest path, least congestion, highest-performing switch, fastest transmission medium, and whatever other factors the switch or router designers want to model.

Not all network connections are designed to be either persistent or transient. When designing a network that is inherently unreliable, different methods must be used. This is exactly the problem that the designers of the Internet were trying to solve. How do you create a highly fault-tolerant network when large portions of the network are disrupted? The solution to this problem was to use packet-switched networks, which send a stream of packets from one endpoint to another. A packet is a specially formatted segment of transmitted data. When you talk about network connections on a packet-switched network, you are describing a virtual circuit; the path is undefined or dynamically assigned and can change at any moment depending upon conditions. One packet in a stream may travel over one route, and the next may travel over another.

Virtual circuits can be created within a connection as a separate channel that carries only a certain type of data. This is the basis for Virtual Private Networks (VPNs), where secured traffic flows from one endpoint to another. To create a VPN, two applications must negotiate a set of connection parameters that define the behavior of the virtual circuit.

Cross-Ref
For more information on VPNs, see Chapter 29.

In describing connections, I have used the terms *persistent* and *transient* to indicate the path definition. The terms used in computer science for these two types of connections are *stateful* and *stateless*. A stateful connection is one in which the connection is defined between two endpoints for an entire session and can be invoked after the session is complete to recreate the original connection. A stateful connection also stores attributes of the connection that will be reestablished. The term stateful is also applied to any process that takes the nature of the contents of communications into account. A firewall performs stateful inspection when it examines not only the headers of packets but also the contents.

Figure 4.5 illustrates the different types of circuits in a graphic form. The endpoints are the circles at the end of the lines, which represent connections or paths. A solid line or circle indicates that the network element is persistent; an empty circle or dotted line indicates that the network element is transient. In the bottom case (private connection), the small solid line is contained within an empty larger line, indicating that the connection is not only transient, but secure.

Figure 4.5 shows five different types of network connections that can be defined.

FIGURE 4.5

Five different types of network connections

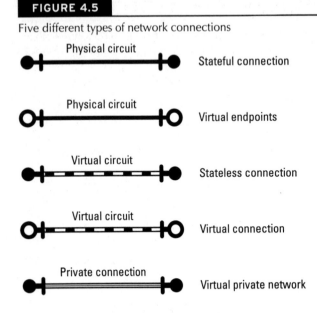

Physical circuit — Stateful connection

Physical circuit — Virtual endpoints

Virtual circuit — Stateless connection

Virtual circuit — Virtual connection

Private connection — Virtual private network

In comparison, stateless connections are those in which the path used is indeterminate and only the endpoints are known and the connection is transient. No details of the connection are retained or managed. An example of a stateless connection is communications using the HTTP protocol over a TCP/IP network. As previously mentioned, packets can travel by any convenient route between the two endpoints. A measure of "statefulness" can be applied to stateless connections without changing the classification of the connection type by recording transient information in a manner that allows the information to be retrieved later. That is exactly what Web sites do when they put a cookie on a computer; it stores information about the user, prior sessions, and other details.

Connections are named objects in all network operating systems and are programmatically accessible in any of the object-oriented programming languages in current use. Network objects have a number of attributes that describe them and that are important in understanding how connections function. Those attributes include the state of the connection, the protocols in use, and other factors. Another defined object related to connections is that of a *session*. A session is a defined period during which a network connection is engaged in a communication of a defined type. For some system functions, the session may be defined as the entire time that a network interface is up and running, sending and receiving traffic. Applications use the concept of a session to set rules such as the allowed bandwidth, the Time to Live (TTL) parameter that packets have, and others. The attributes of connections and sessions allow two systems and devices to negotiate the connection properties.

Simple Network Management Protocol

As networks became more complex historically, the need to discover, manage, and control devices on the network became an important concern. The Simple Network Management Protocol (SNMP) was developed within the framework of the Internet Engineering Task Force (IETF) to provide a means to address these needs. SNMP is an Application layer (Layer 7) protocol that has become the most widely used method for managing network systems.

SNMP has five built-in elements that are part of networked devices:

- **SNMP protocol.** Used to communicate between devices and SNMP-enabled software over TCP/IP networks.

- **Managed objects.** Respondent devices such as Network Interface Cards (NICs), routers, switches, printers, and a panoply of other devices.

- **Agents.** A small software module that is resident (running) on a managed object. It collects data from the object and from network traffic and makes it available to SNMP queries.

- **Management Information Bases (MIBs).** MIBs comprise an object database that stores information about managed objects. Many, if not most, data objects used by SNMP devices are READ-only (the Device Model, for example). Other data objects are READ/WRITE (the Device Name, perhaps) and are therefore variables that are used to manage objects.

- **Management console.** Where data queries are collected using SNMP-enabled software.

SNMP software can communicate with these elements to develop a picture of the network, create an inventory of the device's state or functions, and receive and react to those events. The model used by SNMP is used by other vendors as the model for their own management systems. The Windows Management Interface (WMI) from Microsoft, which is discussed later in this chapter, is one example of a proprietary SNMP implementation.

SNMP network management uses SNMP commands to send and retrieve data collected from the SNMP agents on managed nodes. Figure 4.6 shows how SNMP discovery and management works. A management console collects SNMP responses and stores and displays the information to users. The console can also be used to send SNMP commands that modify device settings. A managed node, labeled as a circled N in the figure, is one that can accept and act on SNMP commands. The circled A represents SNMP agents, which are small software programs that can send and receive SNMP information. SNMP has very broad product support.

Figure 4.6 shows how these different SNMP elements interact with one another.

Control console management software sends and receives SNMP commands from other devices on the network. Console management software is an application that can store device information, display it to a user, and change device settings through user commands. Devices that can initiate and respond to SNMP commands are referred to as a *party*, a name that is formalized within the SNMP version 2 definition. A party is a single identity that has a unique network location. Each party in an SNMP communication has an authentication and privacy protocol that it uses to establish a secure link with other parties. Devices that are SNMP-enabled (entities) may contain multiple parties within them, provided that each is unique. An example of an entity would be a router, where each individual port of the router would be a party. A router can be managed down to each individual port level.

FIGURE 4.6

SNMP network discovery and management

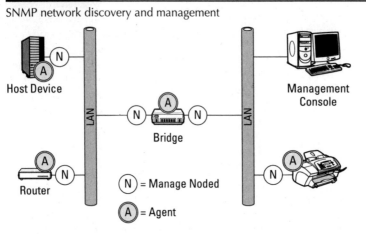

Network management software works by installing small software modules called *agents* on managed devices. Usually the software is installed with deep hooks into the operating system so that the agents are difficult to remove. Agents can also be installed by a vendor as part of the hardware on any device that can be managed, but not all vendors go to the expense or trouble to incorporate SNMP agent software. There is a range of software that can discover, manage, or map network devices using SNMP, including the following: shareware applications that you can download for free from sites like Download.com or Tucows.com; commercial packages such as WhatsUp Gold (www.whatsupgold.com) from Ipswitch; and many of the components of the large network framework management systems, including LANtastic, HP OpenView, IBM Tivoli, CA NSM (formerly Unicenter), Altiris, ZENworks, and many others.

SNMP is a broadcast technology that operates at the upper layer of the network model, the Application layer or Layer 7. Software can send out a request or query to any party that can listen for it, and to which another party can respond. SNMP uses a small command set that should be very familiar to anyone with knowledge of how the HTML protocol works. Commands used by SNMP, such as GETs, are used to communicate with specific agents on managed devices. Variants of these commands, such as GETBULK or GETNEXT, can be used to communicate with multiple devices. Agents also advertise their availability by sending out INFORM or TRAP commands that can be collected by management systems. Any data object that is writable can be changed using a SET command.

The Management Information Bases (MIBs) collect data on a managed node or system. The data that an MIB contains is defined by the device type but is extensible. SNMP makes no demands on the type of information stored on a device, or which device attribute can be a variable. What SNMP specifies is the manner in which information is stored in the MIB files, and the manner in which the information is exposed.

SNMP devices can change states at any time, and so the model requires that a device can advertise a change of state without waiting to be polled on its state. The MIB module on the device stores events that occur and then advertises these events by issuing what is called an SNMP trap for that event. Listening devices can intercept the trap and then request the details if required. SNMP is traveling over packet-switched networks such as TCP/IP, and so a management console can't assume that it has received all of the available traps that have been issued. Therefore, SNMP management software will, at an interval defined in the software, poll each managed device to update its status. Trap-directed polling requests that specific devices update their status, and because both parties in the communication are known, the traps are reliably received and updated. When an important trap is received, the interval between status updates is changed so that updates from the device are done more frequently.

In SNMP, MIB files are organized into a hierarchical namespace, an upside-down tree structure where each node is an object identifier, or OID. Individual OIDs may be READ, SET, or both. The ISO's Open Systems Interconnection (OSI) Abstract Syntax Notation (ASN.1) standard defines the syntax by which a MIB file is queried, and is something that is platform independent, using a set of rules that describe the MIB file called the Structure of Management Information (SMI). You can examine the structure and contents of an MIB file using any number of SNMP-enabled utilities.

Shown in Figure 4.7 is OidView Professional (www.oidview.com), one of the many SNMP utilities that are available to view MIB files, their structure, and the data that they contain. OidView performs SNMP analysis and presents the data in an MIB Browser. Different panes can display a searchable and navigable data tree, data analysis, graphs and traces, captured SNMP traps, and different MIBs from the different SNMP agents located on the network.

The Structure of Management Information (SMI; http://en.wikipedia.org/wiki/Structure_of_ Management_Information) is information collected as text files onto which a structure or schema is imposed. What SMI means in practical terms is that if you are using a management console to perform network discovery for devices, then it doesn't matter if the devices you are polling are on the Ethernet network of the management console or on a network of some other kind. Nor does it matter what operating system you are using or what the device is. The information is simple text, and to use it the management console need only be able to parse the information correctly, something that is very easy to achieve.

Storage networking is a type of heterogeneous networking where storage data is segregated onto a separate network connected with Fibre Channel, while hosts and clients are on a separate Ethernet network. A heterogeneous network is one that supports multiple NOSs on the same network. The two networks are connected through one or more switches so that each network can communicate with devices on each side, and so that storage traffic is separated from data communications. Figure 4.8 shows this type of network.

FIGURE 4.7

OidView Professional is an SNMP management tool.

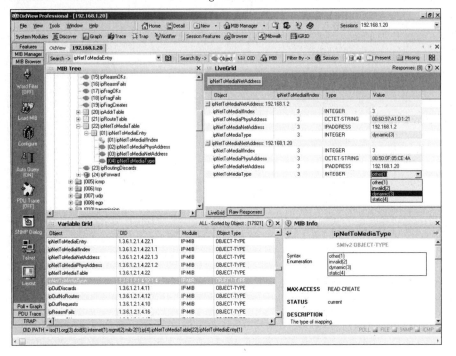

Cross-Ref

For more on storage networking, see Chapter 15.

If you place an SNMP management console on the Ethernet network, it doesn't matter whether the SNMP application software runs on a Windows or a Sun Solaris workstation or server because SMI is agnostic (it doesn't favor a particular NOS). The management console provides what is called out-of-band management for the devices on the Fibre Channel network, which is the in-band network. It is out-of-band because the TCP/IP traffic looks like a different stream from the Fibre Channel data. A management console running software such as StorageWorks from HP can discover both the devices on the Ethernet and storage network at the same time. Not only are switch ports discoverable, but so are Host Bus Adapters (HBAs), as are the intelligent hard drives that are part of storage systems. HBAs are the network interfaces that storage devices connect to. Considering that some storage systems can contain literally hundreds of disk drives, the ability to discover and address each individual disk drive enables very powerful network management tools, such as Storage Resource Management packages, that can reconfigure volumes on the fly. That is the power that SNMP provides to intelligent network software.

FIGURE 4.8

A Fibre Channel Storage Area Network (SAN) attached to a LAN

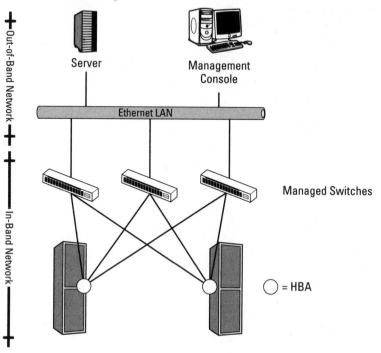

Windows Management Instrumentation

Windows Management Instrumentation (WMI) is a Microsoft extension of the Common Information Model (CIM) as exposed through the Web-Based Enterprise Management (WBEM) network management system. WMI creates a repository of data from managed objects and makes this information available to management software through an API, which is an extension of the Windows Driver Model (WDM). WMI is the interface by which the data repository can be queried, and through which commands and configuration settings can be passed to managed network devices on Windows networks. WMI commands can be applied inside a VBScript or Windows PowerShell script, or they can be entered as a command line.

WMI provides a rich management system that can control a large number of devices and give a detailed description of their current states, but WMI is Windows-specific technology.

WMI's enterprise management framework can take existing data from SNMP-managed nodes and agents and from any data source that works under the Desktop Management Interface (DMI) standard and make the data available to management software under a uniform access model. A number of Microsoft Office applications, servers, and even the Microsoft Internet Explorer extend the CIM mode to add their information to the CIM data repository that WMI manages as a WMI class with associated properties. WMI's repository has its own namespace and its own query language, which is called the WMI Query Language (WQL). The overall CIM repository contains the namespaces for the Active Directory (RootDirectoryDAP), for SNMP (RootSNMP), and for the Internet Information Services (RootMicrosoftIISv2).

Here are some of the many things you can do with WMI:

- Start or stop a process on a network system
- Restart a remote computer
- Compile a list of installed applications on a networked system
- Have a process run at a specified time
- Query the Windows event logs on a networked system

Microsoft exposes WMI in the form of a set of providers. As of Windows Server 2008 and Vista, there are around 100 providers that have been published. In addition to the scripting tools previously mentioned, a wide variety of management software can be WMI consumers, including Microsoft System Center Operations Manager, HP OpenView, BMC Software Distributed Systems Management, and others. WMI provides not only an automation interface, but also a .NET management interface, and for older applications, a COM/DCOM interface. Providers can access WMI remotely with DCOM and SOAP and can consume WMI events.

Mapping

Network mapping is the automated discovery of systems and the connections between them. Different mapping software packages use different techniques to map a network, but one common technique is to start with each subnet that the software knows about and then PING each of the possible network addresses to see which nodes respond. This process enumerates any device that is currently active on the network and is an active discovery method. You can do this kind of mapping using a utility such as nmap on Linux, Microsoft Windows, Solaris, and BSD, and Mac OS X. nmap (www.nmap.org) runs as a command line utility, but there are several graphical front ends such as Zenmap (http://nmap.org/zenmap/), which is shown in Figure 4.9.

There will be nodes on the network that may be unavailable at a particular time, and so an active method won't find devices that aren't active. Nor will it find any nodes that aren't on subnets that the mapping software's system knows about. To find more nodes, various passive exploration methods must be used.

FIGURE 4.9

A Zenmap network scan

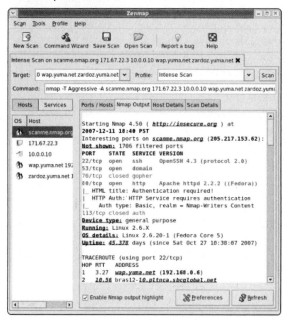

The problem with active network discovery tools is that many operating systems now come with personal firewalls that block their discovery and prevent their detection. If the system is a laptop, then that system won't always be available for discovery, and so any software that intends to build an accurate network map needs to use both active and passive methods to have any chance of building a complete map. Passive exploration looks in places that store network addresses such as router tables and browse lists to extract endpoints from those sources. By contrast an active exploration would have to discover the devices themselves. Those tables provide information on how to discover the entire network, and they extend the discovery process to the additional subnets, within the number of hops from the network's routers that the system wishes to explore.

There are several different techniques used to map networks:

- Active identification of the different points of attachment that devices have on a network.

- Examining packet routing through the mining of routing tables.

- Payload inspection to determine the sending system, as well as any intermediate locations that have added addressing to the packets.

- Mining the data in available Authentication, Authorization, and Accounting (AAA) servers. AAA servers include dial-in, RADIUS, and other remote access servers.

- Network access credentials. By examining user and machine logins, additional mapping can be accomplished.

Many software packages can map networks and include the following: SNMPWalk, Cheops, SNMPutil, WhatsUp Gold, and PacketTrap.

The purpose of network discovery is to map the network; determine what systems, devices, and software are on the network; and improve the network health and security. Network discovery can find unknown systems as well as determine methods for discovering systems on the network that aren't meant to be discovered.

A network map is able to accumulate all kinds of data. When a system is profiled, it is possible to determine which processor the system has (type and ID), what version of the operating system it has (type and install ID), when it was last patched or upgraded, the specific hard drive (type and ID), and so on, in great detail. This information allows you to create an asset inventory of your entire network that you can use for any purpose. Organizations that have network management systems in place with asset management modules, systems such as LANtastic or Altiris, can produce detailed reports of the nature and location of their assets, which can be invaluable in planning, deployment, and utilization.

Summary

In this chapter, you learned about different methods for network discovery and name resolution. These methods are independent of the protocols used, but often determine how protocols are constructed.

Connections are paths with defined endpoints. Different types of connections can be defined, a combination of physical and virtual paths and endpoints.

You learned about SNMP and how it is used to store device information and provide that information to other applications. SNMP can not only provide device information but it can also allow an application to send commands and change the configuration and state of devices. With SNMP, you can map networks and do deep asset analysis.

In the next chapter, you will learn about aspects of network performance related to bandwidth and throughput.

Bandwidth and Throughput

I nformation flows over a network as a series of signals. Those signals can represent either analog or digital data. Groups of signals are defined by various standards to represent different types of data. Some groups can be character sets, and some groups might be the various notes of a song or words in a conversation. It is up to various protocols to encode and decode the data, while other protocols are responsible for transporting and controlling the flow of the data. A collection of data represents information. The bandwidth of a network segment, its throughput, and its capacity are described.

Signals that carry data are transferred in the form of periodic waves. Any periodic function or complex waveform can be described by a Fourier transform, which is a mathematical operation that takes a complex waveform and transforms it into another set of simpler sinusoidal functions and coefficients. This analysis creates a set of terms called *harmonics* that perform curve fitting. This process is needed to store information and recreate it later.

A waveform can be recreated by sampling the wave and splitting it into small components. Sampling theory places a limit on the amount of sampling you can do and still obtain useful information.

Multiple streams of data can be sent over the same network connection using a technique called *multiplexing*. There are many different forms of multiplexing. Some use time division, others frequency division, and a few use polarization division to separate one data stream from another. Multiplexing must be supported by protocols and is responsible for one network type being different from another.

IN THIS CHAPTER

Learn how signals are used to send data

See how to store and recreate complex data

Learn how multiple data streams can share the same connection

Understand resource allocation and traffic control methods

Higher-level protocols are used to control the flow of traffic over a network. For IP networks, this is called *packet shaping*. Traffic control can look at data types, destination, and other factors and change the priority with which data is sent, limit the bandwidth, and perform other actions. The collection of technologies that assign network traffic to network resources is called *Quality of Service* (QoS).

Bandwidth and Capacity

Information is transmitted through a medium such as copper metal in an Ethernet wire by the flow of electrons past a point. The signal is carried by the manner in which the current, the voltage, the frequency, or the phase, or some combination thereof changes periodically with time. It is the variation in the amplitude and/or the frequency of the current that is most often used to turn a signal into data.

The signals that flow over a wire are analog signals, even when they encode for digital signals. A system can send a near perfect square wave for a 1-bit value, but noise, signal contention, and many other factors degrade the signal. The receiving system must measure the signals for their periodicity and for the range of values that the bit falls into to determine whether it represents 1 bit.

Computer networks can use different media to transmit data from point to point. Optical wires transmit light as the signal carrier, Bluetooth and Wi-Fi use radio frequency waves, WIMAX uses microwaves, and so on. The description of the signals is different, but the ideas of bandwidth, throughput, capacity, and other concepts described in this chapter are similar.

Beads flow through a pipe of syrup

The Zen master asks you to close your eyes, take a deep breath, and visualize, if you will, beads flowing through a pipe filled with syrup floating in front of you. (This is the networking equivalent of a Lava lamp.)

Every networked medium has limiting factors that place a ceiling on the bandwidth and capacity of the data flow. If you think of a network connection as a pipe that is filled with some medium (syrup, perhaps) through which some particle or wave flows (the beads), then you can measure the flow of the beads in several important ways that can be used to transmit data that can be interpreted as information. A bead doesn't have enough of a wavelength that it can be measured, but Heisenberg's uncertainty principle defines what that wavelength is.

The diameter of the pipe determines the maximum number of beads that can flow past any point at any one time: that is the bandwidth. The pressure of beads applied affects the speed of the beads up to some maximum level above which the technology that you push with can't go faster. The pressure corresponds to the potential energy you are applying; in a wire, pressure corresponds to voltage. The speed of the flowing beads past any given point gives rise to the observation of a flux, which is the amount of beads per unit time. The flux defines the throughput. The corresponding throughput in a wire is the current, which is the number of electrons that pass a point per unit of time.

Taken together, the maximum bandwidth and throughput represent the amount of beads that the pipe of syrup can carry, which is the capacity of the pipe. Some capacities are practical; the method used to apply pressure just can't go any higher. Other capacities are theoretical; the pipe bursts. Electrically that is equivalent to current flowing through a wire or a transistor creating a defect such as electromigration that destroys the wire or the junction of the transistor that forms a switch. Electromigration results in a hole in the wire as the metal itself moves with the current.

Because a collection of beads represents information, your data rate corresponds directly with the rate at which the beads flow. The rate of beads depends on the bandwidth of the pipe that feeds the flow. Speeds and feeds are fundamental performance metrics that you use to measure the efficiency of any data network.

These are simple concepts, but they apply to any network segment. The different factors determine what you can do on a network, how much data can be carried, when there is too much data for the medium to carry, and so on. There isn't enough room to cover all of the physics you need to know in relation to electricity, optics, and radiotelegraphy (radio messenger), but a simple example of signal theory can help you better appreciate the concepts that follow.

Signaling

Let's say that you have an electric current traveling down a wire over a certain period of time that you want to use to communicate with. The message is a short one: Save Our Ship, which is transmitted using the acronym S-O-S. You encode the message in Morse code, which means that it consists of three short signals for the letter S (dots) and three long signals for the letter O (dash).

Encoding a dot corresponds to a signal of 1 (On) for one time period. A dash is a signal of 1 (On) for two consecutive time periods. A signal that is On corresponds to an amplitude between a certain range of values, while an Off signal has an amplitude of between zero and the start of the On range. Figure 5.1 shows the digital SOS signal that you've just constructed. In the real world, signals aren't perfect square waves and there are certain variations in the shape of each signal that are tolerated.

Figure 5.1 is meant to illustrate some of the complexities of electrical signal. The signal is carried over the time domain, with a periodicity of 8 measured amplitudes (voltage) per cycle. If a time period has an amplitude in the 1 range, it is considered to be ON, and if the amplitude is in the 0 range, it is considered to be OFF. That is the reason why the first S looks different than the second S, but is interpreted as the same data.

FIGURE 5.1

An idealized SOS digital signal

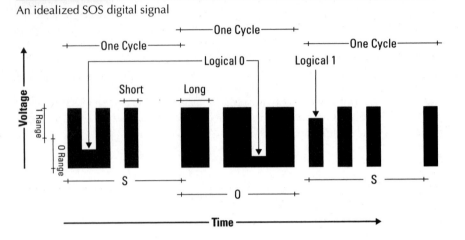

It's easy to represent our SOS as a pictograph, but what if you wanted to be able to mathematically describe the signal so that you could re-create it if you needed to. When Sir Isaac Newton wanted to calculate the area under a curve, he developed calculus to create rectangular slices that he could calculate. The finer the slice, the closer the calculated sum is to the real area. This analysis is called *integration*, and the mathematical representation used is an *integral*.

For a signal with an imposed periodicity (frequency), the problem is somewhat different. You still want to approach the problem by breaking the overall shape into smaller shapes that you can calculate, but here you need periodic time varying function(s) to do so. This is exactly the problem that Joseph Fourier faced when he tried to analyze heat flow. His solution was to break the signal into a large set of increasingly more precise trigonometric functions.

The process by which the signal is broken apart is called a *Fourier analysis*, the equations that describe the result are a *Fourier transform*, and the process by which the signal can be reconstructed is called *Fourier synthesis*. For data signals of the type you are considering here, the functions used are typically the sine and cosine functions.

The general form of a 2π periodic Fourier function is:

$$g(t) = \frac{1}{2}a0 + \sum_{n=1}^{\infty} a_n \cos(2\pi nft) + \sum_{n=1}^{\infty} b_n \sin(2\pi nft)$$

where the frequency f is 1/T, and an and bn are the amplitudes of the nth harmonics. A harmonic of a wave is the frequency of the signal divided by an integer so that the resulting function still retains the same periodicity. The equation above leads to a series of terms based on the value of n. The more terms used in a Fourier series, the closer the curve fits the signal that you are trying to represent. The equation above can be manipulated so that you can solve for the constants for each term you use: an, bn, and so forth individually, but the details are not important for this discussion.

The result of applying multiple harmonics to fit a square wave is shown in Figure 5.2. The square wave is f(t), and the other two curves approximate the square wave. The coarser curve is the fifth harmonic k = 5, and the finer curve is the fifteenth harmonic k = 15.

FIGURE 5.2

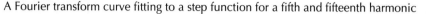

A Fourier transform curve fitting to a step function for a fifth and fifteenth harmonic

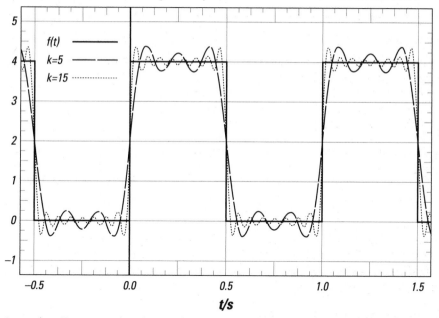

Source: http://commons.wikimedia.org/wiki/Image:Square_Wave_Fourier_Series.svg. This image is in the public domain.

Although the example shown is just one square wave, Fourier analysis can create a representation for a collection of square waves, ramps, or sawtooths, or any other time varying function. You can run a complex audio signal through a Fourier analysis and derive a formula that describes it, or apply Fourier analysis to a spectrum.

How does this all relate to our SOS signal? The frequency of the signal is the number of cycles per unit time that passes a point in time, that is, $f = 1/T$. A computer has no way to determine where one cycle begins and another cycle ends, but the computer does have a clock. Data is sent so that each character is represented by a standard bit length value, called a *byte*.

Last time I checked, computers weren't using Morse code; what they do use is one of many character sets based on published standards. One standard is 7-bit ASCII, which can vary by locale; another standard is Unicode. For American and British ASCII character sets, the bit pattern for an S is 1010011, while the bit pattern for an O is 1000011. If your computer communicates in 8-bit bytes, then the signal is padded with zeros so it reaches the required length. In 8-bit representation, S is 01010011 and O is 01000011 — note one zero is padded at the beginning of each 7-bit sequence to make them 8 bits. A Fourier series can define these bytes in the correct sequence. In Figure 5.2, the byte is 8 bits long, adding extra zeros to the S bits in order to bring them up to the length of the O byte.

A system that uses the amplitude of a signal to encode data is referred to as *amplitude modulation*. In the radio frequency world, AM is the basis for talk radio. Another method for encoding data is *frequency modulation*. Frequency modulation in the radio frequency world gives us FM and NPR. The third method used to encode data is called *phase modulation*. You use a change in the signal's phase to switch a signal on or off. The phase of a wave is the amount of a wave's offset from a reference time.

Figure 5.3 shows an example of these three different modulation techniques and how they are used to encode data by altering the carrier wave. The first figure for amplitude modulation shows a signal is contained in the amplitude of the wave. As you move left to right, the first maximum would represent a 1 or ON signal, and the minimum part of the wave on the right would be a 0 or OFF signal. As the wave moves off the right hand portion of the figure, it is rising, perhaps indicating that another 1 is next. However, the wave could just as well continue with the low amplitude signal. Amplitude measurements in an amplitude modulation scheme are measured at timed intervals.

The middle figure for frequency modulation shows a set of transitions which are from left to right: low frequency, high frequency, low frequency, and finally high frequency. As measured periodically this usually represents the pattern: 0, 1, 0, and 1.

Phase modulation is a little more subtle. In the bottom figure you see two transitions resulting in three different waveforms. The middle waveform is phase modulated, that is offset from the other two waveforms. The transitions of the phases encode the signals that are translated into data.

FIGURE 5.3

Amplitude, frequency, and phase modulation can all encode data.

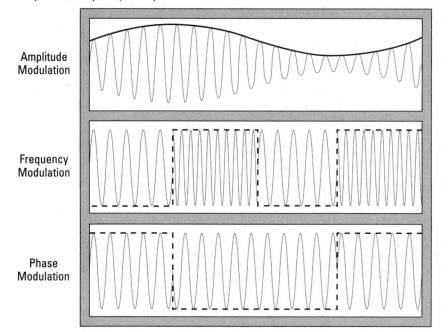

Bandwidth

Bandwidth is a term that can have one of several related meanings. In digital communications the bandwidth of any channel, connection, link, or pipe is the amount of data that may be transferred per unit time. This type of bandwidth measures capacity and is sometimes referred to as the available bandwidth. Bandwidth can also measure throughput, which is stated in terms of available bandwidth or capacity.

In terms of the discussion in this chapter, the bandwidth we are interested in describes the frequency range of signals that are allowed to pass over a circuit usually in terms of cycles per second or hertz. To limit bandwidth, filters may be applied; a low-pass filter limits the low frequencies, and baseband bandwidth is used to define the upper frequency limit.

The amplitude of a signal corresponds to the voltage, which is another way of describing the electrical "pressure" or potential energy at the point the voltage is measured. As the signal travels down the wire, the signal encounters resistance in the wire, and some of the potential energy is converted to kinetic energy. Heat is produced and the signal strength is degraded. This is one of the reasons why there are length limitations on different types of cables and technologies. Frequency has a direct relationship to energy. The physicist Max Planck found that the energy of a photon could be determined using the following formula:

```
E = h n
```

where h is Planck's constant and n, or Nu, is the frequency. The higher the frequency, the higher the energy. Planck's law doesn't apply to the energy of electrons in a wire, but the overall effect of energy loss is to diminish the highest-frequency waves first.

If you analyze signal loss, there is usually a frequency above which the signal drops off rapidly. This is called the *cutoff frequency*. You can also achieve a cutoff by introducing a low-pass filter in the circuit. Low-pass filters are used to limit the bandwidth of a circuit. A low-pass filter reduces noise in signals and allows higher frequencies to be boosted so that their signal-to-noise ratios are higher and it is easier to send a higher frequency of data over a circuit.

The impact of a filter that allows only very low frequencies to pass through it is that only the first harmonic term in the Fourier series may pass through the filter. If that is the case, then the signal is quite degraded and becomes unusable. As the filter limit is raised to higher frequencies, more terms in the Fourier series pass through the filter, and the signal more accurately represents the original signal. In Figure 5.4, raising the pass-through frequency would first let the k = 5 term through; raising it some more would let the k = 15 term contribute.

Noise, resistance, contention, and other factors always place a limit on the frequency of the signal that can pass through the wire. The rate of change per second is called the *baud rate*. In the examples you've seen so far, the amplitudes were normalized to a value of 1. However, if the voltage were high enough to represent intermediate values, then the baud rate would have to account for voltage changes as well. In a system where the signal is at a voltage that allows two logical values, 1 and 2, to be determined, each signal carries two bits worth of information and the baud rate is twice what it would be for a system of just 1 and 0.

Sampling theory

In the previous sections, you saw how you could take a digital signal and describe it in terms of periodic trigonometric functions, such as sinusoids. You also saw how the signal could encode data (ones and zeros) that could be used to convey information (SOS). The process of splitting up data into bits of information is called *sampling*, and the number of bits of information per unit time is the *sampling rate*.

The information contained within a single data point is a function of the bit space. Let's say that you have a signal that changes color in a periodic way and it is the color value that conveys information. The first system you build changes color from black to white through continuous shades of gray. Because the human mind can only differentiate around 1,000 shades of gray under ideal situations, you decide to store the color value at 256 different levels. That corresponds to an 8-bit data point.

The second system is a full-color system. To represent a color value in time, you might describe the color using the RGB (Red, Green, and Blue) color space. For each color, you choose a scale of 256 values, just as you did with the grayscale system. Now you have a bit depth that is 256 x 256 x 256 (28 x 28 x 28) or 224. This color space stores approximately 16.8 million color values. You could have used smaller or larger bit depths, and whether you did so would depend upon the purpose you intended to use the data for.

Sound or music can be sent over a wire and displayed as an analog signal in a waveform. You might ask the question: "How many data samples are required?" The answer again depends upon your intended purpose. For conversations over a telephone, a sampling rate of 8 kHz is sufficient. Higher-quality speech might be recorded at 11 kHz. For music, you might store a signal of lower quality such as AM radio at 22 kHz, while for CD quality, the sampling rate would be 44 kHz.

Now let's consider the sine wave shown in Figure 5.4. How many samples do you need to take in order to determine its frequency? If you sample at once a cycle, and then try to reconstruct the waveform, what you get is a constant value that defines a line. If you increase the sampling rate to 1.5 samples per cycle, you get a sine wave, but at a lower frequency than the sine wave you are trying to describe. At two samples per cycle, you are finally able to store the frequency rate. To better approximate the waveform, you need to sample at least twice the maximum frequency, but the more samples you take, the closer you are to recreating the original sine wave. At 16 samples per cycle, you are close to recreating the original sine wave.

Figure 5.4 shows that at twice the rate of the sine wave, you can store the information necessary to define the frequency. This rate is known as the *Nyquist rate*, and it comes from the 1924 work of Harry Nyquist. He found that you can have a signal with a bounded bandwidth B, and that the signal can be recreated by storing 2B samples per second, which is the *Nyquist frequency*. The original work was with a low-pass filtered signal over a noiseless channel. The reason why a higher sampling rate is oversampling and yields no additional information is because higher frequencies have already been eliminated when they were filtered out.

Nyquist's theorem for the relationship of the bandwidth B to the maximum sampling rate R is as follows:

```
Rs = 2Blog2 BL
```

where BL is the number of values that a bit can have. A voice signal of 262 Hz is C4 or Middle C and is considered the median note of a human voice. The Nyquist theorem calculated that a maximum sampling rate to store this note in digital form (BL = 2) would be 524 bits/s.

FIGURE 5.4

Sampling a sine curve and the Nyquist sampling rate

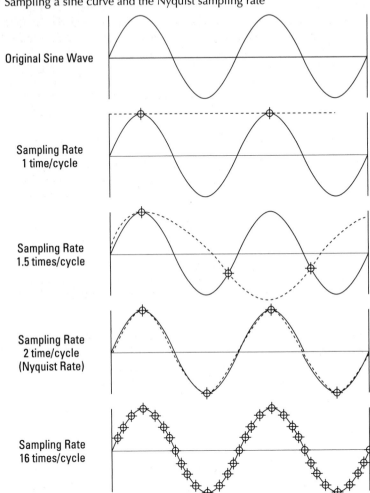

Original Sine Wave

Sampling Rate
1 time/cycle

Sampling Rate
1.5 times/cycle

Sampling Rate
2 time/cycle
(Nyquist Rate)

Sampling Rate
16 times/cycle

In 1948 Claude Shannon published a paper that provided a mathematical proof for Nyquist's theorem and went on to extend the concept by showing that you could reconstruct the original signal from 2B samples. Put another way, sending a signal with a baud rate of 2B is the inverse operation of sampling a signal with a frequency of 2B. The resulting theorem is now referred to as the *Nyquist-Shannon sampling theorem*, and Shannon's work is considered by many scholars as marking the beginning of the field of science known as information theory.

The sampling theorem applies to a noiseless channel. Most channels do suffer from noise and the noise introduces a certain degree of randomness to the data. The amount of noise in a signal is given by the ratio of the power of the signal to the noise, S/N. Because noise is often a minor component of the signal, it is common to quote the S/N ratio as a function of the common log, 10log10 S/N in units of decibels. An antenna that attenuates the noise of a receiver by 10 dB would reduce the noise in the signal by a factor of 10. A fine stereo cartridge that has a 75 dB S/N ratio would have a signal-to-noise ratio of 750 to 1.

Shannon went on to establish that you could calculate the maximum sampling rate for a noisy channel by substituting the term 1 + S/N into the Nyquist theorem for the bit level, as follows:

```
Rs = Blog2 (1 + S/N)
```

The effect of noise comes into play when you are trying to determine the maximum amount of information that a channel can transmit. Consider a channel with a low-pass filter that cuts off all frequencies at about 1000 Hz, and which is subject to Gaussian thermal noise. The S/N ratio is 20 dB; and S/N would be 200/1. Therefore, Rs is calculated to be:

```
Rs = 1000 log2 (1 + 200) = 1000 * 5.30 = 5300 bits/s
```

This calculation shows that the channel described can transmit signals at a maximum rate of 5300 bits/s, regardless of the sampling rate, under ideal conditions. An important realization is that the amount of information conveyed is much more sensitive to the frequency of the signal than it is to the quality of the signal (S/N).

Information theory goes on to relate the assignment of values to signals as a form of negative entropy. That is, a logical sequence of bits requires some energy to be in that state instead of being randomly assigned as it would in a thermal state. Therefore, any data claimed above the maximum Shannon sampling rate would be akin to creating energy. As interesting as this idea might be, the point is that this theory establishes a theoretical maximum data rate for any channel.

Multiplexing

The process by which a transmission medium can be made to carry two or more signals or data streams is called *multiplexing*. Conceptually, a multiplexed transmission is carried over a channel, and the path a channel takes from one point to another describes a circuit. Because a wire, fiber, or radio link is a physical connection that is described as a physical circuit, data channels are often referred to as *virtual circuits*.

Multiplexing requires a device called a *multiplexer* (MUX) that is capable of both separating and combining multiple signals or data streams into individual channels. The multiplexer device is actually a combination of a multiplexer that takes multiple inputs and combines them, and a demultiplexer (DEMUX) that separates the signals into components and sends each signal down the appropriate output.

Previously you learned that there are three different methods used to modulate carrier waves so that they encode data: amplitude modulation, frequency modulation, and phase modulation. Similarly, multiplexers perform time, frequency, or phase division (partitioning) of analog and digital data. These classifications separate one set of computer protocols from another, and one type of computer network from another, in the same way that Linnaean taxonomy allows biologists to separate the tree of life into a hierarchy of domains, then kingdoms, phyla or divisions, families, genera, and species.

Time Division Multiplexing

Time-based multiplexing is referred to as *Time Division Multiplexing* (TDM) and uses time slicing to separate data streams. When different transmitters share the same TDM network, the technology is referred to as *Time Division Multiple Access* (TDMA).

TDM sequences analog data using a device called a *codec*, which samples the data into a stream. At the receiving end, a codec reassembles the data from the slices. You are probably familiar with codecs, as they are used to digitize voice, music, and video, another example of this technology. This kind of sampling is referred to as *Pulsed Code Modulation* (PCM). Other techniques, such as *Pulsed Amplitude Modulation* (PAM), *Pulsed Width Modulation* (PWM), and *Pulsed Position Modulation* (PPM), are used less frequently than PCM to perform digital modulation.

TDM uses different techniques to sequence digital data. The system used on T- and E-carrier lines multiplexes a set of channels together, whereas TDM transmits the multiplexed channels as one large frame consisting of multiple channels (25 for T-1) every 125 msec. There are different standards for TDM frame sequences that add control bits either to the end of the channels (*common channel signaling*) or to the end of the frames (*channel associated signaling*). Channel signaling uses the same time slicing technique shown in Figure 5.5 for TDM, but instead of sending a sequence of channels, it sends a sequence of frames.

Cross-Ref
T- and E-carrier lines are discussed in Chapter 13.

There are many different methods used to compress digital data that is being time multiplexed; some are industry standards, and others are proprietary. One common technique for compression is called *differential pulsed code modulation*. This technique evaluates the amplitude of time slices and determines the difference or delta value between that time slice and the next time slice. The codec sends a data stream consisting of the delta values only. You get data compression because the delta is assumed to never go beyond a certain value. When the sound does vary widely between time slices, the compression scheme uses the next time slices to bring the levels in line with the original waveform.

For example, in a system that stores 256 sound levels, which is 28, you might decide that the levels never change more than 8 levels in any one time slice. Instead of encoding an 8-bit signal, this system would allow you to send only 7 bits of information per slice.

The technique called *delta modulation* stores only step changes of 1 in the value as a single bit. Delta modulation requires a very fast sampling rate in order to accurately describe the original waveform. Other more advanced compression schemes use algorithms to do predictive encoding. You can more aggressively compact signals, but there is a cost in data quality or more overhead to process data more quickly.

Frequency Division Multiplexing

Frequency-based multiplexing uses signal modulation to separate one signal from another; and is referred to as *Frequency Division Multiplexing* (FDM). When a single channel is shared between users using FDM the technology is referred to as Frequency Division Multiple Access. FDMA is used to keep radio signals coming from different transmitters apart, and because cellular telephone networks are designed to have overlapping ranges FDMA finds use in cellular networks.

FDM multiplexing can send either analog or digital data, but as a general rule, it is easier to send digital data over TDM circuits and it is easier to send analog data over FDM circuits. FDM networks are found in wired networks and in microwave technologies. FDM is used on all sorts of wired media, but when frequency modulation is used on fiber-optic lines it is called Wavelength Division Multiplexing (WDM), although they are essentially the same idea. TDM multiplexing is really only practical for carrying digital data.

Figure 5.5 shows a simple example of TDM and FDM. The channels are indicated by the numbers in the boxes. In TDM, channels pass by oscillating between channel 1 and channel 2. The overall data stream is fully utilized, and consists of consecutive packets filling the channels during each time slice. In FDM, the channels are separated into four separate frequency channels and data is alternately sent over each of them.

In FDM although there are guard bands between each of the frequencies in the figure, in real life, many transmission schemes crowd channels together so that they overlap a little. There can also be overlap due to the fact that band filters usually create a sharp edge on a channel. The guard bands are represented by the blank spaces between each of the four frequency channels.

Tip
In FDM, a group is usually considered to be a 4000 Hz band that includes 500 Hz blank guard bands at the start and end of the group. This corresponds to the bandwidth required to carry voice data. A set of five groups is a supergroup, and a mastergroup is either five or ten supergroups.

A comparison of Time Division Multiplexing versus Frequency Division Multiplexing

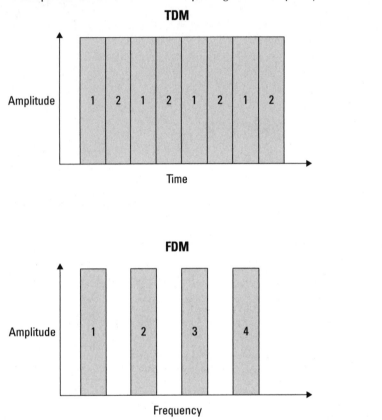

Other multiplexing technologies

Because wavelength and frequency are fundamentally related by the speed of light, you might think that FDM would also be used in optical networks. However, for historical reasons, optical networks refer to frequency multiplexing as *Wavelength Division Multiplexing* (WDM).

You can create a WDM link by placing optical fibers on one side of a prism so that different frequency ranges of light travel down different fibers. The other side of the prism would combine the light so that it travels down a shared optic fiber link. Figure 5.6 shows how WDM is achieved using a prism or a diffraction grating.

Cross-Ref

Chapter 13 describes the use of multiplexing for internetwork links and the protocols that use those techniques.

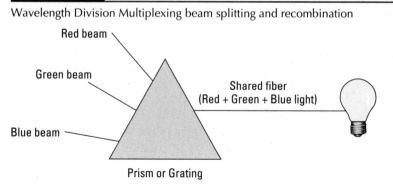

FIGURE 5.6

Wavelength Division Multiplexing beam splitting and recombination

You encounter multiplexing techniques that polarize a data stream in some optical networks. Light can be polarized in a number of different ways, but one common technique is to use an *Add-Drop Multiplexer* (ADM). ADMs typically use a Fabry-Pérot etalon (interferometer) to split or combine light waves. More recent versions of ADMs, called *Reconfigurable Optical Add-Drop Multiplexers* (ROADMs), have become popular on *Metropolitan Area Networks* (MANs). Not all optical networks use polarization. The widely used SONET/SDH optical network uses timed pulses of lasers and LEDs to create TDM communications.

Radio frequency communications can be polarized by passing the data through a phased multi-antenna array to create *Multiple-Input and Multiple-Output* (MIMO) channels. The signal is recombined at a receiving phased multi-antenna array. This technology is similar to the way RADAR is created. MIMO wireless networks are becoming more popular in home wireless networks in order to create higher throughput connections.

Note

Just to make this nomenclature even more confusing, radio frequency multiplexing uses the FDM acronym.

Other forms of multiplexing exist that are important in areas such as cellular communications. *Frequency-hopping spread spectrum* (FHSS) radio communications is perhaps the most famous of these methods. This multiplexing technology works by rapidly switching the carrier wave between a number of different frequencies in a pseudorandom sequence. The transmitting device and receiving device are aware of the order and timing and can tune in, but a spread spectrum transmission would simply appear as transient noise to any narrowband receiver that is tuned to any one frequency. This makes FHSS very secure.

A famous patent in frequency hopping was issued to the composer George Antheil and the actress Hedy Lamarr in 1942 for a system that used a piano roll to switch between 88 different radio frequencies. It was hoped that this system would make it impossible to jam radio-guided torpedoes. The system was never deployed, but became widely known when the *Code Division Multiple Access* (CDMA) system for cellular networks was developed a decade later.

Flow Control

As data flows across a network, there is often a mismatch between the rate at which a system can process data and the rate at which data is being received. These mismatches occur when the receiving system is slower to process and/or cache incoming data than the sending system is at sending the data through the network connection. When the receiving system is the target of data coming in from multiple systems, it's even easier to get a data transfer/processing mismatch. Yet another problem is encountered when a network segment becomes congested, and packets or frames required by the receiving system to reassemble the data cannot be acquired in a timely fashion. The management of data traffic is a problem that is typically addressed in Session layer (Level 3 in the OSI model) protocols using flow control messaging, data caching, session timing schemes, data buffering, and other techniques.

Network flow control can be implemented by devices referred to as *Data Terminal Equipment* (DTE), at switches and routers, and at the circuit level using *Data Circuit Terminating Equipment* (DCE). These devices control the transmission of data by providing a gating function that alters the rates of data flow in one direction or in the opposite direction. A connection must have one of these DTEs or DCEs at each endpoint.

Modems are devices that suffer from flow control problems. A modem negotiates a connection with another modem, ensuring a certain set of protocols are used for the session, a certain data transfer rate, and so on. Modern high-speed modems, at 56 Kbits/s, transfer data at a rate that exceeds the theoretical Nyquist rate when they operate at full speed. They do so by employing compression and other techniques. Data transfer using modems over phone lines have a theoretical limit of around 56 Kbps (the bandwidth of the DS0 telephone channel), but with compression and error correction it is possible to transfer data at a slightly faster rate if the phone line is sufficiently free of noise. However, phone line quality can vary — often by a large amount — and so some mechanism needs to be employed to signal the current condition of the telephone line and the amount of noise that might be encountered. That mechanism is to go through a handshaking routine where the transfer rate and different protocols are negotiated by both the sending and receiving modem.

Most modems use two different forms of flow control. The first method is a set of commands called XON/XOFF that are sent from the modem to the computer. The program that your computer is using to communicate with the modem can also send XON/XOFF messages to the modem. This form of flow control is called *software flow control* (modems can be implemented in software). When a connection is made without a feedback loop like these commands do, it is a form of open-loop flow control. An open-loop flow control mechanism doesn't use communication between the sender and receiver, relying instead on other flow control mechanisms such as resource allocation using resource reservations. You see this type of flow control in ATM networks.

The second system uses control characters or RS 232 and serial port control lines to send control signals and is called *hardware flow control*. Common control signals are *DTR* (Data Terminal Ready), *DSR* (Data Set Ready), *CTS* (Clear to Send), and *RTS* (Request to Send). These are signals that you may see indicated by a set of lights on physical modems. Hardware flow control uses a master/slave relationship. The DTE master sends a signal indicating its condition; then the DCE slave responds. A PC modem connection uses DTR/DSR signals to create a modem session and RTS/CTS signals to control data transfer.

Flow control is also built directly into important protocols. The Internet Protocol (a Network level protocol in the OSI model or the main protocol at the Internet level in the TCP/IP Internet model) creates IP packets that contain blocks that provide a sequence number for reassembly, blocks that indicate packet priority, and so forth. As packets arrive, messages are sent back to indicate if there are any missing packets that are required, if a packet failed its error check, and if a packet took too long to arrive, and when the data has been reassembled completely then the transfer was received correctly. The use of messaging is a form of closed-loop flow control.

The IP protocol is not unique in using a messaging system or in signaling the successful transfer of data. The Frame Relay network protocol (a Data Link protocol), which is used to connect LANs to WANs, creates frames that encapsulate data from packets in the form of variable-sized frames. Frame relay technology has no flow control or acknowledgment messaging. However, frame relay networks offer congestion control for incoming connections and guaranteed throughput mechanisms. Two different control bits in the data header tell the sender when there is congestion, and the sending system reads those bits and adjusts the data rate.

Traffic Engineering

Traffic engineering describes a set of technologies that are used to control traffic on packet-switched networks such as TCP/IP or the Internet. Among the technologies that are used are *packet shaping* (where packets are controlled based on their type of content), *store and forward technologies* (exemplified by the Leaky Bucket Algorithm), and *buffering technologies* (such as the Token Bucket Algorithm). All of these technologies are flow control methods that are used to enforce different Quality of Service levels that both filter and meter network bandwidth to clients.

Packet shaping

A common method that is used to control data rates on a network is called *traffic shaping*, or on an IP network, it is more frequently called *packet shaping*.

Packet shaping isn't just a flow control mechanism that controls data transfer rates. Packets can be categorized on the basis of the protocol they use or the port number that they are destined for. Based on these parameters, rules can be established that alter the way the packets are handled. For example, one ISP examines packets, and if they find that they are BitTorrent packets, they apply a low *Quality of Service* (QoS) to them and send them down the wire as a trickle. BitTorrent can be easily recognized by the fact that the header begins with the character 19 and a 19-byte handshake string.

If a packet is analyzed as part of a *Voice over IP* (VoIP) data stream, then it can be prioritized by an ISP to ensure a certain QoS level. Another ISP (a large phone company, for example) might choose to lower the QoS level so that VoIP doesn't seem as attractive as their phones. This happens to Skype traffic on some networks or to video streaming on networks that are provided by a large cable ISP.

Packet shaping, like any tool, can be used for good reasons or not-so-good reasons. However, without some form of packet shaping, it would be impossible for large public networks to provide the QoS that their service agreements contractually commit them to.

On ATM networks, cells are examined using an algorithm called the *Generic Cell Rate Algorithm* (GCRA) and checked for their compliance to rules that are defined for that particular virtual circuit. A cell is a small, specially formatted packet of data that is transferred on ATM networks and other similar cell relay technologies. Depending upon the arrival rate and variance in that rate, cells are passed through, scheduled, or dropped. GCRA changes the flow control bit settings in the ATM cells to change the data rate. Techniques such as *admission control*, *resource reservation*, and *rate-based congestion control* are used by ATM networks to control traffic flow.

Cross-Ref

Cells are described in more detail in Chapter 13.

Admission control is a mechanism for assigning network bandwidth and latency to different types of traffic entering a network. Resource reservation refers to a system by which network resources are set aside for different application data streams and is commonly used for broadcast technologies. Rate-based congestion control is a technique similar to the traffic light controlled entry lanes on freeways: traffic is allowed onto the network at a steady rate in order to limit network congestion.

On IP networks, packet shaping examines the headers of packets that are flowing through an IP connection, and if the packets match some criteria that you set a rule for, it executes that rule. Packet shaping can limit the bandwidth allowed to a certain datatype or bound to a certain IP address, which is called *bandwidth throttling*. Packet shaping can also be used to change the allowed rate of data transfer and to delay or redirect traffic. *Traffic policing* is differentiated from packet (traffic) shaping in that traffic policing drops packets or marks them.

As you can imagine, packet shaping is a very popular technology with ISPs, who refer to the technology as *network traffic engineering*. You can think of packet shaping as a "Quality of Service" technology if you like, and ISPs tend to describe it in those terms.

Packet shaping is enabled in application software usually running on a network edge device. Some companies, such as Packeteer, offer a PacketShaper appliance. The PacketShaper appliance enforces the various Quality of Service technologies described in the sections on traffic engineering. Packeteer was acquired by Blue Coat Systems in June 2008 (www.bluecoat.com).

Leaky Bucket algorithm

Packet shapers use different methods to store and forward packets. A common scenario places ATM cells or IP packets into a buffer and then uses an algorithm to determine how to transmit them. The buffer, often referred to as a *bucket* in this technology, may use a delay technique or *Leaky Bucket* to create a First In First Out mechanism that takes an inflow at a variable rate and then transmits the data at a fixed (usually lower) rate.

The effect is similar to having some small holes in the bottom of a bucket and then filling the bucket up with water. A packet shaper can control the size of the "holes" of the bucket, and thus the outgoing rate. If the incoming rate overflows the buffer, then the packets flow over the top of the bucket, and they are discarded. Figure 5.7 shows the concept behind the Leaky Bucket.

The Leaky Bucket algorithm provides constant data output.

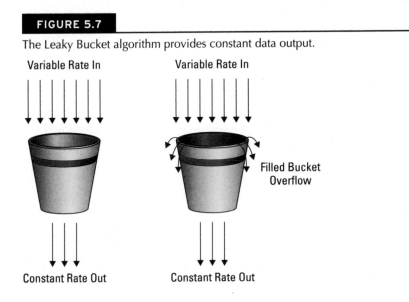

The Leaky Bucket algorithm is simple to implement when the sizes of the incoming packets are constant, the incoming rate is predictable, and the outgoing rate can be efficiently satisfied by the packet size in the bucket. However, in situations where the packet size varies or the incoming rate is bursty (subject to short spurts of high traffic volume), the Leaky Bucket algorithm has a number of inefficiencies, most notably the fact that when high traffic is encountered that is beyond the capacity of the bucket, that extra traffic is discarded. Modifications to the Leaky Bucket that add a byte-counting algorithm improve the Leaky Bucket algorithm's performance.

Token Bucket algorithm

A second buffer mechanism used is called a *Token Bucket*. This packet shaping flow control uses an algorithm that can control how much data is allowed onto the network, and provides the byte-counting capabilities that the Leaky Bucket lacks. The algorithm provides for average and burst transfer rates. Whereas the Leaky Bucket enforces a constant outgoing rate, the Token Bucket allows for more flexibility in the data rate.

The token mechanism acts as follows: A bucket is filled with tokens, which represent an amount of data that can be sent. When data is removed, the token that corresponds to that amount of data is removed from the bucket. When all tokens are gone, data is not transmitted. If there are enough tokens in the bucket, then the data can be transmitted at a bursty rate. If the bucket is full of tokens, then any additional tokens are discarded. These four scenarios are illustrated in Figure 5.8.

In this system, a network administrator assigns how many tokens correspond to how many bytes of data. There is a constant rate of new tokens arriving at the bucket, but the bucket has a limited capacity. When a packet arrives of a certain size, the number of tokens required for that size are removed. If a packet arrives and there aren't enough tokens, then the packet is dropped, held in a buffer, or marked and transmitted.

FIGURE 5.8

The Token Bucket algorithm provides variable data output.

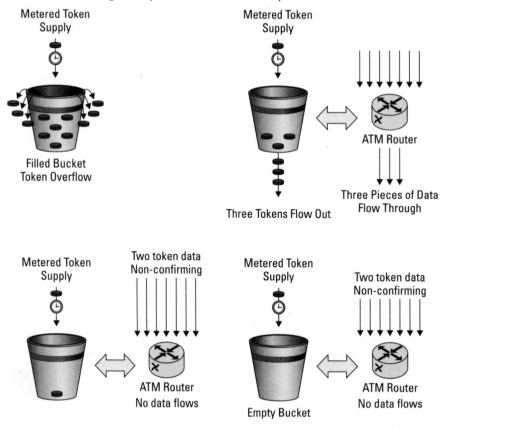

Quality of Service

Quality of Service (QoS) is a form of packet shaping or traffic engineering that guarantees that a certain service will have a certain amount of resources dedicated to it. The classic use of the term *QoS* is to ensure that an application that is in real time and sensitive to delays is given a certain sized circuit over which it can be transmitted. QoS is especially important for VoIP, streaming media, online multiplayer games, and other such applications. QoS methods are only employed when the network is bandwidth limited or congested. QoS technology is being built into network server operating systems such as Windows servers.

QoS is not a metric that is used to measure delays, latencies, signal-to-noise ratios, frequency response, and so on, although the QoS agreement can include these requirements. These sorts of metrics are better classified as a *Grade of Service* (GoS), with QoS reserved for resource access. The two concepts, although related, are often confused.

As an example of QoS services, let's take a look at how they are implemented using the *Asynchronous Transfer Mode* (ATM). ATM networks have several categories of service built into that transfer protocol. These categories are built directly into ATM network adapters and ATM switches to service different classes of subscribers.

Classes of ATM services that are available:

- **Constant Bit Rate (CBR).** This category provides no control over traffic flow and no error checking. CBR is used on T1-carrier connections.

- **Unspecified Bit Rate (UBR).** This category provides no congestion messaging and sets no flow level. Cells move about the ATM network up to the available capacity. When the capacity is exceeded, cells are discarded; if there is additional capacity, more cells are transferred. Any program that does its own flow control and error checking can use UBR. Typical applications that this category attracts are mail servers (e-mail) and FTP servers (background file transfers).

- **Real Time Variable Bit Rate (RT-VBR).** This category is used for applications that deliver data in a form that is non-linear. An example would be videoconferencing, which, due to the way its compression works, creates frames in a non-linear way. RT-VBR ensures that there is enough data to provide the compression algorithm with an adequate queue to run the video smoothly or to ensure that the compression is efficiently used.

- **Non-Real Time Variable Bit Rate (NRT-VBR).** Applications that require traffic flow control but can accommodate a certain amount of variability (called *jitter*) can use this category. Print spooling is an example of an application that can use NRT-VBR.

- **Available Bit Rate (ABR).** This level of service allows data to move through the line at a rate that is dependent upon the available bandwidth. It is meant to accommodate bursty traffic and to allow network capacity to be better utilized at times when traffic is low. Web server traffic is an example of an application that can use the ABR service.

Network service providers may implement a service such as ABR when they have short periods of high utilization, as it can allow them to avoid building additional capacity when the investment isn't required long term. To implement ABR, a messaging system is implemented that informs sending systems when traffic is high and that they need to throttle their traffic back.

Table 5.1 summarizes the different capabilities of ATM service categories.

TABLE 5.1

ATM Service Categories

	Bandwidth Control	Bursty Traffic (Variable)	Congestion Control	Real Time
ABR	Capable	Yes	Yes	No
CBR	Yes	No	No	Yes
NRT-VBR	Yes	Yes	No	No
RT-VBR	Yes	No	No	Yes
UBR	No	Yes	No	No

These different service categories allow ATM network service providers to create *Service Level Agreements* (SLAs) with their subscribers that guarantee access to network resources. The contracts contain a traffic description that may specify bandwidth and/or throughput values in a measurable way. Transfer rates may be measured for *Sustained Cell Rate* (SCR), *Peak Cell Rate* (PCR), *Minimum Cell Rate* (MCR), *Cell Error Rate* (CER), *Cell Loss Rate* (CLR), *Cell Transfer Delay* (CTD), *Severely Errored Cell Block Ratio* (SECBR), *Cell Delay Variation Tolerance* (CDVT), *Cell Delay Variation* (CDV), and *Cell Misinsertion Rate* (CMR). These parameters are measurable and are defined on a connection basis in ATM.

Summary

In this chapter, you were introduced to signaling and information theory. These basic concepts are at the heart of why networks do what they do and how different types of networks are different from one another, and they separate what is possible to do on the network from what is impossible.

Complex data can be described in mathematical terms using techniques such as Fourier analysis. This allows you to store information and recreate the data at a later time. Sampling data provides the means to recreate data. There is a theoretical limit to the amount of sampling that is useful based on the bandwidth of the data.

Networks create channels that allow data streams to share network segments. Channels are created in a number of different ways, based on time, frequency, and polarity. The process of creating channels is called multiplexing, and when you combine data streams it is called demultiplexing.

Traffic control, flow control, and congestion control methods allow a network to provide services of different quality levels.

In the next chapter, you will learn about servers, systems, and appliances. These devices provide the important network services that clients and the network depend on.

Part II

Hardware

Servers and Systems

I n this chapter, principles relating to servers and services on a network are presented. Different server types are considered, a server being described as a software application that provides a service to other networked systems. Because servers come in all shapes and sizes, a process model for a server system is shown.

Right-sizing server services by determining capacity and loading is an important part of having a well-functioning network. Different approaches to capacity planning include maintaining excess capacity, adding capacity as required, or matching capacity to demand. Projects that add server capacity to networks are best handled as part of a solution framework in a phased project. Different methodologies that you can use are described in this chapter.

To improve network performance, you need to be able to define the different levels of service that the network performs. Deconstructing response time into its components, measuring throughput, and defining network reliability, scalability, and other factors allow you to define the performance characteristics of a network.

In this chapter, you learn about different measurable performance data characteristics that you can use to derive fundamental network relationships. These relationships help you to determine which network resource is the bottleneck that is slowing down system performance, and allow you to eliminate those bottlenecks. Modeling networks is briefly described.

The chapter ends with a discussion of adding server capacity, by adding either more powerful systems (scale up) or more servers (scale out).

IN THIS CHAPTER

The most common types of network servers

The range of network services

Measuring network performance

How to model networks and find bottlenecks

Network Server Types

A server is a software program that provides a service to another computer over a network connection. Servers can run on the local system or on a remote system, but the software routine must provide this service to other systems or at least be capable of providing the service. Any service that does not have this shared component is more properly classified as a daemon, which is a local service.

The use of the word *server* is applied very loosely in modern computing. A server is also the name given to a computer that has been configured to run a particular shared application or service. To better enable server functions, most modern servers run a server operating system — what I've chosen to call a *network operating system* in this book. This chapter describes network servers and focuses on the characteristics of shared services and applications.

Often the network server operating system is simply a special version of the desktop version of the operating system, or to be more precise, the desktop operating system is simply a partially disabled, more general-purpose, performance-crippled version of the server operating system. This has been the case with the Microsoft Windows operating systems since the days of Windows Server/Professional 2000, and subsequent server projects such as Windows Server 2003/XP and Windows Server 2008/Vista have continued down this path. Other operating systems, such as Sun Solaris and versions of Linux, make no specific delineation between clients and servers allowing the power of the hardware and the configuration by the user to enable the required features.

Cross-Ref
Chapter 20 covers network operating systems in more detail.

Another use of the word *server* refers to the specific applications that a hardware system runs. A server that hasn't been specifically configured for one application or service function is referred to as a *general-purpose server*. All other servers are described in terms of the major application function that they provide. The most common network server types found today are:

- **File and print servers.** On large networks, file and print servers often represent 25 percent of the servers deployed.

- **Application servers.** Application servers include database servers, Web servers, e-mail servers, and so forth. If the application server runs a branded piece of software, most people refer to the server as an Apache server, Oracle server, and so on. Application servers can usually be as much as 25 percent of the server population on enterprise networks.

- **Backup servers.** Most people are surprised to learn that backup servers are often the third-largest number of server types in an enterprise deployment. It is common to find that as many as 20 percent of all servers are dedicated backup servers.

- **Network servers.** The definition of a network server varies, but if you include services that provide a routing function, system identification such as DNS and DHCP, and similar services, then this class of servers can represent as much as 15 percent of an enterprise network.

- **Domain servers.** Domain servers are essential network servers for most large networks, but they represent perhaps 5 percent of deployed servers.

The percentages mentioned in the bulleted list are based on surveys taken among network administrators across a large population and can vary greatly, depending upon the type of organization and network type. In the list, the total percentage adds up to 90 percent, leaving a category of 10 percent of miscellaneous servers — or simply none of the above.

The server count, and therefore the percentages assigned to different categories of servers, can often be skewed by the deployment of what have come to be known as *server appliances*. A server appliance is a server hardware platform that has been specially configured to run an application or service with minimal human operation. A true server appliance (like a toaster) is one where you take it out of the box, plug in a power cord and network connection, turn it on, and forget about it. Examples of server appliances are routers, gateways, firewalls, print servers, Web servers, and others. The key differentiating factor that defines a server appliance, be it an Oracle 8i appliance or Google Search Appliance (www.google.com/enterprise/gsa/), is the ease of use.

A good example of a network server appliance is the series of DNS/DHCP/FTP/NTP/IPAM/RADIUS server appliances sold by Infoblox (www.infoblox.com). These appliances are security-hardened devices that run a real-time operating system, are zero configuration enabled, and can replace a number of different server types. Figure 6.1 shows the Infoblox-2000 Network Service Appliance.

FIGURE 6.1

The Infoblox-2000 Network Service Appliance can replace a broad range of network servers.

Photo courtesy of Infoblox, Inc.

Servers come in a wide variety of form factors. Common server hardware form factors are stand-alone pedestal and tower systems, rack-mountable standard-width servers, and system frames into which complete servers mounted on long add-in cards called server blades are placed. You will find servers deployed in just about any form factor you can think of, and technology continues to make even smaller form factors possible.

Given that computer servers can be emulated in software — their services abstracted so that they can run anywhere and seem to be local, run inside virtual machines, and be made such that resources can be added or removed as needed — the best way to conceptualize a network server is to consider its function and building blocks. An example of the different units required to model a general-purpose server is shown in Figure 6.2. The parameters shown in the model are those that you can measure or derive.

An operational model of a network server

A_i = Total number of service requests presented

C_i = Total number of service requests completed

K_i = Number of resources used

U_i = Resource utilization

X_i = Resource throughput

(i = RAM, Cache, Disk, CPU)

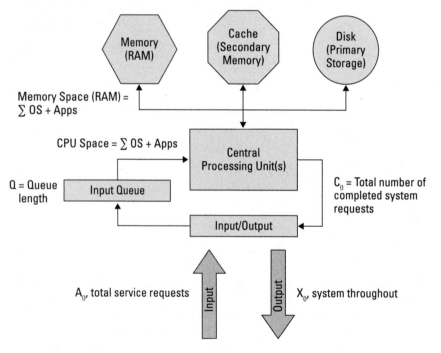

Figure 6.2 shows the different functional units of a network operating system. In this figure the different subsystems that impact performance are shown. A service request is input from a network client A0 and the network server operates on the service request returning system output X0 with a certain efficiency represented by the system's throughput.

A service request is added to the Input queue and then submitted to the Central Processing Unit (CPU) for further handling. The Input Queue may have a certain queue length that is a prioritized number of service requests. As service requests are processed, they are removed from the Input Queue. The ability of the CPU to service requests is a function of its speed and the ability to run the operating system(s) and various applications. As requests are processed, instructions may be stored and retrieved from a set of different memory systems: RAM, cache, and disk storage in order of their diminishing speed and increasing capacity (generally speaking).

Capacity and Loading

The capacity of a network server is its ability to perform a certain workload. Loading measures that portion of a server's capacity that is currently in use. There are many different ways in which capacity and loading of a server may be measured; some descriptions have a mainly theoretical interest, while other descriptions are purely practical. However, while the concepts may be warm and fuzzy, the impact that server capacity has on your network's performance and your company's bottom line is not. Your ability to understand, measure, and modify the capacity and loading of your network services is a fundamental skill.

There are different approaches to capacity planning, and in the next section three different approaches are considered. Capacity planning can be proactive, reactive, or analytical. Each approach requires a different mindset and set of actions. I also cover solution frameworks, which take a stepwise approach based on a team structure that forces organizations to confront project plans and sign off on them step by step to combat large project failures.

Three approaches

Broadly speaking, there are three different approaches to capacity planning:

1. Maintain excess capacity at all times.
2. Add capacity as demand requires.
3. Match capacity to demand.

Each of these approaches has its own pluses and minuses, and each makes certain demands on the resources available. A lead strategy, which is the proactive approach where you always have excess capacity for any demand, requires that you either have resources in place or that you have access to resources. Because a lead strategy is wasteful of permanent resources, many networks that employ a lead strategy use a tiered approach where additional resources are brought to bear as needed.

Networks employ a lead strategy when they anticipate an increase in traffic and it is essential that they be able to react to that change. A general characteristic of a leading strategy is that the business captured is much more valuable than the cost of the resources. For example, a major company such as Amazon must employ a lead strategy, as the ratio of sales dollars to equipment costs is very large.

The second approach adds resources only when required and is called a reactive or lag strategy. Capacity is added only when the need is demonstrated. The downside to a lag strategy is that a certain amount of traffic will not be satisfied until the extra capacity is brought online. It is a characteristic of a lag strategy that the cost of deploying a network resource is usually larger than the loss associated with the lack of the resource. A lag strategy is a conservative approach, based on different assumptions. When demand is measured, the demand can be described either in terms of an average or mean level of traffic or in terms of the maximum level of traffic seen at peak times.

One approach is to have enough resources to satisfy the average or mean level of traffic, or perhaps more reasonably, a traffic level of a standard deviation so that only outliers are left unsatisfied. The standard deviation measures the *probability distribution* of a data set around a mean value. With a low standard deviation, data points cluster closely to the *mean*; high standard deviation has the data distributed over a large range of values.

While a lag strategy is considered conservative, many businesses operate with a lag strategy in order to maximize the use of a particular resource that may be in demand. A good example of this approach is used on packet-switched networks, which is the basis for the Internet and is used by ISPs. The network pipe is a limited resource and the goal of the ISP is to apportion the bandwidth in such a way as to maximize the utilization while promising the highest level of access that can be reasonably expected by a customer. At periods of high utilization, customers are throttled back or access times are increased, but it is rare that a customer experiences an outage. Or so it seems...

The third approach is the one Goldilocks prefers: "Just Right" or right-sizing the network to demand. This is the analytical approach. Here you modify the amount of system resources in an incremental way so that the network's capacity adapts to changing demand. A match strategy requires the implementation of a feedback loop bringing resources to bear as needed, and perhaps releasing those resources when they are no longer needed.

Solution frameworks

It is a sad fact that the majority of all major IT projects fail — and you thought that economics was "the dismal science." For our purpose, failure may be defined as one of the following:

- **Cost overrun.** The project greatly exceeds its initial projected cost due either to specification problems or project creep.

- **Time overrun.** The project greatly exceeds its initial projected length before it is deployed or is never deployed.

- **Specification error.** The project solves a problem that doesn't exist, or the problem doesn't exist once the project is complete.

- **Resource misallocation.** The resources brought to bear are better used elsewhere, perhaps solving one problem while creating more substantial issues.

- **Benign neglect.** The project fails because it loses a champion needed to see the project through to completion.

Network deployment and modification projects are often large projects, and they can suffer from any of the aforementioned defects or any combination thereof. To combat large project failures, there have been several different approaches to managing system development and deployment. These solution frameworks take a stepwise approach based on a team structure that forces organizations to confront project plans and sign off on them step by step. As an example of how you might want to structure a large network project, let's consider two related approaches used in the industry based on focused task groups.

Perhaps the best known of these solution frameworks was developed by the Office of Government Commerce (OGC) of Great Britain. OGC publishes a set of policy guidelines for managing network information technology resources called the Information Technology Infrastructure Library (ITIL; www.itil-officialsite.com/home/home.asp), which has become widely adopted, particularly in the European Common Market countries. Their methodology has been trademarked.

ITIL describes how to apply a set of best practices to network service strategies, designs, and operations, as well as how to provide a level of service as conditions evolve. ITIL has been published through three versions, the most recent being version 3.0, published in May 2007 in five volumes:

1. **Service Strategy.** A service strategy would include a description of the business, a best practices framework, service management description, key processes, and demand management.

Tip
You can lower costs and improve the quality of your project by doing a really thoughtful and detailed project assessment at the beginning of the project. Changes you make later in the project cost exponentially more to fix once the project is under way.

2. **Service Design.** This book describes the network system architecture, business rules, and documentation set. A Service Design Package (SDP) includes a service-level management catalog, business continuity plans, network security scheme, key suppliers, and staffing/role assignment.

3. **Service Transition.** The service transition referred to is the hand-off of prototype systems to production staff for live operation. This book also describes how to conceptualize new projects that modify the existing levels of service, and how to manage assets and configurations as well as configuration changes. Change management, knowledge management, and product release and deployment are tasked to the team that provides service transitions.

4. **Service Operation.** Service operation is described as a set of best practices developed to provide the levels of service that have been placed into the service design. A service operations team provides the day-to-day IT support that working production networks and systems require.

5. **Continual Service Improvement.** The CSI program is a proactive approach to improving a production system while in use. A CSI program would collect user input and feed the more valuable suggestions to one of the other teams for implementation into the product or a next version of the product. Other services covered by this team would include staff training, scheduling, role assignment, and reporting.

The iterative team-based approach used by solution management frameworks is illustrated in Figure 6.3.

FIGURE 6.3

A team-based approach that iteratively conceptualizes, tests, and deploys solutions has the highest chance of success.

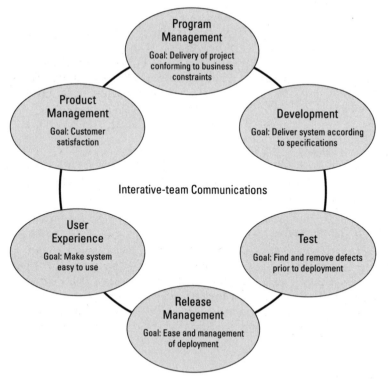

In an iterative team approach, the following groups are created and the project proceeds as each group turns over their part of the project to the next group. The groups include:

- **Program Management.** This team initiates the project and creates the project goals. Their end product is a project plan.
- **Development.** The Development team takes the project plan and reduces it to practice.
- **Test.** The developed project is handed off to the Test team in order to determine that the project works according to specification and without error.
- **Release Management.** The Test team hands off the project to a Release Management team whose task is to roll the project out to the network.
- **User Experience.** A User Experience team works with users to ensure that the project is accepted and works according to user requirements.
- **Product Management.** The Product Management team provides end user support once the project is operational.

Iterative project programs typically include a final analysis of the proposed project and goals with the achieved results by the Program Management team.

As part of the ITIL program, it is possible to obtain a certification in these methodologies from the ITIL Certification Management Board. The OGC (www.ogc.gov.uk/), IT Service Forum International (itSMF; www.itsmfi.org/), Examination Institute for Information Science (EXIN; www.exin-exams.com/), and Information Systems Examination Board (ISEB; www.bcs.org/) all contribute to these certification exams, with the latter two organizations administering the exams. Qualifications awarded include Foundation, Practitioner, or Manager/Masters of ITIL Service Management, ITIL Application Management, and ICT Infrastructure Management.

The Microsoft Consulting Group adapted ITIL's team-based approach for use in their major projects. Their success led Microsoft to incorporate this approach into two different methodologies — Microsoft Operations Framework (MOF) and Microsoft Solutions Framework (MSF). With MOF, the goal is to run the network efficiently, while MSF aims to build the network well.

Microsoft Operations Framework

Microsoft describes the Microsoft Operations Framework (MOF; www.microsoft.com/mof/) as a superset of ITIL, but it is probably better described as being a highly adapted version of ITIL. MOF offers operational guides, templates, assessment and support tools, access to white papers, courseware, and case studies. Microsoft also offers services related to MOF. MOF's emphasis is on how to meld people and processes in complex networking environments. MOF guidance tends to consider distributed and heterogeneous networks. MOF runs using the iterative team approach that was described previously.

Microsoft Solutions Framework

Microsoft Solutions Framework (MSF; www.microsoft.com/msf/) offers solutions that the public can download and use. Among the solutions that can be obtained are product or platform deployments or rollouts such as Windows Server, Exchange Server, Visual Studio Team System, Web and E-commerce services, ERP, n-tiered transaction systems, and operation management systems, among others. Perhaps the best representative solution that you can download is the Microsoft Solution Accelerator for Business Desktop Deployment 2007 (BDD; technet.microsoft.com/en-us/library/bb490308.aspx), which is a solution framework that Microsoft distributes for the deployment of Windows Server 2008/Vista. Many of Microsoft's deployment tools are conveniently bundled in the BDD.

MSF is currently at version 3.0 and includes both Team and Process models; integration into the Microsoft Operations Framework; and project, risk, and readiness management disciplines. When you download one of the business solutions, you will find that it contains a set of guidelines on how to construct different teams and have them interact, what each team's deliverables are, a set of best practices, and a collection of other resources related to the projects being described. The framework presents a set of recipes that you can adapt for your own situation. Figure 6.4 illustrates the relationships between teams and tasks in an MSF solution.

In Figure 6.4 the project starts in the Envisioning stage and proceeds through Planning, Development, Stabilization, and Deployment phases using groups of the type that was described before for an iterative team approach. Each of the diamonds represents a milestone that is defined in the project plan, which for the inner circle is most often represented by hand-off from one group to the next. The outer circle represents concrete tasks and milestones required by the project.

The project proceeds clockwise from the top with both the inner stages path and the outer tasks paths synchronized. An MSF solution doesn't require complete hand-off from one group to another. There may be stages during which two or more groups may still be actively working on the project.

The MSF solution has a set of foundation principles that Microsoft describes as follows:

- **Shared vision.** Each team should have a shared vision for their task and for the project as a whole.
- **Accountability and responsibility.** Each deliverable should be clearly shared and assigned.
- **Open communication.** Keep communication open both inside the group as well as between project teams.
- **Empowerment.** Allow team members to take responsibility.
- **Delivery of value.** Match a need to a set of deliverables.
- **Quality.** Invest in quality, and be quantitative about it. Measure the results.
- **Risk management.** Continually monitor risks and be reactive when problems arise.
- **Learning from experience.** Completed project steps should be subjected to a post-project review.
- **Being agile.** Be open to change based on your experiences.

The group-oriented process embodied in the design of a Microsoft Solution Foundations business solution

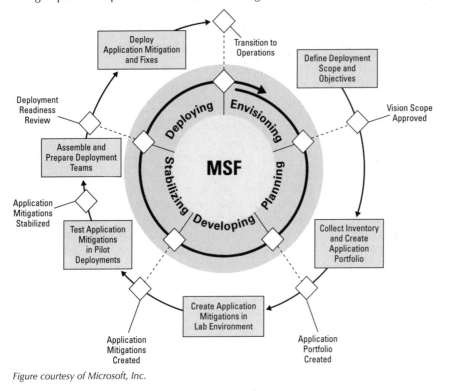

Figure courtesy of Microsoft, Inc.

Server and Systems Sizing

It is essential to understand your servers, services, and systems performance on a quantitative level in order to make good decisions going forward. If the technology is newly deployed, the best approach is to experiment with the system in a testing lab or scenario that provides a realistic diagnostic potential. In some instances, industry benchmarks are constructed using real-world scenarios that may be of use. For example, the Transaction Processing Performance Council's various benchmarks often simulate a real-world scenario such as an E-commerce or data warehousing application. The best metrics are the ones that you develop on your own network using your own systems.

Defining levels of service

To quantify system performance, you need to measure the Quality of Service (QoS) levels in these areas: response time, throughput, availability, reliability, scalability, adaptability, and security.

Several of these factors that are part of QoS, particularly reliability and adaptability, are intrinsic to the technologies that you choose and often need to be designed into the functional requirements for the network from the beginning. Quality of Service or QoS is essentially defined as providing a measured level of service based on an analytical assessment or performance measurement.

Response time

Response time measures the time it takes for a request to be processed. Measuring the response time is equivalent to determining the rate-limiting step in a chemical mechanism. If you know the rate-limiting step, then you have a measure of the current factor that limits your system performance.

For a client/server application such as a browser making a request to a Web server, the response time can be broken into application, network, and server responses, as shown in Figure 6.5. In Figure 6.5 a service request is initiated and starts at the client in the outgoing stack at the top left of the figure. Client response times, network response times, and then server response times all contribute to the latency of the process as the request leaves the client and arrives at the server. Once the server has processed the response, it then sends the response out (Server I/O) and the factors involved in the incoming response components begin. The processes proceed from the top-right Outgoing stack to the bottom-right Incoming stack going right to left. Incoming factors include the network response time involved with the server and then client portions of network handling, and finally end when the client can display the result.

In practice, separating the different components of the response times into times you can measure can be difficult. You might measure the response time as the time between when you press the Enter key or click the OK button and the time the result appears on your screen, or you might measure the network response time as the time it takes for a message such as a PING to be sent to a network node.

FIGURE 6.5

The different components of a response time for a client/server interaction

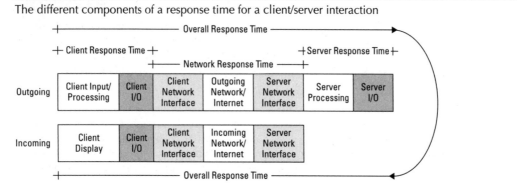

Throughput

A system's throughput is the number of operations or transactions that can be performed per unit time. When throughput is measured, it is important that the operational characteristics be defined in a meaningful way. Throughput may be quantified using the following formula:

```
Throughput = MINIMUM {server capacity, available workload}
```

Throughput can vary greatly under conditions of heavy server or network loading from the average or ideal conditions you might encounter or wish to encounter. A typical throughput curve will rise steadily toward 100 percent utilization, at which point the throughput may decrease as a component of the service becomes the gating factor. For example, many systems cache data to enhance performance or extend memory. At high levels of utilization, disk thrashing may begin eliminating the performance enhancement that the cache was designed to offer. Disk thrashing is a condition of low system performance where the system requires an excessive amount of disk I/O (paging) to service requests because the system has no free RAM to store the data that is required by current processes.

Throughput metrics include:

- millions of instructions per second (MIPS) for CPUs
- I/O per second (IOPS) and kilobytes transferred per second (Kbits/s) for disk drives
- packets per second (PPS) or megabytes per second (Mbits/s) for network segments
- transactions per second for applications
- page views per second
- HTTP requests per second, or kilobytes per second (Kbits/s) for Web servers or sites
- messages per second for an e-mail server
- searches per second or sessions per second for a database

Throughput is a measure of a quantity per unit time and is meaningful as long as the quantity and time are comparable. For example, it is unreasonable to compare metrics for an e-mail transfer of 4 K messages versus one that has a megabyte attachment associated with it.

A well-defined benchmark attempts to correct for these differences by performing a mixture of tasks so that some are performed with low priority, others with high priority, and other factors are varied. For example, the TPC-C V5.10 (www.tpc.org/tpcc/default.asp) executes a mixture of transactions using a typical Online Transaction Processing (OLTP) order entry system that a wholesale supplier would require, including entering and delivering orders, and monitoring the level of stock at warehouses. The benchmark measures the number of orders of this hypothetical system per minute as expressed in the metric tpmC.

Caution

There are lies, damn lies, statistics, and benchmarks. I can't stress enough that a benchmark is only useful when it compares two systems using consistent methodology. A benchmark that measures network performance for small packet transfers will likely be very different from one that measures the performance for large frame transfers. Be vigilant.

Availability

Availability is defined as the fraction of time that a service is available, and is a fundamental network metric for many systems. An online store may seek to have an availability of four nines or 99.99 percent uptime; the system would then be unavailable for over 52 minutes a year. This uptime would be considered to be borderline "mission critical," but would obviously be inadequate for a system that monitors patients in a critical care facility. Availability is a fundamental network design parameter.

Reliability

Reliability is a measure of the probability that the network will perform correctly over time. Many people fail to differentiate between availability and reliability; although these two concepts are related, they are sufficiently different to consider when designing or upgrading a network. A network can be available and still deliver operations that are not reliable. For example, in a packet-switched network under heavy loading, systems may still be available while an increase in the error rate reduces the network's reliability. As the reliability increases, its rate approaches the availability rate.

Scalability

The term scalability is applied to a system that can add additional load without a degradation of performance. Load can be expressed as the number of users, the number of concurrent sessions, or some other factor. If adding more load changes the performance characteristics of a network (usually in a negative manner), the system is considered to not be scalable at the point at which the impact becomes significant.

Adaptability

Adaptability, defined as the ability of a network to be extended to include other services, is a design consideration when installing or upgrading a network.

Security

Security is a combination of providing data access, maintaining confidentiality, and verifying the actions of systems and users.

Quantifying performance

It's good to have a general feeling for the Quality of Service factors that any service installation or upgrade requires; but it is much better to be able to quantify performance using a set of real system metrics to focus in on the tasks required to obtain the desired results. It is considered a best practice to maintain a set of performance logs collected over time in order to determine trends and isolate problems. Analysis of trends allows you to be proactive in upgrading or modifying your network; they allow you to diagnose errors because they serve as baseline measurements, and through event logs they allow you to get detailed information on network conditions.

The following set of data on resource utilization is useful to monitor:

- **CPU utilization.** The average and peak levels of CPU utilization were collected and analyzed to determine trends over time as well as utilization over the typical work week.
- **Memory utilization.** The amount of memory in use, the number of page faults, cache performance, and other factors were collected and analyzed.

- **Disk utilization.** The size of allocated disk space was tracked, as were factors such as disk IOPS, to determine trends over time and over a typical work week. Different disk structures and types were analyzed, including various types of RAID, dedicated storage arrays, and others.

- **Network utilization.** Factors that indicate the level of network performance were collected. These factors include throughput, response times, and collision rates, among others.

Note

Modern network operating systems offer a great variety of performance counters. Only a few are typically running in a default system, so if you need additional types of counters, you may need to install them and/or enable them. Many applications, particularly enterprise server applications, come with their own set of counters that are installed as part of the application's installation process. You may want to consult your operating system and application vendor's documentation to determine which additional counters may be available. Be careful in your use of counters, as enabling them may impact the performance that you are trying to measure. This is particularly true of disk counters.

To obtain this data, different performance counters were turned on at the server, routers, and perhaps at some representative clients. The key observable performance data that you might want to collect is summarized in Table 6.1.

TABLE 6.1

Key Measurable Performance Data

Symbol	Description
Measured Data (operational variables)	
T	Time period of observation
K	Number of resources used
Bi	The time the resource i was busy during T
Ai	The total number of service requests that are presented to resource i during period T
A0	The total number of service requests (of the type being studied) that were presented to the overall system during T
Ci	The total number of returned completed requests from resource i during period T
C0	The total number of returned completed requests from the system during period T
Derived Data	
Si	The mean service time per completion at resource i is: $Si = Bi/Ci$
Ui	The resource utilization of i is: $Ui = Bi/T$
Xi	The throughput of resource i is: $Xi = Ci/T$
li	The arrival rate at resource i is: $li = Ai/T$
X0	The overall system throughput is: $X0 = Ci/C0$
Vi	The average number of visits per request to resource i is: $Vi = Ci/C0$

Source: Performance by Design, by Daniel A. Menasce, Virgilio A. F. Almeida, and Lawrence W. Dowdy, 2004, Prentice Hall.

Performance relationships

Utilization is a key factor in determining the need for additional resources. Once a resource is fully utilized, there is no more capacity available to perform the function (tasks) that the resource is busy doing. Utilization, as you can see in Table 6.2, is defined as $U_i = B_i/T$. To calculate the average time that resource i took to complete a task, you multiply this equation by C_i/C_i, which yields the following equation:

$$U_i = (B_i/C_i) / (T/C_i)$$

Then, because B_i/C_i is the average service time S_i, and T/C_i is the inverse of the resource throughput X_i, you reduce the equation as follows:

$$U_i = S_i \times X_i$$

The relationship derived above is referred to as the Utilization Law, and it states that a resource's utilization rate is the product of the average service time times the throughput. When the completion rate is such that all arrivals are processed during the observation period, $C_i = A$, then $X_i = l_i$ and the Utilization Law takes the form:

$$U_i = S_i \times l_i$$

If the resource that you are studying has multiple instances — for example, multiple connections or wires, multiple processors, and so forth — then the Utilization Law accounts for these instances using the following generalization:

$$U_i = (S_i \times X_i)/m$$

where m is the number of servers that a resource has.

A service request almost always requires multiple uses of critical resources. For example, if you make an HTTP request to a Web server, completing the request might require several READs to obtain the data objects necessary for the response. If the data objects are in cache, then the resource being utilized is RAM; if not, then multiple requests may need to be made from disk(s). When a set of requests are made using a resource, you can define a performance factor called a *service demand*. The service demand D_i is the total average time spent by an average request of the type being analyzed for the resource i. The formula for service demand is then:

$$D_i = (U_i \times T)/C_0 = U_i/X_0$$

or alternatively,

$$D_i = V_i \times S_i$$

This relationship, known as the *Service Demand Law*, states that the service demand is obtained from the visit count multiplied by the service time, or alternatively, the resource utilization divided by the overall system throughput. For any resource derived from multiple instances, you can generalize the equations to the following:

```
Di = Ui,r/X0,r = Vi,r x Si,r
```

where r represents the different classes of service demands, each class being computed individually.

When studying a resource i, you determine that the number of visits to the resource required by the request is 4, and the throughput of the resource is 3.5 requests per second. If this is a disk drive, for example, the 3.5 requests per second are in the form of disk I/O (READ/WRITE) and the units are in IOPS. To relate the resource's throughput Xi to the system's throughput $X0$, you would use the formula:

```
Xi = Vi x X0
```

which generalizes to

```
Xi,r = Vi,r x X0,r
```

This equation is referred to as the *Forced Flow Law*, and applying this law to our example, the throughput of the disk would then be 3.5 x 4, or 14, IOPS.

You can relate the average number of requests, the throughput, and the average time of a request using a formula that is called *Little's Law*, as follows:

```
Ai = Xi x Si
```

Consider the trivial circumstance where a disk subsystem either has a single request or there is no request at all. In this circumstance, the probability that the request is being serviced is equivalent to the disk subsystem's utilization. When there is no request, the probability is equivalent to the disk subsystem's idle time. The equation above is simply a restatement of the Utilization Law.

For a situation where there is a request queue and a certain number of active requests on the disk's subsystem, you can formulate the relationship between the queue length and active requests (Ni), the average time of the request (Ri), and the throughput (Xi) as follows:

```
Ni = Ri x Xi
```

This same equation reshuffled shows that if you know the queue length and the throughput, then you can calculate the response rate as follows:

```
Ri = Ni / Xi
```

Little's Law can be applied to a broad variety of resources and situations when evaluating system performance. However, there are some limitations that you need to be aware of. For Little's Law to function correctly, requests cannot be created or destroyed in the system. A request in the queue that is processed must at some time be completed by the system. The time that any one request spends in the queue isn't relevant; it can be random, Last In Last Out, First In First Out, or the like, as Little's Law is applied to average values.

Consider a client server system with multiple (M) clients accessing a server, as illustrated in Figure 6.6. A client is either processing a request or the client is idle. The average number of clients in the request state is `Mavg` and the average number in the idle state is `Navg`. Because clients can be in either state, the sum of these two averages equals the number of clients:

`M = Mavg + Navg`

The system shown in Figure 6.6 shows multiple client requests made to a server (the bottom set of multiple arrows on the left) and sent to the server on the right. The average time spent by a client in the idle state (Z) is shown by the bar on the left, and the average server response time (R) is shown by the bar on the right. Little's Law separately states that the average number of clients in the request state is related to the system's throughput (X0) multiplied by the server's response time as follows:

`Mavg = X0 x Z`

which states that the average number of requests per unit time or throughput equals the number of completed requests per unit time or system throughput (`X0`).

FIGURE 6.6

A client/server system request/response model

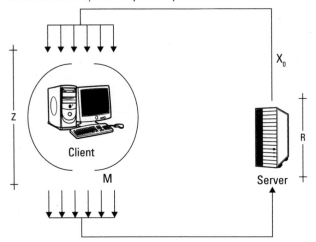

Little's Law applied to the server leads to the relationship:

`Navg = X0 x R`

Combining the two expressions leads to the equation called the Interactive Response Time Law:

`R = (M/X0) - Z`

`or more generally for a multiple system,`

`Rr = (Mr/X0,r) - Zr`

The Interactive Response Time Law then states that the response of the server is equal to the number of clients divided by the throughput minus the idle time.

Table 6.2 shows the five operational laws that have just been described.

TABLE 6.2

Operational Laws

Law	Relationship	Description
Utilization Law	$Ui = Xi \times Si = li \times Si$	Relates utilization to throughput and mean request handling time. The last term is true if all inputs are processed.
Forced Flow Law	$Xi = Vi \times X0$	A resource's throughput is equal to the number of visits (requests) multiplied by the system throughput.
Service Demand Law	$Di = Vi \times Si = Ui/X0$	A resource demand is related to the number of visits times the average request completion time, or to the resource utilization divided by the system throughput.
Little's Law	$Ni = Ri \times Xi$	The queue length and active requests is equal to the t average time of the request times the throughput.
Interactive Response Time Law	$R = (M/X0) - Z$	In an interactive system, the response rate is equal to the number of clients divided by the system throughput minus the idle time.

Source: Performance by Design, by Daniel A. Menasce, Virgilio A. F. Almeida, and Lawrence W. Dowdy, 2004, Prentice Hall.

Eliminating bottlenecks

The whole point of this exercise is to have the highest limit for throughput and the shortest response time possible, within the limits of the technology that you are working in, for any service demand that you are analyzing. To apply the five operational laws discussed previously, you need to be able to isolate the performance characteristics of the resource in question, which in complex network systems can be difficult to do. Still, these equations supply a theoretical framework for performance limits and you need to derive or at least approximate their values in order to input them into any performance model that you want to consider.

If you had to understand an entire network in order to improve performance, you would be faced with an intractable problem. In almost all cases, though, the performance for any service demand is entirely dependent on one subsystem or factor, and in rare instances perhaps two factors. Any factor that gates performance is called a *bottleneck*, and the nature of a bottleneck is that it is the system resource that has the highest utilization and lowest response rate, and has reached the limit of its available throughput. The rationale for improving performance is to successively eliminate bottlenecks until you achieve the desired result. For example, if you have a network containing a set of 10Base-T connections and the speed of the network is gated by these connections, then removing the slowest-performing link simply moves the bottleneck down to the next connection. Replacing all the 10Base-T links, however, would remove that class of bottleneck, revealing the next issue in performance, which might be the hubs that you are using.

Consider four hypothetical resources, A to D, where the utilization and throughput for each have been measured over a range of input. In Figure 6.7, you see a plot of each of these resources mapped over their utilization range. Each of the symbols — plus, triangle, square, and circle — represent measured data points for each of the four resource curves shown. Resources B through D retain spare capacity throughout the input range that was measured. Resource A, however, approaches 100 percent linearly up to a throughput of 7 and greater where it can no longer service the requests efficiently and the curve flattens out. Enhancing the performance of A therefore eliminates this particular bottleneck.

FIGURE 6.7

A plot of utilization versus throughput for four resources highlights resource A as a bottleneck.

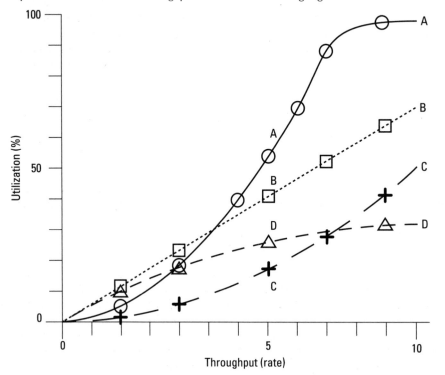

Because the Service Demand Law relates resource demand to utilization and throughput, you can use the experimental quantities you measured to calculate the overall resource service demands as follows

```
Di,r = Ui,r/X0 = A-DS Ui/X0 = UA/X0 + UB/X0 + UC/X0 + UD/X0
```

to obtain the total resource demand of the system based on the overall system throughput that you measure. The resource that is measured to have the highest service demand will have the highest utilization, and vice versa; it is therefore the bottleneck of the system and is governed by the equation:

```
X0 = < 1 / (MAX {Di})
```

This applies to resource A under heavy load in Figure 6.7, and is referred to as the upper asymptotic bound throughput limit under heavy load.

Different types of resources have different levels of concern based on the utilization rates. For disk, you might start to monitor any disk system that is 50 percent utilized, worry about any disk that is 70 percent utilized, and worry harder about any disk that is 80 percent utilized. Many disk operations begin to fail when the disk system is more than 85 percent full. This is particularly the case with databases and graphics, which store copies of the entire data set to disk as temporary files.

You can also consider the number of visits or requests and its relationship to service demand and throughput to make predictions on the nature of the bottleneck resource under light loading, which is a different problem than the one you've just seen for a heavily loaded system. Little's Law is the relationship that provides this connection. In a lightly loaded system with N transactions and no queue, Little's Law predicts that:

```
N = X x R > = (KSi=1 Di) x X0
```

Rearranging this equation and solving for X0 leads to

```
X0 = < N / (KSi=1 Di)
```

which is described as the upper asymptotic bound of throughput under light load. If you combine the two upper asymptotic bounds on throughput together in the same equation, you can derive the following relationship:

```
X0 = < MIN [(1 / MAX {Di}), (N / (KSi=1 Di))]
```

Figure 6.8 illustrates the relationship of the two upper asymptotic bounds on throughput for high and low loading and the impact that upgrading a bottleneck resource has on those relationships. The measured throughput for the original system is shown by the line with plus data points that approaches the heavily loaded system line, which is indicated by the line with triangle data points. In the original system, the throughput can approach this limit. When you upgrade the system and set a new heavily loaded limit line, shown as the line with square data points, the upgraded system can now approach this line as indicated by the upgraded system line with the circle data points.

A system under light load doesn't suffer from these limitations. In a lightly loaded system, the system can scale linearly. The two lines, the original system under light load with star data points and the upgraded system under light load with pentagon data points, scale throughout their range. The upgrade system is able to scale with a higher slope attaining greater throughput faster. Note, however, that there is a limit to the number of transactions that the lightly loaded system can accommodate and that the original system will support up to only six outstanding transactions while the upgraded system will scale up to nine outstanding transactions in the data queue.

FIGURE 6.8

Bounding limits under light and heavy loads for an upgraded resource

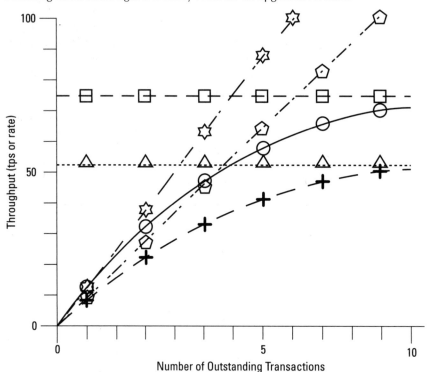

Network modeling

The process for modeling a computer network involves determining the different states that the network can be in, their probabilities, and the relationships between each state and other states. Given six states A to F, what are the relative probabilities that a particular state will lead to the other states? This type of modeling is referred to as a *Markov model* or *chain*, and defines a stochastic process that conforms to the Markov property limitation. In Markov models, the Markov property is that for any present state, transitions to future states are independent of the past states of the system. That is, the past does not determine the future.

Note

The Google PageRank feature is based on a Markov chain.

To build a Markov model, you can start by considering a random walk through the state space, noting the probabilities at each step. The resulting map or graph is a set of nodes representing each state and relationships between nodes that represent transition probabilities. Consider a packet-switched network with four different routers A to D, each interconnected by network segments. Figure 6.9 shows a Markov model representing the probability that a particular message has for navigating the network. Notice that the probability of leaving any one router is 1.0, and the probability of entering any one router is 1.0. You can determine the sum of the probabilities by adding all of the probabilities of arrows leaving the router and all of the probabilities of arrows entering the router. The arrows represent the next hop in the system.

FIGURE 6.9

A Markov diagram for four routers on a network

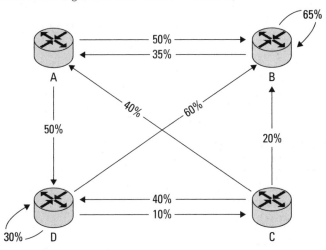

Having established the probabilities for transitions from router to router, you can use the Markov diagram to predict the behavior of this part of the network to solve for problems such as which router or network segment will be used most heavily. To solve these problems, you need to create a set of states to which a Mean Value Analysis (MVA) can be applied. For example, if a path through this router set is described as (Segment 1, Router, Segment 2), then you can fully describe the router space with a set of state transitions as follows:

```
(BA, A, AC), (BA, A, AD), (CA, A, AB)...(AD, D, DB), (BD, D, DC), (CD, D, DA)
```

Because you know the probability for each network segment, you can assign weights to the states or paths described. Some terms will drop out; other terms will be shown to have higher probabilities. The path vectors would then be written as:

```
(0.35 BA, A, 0 AC), (0.35 BA, A, 0.5 AD), (0.4 CA, A, 0.5 AB)...
   (0.5 AD, D, 0.6 DB), (0 BD, D, 0.1 DC), (0.4 CD, D, 0 DA)
```

The terms that are shown as strikeouts in the listing of path vectors are terms that drop out because they have a component that has a zero probability, making that path impossible to follow. Because all of these paths have relative weights, you can add up all of the paths, normalize the values, and obtain solutions to which paths have the highest probability and which router will see the most traffic.

Markov diagrams have a wide application. You could have chosen a set of disks in a disk array, a set of processors, processors and disks, or any other system you like that is not deterministic. Essentially, you use the Markov diagram to look into the black box that Little's Law abstracts processes into.

While Markov models are widely used in many disciplines, they can't be applied to many problems. As mentioned previously, they don't apply to situations where the previous state has an impact on the next state in a system. If one router is significantly slower than the other routers, or if self-loop paths influence the next path chosen, then either those factors must be incorporated into the Markov model or the model will not make accurate predictions. The more factors you add into the model, the more complex the problem becomes, and the more likely it is that the complexity will lead to inaccuracy.

Another problem with the Markov model is that it makes the assumption that the relative probabilities are fairly weighted. If a router has two paths leading out that have equal probabilities (50 percent) and the first packet out takes path B, then the probability that the next packet will take path A is still 50 percent. The probabilities make no specific demand on the path that the next packet takes, even though the population of probabilities will eventually apply. This is referred to as the exponential assumption, that probabilities are exponentially distributed. As an example of how probability can go awry, consider the fact that in the Super Bowl, the NFC team has won the coin toss the last 10 times. Go figure, the odds of that happening (for a fair coin toss) are 1 in 210 or 0.098 percent, even though every single pick by an NFC team still has only a 50/50 chance of being correctly picked

To use a Markov model that accounts for a path with two parts, you could decouple the two segments into individual states, each obeying the exponential assumption. This partitioning would then lead to a more accurate but more complex solution.

In theory, you can construct a Markov model to solve any problem. However, when the number of states rises to a certain level, the equations that solve problems in that state space become computationally onerous and the model no longer can be understood on an intuitive basis. To get around these types of problems, other variations of the Markov models are used, as are other model types. Because the topic of network modeling is more an applied mathematics problem than a networking problem, if you want to read more about performance modeling, you may want to read one of the texts on this area of study.

Server upgrades

Let's consider a specific example of how you can use a Markov model to determine how to upgrade a specific network server. If you have a system of domain servers and notice that those servers are beginning to reach high levels of utilization, you might conclude that these servers must be upgraded. Here are some items that you will need to know in order to calculate the impact of upgrading one component versus another server component:

1. **Maximum load.** The period of highest workload is Monday mornings from 8:30 to 10:00 with a specific measured load level.

2. **Application characteristics.** The application characteristics are crucial in setting RAM requirements, disk sector size, network bandwidth, and other parameters.

3. **Disk performance.** When you match the application's I/O pattern to the disk configuration, you are able to improve performance dramatically and lower disk requirements.

4. **Server/storage abstraction.** By abstracting server functions from storage functions, the system is made more reliable, flexible, and available.

5. **Network performance.** The domain servers generate significant replication traffic that impacts the network, so fewer, more powerful servers are preferred. Replication traffic should occur over dedicated network segments. An availability level of 99.95 percent was deemed satisfactory for this particular network service.

6. **ROI calculation.** An understanding of the Return on Investment (ROI) of the upgrade/expansion project is performed to justify the expenditure. ROI forces you to examine factors that you might not normally think about, such as system and software life cycles, and so this is an important step that you don't want to ignore.

An upsizing project based on these results might have the following phases to it:

- Historical data analysis
- Capacity planning
- System selection and design
- Testing and fine-tuning

- Pilot phase
- Production and rollout

Based on the results of this study, it was determined that the domain servers should be consolidated and their power increased, and that a dedicated connection should be established between domain servers. The question is, what type of server consolidation is a best fit? Server consolidation can:

- **Scale Out.** Increase the processor count by adding more systems
- **Scale Up.** Increase the processor count by deploying fewer, but more powerful servers

The two approaches have very different effects, both on networked server applications and on the network infrastructure. Figure 6.10 shows Scale Out and Scale Up graphically. When you scale out, once the server capacity is taxed, you just add another server to what is called the "server farm." When you scale up to a large server and you max out your server capacity, you add additional capacity to any particular application or task by dedicating more processors on the large server to the task at hand. Both approaches have their own set of benefits and penalties.

FIGURE 6.10

Scale out (left) adds more servers, while scale up (right) adds fewer but more powerful servers.

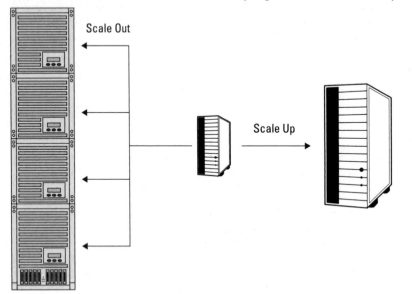

Scale out can be done incrementally and offers more options in terms of vendors and configuration than scale up does. Scale out is usually less expensive because it relies on replicating commodity equipment to achieve additional scale. From a network perspective, scale out maximizes the number of channels and provides better opportunities for applying technologies such as load balancing and failover. The fact that equipment is less expensive and less reliable is offset by the flexibility that scale out offers. Scale out gives you the benefit of working with smaller server units, and achieves availability through redundancy. As a rule, scale out requires more management than scale up does.

If you have an application that doesn't create a persistent connection to a server (is stateless), such as a Web service, then that server service is a candidate for server scale out. The large server farms that run Internet sites, terminal server farms, and other similar types of applications are often architected using this approach. Applications that aren't CPU and memory limited, but are bottlenecked in network I/O, lend themselves to server scale out.

Scale up has its own advantages. When you scale up, you have fewer servers, there are fewer points of failure, and you have a simpler network architecture. This also provides fewer servers to manage, maintain, and upgrade. Large SMP system vendors pay more attention to the quality of their components, are able to run enterprise versions of network operating systems, and offer considerably better support to their customers. Scale up places your eggs into one basket, but a more robust and fault-tolerant basket.

As a general rule, dense SMP systems that support high processor counts and powerful processors don't usually emphasize network I/O. Applications that benefit from enhanced processing but aren't I/O limited benefit from a scaled-up system. For example, a data warehouse application requires the processing of large data sets, but the reported results require modest network connectivity, and so the application is a good candidate for a scale up approach.

Summary

Servers play a central role in networks. They provide the services that other systems need. This chapter focused on how to determine capacity and loading in order to have a well-functioning network. Different project methodologies for adding server capacity were described.

Performance data allows you to derive fundamental network relationships. These relationships help you to determine which network resource is a bottleneck and allow you to figure out how to remove those bottlenecks. Modeling networks using a Markov model was presented.

In the next chapter, the concept of a network interface is described. Network interfaces, just like servers, are hardware, software, and a fundamental network component.

The Network Interface

A n interface occurs where two different media or substances form a boundary. Each of the connections in a network is a network interface, and that interface represents the boundary between the physical transport layers that transfer communication and the layers that prepare data for use with applications. A network interface is addressable, that is, a signal can be sent over physical media meant for that specific interface.

In most networking books, the concept of a network interface isn't clearly defined and is discussed only in relation to various topics. However, I begin this chapter by defining a network interface. Network connections and their properties are important concepts that apply to networks of all types and are also covered in this chapter. From an outside perspective, the network interface is the only representation of a networked device that an outside observer sees.

What Is a Network Interface?

Let's begin by defining what a network interface is. A network interface is the boundary between two different types of networking media. *Network interface* is a loose term that can be applied to any of the following:

- The point where two different networks meet, particularly in a topological or architectural diagram
- A network card, an ASIC (Application Specific Integrated Circuit) chip on a motherboard, a PC Card in a laptop, a USB/Ethernet connector, or some other similar kind of hardware device

- A virtual operating system object that can be manipulated programmatically

- The name given to each network connected to a router, which is an intelligent network switch

- The point at which a terminal connects to a network

- The point at which a switched public telephone network connects to a private telephone network

You may encounter the term *network interface unit* (NIU), which is used to refer to any network interface device that connects devices to or in a *local area network* (LAN). The NIU performs the function of sending and receiving data, as well as translating the communications into a protocol that is capable of being sent to the particular network type that the NIU serves. It is common for an NIU to contain a memory buffer so that if the communications must be resent, the data will still be in the NIU and will not have to be fetched from the sender.

Physical network interfaces

A *network interface card* (NIC), also referred to as a network adapter or less frequently as a LAN adapter, is an example of a physical network interface device. In the ISO/OSI Reference model that you learned about in Chapter 2, a network card is both a Layer 1 and Layer 2 device, spanning both the Physical and Data Link layers, respectively. A NIC's function is to receive communications from the network and to provide the necessary translation services so that the communications can be either forwarded to another network address or transmitted in a form that another networking component can modify so that the data it contains can be prepared for use by an application. A NIC is a type of NIU.

The network card doesn't alter the data being sent, but processes the packets or frames to modify the header or wrapper portion of the data, if required. For most network cards, the processing is directed by the chipset on the card but performed by a system's CPU. Network I/O is one of the key performance metrics that can place a limit on a system's performance.

Busy network interfaces can consume a system's processor resources and bring a computer to its knees. For desktop systems this is rarely a problem, but in high-performance networking where systems are I/O limited, it is a major issue. Web servers rely on network I/O for their performance, and are often I/O bound. Some NICs and advanced motherboards now incorporate special ASICs to offload the processing of the entire TCP/IP stack to a network controller, a technology called TCP offloading. The *TCP Offload Engine* (TOE) is optimized to process TCP headers.

Cross-Ref
Chapter 16 covers TCP offloading in more detail.

Network interface chips are now built into nearly all motherboards because the network chipsets are inexpensive, and on-board networking is a very convenient feature to have. Many high-performance motherboards, such as those used in gaming, workstations, and servers, come with two network interfaces, which provides a number of different configuration opportunities. Three network interfaces are:

- **Redundant.** If one interface fails, you still have a second operational network interface to work with.
- **High performance.** The two interfaces can both be communicating at the same time.
- **Isolated.** Each network interface can be assigned to different networks, which is the essential function of a router.

Logical network interfaces

Network interfaces have both a physical and a logical implementation. Most of the definitions in the bulleted list above describe a physical network interface. However, a network interface can be the logical point of connection between a system and a network. You can think of a logical network interface as being a software module or routine that emulates a hardware device. A logical network interface can accept network traffic, as well as send network traffic; it also behaves as if it is an I/O redirector. Keep in mind that logical network interfaces (or adapters, if you will) still use a system's physical network interfaces to handle network traffic.

One important example of a logical network interface (also called a virtual interface) is the loopback adapter. The loopback adapter is a software routine that emulates an internal NIC card that can accept system requests and reply to those requests. The loopback adapter is used to test whether network functions are operating correctly.

For IP version 4, the loopback adapter is found at

```
127.0.0.1
```

and for IP version 6, the address is

```
::1
```

You can PING these addresses, and they respond when a system's networking function is active. In instances where a system's NIC cards are malfunctioning or improperly configured, some operating systems return the address of the loopback adapter for any PING that initiates from the local system. The loopback adapter is a diagnostic function that isn't accessible from outside of the system being tested.

Modern operating systems implement a network interface as an object whose properties can be manipulated programmatically. Object-oriented programming languages can instantiate (create) a network interface, query the network interface to determine its properties, send data to the interface, or change the properties of the object and therefore change the operating parameters for the interface.

In the Java programming language, for example, you might use the `java.net.NetworkInterface` object class to create network interface instances. You can query a system to enumerate all instances of network interfaces; use the `getInetAddresses()` command to list the IP addresses of a network interface; use other methods to act on an interface; and programmatically alter an interface's properties. These types of commands and network interface objects exist for all other programming languages. The Microsoft .NET Framework also has a rich network interface object that can be manipulated using the C# programming language.

Note

For a brief tutorial on how to manipulate network interfaces with the Java programming language, go to http://java.sun.com/docs/books/tutorial/networking/nifs/index.html. A similar online reference for .NET may be found at http://msdn.microsoft.com/en-us/library/system.net.aspx.

Network Addressing

From a network viewpoint, the network interface is the system, as the interface stores the system's unique address and also provides the means by which network I/O can be directed to and sent away from any system. The address in a network interface is something that must differentiate one specific network card from another, even when both cards are identical models from the same manufacturer.

Physical addresses

In Ethernet networks, that address is a unique 48-bit number that is called the *Media Access Control* (MAC) address. MAC addresses are contained in every single network card; they are a unique address given to it by the manufacturer at the time of its manufacture and encoded in a *read-only memory* (ROM) card. In Ethernet networks, the *Institute of Electrical and Electronics Engineers* (IEEE) defines the standards by which vendors assign their MAC addresses using a unique registry. When you create a virtual network interface, a MAC address is assigned to the interface by the virtualization environment.

The MAC address is a physical address, as it is bound to a device. MAC addresses may be spoofed (faked), but they can't be duplicated.

In order to allow a network interface to seamlessly move from one network to another, each interface is assigned a network address. You can consider this assignment to be equivalent to giving the interface a logical address, and network addresses can be assigned at will. A network address that is assigned permanently to a network interface is called a *static address*. One that is temporarily assigned is called a *dynamic address*. For a network to function properly, no two network addresses on the same network may be the same. Network addresses can be reused on different networks or network ranges, called *subnets*, but duplicates on the same subnet will result in network errors.

A common form used to address a physical network interface is exemplified by the Solaris nomenclature:

```
<driver-name> <physical-unit-number>
```

The interface would then be named

```
hme0
hme1
```

and so on. Other forms of UNIX and variants of Linux use similar schemes, but Windows uses long names for network interfaces.

Figure 7.1 shows the Network Connections dialog box in Windows Vista 64. This dialog box shows that the computer has four network interfaces. Local Area Connection and Local Area Connection 2 are physical interfaces that are 1000Base-T ports associated with the Realtek I/O chipset on the motherboard; one is running and the second is unplugged (which is indicated by the X on the icon). VMnet1 and VMnet8 are virtual network interfaces. VMnet1 is associated with Ubuntu 8.04 (Hardy Heron) running in a VMware virtual machine. VMnet8 is associated with Windows Server 2008 Enterprise Edition running in a second virtual machine.

FIGURE 7.1

Network interfaces appear in the Network Connections dialog box in Windows (in this figure, Vista 64).

Different network types use different addressing schemes, but all network types rely on the assigned network address being unique on a network. When duplicate addresses are detected, the operating system should post an error message, but in some instances you may simply encounter strange network behavior.

Logical addresses

A logical network interface appends an additional identifier to the names given to physical network interfaces. In an operating system such as Sun Solaris, the format would be

```
<driver-name> <physical-unit-number>:<logical-unit-number>
```

The *logical unit number*, or LUN, means that there can be multiple logical network interfaces for the same system. You can configure logical network interfaces or virtual interfaces so that they can be assigned a number of IP addresses, and those IP addresses do not need to be in the same range (subnet) as the physical network interface. This allows a single system to appear as if it is many systems to the network.

Note

LUNs become important when network interfaces are attached to resources connected to servers. Storage servers use LUNs to connect to disk systems and RAID arrays. Because a LUN is a unique network path, its specification provides security features, protocol assignments, and other features that network interfaces offer to computer systems to the data contained on these storage assets.

Instances of LUN naming convention would include

```
hme0:1
hme0:2
hme0:3
```

and so on.

For example, if you run a virtual machine environment such as Microsoft Virtual PC or VMware Workstation, then each of the virtual machines you create can have one or more virtual interfaces. Each of those logical interfaces is not only assigned a unique IP address but can also be assigned a unique host name. That's the case shown in Figure 7.1, where you see two virtual network interfaces: one for Ubuntu and another for Windows Server 2008.

The use of multiple virtual network interfaces can be applied to:

- **Mission critical systems.** Redundant adapters can be configured to fail over when there is a problem with the primary adapter.

- **Improved performance.** Multiple adapters can be load balanced to optimize performance.

- **Application isolation.** An interface can be assigned to a specific application, or instance of an application.

For example, modern Web server software such as Internet Information Services (IIS) from Microsoft, or Apache, allows you to create virtual Web sites, to which a unique logical network interface can be assigned. From the standpoint of a network client, the individual Web servers appear as if they are separate systems on the server.

When you create and use virtual network interfaces, you are creating a software emulation, which has no additional cost. You can access an individual host more directly with a virtual network interface, and that makes it easier to specify tasks such as network backups, or to administer systems on a host-by-host basis.

Keep in mind that all virtual network interfaces still require a physical NIC or similar NIU through which network communication must flow. The more virtual interfaces you create, the heavier the network load can be during production. Also, when you start up a system, each of the network interfaces must be instantiated, which adds more time to the system startup. Network interfaces are complex data objects, and so when you have many network interfaces (both real and virtual), startup time can increase dramatically.

Configuring Network Interfaces

Network interfaces are so central to the successful operation of a computer system that every network operating system has at least two, and usually more, methods for querying, creating, and modifying them. For network adapters that use the TCP/IP protocol, you can query all of your system's network interfaces using the following procedures.

In Windows:

1. Click Start ➪ Run to open the Command Prompt window.

2. Type **CMD**, and then press Enter.

3. Type **IPCONFIG /ALL**, and then press Enter.

A listing of your network adapters, their MAC addresses, network addresses, and status appears in the Command Prompt window, as shown for Windows Vista 64 in Figure 7.2

FIGURE 7.2

The IFCONFIG /ALL command in Windows Vista 64 shows the status of all network adapters.

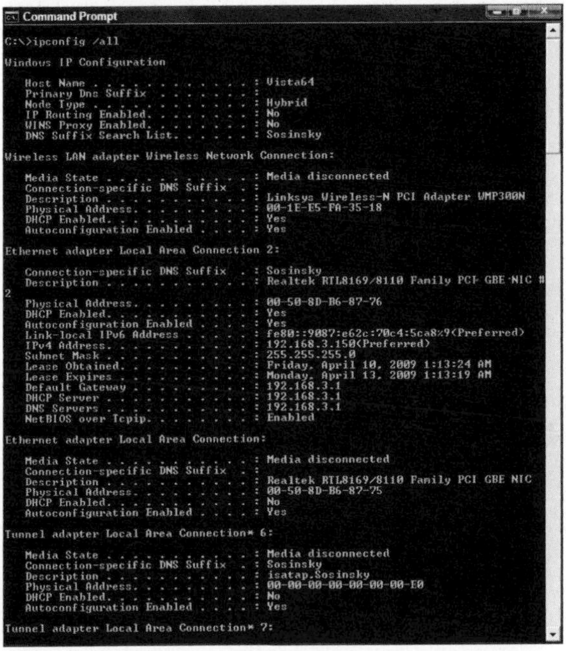

In Ubuntu 8.04:

1. Click Applications ➪ Accessories ➪ Terminal to open the Terminal session window.
2. Type **IFCONFIG**, and then press Enter.

Figure 7.3 shows the output of the Ubuntu Terminal window, with one emulated Ethernet adapter (eth0) and the loopback adapter (lo).

The IFCONFIG command in Ubuntu Linux lists your network adapters.

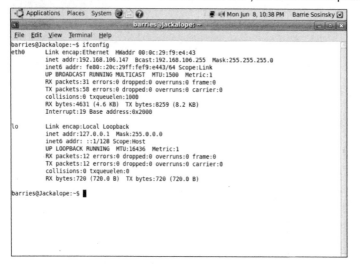

Notice that the physical address, called a MAC address in Windows, is called the HWaddr in Ubuntu, and that it appears on the first line that is returned for each adapter. The second line in Figure 7.3 displays the assigned network address for IP version 4, and the third line is the IP version 6 address.

The IPCONFIG on Windows and the corresponding IFCONFIG commands on Macintosh/Linux/ Solaris/Unix can take a large number of switches and options that can be used to create and modify network interfaces. Although the IFCONFIG commands are very similar from one operating system to another, particularly when it comes to UNIX, Linux, and Macintosh, there are differences between each operating system. Therefore, you should check the MAN pages for these operating systems, or the help page for Windows, to learn more about these commands. Figure 7.4 shows the Ubuntu MAN page for IFCONFIG. A MAN page is the online manual's explanation for that particular command.

Tip

Search engines, such as Google, index the online compilation of operating system manuals. They are particularly good at finding commands. If you type IFCONFIG, for example, several different Linux distributions appear at the top of the returned results. If you want the syntax of the Sun Solaris IFCONFIG command, then type the search term IFCONFIG site:Sun.com.

FIGURE 7.4

The IFCONFIG command MAN page in Ubuntu Linux

```
                           barries@Jackalope: ~

File  Edit  View  Terminal  Help
IFCONFIG(8)              Linux Programmer's Manual              IFCONFIG(8)

NAME
       ifconfig - configure a network interface

SYNOPSIS
       ifconfig [-v] [-a] [-s] [interface]
       ifconfig [-v] interface [aftype] options | address ...

DESCRIPTION
       Ifconfig  is  used to configure the kernel-resident network interfaces.
       It is used at boot time to set up interfaces as necessary.  After that,
       it  is  usually  only  needed  when  debugging or when system tuning is
       needed.

       If no arguments are given, ifconfig displays  the  status  of  the  cur-
       rently  active interfaces.  If a single interface argument is given, it
       displays the status of the given interface only; if a single  -a  argu-
       ment  is  given,  it  displays the status of all interfaces, even those
       that are down.  Otherwise, it configures an interface.

Address Families
       If the first argument after the interface name  is  recognized  as  the
       name  of  a  supported  address family, that address family is used for
       decoding and displaying all protocol  addresses.   Currently  supported
       address  families  include  inet  (TCP/IP, default), inet6 (IPV6), ax25
       (AMPR Packet Radio), ddp (Appletalk Phase  2),  ipx  (Novell  IPX)  and
       netrom (AMPR Packet radio).
Manual page ifconfig(8) line 1
```

Modern operating systems are replete with graphical utilities for working with network interfaces. In Windows, as you have already seen, you can use the Network Connections dialog box to view your network interfaces; and you can get to this dialog box through either the Network Control panel or through network icons in the System Tray. Nearly all common network operating systems have some version of a Network Control panel from which you can start to configure your network adapter and interfaces.

Another method that is used to configure network interfaces involves scripting languages and network management interfaces. SNMP (Simple Network Management Protocol)-enabled hardware can be queried directly for its properties, and can be modified, as can WMI (Windows Management Instrumentation) on Windows. Virtual network interfaces don't have a physical existence, and so they can't be directly managed. A virtual adapter is a creation of an operating system; therefore it is the system object that must be queried. UNIX has a rich *command-line interface* (CLI) for managing system properties, which include network functions. In Windows, a progression of more powerful scripting environments has been introduced over the years, resulting first in the Windows Scripting Host and more recently (with Vista/Windows Server 2008) the PowerShell command-line scripting system.

Bindings and Providers

The collection of software modules that reside between the NIC's Level 2 Data Link layer software and the applications found in the Level 7 Application layer in TCP/IP networking (based on the ISO/OSI networking model) is referred to as the *network stack* or *TCP/IP stack*. As incoming communication is transformed to data, it travels up from Level 3 through to Level 6. When data is outgoing, it is transformed into communications as it travels down from Level 6 to Level 3. The details of this discussion are described in Chapter 2.

In the Windows TCP/IP stack, for example, all of the installed network components are bound to each of the installed network adapters by default. That means that as different types of data and communication traffic passes through the stack, there are different pathways that the data can take. As the stack is traversed, the operating system sends the data and communications to the first module or protocol in the list of components. If that protocol isn't able to correctly handle the information, then the next protocol is sent the information until the entire stack is traversed.

The order in which components are used in the network stack is referred to as the *binding order*, and it is something that you can modify, and by doing so optimize network performance. When an operating system imposes a binding order, it has no idea which protocols you might use, and which you won't. When you don't have the requisite protocol, that particular class of networking doesn't work on your system. The solution to the problem is obvious: you add the component you need to your binding order. When you have protocols that you don't need, you impose unneeded network overhead on your system.

Each adapter stores and maintains its own binding order, and so you can add or remove components and/or protocols from each adapter, as well as change the order in which the components are expressed in the binding order. Not all operating systems allow you to manage the binding order, which is considered to be a more advanced feature, but most network operating systems used on servers do. On a desktop, modifying the binding order probably doesn't change the performance of the system, as most of the time desktops have modest network I/O. However, in systems that are network I/O limited, optimizing the network stack can make a significant difference in system performance, lowering CPU processor loading and improving data throughput. Systems of this type include Web servers, thin client terminal servers (such as Citrix server products and Windows Terminal Server), telephony servers, director- (enterprise-) class switches and routers, and many other server types.

To access the binding order in either Vista or Windows Server 2003, do the following:

1. Click Start ➪ Control Panel ➪ Network and Internet.
2. Click the Network and Sharing Center link, and then click the Manage network connections link.
3. In Vista, press Alt to view the menu (not necessary in Windows Server 2008), click Advanced, and then select Advanced Settings.

4. Click the Adapter and Bindings tab, and then select the connection you want to view or modify.

5. Click Bindings for <*ConnectionName*> and then use the Up and Down arrow buttons to modify the binding order, as shown in Figure 7.5.

FIGURE 7.5

The binding order, as shown in Vista 64

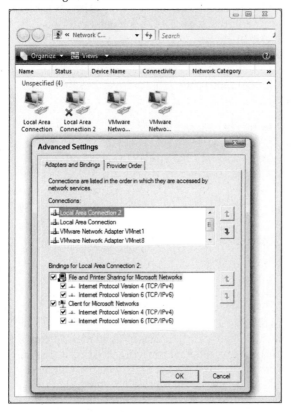

6. Click the Provider Order tab (shown in Figure 7.6) to view or modify the network provider order (NPO); the network interface uses the provider order to prioritize communication with the other devices on the network. You can use the arrow buttons to modify this order.

Changing the order of either the bindings or the providers will affect your interface's performance, so be sure to test the impact of any new settings.

Windows uses the term *network provider* to describe a dynamic link library (DLL) that contains the routines necessary to connect with other network types, such as Novell, which is exposed through a network provider API. Each provider is a client of a Windows network driver and is responsible for creating and managing connections.

The provider order

There's no rule that the network stack must be an operating system function, although that architecture allows new features to be added and code to be optimized more easily than code embedded in hardware. The transition from the Windows XP/Server 2003 core to the Windows Vista/Server 2008 core included a completely rebuilt network stack that exhibited some dramatic improvements in areas such as Server Message Block (SMB) file transfers.

Isolation and Routing

A general-purpose computer or a special-purpose computer that functions as a network appliance can have two or more network adapters. When there is only a single adapter, the system is referred to as *single homed*; with two network adapters it is *dual homed*; and when there are multiple network adapters, the system is referred to as *multihomed*.

There are many good reasons to have multiple network adapters in the same system, among which are the following:

- **Improved performance.** You get additional throughput when you add more network adapters.

- **Fault tolerance.** A system can be configured so that if one network adapter fails, traffic is directed to a backup.

- **Multipurpose Use.** One network interface can be used for network communications, while a second network interface can be used for system management, fault tolerance, or high-performance connections.

  Early dual network-ported motherboards used one high-speed interface and a low-speed interface, such as 100Base-T (100 Mbits/s) Ethernet and 10Base-T (10 Mbits/s) Ethernet, respectively, in combination. Later variants used 1000Base-T (Gigabit, or GigE) Ethernet along with a 100Base-T connection. As high-speed Ethernet chips have dropped significantly in price, it is rare to find a motherboard that offers two network interfaces that doesn't have both as high-speed network interfaces.

- **Routing.** Two or more network adapters define a path or route that can be managed, based on factors you specify.

- **Isolation.** Routing provides two very desirable features that are essential for secure networking: physical isolation and protocol isolation, each of which is described briefly in the sections that follow.

All of these are good reasons to have an additional network interface in any computer. Networking functions are among the most heavily used system components, and they tend to fail more often than many other functions. The older any computer system becomes, the more likely it is that a newer network interface card will add more speed, better security, and most importantly, more up-to-date device driver support. The network interface device driver is a fundamental factor in determining the speed, stability, and compatibility of the network interface in any system.

Physical isolation

In order for one device on a network to discover another device, the network interface of both devices must share the same network address range, or more precisely, be on the same subnet. If you have one computer with an IP address of 4.2.2.1 (which happens to be Verizon's DNS server address) and another computer with an address of 4.2.3.1, then you will not be able to browse the other system on your network; however, if the second system's network address were 4.2.2.224, then you would. This assumes that you are using a Class C subnet mask of 255.255.255.x. That is called physical isolation, and it is a fundamental method that firewalls, gateways, routers, and other devices use for security.

You may have encountered physical isolation if you have configured a firewall, gateway, cable modem, or wireless router on your network. When a vendor ships a device of this type, the device contains two network interfaces. One interface connects to the external network and is configured to accept a dynamic address from a service running on a server on the external network. That dynamic address for TCP/IP networks is assigned from a pool of addresses belonging to the external network. The second network interface in the device is given a private network address by the device's vendor that you need to change. Most often this address is drawn from a pool of private IP addresses that are reserved for use on internal networks and can't be used on a wide area network such as the Internet.

Let's say for the sake of argument that the device's internal LAN interface is set to the Class C network 192.168.1.1 and the computers on your LAN use the IP range of 192.168.3.1 to 192.168.3.255. Your system has an address of 192.168.3.52. That device will not be available to browse from your system using either your network discovery protocol (Windows NetBEUI, for example) or your browser's HTTP broadcast function. To view the device, you first need to change your system's network adapter to the range 192.168.1.x, and then browse for the device.

Now with both devices on the same subnet, you can browse for the device and configure it in the manner that the device vendor allows. Older devices used management utilities for device configuration, and many large servers and systems that play the role of physical isolation still do. However, newer devices and nearly all consumer-level network devices ship with small Web servers and are configured through your browser. Therefore you would open a browser, and enter the following address into the address bar:

```
http://192.168.1.1
```

That address should take you to a login page, which, after you supply the necessary credentials, will allow you to modify the device's LAN interface, which includes the address. If you change the device's address to 192.168.3.2 (which usually requires a device restart), then the device is now visible to members of your network. It will also be available to the system you are using after you change the network interface from 192.168.1.x back to 192.168.3.52.

Tip
Make it a point to change the default login name and password, as well as the default LAN address of a device providing physical isolation. These defaults are known to hackers trying to gain access to networks.

Physical isolation works because communications arriving at the external network interface are only aware of that network interface's address. External communications have no idea what the address of a device on the internal network might be and require a mechanism to identify the internal address that only exists in the routing device. That mechanism might be a network address translation table (called a NAT) in a router, or it could be a forwarding system that is part of a proxy server. A proxy server is a server that receives communications from external devices, acts on them in some way (filtering, caching, anonymizing, or some other function), and then redirects the communications to another system. Internet Security and Acceleration Server (or ISA Server) from Microsoft is an example of a proxy server.

Protocol isolation

Protocol isolation works by using one network protocol for external network traffic and a second protocol for internal LAN communication. With a transport protocol such as TCP/IP, the packets are routable; given enough time and resources, it is possible for an outside user to circumvent different methods of security. Protocol isolation adds yet another layer of complexity to the task presented to intruders. If the internal network is running another network protocol such as NetBEUI from Microsoft or IPX/SPX protocol from Novell, then access to shared resources such as a file share requires the use of communications formatted using those protocols. Because both of these protocols are non-routable, communications in this form cannot originate from an external network.

Protocol isolation is helpful for securing data on the network, but it provides no additional barrier to intrusion from the external network. Unless some means is provided to block TCP/IP traffic, systems that are on the internal LAN are discoverable by other systems. However, because these systems aren't sharing any of their resources over TCP/IP, there are no resources that an external system can connect to. Protocol isolation is best used for devices that don't require TCP/IP to communicate with other devices. An example of this type of system is storage servers running the SAMBA file sharing service, which can use the Server Message Block (SMB) protocol to communicate with servers. Should you want to make a SAMBA file server available to external network systems, you still require a gateway or a network adapter on the internal device with both protocols bound to it.

Bus Interfaces for NICs

Network interfaces come in a wide variety of forms and are used for a variety of different networks. Among the types of network interfaces you will encounter are interface chips found in:

- On-board (on the motherboard) network controller chipsets
- Add-in cards for common expansion buses
- Wired peripheral buses such as USB
- Wireless technologies such as 802.11x or Bluetooth

Network cards follow the current technology of the day. For PCs, the first add-in network adapters were ISA (Industry Standard Architecture) cards. The most common network cards found today are PCI (Peripheral Component Interconnect) cards.

High-performance network cards appear first on the higher-performance bus types, which for PCs today is the PCI-X interface. Therefore, you will find network cards available for PCI-X that include single-channel Ethernet adapters that fit into the small 1X PCI-X slots on a motherboard. 1X-Ethernet cards currently range in price from $20 to $100, and because they offer no compelling performance advantage, they really just represent a replacement of the current generation of PCI network cards by newer technology. PCI-X cards are backwards compatible with the PCI bus, provided that the voltages are compatible. Older PCI cards were 5 volts, while the current PCI Revision 3.0 uses a voltage of 3.3 volts. Therefore any PCI-X card rated at 3.3 volts can be used in a PCI slot. PCI cards can also be used in a PCI-X slot provided that the PCI card has the right voltage and that it can physically fit into the edge connector.

PCI-X has twice the bus width and runs at up to four times the clock rate, but uses the same bus protocol and electrical settings. The theoretical throughput of a PCI-X (1X) bus slot is 1.06 GB/s, which compares to 532 MB/s for the PCI bus. The speed used by either the PCI or PCI-X bus is limited to the speed of the slowest card used. You will find that current motherboards separate their PCI-X slots into separate channels to improve system performance.

PCI-X has a number of additional features that make it attractive, including the ability to restart or hot swap cards, and scalability. Hot swapping allows you to remove and add a card while a system is running, which is important for any server that must be highly available. PCI-X slots come in 4-channel (4X) and 16-channel (16X) versions with theoretical throughput rates of 4.2 GB/s and 17 GB/s, respectively. Therefore you find that server network cards that have multiple ports and advanced interface standards such as InfiniBand or iSCSI that need these higher throughputs come in 4X and 16X form factors.

The expansion card for laptops in widespread use was called a PCMCIA Card, now thankfully shortened to PC Card. The original acronym stood for Personal Computer Memory Card International Association, and the standard is now at PCMCIA 2.0.

The PC Card standard is not a bus standard, per se; it is a packaging standard. PC Cards were first made for memory expansion and were then expanded to modems and even hard drives. However, the most common use for PC Cards has always been for the addition of network interfaces to laptops. There are four standards in use — Types I, II, III, and IV — with the primary difference being the thickness of the card. Type II is the common size for NICs, which are between 5 and 5.5 mm thick, offer either a 16- or 32-bit interface, and usually run at 3.3 volts. At that form factor, PC Cards can support RJ45 Ethernet connections.

In another example of adapting a network adapter to an available computer bus, you can attach a network adapter to a USB port. Wired and wireless Ethernet adapters are both common and valuable devices to have handy. Should your computer networking cease to function properly, you can plug this device into a spare USB port and check to see if it connects properly.

PCI-X bus versus the PCI Express (PCI-E) bus

The PCI-X bus is different from the PCI Express (PCI-E or PCIe) bus, although they are often confused because their names are similar. PCI-E is a full-duplex serial bus that is used for high-speed peripheral devices such as storage arrays or RAID systems. PCI-X is a parallel bus that is a half-duplex bidirectional device. In a half-duplex device, half of the channels must be outgoing and half must be incoming. A full-duplex bidirectional device can communicate with any number of channels incoming or outgoing.

These buses are electrically different, and the cards that they use are keyed differently. The current standard of PCI-E 1.0 x1 offers 32 lanes of up to 250 MB/s for a throughput of 16 GB/s, up to 8 GB/s incoming and 8 GB/s outgoing. The serial architecture makes PCI-E easier to manage, and allows each lane to automatically negotiate the best throughput speed; however, PCI-X is limited to the slowest device speed.

A sample network adapter

The D-Link DGE-560T Gigabit PCI-X adapter shown in Figure 7.7 illustrates some of the common features found in network cards. The 560T fits into a PCI-X 1X slot and allows Ethernet transfer speeds of up to 2 Gbits/s, on either a 16- or 32-bit bus. A 2 Gbit/s throughput corresponds to 0.25 GB/s or 250 MB/s. The card supports a number of management protocols such as SNMP, remote network boot using either Preboot Execution Environment (PXE) or RPL (Remote Initial Program Load protocol), Advanced Power Management, and Wake-on LAN, as well as being hot-plug capable.

FIGURE 7.7

The D-Link DGE-560T PCI-X network adapter

Photo courtesy of D-Link, Inc.

The largest black chip on the card is the network controller. This card is 10Base-T, 100Base-T, and 1000Base-T compatible, and like many multispeed cards has activity lights to indicate its condition. The light above the RJ45 connection is an activity light; it lights up as data is being sent or received. The light below the RJ45 connection is dark when a 10Base-T connection is detected, green when communication is at the 100Base-T level, and yellow when the adapter is operating at 1000Base-T. Many adapters actually have two or three separate lights for this purpose. An interesting feature of this particular card is that it ships with a utility that can detect if there is a problem with the cable attached to the NIC.

If you are running a version of Windows, you should be aware that the Windows operating system can display a network interface activity icon in the System Tray. In Vista, you enable this option in the Notification Area tab of the taskbar and Start Menu Properties dialog box; in Windows XP, it is enabled on a case-by-case basis in the Properties dialog box for each network interface. The icon isn't merely for show, but serves the same function as the activity lights on a NIC card. As shown in Figure 7.8, the network icon is composed of two different computers.

The front computer is the local computer, and it lights up when the network interface is receiving data. The back computer is the remote system, and that icon lights up when your local system is sending data to a remote system. So the animation of the blinking lights in the icon is a good way to analyze your system's network interface function at a glance. Other operating systems have similar utilities, including Performance Monitor applications that allow you to monitor network I/O with much finer granularity.

FIGURE 7.8

The Windows Status Tray Network Interface icon

Network icon

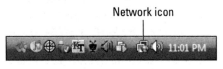

Network drivers

All of these different network interface form factors work because each card or adapter has a network controller chip that can be addressed over the particular bus used. There may be many different NIC vendors, and many different NIC forms, but there are only a few network controller chipsets in use. The software required to communicate with different chipsets and network drivers is often bundled into an operating system's distribution. Operating systems that have an automatic configuration option load the correct driver when the system recognizes that particular chipset. Windows Plug and Play (PnP) architecture is an example of an automatic configuration system.

Unlike graphic cards, where the driver software changes frequently, network drivers don't often change substantially for a particular operating system. It's not uncommon to find that a network driver that works for an older version of an operating system such as Windows Server 2003 will also work for Windows Server 2008. However, it is considered to be best practice to use the latest driver for a NIC. The latest driver is probably considered to be the one that the card vendor — or for an embedded controller, the motherboard vendor — has on their Web site.

Don't assume that the disk in the box with your card or operating system distribution is the most current one. The operational differences between a current and an earlier version of a network driver may be subtle, but they may also be important. You may find that the newer version improves performance, cuts down on error rates, or improves compatibility. This isn't always the case, of course, and some drivers make things worse. But for the most part, vendors tend to improve their software over time.

Modern operating systems use a standard application programming interface, or API, to communicate with NICs. The Microsoft API is called the Network Driver Interface Specification, or NDIS. It was developed jointly by 3Com and Microsoft, at a time when 3Com dominated the Ethernet NIC category. NDIS is conceptually part of the Logical Link Control layer that occupies a sublayer that is part of Layer 2 of the ISO/OSI model, serving as the interface between that layer and the Network layer, which is Layer 3. Below the Logical Link Control layer is the Media Access Control, or MAC, device driver that is part of Layer 1, the Hardware layer. NDIS is part of Windows low-level network plumbing, creating and removing the addressing and wrappers that encapsulate data transmission.

Some Linux distributions ship with software that allows them to use NDIS-compliant network cards, but other operating systems use different network API standards to communicate with NIC cards. On Macintosh systems, Apple uses the Open Data-Link Interface (ODI) that they developed with Novell for their Logic Link Control layer software. ODI is similar to NDIS in that it is meant to be NIC card-vendor neutral.

Other network driver interface software that you may encounter includes the Uniform Driver Interface (UDI), which is a project that is trying to standardize a portable interface for device drivers. UDI may show up in a number of Linux or UNIX variants. The Universal Network Device Interface (UNDI) API is used by motherboard chipset vendors such as Intel to allow a NIC card to be accessed by the PXE protocol by a computer's BIOS. The PXE allows an administrator to remotely manage systems, install new operating systems, and perform system maintenance from a small, independent operating system.

Summary

A network interface is a named operating system object that is configurable through software. Each network interface has a number of associated properties that are unique to that object. Among the properties is a unique physical address, called a MAC address, that is encoded by the NIC or controller vendor. Logical addresses that are meaningful to the particular network type that you use — TCP/IP, for example — are assigned to a network interface.

Network interfaces can be physical devices, as well as logical devices. A logical network interface is created by an operating system for use with virtual machines, as part of software that requires network redirection, and for many other purposes. From the standpoint of configuration, a logical network interface is a complete network interface, except that any logical network interface must still use a physical network adapter to send and receive network traffic.

One aspect of network interfaces that determines their capabilities is the network components that are enabled for use with that interface. This list is called the binding order, and the set of network types that can be used is called the provider order. The order of both determines how data is processed as it comes and goes from the network and travels through the network stack to an application. Both of these orders can be managed and modified.

When you have two or more network interfaces in a computer, it is referred to as multihomed. The ability to have different network addresses on these cards allows computers to be physically isolated from one another. When different network interfaces run different networking protocols or use different network providers, the system has the ability to isolate one adapter from another using protocol isolation.

In the next chapter, you learn about the different types of transport media used to build networks. These include wired cables, wireless connections, and other types of media.

Transport Media

I n this chapter, I cover three types of transport media that occupy the physical layer of a network: wired cables for electrical current, fiber-optic cables for light, and wireless links using mainly radio and microwave frequencies.

Different cable types require different methods for running cable, connecting together, and organization. This chapter describes some of the considerations you need to make when installing a network in a building.

Wired Media

Most people don't pay enough attention to the physical layer of their network. Given that wiring is something that might last 10 to 15 years, it's worth considering which type of wired media will support your network, not only for its present capabilities but also for future ones.

There are four main types of wired media in use:

- **Twisted pair**. Shielded, copper-based, twisted-pair cable. This form of cabling is used in local area networks, particularly older types of networks.

- **Coaxial.** Copper-based coaxial cable. Coaxial cable is thick, multi-wire cable that can be used for both high bandwidth and high connectivity connections.

- **Ethernet.** Unshielded, copper-based, twisted-pair cable. The unshielded twisted-pair wiring is the most commonly used network cable and is used on most versions of Ethernet.

- **Fiber optic.** Glass or plastic-based fiber-optic cable. Optical cable is the basis for high-speed and high-capacity networks.

Each of these cable types offers different connection speeds, has a different bandwidth, and requires different network topologies and physical connections. In the sections that follow, good wiring solutions are discussed and the four wire types are considered in more detail.

Cross-Ref
The physics of signals traveling on wires is described in Chapter 5.

Wiring the physical plant

Good wiring solutions require some preparation, especially when there are many cable runs and when runs must span rooms, floors, and buildings. Many localities have specific building codes for wiring that include standards — such as the use of conduit — that must be met. For that reason, a licensed electrician may be required to install network cable to comply with the codes and to validate the work. Cable runs need to be insulated, and should be routed in a way that makes it easy to adapt to changing systems.

Many networks route their wiring through what is called a *patch panel*, or a collection of patch panels, which is often called a *wiring closet*. The purpose of a patch panel is to allow connections to be quickly modified when systems are moved, or when projects require different connections. An example of a patch panel is shown in Figure 8.1. Good cable management dictates that you adopt a color-coding system so that you can visually tell which cable is for what connection. Administrators often organize these tables into Excel worksheets, and number and label cables at both ends for greater clarity. For groups of cables running to a server rack or into a room, cables are tied together into bundles that make it clear which group they are running to. This organizational system can save a lot of time and frustration later on when you are trying to troubleshoot problems on a network.

Building codes may require that cable be surrounded by an insulator. Insulators can be Teflon (PTFE, also called plenum), Polyvinyl Chloride (PVC), or more frequently, Polyethylene (PE). Teflon is the most expensive of the three but is fire retardant. PVC, although cheaper, will burn and give off toxic gas in a fire. Polyethylene is flammable, but its fumes are non-toxic.

Cabling that is exposed to bending and flexing, tread underfoot, stretched, or crimped is subject to failure. Failure is often the best-case scenario for problems of this type because it is relatively easy (although time consuming) to replace a failed cable. The major problems occur when a network cable fails intermittently. Intermittent failure makes it hard to diagnose the problem, and harder still to locate it. You never know whether the failure is due to hardware or software, a connection setting, a bad port in a switch or router, and so on. Because it is intermittent, the amount of time you spend grows exponentially. Many times, you never find the problem and are forced to simply live with it. So an ounce of prevention is worth a pound of cure.

FIGURE 8.1

A patch panel

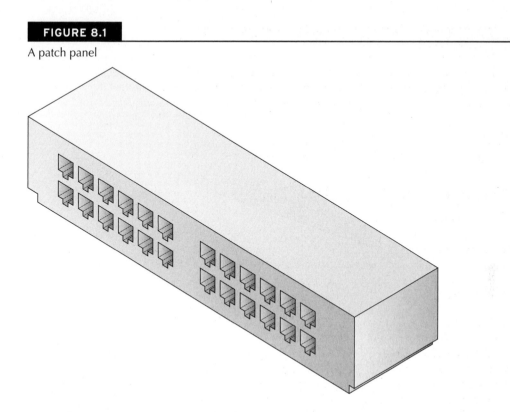

There are many ways to route cable conveniently and safely. If a room has a suspended ceiling, then routing cable above the suspension harness is a good method. You can also buy hangers and special cabling tracks that can be added to ceilings to achieve the same effect. You can use special runners to protect cable that is routed on a floor. In computer rooms, raised flooring serves the same purpose for routing cable as suspended ceilings. Figure 8.2 shows a raceway that uses a two-part design. The lower part holds the wire, and the upper part snaps on to seal the raceway. Alternative designs are open-wire baskets (for hanging), wall mounts, ceiling mounts, and floor runs.

It is also a good idea to route network cables in a conduit. However, you should never use network conduits to run electric power lines with your network cable. Electric lines interfere with the signal in copper network cable by creating a voltage that can degrade the signal or, in severe cases, damage equipment that the network cable is attached to. The dynamo effect that creates a current when a wire is placed near a moving magnet also creates a magnetic field (an applied voltage) when electricity passes by a metallic object.

FIGURE 8.2

An enclosed cable raceway

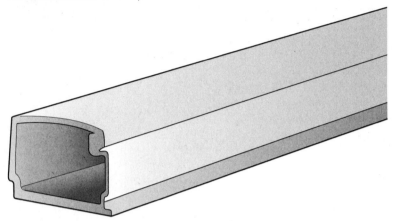

Electric motors, fluorescent lights, motors such as pumps or refrigerators, and any other devices that have high magnetic fields and can cause electromagnetic interference, or EMI. Similarly, devices such as wireless routers, microwave ovens, even wireless telephones can be a source of radio frequency interference, or RFI, which can give rise to spurious signals and degrade communication on network cables. For this reason, cables should be routed away from these various sources or adequately shielded in order to protect the network cable from these outside interferences. Longer cable runs tend to exacerbate these problems, as network signal strength decreases over longer segments.

Twisted pair

Twisted-pair wiring is the most common network cable in use today, particularly unshielded twisted pair. It is used to carry both analog and digital signals. Indeed, the very first telephone transmission by Alexander Graham Bell was over twisted-pair wiring. The wiring used in plain old telephone service (POTS) lines is composed of two sets of twisted-pair wiring, two wires of which are unused. It is these unused wires that allow for the installation of DSL, ISDN, or network connections to run over telephone lines in houses and offices.

Twisted pair is popular because it is relatively cheap to produce and is both insulated and shielded. The twisted wire offers the benefit of averaging out the impact of external magnetic or electrical fields and lowering the amount of crosstalk or interwire signal interference. Twisted-pair wiring offers many of the benefits of coaxial cable. Figure 8.3 shows twisted-pair wiring in its unshielded form, along with the common RJ-45 jack that is used to connect twisted-pair wiring together through couplers

FIGURE 8.3

Unshielded twisted-pair wiring and an RJ-45 male plug

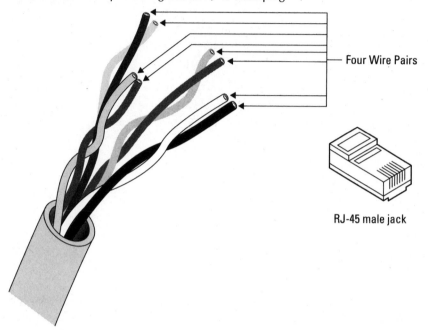

Four Wire Pairs

RJ-45 male jack

Shielded twisted-pair (STP) wiring was introduced by IBM in the early 1980s and is still in use on Token Ring networks. It never achieved the popularity of unshielded twisted-pair (UTP) wiring, probably because of the extra cost of the cables and their bulky nature, which made them hard to work with.

In STP, there are two wire pairs, each pair of which is twisted around its mate. STP shielding is composed of either a foil or braided wire, and must be grounded at one end. When foil is used, the wire may be referred to as *foil twisted pair*, or FTP, but this is an uncommon designation.

While the twisted wire helps to reduce crosstalk in the wires over its run, STP suffers from crosstalk and EMI degradation at the ends of the wire. The more twists per meter, the more protection is afforded against crosstalk and the fewer data errors are incurred. The twist rate is referred to as the *pitch* of the twist (turns per meter) and is usually varied between wire pairs in order to suppress signal degradation.

Note

The acronyms NEXT and FEXT are used to describe Near End Crosstalk and Far End Crosstalk. NEXT measures the interference of two cables in a pair as measured at the same end of the cable. FEXT measures the interference of the two pairs at either end of the cable, with the cable as the transmitter of the signal.

UTP is widely used in many different network types. UTP wiring is constructed from pairs of copper wire that are twisted but not insulated. UTP is the cable used in Ethernet networks and often in telephony applications. When used in T-1 lines, twisted-pair wiring requires that the signal be refreshed by a repeater every 1.8 km (1.1 miles).

UTP categories are an EIA/TIA (Electronic Industries Alliance/Telecommunications Industry Association) standard. CAT 5 is the most common wiring in current use for networks; it was introduced in 1988. CAT 3 is used for telephony, and on older networks as runs from a central wiring cabinet. The colors of the wires are standardized. Most UTP cable conforms to the Underwriters Laboratories (UL) standards and lists the category on the outside of the cable. UTP cable is connected to RJ-45 connectors, which are extended versions of the typical phone plug, with more connections.

Table 8.1 lists some of the more commonly encountered forms of twisted-pair wiring, both UTP and STP, but it is not a complete listing. The various types of backbone UTP cabling used aren't listed. Many backbone UTP cables come assembled from combinations of 25 pair cables.

TABLE 8.1

Twisted-Pair Cables

Category of Type	Maximum Data Rate	Wire Pairs	Application
CAT 1 (UTP)	< 1 Mbps	2	Analog data, POTS telephony, ISDN
Type 1 (STP)		2	Token Ring networks
CAT 2 (UTP)	4 Mbps	2	Token Ring networks
Type 2 (STP)		4	Voice/Data
CAT 3 (UTP)	16 Mbps	4	Voice/Data, 10BASE-T Ethernet, Telephony
CAT 4 (UTP)	20 Mbps	4	Token Ring
CAT 5 (UTP)	100 Mbps - 1 Gbps	4	10BASE-T, 100BASE-T, Gigabit Ethernet, ATM, FDDI
CAT 5E (UTP)	100 Mbps	4	ATM, FDDI
CAT 6 (UTP)	> 100 Mbps	4	Broadband
CAT 6e	10 Gbps	4	Gigabit Ethernet
Type 6 (STP)		2	Token Ring
CAT 7 (UTP)	1.2 Gbps	4	Gigabit Ethernet, VIA, high-speed interconnect, audio/visual
Type 8 (STP)		2	Data
Type 9 (STP)		2	Backbone

The designation of "Types" for STP cable categories is based on older IBM standards for Token Ring networks. These STP cables connect to Multi-station Access Units (MAUs) with IBM data connectors, which are hermaphroditic (male and female) connectors that can be connected to one another with a locking clip. Unconnected token ring cables are a complete self-contained loop, to which is added one or two IBM data connectors and often an RJ-45 jack. STP Type cabling has largely been replaced on Token Ring networks by the more popular and cheaper UTP cabling.

Coaxial cable

Coaxial cable is a packaging method for running cable that is very popular. It was the original cable used in Ethernet networks and is still used almost universally for television connections. Coaxial cable was introduced in 1929 and became the original long-distance cable that AT&T used as their network backbone before the introduction of fiber-optic cable in the 1980s.

The structure of a coaxial cable is shown in Figure 8.4. Every coaxial cable has a central copper wire that is surrounded by an insulator called the *dielectric*. In higher-cost coaxial cable, the copper wire may be coated with silver in order to improve the high-frequency transmission characteristics of the copper. Surrounding the dielectric is a wire braid or foil wrapping that serves to shield the copper wire from EMI and RFI interference. The outer shell of the coaxial cable is usually a plastic casing or plenum (Teflon or Kynar).

FIGURE 8.4

A cutaway view of coaxial cable

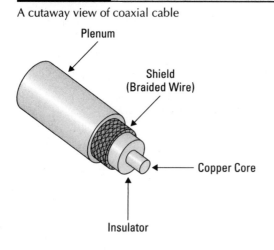

There are many different kinds of coaxial cable in use today, as described in Table 8.2. They vary in terms of their thickness, their ability to carry current, their resistance, and the applications that they are used for. Alternative forms of coaxial cable include Twinaxial (Twinax), which bundles two coaxial cables in the same jacket, and Triaxial (Triax), which bundles three coaxial cables in the same jacket.

The use of coaxial cable for both Thin Ethernet (Thinnet) and Thick Ethernet (Thicknet) applications is very limited. The main use of coaxial cable is in audio/visual (AV) applications such as cable TV, CCTV cameras, and other high-bandwidth applications. Gradually, coaxial cable is being replaced by fiber-optic cable as fiber becomes cheaper.

TABLE 8.2

Coaxial Cables

Coaxial Type	Core Diameter (mm)	Resistance (Ω, ohms)	Application
RG-6	1.0	75	Cable TV
RG-8	2.17	50	10BASE-5 (Thicknet). This was the original cable used for Ethernet, and was replaced by twisted-pair wiring.
RG-11	1.63	75	Cable TV
RG-58/U	0.9	50	10BASE-2 (Thinnet)
RG-58 A/U	0.9	50	Thinnet
RG-58 C/U	0.9	50	Thinnet
RG-59	0.81	75	Cable TV and ARCNET
RG-62	6.4	93	ARCNET and IBM 3270 mainframes (legacy systems)

Transmission lines based on coaxial cable use a tube construction technique that bundles many coaxial cables along with wire pairs inside a protective sheath that is composed of paper wrapping, thermoplastic cement, and a polyethylene jacket. Figure 8.5 shows a diagram of a coaxial cable transmission line. The last Transcontinental Cable System L-carrier standard, introduced in 1972, was L-5. That cable had 22 coax per cable, operated at 57 MHz, required repeaters every 2 miles, and carried 132,000 voice circuits per coax. *Coax* is the term used for the individual inner conductors.

Ethernet wiring

Ethernet cabling uses a nomenclature to describe the different types of cable standards that exist. If you have wired a network with 100BASE-T network cable, each part of the name signifies a different property. The acronym BASE is short for baseband, which describes a signal within a frequency range that can be measured from zero to a maximum level. A system that uses frequency multiplexing can't be described in this way. Baseband is analogous to a low-pass system (a filter with a cutoff), and is the opposite of a pass-band system, where all frequencies in a range are allowed down the wire.

Coaxial carrier cable

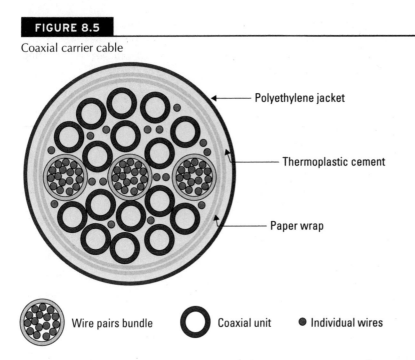

- Polyethylene jacket
- Thermoplastic cement
- Paper wrap

Wire pairs bundle   Coaxial unit   ● Individual wires

The "T" in BASE-T Ethernet means that it uses twisted-pair wiring. The commonly available Ethernet cables are comprised of four wire pairs ending in 8-pin connectors using RJ-45 connectors. This cable type supports any combination of sessions, from four full-duplex to up to eight half-duplex communication. Not all Ethernet runs on twisted-pair wiring. When the standard is designated as BASE-TX, it refers to Ethernet over twin axial cable. 10BASE-2 is a BASE-TX technology and uses BNC barrel-type connectors or T-connectors. Names such as 100BASE-T are used to define a particular Ethernet technology for which an IEEE standard exists. For example, 802.3 (14) is the standard that defines 10BASE-T, and 802.3 (24) is the standard that defies 100BASE-TX.

The CAT system defines a particular wiring type, whereas the standard defines the electrical signals traveling over the wires and the manner in which wires are connected. For example, CAT 5 cable is the current standard for high-speed Ethernet. To make a 100BASE-TX system, you would use a particular type of signaling, and CAT 5 copper wire cabling with two twisted pairs. At speeds beyond 1 Gbit/s, CAT 5E and CAT 6 are becoming more widely used. All Ethernet wire supports wire speeds from its maximum rating down to the slowest speed, 10BASE-T.

Twisted-pair CAT 5 Ethernet has the connections designated by the TIA/EIA (Telecommunications Industry Association and the Electronics Industry Alliance, two trade organizations) using the two standards listed in Table 8.3. Notice that they differ only by exchanging the transmitting (Tx) and receiving (Rx) set of pairs.

Different Ethernet standards specify different line voltages. For 10BASE-T, the two Tx voltages are +/- 2.5 V, as is 100BASE-T. The three 100BASE-TX Tx voltages are +/- 1.0 V and 0 V.

Gigabit Ethernet or 1000BASE-T uses different signaling voltages, depending upon the implementation. For a Pulse Amplitude Modulation (PAM), the three voltages are +/- 2.0 V, +/- 1.0 V, and 0 V. In practice, you might find that the actual voltages are more like +/- 1.0 V, +/- 0.5 V, and 0 V. The wiring of the cable is matched within the host adapter and need not be standard.

TABLE 8.3

TIA/EIA Ethernet Wiring Codes

Standard	Pin Count	Pair	Wire Polarity*	Color
568-A	1	3	Tip	White/green stripe
568-A	2	3	Ring	Green
568-A	3	2	Tip	White/orange stripe
568-A	4	1	Ring	Blue
568-A	5	1	Tip	White/blue stripe
568-A	6	2	Ring	Orange
568-A	7	4	Tip	White/brown stripe
568-A	8	4	Ring	Brown
568-B	1	2	Tip	White/orange stripe
568-B	2	2	Ring	Orange
568-B	3	3	Tip	White/green stripe
568-B	4	1	Ring	Blue
568-B	5	1	Tip	White/blue stripe
568-B	6	3	Ring	Green
568-B	7	4	Tip	White/brown stripe
568-B	8	4	Ring	Brown

EIA/TIA (Electronic Industries Alliance/Telecommunications Industry Association); *Tip is a positive connection, and Ring is a negative connection.

Standard connections are connected so that the pin numbers match through a connection; that is, Tx-Rx to Rx-Tx to Tx-Rx, also called a straight-through connection. Some cables are constructed so that the wires cross from end to end, and so that when the cables are connected, they connect Tx-Rx to Tx-Rx; this is commonly referred to as a crossover cable. For 10BASE-T and 100BASE-T, only two wire pairs are used; 1000BASE-T (GbE) uses all four pairs. A common scheme transmits signals from a node or computer on pins 1 and 2 and receives those signals on pins 3 and 6. When a node connects to a network device, the network device receives signals on pins 3 and 6 and transmits signals on pins 1 and 2.

Tip

When you use a crossover cable in applications that require a straight-through connection, the cable will not work. To quickly differentiate a crossover cable from standard CAT 5 cables, adopt a convention that crossover cables are a particular color (I use red), or carefully label the cable at both ends with a permanent label or marking.

If you wanted a connection between two nodes or computers (or two network devices), then you would need to use a crossover cable as the connection. The one node would send signals on pins 1 and 2, and the other would send signals on pins 3 and 6. The first node would receive signals on pins 3 and 6, and the other node would receive signals on pins 1 and 2. Ethernet NICs can automatically detect the connection type used, and when a crossover is required, supply the necessary signal routing; only the older host adapters lacked this feature.

When connecting one hub or switch to another where a crossover cable is required, manufacturers implement a crossover connection internally as an Uplink or X-connection so that you can connect the two devices with a straight-through cable. You may need to push a button to enable the Uplink feature. Otherwise, if you connect two standard ports of different hubs together, you would need a crossover cable to allow the two hubs to communicate with one another. Many newer hubs and switches do away with Uplink ports and automatically detect the state of the connection, allowing a straight-through connection to function as a crossover cable, a feature referred to as *Auto-Uplink* or *Auto-MDI-X*. MDI refers to a Medium Dependent Interface, and the X means that it is an embedded crossover or internal crossover type. A Medium Dependent Interface is a port on a hub, router, or switch that can connect to another hub, router, or switch without the use of a crossover cable. The reason that this is required is that the standard port connection to an NIC has the outgoing signal from a device going to the input of the NIC and the output of the NIC going to the input of the switching device. MDI-X provides a means to reverse the transmit and receive signals on the wires.

Figure 8.6 summarizes the difference between straight-through and crossover connections with three examples. In the top example (straight-through connection), the signal from one NIC port travels over a straight-through cable to the connecting port or NIC through an uplink port connected to an MDI-X port, which performs the crossover. Some devices contain the crossover wiring internally in the device, as shown in the middle example (internal crossover). Finally, you can use a crossover cable to perform the signal swapping, which is shown in the bottom example (crossover cable link). A crossover cable looks like an ordinary Ethernet cable but has the wired connections transposed. Crossover cables are normally labeled as such on the cable's plenum (plastic jacket).

FIGURE 8.6

Straight-through and crossover connections using MDI and MDI-X ports

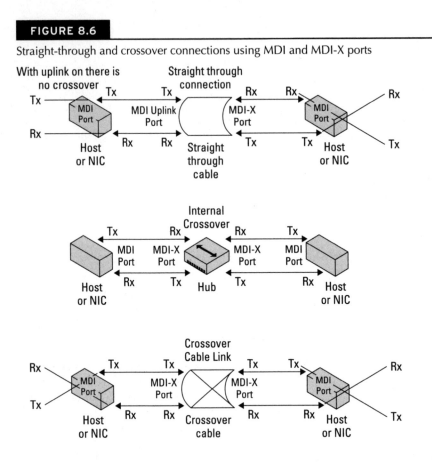

The earlier types of Ethernet used 10BASE-5 or Thicknet and 10BASE-2 or Thinnet. Thicknet was often used for ceiling runs, and was connected to a drop line using either an N connector or what is called a *vampire tap*. A vampire tap literally bites into the cable connecting to the inner core. Figure 8.7 shows a common network segment for these Thinnet/Thicknet segments. These Ethernet connections required that the shielding be grounded on one end and that the cable be terminated on both ends. Transceivers were required at the endpoint of connections that weren't attached to the host controller. The connections were made with a 15-pin D-connector called an Attachment Unit Interface (AUI). Thicknet and Thinnet are more expensive to implement than twisted pair and slower, and so this type of Ethernet is largely of historical interest.

FIGURE 8.7

A Thicknet Ethernet segment and drop connections

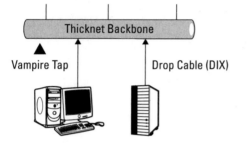

Fiber-optic cable

Fiber-optic cable (sometimes called optical fiber) uses silica, glass, or plastic as its transport medium. AT&T was issued the first patent for optical signal transport in 1934, but practical devices didn't appear until the 1960s. By 1970, Corning Glass Works (now Corning Incorporated) had developed a patented process that dropped the attenuation of fiber-optic cable made from glass from more than 1000 dB/km to less than 20 dB/km. The early 1990s saw the development of much cheaper forms of fiber optics, based on plastic and plastic-clad silica (PCS).

Single-mode fiber is meant to carry a single signal, while multimode carries several different signals. Multimode fiber has a relatively short effective distance because of modal dispersion. Modal dispersion occurs in multimode fibers because the signal tends to spread out over time due to the propagation velocity of the optical signal being different for the different modes. Multimode fiber is used less frequently than single-mode fiber because of the modal dispersion problem.

An optical transmission system is composed of a light source, fiber-optic cable (or another transmission medium), and a detector. The light source must be able to emit a pulse, and when the signal is detected, that represents a 1 or ON condition. The absence of a signal is taken as a 0 or OFF condition. The faster the light can be turned on and off, the more data can be transmitted down the fiber. The two different types of light source that are used to "light a fiber" are light emitting diodes (LEDs) and semiconductor lasers. Light travels down the core from one end to another, reflecting off of the boundaries between layers of different refractive indexes.

Note
When fiber-optic cable is laid down but isn't carrying a signal, it is called dark fiber. The massive amounts of dark fiber-optic submarine cable between the continents that was laid in the 1990s sparked a worldwide computer networking revolution.

Fiber-optic cable isn't affected by EMI or RFI, but is subject to an entirely different set of issues. Perhaps the most important issue with fiber-optic cable is that it is much more fragile than copper cable. Fiber is only glass or plastic, after all. Fiber cable networks can be much more difficult to stage, and they are also a lot more expensive than copper cables.

In the next sections that follow, the nature of data traveling as light through a fiber-optic medium is considered from a theoretical standpoint.

Attenuation and dispersal

The particular type of material for a fiber-optic cable is chosen to allow a certain limited range of light wavelengths to pass through it with little loss of signal over the cable run. This diminishment of the signal is referred to as *attenuation*. Attenuation is the result of both scattering and absorption of the light. Light scattering is the effect of signal loss due to the deviation of some of the light from the intended path. Absorption of light occurs through the transfer of energy to the glass or impurities in the glass resulting in a lower signal strength as the light travels onward.

The attenuation of single-mode fiber-optic cable ranges between 0.25 and 0.5 dB/km. Attenuation is the ratio of transmitted power divided by received power, as shown in the following expression:

Attenuation (dB) = 10 log10 (transmitted power/received power)

The attenuation of the optical signal going down the wire is determined by several factors. At a glass/air boundary, light is refracted or bent so that the signal is bounced internally back into the wire at an angle that is equal to, but opposite, the incident angle. The ratios of the refractive index of the core and clad determine the amount of bending that is allowed, as calculated by

Qc = arc cosine (n2/n1)

where Qc is the critical angle as measured from the center line of the core, above which injected light will not travel down the fiber, n2 is the index of refraction of the cladding, and n1 is the index of refraction of the core. For typical values of n, this might work out to be around 8.5 degrees of angle, a very narrow beam.

You can modify the equation above to account for light entering the core from air by defining an external angle Qext and the refractive index of air, n0 (1.00029) as follows:

Qext = arc sin [(n1/n0) sin (Qc)]

When air is taken into account, the critical angle expands to about 12.5 degrees.

At a certain angle of incidence above a critical value, essentially all of the light is trapped internally in the fiber. Below this angle, there is signal loss. Figure 8.8 illustrates the refraction effect using an LED as the light source that travels down the optical fiber. The core is the glass part, the cladding is a physical enclosure, usually plastic or some other material. The cone with the vertical lines represents the angles of light that can enter the wire and be reflected from the core/cladding interface down the length of the wire to the receiver. Light with a greater angle passes through the interface and is lost in the wire.

FIGURE 8.8

Fiber-optic light refraction

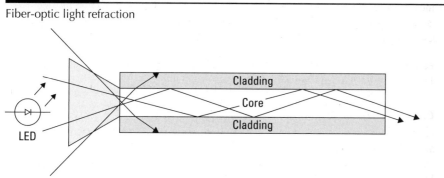

You can create fiber that filters for a small range of wavelengths by using very thin fiber. This is what single-mode fiber optic does. Light travels down the single-mode fiber as if the wire were a wave guide. With multimode fiber optics, there are many different light paths, each of which is defined by different angles of refraction or modes. The different modes travel down the fiber without interfering with one another.

As pulses of light travel down a fiber, they have a tendency to disperse or spread out over distance and interfere with other modes of light traveling down the same fiber. The amount of dispersion is a function of the wavelength and can be decreased by either slowing down the signaling rate or altering the shape of the pulse.

Figure 8.8 illustrates the case for multimode fiber transmission where the difference between the two indexes of refraction changes sharply over a short distance, called a *step index*. If the diameter of the core is smaller and closer to the wavelength of the light, then the light that is able to enter the core is at a very small angle indeed, and tends to travel down the core without refracting. Another technique creates a graded index of refraction that varies gradually from core to cladding. A graded multimode fiber allows a larger number of different angles of light down the core, creating a sharper output signal than a step multimode fiber optic. Figure 8.9 illustrates three different types of light transmission through different fiber-optic lines. In the top scenario a glass core with a very sharp transition or step index is characteristic of a single-mode step index. Light can travel down the glass fiber with little loss; however, this type of fiber only allows light that is highly calumniated to pass through it, which is what single mode means. The term *mode* refers to the different angles of light that can enter the core.

In the figure the wavelength range of the light is illustrated by the three identical parabolas or light pulses on the left. The triangular cone shown to its right illustrates the different angles or modes of light that can successfully pass through the fiber. At the right of the fiber is shown a profile of the index of refraction. The index of refraction is a measure of the ability of a medium to slow the speed of light relative to light traveling in a vacuum. Light is bent or refracted when it encounters materials of different optical density. When light is bent sufficiently it reflects and is transmitted down the fiber and emerges as the output pulse shown at the far right of the three figures. When light isn't sufficiently bent the light is lost from the fiber. The top index profile is of a single step function which reflects the light arriving within the cone shown to the left of the fiber. This single-mode fiber supports only straight-on angles where the light travels down the core without reflections. You need highly focused light sources such as lasers to work with this sort of fiber.

In the middle figure is light transmission through a multimode step index fiber. The index of refraction of the fiber supports a set of different modes and can reflect a broader range of input light angles, as illustrated by the wider cone of light entering the fiber. Unlike the output pulse shown for the single-mode figure at the top, which has an identical shape and some amplitude loss, the multimode output pulse is broadened and flattened out.

In the final scenario shown at the bottom of Figure 8.9, the fiber is a multimode fiber with a graded index. Unlike the two figures above it, which are step functions and reflect narrowly defined angles or modes of light, a grade index will reflect a range of modes and results in a cleaner output signal as shown on the right of the bottom figure. In this more complex scheme, the light is both dispersed and broadened, which is a disadvantage when trying to send signals down the fiber. Step function profiles are a better choice for long transmission lines.

FIGURE 8.9

Single-mode versus multimode transmission

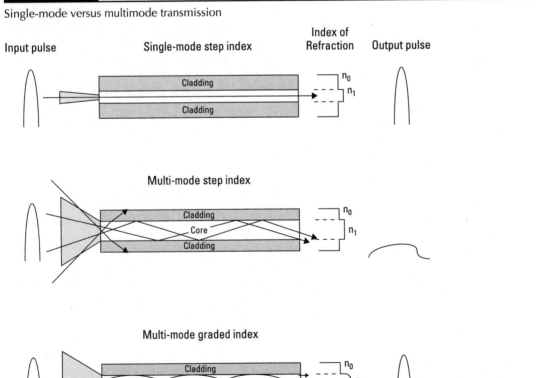

Solitons

One shape that is related to the reciprocal of a hyperbolic cosine allows dispersion effects to cancel each other out in all directions. Pulses that have this shape are called solitons, and they have the property that they can travel vast distances (thousands of Km) without being degraded. Solitons or self-reinforcing solitary waves occur when two or more waves behave like particles and travel with constant shape and velocity.

In the figure, two waves of different amplitude and speed are approaching each other. (Waves with different wavelengths can travel through a medium with different speeds.) They merge, and the larger and faster wave (Wave 1) splits from the merged wave (Wave 1+2) with nearly the same size and shape that it had before it merged with the slower wave (Wave 2). John Scott-Russell observed this type of wave in a canal near Edinburgh in 1834, but it took 50 more years before the mathematical theory could be worked out. You see soliton-like behavior in the tidal bore on the Bay of Fundy. Solitons may also play a role in long-range neural electrical transmission in the nervous system, although this is still a controversial theory. Solitons have been created in optic fibers and studied, but the technology is not yet available and is under research.

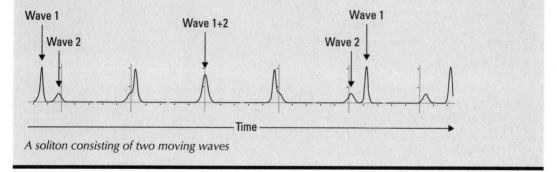

A soliton consisting of two moving waves

Physical description

The core in fiber-optic cables is extruded with a width of either 50 or 62.5 mM (microns), which is the size of a human hair. The conductor is covered in a refractive coating with a lower index of refraction than the core. This refractive coating is called *cladding* and is added to all types of fiber-optic cable. The cladding keeps the light from escaping and reflects the light down the length of the fiber. The fiber and cladding together form a fiber that has a diameter of 125 m. Single-mode fiber has a core with a diameter of 9 m, and cladding is then added to bring the width of the spun fiber up to 125 m. You may see these different types of fiber specified as 50 m/125 m, 62.5 m/125 m, or 9 m/125 m. In any case, the fiber is surrounded by an insulator such as fiberglass, Kevlar, or steel, and then surrounded by a jacket (coating) made of plenum insulator. The combination of the core, cladding, and coating is collectively referred to as the *strand*. Figure 8.10 shows a diagram of a fiber-optic cable.

FIGURE 8.10

Fiber-optic cable

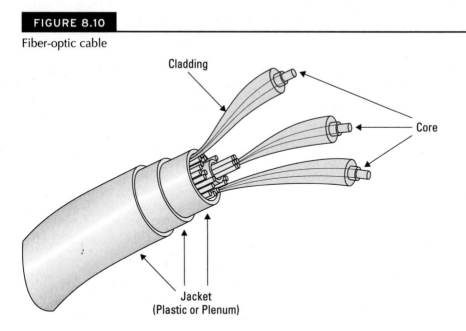

Single-mode fiber has essentially unlimited bandwidth, while multimode fiber has a lower bandwidth. Both have excellent signal quality, but single mode's quality extends over much greater distances. The main attenuation factor in single-mode fiber is chromatic dispersion, while for multimode fiber it is modal dispersion. In chromatic dispersion, light is refracted based on its wavelength; the classic example of chromatic dispersion is white light passing through a prism to create a rainbow of colors. Modal dispersion is where the signal traveling down multimode fibers spreads out in time because the propagation velocity of different modes of light varies along the fiber length. Fiber optic is treated to vary the index of refraction across the diameter of the wire. Some processes create a gradual or graded index; others create a step index. Multimode uses both types of grading, while single-mode fiber uses a step index. As a rule, single-mode fiber optic is universally used, especially where Ethernet wiring is concerned. Multimode fiber optic finds occasional use in Ethernet, analog video, and communications over short distances.

Fiber-optic cable is combined in pairs for duplex communications and then bundled together with additional cables to create bundles of up to 96 strands of single-mode fiber placed inside a tube. Fiber-optic cables can be contained either as loose or tight strands inside a buffer tube. Tight buffer cable is used outside buildings and for longer cable runs because of the physical stability that form factor provides. Other uses for fiber cable include aerial, buried, duct, and submarine cables.

Unlike copper cabling, fiber-optic cable isn't affected by electric, magnetic, and radio frequency interference. Fiber-optic runs also have a much greater bandwidth and longer runs between repeaters than copper cable does. Light sources used are either light emitting diodes (LEDs) or, when longer length runs are required, lasers. The different methods used to modulate the light pulses are

- **Amplitude shift keying (ASK) or intensity modulation.** The output (amplitude) of the source is varied by a modulating signal. Intensity modulation is used with LEDs and in connection links in LANs.

- **Phase shift keying (PSK).** This modulation technique is a digital modulation that changes the phase of a carrier wave using a pattern of binary bits.

- **Frequency shift keying (FSK).** The FSK technique encodes digital information in the changing frequency of a carrier wave.

- **Polar modulation.** In polar modulation the carrier wave's polarity is modified and that variation encodes data.

Table 8.4 compares LED to semiconductor laser-light sources as signal generators.

TABLE 8.4

LED versus Semiconductor Light Sources

Property	Light Emitting Diode	Semiconductor Laser Diodes
Cost	Cheap	Expensive
Light source lifetime	Long	Short
Reliability	High	Moderate
Mode	Multimode only	Single or multimode
Power	Moderate	High
Linearity	High (broader pulse)	Low (sharper pulse)
Coupling efficiency	Moderate	High
Propagation distance	Short	Long
Signal rate	Low	High
Temperature sensitivity	Small	Large

A single-mode fiber cable is used for applications that don't require duplex operation. They can run as long as 3 km between repeaters. Long-distance fiber backbones that are pumped by lasers may only need to have repeaters placed every 100 km or 31.1 miles. Most LAN applications use LEDs, but backbones use lasers. Runs of several kilometers between repeaters are common on fiber-optic cable.

There are several different connector types used with single-mode fiber cables, including SMA screw-on (types 905 and 906), ST (straight tip), and SC (subscriber connector) connections. Many single-mode fiber cables are paired to create duplex communication. The SC connector usually has a square shape with a keyed tab size to ensure that a cable cannot be crossed with its other end during installation. Each proximity connection in a fiber-optic line results in about a 10 to 20 percent loss of signal strength, depending upon the nature of the fiber (glass, plastic, graded, or step). When you fuse two fibers together, the signal loss is much less, but the bond is permanent.

Fiber-optic cable is more expensive than copper cable, for the most part. However, it is widely used in high-speed Ethernet, SONET (optical Token Rings), Asynchronous Transfer Mode (ATM), 10BASE-F, and FDDI networks. The greater bandwidth, longer runs, resistance to EMI and RFI interference, and greater security make them desirable. The enhanced security arises out of how difficult it is to tap into a fiber-optic line. Fiber-optic cable can be tricky to work with. It is finicky, easy to break, hard to terminate, and must be protected using a pipe or conduit. You also need to be attentive to matching the particular fiber-optic cable type to the application for which you want to use it.

Fiber-optic networks

Several network elements dictate the topologies that are allowed in fiber-optic networks. In addition to the wire elements of emitter, transmission medium, and receiver, the connections may require a repeater, or a T-junction as a tap to connect other media to.

T-junctions are either passive or active. A T-junction is a set of fused optical fibers that allow signals to be split or combined. A passive junction passes the signal through with some signal loss, while an active junction amplifies the signal before passing it on. A passive T-junction has two taps that are fused onto the main fiber-optic cable, with an attendant loss of signal strength.

Active T-junctions have an emitting laser diode or light emitting diode (LED) on one side and a photodiode receptor at the other end of the T-connection that leads off the network to a host or node. The straight-through portion of the T-connector is passive, as shown in Figure 8.11. If any component of the active connection were to fail, then the host (network interface for a system) would go offline, but the network portion, which is passive, would remain operational. This makes fiber-optic networks very reliable.

FIGURE 8.11

A fiber-optic T-junction

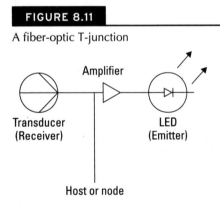

Light traveling down fiber-optic cables can have a long effective run. However, every few kilometers, it is necessary to insert an active fiber-optic repeater to restore signal strength and quality. Early repeaters used optic-electrical conversion to capture the signal, and then used an emitter to retransmit the signal at the desired power. More recent devices are based on optical signal capture, do not perform a conversion, and thus can operate at much higher bandwidths than the older copper wire–based repeaters. A repeater has the same components as the T-junction shown in Figure 8.11, but without the additional tap (connected fiber line) leading off to a host.

Most fiber-optic networks are built with ring topologies. SONET, which is described in Chapter 13, is a prominent example. A break in the ring would remove one of the redundant connections but may not bring the network down. Many ring topologies are built with bidirectional links, making each link in the ring a self-contained loop. Unidirectional link topologies will fail when a single link fails.

In some instances, fiber-optic networks are built with a passive star topology, as shown in Figure 8.12. The passive star is constructed using a central device that is a large silica cylinder, which is an optical hub. Incoming fiber-optic lines are connected in such a way that a portion of the light from each emitter can be seen by each of the receivers. The other outgoing end of the cylinder leads to fiber-optic cables going to the various emitters. Each optical network interface has a transducer to receive signals and an emitter to send signals over the network.

FIGURE 8.12

A passive star with fiber-optic connections

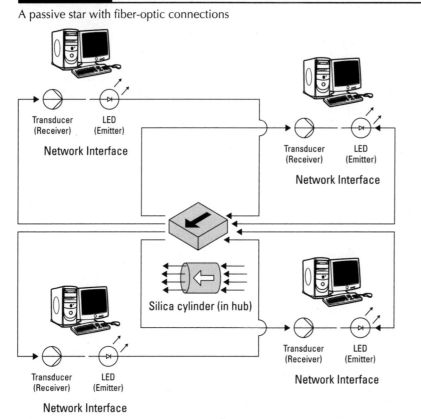

The passive star system allows different network segments and nodes to communicate directly with one another. The hub's construction allows light from any input to be transmitted to any output. The fan-out of a passive star is dependent upon the sensitivity of the photodiode receivers that the network uses.

Wireless

Wires aren't the only medium that can be used for network communications. Signals can be sent through air, thin air, and even the vacuum of space. Somewhere out there in the cosmos, 57 light-years away, another advanced civilization is just tuning into the first episode of "I Love Lucy."

The following sections look at how the electromagnetic spectrum determines the characteristics of different network connections.

Electromagnetic radiation

Frequency and wavelength are intimately related to one another by constraints imposed on radiation by the speed of light. In a vacuum, radiation travels at the speed of light such that

$c = {¦}l$ or $l = {¦} / c$

The relationship of energy to wavelength and thus to frequency is given by the following equations:

$E = h\, l$ or $E = (h\, c) / l$

where ¦ is frequency, l is wavelength, c is the speed of light (3×10^8 m/sec), and h is Planck's constant (6.6×10^{-34} J/sec). In a vacuum, that speed translates into roughly 1 meter every 3 nanoseconds. Radiation travels through a vacuum unimpeded; however, when light travels through different media such as glass or water, the speed is reduced to around two-thirds and one-half of the speed of light, respectively. Electromagnetic waves traveling through conductors such as copper and fiber optics (also glass) are also slowed to about two-thirds the speed of light. Recent research has even shown that you can stop light inside the magnetic containment of a Bose-Einstein condensate, something that may one day be used to store information.

Current technologies use a portion of the electromagnetic spectrum for data communication — radio, microwaves, infrared, visible light, and ultraviolet radiation. The high-energy short wavelength X-rays and gamma rays are too energetic to be economically reasonable and practical. The low-energy long wavelength sub-radio frequencies are too slow to be useful as network connections as that would introduce too much latency into any connections. The International Telecommunications Union (ITU) categorizes the electromagnetic spectrum as divided into the ranges shown in Table 8.5.

TABLE 8.5

Frequency Ranges

Band	ITU Radio Frequency Class	Frequency	Wavelength	Energy (Power)
g (Gamma rays)	-	30 EHz to 300 EHz	10 pm to 1 pm	124 keV to 1.24 MeV
HX (Hard X-rays)	-	3 EHz to 30 EHz	100 pm to 10 pm	12.4 keV to 124 keV
SX (Soft X-rays)	-	30 PHz to 3 EHz	1 nm to 100 pm	1.24 eV to 12.4 eV
EUV (Extreme Ultraviolet)	-	3 PHz to 30 PHz	100 nm to 10 nm	12.4 eV
NUV (Near Ultraviolet)	-	300 THz to 3 PHz	1 μm to 100 nm	1.24 eV to 12.4 eV
NIR (Near Infrared)	-	30 THz to 300 THz	10 μm to 1 μm	124 meV
MIR (Mid Infrared)	-	3 THz to 30 THz	100 μm to 10 μm	12.4 meV
FIR (Far Infrared)	-	300 GHz to 3 THz	1 mm to 100 μm	1.24 meV
EHF	EHF (Extremely High Frequency)	30 GHz to 300 GHz	1 cm to 1 mm	124 μeV
SHF	SHF (Super High Frequency)	3 GHz to 30 GHz	10 cm to 1 cm	12.4 μeV
UHF	UHF (Ultra High Frequency)	300 MHz to 3000 MHz	1 m to 10 cm	1.24 μeV
VHF	VHF (Very High Frequency)	30 MHz to 300 MHz	10 m to 1 m	124 neV
HF	HF (High Frequency)	3 MHz to 30 MHz	100 m to 10 m	12.4 neV
MF	MF (Medium Frequency)	300 kHz to 3000 kHz	1 km to 100 m	1.24 neV
LF	LF (Low Frequency)	30 kHz to 300 kHz	10 km to 1 km	124 peV
VLF	VLF (Very Low Frequency)	3 kHz to 30 kHz	100 km to 10 km	12.4 peV
VF/ULF (Voice Frequency)	ULF (Ultra Low Frequency)	300 Hz to 3000 Hz	1,000 km to 100 km	1.24 peV
SLF	SLF (Super Low Frequency)	30 Hz to 300 Hz	10,000 km to 1,000 km	124 feV
ELF	ELF (Extremely Low Frequency)	3 Hz to 30 Hz	100,000 km to 10,000 km	124 feV 12.4 feV

Radio ranges Long Wave (LW; 153–279 kHz), Medium Wave (MW; 531–1620 kHz), and Short Wave (SW; 2310–25820 kHz) are not part of the ITU specifications.

In music, sound is broken up into ranges, based on the powers of two, called *octaves*. Octaves are a general concept that defines the range of frequencies in the electromagnetic spectrum divided by a power of two. With each 2x increase in frequency, power increases by a factor of 4 or +/- 6 dB/octave (decibels). An amplifier or electronic filter can be said to have a response of an octave if its power or voltage spans the same factor of 4 or +/- 6 dB. An alternative system divides frequencies using powers of ten, defining a range called a *decade*. The response of a factor of 10 or a decade would be +/- 20 dB/decade.

You can detect signals in the electromagnetic spectrum with a range of about 65 octaves (radio to gamma rays). It is theorized that 81 or more octaves exist, from the longest wavelength possible (the size of the universe, perhaps?) down to the Planck wavelength of 1.6 x 10-35 m, at which point the laws governing electromagnetic radiation break down, scale and time are presumed to be no longer measurable, and no information can be exchanged.

Electromagnetic radiation propagates as a periodic or oscillating wave in two coordinate axes, with the wave front moving outwards along the third axis in three dimensions. Consider Figure 8.13, where a point source (the happy sun) is emitting radiation. She is wearing sunglasses because the light being emitted is polarized in one direction (the XZ plane). So polarization simplifies Figure 8.13 by eliminating the other rotational angles of electric and magnetic fields.

FIGURE 8.13

Electromagnetic radiation and wave propagation

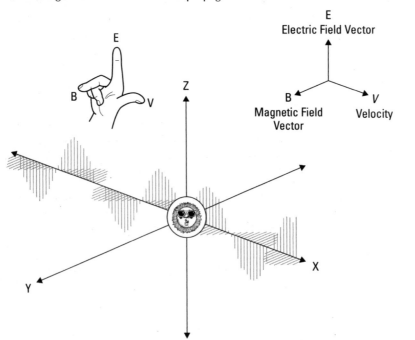

There are several features to notice about this conceptual diagram. The wave is composed of equal amplitude electric and magnetic field vectors that are in phase with one another. Those vectors are displayed in the upper-right coordinates. Electromagnetic radiation obeys what is called the right hand rule. If you examine the right hand in the upper-left corner of Figure 8.13, the thumb points along the direction of motion (V pointed along the X-axis), the index finger points along the direction of electric current (E pointed along the Z-axis), and the middle finger points along the direction of the magnetic field or flux (B pointed along the Y-axis). The three axes indicate motion, magnetic field, and electric field. When polarized, the light travels down the X-axis, the electric field is the oscillation in amplitude in the Z-axis direction, and the magnetic field is along the Y-axis. The right hand rule shows which direction is positive by the way the fingers point. It is useful to keep these ideas in mind as you consider how different emitters and receivers can interpret signals sent over wireless media.

Information and transmission

The electromagnetic spectrum is used to transmit information wirelessly by modulating or changing the waves in some manner. The three most important methods used are

- **Pulse modulation (PM).** PM creates signals by simply turning the light source on and off. When the light is on, it is a logical 1, and when the light is off, it is a logical 0.

- **Amplitude modulation (AM).** AM creates signals by using a change in the amplitude of the wave as its signal. When the amplitude is above a certain threshold value, it is a logical 1, and when it is below that value, it is a logical 0. Usually, AM uses a carrier wave and then adds the signal onto the carrier wave.

- **Frequency modulation (FM).** FM creates signals by alternating the frequency of the wave. When the frequency is above a certain threshold value, it is a logical 1, and when it is below that value, it is a logical 0. FM also uses a carrier wave and then adds the signal onto the carrier wave.

Figure 8.14 shows these three different methods for signaling transmission. In the top signal, the carrier wave is modified by a phase modulation technique. The carrier wave is turned on for a 1 and off for a 0. When the wave switches from 0 to 1, the waveform has a different phase than it had before. Information is carried by the changes in the phase of the signal. Phase modulation is less commonly used than frequency modulation or amplitude modulation.

Shown in the middle signal in Figure 8.14, frequency modulation alters the frequency of the carrier wave depending upon whether the signal is on or off. For an on signal, a higher frequency is used, and for an off signal, a lower frequency is used. The changes in frequency encode information.

Perhaps the easiest modulation to visualize is amplitude modulation, shown in the bottom signal. The waveform's amplitude is above a threshold value when an on state is being communicated and below when an off state is sent.

FIGURE 8.14

Three different modulation techniques for carrying a signal over a wireless link

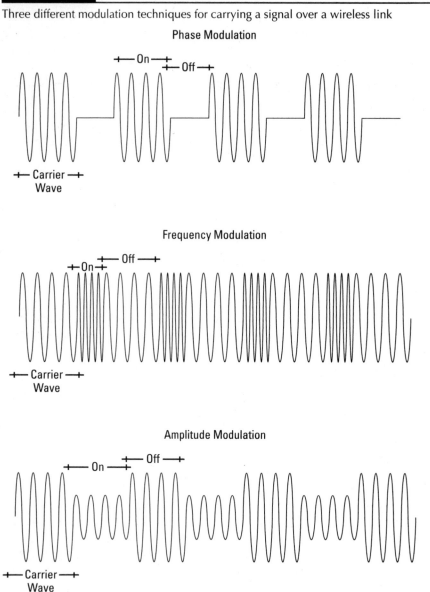

The relationship between the frequency of an electromagnetic wave and the amount of data a wave can carry is a fundamental limit imposed on all systems by signal theory. To get a sense of the absolute limit for signals, the relationship between frequency, wavelength, and the speed of light

can be solved for frequency and then differentiated with respect to wavelength to get the formula shown here:

$$(f/d\lambda) = (c/\lambda^2)$$

Cross-Ref

The relationship of frequency modulation and amplitude modulation to multiplexing signals traveling over a wire is described in Chapter 5.

Because signals are carried by the overall change in the waveform (amplitude or frequency, for example), you are really only interested in how often this equation changes sign. Put another way, you are interested in the number of times per second that the slope of the curve (the differential) changes sign. The equation can be rewritten as a set of finite differences, which provides absolute values, as follows:

$$\Delta f = (c \, \Delta \lambda) / \lambda^2$$

Now consider a wireless radio emitter that provides a signal centered at the 2.4 GHz frequency that is ten 64 Kbits/s DS0 channels wide (five on each size). The band would go from 2.08 to 2.72 GHz. The calculated wavelength for the 2.4 GHz band would be 0.125 m, the difference in wavelength would be 10 units of 64 Kbits/s, or 640 Kbits/s, and the calculation would yield 33.3 Mbits/s. If a wider bandwidth is used, say perhaps 1.28 Mbits/s, then the data rate would be 64.6 Mbits/s. It is usual to have a very low ratio of $\Delta f/f$, and in these two cases, the ratios would be 1.4 percent and 2.8 percent, respectively.

Wireless connections

There are some general factors that influence a wireless connection. Regardless of the frequency or wavelengths used, a wireless data connection still requires three components:

- Transmitter
- Transport medium
- Receiver

Nearly all of the computer network links use air or vacuum as the transport medium. The transmitter and receiver must be reasonably constructed and priced in order to be used. The transmitter used delivers some electromagnetic radiation at some frequency and power. Power correlates with the wave amplitude, which must be large enough for the type of receiver used to detect the signal at the distance required by the connection. Let's consider an example, involving radio transmission.

Radio links

Radio transmission covers a very large range of frequencies, as you can determine from Table 8.5. According to SETI, the following radio astronomy bands are recognized as significant and observed: 3.36-13.41, 25.55-25.67, 73.00-74.60, 150.05-153.00, 406.10-410.00, and 1400.0-1427.0 MHz. The range of 73, 150, and 406 MHz are active for pulsar signals, and the 1400 MHz band is where hydrogen lines fall. That means that radio astronomy is "connecting" using very powerful, extremely distant transmitters, and extremely large antennas and arrays, some on the order of a kilometer in size. The ITU categories for these bands fall in the HF, VHF, and UHF ranges, with wavelengths between 100 m and 50 cm.

Even with the enormously large scale of both the emitter and detector, the vast distance that these radio waves take to make the trip makes the signal vanishingly small. To get a sense of how small the power of these radio waves can be, consider this fact: The total amount of energy collected by all of the radio telescopes since the beginning of radio astronomy is estimated to be less than the energy that is needed to power a flashlight bulb for less than a millionth of a second. That correlates to a heat source emitting these radio waves as its maximum having a temperature of just a few degrees above absolute zero; not much higher than the cosmic background radiation.

Let's scale this radio connection down a bit. AM radio operates between 520 and 1620 KHz, and in the U.S., the highest power allowed is a 50,000-watt transmitter. These radio wave broadcasts can be received by radios approximately 100 miles away during daytime and can penetrate buildings to a certain degree. At night, AM radio waves can be made to reflect off of the ionosphere 100 to 500 km up in the earth's atmosphere; then the signal can be received hundreds of miles away, depending upon conditions.

Radio transmitted omni-directionally loses power as a function of $1/r3$, where r is the radius of the sphere created by the point source.

Radio transmitters can be built to operate at higher frequencies, shorter wavelengths, and more power. The 2.4 GHz Wi-Fi with a wavelength of 12.5 cm (about 5 inches) is powerful enough to penetrate walls. Typical devices may have enough power to be received by another Wi-Fi device 150 to 300 feet away. If you focus the radio transmitter and the receiver so that they are highly directional and focused in one direction, then radio links can be extended to a kilometer. However, focusing the beam and the distance involved reduces the strength of the signal to the point that even intervening tree foliage is enough to interfere with the signal. To get more directional signals requires a more powerful transmission.

Microwave links

Microwave radiation is used to transmit data over long distances because it provides good bandwidth over line-of-sight transmission links. Microwave communication is used for backbone links in cellular networks, as radio relay links for TV and telephony, and as satellite links, and provides a relatively low-cost method for installing high-bandwidth connections.

At a frequency of around 200 MHz, the wavelength of the microwave is under 2 m, allowing a focusing transmitter to narrow the transmission very effectively and a dish antenna to very effectively collect the signal. The line-of-sight requirement means that a transmitter atop a 30-story building would need a repeater about 100 km away.

Tip

You can calculate microwave line-of-sight links using a Google Maps Microwave Link Planning Tool. Go to http:// members.chello.at/stephen.joung/indexDistanceElevation.html and enter the coordinate. With this data in hand, you can set the characteristics of the microwave link at `http://members.chello.at/stephen.joung/ indexMW_Distance20.html`**, and you see how antenna size, frequency, and power affect performance.**

Microwaves are far less effective in penetrating buildings than radio waves because the shorter wavelengths increase the interactions of microwaves with solid material. That's why microwave ovens are effective, but radio frequency ovens are not. RF ovens would require a much higher intensity to heat materials.

As the distance of the microwave link increases, the beam diverges and may be refracted by atmospheric layers. When the signal arrives, the receiver may experience what is called multipath fading, slowly moving in and out of tune. You can experience the same effect in radio transmissions.

If you are in your car listening to a weak radio station and you pull to a stop, you may notice that the strength of the signal can be changed dramatically by moving a few feet forward or backward. That is the result of multipath fading.

In the U.S., the following frequencies have been dedicated to wireless communication:

- 1.7 MHz (AM)
- 27 MHz (FM)
- 43 to 50 MHz (FM)
- 902 to 928 MHz (worldwide open use, cell phones and Wi-Fi)
- 1920 to 1930 MHz (worldwide open use, cell phones)
- 2.4 GHz (worldwide open use, cell phones and Wi-Fi)
- 5.8 GHz (worldwide open use, cell phones and Wi-Fi)

The band between 2.4 and 2.484 GHz is dedicated worldwide for open use. This band, sometimes referred to as the Industrial Scientific Medical band, is where devices such as cell phones and Wi-Fi operate without government licensing. Cell phones operating at 900 MHz and at 2.4 GHz with 100 MW power transmission have a range of about 30 m (100 ft).

Summary

This chapter covered the different wiring standards that you can use to create a network. Twisted-pair and coaxial cable wiring were highlighted, and their application to Ethernet networks was explored.

Fiber optics offers a high-bandwidth network connection. Light from a laser or LED is sent down a glass or plastic fiber, over either a single-mode or multimode link. The principles of light transmission were described.

Wireless communications can transmit radio and microwave frequency radiation across either air or a vacuum. The properties of the electromagnetic spectrum and how it is used to convey information were illustrated.

The next chapter describes how networks intelligently connect devices with one another.

Routing, Switching, and Bridging

Networks require connection devices that can create circuits. Common connection devices such as hubs, bridges, switches, routers, and gateways are described and compared with one another. This chapter explains the two broad categories of networks: circuit switched and packet switched. A circuit is a defined path between two endpoints. Circuit switched networks are stateful and can be described in terms of endpoints and a path. Data travels over the circuit and arrives in sequence. Packet switched networks are stateless. They have endpoints, but the path varies for individual packets based on conditions.

Switching devices can be categorized by the highest level in the OSI data model that they operate on. Hubs and repeaters are the simplest devices; they are simply physical connections. Bridges are devices that span two different network segments, but do not provide protocol translation. A router can connect two different types of networks. Switches and gateways are general terms that describe a variety of different systems.

Circuit versus Packet Switching

Broadly speaking, there are two types of switched networks in use: circuit switched and packet switched. A circuit switched network is defined by a physical or virtual circuit (or connection) that connects two endpoints and has a certain circuit bandwidth. A circuit only needs to be defined for the duration of the message transfer on a circuit switched network. Because switching devices can be used to redefine different connections, a circuit switched network can be reconfigured as needed.

The penultimate circuit switched network is the Public Switched Telephone Network, or PSTN. When you place a phone call to another party, a circuit is created between the two of you for the duration of the call. Circuit switched networks are data networks as well as voice networks. Another example of a circuit switched network is ISDN (Integrated Services Digital Networks).

The best way to think of what a circuit switched network does is to remember that circuit switched networks are stateful. Stateful means that you can define a message transfer in terms of:

- A source
- A destination
- A path of the circuit
- A cost for the path based on time, performance, or some other weighting

In a circuit switched network, you can represent nodes as a graph in graph theory, connections as weighted edges between nodes, and the actual defined or preferred paths through the graph, which are called routes. In real terms, messages are sent from endpoint to endpoint as a complete unit. If you have multiple IP packets (or datagrams), they all travel down the same route on a circuit switched network.

A packet switched network is based on a different concept, that of the best available route. On a packet switched network, individual packets are sent from a source to a destination by the best connection available at the switching device. This type of network is designed for inherently unreliable networks where connections are transient. If a connection drops out, the next packet is sent to a different next hop. A packet switched network cannot guarantee a path. A certain percentage of packets will reach a dead end where, as they say in Vermont, "You can't get there from here," and so some packets will get dropped or returned. Packets will also arrive out of sequence. Therefore, packet switched networks require a mechanism to ensure that all lost packets are re-sent and that packets can be sequenced to retrieve the data that they encode.

Of course, the prototypical packet switched network is the Internet, or more broadly speaking, networks based on the Internet Protocol. Other networks that are packet switched are X.25, Frame Relay, Asynchronous Transfer Mode (ATM), and Multiprotocol Label Switching (MPLS), among others.

The best way to think of what a packet switched network does is to remember that packet switched networks are stateless. Stateless means that you can define a message transfer in terms of:

- A source
- A destination
- The position of the packet in the sequence
- A Time-to-Live (TTL) for the packet, which may be based on a hop count or timeout parameter, and is the time after which the packet expires and is dropped at the next device that receives it.

Note

A circuit is not the same thing as a connection. A connection is a defined transfer of data from one endpoint to another, and it may be stateful or stateless.

Circuit switched networks have their advantages and disadvantages over packet switched networks. A circuit switched network sends an entire message over the same circuit, which can be faster than sending parts of a message over many paths. When a message arrives, the data arrives in sequence and doesn't need to be reassembled. By contrast, a packet switched network makes better use of the network's capacity because it can distribute traffic over many connections. The extra overhead involved to sequence incoming packets and the loss of performance is offset by the more efficient use of the network and the much higher fault tolerance offered by packet switching. Neither model, whether circuit or packet switched, is better than the other; they are simply different.

What both circuit switching and packet switching have in common is that they both have switches that can change the network's topology. To understand modern networks, you need to understand how switches operate. Switches not only control the physical connections between network segments through electrical connections, but different classes of switches also have the intelligence to measure the performance of different paths, determine routes, and optimize the preferred paths or routes to nodes on the network in a stored but dynamic table. Internetworks and WANs would not function without the use of these types of routing devices.

Figure 9.1 summarizes the different types of network switching devices in a single chart. Network switching devices are best characterized by the highest layer of the networking model that they can operate on. Physical layer (Level 1) switching devices have no intelligence; they are simply physical connections or, for a repeater, a physical connection with signal regeneration. Data Link layer (Level 2) devices are characterized as switches or bridges and add the ability to reconfigure connections through device management.

All of the network switching devices so far span networks of similar construction and that usually run the same network protocols. To span networks of different types, additional intelligence is required and devices must operate on higher-level protocols. Two classes of devices become important in internetworking: routers and gateways. Routers connect different network types at the Network layer (Level 3), while gateways connect networks running different protocols at the Transport layer (Level 4). As you ascend the chart of devices in Figure 9.1, they become more capable and more intelligent, more manageable, and also more expensive. In Figure 9.1 the different OSI layers are listed on the left from Level 1 at the bottom to Level 7 at the top. The different network connection devices that correspond with connections at that layer are shown. They are:

1. Physical layer (Level 1). Devices at this level include repeaters and bridges.
2. Data Link layer (Level 2). Devices at this layer include hub, and switches.
3. Data Link layer (Level 3). Devices at this layer are primarily routers.
4. Transport to Application layers (Levels 4 through 7). Devices of this type are called gateways.

All of these devices are discussed in the sections that follow. An explanation for why they are categorized as such is also discussed.

FIGURE 9.1

Different types of network switching devices

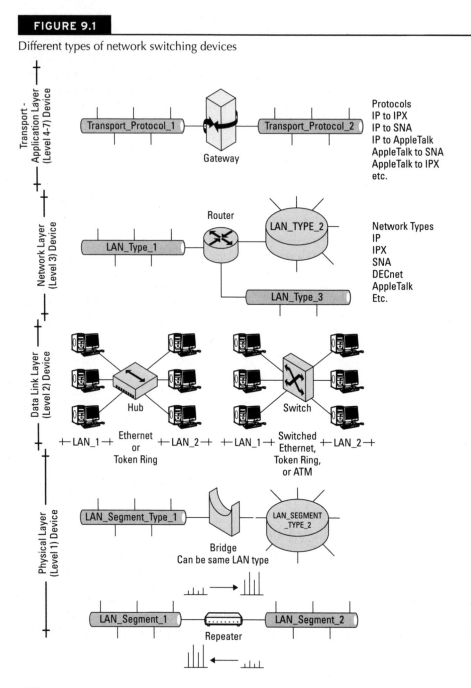

Layer 1 and Layer 2 Connection Devices

Layer 1 and Layer 2 devices form the majority of switching devices sold today. These devices include hubs, repeaters, bridges, and switches. Repeaters (or active hubs) and passive hubs are unmanaged devices. Bridges and switches are more often managed devices. A managed device contains a network management protocol such as SNMP (Simple Network Management Protocol) and can be seen and modified within a network management program. An unmanaged device doesn't allow for remote configuration or diagnosis. The network switch is the most elusive of the devices described in this chapter. A switch is not defined by a standards body and is used by vendors to describe devices with a very large range of capabilities. In the sections that follow, repeaters, bridges, hubs, and switches are described.

Passive hubs

A hub is a simple device that connects network devices together on the same network segment, usually twisted-pair wire or fiber optic cable. A hub is a passive hub when it serves to simply connect one connection to another. It is an active hub when the signal is amplified, and in that case it is most often called a repeater.

In the OSI model, it is a Physical layer (Level 1) device. Hubs play the same functional role that a connector performs, lengthening a network segment by joining two wires together. However, network hubs offer the additional feature of fan-out; they take an input connection and allow it to be connected to 4, 8, 16, or more other connections, with each path through the hub being a separate network segment. Hubs can be passive and simply pass signals through, or they can amplify the signal (repeat) and be classified as active hubs.

Hubs have little or no intelligence, per se, and are unmanaged devices. Every packet coming into the hub goes out through the other connections, and all connected network segments belong to the same collision domain. These two factors mean that traffic flowing through a hub suffers more collisions than through other connecting devices such as switches or routers. It also means that the collision rate tends to increase exponentially as a function of the number of hubs encountered while en route between connection endpoints. As a general rule, 100-Mbits/s Ethernet circuits are limited to no more than two hubs connecting three network segments.

The more modern hubs act as multiport repeaters. When they detect a collision, the hub sends a jam signal to all connected devices to stop transmitting; some hubs act when they detect a significant number of collisions on one port to partition that port so that it can no longer communicate with other connected ports.

Hubs often offer an uplink port, which, when enabled, makes the two hubs function as if they are a single hub. In some cases, a connection between two hubs can be a stack port, which improves the performance of the connection and allows more hubs to be used together. Stack ports use proprietary technology; therefore, you need two hubs from the same vendor to get them to work together. When you combine the ability to stack hubs together with an SNMP chip or VLAN support, the added features allow the hub to be a managed device, and many vendors refer to them as intelligent hubs.

In the past, hubs' main attraction was that they were cheap and reliable; however, hubs are now obsolete and very difficult to find in the marketplace. Although you can still purchase autosensing 10/100-Mbits/s Ethernet hubs, most devices sold today are switches. This is certainly true for any device that connects Gigabit-speed networks. Because most network devices are based on just a few vendors' chipsets, and because there is so little difference now in the cost of adding all of the intelligence of a switch to the chipset, there's no discernable difference between the cost of a hub and that of a switch.

You will find that nearly all devices are sold as switches, even if they use the word hub in their product name. Modern switches are only hubs in the sense that you can turn off all of the features that they offer and simply plug in your devices. The ability of a hub to copy data through broadcast to many connected devices at once is a desirable feature that is emulated in switches by a function called port mirroring.

Repeaters

Repeaters, or active hubs, are Physical layer (Level 1) devices that extend the run length of the physical media by amplifying and retiming the signal before forwarding it. Signals can be degraded over the length of a connection losing their modulation. A repeater recreates the signal and retransmits it in the correct phase and frequency. Repeaters can connect different physical media together, and extend the collision domain without adding any new traffic. Repeaters cannot connect networks using different network architectures together, nor can they filter information. As a signal travels through a repeater, it suffers a small latency called its propagation delay. This factor tends to limit the number of repeaters that can be used on any single segment of a network.

Ethernet has such long run lengths relative to most LAN requirements that repeaters are uncommon. Most wired Ethernet repeaters are sold as "active hubs," and they are sometimes referred to as multiport repeaters. It's rare to find repeaters sold for Ethernet networks, as hubs and switches have become available at more affordable prices. For this reason, wired Ethernet repeaters are deprecated by most organizations. This is not the case for other types of networks.

Tip
When using repeaters, try to use network segments of the same length in order to maximize the amplification feature.

Wireless 802.11x networks have limited coverage, and so it is common to add repeaters to the network to extend network coverage. Although you can buy special wireless repeaters, most of the devices used as repeaters are access points that have been placed in a state called *repeater mode*.

Repeaters become important in network media transmitting light waves. Depending upon the signal attenuation of the media, repeaters may be required at specific intervals throughout the network. This is the case with SONET networks, which are used to transmit much of the telephone data in the United States. As you move to WAN network connections, repeater technology becomes more important.

Switches

A switch is an active device that connects two network segments together at one or more levels of the OSI network model. The term *switch* is applied to a broad variety of devices, and unlike the function of a *bridge*, which is defined by the IEEE 802.1D standard, no such definition exists for a switch. The term switch is more a marketing term than anything else, and is often used when describing a hub, repeater, or bridge when the switch vendor thinks that the term is more valued by the consumer. Indeed, Layer 2 switches are bridges under the IEEE 802.1D standard and are sold as switches by most vendors. Switches have the ability to define virtual circuits that pass through them, but often lack the additional intelligence to provide dynamic reconfiguration of their circuits on the fly without outside intervention. The ability to dynamically reconfigure circuits provides a means to reroute traffic from one input to a different output based on network conditions or as the result of an optimization algorithm.

Switches can be managed or unmanaged. An unmanaged switch cannot be configured over the network, while a managed switch can be. Managed switches usually include an SNMP (Simple Network Management Protocol) agent, Command Line Interface with console, or perhaps a Web browser interface. A smart switch is one that includes a small set of configurable settings and is differentiated from an enterprise-level, fully managed switch that has functions such as the ability to create and store different configurations. Enterprise switches usually have higher port counts and can be stacked into larger manageable units.

When considering switches, you should look for the following features:

- **Ports.** The port count, ability to prioritize ports, and port mirroring.
- **Speeds and feeds.** The port speed and duplexing capabilities affect the throughput of the switch.
- **Link aggregation.** The ability to send data over multiple connections to the same endpoint.
- **SNMP.** The ability to participate in network discovery and management.
- **Filtering.** The ability to segment traffic based on the physical identification of devices (for example, MAC filtering). Network Address Translation, or NAT, is considered to be a function of a firewall or router and generally isn't found in switches, although there are exceptions to this rule.
- **Network Access Control.** The ability of a switch to provide a bridging function between two different networks. This is important for wireless switches, which provide access to Wi-Fi networks.
- **VLAN.** The ability to create a logical group of systems comprised of a single broadcast domain. By segmenting networks into broadcast domains you can greatly isolate network traffic and reduce network utilization providing more network overhead.

You will find switches that have capabilities ranging from the Data Link layer (Level 2) up to the Application layer (Level 7, the top layer) of the OSI network model. Only passive Physical layer (Level 1) devices such as hubs and repeaters aren't called switches by some vendors.

In Ethernet networks, all ports on a hub receive the same broadcast data; there is no segmentation at the hub and all segments belong to the same collision domain. In order to limit collisions, hubs operate in the half-duplex mode over a shared connection. Switches segment communications so that each network segment has its own dedicated bandwidth, runs in its own collision domain without collisions, and can support a full-duplex mode.

Perhaps the most useful way to describe a switch is to define it in terms of the functionality at each of the levels it supports. A Layer 2 switch is one that technically satisfies the IEEE 802.1D standard for a network bridge. The function of a Layer 2 switch is described later in this chapter. Similarly, when a switch uses a Layer 3 protocol, it is serving the function of a router; this function is also described later in this chapter. Dense multiport switching devices, referred to as Director switches, are Layer 3 devices, and are used on different network types, such as PSTN and Fibre Channel SANs, to connect hundreds of devices together. Usually the situation isn't as clear-cut, and a switch can perform services at two or more layers. Switches of this type are sometimes referred to as multilayer switches.

You may encounter two other types of switch devices: Layer 4 and Layer 7 switches. A Layer 4 switch is one that has had network address translation, or NAT, added to it, and performs load balancing between ports. Layer 4 devices can include stateful firewalls, IPsec gateways, and VPN concentrators. Usually, Layer 4 switches are sold as firewalls, as this term seems to have more cachet with the market. Layer 7 switches offer Application layer services and are most often encountered serving as a content delivery server or as an Internet caching appliance. It's rare to find a Layer 7 switch described as such; more often, they are referred to as servers because that is the stronger marketing term.

Bridges

A network bridge is a device that spans two network segments (one subnet) together at the Data Link layer (Level 2). Bridges examine network traffic using the MAC addresses of the destination and not any of the network protocols such as IP, IPX, NetBEUI, and others that are being used. Bridges are also used when you want to connect to different types of physical media, such as 100Base-T and Wi-Fi, or 100Base-T and100Base-TX.

A bridge on an Ethernet network often functions as a transparent network device or adaptive bridge, which means that it compares the MAC address to a forwarding table and then sends the frames on to the destination if an entry exists. When there is no entry or when the table is new, the frame gets broadcast, and when a response is given, that MAC address is recorded in the forwarding table with the associated route. Adaptive switching actually describes the ability of a bridge to switch between three other modes:

- **Frame store and forward.** This method buffers incoming frames, verifies the checksum, and then forwards the message onwards.

- **Cut through.** The frame's envelope is read to determine the destination MAC address, and then forwarded based on the forwarding table entry. No error check is performed.

- **Fragment free.** The first 64 bytes of the frame are read and checked for validity before being forwarded. The idea is that checking the address is almost always good enough to determine if the data is intact or if a collision made the data unusable. The duty of error checking is passed on to devices running higher-level protocols.

Bridges on Token Ring networks use a different method for resolving how to forward traffic, called Source Route bridging. This system broadcasts an All Route (AR) frame that has a certain Time-to-Live (TTL) measured in network segments or hops. As the AR moves around the Token Ring, each bridge registers its location, decrements the TTL counter, and records any new information. When the counter is set to zero, the AR frame is dropped. The system assigns a best route based on the identity of the first AR frame to arrive, ignoring any additional AR frames. Single Route frames that contain the data the network transports are then created with specific destinations and routed to the destination based on AR data stored at the bridge. The system of Source Route bridging tends to distribute data traffic throughout the network and responds to congestion by rerouting traffic over different paths.

Bridges are typically employed when you have two groups of computers for which most of the communication is intragroup, and a smaller portion of the communication is intergroup. An example would be a network with one floor of networked systems for accounting and another floor for engineering. Alternatively, it can separate different clustered groups of systems, such as Linux computers from Macintoshes. When used in this manner, a network bridge improves the performance of both groups by partitioning most of the traffic to half of the entire network, lowering the collision rate.

Nearly all of the devices you can buy that are labeled as a bridge are wireless access points configured to bridge between two networks or network segments. On a wired network Layer 2, switches are set into a bridging mode, and so you may encounter the term network switch as a synonym for a network bridge. In most instances, when the term bridge or network bridge is used on Ethernet networks, the term applies to any network device that conforms to the IEEE 802.D standard. The Spanning Tree Protocol that is described in detail later in this chapter is a routing standard that operates using interconnections described as bridge nodes.

A network bridge is characterized by the following features:

- A bridge doesn't interact with any network protocol at a higher level than Address Resolution Protocol (ARP), Neighbor Discovery Protocol (NDP), or Open Shortest Path First (OSPF), all of which are Link Layer protocols in the TCP/IP network model.

- A bridge separates two collision domains, processing and regenerating packets.

- Regardless of the number of ports available, a bridge has one port that forwards information and another that distributes information. That is, from a network standpoint, a bridge has only one network interface.

- A bridge does not determine routing, but can filter packets based on their destination MAC addresses.

- There are no limits to the number of network bridges on a network, and the limitations placed on network segments do not extend across a network bridge.

- A port is logically part of one bridge only.

- When a port is added to a bridge, it becomes unmanaged because network bridges are self-configuring.

A network bridge or an unmanaged switch is one that doesn't take an IP address and therefore can't be PINGed or respond to network commands. The datagram transfer function of a bridge spanning two different network segments doesn't require that a bridge be managed. However, many devices, such as switches functioning as logical bridges, are managed, have an IP address, participate in SNMP network communication, and can be accessed by commands such as Secure Shell (SSH), TELNET, or RLOGIN. Using these methods, you can work with a managed bridge to set the IP address of the virtual interface, which can communicate with other network interfaces. Traffic from other network endpoints is passed through the managed bridge without interaction.

If you have configured network interfaces on Windows XP or Vista, you might have encountered the Windows network bridge. The Windows network bridge is a software-based or virtual network interface that spans two or more different networks. If you have a wired network and a wireless network and you have a computer with two physical interfaces to both networks, you can use a network bridge to allow computers on both networks to access any network share that you create on that system. The bridge also provides a means for systems on one network to access resources on the other network through the network bridge.

Caution
Do not create a network bridge between a Windows Internet connection and your wired network, because it allows unsecured access to Internet users to your wired network.

To create a Windows network bridge, follow these steps:

1. Open the Network Connections folder.

2. Hold the Ctrl key and click the network connections (interfaces) that you want to add to the network bridge.

3. Right-click a selected interface and select Bridge Connections; if necessary, supply the administrative credentials required. Figure 9.2 shows the Network Connections window in Vista with a network bridge installed.

A network bridge is a virtual network interface and can be manipulated just like any other network interface. You can open its Properties dialog box and add or remove components, including additional network interfaces. To remove an interface from the network bridge or the network bridge itself, you can delete it from the icon's context menu.

FIGURE 9.2

A network bridge and its constituents shown inside Vista's Network Connections dialog box

Although bridging and routing are both methods for directing data on a network, routing refers to methods that are performed at the Network layer (Level 3). A router directs network traffic based on logical assigned addresses such as IP addresses, while a bridge uses only the hardware ID (MAC address). Therefore, routers can determine when different networks are in use while a bridge cannot, which makes routers less prone to errors than bridges. As a general rule, you would use bridges to connect network segments and routers when connecting different networks. Bridges are inexpensive devices, more expensive than hubs or repeaters but less expensive than switches (sometimes) or routers (always). Because bridges buffer frames while they are determining their forwarding status, they have less throughput than repeaters, which simply amplify the signal and forward it.

Routers

A network router is a device that connects two different networks together. Routers separate collision domains, filter and block broadcasts, and determine the optimum path to use to route packets. Because routers operate at the Network layer (Level 3), you may hear routers referred to as Layer 3 switches in just the same way that bridges were referred to as Layer 2 switches. High-performance routers are powerful computers that can perform a considerable amount of data processing.

Routers, as a logical device, have the concept of a multihomed server as their origin. An early router was developed at BBN Technologies (formerly called Bolt, Beranek and Newman) and was eventually replaced by DEC PDP-11 systems configured to route IP traffic. Sun Microsystems popularized the low-cost SPARC servers as routers; when the Internet became commercialized in the 1980s, many ISPs bought Sun servers for that purpose. A startup called Cisco, which turned routers into an appliance, is the dominant switch vendor today.

Routing is included in many server network operating systems, including UNIX, Linux, and Windows servers. The lower cost of Linux makes it very popular as a router. Cisco routers have the Internetwork Operating System (IOS) that was designed specifically for switching and routing, and uses a Command Line Interface. Many of the developments that you read about in this chapter were inspired by Cisco's work. Other vendors that have router operating systems include Juniper Networks (JUNOS) and Extreme Networks (XOS).

Tip

Use a bridge instead of router if your primary aim is to segment traffic but you don't need routing capabilities or the protocol translation functions of a router.

Routing on small networks is not a processor-intensive application, and many people turn their obsolete personal computers into network routers. Among the software packages that you can use to create PC routers are:

- **Quagga (www.quagga.net).** Open source OSPF, RIP, BPG, and Intermediate System to Intermediate System (IS-IS) routers for UNIX, Linux, and Solaris systems based on the Zebra project.

- **SmoothWall (www.smoothwall.org).** An open source Linux distribution that provides an easy-to-use graphical user interface (GUI).

- **Untangle (www.untangle.com).** An open source gateway application that creates a border router on which various anti-spyware, anti-virus software, filters, blockers, and a firewall can be installed.

- **XORP (www.xorp.org).** The Extensible Open Router Platform is an open source router that includes RIP, OSPF, IGMP, BGP, and other routing protocols. Versions of XORP run on Linux, Mac OS X (9.2 and higher), and Windows Server 2003.

You may encounter the composite term *brouter*, which is short for bridge router. A brouter is a device that can function as a bridge or a router. When routable packets such as TCP/IP arrive, brouters perform the function of a router and route them from the source network to the destination network. Any packet with an unroutable protocol, such as NetBEUI, is simply forwarded like a bridge would do.

Routers are characterized by two different functional systems: their control planes and their forwarding planes, which select ports and send data to the correct outgoing interface. The methods used to determine how this is done are based on intelligent algorithms that optimize network performance. Depending on the protocol or protocols that the router supports, different topologies are created. These different aspects of routers are discussed in the sections that follow.

Control plane

Routers are described as having two operating planes: *the control plane*, which determines which port to use to send packets onto their destination, and *the forwarding plane*, which sends a received packet from the incoming to the outgoing interface. The control plane participates with other network devices to construct the routing table used to route traffic; it is also responsible for filtering and blocking behaviors on the router, as well as any Quality of Service (QoS) protocols that the vendor has included. Filtering behavior is based on the destination endpoint.

The control plane stores the routing table, which primarily represents a set of addresses used for unicast communication with other network endpoints. It is possible to hardwire static routes manually in routers, or place rules on the use of different static routes. The latter is sometimes referred to as a floating static route. Some of the entries in the routing table may be for logical groups of systems, which are used for multicast operations. Most routers rely on the routing table or Routing Information Base (RIB) for their routing logic, but some routers also maintain a Forwarding Information Base (FIB) that is placed into fast memory by the control plane for the use of the forwarding plane.

Most networks choose to place the router into a dynamic mode in which the router participates with other routes or switches in determining the network logic that finds the preferred routes through a network. In most routing protocols, the router is assigned a routing priority, which is a major factor in determining what role a router can play, as well as what routes that router participates in.

Routers use physical connections to define routes through a network, but the interface used may also be a logical network interface. Routers have the ability to bind two or more logical interfaces to a physical interface, provided that they support virtual LANs (VLANs). Support for VLANs is based on the IEEE 802.1q standard. Some routers also support tunneling protocols, including the Generic Routing Encapsulation (GRE) and Multi Protocol Label Switching (MPLS) protocols. Tunneling is described in more detail in Chapter 29.

Forwarding plane

The forwarding (or data) plane of a router is the part of the router that examines packets at the inbound interface and transports those packets to the correct outbound interface. Routers often come with multiple forwarding planes connected with a crossbar architecture so that they can forward traffic in parallel. Forwarding planes can come as add-in cards with multiple ASICs for processing; the router itself provides a backplane or chassis into which the cards are placed. The physical structure of many routers is similar to the way blade servers are packaged. One method designed by the IETF's Benchmarking Working Group (BMWG; RFC 2544) to measure performance in routers uses half of the router ports to send packets and the other half to receive them.

This subsystem consults a lookup table that matches the network ID or MAC address to a route stored in the table. As mentioned in the previous section, the forwarding system sometimes uses a Forwarding Information Base stored in memory instead of the Routing Information Base as its lookup to speed up operations. These data stores are searched using algorithms developed for the

IP address space, including binary tree, radix tree, Patricia tree, four-way tree, and a variety of proprietary algorithms that have been developed by the router vendor for their specific hardware.

Routers contain rules on what packets to pass and what packets to filter. Filtered packets are dropped (discarded), and no ICMP (Internet Control Message Protocol) messages are sent back to the source. This is done to make the router opaque to hackers. Should the source or destination address be missing in the router's cache or the router table and the packet not conform to a filter, the router sends an ICMP "destination unreachable" packet back to the source.

Because a router bridges different networks at the Network layer (Level 3), packets that use the same Network protocol can be passed directly through the router without processing, something that is referred to as the router's fast path. However, if the network protocols (IP versus IPX, for example) don't match, then the router has to process the packet to conform to the required protocol. Packets that require additional processing are on the router's slow path.

Routers also perform other functions. They serve as security devices by encrypting packets using the protocols that their technology supports. The part of the router that performs this processing is sometimes referred to as the service plane. To perform these functions, routers operate at the Data Link layer (Level 2) for decoding the packet header, processing and extracting the data contained in the packet, and, if necessary, reading other fields in the packet.

Routers also can enforce QoS requirements, segmenting packets if necessary. When the buffer is full, the router is unable to process additional packets and is forced to drop packets. The methodology used to determine which packets to drop varies by router, but three different techniques are commonly used:

- **Tail Drop algorithm.** This queue-management algorithm measures the cache contents, and when it exceeds a certain maximum level drops all incoming packets until the cache becomes available. Tail Drop (or Drop Tail) does not differentiate between types of packets, source, or any other factor in deciding which packets to drop.

  When the sending system detects that their packets are being dropped by an absence of ACK messages, the sending system goes into slow state until a steady stream of ACK messages are received. The problem with Tail Drop is that when systems begin to re-send packets, they do so all at once, creating a data flood.

- **Random Early Detection (RED).** This is an algorithm that monitors the average queue size and drops packets based on a statistical probability function. RED's statistical behavior means that a source sending a lot of data has a high probability of having its packets dropped, while one sending a few packets will tend to get through. This mechanism avoids the problem of flooding or global synchronization that the Tail Drop method suffers from.

- **Weighted RED and Adaptive or Active RED.** Weighted RED uses the RED method but applies different priorities to packets. Active or Adaptive RED varies the statistical probability function, based on the condition of the queue.

Routing topologies

Routing is the method used to select the path that data is sent over a network. All networks require routing because it is impractical to have dedicated physical circuits for every possible path that data can travel. In a network where traffic flows from a source to a destination through intermediate devices, there can be more than one possible path that can be used. The intelligence brought to bear in selecting these paths plays a major role in the performance of a network.

There are four different broadcast methods used by routing topologies:

- **Unicast.** A message is sent from one node to another node.
- **Broadcast.** A message is sent from one node to all other nodes.
- **Multicast.** A message is sent from one node to several nodes, typically nodes that have requested the message be sent.
- **Anycast.** A message is sent from one node to a group of nodes, and any member of that group can accept the message and act on it. Once the anycast is delivered at a node, the communication is complete.

Figure 9.3 shows the four different broadcast topologies. Each oval is a separate network or subnet.

Routing is essential not only because you can't physically create all of the possible paths but also because you can't just simply throw hardware at the problem. Consider the circumstance where finding that traffic between two endpoints is high, a network installs a backbone of similar capacity, but that is shorter and faster. Switches detect this new connection and recognize that this connection is now the lowest-cost route. All traffic is then sent over the new backbone, saturating it and reducing overall network performance. This is called Braess's paradox: extra network capacity is consumed when traffic always uses the least-cost path, and in some cases, reduces system performance. This is as true with networks as it is with traveling Boston's Route 128 or San Jose's Route 101 at rush hour. It is counterintuitive, but it has been demonstrated that closing busy roads often has the effect of distributing traffic, leading to better efficiency.

Braess's paradox arises out of a game theory developed by John Forbes Nash, the Princeton physicist who won a Nobel prize for his work. Any system of multiple actors, each acting in their own best interest when taking into account the actions of the other actors such that no actor can change their strategy unilaterally to gain improvement, is called the Nash equilibrium. As you can see from the previous paragraph, systems in Nash equilibrium do not always result in the best cumulative outcome. To get the best individual results, groups must deviate from the Nash equilibrium.

This is where routing comes in. To be efficient, routing must be dynamic. In a dynamic system, the network responds to events in order to continue to operate and will make selections for groups of systems that the individual systems themselves wouldn't have the intelligence to make. For example, if a backhoe inadvertently breaks a buried telephone trunk line, an adaptive routing protocol would reroute traffic over a different path. Or if a short, high-speed line becomes available, a dynamic routing scheme would distribute traffic so that congestion is balanced against overall system performance. In individual cases, the path taken would be longer, but overall, the system's efficiency would be optimized.

FIGURE 9.3

The four different broadcast topologies

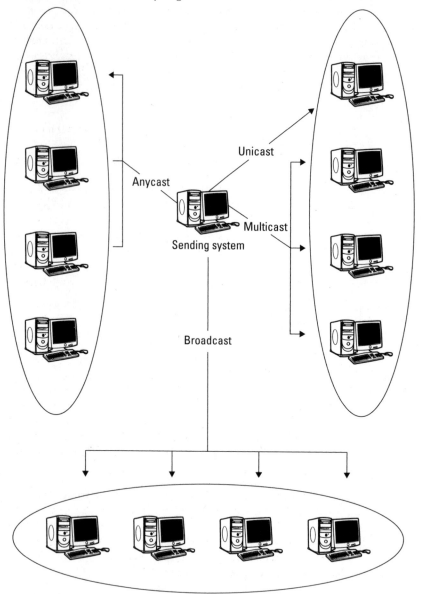

Optimization methods

On very small networks, you can manually set the preferred paths between endpoints in a simple array called a routing table. The approach isn't practical for networks of any size, and so instead they use routes that either have been computed or are computed on the fly as needed. The PSTN used a system where tables of pre-computed preferred routes are stored, along with a set of backup routes to use when the primary route fails. As the telephone network has developed, it has begun to adopt adaptive routing technologies where the routing tables are generated by the routing protocols, thereby acting automatically to reroute traffic. On the Internet, the routing system is rather different; routing is entirely dynamic.

Routing systems operate either between autonomous systems or within them. An autonomous system (AS) is a collection of systems sharing a unified administration structure. They can be a network, a group of networks, an ISP's network range, or the entire Internet. Routing protocols that connect autonomous systems are called gateway protocols. An interior gateway protocol (IGP) is used to route packets on any collection of connected IP addresses, known also as an AS. IGPs are exemplified by RIP (Routing Information Protocol), Cisco's IGRP (Internet Gateway Routing Protocol), OSPF (Open Shortest Path First protocol), and IS-IS (Intermediate System to Intermediate System protocol). Exterior gateway protocols (EGPs) are used to determine the routing between two or more autonomous systems. The class of EGPs included the original EGP (now obsolete) and BGP (Border Gateway Protocol) and also can include backbone routers in the OSPF system. These different routing and gateway protocols are explained in the sections that follow.

Distance vector routing

A distance vector (DV) algorithm assigns a cost to use of each network connection based on the number of hops. Messages are routed based on the lowest hop count of the individual connections summed over the route taken. Each node in the network constructs a distance table with its nearest neighbors, which then share that table with their neighbors. DV routing is very common on packet switched networks and forms the basis for both the Routing Information Protocol (RIP v1 and v2) and the proprietary Cisco Interior Gateway Routing Protocol (IGRP). Two other protocols use aspects of the DV methodology: the Border Gateway Protocol (BGP), which is the core protocol for routing on the Internet, and the Exterior Gateway Protocol (EGP), which is an older and now obsolete routing method.

While some protocols, such as the Spanning Tree Protocol (a Layer 2 protocol described later in this chapter), operate in such a manner that they detect network loops and eliminate them, distance vector methodology does not. Routing tables are created based on the path of delivered packets optimized over specific connection segments. A Bellman-Ford algorithm is applied to the distance vector table to optimize the calculated routes, and preferred routes are communicated with neighbors who update their routes based on new information.

The Bellman-Ford algorithm

The Bellman-Ford algorithm uses a shortest-path calculation over weighted edges. It was developed by Richard Bellman in 1958 and Lester Ford Jr. in 1956, independently of one another. Most protocols that use Bellman-Ford use a distributed version of the protocol. The Distributed Bellman-Ford (DBF) uses three different mechanisms to populate the routing tables at each node:

1. **Start state.** Each router has a table listing the path or vector with the shortest hop count to directly attached networks, with entries in the form (Destination, Distance, Successor). A Successor is the router or node that is one step closer on the path to the destination, and is a nearest neighbor. Destination can be a simple hop count, a weighted cost based on throughput or connection speed, or some other factor.

2. **Send.** Each node sends its path vectors (Destination, Distance) to its immediate neighbors, periodically (a second to a minute) and immediately upon detection of an entry change.

3. **Receive.** On a network, each router calculates the least-cost path to other destinations based on the information it receives from its nearest neighbors. After the update, each router returns to Step 2 and sends its new information on to its nearest neighbors.

In Figure 9.4, the Bellman-Ford algorithm is illustrated. In the figure, the top routing table is populated with nearest neighbor information. Because there is no way for router A to know the shortest route to router E, the vector entry is left blank (NA or Not Available). The middle routing table shows the first update going from D to B. Now router B can fill in a vector for the path from router B to router E of 5, although it is still unknown if this is the least-cost path B to E. Until the E-C vector is populated, router B can't know that BDE is indeed the lowest-cost path, at a cost of 5, because BCE has a cost of 8. The bottom routing table shows the router table after nearest neighbor updates, E to C update, and enough rounds of nearest neighbor updates needed to populate the table with lowest-cost vectors (shown in Figure 9.4).

The routing table that is stored at each router is shown in Figure 9.5 and is somewhat different than the least-cost path shown in Figure 9.4. As an example, consider router B and its routing table, consisting of vectors with their entries (Destination, Distance, Successor) shown in table form. In this table the row is the destination, the column is the successor, and the distance is the values in the grid cells. Notice that many of the entries are not populated with the least-cost path.

Consider what happens when the B-D link breaks, as is shown in Figure 9.6. The break is detected by both routers B and D, and an immediate update is triggered, followed by nearest neighbor updates. Multiple vectors in the table are altered by this update, each of which is shown with its cell's borders made bold.

FIGURE 9.4

The Bellman-Ford algorithm's mechanism for populating a router table

1. Starting step, get vectors from nearest neighbors

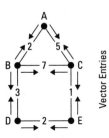

Distance

Vector Entries	-	A	B	C	D	E
	A	0	2	5	NA	NA
	B	2	0	7	3	NA
	C	5	7	0	NA	1
	D	NA	3	NA	0	2
	E	NA	NA	1	2	0

2. Update vectors from D to B, repeat step 1

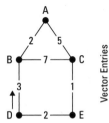

Distance

Vector Entries	-	A	B	C	D	E
	A	0	2	5	NA	NA
	B	2	0	7	3	5
	C	5	7	0	3	1
	D	NA	3	NA	0	2
	E	NA	NA	1	2	0

3. After multiple updates lowest cost vectors are populated

Distance

Vector Entries	-	A	B	C	D	E
	A	0	2	5	5	6
	B	2	0	6	3	5
	C	5	7	0	3	1
	D	5	3	3	0	2
	E	6	5	1	2	0

FIGURE 9.5

The routing table for an individual router, shown here for router B

Router B's routing table

Next Hop

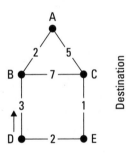

Destination	-	A	C	D
	A	2	12	8
	C	7	7	10
	D	8	10	3
	E	8	8	5

FIGURE 9.6

The impact of a broken link on a Bellman-Ford routing table

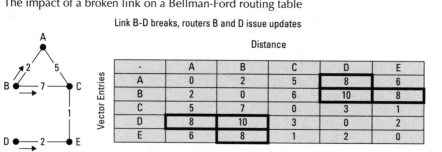

Link B-D breaks, routers B and D issue updates

Distance

-	A	B	C	D	E
A	0	2	5	8	6
B	2	0	6	10	8
C	5	7	0	3	1
D	8	10	3	0	2
E	6	8	1	2	0

Vector Entries

Count-to-infinity

In a distance vector system, any change in the dynamics, such as a link or device failure, is detected during regular updates, and the entries for that link or device are either modified or deleted. The change then ripples through the adjoining nodes' tables. Because only neighbors update, the progression is slower than updating the entire network at once and requires less bandwidth and a smaller amount of processing. It also means that until the downstream nodes learn of the change, they are still communicating the original configuration's validity. This problem is often referred to as the count-to-infinity problem.

Consider a sample network path, A-F, with each segment or hop costing one unit for packets to traverse. This is illustrated in Figure 9.7. The link A-B fails, and B, being the nearest neighbor, detects the problem. At the first update, B gets an update from C and, realizing that C has a route to A with a hop count of 2, B updates, or reactualizes, its routing entry to add the cost of the B-C route to C's cost and puts the value of 3 into its routing table entry, believing that the lowest-cost route to A now goes through C. C still believes that B is the lowest-cost path to A, and so when it looks at B's entry (now at 3), it readjusts its value to 4, and all of the downstream neighbors adjust their values as well. Update 3 performs the same legerdemain that Update 1 does, B looking at C and adding C's value to the hop count of B-C. The process continues on counting to infinity and eventually would immobilize the network. Count-to-infinity is circumvented by the use of a technique in Bellman-Ford called *relaxation*, where a test is performed periodically to determine if a shorter path exists than the one in the routing table entry.

Routing Information Protocol

The earliest and best-known protocol using the DV routing algorithm is the Routing Information Protocol (RIP) that is used as an interior gateway protocol on both LANs and WANs. The original version was defined by IEEE RFC 1058 in 1988; version 2 was defined in RFC2453, and RIP became the original routing protocol used on the Internet. RIP uses a hop count as its cost metric. The maximum number of hosts is limited to 15, and the Time-to-Live for any one path is 180 seconds. RIP slightly randomizes updates so that the system isn't overloaded when too many routers update at once.

FIGURE 9.7

The count-to-infinity problem

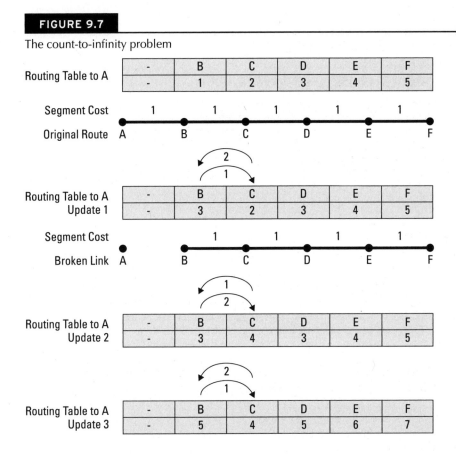

RIP was widely used, but is considered to be less effective than other link state routing protocols such as the OSPF and the OSI protocol IS-IS. A version of RIP exists for IPv6, called RIPng, which has several methods in place to ensure that obsolete or incomplete information doesn't propagate in the system. One rule, called *the split horizon*, prevents any router from advertising a route back to the router that it learned about the route from.

Split horizon effectively eliminates the count-to-infinity problem and suppresses the formation of network loops. In a network branch, with a message starting at router 1 and going through routers 2, 3, and 4 to get to router 5, a router with a higher number will never advertise the route to a router with a lower number. Should link 2-3 break, router 2 is prohibited from returning the packet back to router 1, which would form a loop.

A variation of the split horizon rule, called *split horizon with poison reverse*, actually marks routes back as unreachable, which is really only useful on a network where redundant pathways exist. The vector entries for the reverse routes are removed from the routing tables, whereas for split horizon, backwards routes are simply timed out. Poison reverse significantly increases the size of routing information exchanges, which is a disadvantage over slow network links such as WANs. In addition to RIP, IGRP, Enhanced Interior Gateway Routing Protocol (EIGRP), and VPLS (Virtual Private LAN Service), all use some form of split horizon.

Destination-Sequenced Distance Vector Routing

The Destination-Sequenced Distance Vector Routing (DSDV) protocol is a variation of the DV system for routing on ad hoc Wi-Fi or mobile networks. DSDV adds an additional parameter to the routing table, a sequence number that is assigned to a given link and generated by the destination of the link and communicated back to the emitter. The entire routing table is transferred occasionally, while updates to the table trigger incremental vector transfers. The sequence number is usually an even number, or if a link is not detected from an update, then an odd number is used. An update for an existing link with a different lowest-cost route overwrites the route but not the sequence number. Every so often, routes that have not been used are purged from the table. DSDV was developed some time ago but never achieved commercial success. The Ad hoc On-Demand Distance Vector (AODV) Routing protocol that was developed for MANETS (Mobile Ad hoc Networks) is based on DSDV. AODV may find application in cell phone networks.

Link state routing

The concept of link state routing is that each router informs the network about its neighbors. A link state routing system creates a topological map (graph) of the network at each router, centered at that router. These maps are used to calculate the shortest path, usually by applying Dijkstra's algorithm to calculate the shortest path over several links. While distance vector protocols work by sharing routing tables, a link state protocol only transfers information about the best next hops between neighbors. Whenever a link state changes (up to/ down from), an update is triggered and the information is sent to all nearest neighbors.

Link state routing works by using the following procedure:

1. Broadcasts over each port of any new router on the network establishe who its nearest neighbors are through their responses and record their information in the routing table.

2. Each route is given a sequence number by the link state routing algorithm.

3. A link state advertisement (LSA) is broadcast automatically every so often to neighbors, containing the information about nearest neighbors stored in the routing table.

4. If the sequence number of the announcement from a node hasn't been recorded, the new information is recorded in the routing table by the link state routing algorithm; if the information has a higher sequence number for an existing link, the new information, including the higher sequence number, overwrites the previous information.

   Steps 3 and 4 are repeated over the entire routing domain. Updates are sent by unicast to nearest neighbors, and occasionally link state exchange messages called HELLO packets are sent to ensure system integrity.

5. The link state algorithm then examines all stored valid links and creates a map of the network centered on the router the algorithm runs on. Valid links are those for which both endpoints have reported each as a nearest neighbor.

6. The accessibility of links is tested again when the link state algorithm repeats Step 1 and starts the sequence again.

7. A Dijkstra algorithm is then run on the router over the link information in the routing table to determine the shortest route between endpoints and records the information in the routing table.

The link state routing table is a hierarchical tree consisting of a set of least-cost paths connecting all of the network nodes. For any given destination, the next hop selected is the one that is the first node from the root of the hierarchy traversing the path down to the desired node. That is, if the source node is on the same branch as the destination, the route is direct. If they are on different branches, the best route travels through the node and then down the branch containing the destination node.

The most common link state routing protocols are:

- Open Shortest Path First (OSPF)
- Intermediate System to Intermediate System (IS-IS)
- Novell NetWare Link Services Protocol (NLSP)
- Apple Routing Table Maintenance Protocol (RTMP)
- Cisco Internet Gateway Routing Protocol (IGRP)

Depending upon the protocol, the least-cost route or shortest path can be based on line speed, available bandwidth, the actual cost in dollars to use a line, or other priorities that you can define. Link state routing methods are preferred for large networks because they respond faster to changes than distance vector methods do, and they are the dominant routing protocol on the Internet and with ISPs.

Dijkstra's algorithm

Dijkstra's algorithm is a pathfinder mechanism that is easier to visualize than it is to describe. The process builds two tables: a link cost table and a routing table. Link cost is a complete list, while the routing table is the result of an iterative process that provides the shortest path from A to any other node. Dijkstra's algorithm forms the basis for a number of protocols, referred to as Shortest Path First (SPF).

The description that follows refers to Figure 9.8 and shows how the topological map for node A is built. The process starts by initializing all routes to an unknown state, marked as infinity in the drawing. In Step 1, node A contacts its nearest neighbors to get their link costs. All nearest neighbors have their link cost tables updated with the information provided by A, and because A-C, A-E, and A-F are all the lowest-cost paths, they are marked in the routing table as such. In Step 2, node F discovers its nearest neighbors and updates its link cost table. F notices that the link cost for A-E is longer than the link cost for A-F-E, and therefore takes the route A-E out of the routing hierarchy. In Figure 9.8, links found in the routing table are in bold, and any link that is not in the routing table is shown as a thin line. F's results also indicate that the link cost for C-F is greater than the link cost for C-A-F, and so C-F is removed from A's routing table as well. Once all F's link information is discovered, all of the nodes have their link cost tables updated.

FIGURE 9.8

Dijkstra's algorithm example

Step 1 – A discovers its neighbors

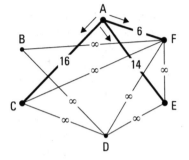

Step 6 – A - E update, D discovers its neighbors

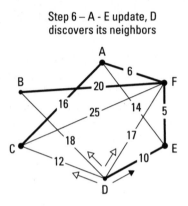

Step 2 – A, C, F update, F discovers its neighbors

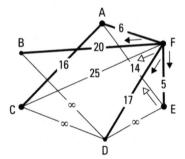

Step 5 – A - E update, B discovers its neighbors

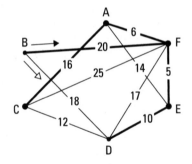

Step 3 – A, B, C, E update, C discovers its neighbors

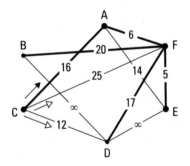

Step 4 – A - E update, E discovers its neighbors

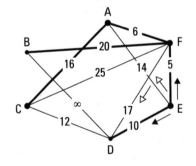

In Step 3, node C begins its discovery process. C finds that A-C is the lowest-cost route. C-D-F-A is longer than C-A. The link C-D therefore remains unused in A's routing table. Similarly, the route C-F-A costs more than the route C-A, and so C-F also remains left out of A's routing table. C's discovery process adds no additional routing to A's table but does extend the entries in the link cost tables.

Step 4 shows the E node discovery results. E results indicate that the path D-E-F-A is shorter than D-F-A, and so the path D-F is removed from A's routing table. The additional information about D-E's link cost is then added to all nodes' link cost tables. Similarly, Step 5 discovers the link cost of B-D but is similarly unable to add any better low-costs paths to A's topological map. At this point, all of the link costs in the graph are known and the routing is complete. The process is finalized by D's discovery process in Step 6, which confirms the information you already have.

The important thing to realize about Dijkstra's algorithm is that it is always expanding out from its starting point, adding more nodes as time goes on. The iterative process involved ensures that eventually the routing table is populated with the shortest least-costs paths, even if other paths were used at an earlier time.

Issues arise with Dijkstra's algorithm when a link fails or a node becomes unavailable and the topological map varies at different nodes. In this case, network loops can form. This is the problem that the HELLO packets are designed to solve. Also, variations in the implementation of link state algorithms add additional concepts such as areas and other wrinkles that make the calculations more complex, but less susceptible to the network loop problem.

Open Shortest Path First

The Open Shortest Path First (OSPF) protocol is the most widely used example of a link state routing protocol. It is in wide use as an interior gateway protocol on the Internet and many other networks. The latest version of this public protocol was version 3, as specified in RFC 5340 released in 2008, and includes support for IPv6.

The Open Shortest Path First algorithm operates similarly to Dijkstra's algorithm but adds a system of designated (primary) and backup routers. Routers are selected for these roles based on their priority number; routers with a priority of 0 cannot be designated or backup routers. The designated router for an area is responsible for sending Link State Advertisements (LSAs) to all other area nodes. OSPF routing packets on an OSPF routed network have a nine-field header, illustrated in Figure 9.9. OSPF packet types include HELLO, database description, link state request, link state update, or link state acknowledgment.

OSPF is used on autonomous systems (AS). Autonomous systems are one or more networks under a common administrative structure. OSPF functions not only as the interior gateway routing protocol for the AS, but it can also send and receive routes from other autonomous systems. Each network in the AS is an area within a hierarchy defined within the AS, each area being a collection of contiguous hosts. In OSPF, a routing domain is an alternative description for all systems in an AS that share the same topological map. OSPF partitions areas into separate topologies so that each area is kept unaware of another area's routing traffic. This system is meant to lower the amount of overall network traffic and speed up the discovery process of shortest routes for an individual area.

FIGURE 9.9

The structure of an OSPF packet

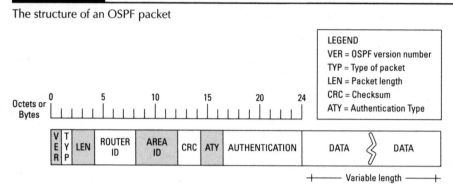

Collections of areas are connected by OSPF border routers in an OSPF backbone. The backbone itself is organized as an OSPF area, and routing information for that area is also separate from the areas the backbone connects. It is possible to organize an OSPF backbone so that the backbone is composed of two or more unconnected groups. The backbone is made contiguous by defining a virtual link through routers in a non-backbone area to serve as the connection between backbone groups. The backbone of an OSPF system composed of border routers communicates with other exterior gateway protocols (EGPs) such as the Border Gateway Protocol (BGP) or the Exterior Gateway Protocol (EGP). Figure 9.10 shows an OSPF network with several areas, a backbone, and a virtual link.

Intermediate System to Intermediate System Routing

Intermediate System to Intermediate System Routing (IS-IS) is the second-most widely used link state protocol used on packet switched networks. IS-IS tends to be employed on large ISP and enterprise-class networks as an interior gateway protocol for a network or autonomous system where it has a dominant position, and connects through exterior gateway protocols to other autonomous systems.

IS-IS was developed at the Digital Equipment Corporation as part of DECnet in the late 1980s and was published as the ISO standard, ISO/IEC 10589.2002. Because IS-IS isn't a public standard, it isn't used on the Internet, although the IETF republished 10589.2002 as RFC 1142 in 1990. The original version of IS-IS was extended to support IP routing over TCP/IP networks and is referred to as Integrated IS-IS in older literature.

IS-IS competes with OSPF and is also based on Dijkstra's pathfinder algorithm. Although they have many overlapping features, IS-IS is considered to be somewhat more stable than OSPF, while OSPF has better performance optimization features. The extra features in OSPF add additional messaging overhead and probably contribute to the fact that IS-IS scales better than OSPF.

FIGURE 9.10

An OSPF routing network with several areas and a backbone

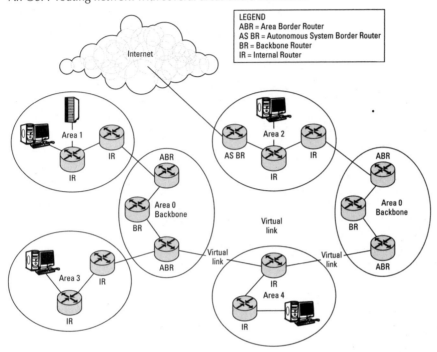

IS-IS defines three different routing area types: Level 1 (intra), Level 2 (inter), and Level 1-2 (intra/inter). Level 1 and 2 routers can only exchange information with routers of the same level, while both can exchange information between Level 1-2 routers. Unlike OSPF, which uses a backbone (Area 0) for inter-area exchange and allows for an area border router to be a union point of two areas and part of both, IS-IS does not use a backbone and areas in the network never overlap.

Path vector routing

Path vector routing is the last of the three main approaches to building routing tables in networks, the previously discussed distance vector and link state routing being the other two. Path vector routing is a derivative of the distance vector routing methodology. In the path vector system, a node gets distance vectors for a destination from its neighbor node, along with the entire path needed to reach that node. Knowing the path allows the algorithm to more easily detect and react to network loops than the distance vector method. In this system, a node stores two tables: a path table for the current path to any node and a routing table with the identity of the next hop for those routes.

A path vector example

Let's consider a simple example of the path vector approach, as shown in Figure 9.11. Vectors take the form:

(Destination, Cost, Path Node Count, Path Node List | ...)

where each | character separates one vector from another.

A sends a HELLO packet in Step 1 and learns about its neighbors, as does C. C then sends its vectors to node A, and in Step 3, A rebuilds its routing table based on the new information. C's vectors allow A to define a route to D but do not alter any of the other known routes, as shown in the lower-left table in Figure 9.11. Condensing several steps into one, all nodes learn about their neighbors using a HELLO packet in Step 4. Now when E sends its vectors to A, as shown in Step 5, A is able to build a routing table to all nodes in the figure. The new information from E adds a route to B (AFB) and changes the routes to C (to AFB) and to D (to AED). In the final Step 6 A is able to communicate its routing table shown in the lower right with all of the other nodes.

In the path vector routing system, one or more nodes in a network, called *speaker nodes*, store the routing table for other connected nodes, and distances are calculated by the speaker nodes. Speaker nodes then advertise the paths available to reach them to other speaker nodes. Path vectors try to minimize the number of domains traversed by messages, which makes this method suitable for routing across autonomous systems. The widely used Border Gateway Protocol is based on the path vector routing methodology.

Of the three methods distance vector, path vector, and link state, only the path vector protocols are practical for inter-domain routing. In distance vector routing, every additional hop a message must traverse greatly raises the possibility that the path chosen may be out of date and dysfunctional. Link state routing requires that the network tolerate heavy broadcast traffic, and that significant computing resources be used to assemble the network maps at each node.

The Border Gateway Protocol

The Border Gateway Protocol (BGP) is a highly scalable exterior gateway routing protocol for use between autonomous systems based on the path vector protocol described in the previous section. BGP is the protocol used to route traffic on the Internet, replacing the Exterior Gateway Protocol (EGP). EGP was the original Internet routing protocol developed by BBN Technologies in the early 1980s. The current version of BGP is version 4, which was specified by RFC 4271, published in 2006.

Unless you are an ISP or work in a very large network, chances are that you won't get hands-on experience working with BGP. However, because BGP powers the Internet, it is worth understanding some of the details of this important protocol. BGP is the only routing protocol that operates natively using TCP as its transport protocol, exchanging packets over port 179. BGP deployments are divided into two different types: the Exterior Border Gateway Protocol (EBGP) and the Interior Border Gateway Protocol (IBGP). A BGP router that is inside an autonomous system (AS) is an IBGP router, while a router that is between autonomous systems is an EBGP router. Any router inside an AS that communicates with another AS is called a border or edge router. By contrast a core router is one that operates on the Internet backbone.

FIGURE 9.11

An illustration of the path vector routing mechanism

1. A HELLO to neighbors
(Destination, Cost, Path Node Count; Path Node List | ...)
(C, 3, 1; AC | E, 2, 1; AE | F, 1, 1; AF)

2. C to A
(Destination, Cost, Path Node Count; Path Node List | ...)
(C, 0, 1; C | A, 3, 1; AC | D, 2, 1; CD | F, 6, 1; CF)

3. A to C, E, F
(Destination, Cost, Path Node Count; Path Node List | ...)
(A, 0, 1; A | C, 1, 1; AC | D, 5, 2; CD | F, 1, 1; AF)

4. All nodes exchange HELLO packets

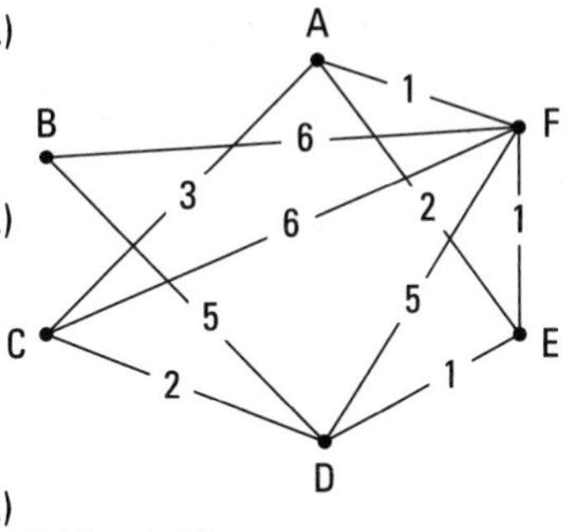

5. E to A
(Destination, Cost, Path Node Count; Path Node List | ...)
(E, 0, 1; E | A, 2, 1; AE | B, 6, 2; BDE | C, 3, 2; CDE | D, 1, 1; DE | F, 1, 1; EF)

6. A to B – F
(A, 0, 1; A | B, 7, 3; AFB | C, 3, 2; AD | D, 3, 3; AED | E, 2, 2; AE | F, 1, 2; AF)

A's Routing Table (after Step 3)

Destination	Cost	Path Vector
C	3	AC
D	5	ACD
E	2	AE
F	1	AF

A's Routing Table (after Step 5)

Destination	Cost	Path Vector
B	7	AFB
C	3	AC
D	3	AED
E	2	AE
F	1	AF

Top ISP routers are currently storing BGP routing tables of around 150,000 routes, and so if you have a fast connection such as a T1 line to AT&T, Comcast, or Sprint, you would have to download 150,000 routes from each service you are connected to. BGP partitions routes by attributes or route parameters so that routing may be more efficiently managed. Attributes that are stored include:

- **Route cost or weight** (as Cisco refers to cost)
- **Next hop.** The first node on the path to the advertising router
- **Origin.** Where the routing information came from, EBGP or IBGP

- **AS_path.** The identity of the AS from which the route advertisement came

- **Local exit preference.** The preferred exit point from the AS

- **Multi-exit discriminator** (a Cisco attribute)

- **Community designation.** This can be no-export, no-advertise, or Internet (advertise to all)

As you move down the Internet hierarchy, the Classless Inter-Domain Routing (CIDR) protocol is used to further partition the routing tables so that related address blocks can be routed as a single unit to other BGP routers. The CIDR system, described in more detail in Chapter 18, replaces the older notion of network classes.

Network loops

One way to bring down a network is to create a network loop. You can do this by plugging an Ethernet cable into two ports on the same switch or router, or by inadvertently creating a loop with multiple switches and routers — hubs don't suffer this problem. Although the circuit has been shown with three routers, you could use any combination of computers, switches, or routers as endpoints in the circuit.

Suppose you have the circular path shown in Figure 9.12. In the complete circular circuit shown in the upper-left diagram, Router_1 sends packets to Router_3 with Router_2 as the intermediary. If the connection between Router_2 and Router_3 breaks, Router_2 will return traffic meant to flow over that broken connection. Router_1 does not know about the break, and when Router_1 sends packets to Router_3 through Router_2, the packets are returned. Router_1, being ignorant of the broken connection, but still believing that the path Router_1-Router_2-Router_3 is the lowest-cost path for transmission, resends the traffic back to Router_2. Traffic between Router_1 and Router_2 bounces back and forth in an infinite loop, and the connection is quickly saturated, as shown in the upper-right scenario labeled as an infinite loop in Figure 9.12. This is the problem that routing algorithms are created to solve.

Let's take this one step further. In the circular path described, both the connections between Router_1-Router_3 and between Router_2-Router_3 fail concurrently as shown in the diagram on the lower left labeled infinite loops. Having two wires fail at the same time is a very uncommon event, but the same result is achieved when Router_3 fails, which is a common event. Now, traffic that would flow from Router_1-Router_2-Router_3 ends at Router_2, where the message is returned. If Router_2 believes that the lowest-cost path to communicate with Router_3 is Router_2-Router_1-Router_3, then traffic along that route ends at Router_1, where it is returned. This routing loop would continue until a routing protocol determines that Router_3 is unreachable. This is the situation depicted in the lower-left example in Figure 9.12.

FIGURE 9.12

Routing failures, infinite loops, and failure cascades

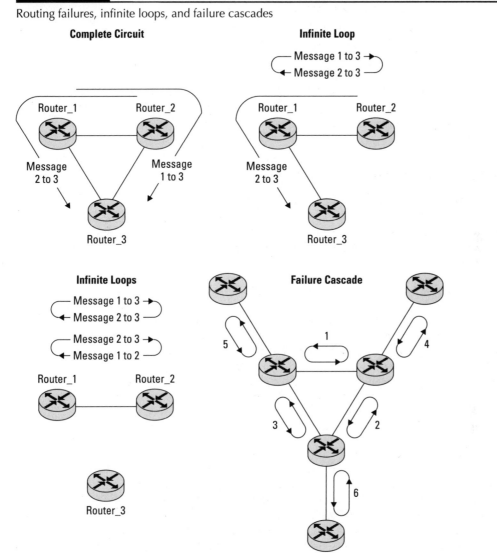

It is at this point where you cross over into the Twilight Zone of computer networking, a failure cascade. At the bottom-right example in Figure 9.12, an infinite loop occurs at the connection labeled 1, which then saturates. The traffic on adjacent connections labeled 2 and 3 begins to pile up, and they develop infinite loops of their own. As connections fail, the effects spread outwards.

A cascade of failing links ripples through the network, expanding out through connections 4, 5, and 6... and beyond. The entire network is down, and the only way to diagnose the problem is to divide the network up into segments, locate the error, and continue segmenting until you isolate the problem to a single device or connection. This is, in essence, what routing protocols do in software.

The Spanning Tree Protocol

The Spanning Tree Protocol (STP), as specified by the IEEE 802.1D standard, is an adaptive routing technology that solves the problem of network loops through adaptive and dynamic routing. STP is a central technology used on switched networks and establishes routes by creating virtual circuits, eliminating any network loops that it can detect. Connections are made at bridge nodes. Switches are commonly used for the connection points, and they are configured to serve the role of a bridge. Routers can also be set into a bridging mode to function in this capacity. However, the extra intelligence added to routers can be applied to different systems of routing.

The STP algorithm (DEC STP) was invented by Radia Perlman in 1985, while at Digital Equipment Corporation (now at Sun Microsystems), and predates the development of the World Wide Web. STP operates at the Network layer (Level 2) of the OSI model, above the Physical layer and inside devices such as switches and routers.

In a hierarchical network, the root node is connected to a certain number of Level 1 nodes, and the network continues to fan out. A hierarchical topology is a tree, albeit an upside-down tree where branches are linear and where the failure of any node or connection to a node in a branch renders the nodes at lower levels in the hierarchy inaccessible. A purely hierarchical topology also means that if a node in one branch wants to communicate with a node in another branch, it would have to traverse a path up the tree to the root node and back down to the target node. For these two reasons, only very small networks can be structured in a pure hierarchy.

The solution to these problems is to build cross-links between different branches. Cross-links provide shorter paths and thus better performance, and they provide a certain measure of redundancy because there are now multiple paths through the network for most connections you might want to make. Cross-links also provide a mechanism to create network loops.

In graph theory, a spanning tree is created by using an algorithm to compute a set of paths through a system of connected nodes such that every node is on at least one branch of the tree, but that no loops are defined. Nodes serve the function of a topological bridge, and therefore are often called bridges. Figure 9.13 shows a spanning tree. The solid lines represent branches of the spanning tree, while the dashed lines represent routes left out of the spanning tree.

There are many different ways that you can compute a spanning tree. In one scheme, each edge is given a weight (a weighted graph) and the spanning tree computes the paths through the system that has the lowest weights, thus providing what is called a minimum spanning tree, or alternatively, a minimum-weight spanning tree. In multi-domain systems, a union of minimum spanning trees is called a minimum spanning forest.

Other optimizations are possible, such as the minimum spanning tree with the most edges, the minimum diameter, fewest leaves, or minimum dilation. An edge is the path between two nodes calculated by the spanning tree algorithm. Leaves are each of the branches of the tree. The diameter is the number of switches traversed to link two switches in a bridged network together. Dilation represents the difference between the shortest path between two nodes in the tree and the path that the spanning tree algorithm calculates.

FIGURE 9.13

A spanning tree

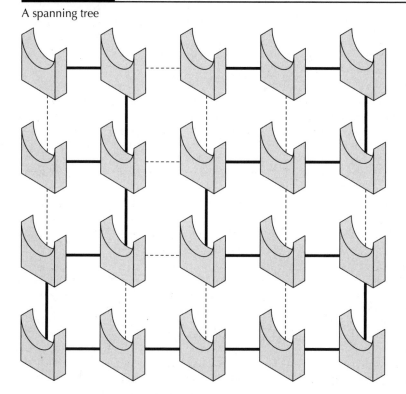

Node/bridge hierarchy

In a network system, the goal is to define a spanning tree such that there are no loops, but that enough redundancy exists in the system to provide access even when a node or connection fails. Instead of using weighted edges, the notion of a least-cost path is used. To compute the least-cost path, the system defines two parameters:

- Node Priority
- Node Identifier

The cost, or weight, of a node is then computed using a combination of the two parameters. In the Spanning Tree Protocol, the node priority is considered first; the node with the lowest priority number is deemed to be the highest priority and takes precedence. Nodes are then compared using their MAC addresses, and the MAC address with the lowest value takes precedence over a node of the same priority. To set a node as the root (root bridge), the priority should be set below 10, while most devices using STP come with their priority set high. For Cisco switches/routers, their priority out of the box is set to 32768.

The STP algorithm computes a path through the system such that messages that travel from any endpoint to the root bridge do so over the least-cost path. The cost of a path is the total of the costs of each of the segments that the path traverses. Because each bridge point in the system has a configurable priority, the STP can change the least-cost path based on conditions. In computing a least-cost path, the following two rules are used:

- Determine the least-cost path from each bridge node.
- Determine the least-cost path for each network segment.

In a switch/router, the port connected to the least-cost path to the root is the root port; the port connected to the least-cost path to a network segment is called the designated port of that segment. For the purposes of this discussion, you can take the definition of a network segment to be a collection of nodes that are connected by the same Physical Layer system that share the same security model. Thus two subnets sharing the same LAN would be two segments, as would two different workgroups/domains.

Once the STP algorithm calculates the root and designated ports, any other active port then becomes a blocked port. It is often the case that two or more paths to the root from a bridge have the same lowest cost. In that case, the path through the bridge node with the lowest bridge ID becomes the root port. When there exist two or more bridges on the same network segment that have the least-cost path to the root, the designated port becomes the one on the bridge that connects to the bridge with the lowest bridge ID.

Figure 9.14 shows a network system to which the Spanning Tree Protocol has been applied. To simplify the analysis, each network segment is assumed to have the same unit cost. The following analysis leads to the STP diagram that you see in Figure 9.14:

1. The bridge node with priority 8 has the highest priority (lowest number) and becomes the root bridge. The root node is not necessarily the highest-capacity or most powerful device; typically, it is one that is most centrally located. Generally, the root node chosen is one that is the least modified or disturbed; for this reason, switches on network backbones are often chosen as a root node. Note that the root bridge is the only bridge in the network that does not have a root port.

2. Two paths lead to bridge nodes with priorities 10 and 12. Because 10 has the highest priority, it connects to the next-highest bridge node, which is 22.

3. Of the two nodes that are unconnected with values of 12 and 22, 12 now has precedence. The highest-priority node that 12 can physically connect to without creating a loop is 45, and that connection is made.

4. The two unconnected nodes compared now are 22 and 45. Bridge node 22 is connected to 50, the next-highest priority node.

5. Because the two bridge nodes compared at this point are 45 and 50, 45 takes precedence. The highest-priority bridge node that it can physically connect to is 125.

6. The three remaining bridge points are 77, 96, and 200, and they are connected in sequence. They become endpoints of each of the branches of the spanning tree.

FIGURE 9.14

A network system to which the Spanning Tree Protocol has been applied

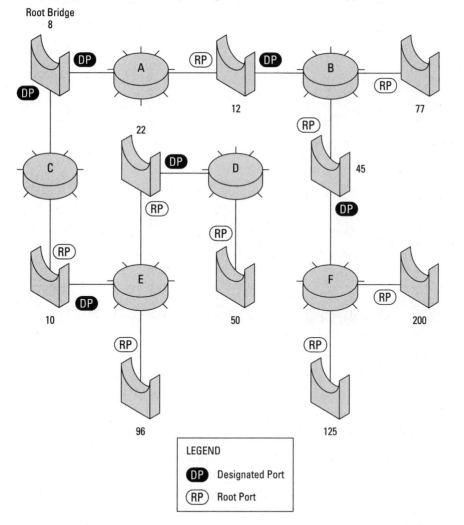

It is still possible that the algorithm may not be able to break a tie to determine which of two or more bridges rank higher in the STP hierarchy. The situation arises when two bridges are connected to one another by two or more links. The selection is then made based on the port priority, and this port is assigned to be either a root or designated port.

Network segment costs

Figure 9.14 makes the assumption that each network segment has the same cost of traversal, which is generally not the case. As was stated in the previous section, the network segment cost is one parameter used to determine the least-cost path. Some network connections are fast, and some are slow. Even in relatively simple networks where bridge points connect to Fast Ethernet, there may be bridge points that connect to wireless devices. In order to optimize the Spanning Tree Protocol, the cost of the network segment is calculated based on the IEEE 802.1D standard from 1998. This standard was amended in 2001 by 802.1t to allow for more granular calculations. Table 9.1 shows the standard segment costs.

TABLE 9.1

STP Network Segment Costs

Segment Throughput	Segment Cost 802.1t	Segment Cost 802.1D
10 Gbits/s	2,000	2
2 Gbits/s	10,000	3
1 Gbits/s	20,000	4
100 Mbits/s	200,000	19
16 Mbits/s	1,250,000	62
10 Mbits/s	2,000,000	100
4 Mbits/s	5,000,000	250

Dynamic optimization

In the example presented, all of the bridge nodes' priorities and network segments were assigned prior to applying the STP. The addition of a network discovery method greatly improves the value of the STP and allows it to adapt to changing network conditions. One method used for discovery is called the Bridge Protocol, and it works by multicasting special frames called Bridge Protocol Data Units (BPDUs) that contain information about current path segment costs and available bridge node IDs. With this updated information, the root path on the network can be adjusted. Figure 9.15 shows the format used for a BPDU frame. The different fields in the BPDU contain information about the bridge ID, priority of the bridge, and the MAC address used by the switch. Other fields set the priority of the path and other parameters, such as the weight of the path (cost of path).

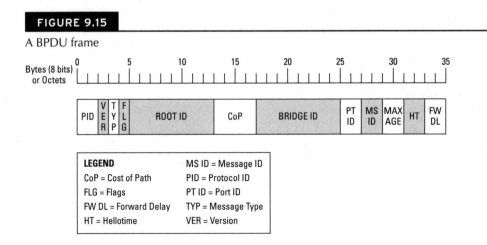

FIGURE 9.15

A BPDU frame

LEGEND

CoP = Cost of Path	MS ID = Message ID
FLG = Flags	PID = Protocol ID
FW DL = Forward Delay	PT ID = Port ID
HT = Hellotime	TYP = Message Type
	VER = Version

Switches and routers, which are the devices that serve as bridge nodes in modern networks, multicast a BPDU frame that includes the MAC address of the port that is the source, and an STP multicast address that, by convention, is set to 01:80:C2:00:00:00. Frames are sent out every few seconds and essentially provide a network heartbeat that STP uses to update its routing tables. The default setting for a standard exchange is every 2 seconds (called the "hello time"), but this is adjustable.

The Bridge Protocol defines three different types of BPDUs:

- Configuration (CBPDU)
- Topology Change Notification (TCN)
- Topology Change Notification Acknowledgement (TCA)

Any time a new device is added to a network port, that port enters a listening state where it detects the different BPDUs and learns about the network configuration. Devices are any endpoint that has a network interface. The default listening state is 15 seconds and is followed by a learning state of an additional 15 seconds. The total of listening and learning is a configurable value known as the forward delay, which is meant to allow the new device time to receive information from the root bridge. With a device such as a computer, server, or printer that cannot operate as a bridge when the port comes out of the learning state, it enters a forwarding state and starts to transmit BPDUs.

When a new bridging node is added to an existing port on a bridge node, a different procedure is followed. Any new switch or router could introduce a network loop into the topology, and therefore the port stays in the blocking mode after the listen/learn cycle completes. The port sends a Topology Change Notification (TCN) frame to the network's root bridge. When the TCN is detected at the root bridge, the change is recorded and a determination is made as to the appropriate port status. The root bridge then acknowledges back to the new port with a TCA frame that determines the port's status. From then on, the new port multicasts BPDUs at the standard regular intervals so that all other bridging nodes update their routing tables appropriately. The root bridge modifies its standard BPDUs to indicate that a change is in progress and then multicasts the change to all other bridge nodes in the system; those root bridges update their routing tables and then acknowledge that the change was made.

At any one time, a bridge node's (switch/router) port may have one of the following five states:

- **Listening.** Incoming BPDUs are received and processed with no frames sent.
- **Learning.** The port adds the addresses of bridge nodes to its routing table but does not forward any frames. A learning port has been incorporated into the active topology.
- **Forwarding.** The port can both send and receive data from the network, and STP continues to process any incoming BPDUs for changes. All ports in a root bridge and any root port are always in forwarding mode, and any designated port on a single LAN segment must also always be in forwarding mode.
- **Blocking.** The port is configured so that it can neither send nor receive data, but it does receive BPDUs and can change states if necessary. Any port in a bridge node that connects to other bridge nodes and isn't either a root port or a designated port must be blocked.
- **Disabled.** Ports can be disabled in software (using SMTP commands, for example), but not using STP.

Rapid Spanning Tree Protocol

As originally conceived, the Spanning Tree Protocol could take up to a minute to reconfigure when a topology change is signaled. While this worked in 1995, by 1998, STP was required to compete with Data Link Level (Layer 3) protocols such as Open Shortest Path First (OSPF) and the Enhanced Interior Gateway Routing Protocol (EIGRP), which could reconfigure an alternative path through the system much faster than STP. For that reason, the IEEE defined what is called the Rapid Spanning Tree Protocol (RSTP) in the 802.1w standard released in 1998. In 2004, the IEEE bundled together the 802.1D, 802.1t-2001, and the 802.1w standards into a single 802.1D-2004 standard that includes them all. Many of the changes added to RSTP were part of Cisco's implementation of STP for switched Ethernet networks.

RSTP is based on STP, but makes some significant changes to the original protocol that allow a bridge node to reconfigure on the order of less than a single hello time (2 seconds) when a root node failure occurs.

Caution
The use of more than one type of STP can lead to unpredictable and undesired results.

In RSTP, blocked ports are separated into two additional states: alternative ports and backup ports. An alternative port is one that is receiving BPDUs from another bridge node of higher priority and is port blocked. A backup port is a port that is receiving BPDUs from the same bridge and is port blocked. The definition allows for a more rapid assignment of an alternative path to the root bridge when the root port fails. The backup port provides a redundant connection to the same network segment, but does not provide a connection to the root bridge. In other respects, the same criteria are used to calculate the topology in RSTP that is used for STP. Figure 9.16 illustrates an example of alternative and backup ports.

FIGURE 9.16

Examples of an alternative and a backup port

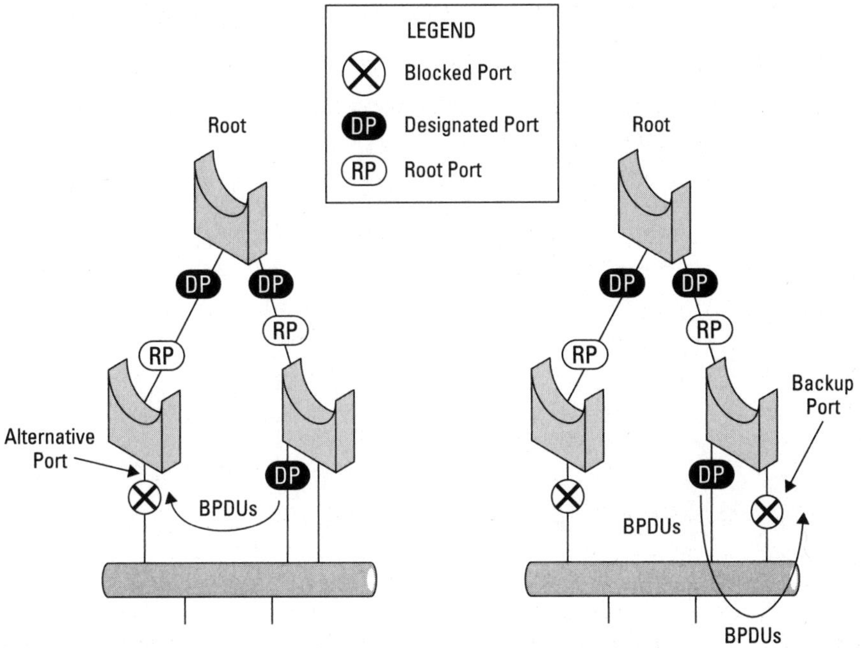

The BPDU frame for RSTP was changed to allow for a faster aging of information, with BPDUs required as a keep-alive or heartbeat between bridge nodes. When three hello cycles pass without a BPDU, a failure is registered and the bridge node sets a flag in the BPDU frames it sends that indicates the failure and asks a lower-priority bridge to accept that node as its root bridge. A bridge receiving the proposal that has no other path to the root bridge and recognizes the higher-priority bridge will then reset its root port to the one connected to the proposing bridge node. However, if the proposed-to bridge still has a functioning path to the original root bridge, it then sends a BPDU to the proposing bridge node, informing it of the status of the original root and updating its routes, and STP reconfiguration is performed at the proposing node.

Figure 9.17 shows the proposal concept and demonstrates how the links fail over. The top-right figure shows the original configuration. When a link breaks, as is the case in the top-middle figure, Node A proposes to Node B that it be made the Root node. Because B still is in contact with the Root, the proposal is declined and A is given B's routing information. The failover results in the reconfiguration is shown on the lower left with A's path through B to the Root.

In the case of two broken connections, the response to the proposal is different. When A makes the proposal to be the Root, B no longer knows it has a connection to the Root and therefore accepts the proposal. The result is shown in the figure on the lower right with A containing the Designated port and B having the Root port. The failover results in the direct link between A and B.

FIGURE 9.17

RSTP failover reconfiguration

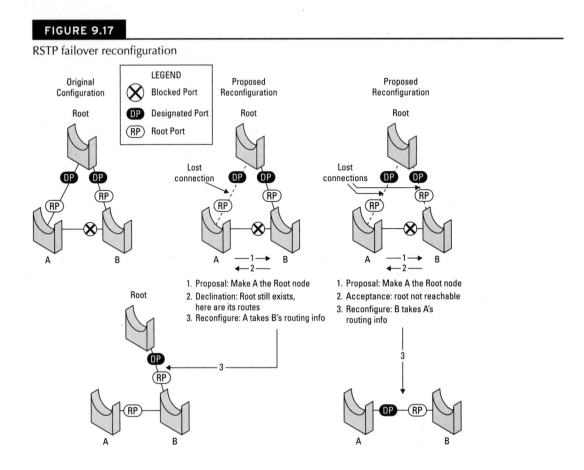

In a network that is routed by RSTP, any port that is connected to an end station cannot create a network loop because all end stations are by definition single-homed. All ports of this type are labeled as edge ports and put into a forwarding state without having to cycle through the standard STP listening and learning modes. Edge ports remain edge ports even when RSTP recalculates and juggles the topology of the spanning tree. Should an edge port receive a BPDU frame, the edge port converts instantly to a spanning tree port.

An instant conversion to a forwarding state can also be performed on ports that have point-to-point links. Ports that are operating in full-duplex mode are taken to be a point-to-point link; half-duplex mode ports are considered to be a shared port. Because nearly all modern switches operate their ports in full-duplex mode, RSTP can convert these ports very quickly to the forwarding state. Fast transition in RSTP occurs because the proposal/acceptance mechanism can ripple through the network, changing ports one link at a time.

Figure 9.18 illustrates the fast transition that RSTP makes possible. In this scheme, the proposal to designate the Root port labeled 1 in the figure on the left side is responded to with an agreement labeled 2. Router 2 then begins a synchronization, which creates a Root port for the Root to 1 connection, blocks two of the ports, and specifies which port will be the Edge port. The proposal to designate the Root port then travels down the network without having to communicate back up to the Root. This makes the transition very fast.

FIGURE 9.18

The RSTP proposal/acceptance fast transition mechanism

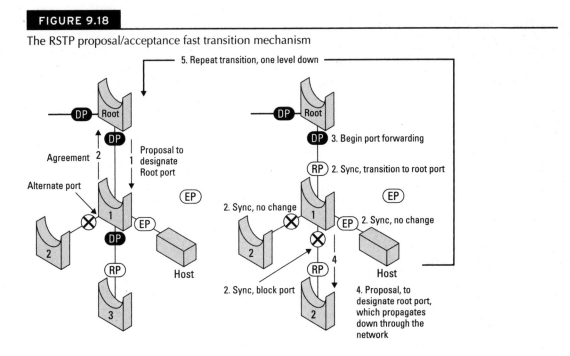

RSTP also handles new links differently from STP. In a network system, if you add a link from the root bridge node to a secondary (or lower-hierarchy) node, you create a network loop. STP, sensing this loop, blocks the ports on the root bridge node and the primary node, placing those nodes into a listening state. STP also disables the new link until it can compute the new topology. The primary node now listens directly to the root bridge node and they exchange information. The primary node then sends BPDUs through the network down to the secondary node where the new link was added, and that node blocks its port leading to the primary node, and returns a BPDU back to the root node. Upon receipt of the BPDU, the root node adopts the new technology, enables the new link, and maintains the block on the port leading to and coming from what was the primary node. The primary node connected to the new network link then becomes the secondary node. The problem with this scenario is that there is a latency of twice the forward delay to enforce this change.

The same situation, as handled by RSTP, works somewhat differently. RSTP detects the new link and blocks the ports between the root and the primary node, as before. Now the root node sends a proposal to the primary node for a reconfiguration, at which point the primary node places a block on all designated ports, called a sync operation. The primary node then signals to the root node to unblock its port and place it into forwarding mode. This transition happens very quickly. Now the blocks are one level down from the root/primary link. The process is repeated, moving the blocks for ports on the router one more level down until the blocks reach the port for the secondary node with the new link connected to it. The end result of the RSTP is the same state as before, but instead of waiting for messaging to travel down the branch and return as STP does, RSTP initiates a set of individual transitions that are very fast. The more intermediate bridge nodes there are between the root node and the new link, the greater the difference in performance that RSTP offers.

RSTP is even more aggressive when it comes to propagating topology changes. In STP, when a node changes its topology, the information flows from that node to the root node where it is then sent back down to all of the other system bridge nodes. In RSTP, the originator of the topology change floods the change state throughout the network, essentially eliminating the latency incurred while the information travels to the root node.

You may encounter some proprietary STP variants when working with Cisco Catalyst switches. When routing over virtual LANs (VLANs), Cisco uses a spanning tree for each VLAN (IEEE 802.1Q) and calls their proprietary protocol the Per-VLAN Spanning Tree (PVST), or PVST+ when tunneling across other routing schemes is added. The Multiple Spanning Tree Protocol (MSTP), as defined in IEEE 802.1s/Q, extends RSTP to VLANs, creating a spanning tree for each VLAN group. Cisco's version of MSTP is called Multiple Instances Spanning Tree Protocol (MISTP). Another Cisco protocol called Rapid Per-VLAN Spanning Tree (R-PVST) combines RSTP and PVST to create one spanning tree per VLAN.

Onion Routers

You know the drill, because you've seen the movie. The bad guys send messages to the good guys, which the good guys trace to a server in New York City. As the good guys get ready to chase the bad guys, the next message comes in from a server in Singapore, and the third message comes from Berlin. Every message after that comes from another server, making the location of the sender impossible to determine. Anonymous communication over the network is the idea behind onion routers.

In an onion router system, network messages are multiply (triply) encrypted at the source and sent randomly through an IP network of routers (onion servers), where each router removes one layer of encryption — just as you can peel the layers off an onion. The Entry Point server is chosen from a smaller set of onion router servers called Entry Guards and then randomly chosen from this set. Each of the three servers, the one chosen randomly from the Entry Guard group and the other two chosen randomly from available onion router servers worldwide, then use their public key to remove one layer of encryption at a time.

When the message arrives at its destination, the message is unencrypted but the receiver has no knowledge of where the message came from or what path it took to get there, only the last server to forward the data on. Not only is the receiver in the dark, but all of the intermediate nodes between the encryption source and the exit node also have no idea of the source, contents, or destination of the packets, making it impossible for anyone inside the onion network to be able to compromise the communication.

Figure 9.19 shows how The Onion Router (Tor) system works. The Sending System gets a list of Tor servers from the Tor Directory Server (1). It then selects an entry server from a short list and sends the data to it triply encrypted (2). The Entry Server removes one layer of encryption and then passes the data along to a randomly chosen server (3), which removes another layer of encryption. That second server sends the data to a third server (4) where the final layer of encryption is removed and the data is sent unencrypted to its destination, the Receiving System (5).

FIGURE 9.19

The Onion Router system for maintaining data anonymity

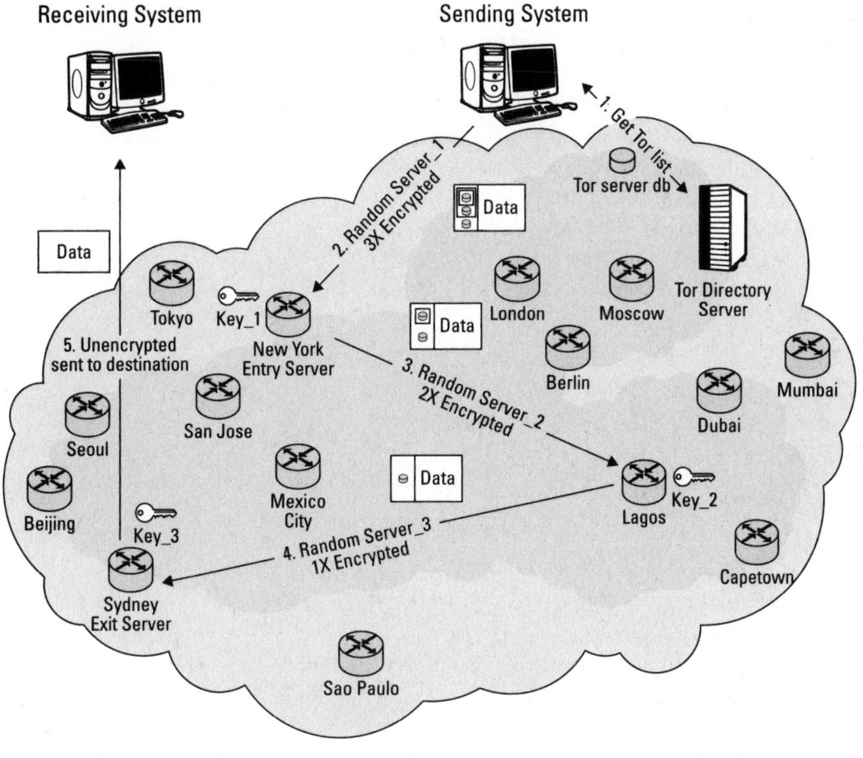

The goal of Tor is to be able to prevent what is called traffic analysis attacks. In a traffic analysis attack, groups of messages are examined at both endpoints of the message path to determine which servers exist on the system and to look for traffic patterns. The greater the number of messages examined, the better. The state of the messages can be either encrypted or unencrypted, as the goal is to be able to intercept the messages that you are interested in. Decryption can be performed later; or more often, the goal of the exercise is to be able to interrupt the communication.

One type of attack that can be performed once the communication is intercepted is to create a Secure Shell link to the victim and examine the timing of the messages that are returned. The time interval between each character is statistically analyzed using a hidden Markov model, which can be used to deduce passwords. Tor systems are built to make this sort of attack very difficult, but apparently not impossible. Also keep in mind that the traffic exiting the onion router system is unencrypted and can be compromised, just as any other messages can be.

Tor

Onion routing describes a technology that presently has one example, the open source Tor project. As you can imagine, secure communication is of primary importance to the military. The original developers of the first onion router were funded by the United States Navy Research Laboratory. A second-generation project called The Onion Router (Tor) was funded initially by the Electronic Frontier Foundation (www.eff.org) in 2004, and in 2006 became an open source project called The Tor Project (www.torproject.org) as part of a non-profit foundation.

Although onion routers represent a concept that anyone can implement, the Tor network is the only one based on this concept that has been reduced to practice. There are currently over 1,800 listings of Tor servers worldwide in one of the directory servers, although the number of servers active at any one time varies greatly.

Tor clients

Tor traffic originates on an onion proxy that is installed on the sending system. The proxy consults a Tor directory and negotiates a virtual circuit through the network. The onion proxy software is a SOCKS interface; therefore, any application that can create a socket can use the proxy to send traffic through the Tor network over that virtual circuit. The message is then multiplexed and sent on its way. Among the applications that can use SOCKS are browsers, IM (instant messaging), and IRC (Internet Relay Chat) clients.

To fully configure a Tor proxy client, you need the following applications:

- **Privoxy (www.privoxy.org).** The Privoxy application is a filtering, non-caching Web proxy. It can help maintain privacy, manage cookies, alter Web page data, intercept pop-ups and banners, and more. This freeware program was based on Internet Junkbuster and is at version 3.0.10.

- **Tor (www.torproject.org).** The Tor client provides the Tor protocol and other components that let you use the Tor network.

- **Torbutton (https://torbutton.torproject.org).** The Tor button installs in Firefox and can turn Tor on and off.

- **Vidalia (www.torproject.org/vidalia/).** The GUI for Tor lets you monitor, control, and modify a Tor setup.

The developers of Tor make installation of these programs easy by bundling them together within a single installer. To obtain the Tor clients, you can go to these Web sites:

- **Windows installer:** www.torproject.org/docs/tor-doc-windows.html.en

- **Mac installer:** www.torproject.org/docs/tor-doc-osx.html.en

- **Linux/BSD/UNIX installer:** www.torproject.org/download-unix.html.en

Once you install the Tor client, you should test to see that it is correctly installed. One way to do this is to access a hidden server (described in the following section) on the Tor network. Enter **http://duskgytldkxiuqc6.onion/** in your browser, and after a transfer time of up to a minute, the Tor network should resolve the address for you.

Hidden services

Tor servers form a private Tor domain with the .onion suffix. The private domain allows hidden services running network applications, such as a Web publishing server or an Instant Messenger server, to be configured to run "hidden" on the Tor network. Each of these services run independently of one another and are distributed across the Tor network. Tor allows users to configure their own hidden services and make those services available to others anonymously. When a Tor user uses a hidden service, neither the sender nor receiver is aware of either the network identity of each other or of the server that processes their requests.

To create a hidden service, you need a working Tor client and Web server. Tor's developers recommend Savant or Apache on Windows, or thttpd on UNIX or Mac OS X. The Web server must bind port 5222 to the local host. This binding ensures that an outside system is not able to ascertain that the service is running on your system. The Web server should be run as a separate instance from any other Web servers, especially Web servers that are exposed to the Internet or an intranet.

Figure 9.20 shows a schematic of how hidden services work. An installed hidden service advertises for clients by broadcasting its availability (1) using the hidden service protocol through random paths (virtual circuits) to servers and by storing its information and public key in the Tor Directory Server. Those servers accept the role of being an Introduction Point and store a public key for the hidden service (2). Because the path taken between the hidden service's server and the Introduction Points consists of random virtual circuits, there is no way for a client to be able to associate the two systems with one another or to learn the hidden server's IP address.

A Tor client learns about hidden services from the Tor Directory Server (3) and creates a Rendezvous Point. Then the Tor client communicates with one of the Introduction Point Servers (4). A Rendezvous Point contains both a public key and a cookie that are used to encrypt/decrypt information as well as supply information that allows the data to be forwarded from the hidden server to the Tor client. Once the Introduction Point transfers the Tor client's information to the Hidden Service Server, the virtual circuit shown as 7 with a large arrow is created. The system separates the Introduction Point from the Rendezvous Point, and by doing so ensures that the Tor client's information remains anonymous.

FIGURE 9.20

Hidden services on the Tor network

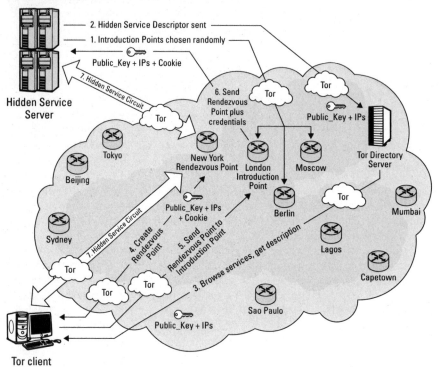

The hidden service creates a hidden service descriptor with the public key, includes a description of the service, and then signs the hidden service descriptor with a private key. This hidden service descriptor is sent by as an encrypted message to a Tor directory server, and then replicated throughout the network, which hides the location of the service. The directory server creates an automatically generated domain name *<HiddenService>*.`onion` for the service, which can now be browsed by a Tor client. At this point, the configuration of the hidden service is complete.

When a client wants to learn about a hidden service, it downloads the hidden service descriptor from the Tor directory server. That descriptor contains the list of the Introduction Points and the public key. The client then connects to a random Tor server, requesting that the server act as a Rendezvous Point, and sends that server a cookie with a one-time secret. The hidden server's public key is then used to encrypt an Introduction message that contains the Rendezvous Point address and the cookie with the one-time secret. All of these exchanges pass through the Tor system in the usual manner.

The hidden server then uses the information contained in the Introduction message to build a circuit to the Rendezvous Point, and sends the one-time secret to that system to validate its connection to the Tor client. The Rendezvous Point sends a "connection established" message to the Tor client. With the virtual circuit between Tor client and hidden service server using the Rendezvous Point as a relay encrypted communication travels in both directions from client to server. This circuit has a set of six relays, of which three relays were chosen by the client's virtual circuit, three more relays were chosen by the server's virtual circuit, and the Rendezvous Point was a commonly chosen relay point.

Gateways

A network gateway is a device or program that allows different types of networks to communicate with one another. Gateways translate addresses, network protocols, and data. Sometimes you purchase a gateway as an appliance, while in other instances you might install gateway software on a computer and have that computer serve the linking function. An example of a software gateway would be a program that takes the data from an order entry module on a Web site and transmits that information to a credit processing service, called a credit card gateway. Another example of a gateway is a firewall or proxy server. In any network interface for TCP/IP networks, the address of the gateway must be specified. Mail and host gateways are also common.

Gateways are therefore something of a marketing term, and need to be considered in this broader context. A router has different aspects of a gateway in it; even an Internet connection-sharing function on a computer serves the function of a gateway. What separates a gateway from other network connection devices like routers is its ability to function at higher levels of the OSI network model. Gateways either operate at the Transport layer (Level 4) or more often, at the Application layer (Level 7), the top layer of the hierarchy — routers may operate at Level 4 but never at Level 7.

Summary

In this chapter, you learned about switching devices. Switches are required on both circuit switched networks and packet switched networks, and both network types were described conceptually in some detail.

Switching devices can be separated by the highest-level protocol that they operate with. Hubs and repeaters are physical connections. Bridges span two different network segments at the Network layer, but do not provide protocol translation. A router can connect two different types of networks because it can operate at the Transport layer. Switches and gateways are general terms that describe a variety of different systems.

The basis for routing was covered in detail in this chapter. The difference between core routers, edge routers, and border routers was also explained. You learned about The Onion Router (Tor) system and how it can be used to preserve anonymity.

In the next chapter, the various types of home networks are described.

Part III

Network Types

Home Networks

Home networking is becoming more advanced, easier to use, and more prevalent. The major reasons people install home networks are to share Internet connections, resources, and network applications.

Home networks tend to be a mixture of different technologies. If you need to have mobile devices, then Wi-Fi networks will be one part of the mix. The two essential decisions you make concerning your home network are how to connect to the Internet and how to bridge different areas of your home together.

In this chapter, some of the common choices for home networking media are discussed in terms of their suitability. Ethernet, HomePNA, and HomePlug networking are described.

HomePNA is a phone line technology, while HomePlug is a power line connection technology. HomePNA and HomePlug are relatively new, and offer higher speeds than older technologies. With HomePNA, you connect devices by plugging adapters into a phone outlet. HomePlug uses adapters to allow devices to plug into your power lines. The Power over Ethernet standard is also described; this standard allows you to have mobile devices wherever an Ethernet cable can be run. These technologies are convenient alternatives to connecting areas of your home by pulling Ethernet cable through the wall.

Different broadband connection technologies are described in this chapter. Common technologies currently being offered — ISDN, DSL, cable modems, satellite connections, and fiber-optic connections — are described.

Home network servers offer the potential for managing your home network from a central location, as well as being able to share important network services. Microsoft Home Server is described briefly. Other home network appliances of this type have come to market but have not gained traction in the marketplace.

Features of a Home Network

Home networking has experienced something of a renaissance over the last couple of years. Part of the current interest is due to people staying home more for entertainment, in part due to the proliferation of home computers, and part due to the public becoming more knowledgeable about networks. The advancement in home networking is also due to a number of new technologies that have been brought to market, and the fact that several other leading-edge technologies are also maturing. You see this trend in the home network market with the introduction of home servers, high-speed networking components, more sophisticated firewalls, and many other technologies. In this chapter, you see different types of wired technologies that you can use in your home to connect one device to another, often very conveniently over phone or power lines.

Most people create home networks to allow for the following functions:

- Share an Internet connection between two or more systems
- Share resources such as storage, printers, and other peripherals
- Back up systems remotely
- Transfer audio/video content for home entertainment purposes
- Use Voice over IP (VoIP) telephony
- Allow for system mobility for laptops, PDAs, and other mobile devices
- Play multiplayer games using computers or gaming consoles

These needs make certain choices entirely predictable:

- If you need mobile connectivity, you should opt for Wi-Fi on your network in the locations where you move devices around.
- If you want to transfer large files, then you need to examine the throughput of the links that will carry the traffic. As a general rule of thumb, AV multimedia content requires at least 100 Mbits/s throughput to be practicable, and the more the better.

- If you have different unconnected areas in your home, consider how you connect them. Common choices for connecting different areas in the home are to pull Ethernet cable, phone line, or power line connections, or to bridge the distance with Wi-Fi.

- Sharing an Internet connection argues for the use of a security appliance such as a firewall/gateway/router or a server or appliance that provides a function such as Network Address Translation (NAT). Placing a firewall between the Internet and your home network is the single best investment you can make to safely share an Internet connection.

- Networked resources such as printers, file shares, and other peripherals are supported in all of the commonly used desktop operating systems. Depending upon the granularity of access required, you may be satisfied with peer-to-peer network access; for a greater numbers of systems, and finer control, you may want to consider a server or server appliance with a central security system.

Common choices for home network connectivity are:

- Ethernet (wired/RF over wires)
- Wi-Fi based on IEEE 802.11x (wireless)
- Phone line (wired) based on HomePNA, for example
- Power line (wired) based on HomePlug, for example
- Bluetooth (wireless/RF)

Wireless technologies are very popular in home settings because of their flexibility, and so most home networks include wireless access. Wireless technologies such as Wi-Fi and Bluetooth are described in detail in Chapter 14, but are mentioned to provide context in this chapter. Most people opt for a mix of technologies in their home networks. Table 10.1 shows some of the common technologies in use on home networks and compares important characteristics such as speed or throughput, technology types, cost, reliability, security and privacy, along with a summary of pros and cons of each.

TABLE 10.1

Home Networking Technologies

Type	Throughput/Range	Used With	Cost	Reliability	Security and Privacy	Pros	Cons
Ethernet (802.3, 802.5)	1 Gbits/s over Cat5e cable. Range 500 ft. or 164 m for 10Base-T. Others vary.	AV, C, R, and S	High	High	High	Fastest method used. Widest standard and largest number of devices sold. Greatest flexibility.	Expensive, especially as a retrofit. Requires dedicated wiring. Installation can be involved.
Bluetooth (Bluetooth Special Interest Group, or SIG)	1 Mbits/s over RF range of 30 ft. (10 m)	C, CD, and M	Moderate	Good	Moderate	Self-configuring and mobile. Low cost. Supported by computers, peripherals, and handhelds. A small amount of setup is required.	Low speed and small range.
Wi-Fi (IEEE 802.11x standards)	600 Mbits/s for 802.11n, 54 Mbits/s for 802.11g over either 2.4 or 5 GHz RF bands. Range 300 ft. for 802.11n omni-directional, 2 mi. with highly directional antennas.	AV, C, M, and R	Low to high	Good	Moderate	Standards-based, large number of devices available. Flexible, newer standards are fast. Good interoperability.	Costly, and limited range. Subject to interference and noise. Requires some setup.

Type	Throughput/ Range	Used With	Cost	Reliability	Security and Privacy	Pros	Cons
HomePNA phone networking (HomePNA Association 3.1 and ITU G9954)	320 Mbits/s over phone lines. Range 1,000 ft. or 333 m.	AV, C, CD, R, S	Low	High	Good	Can be fast, uses wiring in place. Low cost. Minimal installation.	Devices still require network connectivity.
HomePlug power line networking. (IEEE P1901)	200 Mbits/s for AV, 14 Mbits/s for 1.0. Range ca. 3,000 ft. or 1,000 m.	AV, C, CD, M, R, and S	Moderate	Low to moderate	High	Fast, uses power line wiring in place. Very convenient. Minimal installation.	Very difficult transmission environment. Requires that power lines be locally available.

Legend: AV = Multimedia, C= Communications, CD = Control devices, M = Mobile devices, R = Resource sharing, and S = Scheduling.

Broadband Connections

The word broadband has many different meanings. It can refer to a wide spectrum of frequencies over which communications are sent, or it can apply to a high-speed connection to a network or the Internet. It is as a high-speed feed for the Internet that most home users would apply the term. Broadband penetration as a percentage of the population is considered by many economists to be a leading economic indicator.

By one definition, broadband is defined by the throughput through the system, with the lowest transmission speed being several times higher than is possible to achieve with a dial-up modem. The United States Federal Communications Commission in 2008 defined a broadband connection as one that has a download throughput of over 768 Kbits/s. In Europe, the International Telecommunications Union Standardization Sector set the base for broadband at 1.5 Mbits/s, or the speed of primary rate ISDN.

The minimum requirement for broadband tends to rise over time. The definition in terms of download speed is made intentionally because most people's broadband connections are much faster downloading than uploading content; that is, most broadband connections are asymmetric.

When an ISP rates its broadband connection speed, it typically does so under favorable conditions. Many services that share bandwidth among a group of subscribers, such as a neighborhood or apartment building, tend to slow down considerably at times of high usage. To combat this problem, many ISPs have resorted to techniques such as traffic shaping, throttling, or transfer limits in order to maintain an acceptable performance.

The most common broadband connections in the United States at the moment are based on digital subscriber line, or DSL, technology and cable modems. Fiber-optic networks are in the process of being rolled out by several companies and are available in limited geographical areas.

Among the broadband technologies in common use are:

- **Integrated Service Digital Network (ISDN) telephone-based data service.** ISDN is sold either in a basic rate format (ISDN-BRI) with two channels of DS0, 64 Kbits each, for a total of 128 Kbits/s, or as a primary rate format (ISDN-PRI) with 23 DS0 lines having a bandwidth of 1.544 Mbits/s. In Europe, ISDN-PRI involves 30 DS0 channels and has a bandwidth of 2.048 Mbits/s. ISDN has become less popular as consumers opt for either DSL or cable modem technologies.

    DS0 is a holdover from phone line systems; it represents the allocation of a 64 Kbits/s channel for voice communications.

Cross-Ref

ISDN and DSL are is described in more detail in Chapter 13.

- **Digital Subscriber Lines (DSLs).** DSL uses telephone lines to provide digital services and Internet connectivity to customers. Most DSL sold is Asymmetric DSL, or ADSL. Download throughput over DSL lines ranges from 256 Kbits/s to 2.4 Mbits/s; upload speeds of 128 Kbits/s to 256 Kbits/s are typical for this technology.

- **Cable modems.** This technology is popular in North America, Europe, Australia, New Zealand, and parts of Central America. Typical throughput using a cable modem varies between 1 Mbits/s to 6 Mbits/s for downloads, and between 128 Kbits/s and 768 Kbits/s uploads. The technology is theoretically capable of supporting speeds as high as 30 Mbits/s. Cable modems use a shared connection among local users, and so speeds depend on the level of activity at any one time.

  Cable modems are network bridge (Data Link layer, or Level 2) devices that connect home networks to the Internet through a cable television system. On the network side, cable modems support Ethernet, and on the cable side, they support DOCSIS (Data Over Cable Service Interface Specification) as the Physical layer technologies. DOCSIS was created out of Motorola's CDLP (Cable Data Link Protocol) Physical layer technology and the MAC layer created by LANcity for use with NTSC broadcasts. In Europe, a version of the technology compatible with the PAL broadcast standard, called EuroDOCSIS, is used.

- **Satellite connections.** The use of satellites to provide Internet access is popular in rural areas where it is impractical to run different forms of cables. Systems use geostationary orbit satellites that are as high as 22,236 mi. (35,786 km) above sea level on the Earth, or 42,164 km from the Earth's center. An antenna must be fixed to the direction of the satellite.

  Communications through satellites suffer a considerable latency (about 200 milliseconds) because of the distance involved. As a general rule, download throughput is competitive with other broadband technologies, between 256 Kbits/s and 2.048 Mbits/s, but much slower for uploads, between 64 Kbits/s and 128 Kbits/s. The latency and slow upload speeds have tended to limit the use of satellite broadband technology.

- **Fiber-optic connections.** Fiber-optic broadband connections are now being offered in the United States by companies such as Verizon (FiOS), SBC, and Qwest, among others. These connections allow Internet access, telephone, and TV services to be delivered to consumers who are using a fiber-optic connection. The service can be sold in a number of different speeds, ranging from 10 Mbits/s to 50 Mbits/s download, and 2 Mbits/s to 20 Mbits/s upload.

Wireless Connections

Wireless connections are a very convenient method for networking various devices on a home network. Some home networks rely entirely on wireless connections for all devices, but most use wireless connections for devices that are mobile in a home or as links between areas of the home that aren't conveniently wired together. Many ISPs provide broadband routers with wireless capabilities as part of their service.

Nearly all wireless networking devices sold for the home market are based on one of the IEEE 802.11 standards, which define a set of technologies that use public radio frequency bands that fall in the 900 MHz to 5 GHz frequencies. The technology goes under the trademark Wi-Fi, an industry trade group that manages the standards and ensures that chipsets and the devices that use them are interoperable.

Cross-Ref

Chapter 14 describes wireless network technologies in detail. It is entirely devoted to the Wi-Fi standard and goes into great detail on the nature of each of the standards, how the bands are utilized, and how to build Wi-Fi networks or links from different components. Chapter 14 also describes the different methods used to encode Wi-Fi signals, as well as how Wi-Fi connections need to be configured.

Wired Connections

In the previous section, your home network's broadband connection to the Internet was considered. If you connect a wireless router to your Internet connection and all of your devices are wireless, or if you were lucky enough to move into a new house that is wired for Cat5e or Cat6 cable in every room, then your work is done. Most people aren't so lucky. The most common situation is that you have devices scattered around in different areas of your home and you've networked those areas individually, but are faced with the problem of connecting the areas together. Different areas in a home exist when you have rooms that aren't connected together by a network connection, for example an upstairs bedroom, a den on the first floor, and an office in the basement.

You could decide to have an electrician come in and pull cable through the wall to connect those areas together, or do it yourself. Pulling cable is difficult and often expensive, but it does provide the fastest speed connections when you are done. There are many homes in which pulling cable simply isn't practical or even worthwhile. In the sections that follow, different alternatives are presented that show how you can use wiring that is already in your home and in place (phone lines and power lines) to provide the missing links that connect up all of those separate networked areas. Among the technologies that are described in the following section are Ethernet wiring, HomePNA phone line connections, Power over Ethernet (PoE), and HomePlug Powerline networking over power lines.

Ethernet

Direct Ethernet connections to WANs are uncommon in the area of home Internet connections. However, this technology is offered as a business service and may someday become available for consumers. The IEEE 802.3ah standard defines a set of protocols for Ethernet used on first or last mile connections.

Ethernet in the First Mile (EFM) can be used over:

- **Copper wire.** EFM over Copper (EFMCu) is used over voice-grade wiring and can be aggregated into multiple concurrent connections. The two types of EFMCu defined are 2BASE-TL and 10PASS-TS.

- **Long wavelength fiber.** Ethernet can connect using either single or dual strand fiber.

- **Point to Multipoint (P2MP) fiber.** Ethernet connections of this type are sold under the name Ethernet over Passive Optical Networks (EPON).

IEEE's EFM standard also describes how to install, manage, and administer Ethernet connections, as well as how to have these technologies interoperate with other commonly used technologies. EFM EPON development is now part of the IEEE Metro Ethernet Forum group; they are currently working on a 10 Gbits/s version of EPON called XEPON.

Cross-Ref
Ethernet is discussed further in Chapter 12.

Phone lines

For many years, vendors have offered devices to network computers over phone lines in buildings. One early system called PhoneNet, from a company called Farallon (now Netopia), allowed Macintoshes to network without having to use Apple LocalTalk. This technology worked by using the spare wiring in the telephone line as its physical medium. This was back in the days when a single telephone line was all that anyone ever had coming into their house. Now it seems that anything that moves has a phone number attached to it, and there is no such thing as a spare set of phone wires.

The latest versions of phone networking are designed to work over the telephone wires that are in use. They do this by working at frequencies that aren't in use for voice communication. They also use different modulation technologies to ensure that the data arrives correctly at its destination. The most widely used phone line networking technology in current use is HomePNA. If you are familiar with the older phone line networking technologies that poked along at 10 Mbits/s on a good day, you may want to take a look at the latest HomePNA standard; it was built to transfer large multimedia files at relatively high speeds.

Figure 10.1 shows different devices in a home network using HomePNA network technology. In this figure a HomePNA router is connected to the Internet and to an Ethernet line. That router provides Internet access to other devices on the network by connecting through Ethernet/PNA adapters that plug into existing telephone lines. In each of the different areas of the home an Ethernet/ PNA adapter is plugged into a phone outlet and Ethernet is connected to networked devices. Three different areas of the home are shown connected to the PNA network — Area 1 with a set of wired devices, Area 2 with devices connected through a wired hub, and Area 3 where a wireless access point serves wireless clients in that area of the house.

Telephone line networking is extremely convenient. You can connect up to the telephone line directly from a telephone network interface or through an Ethernet-to-telephone connector or bridge. It doesn't matter what kind of phone service you have; telephone networking uses the telephone wires as its physical medium and works regardless of the phone service type. However, the phone lines used must be on the same circuit. If you have an additional phone line or lines installed, you will need to use one of those lines for each of your network connections.

FIGURE 10.1

HomePNA allows you to connect your network using standard telephone lines without any additional modification needed.

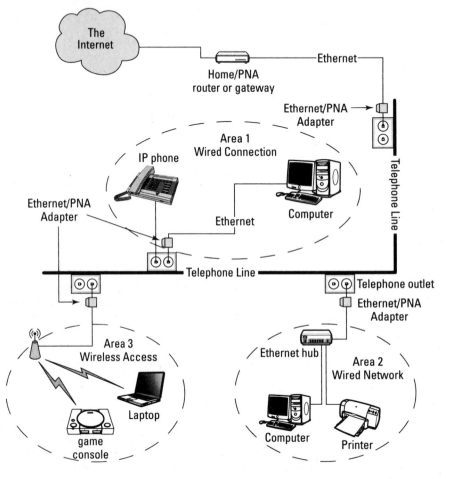

A current generation of home phone networking products is organized around the HomePNA 3.1 standard, created by the HomePNA (Home Phone Networking Alliance) industry alliance (www. homepna.org) that delivers IP services such data, VoIP, and IPTV (the so-called "triple play services" shown in Figure 10.2) over existing coaxial cables and telephone lines. The International Telephone Union (ITU) G.9953 standard, ratified in January 2007, is based on HomePNA 3.1.

In Figure 10.2 a graph of power versus frequency for signals traveling over a phone line is shown. HomePNA networking supports triple play networking because it is able to support different technologies such as telephone signals (a narrowband service) as well as DSL and Ethernet over distinctly different frequencies. The signals carried over the same physical medium do not interfere with one another.

FIGURE 10.2

Phone networking separates voice, Internet, and home network traffic into three distinct bands over the same wire.

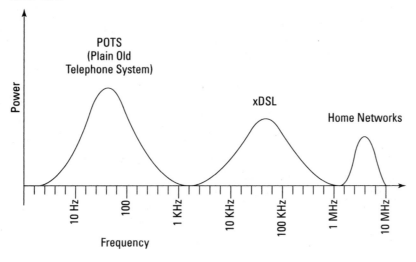

The HomePNA standard is based on work done at Broadcom and Copper Solutions. Broadcom sells the two custom ASIC chip sets needed to communicate with other devices as part of the core reference architecture. The Broadcom MC4100 analog front-end is a transceiver or digital-analog converter that converts signals sent to or received from the phone line, and the Broadcom BCM4210 PCI/MSI controller chip sends data to or reconstructs the data at the transceiver. HomePNA uses Frequency Division Multiplexing (FDM) to send signals over the same two wires that a phone service uses.

Connections are made from an RJ-11 wall jack to computer systems that are equipped with a HomePNA network adapter. This adapter takes the form of an add-in PCI or PC Card, or a USB device. Connections can be up to 1,000 feet, and up to 50 devices are supported. HomePNA states that the building can be no bigger than 10,000 square feet (929 square meters). Version 3.1 has a projected throughput of up to 320 Mbps over coaxial cable, with current devices offering up to 128 Mbits/s. HomePNA is mainly aimed at ISPs and telephone companies, as it allows remote management and diagnostics, QoS, and features such as unified billing. HomePNA claims that the system is compatible with 99 percent of the homes in the United States. In instances where telephones or fax machines generate too much noise, those devices should be connected to a low-pass filter, just as you would for any DSL connection.

Among the products tested and certified are set-top boxes, ADSL and VDSL residential gateways, Ethernet-HomePNA 3.1 bridges, and residential gateways with a Wi-Fi access point included. You can find the current list of certified products at the following Web page, with links to their manufacturers: www.homepna.org/en/certification/member_products.asp.

Power over Ethernet

Power over Ethernet (PoE) connects devices over Ethernet, and provides both data and power from one device, called the Power Sourcing Device (PSD), to the other device, called the Power Device (PD). This makes the PD mobile as it can be plugged into an Ethernet port without requiring a nearby power socket. This technology was developed at Cisco and first released in 2000 as "inline power." PoE's primary goal was to create a technology that would make it easy to use IP telephony devices, wireless access points, Web cams, and other appliances wherever a network exists.

PoE became an IEEE standard with the release of the IEEE 802.3-2005 (802.3af) specification, and nearly all devices made since that time conform to this standard. The part of that standard relating to PoE is referred to as 802.3af. PoE devices span a range, from simple wall plug adapters that connect a power outlet to one or two Ethernet RJ-45 connections up to Enterprise-level switches that can be connected through up to 48 PoE Ethernet cables to devices or systems. PoE relies on the wiring that most likely already exists in place in homes and buildings. No power main voltages are exposed. Should a building suffer a power outage, the PSD can be kept active by being backed up by a UPS (uninterruptible power supply) and connections will remain active. PoE connected devices can be moved to any networkable location, and in the case of wireless LANs, this makes it easy to reconfigure your Wi-Fi network's coverage.

The 802.3af standard transfers data and power over the two unused pairs of the four wire pairs in CAT3/CAT 5e wiring. PSDs and PDs can be run over either the signal pair or the spare pair of the Ethernet cable, but not both. Any connection can use one of these two configurations, supplying 13W of power with a voltage at 48V. Figure 10.3 shows these two different configurations, one sending power over spare pins and the other showing power over data pins.

sends a small voltage over each of the Ethernet cables and detects the 25k ohm resister that is present in the transmitter (TX) and receiver (RX) of the PD. When detected, the entire 48V is then sent down that wire with a signal. At first, the current to the PD is limited, and when the discovery process is completed, full power is applied. As part of the discovery process, developers can include a negotiation that sets the amount of current that the PD supplies.

HomePlug Powerline

HomePlug devices use the power lines in a building to connect Ethernet devices together, sending data over the power lines. Depending upon the modulation in use, the throughput for this technology is between 1.0 Mbits/s and 13.8 Mbits/s. There are two versions of the HomePlug standard: HomePlug 1.0 and HomePlug AV. HomePlug AV is meant to support audio-visual applications such as HDTV over the network and achieves speeds of 200 Mbits/s.

FIGURE 10.3

The two different configurations possible with Power over Ethernet

Power Over Spare Pins

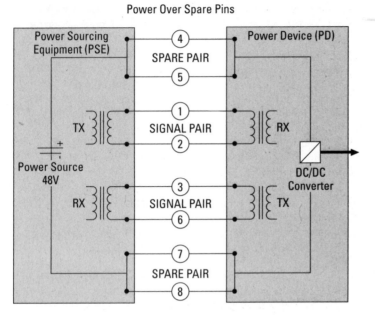

Power Over Data Pins

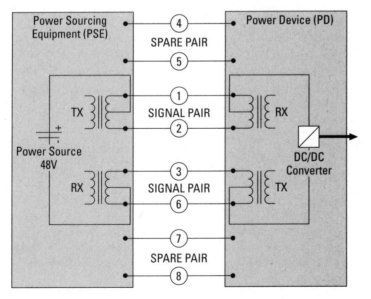

PoE connected devices can be managed through SNMP (Simple Network Management Protocol), and remotely restarted or turned off. While in discovery, the PSE (power sourcing equipment) HomePlug is based on the HomePlug Powerline Alliance's specification, and not on the 802.3af standard. The IEEE is developing a standard called IEEE P1901 that may unite HomePlug's technology with its competitors, which include Panasonic and the Universal Powerline Association.

Figure 10.4 shows how Powerline networks can be used to connect different areas of the home together. The technology for Powerline uses an identical topology shown previously for HomePNA networks. A HomePlug router connects the Internet to the powerlines in your home or building over an Ethernet connection using Powerline Ethernet Bridge devices that are plugged into a power outlet. Each area of the home is connected to the network using another Powerline Ethernet Bridge.

Powerline uses network routers, bridges, and other adapters to connect areas with different needs. A typical arrangement plugs a wall socket adapter into the electrical outlets of a home and connects that wall plug through USB or Ethernet to the devices that are part of the network. Wireless access points are sold using Powerline technology. This type of home network connectivity is relatively new. Look for the next generation of Powerline devices that run at the faster network speeds. Also, you should be aware that older home wiring can limit the use of Powerline, and that the technology is sensitive to interference. Either test your wiring or ensure that if these adapters don't work in your home network that you can return or replace them with different models before purchasing.

The fact that you can send data over power lines is quite amazing, as power lines are full of random noise and fluctuating conditions. The loads at each connection have different impedances, and the conductors often vary from place to place. A power line signal's amplitude and phase can vary with frequency, often dramatically, so that some frequencies are attenuated dramatically while others are not attenuated at all. Channel conditions can also change with time, depending upon the load being driven through the line. Many devices also create interference on a power line. Halogen lights, brush motors, and switching devices put oscillations or spikes into the line at different places that can mask signals.

Note

HomePlug adapters must be plugged directly into the socket. Plugging them into a power strip interferes with the RF signal transmission.

HomePlug modulation

HomePlug uses a transmission technology called Orthogonal Frequency Division Multiplexing (OFDM). It is the same technology used in DSL, wireless TV, and Wi-Fi 802.11a and 802.11g networking.

OFDM creates data channels by slicing up the spectrum into narrow bands, which for HomePlug is a set of 84 equally spaced subcarrier bands centered between 4.5 MHz and 21 MHz. The signal is sent through several adjacent channels so that the subcarriers overlap and are orthogonal to one another. Different modulation techniques are used; for HomePlug, it is mainly DBPSK (Differential Binary

Phase-Shift Keying) and DQPSK (Differential Quadrature Phase-Shift Keying). Each channel's signal strength should drop off as a constant to a set of flat and fading channels. From the strengths of parts of the signal, the whole signal can be determined, without the use of electronic equalization to restore the signal shape. It can be restored mathematically using forward error correction and data interleaving. Forward error correction (FEC) is a method for sending redundant data in a transmission to provide an error check that the data received is correct. Data interleaving is a technique that sends data over a variable time period so that adjacent errors in the data stream may be corrected.

FIGURE 10.4

A Powerline network connecting three different areas of the home

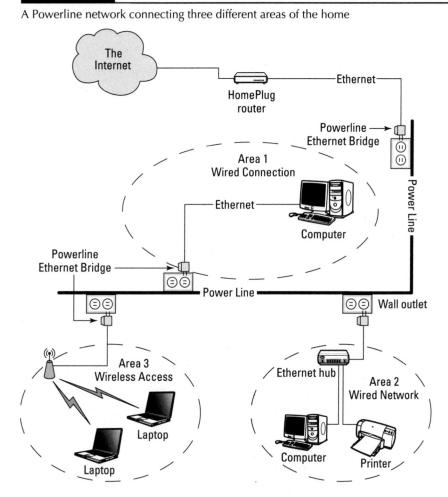

Because the power line conditions vary at different locations, the HomePlug technology measures the transfer rates of individual subchannels and turns off any subchannels that are heavily attenuated or impaired, a process that is called *Tone Allocation*. Depending upon the characteristics of the connection, different modulations such as DBPSK 1/2, DQPSK 1/2, and DQPSK 3/4 can be chosen, and that, combined with Forward Error Correction, greatly lowers the transfer error rate. This technology is called channel adaptation, and it is essentially a link optimization technology.

Because a link is essentially point to point, different techniques need to be applied when using HomePlug for broadcast transmissions. What is done in this case is to use the DBPSK modulation, send multiple copies of each bit down the wire at different times and at different frequencies, and apply error correction to all of that data, which HomePlug calls ROBO modulation. The structure of the frames that are sent is also modified for the channel adaptation done in ROBO.

Frames and sequences

The HomePlug Medium Access Control (MAC) protocol is based on the Ethernet IEEE 802.3 frames, both of which are long frame formats, which is why there is a high compatibility between HomePlug and Ethernet networks, with little additional processing required. HomePlug's MAC encrypts the frames entering HomePlug devices from Ethernet networks, and appends them to the HomePlug header before they are sent over power line connections. HomePlug frames are then sent to the receiving device. The receiving device reassembles the segmented frames and then decrypts the data before sending it on. If the Ethernet frame is encrypted (with IPsec, for example) before it enters the power line connection, it remains encrypted when it leaves the receiving device.

HomePlug uses both a messaging frame that is called Short Frame, and the Long Frame for data encapsulation that was described in the previous paragraph. The structure of these two frames is illustrated in Figure 10.5. Message frames are used to indicate whether frames have arrived correctly, whether data needs to be retransmitted, and for other purposes. Long frames contain start of frame and end of frame sections with a number of control fields. Since frames must be a sandard size, data is padded (PAD) to length. The FCS field contains error correction data.

The Short Frame is used to initiate a Stop and Wait automatic repeat, or ARQ, which is used to get the transmitting device to resend data that did not pass its error correction validation. Short Frames use a Response Delimiter, which has a Preamble and Frame Control information field. The Preamble is a spread spectrum signal, which signals the start of the delimiter. Frame Control information encoded in HomePlug's Turbo Product Code is used to allow detection of this message at very low amplitude, several dB below the ambient noise according to their specification. The Long Frame's Payload (data) is also indicated through the use of this special delimiter field, and the encoding can vary, based on the channel adaptation method used.

As is common for 802.3 frame types, the first 17 bytes of the Frame Header contain the source address, the destination address, and the segmentation number to be used for sequencing the frames. The reason that the very first bytes have addressing in them is that even if part of the frame is corrupted, the first bytes provide the means to send a message back for the frame to be resent. The payload is padded (PAD) to bring it to standard length. FCS is the Frame Control Sequence used.

FIGURE 10.5

Long and short HomePlug frames

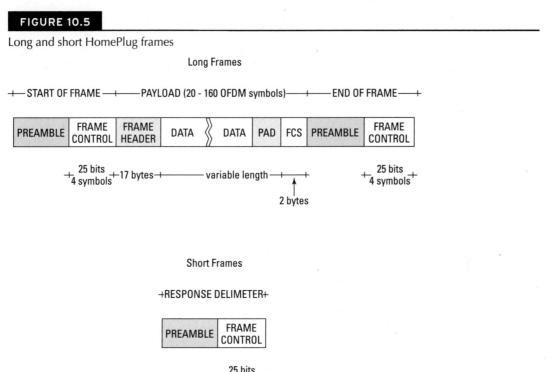

As frames are sent over a power line, a form of Carrier Sense Multiple Access with Collision Avoidance (CSMA/CA) is used to provide traffic flow control and lower the collision rate. CSMA/CA listens using both Physical Carrier Sense (PCS) and Virtual Carrier Sense (VCS) for an idle period before transmitting additional frames, with HomePlug providing a prioritization scheme along with a resolution mechanism. PCS is a Physical layer protocol used to detect the preamble. VCS is a MAC layer protocol and uses the information in the delimiter to determine the following:

- **Start of Frame delimiter.** The type of response required, frame length, priority, and tone map index or channel adaptation used to send it.

- **End of Frame delimiter.** The type of response required and the priority.

- **Response delimiter.** A response (Resp) can require an ACK (acknowledgment), NACK (negative acknowledgment), or FAIL response (negative acknowledgment due to resources), and also includes the priority of the preceding frame.

Priority resolution is based on assigned user priorities for application classes, and has a backoff algorithm that detects contention and lowers priorities appropriately. This system allows HomePlug to offer several different Quality of Service features that support streaming applications such as VoIP, multimedia, and other technologies.

Security

Each device comes with a label showing the master password given to it by the manufacturer; that password provides access to create other passwords. To access the encryption features of a HomePlug device, you need to install the software that came with that device. Most of these devices come with software for Windows. If you are using a Macintosh or Linux computer, check to see if this software is available for your operating system, or is browser based.

The security scheme used is based on a 56-bit Data Encryption Standard (56-bit DES) technology. A HomePlug station (the connection endpoint) stores a table with encryption keys and the Encryption Key Select (EKS) values used to encrypt frames. EKS is an index value used to identify an encryption key; the EKS value is stored inside the frame header and used by the receiving station for key selection for the decryption. For each network, an individual shared Network Encryption Key is used and an associated EKS is on every station in the network.

Note that the optimization of the channel selection done in channel adaptation provides an additional level of security.

Home Network Servers

Home network servers are created to serve the needs of small networks of users in a residential environment. Home servers are engineered to be easy to use and to support a range of functions needed for networks of this type. The small number of computers on a home network means that the hardware needs of a home server are usually modest. Many people turn older computers into home servers, and many vendors use older or more limited versions of the network server operating systems as the basis for a home server. The Microsoft Windows Home Server is based on the Windows Server 2003 operating system, has some administrative features turned off, and comes with a number of wizards included to make configuration easier. Many home servers are sold as appliances, and are based on Linux distributions or BSD UNIX.

Many home servers include the following elements:

- Network addressing services such as DHCP and DNS
- Firewall or proxy services for Internet connections
- Web servers for use by computers on the network for an intranet, and in rarer instances, for Internet use

- Resource sharing of storage (file sharing), printers, and other peripherals
- Remote access capabilities that allow users to connect from outside
- Media streaming capabilities for audio/visual files
- An e-mail or instant messaging (IM) server
- Network security
- Application software for the home, such as group calendars, to-do lists, and more

As a category, home servers have had only a very tiny impact on the market. In the two years that Microsoft Home Server (`www.microsoft.com/windows/products/winfamily/windows homeserver/default.mspx`) has been available, it is estimated that less than 100,000 home servers have been sold.

Over the past decade, several home server appliances have appeared in the marketplace, none of which has fared as well as Microsoft Home Server. One example of a home server appliance is the Toshiba Magnia, which was released in 2001 and based on Red Hat Linux. This appliance provided a browser administrative interface, DHCP, DNS, FTP, a Web server, print server, firewall, filtering, and Web caching, all in a package the size of a laptop. Some other examples of appliances in this category were the Sun Cobalt Qube, EmergeCore Network's IT-100, Mirra Personal Server, Greencomputer Innovation's PowerElf II, IOGEAR BOSS, Tritton Technologies ASAP, and Chili Systems ChiliBox; all were aimed at the Small Office Home Office (SOHO) market. Of this list, only the IT-100 is still available.

The idea of having a home server on your network makes sense, even if it hasn't been a market success. It may well be that people who are technically inclined simply opt for standard versions of networked server operating systems such as Windows Server, Solaris, Red Hat Linux, or something else. Still that doesn't stop people from trying to introduce new products in this area. One group of Ubuntu devotees have gotten together to start a Ubuntu Home Server project (`www.ubuntuhome server.org`), but this project is still in development. Other rumors I've read are that Apple is developing a competitor for the Microsoft Home Server, but one never knows with Apple.

As it stands now, Microsoft Home Server is the only real game in town, and it is certainly worth considering if you are interested in centralized home network services. Home Server is a very smooth product, and over 60 third-party products have been built to support it. Just the network backup service, mirroring, and the ability to aggregate all of the disks it can see make this product a worthwhile investment for any home network of four computers or more. HP, Acer, Shuttle, and Via all offer Windows Home Server appliances. Figure 10.6 shows the Microsoft Home Server storage console.

FIGURE 10.6

Microsoft Home Server uses any disk it can find for storage.

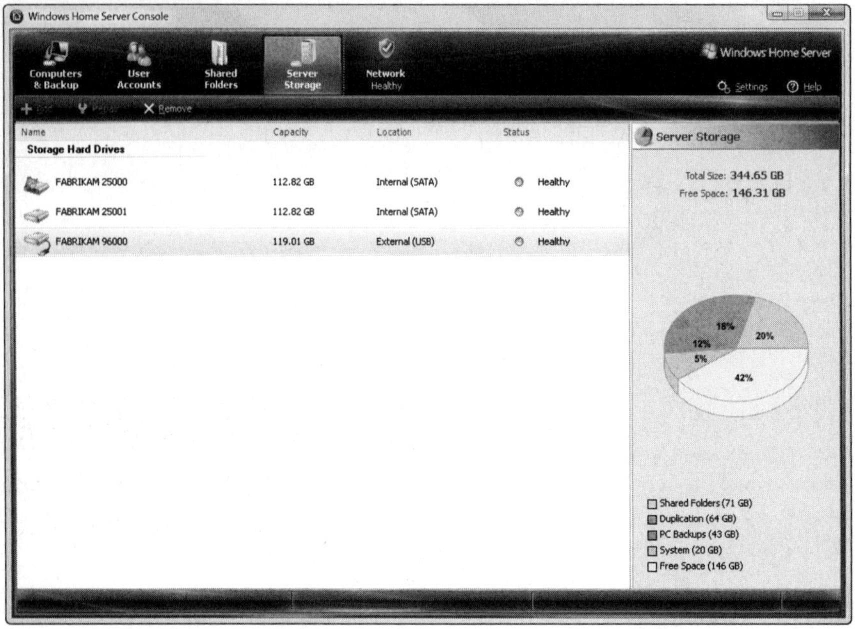

Summary

In this chapter, home networks were described, and their common features were listed. Home networks let you share resources, which is a great savings of time and money. Usually home networks use different technologies mixed together for maximum convenience, and minimum cost and complexity.

This chapter focused on two essential home network problems: how to connect to the Internet and how to bridge different areas of your home together. Ethernet, HomePNA, and HomePlug networking were described. Wi-Fi was briefly described.

In the next chapter, peer-to-peer networking technologies are described. This category of networks also includes networks based on different computer bus standards.

Peer-to-Peer Networks and Personal LANs

Personal Local Area Networks, or pLANs, are networks that have a small number of users and/or cover a small physical area. In this chapter, you look at several different technologies that implement networks of this type.

You also examine peer-to-peer (P2P) networks. A workgroup is an example of a P2P network that is composed of a dozen or less members. P2P networks can also be created by distributed applications. For a system to be P2P, all nodes must be both client and server; there is no central network management or services, and no routing function exists.

Peer-to-peer networks exist in many types. A pure P2P network is one that has no central service of any kind. A hybrid P2P may have a central index or lookup function, but the peers perform all of the data sharing between themselves.

In this chapter, you examine some of the more famous examples of P2P networks and the impact that they have had on network application architecture. Among the examples you look at are the pure P2P Gnutella and Freenet file sharing systems that use peer-to-peer discovery and an ad hoc mechanism to retrieve data. Napster and BitTorrent are given as examples of hybrid P2P systems.

The security and anonymity afforded by friend-to-friend (F2F) networks are considered.

Some computer buses play the role of personal networks. The three that are examined from a network and architecture viewpoint are the Universal Serial Bus (USB), FireWire (IEEE 1394), and Bluetooth. USB uses a tree structure,

IN THIS CHAPTER

Personal Local Area Networks

Peer-to-peer (P2P) network models

Large P2P systems

Computer buses that can connect many devices

FireWire uses a daisy chain, and Bluetooth relies on an ad hoc form of networking called a piconet or scatternet.

Peer-to-Peer Networks

A peer-to-peer (P2P) network is one in which all nodes can be a client and a server, as well as have direct connections to one another; it is also a network on which there is no central point of management. The term is applied equally to a network of computers that share a common LAN, as well as to distributed software applications sharing resources across a LAN, or more frequently a WAN.

Peer-to-peer networking's prime attraction is that it can share distributed resources, thus avoiding duplication and additional cost. One or more computers can share files, printers, optical drives, and other resources. Distributed software can make vast amounts of data ubiquitous or can allow projects with enormous processing requirements to be accomplished on many computers.

The first personal computer networks were P2P networks. The first personal computer to ship with P2P networking was the Macintosh Plus in 1984. For Microsoft Windows, the first networked version, released in October 1992, was called Microsoft Windows for Workgroups 3.11. WfW, as it was then abbreviated, used SMB (Server Message Block) Application layer file sharing, NetBIOS Session layer identification, and NBF/IPX (NetBIOS Frames and Internetwork Packet Exchange) as the Transport layer protocols. WfW's network program was VSHARE.386, which was a virtual device driver that performed file locking. For most networks of any size, the introduction of low-cost networked operating systems such as Windows NT has made P2P networks mainly a small office or home technology.

Peer-to-peer networking lives on in Windows in each of its desktop versions as the "workgroup feature," although the protocols and capabilities have changed radically over the years. Workgroups usually begin to have performance issues when they reach anywhere between 12 and 20 connections. For Windows XP and Vista, Microsoft has set a connection limit of 10, although this is an artificial limit.

When you log into a Windows workgroup, your security is maintained by your local system, and your files are local. The resources that you publish on the network are referred to as *shares*, and an administrator on a peer can set the security for that resource based on users and groups. This arrangement isn't nearly as secure as having a central authority managing security, and most networks that need security move to a client/server network, preferably with a directory service installed. The options that you have in a Windows workgroup, for example, are limited compared to a domain.

However, a server adds significant cost and complexity, which is why there are still a lot of workgroups in use. It can be argued that the lack of security, poor performance, and distributed management, as well as lack of central resource protection, make P2P a more expensive technology over the lifetime of the network; however, workgroups definitely have a lower barrier to entry.

Software can also be distributed using a peer-to-peer model. In this model, all nodes that have the software installed are peers and can see all other peers. In the sections that follow, you will see the different types of peer-to-peer networks, with examples of some of the better-known products in that area.

Peer-to-peer software has had a tremendous impact on the architecture of modern software. This kind of software can make vast amounts of data available, often for an insignificant price. In some instances, peer-to-peer software can be assembled in a common task into a powerful distributed network that can perform the work of a supercomputer such as solving complex protein folding problems, looking for aliens in outer space, and other computationally intensive tasks.

Pure P2P networks

Pure P2P networks are those in which all network services are provided on a peer-to-peer basis. For a network to be considered a pure peer-to-peer system, it must have the following traits:

- All peers are both clients and servers.
- There are no network servers available.
- Clients can manage their own services; there is no central management console.
- There is no router function; every peer can see every other peer.

A Windows workgroup is an example of a pure P2P model system. There are also some applications that use the pure P2P model. Applications that use this model tend to be file and content transfer utilities, streaming media, IRC chats, and telephony.

Small world networks

A small world network is one where most of the nodes on a network aren't nearest neighbors, but in which any node on the network can connect to any other node through at least one, and usually more, paths. These types of networks can be analyzed by graph theory, and they form the basis for a wide variety of systems, including social systems and computer networks. The theory that everyone is related by no more than six degrees of separation, commonly referred to as the Kevin Bacon theory, is an example of a small world network. Short-term memory is known to use a small world network of neurons. Pure P2P networks are another example of this network type.

A totally randomized small world network has the smallest average "shortest paths." Most small world networks are not random and tend to form higher-traffic paths among a group of nodes. Also, there is usually at least one short path that connects any pair of nodes. Small world networks are populated with a large number of hubs, which are nodes of high connectivity; and a much smaller number of edge nodes. When a small world network has a higher number of hubs than you might expect, this is called a fat-tailed distribution.

Gnutella

Perhaps the best-known pure P2P application is the popular Internet file sharing system called Gnutella. The name comes from the developers' love of the hazelnut-and-chocolate spread called

Nutella and their intent to release the software under the GNU general license. Gnutella was released to circumvent some of the problems that Napster was experiencing. (Napster is discussed later in this chapter.) Gnutella is a system that allows peers to view files on other peers' computers without the need for a central database.

There are many systems that use Gnutella, as well as a large number of Gnutella clients for all available platforms. The most popular clients include BearShare, Gnucleus, LimeWire, Morpheus, WinMX, and XoloX.

When you launch a Gnutella client, it first searches for one or more available peers. Sometimes the software comes with a listing of possible peers, and other times the client is configured to consult a Web cache. In early versions of Gnutella, the client first searches for another peer, and will continue to look for more clients up to a small limit that is usually around five systems. Each node also has five known peers so that when a request for a file goes out, the request can be forwarded to all peers within seven hops of the first peer, within the limit of the request's Time to Live (TTL) parameter. This fan-out can connect to up to 78,125 systems if necessary. Any systems that respond to the recognition ping by the first peer with a pong are listed in a table that is stored by the Gnutella client for later use.

Figure 11.1 shows Gnutella's very simple but effective pure P2P architecture. The figure shows that the system is a tree structure that fans out seven levels deep. A message can travel up to seven hops, illustrated by the dark tree shown on the left-hand side of the figure. The other trees and the ellipsis symbols illustrate that the actual network fans out to accommodate the additional levels. Space precludes showing all of the nodes. All of the peers in this figure are connected.

Some programs that use Gnutella use a system of leaf nodes that connect to three ultrapeers. Each of these ultrapeers can connect to 32 more ultrapeers. Up to four hops are allowed. The fan-out for this system is enormous; I calculate it as 4.38 x 1048. Peers use the Query Routing Protocol to exchange a Query Routing Table (QRT) containing hash values, and at the ultrapeer level, those peers merge the tables together. The query from a client travels down the chain until a hash value matches, at which point the peer that was responsible for the hash entry is contacted for a file match.

Once a match is located, the requesting peer contacts the peer with the content and they negotiate the file transfer. If the content peer is behind a firewall and can't respond to a request to transfer the file to the system outside the firewall (a pull request), then the requesting system sends a message asking the content peer inside the firewall to initiate the transfer (a push request). If that still doesn't work, then a push proxy (often the ultrapeer) is used as an intermediary.

Gnutella makes no requirements about the types of files that can be shared. It also isn't easy to trap Gnutella requests because they are ad hoc and the links can be transient. The distributed nature of the system and the lack of a central authoritative database also mean that it suffers from fewer performance problems and bottlenecks.

FIGURE 11.1

The Gnutella file sharing system uses a pure P2P hierarchical structure for queries and data transfers.

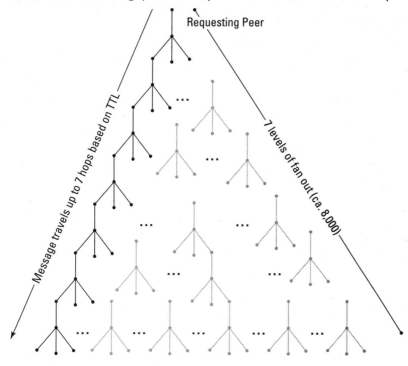

Note

The file sharing system Kazaa uses a system of pure P2P fan-out similar to the one that Gnutella uses.

Freenet

Another example of a pure P2P system is the open source project called Freenet that is available under the GNU license. Freenet uses a key-based routing protocol in place of the distributed hash tables that Gnutella uses. The algorithm examines the keys and connects to those nodes that are closest to the requesting system or connecting peer. A key is a hash function that is based either on content or location; Freenet uses both.

Unlike other P2P systems, Freenet creates a distributed storage system or cache and populates that cache with content. Typically a peer donates about 10GB to the system. The act of adding a file or Web page to the cache is called *insertion*. The user does not control what is stored in his cache. Varieties of Freenet are Darknet, where users are connected to a selected number of trusted users or networks, and OpenNet, where no restrictions are made. Darknet can still fan out to fantastically large limits but must retain their trusted connections. Freenet is still under development but exists in stable forms that are in use.

Hybrid P2P systems

A hybrid peer-to-peer network is one where clients are peers but some central services still exist. Hybrid P2P networks are widely used for distributed Internet applications, and have played a large role in popularizing these types of networks.

Peer-to-peer networks that are created by links in which any two nodes know about the existence of their peer before they form the connection are called *structured networks*. The hybrid P2P file sharing networks that follow, Napster and Torrents, are examples of this type of network. A structured network requires some kind of global protocol for maintaining pointers to content and systems. Many P2P networks store this information in a distributed hash table (DHT) of some kind.

Napster

The music sharing service Napster started out as a P2P network designed by Shawn Fanning while he was a student at Northeastern University. His system created a central server on which the locations of MP3 songs were indexed and stored in a central database. This music was distributed on client system file shares, and when you selected a song from the database your file transfer was from its location on a peer client to your system. The software was commercialized and the company took Shawn's nickname, Napster, which came from his '50s-styled hairdo.

Napster became wildly popular and led to rampant music sharing, which became the object of a music industry lawsuit that argued copyright infringement. At its peak in February 2001, Napster had 24 million unique users worldwide. Napster's argument was that they were simply a listing service and that the act of file copying was done without their permission. Eventually the service was closed by court order.

The company's logo and brand were purchased and repositioned as a pay-for-download service, first by Roxio, and then in 2008 by the Best Buy retail chain. It has never recaptured its former level of usage. However, Napster did illustrate to everyone how powerful a hybrid P2P architecture can be. Today there are many companies, particularly on the Internet, that use this model.

Torrents

BitTorrent is a hybrid P2P file sharing protocol developed using the Napster model. The protocol is widely used and, according to a number of studies, represents a significant percentage of current Internet traffic worldwide. The site isoHunt.com maintains a BitTorrent search engine that currently has a million indexed torrents listed. In 2008, isoHunt was able to document more than 1 petabyte of torrent traffic. Other popular torrent indexes are TorrentBox, and isoHunt.com. The BitTorrent protocol was developed by Bram Cohen and is made available by his company, BitTorrent.

There are numerous BitTorrent clients that you can download. The site About.com has a listing that ranks their users' top seven client software applications. They are:

1. mTorrent (www.utorrent.com), shown in Figure 11.2
2. BitComet (www.bitcomet.com)

3. ABC (pingpong-abc.sourceforge.net)

4. BitLord (www.dailysofts.com/program/907/29391/Bitlord.html)

5. Vuze (www.vuze.com)

6. The original BitTorrent client (www.bittorrent.com)

FIGURE 11.2

mTorrent is currently the most popular BitTorrent client. The peer list view appears in the lower half of the application window.

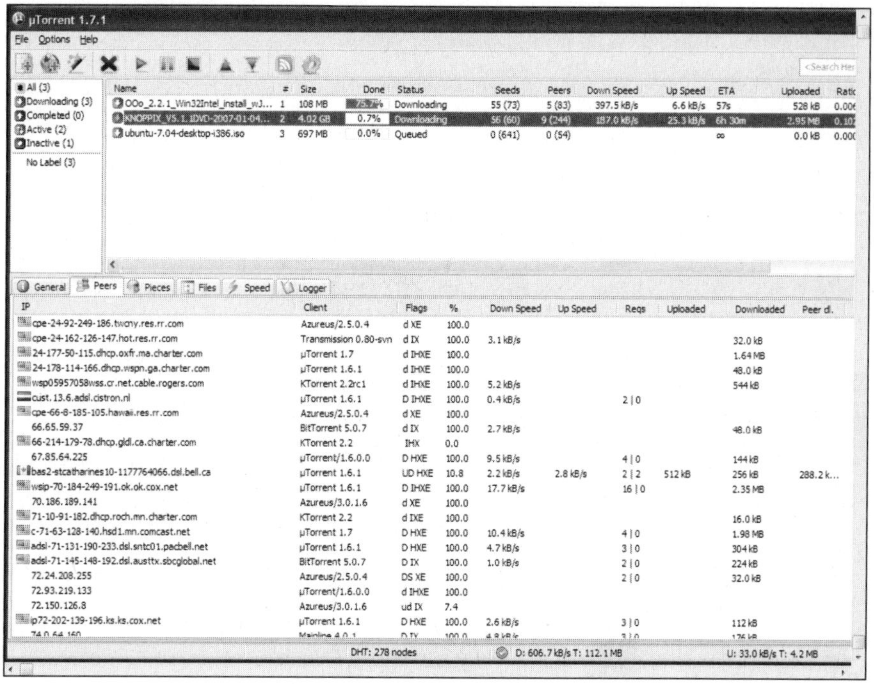

When a client wants to share a file, the software creates a .TORRENT file that contains information about the file and about the server that will store the metadata pointing to the file. That .TORRENT file is then transferred to the Torrent server, which is called the *tracker*, where it is indexed in a database. The second client comes along and queries the server for the file to learn about its location. After the .TORRENT file is transferred to the second computer so that the location of the file is known, the peer-to-peer transfer of the file begins. The first client with the file is the initial *seeder*, and any client that provides a complete copy of the file is also called a seeder.

Eventually any file of interest is populated to many clients, often geographically dispersed clients. It no longer becomes necessary to download the entire file from a single client, and so the

.TORRENT file directs the client to download pieces of the file from multiple clients. Multiple clients sharing a torrent are referred to as a *swarm*. This helps distribute the load off of any one system. Figure 11.3 shows the P2P architecture that BitTorrent uses and illustrates the steps that BitTorrent follows:

1. Client to Tracker: Which computers have the movie file or pieces of it?

2. Tracker to Client: You can find the pieces here.

3. Tracker to Swarm: Send and receive file pieces from the client.

4. Seeds to Client: File is on the way.

5. Swarm to Client: Here are some of your missing pieces.

FIGURE 11.3

The BitTorrent architecture

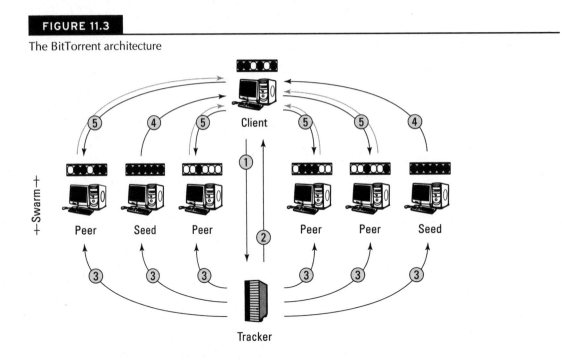

In Figure 11.3 the different steps shown in the previous list are illustrated. A streamed file, which in the figure is represented by a movie reel above the computer, is stored on the seed system as a complete file with all of its constituent frames (represented in black). Peers in the system only have a subset of the frames, as illustrated by the missing frames (represented in white) in the movie reel. As the BitTorrent sends the movie to the client system, the peers send their portions of the movie to the client, eventually resulting in the entire movie file being transferred.

You can imagine that this technology doesn't make the entertainment industry very happy, to say the least. Nor is it popular with ISPs because it was estimated by CacheLogic (an Internet traffic analyst firm in Cambridge, England in 2005) that *BitTorrent accounts for 35 percent of all Internet traffic*. Many ISPs use packet-shaping tools to sniff traffic and filter out BitTorrent packets.

If BitTorrent used a single well-known port, then it would be easy for providers to simply block that port. However, BitTorrent doesn't use port 80, which browsers use for HTTP data. Instead, BitTorrent breaks up the data and uses a few TCP ports to download data in a random or least-used sequence. This approach makes the torrent more efficient and harder to block; however, it adds extra overhead (particularly at the start of the torrent) as those multiple torrents are established. The protocol doesn't yet support streamed content because of this fragmented download approach.

The BitTorrent system breaks files up into a set of equal slices up to 4MB in size. To each piece is added a checksum, which is checked upon arrival and resequencing. BitTorrent has a number of competitors; some use a metadata server called a *tracker*, while others don't. In the trackerless services, the peer clients distribute the metadata amongst themselves. Trackerless systems are pure P2P systems, and not a hybrid like BitTorrent is.

BitTorrent by itself is not illegal. It is simply a method for sharing files. It is up to the application that uses BitTorrent to police itself. The BitTorrent company has licensed the software to many multimedia companies for use in distributing their own copyrighted content. The popular World of Warcraft massive multiplayer online game is a torrent service. There are also efforts underway to incorporate RSS feeds and podcasts into BitTorrents in order to share the cost of distributing these media types.

BitTorrent sites offer tremendous services, both legal and illegal. That aside, there are some aspects of these sites that you should be aware of. When you use BitTorrent, your system's address is known and you can be tracked either as a *seeder* (the one that does the seeding) or as a *seedee* (the one that receives the seeds). BitTorrent is also a bandwidth hog and requires a broadband connection.

To discourage people who download files but don't allow their computer to be a seeder, called *leeches*, the BitTorrent system can monitor the share ratio. If a peer has a ratio of less than 1 bit downloaded for every bit shared, it can withhold the final seed or take another action. To throttle a client is to "choke" them. A *lurker* is someone who downloads files but does not add any new content to the system. Lurkers do seed the system with the content that they download.

Given the flood of data stored in torrent systems, it is impossible for these services to monitor content. It's not uncommon for malicious users to upload files with nasty business in them. So be sure that you trust the sites you download from if you use this technology, and test any files appropriately.

In honor of September 19th, Talk Like a Pirate Day, it is difficult to leave the topic of P2P software without mentioning those counter-culture heroes at The Pirate Bay. The Pirate Bay (thepiratebay. org) is a Swedish Web site that is reportedly the world's largest BitTorrent tracker and one of the world's top 100 visited Web sites. It is also one of the most contentious, and ultimately one of the most amusing to follow. While current plans by the pirates to buy their own island nation seem to have run aground, one never knows where the skull and crossbones will wave.

Friend-to-Friend Networks

An anonymous peer-to-peer network is one in which the identification of the user is kept hidden. Because peer-to-peer networking requires that nodes be able to connect to other peers, anonymity requires that the peer be hidden in some manner. Most often, this is done through a routing technique.

There are many reasons that people use anonymous P2P networking. They may want to maintain their privacy, prevent tracking, keep their information out of the public domain, avoid censorship, or escape controversy. Whatever the reason, anonymous P2P is not only of interest to people but to organizations and governments, as well.

The Freenet file sharing system that you read about is a popular one on which to implement anonymous networking. When that network is an OpenNet network, all peers are seen by all other peers. That type of network is difficult to be anonymous on. The Darknet network type is one where only trusted links are allowed. Sometimes, this kind of network is called a friend-to-friend (F2F) network.

F2F networks authenticate their links using passwords or digital signatures. An F2F network can be more secure because the link is protected cryptographically, and the link's bandwidth can be controlled and protected. However, an F2F link requires extra setup and perhaps teardown, and may not be available when it is needed.

Consider the situation where you have three nodes connected by two F2F links. The middle node is a friend of both endpoints, and no trust relationship exists between the endpoints. Data that is sent from endpoint to endpoint can be hidden from each by the middle node. Networks of this type can remove the original source's IP address prior to sending the packets on to their destination. This makes the middle node essentially a proxy for both endpoints.

When you have a network where a link such as the one between endpoints appears to be a combination of one network link that is known and another that is unknown, this type of link is called an *overlay*. An overlay network is one where it appears that one network is built on another network. Nodes are connected by virtual links, often through multiple physical links. The use of dial-up networking to connect through the phone company to the Internet is an example of an overlay. Overlay is a common characteristic of peer-to-peer networks. Gnutella and Freenet are examples of overlay P2P networks.

Bus Networking

A computer bus is a physical connection to peripheral devices. It is either something that is built into a computer or that can be added to a computer through the use of an add-on card or a peripheral device. The term *computer bus* used to imply that only a few devices were connected to that physical subsystem. For example, the Small Computer System Interface, or SCSI, in its initial forms was limited to only 8 devices, of which the host was one. Later versions of SCSI could accommodate up to 16 devices. However, most people populate SCSI buses with only a small handful of devices.

Several computer buses allow you to attach a large number of devices, or nodes. This makes them the equivalent of a computer network, albeit one in which the whole network stack is contained in the computer itself. The bus provides the physical layer, and any data linking or network software is part of the bus driver software.

In the sections that follow, you'll look at three popular computer buses — the Universal Serial Bus (USB), FireWire (IEEE 1394), and Bluetooth wireless networks — and consider how these standards enable networks that you could classify as Personal Local Area Networks (pLANs).

Universal serial bus

The universal serial bus, or USB, is almost universally used for peripheral connections. After 1999, you'd be hard-pressed to find a motherboard that didn't support this bus standard. The USB serial bus is theoretically capable of connecting up to 127 devices per host controller, although in practice the limit is quite a bit less than the address space allows. USB-IF, the USB Implementers Forum (www.usb.org), is the industry group that develops the standard. USB has gone through two major versions, 1.0 and 2.0; USB version 3.0 has been demonstrated and devices are expected to be available at the end of 2009.

The main attraction of USB is that devices are hot swappable and offer plug-and-play ability. Hot-swappable means that you can physically remove an active device and replace it with another device while the system is running. The standard allows for powered and non-powered devices and can be used to support input devices, output devices, network interfaces, and external expansion cards. USB is a low-power bus and can trickle-charge, or slowly recharge, devices. A version of the USB port called PoweredUSB adds an extra four pins to supply 6A at 5 V, 12 V, or 24 V to devices. Any device that requires significant amounts of power requires its own power adapters.

A USB is controlled by a root host controller, which attaches to devices to create a pLAN with a hierarchical star topology, as shown in Figure 11.4. In these topologies any device that connects to two or more USB devices is a hub, the endpoints are USB devices, and the lines represent the individual USB connection (wires). If you attach another USB host controller, you can create fan-out in the bus structure with up to five levels allowed. Additional host controllers are called *hubs*. The device limit of 127 applies to each host controller individually. Host controllers are found as chips on a motherboard, add-in PCI cards, or in USB hubs. The technology is ubiquitous and inexpensive, and so controllers are found on a wide variety of devices.

USB devices connect to the host controller using a set of logical channels that are called *pipes*. Unlike computer networks, only the end of the pipe on the device side is referred to as an endpoint. Each device can create 32 active unidirectional pipes, with a limit of 16 pipes in and 16 pipes out. One endpoint, called *endpoint zero*, is reserved for device control, and any group of endpoints sharing a common purpose is referred to as a *group*.

FIGURE 11.4

The tiered star shares elements of a daisy chain and star topologies.

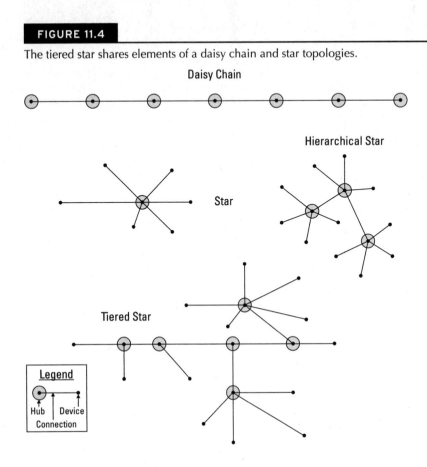

When you connect a device to the USB bus, the host controller gets a signal to poll devices on the bus and enumerate them. The newly connected device is reset, and when it is recognized again, it is configured and assigned a unique 7-bit address. On a serial bus, there is one data path, and so device traffic is queued by device in a sequential (round robin) order.

USB host devices in USB 2.0 create what is called the Enhanced Host Controller Interface (EHCI). The interface supports device classes that are supported in the operating system. This allows operating system vendors to create a generic set of drivers that work with a broad range of devices automatically.

Version 2.0 supports the high-speed mode of 480 Mbits/s, as well as legacy 1.0 devices at the full speed of 12 Mbits/s and at the low speed of 1.5 Mbits/s. Version 3.0 supports the super-speed rate of 4.8 Gbits/s. These are speeds measured under favorable conditions; most current USB 2.0 devices attain about 65 percent of the rated speed. The USB cable is a twisted-pair wire supporting half-duplex communication, which can be captured by USB protocol analyzers when diagnostic work is being done.

USB data is transmitted as frames that are in 8-bit multiples, and begin with a synchronization header and end with a short end-of-packet signal. Communications begin with packets sent from the host controller to devices. If this is the host controller at the highest level of the bus, then the path is through the root hub. Devices respond to the host's communication by returning handshake packets that the host can acknowledge. Communication uses token, data (two types), and pre-packet types. The USB network uses what has been called a "speak when spoken to" model, with the host controller directing all communications.

USB cables have connectors that come in six varieties: Type A, Type B, Mini-A, Mini-B, Micro-A, and Micro-B. Type A and B have four pins, while Mini-A and -B and Micro-A and -B have six pins. There are both male and female connections. (The male plugs are shown in Figure 11.5.) You can find cables that mix and match these connections. The B plugs are used on the device side. The reason that these cables are usually two-sided is to prevent users from creating USB loops, which would cause the bus to fail. The smaller mini plugs are used on small devices such as cell phones and cameras. Micro-USB is meant to replace the mini plugs. USB 3.0 connectors will come in one version that is similar to USB 2.0 Types A and B, and another with five pins. Optical cables and connectors are expected to be released as part of the 3.0 standard.

FIGURE 11.5

USB male connector types

Type A

Type B

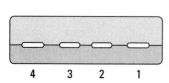

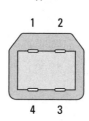

Mini-A

Mini-B

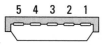

Micro-A

Micro-B

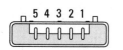

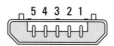

Standard USB cables are limited to around 5m, or 16.4 feet, in length because longer distances lead to unacceptable signal loss. It is possible to find repeaters that can boost signal strength, and using them allows you to significantly increase the cable length. These repeaters are actually mini-USB hubs connected to a USB cable. You can chain up to five USB hubs together and get an aggregate distance of 30m. For USB version 3.0, the cables change significantly; they look like Ethernet cables, are limited to 3m, and support full-duplex operation. You can find USB wireless hubs available from vendors, but they are proprietary. The USB-IF is currently working on an ultra-wide-band wireless connection that should achieve rates of 480 Mbits/s.

FireWire

FireWire is the Apple brand name for the IEEE 1394 serial bus standard. IEEE 1394 provides a high-speed alternative to USB 2.0, making it very popular for devices like digital scanners, digital audio and video peripherals, and hard disks. As such, it has replaced SCSI as a more convenient bus to work with and configure. While FireWire appears on many PC motherboards and can be added on, this bus standard isn't nearly as popular on PCs as it is on the Macintosh, where it was introduced. Other implementations of IEEE 1394 are Sony i.LINK for digital video cameras and Lynx from Texas Instruments.

The FireWire bus can link up to 63 devices in a hierarchical tree topology. In a tree, there is one root node that takes the highest of the ID numbers. During a bus reset, devices on the bus are assigned by a Depth First Search (DFS), with each device assigning itself an address. Figure 11.6 shows an example of this tree traversal algorithm. Notice that the longest limb is assigned first, and then the algorithm moves backward up the tree. In this figure the search begins at the root node 1 and proceeds down the first branch 2 through 8 looking for a match. If no match is found, the algorithm begins tracing each of the other branches sequentially from top to bottom in the order of 9 then 10 through 14, and finally ending at 15.

DFS was chosen as the enumeration technique because it is simpler to implement than a Breadth First Search (BFS), and although it isn't an optimized search technique, the small size of the IEEE 1394 bus allows for the use of DFS.

Devices on IEEE 1394 are peers and are hot swappable and self-configuring (plug and play). FireWire enumerates devices based on their IEEE EUI-64 identification number, rather than using IEEE's 48-bit standard for Ethernet MAC addresses. The former is a superset of the latter, adding additional information that identifies the device type and protocols.

FireWire has gone through several standards since 1995. The original FireWire 400 (IEEE 1394-1995) and the enhanced version (IEEE 1394a-2000) are the most common device types. FireWire 400 allows for half-duplex communication at theoretical rates from 100 to 400 (S100 to S400) Mbits/s over cables that can be up to 4.5m in length.

FIGURE 11.6

The Depth First Search algorithm used to enumerate the FireWire bus

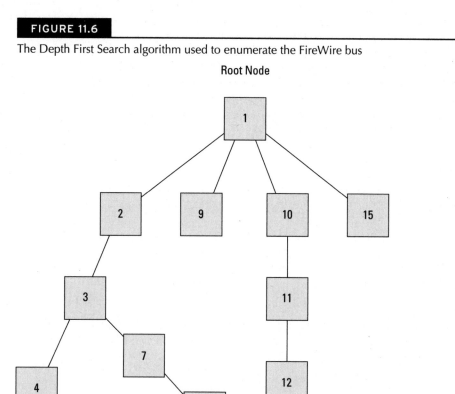

Just as with USB, it is possible to extend the bus in a daisy chain up to a limit of 16 connections; FireWire has a much higher power requirement than USB and requires active repeaters — essentially FireWire hubs. The most common connection, a six-circuit FireWire 400 circuit, carries anywhere from 25 to 30 volts and allows a device to draw up to 8 watts from the circuit. This is enough to power moderate peripheral devices such as scanners and printers, which is considered to be an attractive feature to most users. Figure 11.7 shows the FireWire 400 connectors.

FIGURE 11.7

Six- and four-pin FireWire 400 connectors

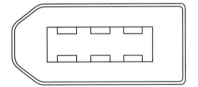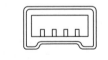

The demand for FireWire has been a fraction of the demand for USB. USB 2.0 runs a little slower than FireWire 400 due to a higher protocol overhead on USB. FireWire 800 runs at 3200 Mbits/s, while USB high speed runs at 25 percent that speed, at 480 Mbits/s. However, speed isn't the issue. It would seem that the cost of the bus devices are part of the problem, as is the fact that FireWire tends to be used for one or two powered devices. It is rare for a FireWire bus to be populated by more devices than that. The USB industry grew faster, and now those devices are the dominant peripheral bus or pLAN available.

FireWire has supported networks between computers using direct connections (peer-to-peer) or when a FireWire hub is connected. Devices can use IP v.4 or IP v.6 addressing. Among the operating systems that support or supported FireWire networking are Mac OS X, Free BSD, Linux, and Windows ME/2000/XP and Server 2003. Microsoft dropped FireWire network support in 2004. Even Sony's PlayStation 2, which first used an i.LINK connector for networking, has found that most users have switched to Ethernet adapters.

To combat these trends, the last released standard, called FireWire S800T (IEEE 1394c-2006), which appeared in June 2007, offers Ethernet interoperability. The port speed is 800 Mbits/s over twisted-pair Category 5e cable with RJ-45 connectors. This is the same cable used for Gigabit Ethernet, and the standard allows both Ethernet and FireWire devices to be auto-recognized and use that port. This standard, while quite intriguing, isn't yet expressed in any products that you can buy. If it can gain traction, it may make FireWire more attractive in the marketplace.

Bluetooth

Bluetooth is a personal wireless LAN technology that creates secure connections to devices within a small distance. Bluetooth is best known for its use in cell phone connections to wireless headsets, but the technology is also used in desktop printers, keyboards, PDAs, GPAs, bar code readers, and other peripheral devices. Devices on a Bluetooth network can see and talk with other Bluetooth devices. The Bluetooth standard is developed by the Bluetooth Special Interest Group (www.bluetooth.com).

Note

Harald Bluetooth was a tenth-century Danish king who united much of Norway, Sweden, and Denmark — three countries in close proximity.

The technology used for Bluetooth is similar to cellular phone technology; it is called frequency-hopping spread spectrum. The technology uses the 2.45 GHz band in the United States and in Europe. This band is considered to be an "open" band, and so many devices transmit on it. This is the same frequency range used by the 802.11g wireless standard, many cell phones, and other devices. Oddly enough, microwave ovens emit radiation in this frequency range, and they can interrupt 802.11g phones as well as Bluetooth.

The exact range is 2400 to 2483.5 in the United States, which is split into 79 separate 1 MHz channels. In Japan, the spread is 23 separate 1 MHz channels. Bluetooth uses a technique called Gaussian Frequency-Shift Keying (GFSK) to make physical connections between devices with a transfer rate of up to 1 Mbit/s.

Bluetooth devices contain transceivers that are categorized into three classes:

- Class 1 — 100 mW with a range of 100m

- Class 2 — 2.5 mW with a range of 10m

- Class 3 — 1 mW, with a range of only 1m

These three standards are used by transceivers that are omni-directional wireless transmitters. The low power output means that Bluetooth signals cannot travel through walls. Cell phones, by comparison, emit signals of over 3 watts. Connecting a device in a network class rated for a shorter-range communication (such as a Class 2 device) to a longer-ranged device (Class 1, for example) extends the range of the shorter-range device somewhat.

Connections

To create a Bluetooth network, called a *piconet*, you need to have a Bluetooth hub that has its own transceiver. A piconet (see Figure 11.8) is defined as an ad hoc network of Bluetooth devices, both active and passive. Generally, it is a network that is decentralized and on which any node will forward data to any other nodes. The term *scatternet* has also been used to describe networks of this type. Many laptops and some devices such as the Logitech diNovo keyboard come with a Bluetooth hub built into them. You can also purchase Bluetooth hubs that plug into USB ports, are PC cards (PCMCIA), or are PCI expansion cards. A Bluetooth network allows for only eight connected peer devices.

Clients can join the network and leave the network at any time. Wireless networks are often created as ad hoc networks. The task of defining connections is made dynamically using an adaptive routing function.

FIGURE 11.8

A Bluetooth piconet

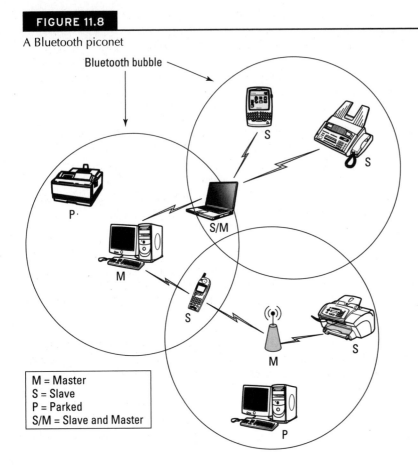

M = Master
S = Slave
P = Parked
S/M = Slave and Master

The network can be aware of up to 28-1, or 255 devices. A piconet or scatternet can have eight devices, one master and seven slaves as indicated in Figure 11.8. A device can be a master in more than one piconet, and devices can be both masters and slaves on two or more piconets. When registered devices are not active they are in the "parked" mode, indicated by devices marked P in Figure 11.8. When a device is on, it initiates device discovery to see which devices are within communication range. To connect to a network, a device must have a name, an address in the form ##.##.##.##.##.## (six number pairs), and a Bluetooth passkey (PIN). The passkey is a shared secret password that the remote device provides, which can be used to cryptographically authenticate each of the endpoints in the connection. This is a unique identification number that is provided by the manufacturer of the device at the time of fabrication and is dependent upon the device category. That ID isn't used as part of the Bluetooth handshake; the user-assigned friendly name is used instead.

Data is transferred over a Bluetooth network in the form of packets up to 2,745 bits in size. About 80 percent of these packets are the payload or data, and those remaining are used for the header and for protocol settings. Communication begins when a device chooses one of the 79 random channels and starts sending data. Channels switch every 625 microseconds, or at a rate of nearly 1,600 cycles per second. A packet can be sent on up to five different time slices. Should another device pick the same channel, the error-checking routine recognizes that it is the wrong data and has the devices retransmit the packets.

Because the chances for the first collision are 1 in 79 (1.3 percent), the chances for two or more collisions are miniscule. The second collision would have 1 chance in 792 (0.016 percent), the third would have 1 chance in 793 (0.000021 percent), and so forth. However, you can see how much the odds change when the Bluetooth bus is fully populated with eight devices. Then the odds would be 7 chances in 79 (8.9 percent), 7 in 792 (1.6 percent), and 7 in 793 (0.00014 percent). It is the availability of frequency channels that limits the device count.

Bluetooth connections can be either full duplex or half duplex. In full duplex, a device can send and receive, but in half duplex it can only do one or the other. Full-duplex devices, such as a phone, transmit and receive voice at the rate of 64 Kbits/s. With that speed for a transfer rate, it is possible to have multiline phones that support multiple conversations. A half-duplex Bluetooth connection from a computer to a printer is much faster, up to 721 Kbits/s. When a computer-to-printer connection uses two half-duplex channels, they both operate at up to 432 Kbits/s.

Bluetooth connections can be categorized as either Synchronous Connection Oriented (SCO) or Asynchronous Connectionless Oriented (ACO). For the synchronous type (SCO) of Bluetooth connection, a master-slave relationship is formed; one master device can connect with up to three slave devices, with each connection having a data rate of 64 Kbits/s. These devices don't experience collisions during an exchange because the master device coordinates the channels that are used. The asynchronous type of connection (ACO) allows the master device to connect with only one slave, but still retains the property that the master initiates and manages all data that is exchanged.

Profiles

Bluetooth devices use a system of profiles to establish their device characteristics so that the network provides the necessary services to them. Devices must transmit the name, class, a list of services, features, manufacturer, clock offset, and the version of Bluetooth that the device uses upon demand. Different profiles enable different protocols and contain information on the format of data that can be exchanged, as well as what is required from devices that are managed by a different profile. Perhaps the best way to think of a device profile is that it is a description of a Bluetooth network interface.

There are around 28 profiles defined by the Bluetooth SIG, with an additional 4 that are at review stage. As an example, let's look briefly at a couple of the networking profiles. When you have an older Bluetooth device that connects to a LAN, such as a Bluetooth hub, it might use the LAN Access Profile, or LAP. LAP allows a device to connect to an IP network through any physical connection. LAP specifies the use of the PPP over the RFCOMM (Radio Frequency Communications) Bluetooth protocol.

A more recent device might connect to the same network using the Personal Area Networking (PAN) profile, which employs a different Network layer (OSI Level 3) protocol. Or perhaps you have a laptop that connects to a network through a Bluetooth phone. In that instance, the profile used would probably be the Dial-Up Networking (DUN) profile, which is similar to the Serial Port Profile (SPP) and uses the common modem AT command set and PPP. This is information that is negotiated between the two endpoints of a Bluetooth connection and ensures that the correct data types are used.

Summary

In this chapter, you learned about small networks called Personal Local Area Networks, or pLANs. They are small in terms of users and/or area of coverage.

Peer-to-peer (P2P) networks can also involve a small number of users, and sometimes a small geographical area. A workgroup is an example of a P2P network that is composed of a dozen or fewer members. P2P networks can also be distributed applications deployed on many systems and over a large area.

You learned about both pure P2P and hybrid P2P systems. Some of the examples that you looked at were Gnutella, Freenet, Napster, and BitTorrent.

Some computer buses play the role of personal networks. The three that were examined from a network and architecture viewpoint were the Universal Serial Bus (USB), FireWire (IEEE 1394), and Bluetooth.

In the next chapter, you will move up the network food chain to local area networks. Chapter 12 looks at various ways of creating local area networks from the standpoint of software, addressing, and factors that aren't related to hardware.

Local Area Networking

This chapter surveys the major classes of networks that are used to create Local Area Networks (LANs), with the exception of wireless LANs. It describes the different technologies and how they are implemented. The network types described are Ethernet, Token Ring, Fiber Distributed Data Interface (FDDI), X10, and different industrial automation bus standards. The many IEEE 802.x standards that have codified these different network types are also listed.

Ethernet is an example of a frame-based broadcast network. Frames are constructed that include standard fields for source and destination addresses, synchronization, error checking, and more. The construction of an Ethernet frame is fully described. Ethernet frames sometimes arrive at the same time, resulting in a collision. Ethernet uses Carrier Sense Multiple Access with Collision Detection (CSMA/CD) to detect and correct data loss that results from collision.

Token Ring networks use a different method for network access. On these networks, endpoints get the chance to broadcast on the network when they receive a special token frame. Token Ring networks are now largely an IBM technology. FDDI networks are token rings that use optical fiber to create high-speed systems. They have been widely deployed in the past, particularly in the telecommunications industry.

The X10 RF over power-line networks allows you to automate a home. The signaling technology is explained, and related automation networking standards are briefly introduced.

Industrial automation networks are described. Those networks aggregate the data from sensors, actuators, switches, valves, and other devices and make that data available to a control station with a Human Machine Interface

IN THIS CHAPTER

Introduction to LANs

How broadcast technology solves some network issues

How Ethernet works

Token Ring and FDDI networks

How industry creates network automation systems

Automate a home using RF over power lines and X10 networks

system. Process control systems that include the Modbus device bus, Programmable Logic Controllers, OLE for Process Control (OPC) data interchange, and Supervisory Control and Data Acquisition (SCADA) systems are detailed.

Introduction

Local Area Networks, or LANs, are networks that are limited in scope, private, and have a limited number of administered entities such as domains and subnets. The characteristics of a LAN are best summarized by these factors:

- Topology
- Transmission media
- Technology standards
- Size
- Management characteristics

In Chapter 3, different topologies are described, Chapter 8 discusses media, and Chapter 30 describes management technologies. In this chapter, you learn about technology standards and network sizes, in terms of node counts, connections, and run lengths. A few of the most important LAN network standards are discussed in this chapter, including:

- Ethernet, the dominant network broadcast standard
- Token Ring, a method for synchronized network access
- Fiber Distributed Data Interface (FDDI), a high-speed Token Ring network protocol
- X10 power-line radio frequency (RF) networks, and other home automation network types
- Industrial automation bus and data exchange standards

These five LAN network types serve to frame the subject of what a LAN is, how you design a LAN, and how data on a LAN is processed. Wireless technology is also popular in constructing LANs and is becoming increasingly popular as time goes by. To completely explore the subject of modern-day LANs, you would have to include the different Wi-Fi network standards in use today. However, to keep this chapter to a reasonable length, Wi-Fi networks are covered in Chapter 14, where the topic is expanded and more fully explored.

In order for different types of Ethernet components to interoperate, they must be based on tested industry standards. Most of the Ethernet standards are the result of efforts of committees of the IEEE (Institute of Electrical and Electronics Engineers, pronounced "eye triple E"). In the next section, you will learn about the different versions of IEEE standards that have been and are now in use. A fundamental feature of a network is the area over which communication can be transmitted without requiring modification, called the broadcast domain. Broadcast domains and their relationship to Ethernet networks are explored in the section that follows the IEEE standards.

The IEEE 802 LAN standards

As LAN standards have been developed, the IEEE has created a set of standards that mirror the real-world networks in use. These Ethernet standards can arise out of the work of a single vendor, such as the Token Ring technologies from IBM, a small group of vendors, such as the DIX (DEC, Intel, and Xerox) group that created Ethernet, or the result of an industry working group of some type.

Whenever possible, IEEE committees generalize the specification of the standard so that as many other vendors' products can interoperate as possible. So while the IBM Token Ring technology might require a specific medium, the IEEE standard would generalize this requirement. These different standards go through a proposed stage where different aspects of the standards exist fully specified as Request for Comment documents, or RFCs. Many RFCs live very long lives, eventually being modified or replaced by other RFCs. IEEE eventually formalizes some of these standards, and when it does, it publishes the standards as a set of reference manuals based on the standard's components.

This has resulted in a set of 15 (and growing) standards that have been created or are in development from work that now spans nearly 30 years. These standards are summarized in Table 12.1. Each standard may have multiple substandards, and some of these substandards get reduced to practice and are commercially viable, while many other substandards are not. If you have followed the development of Wi-Fi standards over the past decade, you will remember that the 802.11 standard has produced the 802.11a, 802.11b, 802.11g, and 802.11n substandards.

Broadcast channels

LANs all face the central problem of how to broadcast over a shared network. The solution to this problem is the fundamental decision that separates one type of LAN from another. Because point-to-point network connections involve an exponential number of circuits, this approach to building networks isn't practical. You could use switches to build circuits, the way you do when you create a virtual link (point to point) over a WAN. However, populating a network with a large number of switches on a single network isn't practical either.

In Chapter 5, you learned about the concept of a channel. A channel is a defined state of a network that allows information to pass through it, as implemented in the Medium Access Control portion of the Data Link layer. Channels can be single or multiple; they can also be dedicated, multiple access, or random access. In networks that use virtual channels such as telephony, techniques such as Frequency Division Multiplexing (FDM) slice up the bandwidth into portions that are assigned to each user. Traditionally, for voice, those slices are called DS0, and if you recall from previous discussions they are allocated in chunks of 64 Kbits/s.

TABLE 12.1

IEEE 802 LAN Standards

Standard	Application	Substandards
802.1	LAN/MAN Bridging and Management	802.1b, LAN/MAN Management; 802.1D, MAC Bridges; 802.1e, System Load Protocol; 802.1f, Definitions and Procedures for IEEE 802 Management Information; 802.1G, Remote MAC Bridging; 802.1H, Ethernet MAC Bridging; 802.1Q, VLANs; 802.1x, Port-based Network Access Control; 802.1AB, Station and Media Access Control Connectivity Discovery (LLD); 802.1ad, Provider Bridging; 802.1AE, MAC Security; 802.1af, MAC Key Security; 802.1ag, Connectivity Fault Management; 802.1ah, Provider Backbone Bridge (PBB); 802.1aj, Two Port Mac Relay (TPMR); 802.1ak, Multiple Registration Protocol (MRP); 802.1ap, MIBs; 802.1aq, Shortest Path Bridging (SPB); 802.1AR, Secure Device Identity (DevID); 802.1AS, Time and Synchronization for Time Sensitive Applications in Bridged LANs; 802.1Qat, Stream Reservation Protocol; 802.1Qau, Congestion Management; 802.1Qav, Forwarding and Queuing Enhancements for Time Sensitive Streams; 802.1Qaw, Management of Data Driven and Data Dependent Connectivity Faults; 802.1Qay, Provider Backbone Bridge Traffic Engineering (PBB-TE); 802.1Qaz, Enhanced Transmission Selection; 802.1BA, Audio Video Bridging (AVB) Systems.
802.2	Logical Link Control	No sub-standards. LLC manages data link communication and link addressing. It defines Services Access Points (SAPs), and provides sequencing.
802.3	CSMA/CD	Ethernet standards. Table 12.2 lists the 802.3 sub-standards.
802.4	Token Bus	802.4a, LAN: Fiber Optic Token Bus
802.5	Token Ring	802.5a, LAN: Station Management Supplement to 802.5; 802.5n, Unshielded Twisted Pair at 4/16 Mbps; 802.5q, LAN: Part 5: Media Access Control Revision; 802.5, LAN: Dedicated Token Ring Station Attachment.
802.6	Distributed Queue Dual Bus (DQDB)	802.6bm, Premises Extension of DS3-Based 802.6 MAN; 802.6e, Eraser Node for DQDB MAN; 802.6g, Layer Management for 802.6 MAN; 802.6i, Remote LAN Bridging Using 802.6 MAN; 802.6l, Point-to-Point Interface for Subnetwork of MAN; 802.6m, Subnetwork of MAN.
802.7	Broadband LAN	
802.8	Fiber Optic LAN/MAN	

Standard	Application	Substandards
802.9	Integrated Services	802.9a, Supplement to Integrated Services LAN: 802.9 Isochronous with CSMA/CD MAC; 802.9b, Support for Functional Specifications for AU to AU Interworking 802.9; 802.9c, Supplement to 802.9: Management. Object Conforming Statement; 802.9d, Supplemental to 802.9: Protocol Implementation Conforming Statement; 802.9e, Asynchronous Transfer Mode (ATM) Cell Bearer Mode; 802.9f, Remote Terminal Line Power for Integrated Services for Terminal Equipment (ISTE).
802.10	LAN/MAN Security	802.10, Standard for Interoperable LAN Security (SILS); 802.10a, Interoperable LAN Security (SILS) - The Model; 802.10c, SILS - Key Management; 802.10d, SILS - Security Management; 802.10g, Standard for Security Labeling Within Secure Data Exchange; 802.10h, Support to Interoperable LM Security: PICS Proforma/Secondary Data.
802.11	Wireless LAN	802.11a, 5 GHz, 54 Mbits/s; 802.11b, 2.4 GHz, 11 Mbits/s; 802.11c, Bridge operations procedures; 802.11d, International roaming extensions; 802.11e, QoS Enhancements; 802.11g, 2.4 GHz, 54 Mbits/s; 802.11h, Spectrum Managed 802.11a (Europe); 802.11i, Enhanced Security; 802.11j, Extensions for Japan; 802.11k, Radio resource management enhancements; 802.11m - Maintenance of the standard; 802.11n - Higher throughput improvements using MIMO (multiple input, multiple output) antennas, 5 GHz or 2.4 GHz, 600 Mbits/s (over 4 x 40 MHz channels); 802.11p, WAVE - Wireless Access for the Vehicular Environment (such as ambulances and passenger cars); 802.11r, Fast roaming (in progress); 802.11s, Mesh Networking, Extended Service Set (ESS) (in progress); 802.11T, Wireless Performance Prediction (WPP) - test methods and metrics; 802.11u, Interworking with non-802 networks (for example, cellular) (projected); 802.11v, Wireless network management (projected); 802.11w, Protected Management Frames (projected); 802.11y, 3650-3700 MHz Operation in the U.S.; 802.11z, Extensions to Direct Link Setup (DLS) (in progress); 802.11aa, Robust streaming of Audio Video Transport Streams (in progress).
802.12	High-Speed LAN	802.12a, Operation at Greater than 100 Mbits/s; 802.12b, 2-TP PMD Medium Dependent Interface and Link Specifications; 802.12c, 100 Mbits/s Operation: Full Duplex Operation; 802.12d, 100 Mbits/s Operation: Redundant Links.
802.13	The LAN to Nowhere	This standard was never defined for the same reason that there are no thirteenth floors in buildings: Triskaidekaphobia.

continued

TABLE 12.1	(continued)	
Standard	**Application**	**Substandards**
802.14	Cable TV-Based Broadband Communication Networks	
802.15	Wireless Personal Area Networks (WPANs)	802.15.1, Bluetooth; 802.15.2, Coexistence for WPAN and Wireless LANs; 802.15.3, High-Rate WPANs.
802.16	Broadband Wireless Access (WiMAX2, or WirelessMAN)	First mile, last mile connections. 802.16e, Mobile; 802.16f, MIB definition; 802.16g, Management Plane Procedures and Services; 802.16h, Improved Coexistence for License Exempt Operation (in progress); 802.16i, Mobile MIB (in progress); 802.16j, Multihop Relay Specification (in progress); 802.16k, Bridging; 802.16m, Advanced Air Interface (proposed).
802.17	Resilient Packet Ring (RPR)	Used in high-speed SONET networks; 802.17b, Spatially aware sublayer (SAS).
802.18	Radio Regulatory	
802.19	Coexistence	
802.20	Mobile Broadband Wireless Access	Standard for Local and Metropolitan Area Networks, Standard Air Interface for Mobile Broadband Wireless Access Systems Supporting Vehicular Mobility, Physical and Media Access Control Layer Specification.
802.21	Media Independent Handoff (MIH)	Enables information exchange between cellular, GSM, GPRS, Wi-Fi, Bluetooth, 802.11, and 802.16 networks through a set of handover mechanisms. MIH is similar to Unlicensed Mobile Access (UMA), a roaming and handover protocol that works between GSM, UMTS, Bluetooth, and 802.11 networks.
802.22	Wireless Regional Area Networks (WRAN)	WRAN transmits over white spaces in the TV frequency range. This is a new group with a proposed technology.

1. Merged and abandoned standards are not listed. 2. WiMAX stands for Wireless Interoperability for Microwave Access; it is called Wireless Broadband, or WiBro, in South Korea.

FDM is fine for network traffic that is predictable, where there are only a few users at any one time, and the data is cached or buffered en route to accommodate traffic fluctuations. Once the number of users grows, the traffic load becomes unpredictable, the size of the data being transmitted varies, and traffic becomes bursty; the FDM model is no longer efficient. Time Division Multiplexing (TDM) sets network allocation using time slicing, and for all of the same reasons it fares no better than FDM. These are the reasons that all modern LAN technologies adopt a broadcast model. Information is sent onto the LAN where it competes with other pieces of information until it gets to the destination specified.

Broadcast communication uses the concept of a "channel" to describe a path or multipath that exists over a physical medium. A multipath is a routing technique that can use multiple alternative pathways through an existing network. A channel can be assigned in any of the following ways:

- **Unichannel single sequential access.** There is one channel and it is shared among many stations, one at a time (time slotted), based on a predetermined order. This scheme ensures that data doesn't contend with other traffic on the network, but is inefficient as there is no prioritization of the data being sent.

  Unichannel technologies aren't efficient for full-duplex operations, but are fine for half-duplex operations. However, there is no additional channel for sending a message between endpoints, which introduces some inefficiency into the system.

- **Unichannel tokenized access.** The token scheme uses a metaphor of passing the baton from one station to the next. The station with the token gets network access and then uses an algorithm to determine whether to use the access rights or pass it along. Tokenized networks do not suffer contention, and they allow for very large data transfers; however, they run at slower speeds than other broadcast methods.

- **Unichannel multiple access with collisions.** All stations broadcast data onto the network; there are no time slots or master clocks. When two pieces of data arrive at the same time at the same end station and a collision occurs, collision correction mechanisms force retransmission of the data.

- **Carrier sensing.** Stations broadcast onto the network when they determine that the network is quiet. This reduces, but does not eliminate, collisions and is more efficient than a situation where no carrier sense detection technology is used.

- **Multichannel broadcast.** A multichannel broadcast offers the most throughput and is more efficient for full-duplex operations. On a multichannel network, one channel can be sending data while the other is either controlling the process or messaging, which adds extra efficiency. Multichannel networks require additional buffering and caching, and extra coordination. They also allow for dedicated channels.

Ethernet

Ethernet is the dominant wired network technology in use on LANs today. The standard defines frames broadcast over Physical Layer media and Data Link Layer signaling methods based on Carrier Sense Multiple Access with Collision Detection (CSMA/CD). Ethernet is defined by the IEEE 802.3 standard. Nodes on an Ethernet network are identified by the globally unique 48-bit MAC address. There are two classes of network nodes on an Ethernet network:

- **Data Terminal Equipment (DTE).** This category includes any component that represents the target or source of an Ethernet frame. Computers, servers, printers, and other devices of this kind are sometimes called *end stations*.

- **Data Communications Equipment (DCE).** Any network device that receives and forwards Ethernet frames is a DCE. This includes switches, routers, bridges, repeaters, and any network interfaces such as NICs or modems.

Note

A packet transmitted over a wire is called a frame.

Ethernet was developed at Xerox PARC in the 1970s where the CSMA/CD protocol was created by Robert Metcalfe, David Boggs, Chuck Thacker, and Butler Lampson. (Metcalfe went on to found 3COM.) The name Ethernet arises from the idea that the network was similar to the *ether*, derived from the Greek personification of the pure air or sky. In the development of science, various ethers are promoted as a transport medium for electromagnetism, light, gravity, as well as where matter disappeared to in early chemistry, and a host of other unexplained phenomena.

Cross-Ref

In Chapter 8, the various wiring standards used by Ethernet are described.

The Ethernet prototype ran at 3 Mbits/s and was designed to provide high network throughput even when the network was heavily loaded. In 1980, Digital Equipment Corporation, Intel, and Xerox created the first released version, Ethernet 1.0 (dubbed the DIX standard), which ran at 10 Mbits/s. The 802.3 standard is based on Ethernet 1.0.

An early version of Ethernet, called StarLAN, ran over unshielded twisted pair (UTP) and served as the basis for the early LANs, eventually categorized as 1BASE5 Ethernet. In the early 1980s, StarLAN was unique because you could use a standard RJ-45 telephone connector to use the wiring in a building as the network medium. Today this method is commonplace. The 10BASE-T adopted StarLAN's modulation scheme, its link detection, and its wiring assignments.

Cross-Ref

10BASE-T is covered in Chapter 8.

The name 10Base-T indicates both the speed of 10 Mbits/s and the transmission medium, which is twisted pair. For 100Base-T4, the speed would be 100 Mbits/s and the medium would be four twisted-pair cables. The 1000Base-LX refers to Ethernet using a long wavelength traveling over fiber optic cable. Ethernet uses the term *Base*, which is short for Baseband, a signal-filtering mechanism that is described in Chapter 5. Today Ethernet travels over broadband connections, with multiple data paths defined by frequency or amplitude without regard for the signaling rate, but it is rare to see the term 100Broad used even when high-speed connections are used, even though it is appropriate. The two other signaling methods of wideband and narrowband do not apply to Ethernet.

In Table 12.2 the various forms of 802.3 Ethernet standards are listed. The 802.3 standard codifies the important types of wired Ethernet that are so important for modern local area networks. The numbers in parentheses indicate the theoretical throughput that each standard has.

TABLE 12.2

802.3 Ethernet Standards

Substandard	Date	Purpose
Experimental Ethernet	1972	2.94 Mbits/s (367 KB/s) over coaxial cable (coax) cable bus
Ethernet II (DIX v2.0)	1982	10 Mbits/s (1.25 MB/s) over thin coax (Thinnet); frames have a Type field. This frame format is used on all forms of Ethernet by protocols in the Internet protocol suite.
IEEE 802.3	1983	10BASE5 10 Mbits/s (1.25 MB/s) over thick coax (Thicknet); the same as DIX except that the Type field is replaced by Length, and an 802.2 LLC header follows the 802.3 header.
802.3a	1985	10BASE2 10 Mbits/s (1.25 MB/s) over thin coax (Thinnet or cheapernet)
802.3b	1985	10BROAD36
802.3c	1985	10 Mbits/s (1.25 MB/s) repeater specs
802.3d	1987	FOIRL (Fiber-Optic Inter-Repeater Link)
802.3e	1987	1BASE5 or StarLAN
802.3i	1990	10BASE-T 10 Mbits/s (1.25 MB/s) over twisted pair
802.3j	1993	10BASE-F 10 Mbits/s (1.25 MB/s) over fiber optic
802.3u	1995	100BASE-TX, 100BASE-T4, 100BASE-FX Fast Ethernet at 100 Mbits/s (12.5 MB/s) with autonegotiation
802.3x	1997	Full Duplex and flow control; also incorporates DIX framing, and removes the DIX/802.3 split
802.3y	1998	100BASE-T2 100 Mbits/s (12.5 MB/s) over low-quality twisted pair
802.3z	1998	1000BASE-X Gbit/s Ethernet over fiber optic at 1 Gbit/s (125 MB/s)
802.3ab	1999	1000BASE-T Gbit/s Ethernet over twisted pair at 1 Gbit/s (125 MB/s)
802.3ac	1998	Maximum frame size extended to 1522 bytes (to allow "Q-tag"); the Q-tag includes 802.1Q VLAN information and 802.1p priority information.
802.3ad	2000	Link aggregation for parallel links
802.3ae	2003	10 Gbits/s (1250 MB/s) Ethernet over fiber; 10GBASE-SR, 10GBASE-LR, 10GBASE-ER, 10GBASE-SW, 10GBASE-LW, 10GBASE-EW.
802.3af	2003	Power over Ethernet
802.3ah	2004	Ethernet in the First Mile
802.3ak	2004	10GBASE-CX4 10 Gbit/s (1250 Mbits/s) Ethernet over twin-axial cable
802.3an	2006	10GBASE-T 10 Gbit/s (1250 MB/s) Ethernet over unshielded twisted pair (UTP)
802.3ap	2007	Backplane Ethernet (1 and 10 Gbits/s [125 and 1250 MB/s] over printed circuit boards)

continued

TABLE 12.2	*(continued)*	
Substandard	**Date**	**Purpose**
802.3aq	2006	10GBASE-LRM 10 Gbits/s (1250 MB/s) Ethernet over multimode fiber
802.3as	2006	Frame expansion
802.3at	2008	Power over Ethernet enhancements
802.3av	2009	10 Gbits/s EPON (Ethernet Passive Optical Network)
802.3az	2007	Energy-Efficient Ethernet
802.3ba	2009	Higher-Speed Study Group. 40 Gbits/s over 1m backplane, 10m Cu cable assembly (4x25 Gbit or 10x10 Gbit lanes) and 100m of MMF and 100 Gbits/s up to 10m or Cu cable assembly, 100m of MMF or 40km of SMF, respectively.

Ethernet encodes its information in a timed sequence of signals that are distorted as they travel over the network. Sometimes the receiving system must filter the incoming data, compensate for drift (baseline wander), or synchronize the data to the correct clock rate in order to extract the data from the incoming signal. Different encoding schemes are used to fix these problems. Early Ethernet used Manchester encoding (described later in this chapter), while GigE moved to a system using forward error correcting codes. Only bit errors are detected by Ethernet; other errors are passed up the protocol stack for further error checking.

Ethernet frames

Frames are chunks of data that are packaged for transmission over a network. They are created in software at the Data Link layer where the data may have to be fragmented or padded to reach the appropriate size for that frame's format. The data portion, sometimes called the *payload*, is wrapped or encapsulated with a number of starting and ending bits that represent additional information on what the data is, where it comes from and goes to, error checking or diagnostic features, and more. Ethernet frames are the prototypical example of the use of frames on a network. You don't need to be on a packet-switched network like TCP/IP and the Internet to use frames, although that is probably the best-known example.

Frames are helpful because they provide a context in which a receiving system can understand the data that is being sent and interpret it. From the standpoint of any system listening to the network, signals are being received nearly all the time, depending upon current network utilization. A starting sequence, once recognized, provides the timing and synchronization required to know when the first bit starts and how long the frame is. The following features are characteristic of nearly all frame structures that you will encounter:

- Frames have a purpose: some transmit data, others give commands, and others provide information or messages.
- Frames have starting and ending sequences or fields called delimiters.

- Frames generally contain a character count field that indicates the size of the frame and is part of the error-checking mechanism. Some frames are defined to be of uniform length and don't require a character count field, as it is built into the standard.

- Data fields may be variable or fixed length, and may or may not be required, depending upon the frame's purpose. It may be necessary to pad the data field (usually with zeros) to achieve a certain field length, also referred to as *bit stuffing*.

- An error-checking sequence is included that is used to determine the validity of the data sent.

Error checking is a critical function in frame transmission, as there is no other way to be completely certain that a frame arrived correctly at its destination. On a frame network, different frames are meant to be separated by a quiet period between frames, but that is not a reliable frame delimiter. If two frames arrive at a destination at roughly the same time (a collision), it may appear that they both belong to the same frame — that is, until the data is error checked. Even with error checking, some errors creep into the system, but those additional errors (usually in the data itself) are left to the higher-layer protocols to diagnose.

You are used to 8-bit character assignments based on translation tables such as ASCII, but this octet size is just one possible way of representing characters. Larger character sets use wider bit representations, with Unicode being a prime example. There is no reason why 8-bits or even a multiple of 8-bits are used as characters or words, and from a network standards perspective, there needs to be flexibility when it comes to the number of bits. That is one reason why frame data is delimited and bit stuffing is used to bring the data up to a required length.

Figure 12.1 shows the portion of the OSI reference model that corresponds to the various Ethernet networking component protocols. Ethernet defines protocols at the OSI Physical level (Layer 1) and the OSI Data Link Layer (Level 2). Different Physical layer protocols are used depending upon whether the wiring used is copper-based or fiber-based media. While both media types use the same MAC addressing, the different sublayers that connect the medium to the MAC layer vary based on media type, as shown on the right of the figure.

FIGURE 12.1

Ethernet layers and their relationship to the OSI model

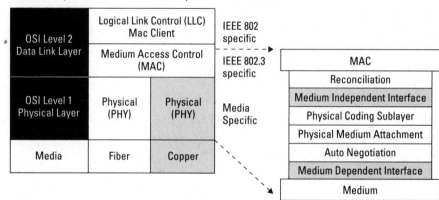

The Medium Access Control (MAC) layer is where data encapsulation and media access control is performed. This includes frame sequence, assembly, and error detection, both during reception and after verification. The MAC portion initiates frame transmission and provides the means to retransmit frames when errors occur.

The Logical Link Control shown is the MAC client and applies when the end station is a Data Terminal Equipment (DTE) node. Above the MAC client are the upper-layer protocols such as TCP/IP and others. However, if the MAC client is a bridging unit or Data Communications Equipment (DCE) device, then there are no upper-layer protocols, and the connection is Ethernet-to-Ethernet.

Frame structure

Ethernet frames consist of up to 11 different fields transmitted serially without any spaces or gaps. Figure 12.2 shows the structure of an Ethernet 802.3 frame with 11 fields that serve the following purposes:

- **Preamble (PRE).** A sequence of 7 bytes of 10101010 that serves to alert receiving end stations that a frame follows. The alternating pattern helps to synchronize the medium-dependent interface of the Physical Layer.

- **Starting Delimiter (SD).** The start-of-frame delimiter is the 1-byte sequence 10101011 with the final two ON bits of 1 indicating that the next bit starts the Destination Address field.

- **Destination Address (DA).** A 6-byte field that indicates the end station or group of end stations (multicast) to which the frame is directed. The first bit is a 0 when the address is to a single end station or a 1 when it is directed to a group. The final bit is a 0 when the address is globally administered or a 1 when it is locally administered. The middle 46 bits are the unique MAC address of the destination: an end station (unicast), group of stations (multicast), or all stations (broadcast).

- **Source Address (SA).** A 6-byte field that indicates the sending station. The first bit is always 0, and the address is 46 bits long.

- **VLAN Type ID (VT).** This optional 2-byte field specifies that the frame is a VLAN frame. (VLAN is discussed later in this section.) For VLAN to operate, all the end stations involved require that this feature be operational.

- **Tag Control Information (TCI).** This optional 4-bit field for VLAN gives the priority of the frame and the VLAN group ID that the frame is meant for.

- **Length/Type (LT).** A 2-byte field that indicates the size of the data field (46 to 1500 bytes) or that can be used to give the frame type ID for an optional format by using a value greater than 1536.

- **Data.** The payload being transmitted, from 46 to 1500 bytes. When the data is smaller than 46 bytes, it must be padded with zeros in order to bring the length up to 46 bytes.

- **Padding to Length (PAD).** The PAD portion of the Data field adds enough non-data characters (typically zeros) to bring the frame up to the standard length.

- **Frame Check Sequence (FCS).** A 4-byte field that has a 32-bit CRC (Cyclic Redundancy Check) value used to check for errors. Figure 12.2 shows the bits that are used to generate the CRC as indicated by the bar at the top of the figure labeled FCS Generation Span. The fields below that bar are used to generate the CRC value and placed into the FCS field just to the right of the included fields. Since the FCS Generation Span plus the FCS field are used in error detection, the second bar from the top labeled FCS Error Detection Coverage (CRC) indicates the portion of the frame used for error checking.

- **Extension.** The 12-byte Extension field is a non-data field used to make it easier to send Ethernet frames over Gigabit Ethernet networks. It is set to 416 bytes for 1000Base-X and 520 bytes for 1000Base-T.

FIGURE 12.2

The structure of an Ethernet (802.3) frame

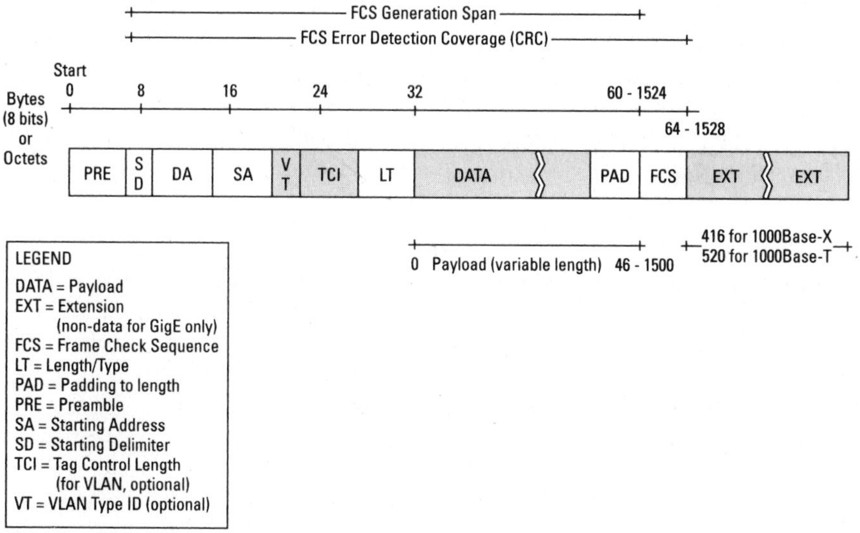

Ethernet frames vary, depending upon the type of Ethernet network, although all follow the general format shown in Figure 12.2. Among the various versions of Ethernet frames that have been used are Novell's Raw 802.3 frame (no LLC header), IEEE 802.2 LLC, 802.2 LLC/SNAP, and Ethernet II (version 2). To support these different versions, the Length/Type field (also referred to as the EtherType field) is added into the MAC header just after the Source Address field. With the EtherType field specified, it is possible to have different versions of Ethernet running over the same network concurrently.

Burst mode

With the advent of Gigabit Ethernet, a high-speed burst mode was added to CSMA/CD. In burst mode, a sequence of bursts is transmitted up to about 8192 bytes (65,536 bits), enclosing multiple frames separated by interframe gaps (IFGs). Using frame bursts, a source can control the network longer and get up to three times more throughput for small frames than GigE could normally attain. Only GigE can be bursty; slower versions of Ethernet do not support the Extension field that maintains control of transmission by suppressing other stations from sending data. Figure 12.3 shows a GigE frame burst, with the carrier cycle indicated by the longest length that can carry a maximum burst.

FIGURE 12.3

Gigabit Ethernet burst mode

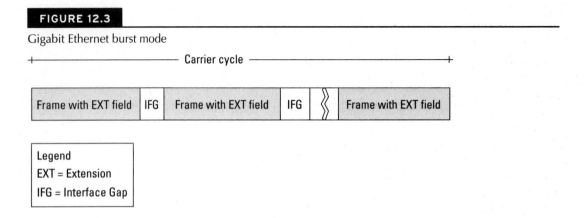

VLAN frames

A VLAN, or virtual LAN, is a set of nodes that are grouped into a logical broadcast domain that is independent of their physical locations. Data sent from a node on one network to a node on another network appears as if the remote network is part of the local network. VLAN traffic can be prioritized, grouped, and administered from a single console. A VLAN is a Layer 2 definition of a segregated grouping and is used to create the equivalent of subnets on Layer 3 of IP networks.

Cross-Ref

Products based on a VLAN are described in Chapter 16.

To support a VLAN's features, two fields are inserted into the Ethernet frame just before the Length/Type field (EtherType). The first field is the 2-byte VLAN Type ID field, which identifies the frame as a VLAN frame; the second field is the 2-byte Tag Control Information field, which contains a priority number from 0 to 7 (highest) and the VLAN ID (group identifier). When Ethernet frames are tagged with VLAN fields, all nodes participating in the VLAN must have that option installed.

Carrier Sense Multiple Access with Collision Detection

Carrier Sense Multiple Access with Collision Detection (CSMA/CD) is a half-duplex communications protocol that used to allow the traffic from many nodes to broadcast over a common medium concurrently. It was meant to be an alternative to token-based networks and to allow a network to be used as close to its capacity as it could be. Because it is possible to have two or more stations send an Ethernet frame that overlaps, the receiving station may not be able to detect the different bit streams, and an error occurs. This type of error is referred to as a *collision*. CSMA/CD provides for error detection and recovery when collisions occur.

The name is derived from the following:

- **Carrier Sense.** This provides the rules needed so that end stations can determine the start and end of frames based on transmission gaps.

- **Multiple Access.** Any station can transmit on the network when it detects that the network is quiet.

- **Collision Detection.** When two (or more) sending stations detect that a collision has occurred, they must resend the frame after a period of time that is determined by a back-off algorithm that generates a pseudo-random number.

Ethernet CSMA/CD networks exist in one of three states:

- **Transmission.** Data is traveling from source to destination over the network.

- **Quiescence (idle).** No data is in transit.

- **Contention (collision).** Data from two sources are traveling over the network at the same time.

Collisions on Ethernet networks occur all of the time; the higher the network utilization, the higher the percentage of frames that are involved in collisions. However, it has been demonstrated that Ethernet can still attain a throughput of 90 percent of its theoretical carrying capacity because of the use of recovery that CSMA/CD provides.

Longer network runs lead to time differences in the detection of collisions by different stations. It is this fact that sets the maximum run length for Ethernet, which is balanced by the frame size that was chosen. When Ethernet moved to faster standards (100 Mbits/s and greater), the time delay for collision detection shrank, and this balance of run length and frame size needed to be altered. For 100 Mbits/s Ethernet, the decision was made to keep the frame size the same and reduce the run lengths, while for 1 GigE, the run length was kept the same as 100 MHz, and an extension field was added to the end of the Ethernet frame. This non-data Extension field makes it appear as if the frame is larger than it is, and was set to 416 bytes for 1000Base-X, and 520 bytes for 1000Base-T. Table 12.3 summarizes frame sizes and connection lengths for different Ethernet speeds.

TABLE 12.3

Ethernet Frames versus Run Lengths1

Factor	10 Mbits/s	100 Mbits/s	1000 Mbits/s
Minimum frame size	64 bytes	64 bytes	416 bytes for 1000Base-X and 520 bytes for 1000Base-T
Maximum collision diameter2	100 UTP	100 UTP 412m fiber	100m UTP 316m fiber
Maximum distance allowed between repeaters	2500m	205m	200m
Number of repeaters allowed in a path	5	2	1

1. Calculated for half-duplex operation. 2. The maximum collision diameter is the longest distance between any two stations (DTEs) in any collision domain.

To transmit an Ethernet frame using CSMA/CD, the following sequence occurs:

1. The frame is prepared for transmission.

2. The carrier (medium) is sensed for activity by the sending station.

3. If the medium is idle, then transmission occurs. If the medium is busy, then transmission is delayed for a period that is determined by the protocol, which in Ethernet is called the interframe gap (IFG), interframe spacing, or interpacket gap (IPG).

4. The sending station monitors the wire to determine if the bits it receives back are the same as the bits it sent, which is a test for a collision. When collisions are detected, the sending system or systems stop transmitting and perform a collision remediation scheme, as described in the next procedure. The mechanism in this step is important because it limits the amount of time that a wire is captured by any one sending station.

5. Upon acknowledgment from the end station, the sending station ends transmission and sets the CSMA/CD counters to zero.

The IFG is the minimum idle time that must be observed on an Ethernet network before a device is allowed to send a frame. This quiet period allows other devices to reset their network stacks so that they can receive the frame that is about to be sent. The length of the gap is protocol dependent. Typical values are:

- 10 Gigabit Ethernet (10 GigE) — 9.6 nsec (nanoseconds, 10-9 seconds)

- 1 Gigabit Ethernet (1 GigE) — 96 nsec

- Fast Ethernet (100 Mbits/s) — 960 nsec

- Ethernet (10 Mbits/s) — 9.6 msec (microseconds, 10-6 seconds)

These numbers are not inviolate. Network interface card vendors with faster chip sets often reduce the IFG to improve data throughput. The Intel EtherExpress PRO/100B NIC is an example of a card that uses this feature. Network repeaters, devices that amplify signals for longer-distance transmission, also shrink the IFG. As frames arrive at their destinations, network conditions can also act to reduce the IFG due to transit of a repeater, packet assembly en route, or network congestion. The IFG can tolerate a reduction that is equivalent to 40 bit times (5 bytes) for 10 GigE, 64 bit times (8 bytes) for 1 GigE, or 47 bit times for 10 Mbits/s Ethernet.

Upon detection of a collision, CSMA/CD performs the following steps:

1. Sends additional packets so that all receivers detect a collision.
2. Raises the CSMA/CD counter.
3. At maximum transmission, attempts ceiling abort transmission.
4. Pauses for an amount of time, based on how many collisions were detected.
5. Starts over transmitting the frame, as is described in the previous procedure.

Full-duplex operation

Faster versions of Ethernet have tended to switch from CSMA/CD half-duplex communication to full-duplex communications. In a full-duplex connection, data travels in both directions without collisions. This allows for faster transmission, smaller Ethernet frames due to the elimination of the Extension field, and a network bandwidth that is roughly two times greater. Frames sent over a full-duplex point-to-point connection are separated by interframe gaps (IFG), just the way they would be on a half-duplex network, and frames are transmitted as they become ready at the sending station.

To make full duplex practical, Ethernet has to enforce flow control at the switch or router so that network congestion is avoided, and separate frame buffers must be established for data traveling in each of the two directions. A pause frame is transmitted at the receiving node and sent to the sending station when the rate of dropped packets is detected beyond a certain threshold. Pause frames are constructed so that they are unique and can't be processed beyond the MAC client layer.

Full-duplex communications and flow control can be used on any type of Ethernet and at any speed. In order for this method to be implemented, the link involved must have the appropriate physical layer equipment needed to support the full-duplex mode.

Token Ring Networks

In a relay race, one runner passes the baton to the next runner, who then runs to the next station and hands the baton off once again. In a token-based network, the baton is a token frame that gives the right to send data on the network from one node to the next. The time that any one node has control over traffic is short. Because there is only one node that is communicating, token-based networks don't suffer from the inefficiencies of collisions and dropped data, and they can send data in much larger chunks than Ethernet can. In order to have periodic or cyclic data access, token-based networks are always built as topological rings, as shown in Figure 12.4.

On the left in Figure 12.4 is a single token ring wired into a single MAU or Multiple Access Unit. A MAU is a routing device with an In port, a number of additional ports (numbered 1–6 in the figure), and an Out port (shown on the right). Each dot is a node having two wires, one for incoming and another for outgoing data. Data traffic travels in one direction around the ring. You can expand a token ring by adding multiple token rings together as shown in the figure on the right.

FIGURE 12.4

A token ring's logical topology (left), and four rings concatenated together (right)

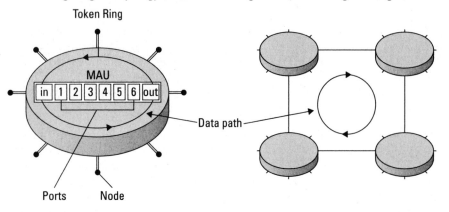

IBM developed Token Ring networks in the late 1970s at the same time that Ethernet was being developed at Xerox PARC and that ARCnet was being deployed. The original Token Ring standard has a line speed of 4 Mbits/s compared to the 10 Mbits/s Ethernet of the time. In 1989, a 16 Mbits/s Token Ring standard was introduced. Token Ring networks had a competitive performance advantage over Ethernet early on because, even though they ran at slower speeds than Ethernet, they could transmit much larger packet sizes, resulting in greater throughput.

That early advantage of Token Ring networks over Ethernet was squandered by the higher prices of the switches and network adapters, and by the fact that all competing Token Ring technologies, such as the ones Apollo Computer and Proteon introduced, wouldn't interoperate with IBM's version. The IEEE 802.5 standard is based on the IBM Token Ring but generalizes it so that it isn't dependent upon a particular media type or topology.

ARCnet largely disappeared from the LAN marketplace in the mid-1980s, displaced by Ethernet, although it remains in limited use in the embedded systems market. Fast Ethernet (100 Mbits/s) also overtook Token Ring technology. By the time Fast Ethernet appeared, switch vendors had developed methods to significantly reduce collisions on Ethernet networks. The lower cost of implementing Ethernet removed Token Ring technology's chance to dominate the LAN marketplace. Today, you are hard-pressed to find Token Ring technology anywhere outside of an IBM-based shop. However, Token Ring technology has played an important role in the development of network technology and continues to have an influence on the development of future network technologies, and so a brief discussion on how it works is valuable.

Token Ring networks are logical rings in the sense that the wiring is looped from the point of attachment back to the switch. In the case of IBM's Token Ring, the switch is called a Multiple Station Access Unit (MAU or MSAU). If you were to install a Token Ring network, you would begin by locating the MAU in a central location such as a wiring closet, and then run a wire from the MAU to each of the hosts (called end stations) on your network.

The network is a physical star topology, with spokes radiating outward from a central hub. The "ring" of the Token Ring network is implemented inside the MAU. Each host is connected by a Type-1 twisted-pair wire called a *lobe cable*, a hermaphroditic connector which, taken together, is IBM's Structured Cabling System. Token Ring networks span the OSI data model from the Physical Layer through the Network Layer to include Data Link Layer components. Each MAU has an input port and an output port, which can be used to expand the token ring.

Figure 12.5 shows a set of four token rings that have been concatenated together to form a larger network. Each MAU can connect to six end stations, but for clarity, only two are shown connected to a MAU. Figure 12.5 is the physical implementation of the topological figure shown on the right side of Figure 12.4. Note that there are patch cables that extend the Token Ring. Those patch cables run from each MAU and connect all four MAUs. Data travels in one direction on the patch cable, but in two directions in the lobe cables. An exploded view of the lobe cable is shown in the lower center of Figure 12.5.

The token in a Token Ring network is a 3 (8-bit) byte frame that is passed from one node to another. When a node has network control, it can send a data frame. When that data is correctly received at the destination node, that node converts the data frame to a token frame and transmits that token frame to the next node on the network. While the data/command frame is circulating, no other tokens can be on the network unless the network supports a feature called *early release*. On a 4 Mbits/s Token Ring network, only a single token could be passed, but on the 16 Mbits/s standard, several tokens could be circulating on the network concurrently. The system essentially eliminates frame collisions, which makes it a very robust network with predictable data delivery.

FIGURE 12.5

A network of four concatenated token rings

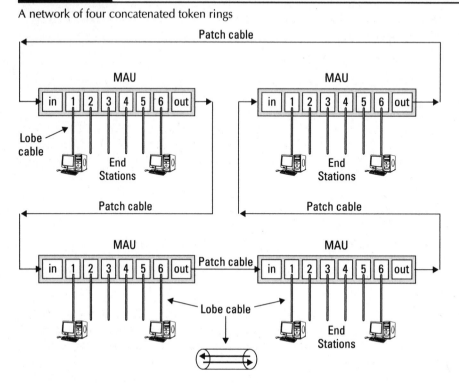

Token rings implement traffic control using a priority bit, set to between 0 and 7. When a node receives a token that has a priority that is less than its own, the node changes the priority bit and retransmits the token. The token passes around the network until it reaches a node with the highest priority setting. At that point, the token is changed to the highest setting, and sent around the ring until it returns to the highest-priority node, which then receives a data frame. After the data has been received, the token's priority is reset to the value it had when it first arrived at the node with the highest-priority setting. In this manner, nodes are serviced based on their priority settings.

Figure 12.6 shows the structure of a Token frame, a Data or Command frame, and an Abort frame. The Data or Command frame carries a payload that can be any size up to 18,200 bytes. The Starting Delimiter (SD) field, shown at the bottom of Figure 12.6, shows the different values that it stores. Those values set the priority that the data transmission has, which is used to control which source has access to the network at the moment. The SD field also provides the token, as well as the values required to provide the Quality of Service functions provided by the value of the Monitor value as well as the Reservation value.

Token ring frames use a time-based encoding method called *Manchester encoding*, which maintains clock rate by providing a data transition (1 to 0 or 0 to 1) at a regular interval. To create a Manchester code, you would perform an XOR (exclusive OR) of the clock and the data, as shown below for a four-digit number:

Data String: 1100

Clock String: 1010

XOR Manchester code: 0110

Manchester encoding has also been used in Ethernet but has given way to differential Manchester encoding (Conditioned Diphase), where the data and the clock signals are synchronized. In differential Manchester encoding, it is the transition itself that encodes the logical value. The strings are combined as follows:

Data String: 11001100

Clock String: 10101010

Differential Manchester code: 10100101

Differential Manchester encoding is part of the 805.2 Token Ring protocol specification and is used in IBM's Token Ring.

Because there is always the possibility of network errors, an end station called an *Active Monitor* is always evaluating the state of the token and correcting any errors it detects. Because this is a mission-critical function on a Token Ring network, a backup or standby monitor can be deployed. When two token rings are joined, one monitor is selected to be the active monitor, and only that station monitors the network. Election of a new active monitor can also be initiated when there is no signal on the network, when the active monitor isn't detected, or when a token frame isn't detected within a certain time period. Any end station can be a monitor, as it is built into the Token Ring protocol.

The Active Monitor plays a critical timing role in a Token Ring network. It runs the network clock, inserts a buffering delay, suppresses token circulation when a data/command frame is being sent, and ensures that tokens are indeed circulating. A Token Ring algorithm called *beaconing* tests the network and creates a beacon frame when a fault is detected. Beaconing can initiate an auto-reconfiguration, which is essentially a diagnostic or reboot of the MAU. During a beaconing operation, data cannot be passed over the token ring.

Token Ring networks are not the only networks that use tokens. FDDI networks, which are described in the next section, are the other major example of token-based networks.

FIGURE 12.6

Token Ring frame structures

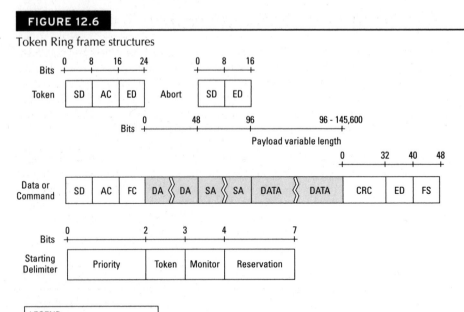

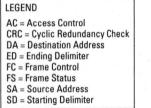

LEGEND

AC = Access Control
CRC = Cyclic Redundancy Check
DA = Destination Address
ED = Ending Delimiter
FC = Frame Control
FS = Frame Status
SA = Source Address
SD = Starting Delimiter

Fiber Distributed Data Interface Networks

Fiber Distributed Data Interface (FDDI) is a Token Ring network protocol that is used to create high-speed Local Area Networks. The protocol is specified as the IEEE 802.4 standard, and the technology is the ANSI standard X3T12. FDDI is differentiated from 802.5 Token Ring networks by its use of a timing mechanism for token exchange. FDDI uses optical fiber as its physical medium; a related technology using the same protocol but with copper wire is referred to as CDDI. Figure 12.7 shows how different portions of the FDDI protocol correspond to the OSI reference model.

In Figure 12.7 the two OSI layers are labeled in the left column above the Media layer. The Token Ring protocol has the SMT spanning the Physical Layer and part of the Data link layer. By contrast, although the Logical Link Control layers for FDDI and Token Ring protocols are the same, the Station Management Task portion of Token Ring is split into a MAC layer and into different and separate Physical layer protocols. Depending upon whether FDDI uses fiber- or copper-based media (wiring) the protocols are PMD and PHY or TP-PMD and TP-PHY, respectively.

FIGURE 12.7

The relationship of the FDDI protocol to the OSI model

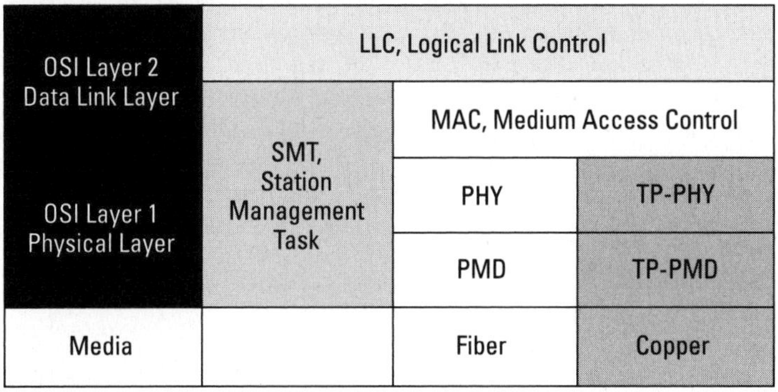

OSI Layer 2 Data Link Layer	LLC, Logical Link Control		
	SMT, Station Management Task	MAC, Medium Access Control	
OSI Layer 1 Physical Layer		PHY	TP-PHY
		PMD	TP-PMD
Media		Fiber	Copper

LEGEND

PHY = Physical, signal timing and encoding

PMD = Physical Medium Dependent Interface, converts electical signals to light waves

SMT = Station Management Task, includes Ring Management (RMT), Configuration Management (CFM), Connection Management (PCM), Physical Configuration (PCM), and Entity Coordination Management (ECM)

TP = Twisted Pair

There are two types of devices that are defined on an FDDI network:

- **Stations.** Stations are computers, printers, and other active devices. They can be Single Attached Stations (SAS) or Dual Attached Stations (DAS).

- **Concentrators.** Concentrators are devices that connect an SAS to the FDDI network. When connected to a ring, concentrators are Dual Attached Connectors (DACs) and have three port types: A (Primary ring), B (Secondary ring), and M (Master). Concentrators can also be Single Attached Connectors (SACs), and through their M port, connect to the single Slave (S) port of a SAS.

There are three different connection types:

- **Single Attached Stations (SAS).** SAS devices.

- **Dual Attached Stations (DAS).** DAS are ring connected and must be operational for the ring to be fully functional.

- **Dual Homed.** Dual homed has a concentrator or DAS connected to two other concentrators. It is equivalent to two SAS links.

As shown in Figure 12.4, where the token ring exists within an MAU, FDDI rings also are implemented inside Dual Attached Concentrators. This allows for a simple stand-alone FDDI ring structure. If you have a Dual Homed concentrator, then you can create fault-tolerant paths to Dual Attached Stations. Both of these scenarios are shown in Figure 12.8. M-S connections can be either fiber optic or UTP cabling. In Figure 12.8 the primary ring is indicated by the dark lines in the figure while the secondary ring is indicated by the gray lines. Data travels in the directions indicated by the arrows at the head of the line.

FIGURE 12.8

A stand-alone concentrator versus a Dual Homed concentrator

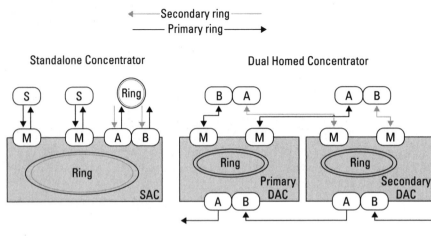

To add more nodes to an FDDI network, you connect the one or more AB ports on a root concentrator to other concentrators and iterate this connection; this creates a hierarchical tree of concentrators. You can also create a ring of trees by replacing a root concentrator with a dual FDDI ring structure. The ring-of-trees topology is often used for campus-wide LANs. In many instances, FDDI networks are connected to Ethernet networks to create a mixed network type. Mixed networks require that FDDI/Ethernet IP routers be placed as the edge devices separating the three network types — tree of concentrators, ring of trees, and mixed FDDI/Ethernet networks.

Figure 12.9 shows these three topologies. The three different network types illustrate different approaches to utilizing FDDI in increasingly larger types of network. FDDI can be used as a backbone of concentrators as shown in the Tree of Concentrators topology. The Ring of Trees topology allows for a hierarchical fan out of FDDI with each concentrator on the main ring serving the function of a root in its particular tree. Each level in the Ring of Trees is referred to using the name Primary, Intermediate, and Horizontal distribution frames. You can also create a mixed FDDI/ Ethernet network by combining an FDDI ring with connections to Ethernet networks through FDDI/IP routers.

FIGURE 12.9

Three different types of FDDI network topologies: Tree of concentrators, ring of trees, and mixed FDDI/ Ethernet network

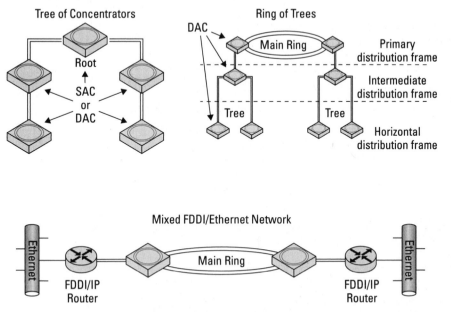

FDDI has been widely used in the telecommunication industry as a core network system but is being displaced by high-speed Ethernet, as have other Token Ring networks. Version 2 of the FDDI standard (FDDI-II) added circuit switching to this network type. There has been a considerable investment in FDDI networks in the past, and they are used for both voice and video transmission. FDDI networks are now often connected to Synchronous Optical Network (SONET), which is used as a backbone for modern high-speed networks.

Cross-Ref

SONET is described in Chapter 13.

FDDI is constructed using two token rings, each sending data in opposite directions; these dual-ring networks are often deployed in room-sized LANs. The primary ring runs at 100 Mbits/s and the counter ring either performs backup or adds another data channel to the network that extends the throughput of the network to 200 Mbits/s. FDDI network interfaces on FDDI routers connect to both rings, making them dual-homed or dual-attached systems. Hosts connecting to an FDDI network are single attached. As is the case with other optical networking systems, devices called concentrators allow multiple hosts to communicate through the network using a single fiber connection.

If the second token ring is configured to be a backup, and ring connections are dual homed, then the network can fail over to the secondary ring should the primary active token ring suffer a broken connection. Figure 12.10 shows an FDDI network that has suffered two points of failure: a failed cable and a failed Dual Attached Station (DAS). One point of failure leaves the network functional; a second point of failure divides the network into two smaller networks.

FIGURE 12.10

FDDI is a highly fault-tolerant high-speed LAN; even two faults simply segment this basic dual-ring network.

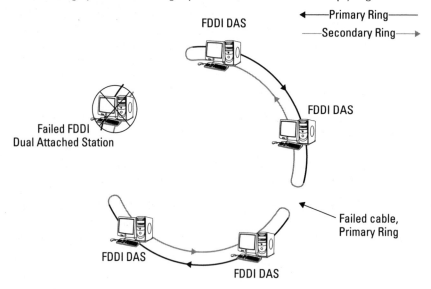

FDDI is notable for its combination of speed, potential long-distance connections, and high host connection count. FDDI can connect to 500 DAS or 1000 SAS nodes. Optical cable runs for an FDDI link can be up to 125 miles (200 km) and are for networks that have thousands of connected users. The rings themselves can be half that distance, 62 miles (100 km). This distance is the reason that FDDI is a very popular Metropolitan Area Network (MAN) technology.

CDDI (FDDI over copper wire), by comparison, has a maximum rated throughput of 16 Mbits/s, and a maximum connection length of 250m for shielded twisted-pair (STP), or 72m for unshielded twisted-pair (UTP) wiring.

Automation Networks

Networks don't just exist to connect computers, although the bulk of this book is dedicated to computer networks. Networks exist to connect a wide variety of devices. Cars and planes have networks, which are LANs with a set of connected computers, a host of sensors, and other devices that make them very sophisticated systems. You only have to watch a mechanic hook up an automobile diagnostic handheld computer to appreciate how useful networked components are.

If you have been interested in smart houses, you may be familiar with the X10 standard for home automation, which is described in the following section. Go into any modern high-rise building and you will probably find that the HVAC (Heating, Ventilation, and Air Conditioning) and lighting systems are computer controlled, often from a single console or computer. More generally, you will find that network systems are built to sense and control all manner of industrial equipment. Automotive assembly-line robots, pharmaceutical plant recipes, railroad train movement, package tracking, and other activities form networks that rely on control functions to operate.

All of these automation networks find different ways of abstracting networked devices from the software that is used to detect and control them. Some networks connect sensors, switches, valves, and activators to network hubs or switches that can recognize the output of device drivers on network devices. If you connect those switches to a computer or a network of computers, software can be used to analyze the signals and send commands that control these devices. Systems of this type are sometimes referred to as Human Machine Interface (HMI) systems, or alternatively, Supervisory Control and Data Acquisition (SCADA).

The methods that these computers use to discover network devices are often industry standards that you've already learned about, such as SNMP. The devices used to aggregate automated device signals and distribute commands, sometimes referred to as Programmed Logic Controllers, may communicate using proprietary software or open standards such as Sun's Java, Microsoft's OLE, DCOM, or even .NET Framework components.

Many of these types of networks are proprietary to the manufacturers that build these systems, but there are some network types that open standards. In the sections that follow, you'll learn about some of the more successful open standards, how they are implemented, and where they are used.

X10 and home automation

The X10 standard is an open standard for signal communication and control of devices over power lines. It is widely used to automate homes by creating home automation networks that have been dubbed *smart homes* or *domotics*. X10 defines a protocol for radio transmission signals over a carrier wave. Very short low-power RF bursts are transmitted synchronously with the power line signal such that the signal which corresponds to the power wave's inflection points (zero amplitude) is a logical one, and any inflection point without a signal is a logical zero.

Because the signal is at a higher frequency than the carrier wave, the signal is actually repeated two times between inflection points, between 0 and π, and two more times again between π and 2π. Those additional signals are used for timing and aren't measured as an X10 signal, although they do play an important role. Many encoding schemes don't simply rely on a signal being recognized as a 1 or 0. Instead, what they do is to have two signals, the first bit of which is the signal and the second bit of which is a synchronization bit. To generate a 1, not only must the first bit be a 1, but the second bit must also be a 0; that is, a High-Low signal pair is recognized. For a 0, the first bit would be 0 and the second bit would be 1 — a Low-High signal pair. It is that transition that makes the bit boundaries easier to locate and less prone to error. Figure 12.11 shows the carrier wave and signal, with a 1 msec bar indicated as part of the legend below the figure.

If you have an X10 controller, either a remote control or a virtual button on a console, and you press a button, a binary code is transmitted over the power line. The code is a set of three binary identifiers: a START CODE (4 bits, 1110), HOUSE CODE (8 bits), and CONTROL CODE (10 bits), which defines an X10 frame. The CONTROL CODE can be a NUMBER CODE or FUNCTION CODE and uses alternating inflection points to encode its binary signal, ignoring the bit in between. Figure 12.12 shows a sample encoding, which requires 11 full cycles and illustrates the full length required by a CONTROL CODE for transmission. The different lengths and spacing of the codes make them all unique and make it possible for a translation table to be built.

The X10 standard has a complete set of the codes sent twice back to back, a space of three power line cycles, and a repeat of the codes. Also, any time commands are used that are sent to different devices, there must be three cycles of null bits transmitted. The codes for bright and dim settings are meant to be sent continuously with no spacing between the codes, and with at least two and preferably more repetitions. Table 12.4 shows the X10 translation code.

X10 works by plugging a receiver unit into a power outlet in your house, and then plugging the device being controlled into the X10 receiver. Devices can be lights, televisions, temperature controllers, fans, and other household appliances. Different devices require different types of X10 modules. In some cases, modules are designed so that they have local control and can be turned on by a physical switch. Many light modules also have a feature called *local dimming*, which allows for the light to be turned on and off through progressive settings. Figure 12.13 shows some of the devices that can be controlled in an X10 network inside a home. For example, the hose shown at the lower right of the figure is controlled by a metering switch that is plugged into an X10 switch.

FIGURE 12.11

X10 radio signals on a power line carrier wave

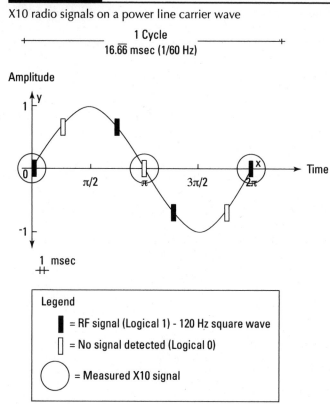

Legend

▮ = RF signal (Logical 1) - 120 Hz square wave

▯ = No signal detected (Logical 0)

◯ = Measured X10 signal

FIGURE 12.12

An encoded X10 signal. The intermediate timing signals have been omitted for clarity.

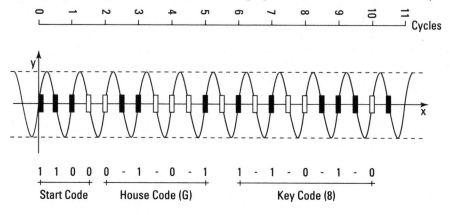

1 1 0 0   0 - 1 - 0 - 1   1 - 1 - 0 - 1 - 0

Start Code   House Code (G)   Key Code (8)

FIGURE 12.13

Some of the devices inside a home that can be controlled by an X10 network

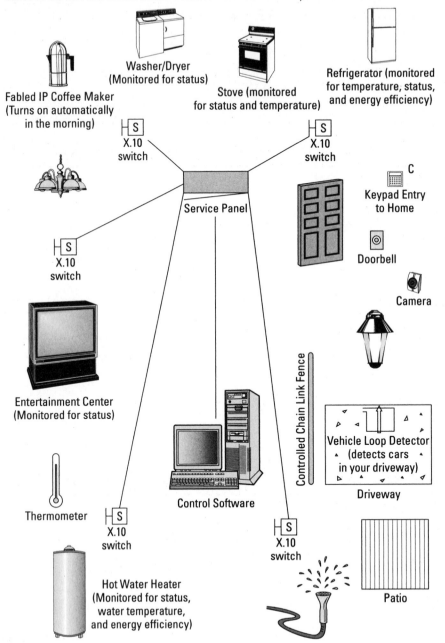

Each X10 receiver is assigned a unique address so that it can receive signals. The X10 transmitter can be a remote control keypad, or it can be a software program on a PC that is interfaced to the X10 system through a transceiver that is also plugged into a power outlet. When a keypad is used, it uses one of the command codes shown in Table 12.4 to communicate with specific devices.

TABLE 12.4

X10 Command Codes

Code	Bit 1	Bit 2	Bit 3	Bit 4	
START	1	1	1	0	-
House Code	**Bit 1**	**Bit 2**	**Bit 3**	**Bit 4**	
A	0	1	1	0	
B	1	1	1	0	
C	0	0	1	0	
D	1	0	1	0	
E	0	0	0	1	
F	1	0	0	1	
G	0	1	0	1	
H	1	1	0	1	
I	0	1	1	1	
J	1	1	1	1	
K	0	0	1	1	
L	1	0	1	1	
M	0	0	0	0	
N	1	0	0	0	
O	0	1	0	0	
P	1	1	0	0	
Key Codes	**Bit 1**	**Bit 2**	**Bit 3**	**Bit 4**	**Bit 5**
1	0	1	1	0	0
2	1	1	1	0	0
3	0	0	1	0	0
4	1	0	1	0	0
5	0	0	0	1	0
6	1	0	0	1	0
7	0	1	0	1	0

continued

Key Codes	Bit 1	Bit 2	Bit 3	Bit 4	Bit 5
TABLE 12.4 *(continued)*					
8	1	1	0	1	0
9	0	1	1	1	0
10	1	1	1	1	0
11	0	0	1	1	0
12	1	0	1	1	0
13	0	0	0	0	0
14	1	0	0	0	0
15	0	1	0	0	0
16	1	1	0	0	0
All units off	0	0	0	0	1
All lights on	0	0	0	1	1
On	0	0	1	0	1
Off	0	0	1	1	1
Dim	0	1	0	0	1
Bright	0	1	0	1	1
All lights off	0	1	1	0	1
Extended code	0	1	1	1	1
Hail request1	1	0	0	0	1
Hail acknowledge	1	0	0	1	1
Preset Dim	1	0	1	-	1
Extended Data Analog	1	1	0	0	1
Status On	1	1	0	1	1
Status Off	1	1	1	0	1
Status Request	1	1	1	1	1

1. Three blank cycles between each pair of transmissions is required, except for dim and bright.

In software, devices can be programmed up to the limit of the sophistication of the program. They can be used to control home theaters with custom-made interfaces, run event schedules, log events, send messages upon events, and almost any other action you can think of. Among the best-known home automation software programs are Central Home Automation Director (CHAD) Software, HAL 2000 Voice Control Software, Home Controls, HAI Web-Link, HomeSeer Software, Indigo, PowerHome, Smarthome Manager PLUS, Superna ControlWare, and Thinking Home.

The X10 protocol also allows for radio frequency devices such as keypads, keychains, burglar alarms, IR switches, and other devices. In the U.S. the radio frequency is 310 MHz, and in Europe it is 433 MHz. A radio receiver provides the bridge needed to transmit X10 commands over the wired network. Some of the devices that can be on an X10 network are shown in Figure 12.14.

Devices inside and outside a house that can be controlled by X10

Tip

Perhaps the best-known commercial Web site for home automation products is www.Smarthome.com.

While X10 is the best known of the home automation networking systems, there are many other systems in use that you might want to consider. These alternatives include INSTEON, UPB, ZigBee, and Z-Wave. Table 12.5 lists some of the standards used in home networks and compares them to different computer standards.

TABLE 12.5

Common Home Automation Networks

Network Type	Medium	Throughput	Connection Limit
Bluetooth	RF	1 – 10 Mbits/s	10 – 20m
Ethernet	UTP or fiber optic	10 Mbps – 1 Gbits/s	100m – 15 km
HomePlug	RF over power lines	14 – 200 Mbits/s	200m
HomePNA	Telephone line	10 Mbits/s	300m
INSTEON	RF over power lines		
IRDA	Infrared	9.6 Kbits/s – 4 Mbits/s	2m (line of sight)
LonWorks	UTP, RF over power lines, RF, IR, or Ethernet	1.7 Kbits/s – 1.2 Mbits/s	1,500 – 2,700m
Wi-Fi (IEEE 802.11)	RF	11 – 248 Mbits/s	30 – 100m
X10	RF over power lines	50 – 60 bits/s	500m
Z-Wave	RF	9.6 – 40 Kbits/s	30m
ZigBee	RF	20 – 250 Kbits/s	10 – 75m

In Table 12.5 the different types of home networking automation systems are described. Networked automation also plays an essential role in industrial systems as well. In the section that follows, different process control systems for industry are described.

Process control systems

Industrial automation networks that control processes are most often built with some form of distributed control system (DCS). An industrial process control might include controlling oven temperatures in a bakery, part delivery on an assembly line, lights on a factory floor, or any other controllable feature of a plant or factory. Elements of the network are deployed at the point of service for the devices that they monitor and/or control. These network elements provide output through a bus to an aggregation/translation device where the signals from the different elements can be converted into a form that is compatible with the network that the control system is on. DCS systems are used in chemical plants, electrical power grids, HVAC, oil refining and transportation, pharmaceuticals manufacturing, sensor networks, vehicles, water treatment and management, and hundreds of other industries.

The best way to think about a DCS system is that there are usually two networks involved, connecting three layers of devices. The distributed part of the system is the group of sensors, controls, actuators, and other devices that are performing their role in the systems that the network is meant to control. This defines what can be called the device layer.

Figure 12.15 shows a process control system. In this type of system, a control console or SCADA system (Supervisory Control and Data Acquisition) is used to interact with the automate system. The SCADA typically shows a graphical HMI or Human Machine Interface display indicating the current state of the system and allowing an operator to make modifications. Commands go to the PLC or Programmable Logic Control, as does the input and output of data from connected devices. The PLC connects to devices that send data (output devices) or that take data (commands) such as the input devices shown. This is a distributed architecture with a top level network such as Ethernet, a device bus, and a layer of devices.

Simple processors or ASICs in these devices transmit what are called field signals, and many receive and process controls using a wire protocol that the devices understand. These field signals that are transmitted can be analog or digital values, Booleans (ON or OFF, 1 or 0), arrays of values all updating in real time; data can flow out of many devices in a flood in such a large amount that only a small percentage of the signals may be sampled. Many sensors sample their circuits and output values at a rate in the millisecond range, creating hundreds of values per second. Software that collects the data and graphs it or creates a historical log file for later replay or analysis will usually discard most of the data, and sensors send and sample it in manageable intervals.

The device layer is connected through a device bus to a module that serves to multiplex/demultiplex the field signals. These modules go by a number of names, depending upon the protocol, technology, vendor, and other factors. One common type of aggregation device is a Programmable Logic Controller, or PLC. PLCs are special-purpose computing devices with extensive I/O capabilities. They were developed in the late 1960s in an effort to integrate automation in the automobile industry in a way that would expose devices to a multivendor solution.

PLCs are real-time devices that take the input from distributed devices and make that data available to control systems. Some PLCs have internal logic that allows them to maintain a steady state using a feedback loop created with the data from a connected device. For example, if you had a reactor that required a certain temperature, the PLC would read the field data from a temperature sensor and then adjust the voltage to a heating element appropriately.

A PLC often serves as the interface between two or more heterogeneous network types. PLCs allow for multiple I/O connections, can read analog or digital data, respond to limit settings, and can control motors, cylinders, relays, solenoids, and many other devices. The "programmable" portion of the name refers to the ability of these devices to accept commands from other devices. PLCs may be configured with RS 232 or RS 485 serial ports, RJ-45 Ethernet, and other connections. Most PLCs are not only configurable, but also expandable. They come as chassis into which you insert PLC modules with the interface that you need.

FIGURE 12.15

A process control network with three different network layers

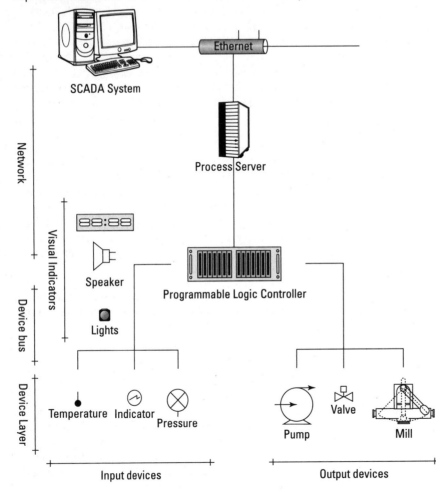

PLCs often communicate with devices using a protocol such as Modbus or DF1, or with a variety of field buses such as DeviceNet or Profibus. There are many proprietary protocols and buses that are in use. Among vendors of PCL systems are ABB, Allen-Bradley, IDEC, Honeywell, Omron, General Electric, Mitsubishi, Siemens, and others.

Not all DCS systems rely on PLC-type devices. Some technologies require extremely high speed control signals that PLC devices can't keep up with; aircraft controls are a good example. Some automation tasks are repetitive and can be automated using mechanical timing devices at much lower cost. Devices called Remote Terminal Units (RTUs) were used in place of PLCs and have very similar characteristics, but RTUs lack the ability to be as extensively programmed as a PLC and are now less commonly used. Increasingly though the functions of PLCs and RTUs are merging.

These days, the differences between DCS, PLC, and RTU-based systems are rather hard to discern. I tend to associate DCS systems with large, expensive, and proprietary industrial automation networks. Some of the projects can run into the millions of dollars. PLCs tend to work with the newer open system standards that are vendor independent. "Open" automation systems are not open in the usual sense in that they are not platform independent. That is, with open standards, while you can mix and match hardware and software vendors, the technology is locked onto a particular network interapplication communication architecture. One technology is Microsoft's OLE for Process Control (and later DCOM), which spawned the OPC standards for automation systems. Automation systems have been built around Java, the .NET Framework, and other standards.

The third part of a DCS system, beyond the devices and the device bus, is the network containing the control software, which includes the SCADA software. SCADA software can be implemented as command line software but is more typically developed into graphical displays called HMIs that can be secured and locked in a manner that allows an operator to observe, maintain, or control systems at the level of access and privilege that the developer allows. A SCADA system built on top of an operating system such as Microsoft Windows would make full use of the modern object-oriented programming, offering fine granularity of control: users and groups, object security ACLs, scripting, and other features.

In the next sections you learn about two of the more important and commonly used device buses: Modbus and BACnet, as well as the OPC standards for data communication over Windows networks.

Modbus

Modbus is the most commonly encountered serial data communications protocol in use on automation networks. This open standard was first published in 1979 by Modicon (now part of Schneider Electric) for use with their PLC systems. Versions of Modbus exist for serial port links and Ethernet, and the protocol can be transported over a TCP/IP network. There are variants of Modbus in use, including a lightweight version Modbus RTU (which encodes data in binary), Modbus ASCII (which translates data into readable but verbose text), Modbus+, or MB+ (which is Modicon's proprietary version of the protocol), and Modbus/TCP for Ethernet. The different types of network connections for these different versions of the Modbus protocol and network types are shown topologically in Figure 12.16.

In Figure 12.16 the Modbus protocol can be run over different network types. At the top the horizontal TCP/IP network (usually Ethernet) runs Modbus. Three switches above this network connect left to right to a control station (HMI) and to different devices, PLCs, and network storage systems (drives). Modbus can also run over other network types. Shown on the left, Modbus has been deployed over a MB+ network, in the center it is deployed over a serial bus network RS 232, and finally on the right Modbus is deployed over the two-wire half-duplex multipoint serial network designated as RS-485.

FIGURE 12.16

Different types of Modbus networks and the connections that they support

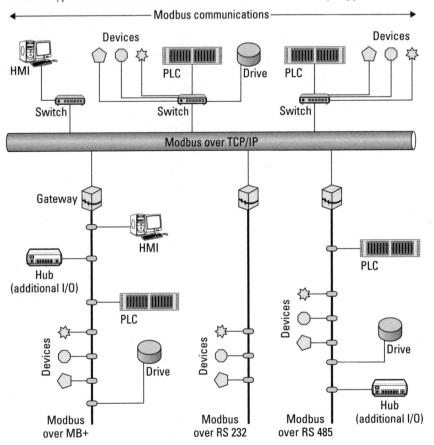

All forms of Modbus data use checksums to validate the data sent and require that the data stream be sent without gaps in the data. Therefore, Modbus devices that receive data over the wire must buffer out the gaps before either acting on the data or retransmitting it. Figure 12.17 shows a general Modbus frame. Address and Error Check are transport data that is added by the Transport layer protocol to create the Application Data Unit (ADU) frame. Contained within the ADU is the simple Protocol Data Unit (PDU), which is independent of the communication layers. The function code field is a set of values from 1–255 that tell a server what type of action to perform on the data that the frame contains. The data field is sent from client to server devices and contains additional information that the server uses to perform the action. The data can be items such as discrete or register addresses, number of quantity of items, and field byte counts, among other things. The data field can also be left out, indicating that the server's action is the default action and does not take any additional input.

FIGURE 12.17

A general Modbus frame

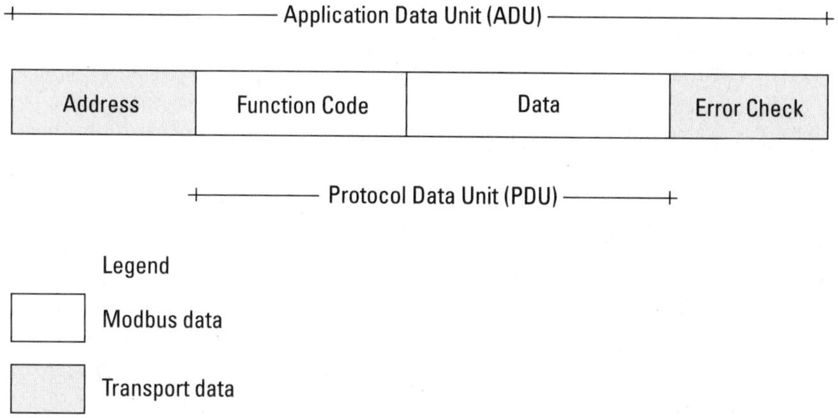

Legend

Modbus data

Transport data

On a Modbus, bus devices are assigned a unique address, with up to 247 devices on a single Modbus. Depending upon the Modbus type, devices can be in a master/slave relationship, or if they are on Ethernet, a peer-to-peer relationship. A master system is the only one that can initiate commands on the bus. Typical commands alter a value setting at the PLC or RTU, read or set a value stored in a register (address in memory), read a value in real time from a port I/O, and perform other actions.

Note

To read the Modbus protocol specification, go to www.modbus.org/specs.php.

The data types used on Modbus (and other wire protocols) are:

- Floating point
- Boolean
- 8-bit and 32-bit data (32-bit is a Modbus extension)
- 32-bit Integer
- Exponential multipliers
- Mixed data

- 16-bit Word
- Binary Large Object Binary (BLOB) data (on other buses, but not Modbus)

If you had a switch that could be either open or closed, then that switch would store its condition as a 1 or 0 in its assigned register. To change its state, the supervisory station would issue a command to switch the value to 0 or 1, respectively. That value would then generate an action such as a voltage change that forces the switch to open and close.

BACnet and LonTalk

The Buildings Automation and Control Networks data protocol, called BACnet, is an alternative to Modbus. This is an open standard that is supported by ANSI, ASHRAE (American Society of Heating, Refrigeration and Air Conditioning Engineers), and ISO. The BACnet standard predates Modbus, and when it was released in 1996 it was adopted by a number of vendors in the building automation industry.

BACnet was designed to be an object-oriented protocol with both device and object name and attribute discovery built in. The defined object types include the following: Analog Output and Value; Binary Input, Output, and Values; Event Enrollment Command; Device; File; Multistate Input and Output; Notification Class; Program; and Schedule. BACnet communications can be transported over ARCNET, BACnet over IP, Ethernet, Point-to-Point (P2P over RS 232), Token Ring (Master-Slave over RS 485), and LonTalk. BACnet is vendor independent and does not require any special hardware support.

LonTalk protocol predates both Modbus and BACnet and, although it was once a proprietary protocol of the Echelon Corporation, it is now an open ANSI standard. It is often mentioned as an alternative to both of these other protocols and is used in industrial, home, transportation, and building automation. The name comes from Local Operating Network, and the protocol depended upon an ASIC called the Neuron Chip. There are now multiple processors that are sold that support LonTalk.

OPC

Microsoft's Object Linking and Embedding interapplication communications technology became the basis for the automation control industry OLE for Process Control (OPC). The process control industry developed OPC standards to exchange process data using Windows servers and clients. The OPC standards are developed by the OPC Foundation (www.opcfoundation.org) and define a set of methods (interface and protocols) for accessing data from devices on a network. OPC provides an open ("Microsoft-centric") standards-based approach for connecting data sources such as PLCs, controllers, I/O devices, databases, and so on with HMI client applications for graphics, trending, alarming, and other applications.

As Microsoft's networking technology moved from the Common Object Model (COM) to Distributed COM (DCOM), the OPC standard evolved with it. Applications using OPC were expressed as a set of ActiveX controls that could be added to a container object. Today, OPC embraces the .NET Framework with a version of OPC called OPC-Universal Access, or OPC-UA, that is under active development.

A number of versions of OPC exist, including:

- OPC Data Access (OPC-DA), which is used to connect to real-time data from devices
- OPC Alarm & Events (OPC-AE), which allows event data to be processed
- OPC Historical Data Access (OPC-HDA), which is an event- and data-logging standard
- OPC Batch, which is the standard used to automate batch processes
- OPC Data eXchange, which is used for server-to-server communications, monitoring, configuration, and management
- OPC Commands, which sends control commands to devices
- OPC XML-DA, which defines an interchange format for real-time data
- OPC Security, which is a technology for securing OPC data selectively from clients
- OPC Complex Data, which allows for communication of binary data and XML
- OPC Unified Architecture, which is the newest technology based on the .NET Framework

The three most important standards are OPC-DA, OPC-AE, and OPC-HDA.

OPC provides the interface between client and server applications by providing a universally supported and well-documented mechanism to communicate data from a data source to any client application. The standard includes the methods used to pass the data, as well as specific information on other attributes to supplement those data, such as range information, data type, quality flags, and date and time information. OPC servers collect the data from OPC devices aggregated at a PLC and make that data available to clients on a network. Figure 12.18 shows what an OPC network looks like.

In Figure 12.18 a three-tiered OPC network is shown. The topology is similar to the one you saw in Figure 12.15, except that the three different levels are inverted in this figure. At the bottom level is shown the client layer with an HMI (Human Machine Interface) control system. The alarm event viewer displayed on the monitor is shown at the bottom right. The client accepts event data and sends commands over the LAN to a variety of OPC servers that represent the middleware layer. In the OPC Server layer are shown an OPC Data Access (DA), Horizontal Data Access (HDA), Alarms & Events (AE), and Universal Access (UA) servers. Those servers take data from the Device layer or send commands from the Client layer to the Client layer and Device layer systems, respectively.

FIGURE 12.18

An OPC client/server network

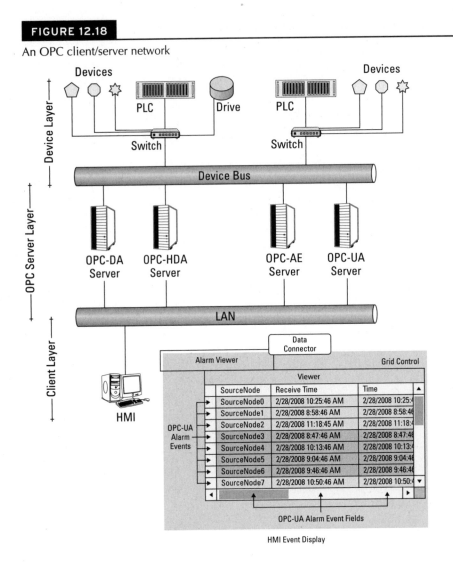

HMI Event Display

The developing OPC-UA standard unites OPC-AE, OPC-DA, and OPC-HDA (Historical Data Access) into a complete specification. OPC-UA adopts a Service-Oriented Architecture (SOA) with an application model, namespace, and security scheme based on the Windows .NET Framework Architecture. OPC-UA has the following features:

- Data buffering, where data is transmitted and acknowledged so that its delivery is ensured.
- Data redundancy with alternate pathways, failover to mirrors, and other technologies.

- Heartbeat signals that provide a timing function that establishes the state of a connection and additional actions.

- A Security Model, which defines an access mechanism to OPC data based on authentication and authorization, and which uses encryption and access through a certificate and signature model.

- An Address Space Model that allows data sources and their values to be mapped.

- Backward compatibility to Data Access, Alarms, and Conditions, and Historical Access servers.

- Services and Service Mappings that allow data sources to be managed by a network or internetworking service model. Communication is through a set of OPC-UA APIs (for .NET, Java, and so on) that allow applications to access these services.

Summary

In this chapter, you learned about different types of Local Area Networks and the technologies behind them. Ethernet, Token Ring, FDDI, X10, and different industrial automation bus standards, as well as all IEEE 802.x standards were detailed. Ethernet is a frame-based broadcast network. You learned why frames are used, and how they are constructed.

Token Ring networks use a special token frame to give network access to end stations. Fiber Distributed Data Interface (FDDI) networks are token rings that use optical fiber to create high-speed systems.

This chapter also looked at different automation networks. X10 RF over power-line networks can automate a home. Industrial networks use different technologies. Those networks aggregate the data from sensors, actuators, switches, valves, and other devices and make that data available to computers running monitoring and supervisory (control) software.

In the next chapter, you learn about Wide Area Networks, or WANs. WANs are characterized as being a collection of networks (internetworks) or networks with long-distance links.

Wide Area Networks and Backbones

A Wide Area Network, or WAN, is a collection of networks connected through a public service or covering a large geographical area. To enable a WAN requires a routing or switching technology and a set of protocols that create paths from one point to another. There are four kinds of WANs: circuit switching, packet switching, cell relay, and leased lines.

The Public Switched Telephone Network (PSTN) is used as an example of a circuit switching network. The PSTN is built hierarchically. Different methods for connecting to the PSTN for data services are described. In particular, two of the most popular connection types, ISDN and DSL, are described in detail. The backbone technologies for connecting networks are through T- and E-carrier networks. Different standards and grades exist, and the higher-speed grades require optical fiber cables. SONET/SDH is the most popular protocol for data transfer on these backbones. Data that flows over SONET can be in the form of Asynchronous Transfer Mode (ATM) or Packet over SONET (PoS).

Packet switching networks define endpoints but not the routes. IP networks are built from packet switching, with the Internet being the prime example. Protocols such as X.25, Frame Relay, and ATM, which are used on packet switching networks, are described in this chapter.

The Internet is an internetwork or group of internetworks that consist of predominantly TCP/IP traffic. The connection points of the Internet are Internet Exchange Points (IPX). The Internet2 Network, a high-speed next-generation 10 Gbits/s backbone, and the capabilities it enables, are briefly described.

What Is a WAN?

A Wide Area Network, or WAN, is a network of networks, or internetwork, that has a broad geographical reach. WANs link Local Area Networks (LANs) together through the use of links maintained by a public service provider. When a WAN is confined to a small geographical area such as a business park or university, it is sometimes referred to as a *Campus Area Network* (CAN). WANs defined by their coverage of a city are called *Metropolitan Area Networks* (MANs). The name WAN is often used interchangeably with CAN or MAN to indicate the multi-network aspect of the internetwork. The telephone system is a WAN. The Internet is the ultimate example of a WAN.

There are two essential aspects of WAN technology that you need to be familiar with. The first is the manner in which LANs are linked and data is transferred, the connection type. When an interconnection is high capacity, it is call a *backbone*; the term is also applied to any circuit within a LAN that offers high capacity. The second function is switching and routing. Routers are used throughout networks, but the routers at the boundaries of networks, edge routers, are essential to determining the characteristics of a WAN. This chapter describes the various network protocols for the ISO/OSI Data Link layer and Session layer protocols (Levels 2 and 3).

Connections can be made over a variety of media and using a variety of different protocols. A key differentiation is whether the WAN uses the concept of a state in the form of a circuit or path and a mechanism for switching paths as the need arises; this is referred to as a *circuit switching network*. As a rule, the need to create dedicated circuits makes this type of network more expensive than networks where virtual circuits that are constructed on the fly are used.

Alternatively, a WAN can use a stateless mechanism where only the endpoints of the connection are defined and the route or path through the system is determined by an intelligent routing function. This type of WAN is a *packet switching network*, a packet being an encapsulation technique for data of different types. Similar to packet switching is cell relay technology. In a cell relay network, data and its formatting and addressing are divided into small, fixed-length data called *cells*, which are then sent over a switching or virtual circuit.

WANs can be divided into four broad categories:

- **Circuit Switching.** This is the type of WAN used by the phone company. It uses dedicated circuits between endpoints. There is overhead involved in provisioning the connection. Protocols that use this type of network include PPP (dial-up), ISDN, and DSL.

- **Packet Switching.** A packet switching WAN creates virtual circuits to send packets from one host to another, which allows many systems to share the same links. Transmission can be unicast (point-to-point) or multicast (point-to-multiple points). Protocols of this type include X.25, Frame Relay, and PoS.

- **Cell Relay.** Cell relays are similar to packet switching but use smaller fixed-length cells for data transport. The technology relies on synchronization techniques, which tend to make this slower due to overhead. The protocol most associated with cell relay is ATM.

- **Leased Line.** A leased line is a dedicated connection between two endpoints. Because traffic must come from a defined source and go to a defined destination, these WAN links are secure, often fast, and tend to be expensive. Lease lines use Data Link protocols as their control mechanisms.

No single network type dominates all WAN technology. The mixture is a compromise of cost, distance, reliability, and complexity. As a result, a host of technologies have been employed to enable WAN connections. Many were designed for the telephone company and then adapted to provide data services. Some technologies were fresh attempts to create high-speed networks. Others aimed at providing new services while retaining backwards compatibility to older standards.

Circuit Switching Networks

Circuit switching networks were the first type of WANs to be widely used. They arose from networks that carried voice communication, were analog, and generally involved low data throughput. The telephone system is the best example, but even earlier, you could consider telegraph lines to be a circuit switching network. Circuit switching networks today transfer both analog and digital data through a defined connection path. A network can also assign circuits to individual paths to an endpoint; that kind of network is referred to as a *dedicated circuit network*, as shown on the right in Figure 13.1. Alternatively, a network can create circuits as required from a set of available potential connections, which is referred to as a *virtual circuit network* (as shown on the left in Figure 13.1). The dedicated circuit is a set of defined stateful connections, whereas the virtual circuit creates circuits on the fly and tears them down when the data is passed through those connections.

Figure 13.1 shows the difference between these two network types. LANs can connect to the service provider using modems, multiplexers, channel service units (CSUs), or data service units (DSUs). CSUs and DSUs are network interfaces to the WAN.

Circuit switching networks build a circuit between two endpoints prior to data transfer; they use a cloud architecture where the path through the network can be drawn from a pool of available possible connections. Data is sent and received over that path, which is also referred to as a *channel*. Even though multiple data sources can be multiplexed so that they can be delivered on the same circuit over different channels, all circuit switching networks suffer from a certain degree of inefficiency due to the fact that some connections and channels are always idle. Weighted against that deficiency is the fact that a named connection imparts a certain guarantee of service without, or perhaps in addition to, any higher-level protocols that are used.

Some packet switching networks, which are covered later in this chapter, can behave as if they are circuit switching networks by creating a virtual circuit.

There is a latency involved with circuit setup (the call) and teardown that must be suffered over a circuit switching network. Most higher-speed circuit switching networks use control signals over a dedicated channel or channels to manage traffic, but it isn't a prerequisite. Low-speed networks, such as the plain old telephone service (POTS), do not reserve channels for signaling or data control.

FIGURE 13.1

Virtual circuits versus dedicated circuits in a circuit switching network

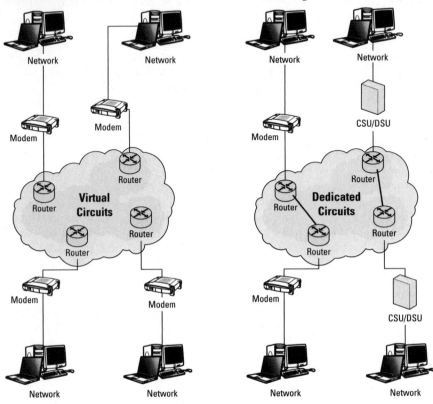

The Public Switched Telephone Network

Digital service networks also allow circuit switching networks (such as POTS) to interoperate with packet switching networks such as TCP/IP. Both networks can be used for telephony, but their requirements are different.

The network of circuit switching telephone networks is referred to as the *Public Switched Telephone Network*, or PSTN. PSTN interoperability is governed by the ITU-T standard; the telecommunications numbering plan that codifies telephone numbers uses the ITU-E.164 standard.

In the United States, the telephone network was controlled by AT&T until the early 1980s. AT&T organized the U.S. telephone network into a hierarchical structure that included five levels or classes. The telephone exchange represented the three-digit prefix for a seven-digit phone number, and was managed from end offices in Class 5. There were approximately 20,000 end offices at that time. Toll centers in Class 4 concentrated exchanges into primary centers in Class 3, where area codes were managed. Further concentration occurred in Class 2 Sectional centers, finally ending up at a regional center in Class 1. Class 1 centers were connected to the International Gateway Exchange. Each of these different office levels are switching centers. These categories are shown in Figure 13.2.

On January 1, 1984, AT&T was broken up to create the Regional Bell Operating Companies (RBOC), a set of seven companies called the Baby Bells. The original companies were:

- Ameritech
- Bell Atlantic
- BellSouth
- NYNEX
- Pacific Telesis
- Southwestern Bell
- U S West

There were two additional Bell System members that were non-RBOC companies: Cincinnati Bell and SNET, both of which AT&T owns minority interests in.

This breakup altered the nature of the Class 1 to 3 layers of the AT&T network so that today these layers aren't particularly relevant to phone internetwork architecture. Class 4 and Class 5 are still in use. After the breakup, the RBOCs worked together to create a number of new networking protocols that they could use as a group. Many of them were created by Bellcore.

Note

To read about the divestiture and evolution of the Regional Bell Operating Companies in more detail, go to http://en.wikipedia.org/wiki/Bell_System_divestiture.

Today the United States phone network has undergone considerable consolidation, and the following companies exist:

- **AT&T.** This was originally Southwestern Bell, which acquired AT&T and renamed itself. It also acquired BellSouth.
- **Qwest.** U S West was acquired by Qwest.
- **SBC.** Southwestern Bell changed their name to SBC and acquired Ameritech and Pacific Telesis.
- **Verizon.** They were originally Bell Atlantic and changed their name. They acquired GTE and NYNEX.

FIGURE 13.2

The original AT&T network system architecture

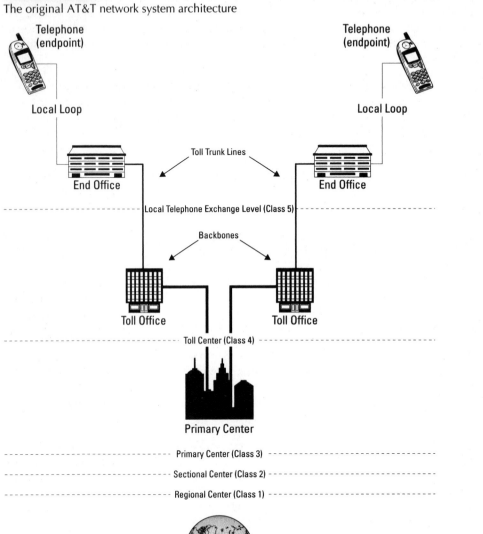

In a circuit switching network, a connection is made between two hosts as endpoints that remain in place while data is transferred. Depending upon network conditions, that circuit would likely be different every time you made a connection, but it would stay intact for the duration of the exchange. Circuit switching networks are stateful, and so their capacity is limited by the number of circuits that a system has. Each physical circuit has a limited number of connections that it can support, which can be large, but is limited.

On a packet switching network, data is fragmented and packaged into packets, and a virtual connection is made between two hosts as endpoints. The path that any single packet uses to travel to its destination is not important and can be individually different; what matters is the faithful reassembly of the data by the host. A packet switching network is stateless; their capacity is limited by the speed of the data transmission and by the efficiency of the methods used to encode the data.

The next two sections describes two of the more commonly used technologies for connecting networks to circuit switched networks: Integrated Services Digital Network (ISDN) and Digital Subscriber Line (DSL). Cable networks are also covered.

Integrated Services Digital Network

An Integrated Services Digital Network, or ISDN, is a telephone network service that is a means of sending digital data over circuit switching telephone networks. ISDN allows phone companies to support both voice and data communications over the same lines, thus making it an integrated service. When purchasing an ISDN connection, the user purchases data pipes in 64 Kbits/s slices; with IDSN, connections to the Internet are typically 128 Kbits/s in both directions.

ISDN connects to the PSTN network through either an ISDN modem or a network terminator (NT-1 or NT-2) and a terminal adapter (TA). The network terminator serves the function of a hub, and the TA serves the function of a NIC for the connection. ISDN is a dial-up technology; when you want to access the network, the ISDN modem dials the service and connects to the remote router, providing its Service Profile Identifier (SPID).

ISDN was one of the earliest forms of broadband connections for the home market but required that the customer be within 18,000 ft (3.4 mi or 5.5 km) of a central phone office. At distances farther than that, a repeater must be used, which makes the cost of providing the service to individual consumers expensive.

ISDN networks defined the following three interfaces:

- **Basic Rate Interface (BRI).** A 144 Kbits/s connection to copper telephone wire, BRI is segmented into two 64 Kbits/s data-bearing channels (B channels) and one 16 Kbits/s control or signal channel (Delta or D-channel). This format can be found in two- and four-wire connections, as a serial connection to a digital modem, or between a device and a TA.

- **Primary Rate Interface (PRI).** This is a 1,544 (23B) or 2,048 (30B) Kbits/s service that is carried over either T1 or E1 networks, respectively, using a single D-channel for its signal control path. PRI is used worldwide and is often used to connect the telephone network to PBX systems.

- **Broadband Integrated Services Digital Network (B-ISDN).** This was developed as an extension of ISDN in the 1980s. At the time, it was devised to support sending multimedia content such as video on demand and television, and as a high-speed data service for companies and scientific organizations such as universities and research labs. B-ISDN uses ATM for switching and SONET for high-speed networking. Neither ISDN nor B-ISDN achieved market success. B-ISDN is rarely used these days by any carriers.

ISDN can aggregate B channels into what are called *H channels*, as follows:

- H0 aggregates 6 B channels to 384 Kbits/s
- H10 aggregates 23 B channels to 1.47 Kbits/s
- H11 aggregates 24 B channels to 1.54 Kbits/s
- H12 aggregates 30 B channels to 1.92 Mbits/s

H12 is only available on E1 networks, mostly in Europe.

When ISDN was introduced in the 1990s, it was expected by the telephone industry to be the way most consumers would connect to the Internet. It did achieve some success in the United States, and more success in Europe, but nothing compared to early expectations. The PRI interface is widely used for telephone communications on telephone networks themselves, but the BRI circuits, which were optimized for data transfers, are more expensive and less popular than Digital Subscriber Line (DSL).

All of the forms of ISDN described in this section fall under the category of narrowband ISDN (N-ISDN). That differentiates these technologies from broadband ISDN (B-ISDN), which was discussed previously.

Digital Subscriber Line

Digital Subscriber Line, or DSL (originally Digital Subscriber Loop), is one of the most popular methods in use today for connecting to the Internet through the phone system, rivaled only by cable modems offered by digital cable TV networks, and perhaps WiMax (802.16) in the future. DSL was introduced in 1998 and has largely replaced ISDN.

The most common version of DSL in use is Asymmetric DSL (ADSL), but occasionally Symmetric DSL is encountered. ADSL operates at anywhere from 256 Kbits/s up to 6.31 Mbits/s, the speed of which is a function of the level of service you purchase from a provider and the line condition. Speeds are more typically found in a range between 512 Kbits/s and 1.54 Mbits/s for downloads and 128 Kbits/s for uploads. The assumption made with ADSL is that most of the time, users want to download information. By skewing the line so that downloads are faster, the service provider is speeding up the overall service and improving customer satisfaction.

One important factor that influences DSL is the distance that the subscriber is from the repeater or local office. DSL requires that the subscriber be within 18,000 ft (3.4 mi or 5.5 km) of a central phone office, which is the same requirement that ISDN has. This distance can be extended by the phone company if they install an optical fiber cable from the repeater or office to the loop. The phone company can also install bridge taps to increase the service length of their DSL loops. Another factor in performance is the quality of the copper wire; larger gauges are better because there is less loss to resistance.

With ADSL, the download speed is faster than the upload speed, while for SDSL, the speed in both directions is about the same. DSL first appeared over ISDN lines, a technology that is now referred to as IDSL. ADSL can not only be used on a telephone line but also works on an ISDN connection using BRI circuits.

DSL operates over the local loop on a phone line (plain old telephone system, or POTS) by sending data at a higher frequency than voice does. That higher frequency means that it doesn't interfere with voice data when they are both sent down the line to a DSL Terminal Adapter (commonly called a DSL modem). A DSL modem is more properly called an ATU-R transceiver and can connect to a firewall, router, or gateway, or a computer using either its Ethernet or USB connection. In most instances, people opt to use the Ethernet connection.

Typically, voice is below 4 kHz and data is above 24 kHz. To ensure that data transmission doesn't affect the phones connected on the same phone loop, a low-pass DSL filter is placed between any phone and the wall connection. This filter screens out all signals above 4 kHz (the upper limit of DS0, the voice band).

Some DSL types require the installation of a splitter, while others do not. The terms DSL Lite, G. Lite, and Universal ADSL refer to splitterless DSL technologies that can be split in the telephone office. For systems that require splitters, there are two main methods used. The Carrier Amplitude/ Phase (CAP) system shown in Figure 13.3 divides the phone signals into three bands:

- Conversations are carried in the 0 to 4 kHz band (just like POTS).

- The upstream channel is carried over the 25 to 160 kHz band.

- The downstream channel (from the server to the user) begins at 240 kHz and goes up to a point that varies, depending on a number of conditions (line length, line noise, number of users in a particular telephone company switch) but has a maximum of about 1.5 MHz.

An alternative, called the *Discrete Multitone* (DMT) system, uses an entirely different scheme, as shown in Figure 13.4. DMT divides the spectrum into 247 equal 4 kHz channels and then monitors each channel to ensure that the signal on that channel is good. As conditions change, DMT moves signals to different channels to optimize throughput and quality. The lower frequencies in the spectrum around 8 kHz are used for bidirectional traffic. CAP requires a lot of processing to operate, but makes much more efficient use of the bandwidth than the MDT system does. Most ADSL providers use the DMT systems on their lines.

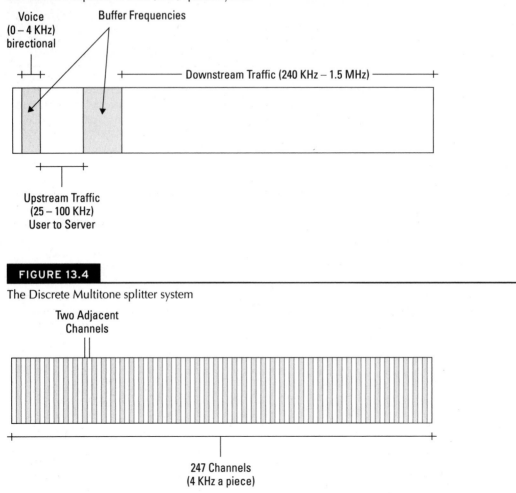

FIGURE 13.3

The Carrier Amplitude/Phase (CAP) splitter system

FIGURE 13.4

The Discrete Multitone splitter system

Table 13.1 summarizes the different forms of DSL that are available worldwide, along with their speeds, requirements, and limitations.

As cellular technologies become more popular, more people in the United States are choosing not to have landline phones in their homes. This has led the Federal Communications Commission (FCC) in the U.S. to mandate that telephone companies provide DSL service, regardless of whether phone service is chosen. The use of a phone line for DSL without a phone is referred to as either *dry-loop DSL* or *naked DSL*.

TABLE 13.1

DSL Types and Characteristics

DSL Type	Description	Data Rate (Downstream, Upstream)	Distance Limit	Application
ADSL	Asymmetric Digital Subscriber Line	1.544 to 6.1 Mbits/s downstream; 16 to 640 Kbits/s upstream	1.544 Mbits/s at 18,000 feet; 2.048 Mbits/s at 16,000 feet; 6.312 Mbits/s at 12,000 feet; 8.448 Mbits/s at 9,000 feet	Used for Internet and Web access, motion video, video on demand, and remote LAN access.
CDSL	Consumer DSL from Rockwell	1 Mbit/s downstream; less upstream	18,000 feet on 24 gauge wire	Splitterless home and small business service; similar to DSL Lite.
DSL Lite (G.Lite)	"Splitterless" DSL without the "truck roll." *Truck roll* is the use of a dispatched truck and technician to install or modify equipment on site.	From 1.544 Mbits/s to 6 Mbits/s downstream, depending on the subscribed service	18,000 feet on 24 gauge wire	The standard ADSL; sacrifices speed for not having to install a splitter at the user's home or business.
HDSL	High bit-rate Digital Subscriber Line	1.544 Mbits/s duplex on two twisted-pair lines; 2.048 Mbits/s duplex on three twisted-pair lines	18,000 feet on 24 gauge wire	T1/E1 service between server and phone company or within a company; WAN, LAN, server access.
IDSL	ISDN Digital Subscriber Line	128 Kbits/s	18,000 feet on 24 gauge wire	Similar to the ISDN BRI service, but data only (no voice on the same line).
RDSL	Rate-Adaptive DSL from Westell	Adapted to the line, 640 Kbits/s to 2.2 Mbits/s downstream; 272 Kbits/s to 1.088 Mbits/s upstream	Not provided	Similar to ADSL, the speed varies based on the length and quality of the phone line.

continued

TABLE 13.1	*(continued)*			
DSL Type	**Description**	**Data Rate (Downstream, Upstream)**	**Distance Limit**	**Application**
SDSL	Symmetric DSL	1.544 Mbits/s duplex (U.S. and Canada); 2.048 Mbits/s (Europe) on a single duplex line downstream and upstream	12,000 feet on 24 gauge wire	Same as for HDSL but requiring only one twisted-pair line. Requires exclusive use of the phone line for data, and so is mostly used for dedicated DSL.
UDSL	Unidirectional DSL proposed by a company in Europe	Performance of UDSL is some-where between ADSL and VDSL at longer distances; four times VDSL at short distances in some locations	Not known	Similar to HDSL. Introduced by Texas Instruments, this is a relatively new format.
VDSL	Very high Digital Subscriber Line	12.9 to 52.8 Mbits/s downstream; 1.5 to 2.3 Mbits/s upstream; 1.6 Mbits/s to 2.3 Mbits/s downstream	4,500 feet at 12.96 Mbits/s; 3,000 feet at 25.82 Mbits/s; 1,000 feet at 51.84 Mbits/s	ATM networks; fiber to the Neighborhood. Very fast, but works over short connec-tions.

Source: http://whatis.techtarget.com/definition/0,,sid9_gci213915,00.html.

DSL can be used on either bridged networks or routed networks; of the two, bridged networks are more common in homes. On a bridge network, a group of subscribers in the same locale share a single subnet. When traffic is high, bandwidth to individuals can be affected. To prevent this, DSL providers tend to implement usage limits; the higher-speed versions of DSL that are more likely to be used by businesses, such as HDSL and VDSL, tend to be routed networks. In these instances, DSL is more likely to be connected to DSL routers or DSL gateways, which add features such as routing control, firewalls, and other services.

As local loops of DSL subscribers are aggregated, they are connected to the backbone networks of the telephone network by connecting a Digital Subscriber Line Access Multiplexer (DSLAM). This device typically is placed in phone company offices, and multiplexes the input of multiple DSL loops into ATM, Frame Relay, or IP protocols. Some DSLAMs offer a mixture of multiplex conversions. DSLAMs are required on both ends of the communication, so that at the receiving end there must be a DSLAM to demultiplex the signals and route them.

Unlike the case with cable modems, where users share a common connection and are therefore affected by their neighbors' usage, ADSL provides a dedicated connection from the user to the DSLAM. The performance of one ADSL user does not impact the performance of another user on the same loop.

Cable network

Cable modem Internet connections are often compared to DSL services. Cable companies use hybrid fiber coaxial cable (HFC) networks to provide both fiber and coaxial connections to the customer. The coaxial portion carries the television service, and the fiber optical cable carries the data connection. Cable modems generally follow the Data over Cable Service Interface Specification (DOCSIS) standard, but implementations vary by cable provider.

Cable networks are shared multipoint circuits, which means that data is shared over the particular circuit. Security can be an issue on these networks, as your data is potentially viewable by neighbors. The performance of cable modems can be theoretically as high as 27 and 35 Mbits/s downstream, and 2 to 10 Mbits/s upstream. With typical loading, a cable modem usually performs around 2 Mbits/s downstream and 200 Kbits/s to 2 Mbits/s upstream. Cable networks' WAN features use the other technologies described in this chapter.

T- and E-Carrier Networks

Both circuit switching and packet switching networks use the concept of a channel to increase the capacity of the network. A channel is a path over a transmission medium that is either physically separated by using a multi-wire cable, or electrically separated by applying techniques such as Time Division Multiplexing (TDM, or time slicing) or Frequency Division Multiplexing (FDM). FDM over optical media is called *Optical Division Multiplexing* or *Wavelength Division Multiplexing* (WDM), which separates light with a diffraction grating.

With FDM, the available frequency spectrum is divided into discrete ranges, and all of these ranges become logical channels. AM radio provides an example of FDM, with each station representing a channel. Some countries allow AM band radio stations to create logical channels on the same frequency and to switch rapidly between the channels, which is an example of TDM. When you use Stereoscopic Liquid Crystal shutter glasses to view 3D video, the screen rapidly displays right and left images sequentially, an example of a two-channel TDM technology.

The L-carrier and coaxial cable connections used in mid-twentieth-century telephone networks could carry thousands of multiplexed voice connections over long distances using FDM. Over shorter distances, Bell used twisted-pair cables, such as the Bell System K- and N-Carrier media, that could enable 12 (double sideband) or 24 (single sideband) connections over four wires. To ensure signal quality, twisted-pair media required that the signal be amplified by repeaters every 10 km (6 mi) or so. DSL's use of Discrete Multitone (DMT) frequency switching is another example of FDM.

Modern telephone networks tend to use TDM. TDM is the method used in the Pulsed Code Modulation (PCM) systems, which are also referred to as Plesiochronous Digital Hierarchy (PDH) systems. PCM is the technology used on most digital networks today.

On a T1 line that uses the DS1 format, the T1 carrier is composed of 24 multiplexed channels. The point at which an analog signal is translated to a digital signal in the phone network is called a *codec*. Although different codecs multiplex in different ways, a common scheme is to have the different analog signal sampled consecutively and then interleaved into channels 1 to 24. The entire set of channels is then packaged into a frame, and that frame is then transmitted. The size of a frame is a function of the technology used. For an 8-bit signal, the frame would be 192 bits, plus one extra bit for framing code, or 193 bits. At a frequency of 125 μsec, the data rate would be 1.54 Mbits/s. An E1 line, by comparison, transmits 32 channels of 8-bit data sampled at a data rate of 2.05 Mbits/s and reserves of these channels for synchronization when data is transmitted instead of sampled audio.

As telephone lines converge, multiple T1 streams can be consolidated into higher carrier formats through the use of TDM. The scheme used in the United States is as follows:

- A stream of four T1 lines running at 1.54 Mbits/s concentrated into one line would form a T2 stream with a data transfer rate of 6.31 Mbits/s.

- When you concentrate six T2 streams into a single stream, you form a T3 stream that transfers data at the rate of 39.96 Mbits/s.

- Finally, seven T3 streams can be concentrated into a single T4 stream that would run at 274.18 Mbits/s.

Figure 13.5 illustrates this progression.

FIGURE 13.5

Consolidating T1 streams into higher order carriers

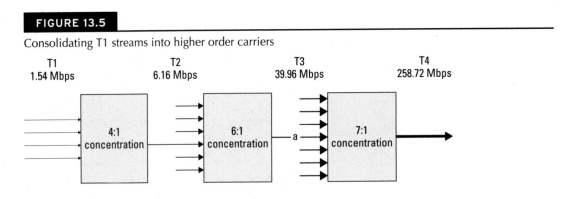

In Europe, the standard high-speed interconnect is called an *E-carrier*. It's a standard of the European Conference of Postal and Telecommunications Administrations (CEPT) and is analogous to the T-carrier standards used in the United States. T-carrier is a standard of the ITU-T. Table 13.2 compares T-carrier and E-carrier lines. E1 and E3 are the versions that are in common use, with E1 typically run over twisted-pair cables.

TABLE 13.2

T- and E-Carrier Speeds

T-Carrier Level	E-Carrier Level	DS Level	Throughput	Voice Channels (Circuits)
FT1	E0	DS0	64 Kbits/s	1
T1		DS1	1.54 Mbits/s	24
	E1		2.05 Mbits/s	30
T2		DS2	6.31 Mbits/s	96
	E2		8.45 Mbits/s	120
	E3		34.37 Mbits/s	480
T3		DS3	44.38 Mbits/s	672
	E4		139.27 Mbits/s	1,920
T4		DS4	274.18 Mbits/s	4,032
	E5		565.15 Mbits/s	7,680

T-carriers are used in the U.S.; E-carriers are used in Europe. FT1 stands for Fractional T1 line.

In digital telephone networks, PCM is used to carry multiple calls of four-wire, twisted-pair copper cables (either E-carrier or T-carrier) or fiber optic cable. Synchronous Digital Hierarchy (SDH) networks and the related, better-known Synchronous Optical Networking (SONET), use TDM to transmit over optical fiber. SONET is important for trunk lines on the Internet, as it allows several ISPs to transmit over the same optical line. The wireless GSM telephone system also uses TDM technology.

Synchronous Optical Networking

Synchronous Optical Networking, or SONET, is a high-speed TDM Physical Layer or wire standard (like the Internet Protocol). It is used for sending telecommunications data in the form of light over fiber optic cables on a circuit switching network. The digital data is created by pulsed lasers or by light emitting diodes (LEDs). SONET is used in the telephone system for their trunk lines, and with the use of a SONET chipset and an adapter board, you can connect a computer to a SONET network.

SONET arose from research done by the Baby Bell company Bellcore in 1985. A few years later, the CCITT's (International Telegraph and Telephone Consultative Committee) version of SONET became known as Synchronous Digital Hierarchy, with only a few additional extensions added. SONET is used in North America, while SDH is used worldwide, and the two can be used over the same network.

SONET/SDH also specifies wire standards for bitrates, jitter, isolation, and signal correction, as well as a set of network management protocols such as the TL1 telecom language. SONET/SDH devices are managed using framework applications with SNMP or another management protocol.

Note

Frame Relay, ATM, and Packet over SONET are each described in more detail in their own sections in this chapter.

SONET was designed to send voice data that could completely fill an entire 64 Kbits/s segment. With data of variable sizes such as packets, the TDM time slicing fills whatever remains in a DS0 segment with arbitrary data when the circuit isn't 100 percent utilized, leading to inefficiencies. The solution to this problem was the development of Frame Relay technology, which used statistical multiplexing to combine data and fill the SONET segments.

Frame Relay doesn't provide satisfactory QoS services and can't support higher-speed networks. To solve these problems, carriers have turned to ATM, which has enough QoS to provide connection quality and which could scale over fiber optic carriers. ATM is currently used on most SONET networks and satisfies the requirements of the slower optical carriers. However, on faster carrier grades, ATM suffers from overhead associated with translation of other transport protocols, such as Ethernet, into its cell structure. When a frame doesn't coincide with a cell boundary, the rest of the cell is padded to fill the cell; this creates an overhead called *cell tax*. At high speeds, ATM's efficiency falls off.

On the higher-speed optical networks that will be the WAN backbones of the future, the expectation is that ATM will be deprecated in favor of the PoS protocol. ATM and PoS can run on the same SONET network, as they are not mutually exclusive.

SONET architecture

SONET networks are implemented as a ring structure. A SONET connection is called a *path*, and each part of the connection is called a *section*. In order to keep the signal strength high, repeaters are used. The system relies on signal multiplexers at the sending and receiving ends at a minimum, and if different networks connect, at the point of connection. Each connection between a multiplexer is called a *line*. Figure 13.6 shows a diagram of a path.

FIGURE 13.6

A SONET path, line, and section

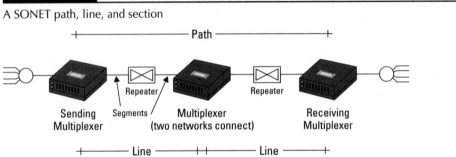

SONET/SDH uses three different network topologies (see Figure 13.7):

- **Linear Automatic Protection Switching (LAPS).** APS or 1+1 has two pairs of bi-directional fibers. Switching is done on a line-by-line basis, based on negotiation.

  In Figure 13.7, the arrows indicate the direction of the path. The primary path is shown as a black line with a black arrow; the secondary or failover path is shown as a dotted line with a white arrow. The LAPS circuit contains two failover switches that route traffic over the alternate path when failure occurs.

- **Unidirectional Path Switched Ring.** SONET UPSR consists of redundant data paths sent around a ring structure. One circuit is working and one is standby, with both in the same direction. When the working circuit is interrupted, the standby circuit takes over. In SDH, the analogous technology is called Subnetwork Connection Protocol (SNCP), but is a mesh instead of a ring.

- **Bidirectional Line Switched Ring.** BLSR is a two- or four-fiber network with a ring structure that transmits redundant information. In the two-fiber configuration, each ring is both working and standby, with one circuit being the data channel and the other being the redundant path. In BLSR both rings are in use, both working and standby, whereas in unidirectional one ring is in standby mode.

Framing

SONET circuits transfer data at a steady rate in multiples of 64 Kbits/s. A 64 Kbits/s segment is referred to as a *DS0 line*, and that is the standard throughput of a voice phone wired into homes.

The synchronization feature in SONET is maintained by a system of atomic clocks located throughout the system. Data travels over the SONET network as a collection of frames with encapsulated data such as Asynchronous Transfer Mode (ATM) or Packet over SONET/SDH (PoS), with the definition of the frames being slightly different for the two different versions of this standard.

SONET data is heavily multiplexed and can mix different communication types together into a virtual path envelope (container). SONET STS-1 (Synchronous Transport Signal Level - 1) operates at 51.84 Mbits/s, while the equivalent SHD standard STM-3C (Synchronous Transport Module - 3, concatenated) operates at three times the speed, at 155.52 Mbits/s. The main difference between SONET and Ethernet T1-4 streams is that SONET has a lower latency passing through switching equipment. For T1, that latency is 125 μsec, while for SONET/SDH the latency is 32 μsec. When SONET/SDH data travels over optical cable, the term OC-1 is used in place of STS-1, and the signal is in the OC-N format. An OC-3 standard contains three streams of STS-1 data.

Note
An octet is a group of 8 bits. A byte is often 8 bits, but not always. Often both terms are used interchangeably.

FIGURE 13.7

SONET topologies

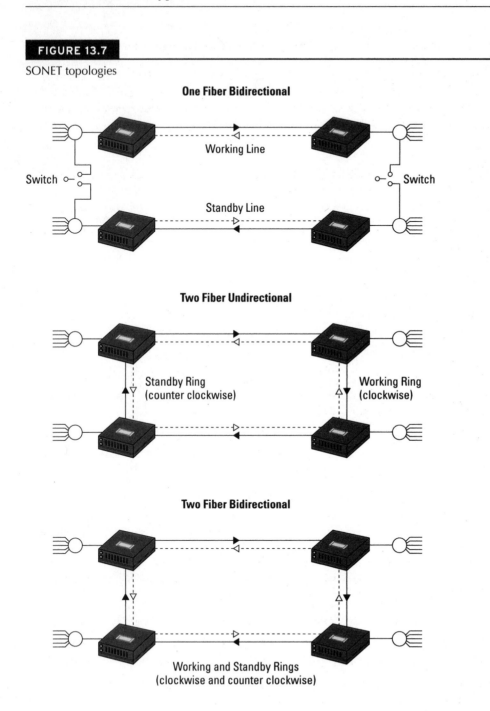

Chapter 17 discusses the structure of TCP packets, where a packet consists of a header portion with multiple sections followed by the TCP data as the payload. SONET frames use a different structure, where the overhead portion of the frame is interwoven with the data or payload. SONET and SDH use slightly different frame structures. Taking SONET STS-1 as an example, a frame consists of 810 octets, with a pattern of 3 octets of overhead followed by 87 octets of payload repeated nine times. For STM-3, the pattern components are three times larger. Figure 13.8 shows a SONET frame.

FIGURE 13.8

An 810-octet SONET frame

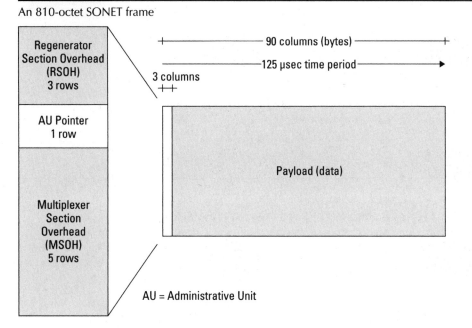

The synchronization feature is such that every 125 μsec, a frame passes by a specific point on the network, and at 8-bit/125 μsec, the transfer rate would be 64 Kbits/s, the DS0 standard. Because both standards use the same clock rate, the signals from SONET and SHD are interoperable. Table 13.3 shows the different SONET/SDH speeds, which are obtained by concentrating the following streams:

1. Three STS-1 lines are sent through a 3:1 multiplexer and one STS line is output.

2. Four STS-3 lines are sent through a 4:1 multiplexer and one STS-12 line is output.

3. One STS-12 line is sent through a scrambler.

4. The output from Step 3 is sent through an electro-optic converter.

5. An OC-12 signal is sent down the fiber.

Refer to Figure 13.5 for an example of how multiple lines are concentrated for higher levels of throughput using T standard lines.

TABLE 13.3

SONET/SDH Standards versus Carrier Levels

SONET Optical Carrier Level	SONET Frame Format	SDH Frame Format	Bandwidth (Kbits/s)	Throughput (Kbits/s)
OC-1	STS-1	STM-0	50,112	51,840
OC-3	STS-3	STM-1	150,336	155,520
OC-12	STS-12	STM-4	601,335	622,080
OC-24	STS-24	-	1,202,688	1,244,160
OC-48	STS-48	STM-16	2,405,376	2,488,320
OC-192	STS-192	STM-64	9,621,504	9,953,280
OC-768	STS-768	STM-256	38,486,016	39,813,120
OC-3072	STS-3072	STM-1024	153,944,064	159,252,240

At the moment, the highest transfer rate commonly available with this kind of technology is OC-192 or STM-64, which can attain transfer rates of up to 10 Gbits/s. This is comparable with Gigabit Ethernet. STM-256, operating at 40 Gbits/s, is being introduced. To attain higher speeds, SONET data can be made to travel over several different wavelengths on a fiber pair using technology called *Wavelength Division Multiplexing* (WDM). The undersea fiber optic cable laid in quantity during the 1990s used a form of WDM called Dense Wave Division Multiplexing (DWDM).

Packet over SONET

Packet over SONET, or PoS, is a packet transport protocol that uses a Point-to-Point (PPP) connection. It is anticipated that PoS will become the dominant transport over SONET/SDH over backbone fiber optic networks that run at high speed. This standard was developed by Cisco Systems, is supported by their high-speed routers, and is enabled in hardware. A significant amount of PoS traffic runs on OC-192 SONET rings.

PoS is a Data Link level (Layer 2) protocol in the ISO/OSI network model. PoS packets are encapsulated in SONET frames, and technology provides for alarm levels, performance monitoring, reliability switching, and synchronization. The PoS packet format makes it much easier to integrate Ethernet IP traffic into PoS frames, with lower header overhead.

PoS can run over SONET networks concurrently with TDM voice and ATM, provided that they use different time slots and suffer no contention. This independence has a number of benefits. For example, ATM can be used to provision Digital Subscriber Lines (DSL), digital cable, and traffic over Permanent Virtual Circuits (PVC) or Switched Virtual Circuits (SVC). All of these different inputs to ATM can be aggregated by ATM to the PoS routers, which then feed the input to the IP backbone optical fiber network. A Cisco 12000 series router is capable of ATM – PoS translation. Figure 13.9 shows this aggregation process.

Notice in Figure 13.9 that the Point of Presence (POP) links between the PoS and ATM routers are made into a fabric and are redundant. POP, being a point-to-point technology, is subject to failure and needs to be made redundant in order to ensure reliability. Backbone traffic is mission critical and cannot fail.

PoS routers can be connected to backbones in the following ways:

- Through a SONET multiplexer
- Through a Dense Wavelength Division Multiplexer (DWDM)
- Directly to a dark fiber backbone

When dark fiber is used, a laser or LED must be provided at the sending end, and a photodiode receiver must be provided at the receiving end. If the run is long enough, a SONET regenerator needs to be added in the line. An example of a SONET optical regenerator for an OC-48 backbone is the Cisco 15104. This procedure is given the name "lighting the fiber."

PoS frames have some specific requirements:

- **High order containment.** PoS frames must be properly encapsulated by SONET transport signals.
- **Octet alignment.** The data packet octet boundaries must align to the STS octet boundaries.
- **Payload scrambling.** Data in the payload portion must conform to rules that require a certain density of ones in the data. The requirement is needed for timing recovery and for network synchronization.

The high order containment process does the following three things:

- Encapsulates an IP datagram into a PPP frame
- Encapsulates PPP frames into a High Level Data Link Control (HDLC) frame
- Encapsulates an HDLC frame into a SONET/SDH frame

FIGURE 13.9

Aggregating ATM traffic to a PoS router

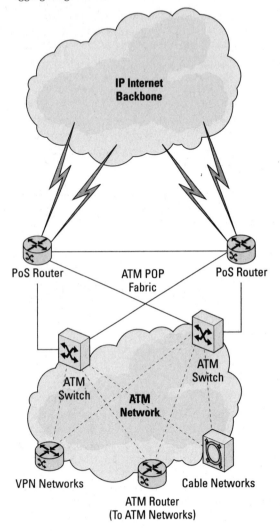

Packet Switching Networks

Packet switching networks work by segmenting data into pieces called *packets* that are variable in length and are encapsulated with addressing and formatting information in a header portion of the packet. On a packet switching network, the endpoints for communications are defined, but the route packets taken between those endpoints may or may not be defined, depending upon the technologies used.

Note

For a list of packet switched networks, go to http://en.wikipedia.org/wiki/Packet_switched_network.

Ethernet and the IP protocols are connectionless; the route the packets take is irrelevant. Some packet switching technologies use virtual circuits, while others may use permanent virtual circuits. The protocols that use connections are TCP (described in Chapter 17), X.25, ATM, and MPLS, all of which are described in the sections that follow.

Packets are created in a certain order or sequence, and they need to be reassembled in that sequence. To ensure that packets are correctly assembled, packet switching protocols use a number of different mechanisms. Each packet carries a sequence identification, and packet switching networks usually employ a messaging system when a packet needs to be re-sent. The validity of the packets is determined by error-checking mechanisms, at the end of each segment of the route and/ or the point at which the data is reassembled (the endpoint).

Packet switching can employ an additional data construct called a *datagram*. Datagrams are part of a packet, a collection of packets, or some combination that is encapsulated within an envelope used to send and control the data communications. Multiprotocol Label Switching (MPLS) is one technology that uses datagrams.

Packet switching has an advantage over circuit switched networks in that it can more fully utilize network bandwidth. Packets can be routed over segments based on current conditions. The low latency involved in transient and often short connections (such as hops) makes packet switching faster to initiate than circuit switching technologies.

X.25 Networks

X.25 is a digital packet switching protocol that was developed in the 1970s, prior to the Internet, as an ITU-T standard. X.25 was deployed on telephone grids before being replaced by faster networks that used ISDN, ATM, ADSL, and PoS starting in the 1990s. It has been displaced by the IP protocol. In the OSI model, the X.25 protocol provides services at Layers 1 to 3 (the Physical, Data Link, and Network layers). The Physical layer standard supporting X.25 is X.21.

Today, X.25 is used on legacy networks in developing countries, in Europe in some point-of-sale systems, for GPS tracking, and on wireless packet radio networks, such as the related AX.25 standard. X.25 is therefore largely of historical interest. Networks such as CompuServe, Telenet, Euronet, and Tymnet were built with X.25.

The X.25 architecture creates virtual calls that connect the Data Terminal Equipment (DTE) of the user or subscriber with Data Circuit Terminating Equipment (DCE) on the X.25 network. A DTE is usually a computer or a terminal, while a DCE can be a modem that is connected to the network. To a user, X.25 appears as if it is a point-to-point connection. X.25 defines both switched and permanent circuits — Virtual Calls (VC) and Permanent Virtual Circuits (PVC), respectively.

Note
DCE is also called Data Communications Equipment or Data Carrier Equipment. It is typically a computer or device that performs signal conversion, encoding, and synchronization.

X.25 networks connected to asynchronous devices such as modems, terminals, and printers by sending data through a gateway device called a Packet Assembler Disassembler (PAD) device. The protocol used by a PAD was defined as X.3, between a terminal and PAD as X.28, and between a PAD and the network as X.29. For this reason, PADs were also called "Triple X" devices. PADs are a common element on all packet switching networks where they mediate the differences between the sending device's speed and the receiving device's speed. PADs must be on both ends of the connection.

X.25 was built to be a reliable data connection, and implemented various mechanisms to ensure that packets arrived correctly and in sequence at their destination. It included features that IP networks have carried forward: error correction, flow control, and messaging. These features limited X.25 to speeds of only 64 Kbits/s or DS0, which is the basic speed for voice data.

Switched Multi-megabit Data Services

The Switched Multi-megabit Data Services, or SMDS, were developed by Bellcore in the early 1990s as a means for connecting LANs to MANs. At the time, the Regional Bell Operating Companies (RBOCs) could only create networks in a relatively small area that they referred to as *Local Access and Transport Areas* (LATA).

SMDS predates the development of Asynchronous Transfer Mode (ATM). Billed as a connectionless packet switching service, SMDS split datagrams into cells and sent those cells across SONET/SDH rings, allowing MANs to achieve a radius of 30 mi, or 50 km. The technology was part of the IEEE 802.6 standard that included the Distributed Queue Dual Bus (DQDB) technology.

The RBOCs and GTE deployed SMDS in the United States for several years, but the technology never became pervasive. In Europe, SMDS had more success. It was sold in those markets as Connectionless Broadband Data Service (CBDS) and was popular in countries that were both mainly metropolitan and small. However, by the mid-1990s, SMDS was replaced by Frame Relay, and by faster networks that ran Ethernet protocols such as PoE. IEEE has deprecated the 802.6 format, and SMDS is largely of historical interest.

Asynchronous Transfer Mode

Asynchronous Transfer Mode (ATM) is a medium-speed connection-oriented network protocol. This protocol operates at the Data Link layer (Level 2) to define a data transfer format called a *cell*, and at the Physical layer (Level 1) to define a digital switching technology that connects endpoints together using a virtual circuit. ATM was meant to be a format that could run over both packet switching and circuit switching networks, as its features are compatible with both.

ATM is usually implemented in hardware in switches and NICs, and the technology is central to the SONET/SDH backbone of the telephone network that was described earlier. ATM is also the technology used in Broadband Integrated Services Digital Networks (B-ISDNs), which are widely used for multimedia applications and for ADSL. The cost and complexity of ATM has prevented its use on LANs.

ATM is designed to process real-time data such as voice and video. To do this, the cells that travel over an ATM network are designed to be 53 bytes wide. This uniform, small size results in an evenly spaced, high-speed data stream delivered to the codec that performs the digital-to-audio conversion, or vice versa. Datagrams that travel over ATM, regardless of the size, are broken up into 48-byte chunks, and a 5-byte ATM routing header is added for addressing and sequencing during assembly.

If a cell is lost in transmission or late, the codecs used for real-time processing in segmentation and reassembly (SAR) hardware are designed to transmit silence for audio or the previous frame for video, or to use some other method to make up for the missing data. The small size of the cells means that there is little discernable difference in the output; the missing audio would show up as brief noise, and the missing video frame can't be recognized by the human brain at normal play-back speeds. The result of using ATM is that it can reduce jitters to less than 5 percent of a packet switching network at network speeds that were common at the time that ATM was developed.

ATM uses virtual circuits to define a connection. This is implemented as an 8- to 12-bit Virtual Path Identifier (VPI) and a 16-bit Virtual Channel Identifier (VCI) in the cell header. As a cell moves through an ATM network, each switch changes the two identifier values to move the cell along the circuit's route. Unlike TCP/IP, where the route is irrelevant and only the endpoints matter, ATM cells travel the same route, which is why less overhead is needed to manage the data stream.

ATM's developers used slightly different cell headers to separate cells used over WAN links from cells moving within the same LAN. Because LANs don't require the additional network information, the GFC is omitted. However, because ATM is rarely used on IP LANs, most cells use the User Network Interface cell format. Figure 13.10 shows the UNI and NNI side by side.

Even though ATM is a lower-overhead protocol, it does have some mechanism in place to control traffic. ATM contains four bit parameters that enforce transfer rates: Constant Bit Rate (CBR), Variable Bit Rate (VBR), Available Bit Rate (ABR), and Unspecified Bit Rate (UBR). Setting these Quality of Service (QoS) parameters collectively comprises what ATM calls a *traffic contract*. A traffic contract controls the queuing and flagging of cells, which are referred to as *traffic shaping* and *traffic policing*, respectively. The VBR parameter is used by ATM to define burst mode. The receiving system does send a short message to the sending system when the packet arrives correctly.

FIGURE 13.10

The cell structure for ATM on WANs (left) and on LANs (right)

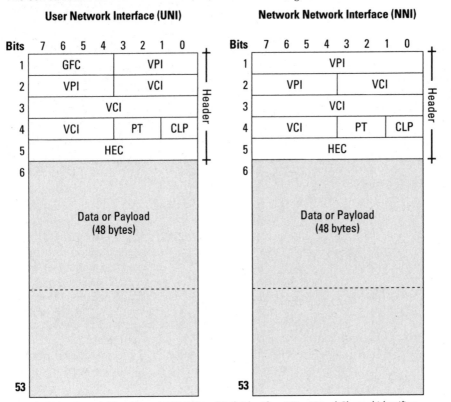

Legend: GFC = Generic Flow Control; VPI = Virtual Path Identifier; VCI = Virtual Channel Identifier;
PT = Payload Type; CLP = Cell Loss Priority; HEC = Header Error Control (CRC)

It's been 20 years since ATM was first developed by the ATM Forum and the ITU, and network technology has improved greatly since then. At the current speeds achieved by technologies such as 10 GbE over fiber, the transmission of packets, even full-sized 1600-byte packets, is very fast — on the order of 1.3 msec. That speed reduces jitter significantly and tends to make ATM very expensive to implement. On high-speed IP backbones over optical fiber operating at speeds greater than OC-3, the common technology used for data transfer is Packet Over Ethernet (PoE). Although ATM will be used for many years to come, it is clear that other technologies will replace it on high-speed backbones of the future.

Frame Relay

A Frame Relay service (see Figure 13.11) is a virtual leased line that provides a point-to-point connection between two network nodes, or between a set of nodes at two different sites. Frame Relay is a Layer 2 Data Link protocol. In a Frame Relay system, frames are routed from one node to the other based on the logic of the router or switch. The frame forwarding system operates like a relay race in the sense that frames are sent to the destination in a series of intermediate steps. Frame Relay systems are popular for sending voice and data between LANs over a WAN connection.

A DCE, or Data Circuit terminating equipment, is a modem, switch, router, or other networked device that sits between Data Terminal Equipment (DTE) on a data transmission circuit. A DCE manages line clocking, data coding, and signal conversion. Although many DCEs are separate devices and require attachment to a network interface on both ends of their connections, some systems build DCEs into their network interface. In the oldest network scenarios, a DTE was a computer and a DCE is a modem.

FIGURE 13.11

A Frame Relay system

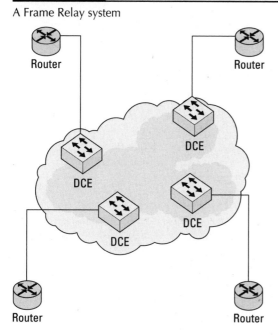

Typical frames in a Frame Relay are 1600 bytes long, with a 10-bit ID number that identifies a particular virtual circuit from one host at a site to another host at a different site. The lease type places a limit on the size of the packets, the circuit provides a limit to the burst speed or maximum transfer rate, and the service contract places a limit on the average data transferred in a particular time period. The performance of Frame Relay running on T-1 lines falls between ISDN (128 Kbits/s) and ATM (155.5 Mbits/s).

A virtual leased line is different from a permanent leased line in that a leased line is dedicated to the lessee who can send data over the line at the full rated speed. A virtual leased line allows the lessee to share the capacity of a circuit in the manner described in the previous paragraph. Another way of looking at this is that virtual leased lines are essentially level-of-service agreements. Virtual leased lines usually cost a fraction of what a leased line costs. Frame Relay networks are meant to improve network utilization rates for service providers, and work well, provided that the service provider doesn't overload the system with too many subscribers.

Frame Relay technology has very little overhead; there is no flow control or acknowledgment messaging used. However, Frame Relay networks do have congestion control, which includes Admission Control for incoming connections, Committed Information Rate (CIR) for guaranteed throughput, Committed Burst Size (BC) for the largest rate allowed, and Excess Burst Size (BE) for an additional rate that will be attempted but not guaranteed. Two different control bits in the data header can be set to 1 (On) when there is congestion to control network actions; they are Forward Explicit Congestion Notification (FECN) and Backwards Explicit Congestion Notification (BECN). Those bits can then be used to adjust the data rate.

Unlike the older protocol X.25, which transports analog data, and on which Frame Relays are based, Frame Relay uses fast packet technology and does no error correction. When a frame fails the error checking routine, it is dropped. The Frame Relay service has a bit Command/Response (C/R) flag in the header, but the C/R flag is application specific and the Frame Relay service makes no demands on how or if it is used.

The technology relies on applications at each end of the virtual circuit to determine if a frame is missing and needs to be resent. It is the host's Transport and Session protocols that provide the messages used for control and context in which frame delivery can be understood. You can apply a priority flag to frames to implement QoS on Frame Relay networks.

Frame Relay services aren't universally used as WAN connections; indeed, their use is diminishing as broadband connections over dedicated lines such as DSL or cable modems are installed. Those lines, along with Virtual Private Networks (VPNs), use a different type of service called *Multi Protocol Label Switching*.

Multi Protocol Label Switching

The Multi Protocol Label Switching (MPLS) protocol provides an alternative method for managing packets, frames, and cells on a variety of different network types. The protocol operates at both Layer 2 and Layer 3, the Data Link and Session levels of the ISO/OSI model, and can be used on both packet switching and circuit switching networks. MPLS is an IETF standard that provides Quality of Service features such as prioritization and service level control.

MPLS labels are applied to packets at the edge router of a network, called the *Label Edge Router* (LER). A label is a collection of routing information added to the header that includes the destination address, the allowed bandwidth and delay tolerated, the source IP address, the socket number used, and other service information. The information is entered after consulting the routing table of the LER. With this information, the LER assigns a Labeled Switch Path (LSP) to the packets and then places them into appropriate queues on the Label Switch Router (LSR). The information contained by MPLS labels makes MPLS traffic much more fault tolerant than SONET/SDH is.

The system of labeling is referred to a *Penultimate Hop Popping*, adding a label is called a *push*, and removing a label is called *pop*. When a packet arrives at a LER with a label on it, the LER adds a second label to that packet. As packets arrive at their interim destination, that additional label is removed, or popped; and when the packet arrives at its final destination, the last label is popped.

MPLS seeks to be the logical replacement for ATM networks, replacing all of the overhead involved with splitting data into cells and then having to signal and synchronize the traffic, which the speed of optical networks now makes unnecessary. As a Layer 2 to 3 protocol, MPLS offers a service that is similar to using datagrams and can be used for IP packets, as well as Ethernet, ATM, and SONET frames. MPLS relies on high-speed switches for its performance, and so it should come as no surprise that Cisco Systems was one of the main original developers of this "tag switching" technology; Ipsilon Networks was the other company involved, and was mainly responsible for the IP portion of the protocol.

MPLS finds an application on large, IP-based networks as a Quality of Service protocol, or as Cisco calls it, a Class of Service (CoS) application. It supports IP v.4 and v.6 and can be employed on ATM, Frame Relay, and T1 connections. The speed advantage of MPLS is no longer its main benefit, as network speeds have made switch speeds less important. The QoS support of data such as VoIP that requires high network efficiency (low latency) and other technologies with this requirement is the primary reason that MPLS is used.

The Internet and Internet2

The Internet is a WAN composed of many other WANs. It is an internetwork of internetworks, if you will. About 95 percent of the protocols used for data transport on these networks are TCP/IP traffic. Those technologies are described throughout this book. One aspect of the Internet is worth considering from a WAN viewpoint: the connection points where different WANs are routed. The next section describes Internet Exchange Points in some detail.

As the Internet became more commercial, open, and congested, its initial purpose to support research and development at universities and laboratories became difficult. A number of newer networks have been developed that are building a next-generation Internet, also known as the Internet2 Network. A similar project in the UK is called JANET, and there are also projects of this type in Europe. The Internet2 Network enables a number of advanced applications and technologies and serves as a test bed for future development of the public commercial Internet.

Internet Exchange Points

The original points of connection for large networks on the Internet in the United States were called Network Access Points (NAPs). The National Science Foundation (NSF) maintained the first NAP, and as the system expanded, three more were added that were managed by Sprint, Ameritech, and Pacific Bell. They were located in Washington, Chicago, California, and New Jersey. As the number of NAPs grew, certain urban areas with multiple ISPs established what became known as Metropolitan Area Exchanges (MAEs).

As the system expanded, the private sector greatly increased the number of network-to-network links. Today the points of connections between service providers and national networks are called Internet Exchange Points (IXP or IX), and the terms NAP and MAE are rarely used. An IXP is a switching facility managed by an ISP where traffic is exchanged between networks based on an exchange system called a *mutual pairing agreement*. IXPs route traffic from and to other IXPs without additional charges being imposed for the transit through the exchange. Data delivered to a receiving network upstream is billed for service, typically on the basis of the amount of traffic and level of service.

The proliferation of IXPs to provide internetwork connections provides the routing function that makes the Internet efficient and fault tolerant. The system of IXPs has another benefit as well. Each IXP connection is independent of the other IXP connections. If an ISP has a slow connection to another country, but fast connections internally, then their internal communications can run at full speed. The connections between countries separated by oceans are made using undersea or submarine optical fiber cable. Figure 13.12 shows the Internet Exchange Directory on the Packet Clearing House Web site (https://prefix.pch.net/applications/ixpdir/), which lists IXPs by country along with their statistical data.

IXPs have a function that is purely switching. Any traffic shaping, filtering, or control over routing is controlled by the ISPs that participate in an exchange. The peering relationship between two ISPs connected through an exchange is defined by the Border Gateway Protocol (BGP), which builds a table of routers that serve as the entry points to various IP networks. Networks reached over this system are referred to as *Autonomous Systems* (AS), and the routes are called *path vectors*. AS are a collection of IP-connected routing prefixes that the ISP controls.

Not all traffic on the Internet flows through IXP facilities. Many ISPs have direct connections to one another. In those instances, it is only when the direct connection fails that traffic between the two ISPs is sent through the exchange. For ISPs that have no relationships, data exchange through IXPs is the only mechanism available.

As of October 2008, the top ten Internet Exchange Points in terms of traffic are listed in Table 13.4, based on a compilation of available sources. The highest-rated U.S. IXP isn't shown on the chart. It was the New York International Internet eXchange (NYIIX), which was rated twelfth. NYIIX had 98 members, a maximum throughput of 23 Gbits/s, and an average throughput of 15 Gbits/s. This list is not definitive and is subject to seasonal changes. It is also noted that IXPs in the U.S. often don't disclose their traffic volumes.

FIGURE 13.12

The Packet Clearing House is a resource for locating IXPs.

TABLE 13.4

Top Ten Internet Exchange Points

Name	Location	Connected Members	Maximum Throughput (Gbits/s)	Average Throughput (Gbits/s)
Amsterdam Internet Exchange (AMS-IX)	Amsterdam, Netherlands	300	419	280
Deutscher Commercial Internet Exchange (DE-CIX)	Frankfurt am Main, Germany	250	428	210
London Internet Exchange (LINX)	London, United Kingdom	221	256	157
Japan Network Access Point (JPNNAP)	Tokyo, Japan	88	183	129
Netnod Internet Exchange in Sweden (Netnod)	Stockholm, Sweden	53	103	104

continued

TABLE 13.4 *(continued)*

Name	Location	Connected Members	Maximum Throughput (Gbits/s)	Average Throughput (Gbits/s)
Japan Internet Exchange (JPIX)	Tokyo, Japan	107	73	55
Spain Internet Exchange	Madrid, Spain	43	72	61
Hong Kong Internet eXchange (HKIX)	Hong Kong, China	76	47	34
Budapest Internet Exchange (BIX)	Budapest, Hungary	52	35	26
Polish Internet eXchange	Warsaw, Poland	76	35	18

According to the site InternetWorldStats.com, as of June 2008, 1.46 billion of the world's 6.68 billion people were connected to the Internet, or about 21.9 percent. A recent estimate by the Discovery Institute of the amount of traffic that will flow over the Internet annually by 2015 predicts that it may reach one zettabyte, which is one million, million, billion bytes (1021), or 1000 exabytes. This is a factor of 50 times the size of traffic in 2006, which was 20 exabytes.

Internet2

The Internet2 Network is a consortium of schools, corporations, research organizations, and government agencies that share in the use and development of an advanced internetwork. The goal of the project is to create a system for supporting leading-edge research, enabling next-generation technologies, and transferring the technologies to the public Internet. Among the technologies currently on The Internet2 Network are rich media libraries, video conferencing, advanced middleware, virtual laboratories, tele-immersion, tele-health, long-distance learning applications, and many more.

Internet2 is the trademark of the organization that created the first of these advanced network backbones, the Abilene Network. The Abilene Network connects all 50 of the states in the U.S. with a 10 Gbits/s pipe. Another project by this group established the National LambdaRail (NLR) regional optical network, which is an OC-192 optical backbone. Most of the articles written about Internet2 were written about the Abilene Network and not the consortium. Today, Internet2 has adopted the name "The Internet2 Network" as the new name for the Abilene Network. Figure 13.13 shows the current extent of The Internet2 Network as of May 2009. Note that the Internet2 is a backbone service and doesn't cover the entire United States.

FIGURE 13.13

The Internet2 Network

Source: Internet2: http://www.internet2.edu/pubs/networkmap.pdf

Summary

In this chapter, you learned about WANs and their characteristics. Routing and switching technology and the protocols required were also described.

The Public Switched Telephone Network (PSTN) is a circuit switching network that can support both voice and data services. The most popular connection types, ISDN and DSL, were described in detail.

The backbone technologies for connecting networks are through T- and E-carrier networks. SONET/SDH is the most popular protocol for data transfer on these backbones. Data that flows over SONET can be in the form of Asynchronous Transfer Mode (ATM) or Packet over SONET (PoS).

Packet switching networks are used for TCP/IP networks. Protocols such as X.25, Frame Relay, and ATM are used on packet switching networks. You also learned about how the Internet is connected by Internet Exchange Points (IXPs). The Internet2 Network was also briefly described.

In the next chapter, you learn how to create wireless networks.

Wi-Fi Networks

The IEEE 802.11x wireless networking standards known as Wi-Fi have sparked a revolution in computer networking over the last decade. In this chapter you will learn about the different standards, their performance characteristics, and how you can create networks or network links with this technology. Wireless networks support two different types of architectures: ad hoc and infrastructure modes.

The commonly used standards are all radio frequency communication links over public bands in the 2.4 GHz or 5 GHz frequency range. Wi-Fi separates the bandwidth into channels and then uses a form of spread spectrum transmission that either creates a direct sequence of overlapping transmissions or transmits using a frequency-hopping scheme. This chapter presents both Direct-Sequence Spread Spectrum (DSSS) and Frequency-Hopping Spread Spectrum (FHSS) in detail. Signals are encoded onto the carrier waves that DSSS and FHSS create using a number of different modulation technologies that you learn about in this chapter. In particular, Phase Shift Keying methods are popular.

The 802.11x frames are similar to Ethernet frames and are described here. The main method for sending frames uses Carrier Sense Multiple Access with Collision Avoidance. Methods for handshaking, traffic control, and connection management are described.

Access points, gateways, and routers are the wireless devices that are used by wireless clients to connect to networks. The characteristics of these different devices are described. Methods for extending networks, including repeaters, distribution systems, and special antennas (such as smart antennas) are touched upon in this chapter.

Software that you can use to discover wireless network devices and learn about wireless traffic are surveyed. This chapter also presents the different forms of wireless network security methods in common use today.

Wireless Networking

The dominant form of wireless networking uses radio frequency transmission over either the 2.4 GHz or 5 GHz bands of the electromagnetic spectrum. These bands were chosen because they are in the public domain, and because they can accept the introduction of ad hoc network links that wireless networks create without disruption of other systems. It is safe to say that the emergence of the 802.11x family of standards has been as revolutionary to computer networking as cellular phones have been to the telephone industry. There are four main standards of 802.11 wireless equipment on the market in wide use today: 802.11a, 802.11b, 802.11g, and 802.11n. Products based on the 802.11n standard are finally becoming popular after a relatively long gestation period in which products were based on draft standards.

The 802.11 networks formed using direct point-to-point links between two stations, or STAs, are called ad hoc networks and implement a set of services called the Independent Basic Service Set (IBSS). An ad hoc network can be formed from a set of STA links such that a closed loop is formed between the STAs. Ad hoc mode is sometimes referred to as peer-to-peer (P2P) mode. A network formed between stations and a transmitter/receiver called a wireless access point (AP) is referred to as an infrastructure network, and it implements a set of services called the Basic Service Set (BSS) and assigned a BSSID. Figure 14.1 shows these wireless network components.

Both ad hoc and infrastructure networks create a named network security object called the Service Set Identifier (SSID). The SSID is the wireless network's name, and SSIDs are used the same way that a network domain is used. When you initialize the first P2P client on the ad hoc network, you are asked to name the network. Similarly, when you set up your wireless access point, or a similar device such as a wireless router or gateway, you are asked to create an SSID.

The first P2P client, or the AP that created the wireless network, issues what is called an 802.11 beacon frame, advertising the network to potential wireless clients. Clients are then asked to provide the password needed to access the wireless network. In cases where no password was created, the wireless network is unsecured and any wireless client can simply join the network.

When two or more wireless networks are joined through area connections provided by overlapping access points, the network is referred to as a distribution system (DS). A DS is characterized by the ability to take a wirelessly connected STA attached to one access point and move it to a location where it can connect to another access point on the DS. When one STA communicates with an STA linked to a different AP, the communication requires a functional AP-AP bridge link; STAs do not connect directly with one another.

FIGURE 14.1

Logical 802.11 wireless network types — ad hoc and infrastructure network

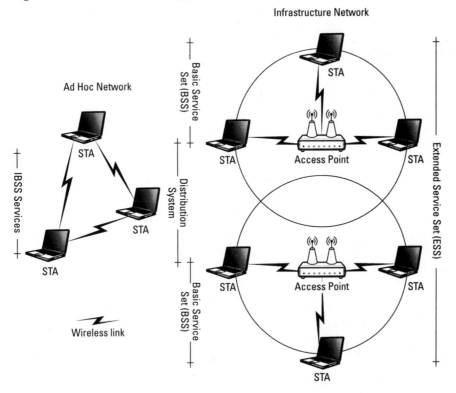

When you have two or more wireless APs that communicate with one another, they must be part of the same subnet or network, and they implement what is called an Extended Service Set (ESS) and are assigned an ESSID. Although the DS illustrated in Figure 14.1 is an AP-AP connection, many wireless 802.11x infrastructure mode networks use wired networks as the DS. When a wired/wireless network is considered, the ESS spans the part of the network that includes the AP and its connected clients and does not extend to the wired network. When two Extended Service Sets share the same ESSID, a wireless client can roam from one to the other without reconfiguration.

Figure 14.2 shows the corresponding diagram for an infrastructure network with a wired network connected to a set of access points.

FIGURE 14.2

A wireless/wired heterogeneous network

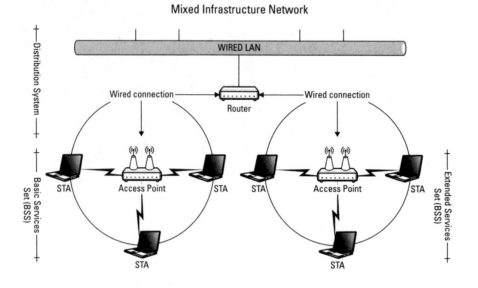

Mixed Infrastructure Network

Wi-Fi networks

Wi-Fi is the trademark of the Wi-Fi Alliance and the generic name given to a set of technologies based on the IEEE 802.11x standards. Wi-Fi is meant to evoke a connection to Wireless Fidelity, just as Hi-Fi represents the idea of High Fidelity. Wi-Fi was created by the Interbrand Corporation in 1999 to replace the name IEEE 802.11b Direct Sequence, and it remains a brand name with no real relationship to the technology that it describes. The Wi-Fi logos have a yin-yang design that is meant to indicate the interoperability of the standards.

Wi-Fi is the predominant form of wireless networking for computers, and its standardization by the IEEE has made it nearly ubiquitous in the marketplace. If you purchase a wireless laptop, printer, streaming media server, or any of a host of devices, then it is almost certain that they contain some version of the 802.11 standards; and there is a relatively good chance that that device will interoperate with other wireless network devices you already own. There are some interoperability issues, and in this chapter you will learn what they are.

Wi-Fi isn't the only wireless technology in use. Many wireless technologies in cellular telephones, video games, remote controls, and other devices offer wireless connections based on Bluetooth, IR, radio, and a few other types of technologies. For the most part, these additional technologies are connection-oriented, which is why this chapter describes 802.11 networks in detail. The one exception, Bluetooth, is described in Chapter 11, where personal LANs (pLANs) are discussed.

IEEE 802.11x Standards

Each of the different 802.11x standards specifies a different modulation scheme and a different bandwidth that it operates at. Every standard uses the concept of a channel to separate one set of connections (a network or subnet) from another. For example, the 2.4 GHz band (S-Band ISM) used by 802.11b/g actually spans the range from 2.400 to 2.4835 GHz and is divided up into a set of 13 channels, each channel occupying 22 MHz with a space of 5 MHz between each channel. The channels are numbered from 1 (2.400 to 2.422 GHz) up to channel 13 (2.4823 to 2.4835 GHz). The highest signal is at the center point of each band, which would be 2.411 GHz for channel 1 and 2.472 GHz for channel 13.

There is some variation in the use of the different channels on a per-country basis worldwide, but not as much as there was a few years ago. The United States and some of the Central and South American countries allow the use of channels 1 to 11 in the 2.4 GHz band, while forbidding the use of channels 12 and 13, as well as a fourteenth band that is sometimes added at 2.4835 GHz (the top of the 2.4 GHz range). Japan and now France support the use of all 14 channels, but most of the rest of the world allows the use of only the 13 official bands.

In the 5 GHz band (C-Band ISM), where 802.11a and optionally 802.11n operate, the spectrum is divided into 42 channels. Figure 14.3 summarizes the current usage of the different channels by country. Be aware that these assignments can change over time.

The size of the 2.4 GHz channels arises from their power distribution, which must be attenuated by 50 dB (reduced in amplitude) from the center frequency of the channel to the edges, 22 MHz on each side. The separation of the channels is 5 MHz, which means that each channel overlaps four channels to either side. Figure 14.4 illustrates the overlaps of different channels in the 2.4 GHz radio band.

This effectively means that of the 13 or 14 channels in the 2.4 GHz band, only 3 channels may be assigned to physically adjacent wireless networks. In the United States, those channels are usually assigned as 1, 6, and 11. In Europe, the 1, 5, 9, and 13 channels are assignable.

As transmitters get farther away from one another, their ability to impact another receiver on an adjacent channel diminishes. So, while 1, 6, and 11 can be operating in the same room without problems, a transmitter on channel 1 on one side of a building might not impact another using channel 4 on the other. Still, it's best to observe the recommended assignments and not try to finesse the overlap problem.

FIGURE 14.3

The 802.11 channels in use worldwide

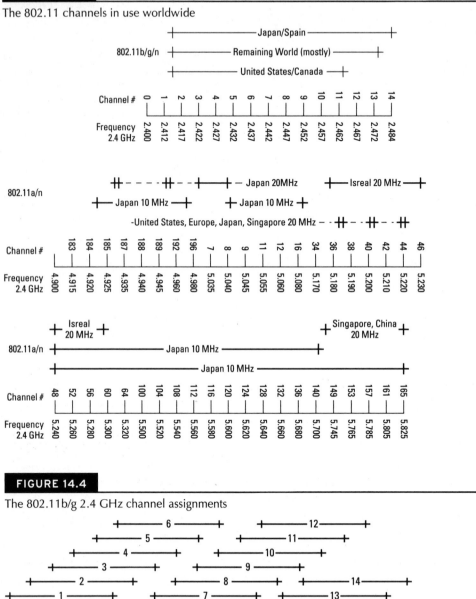

FIGURE 14.4

The 802.11b/g 2.4 GHz channel assignments

Frequency in MHz

The scheme used in Figure 14.5 shows how you can lay out a set of access points so that channel numbers that are close to one another have little overlap. Using this methodology, it is possible to extend the coverage area without suffering much channel interference.

FIGURE 14.5

How wireless network numbers overlap

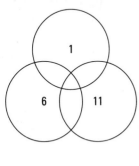
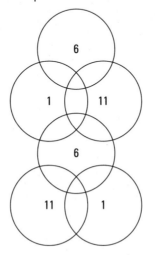

802.11 legacy

The original 802.11 standards, now referred to as simply 802.11 legacy mode, were released in 1997. They specified three different wireless connection types:

- **Diffuse Infrared.** When connected over a diffuse infrared link, speeds of up to 1 Mbits/s were achieved.

- **Radio Frequency with FHSS.** In the 2.4 GHz band, 802.11 could operate at 1 or 2 Mbits/s using Frequency Hopping Spread Spectrum (FHSS) modulation.

- **Radio Frequency with DSSS.** In the 2.4 GHz band, 802.11 could operate at 1 or 2 Mbits/s using Direct Sequence Spread Method (DSSS) modulation.

Products based on 802.11 legacy became obsolete when the 802.11b standards were introduced.

Note

In order to carry a signal over a radio frequency, a modulation technology must be used, as is discussed in some detail in Chapter 5.

The 802.11b and 802.11g standards both use DSSS modulation over the 2.4 GHz Industrial Scientific and Medical (ISM) radio band. The 2.4 GHz band is crowded with other devices such as microwave ovens, phones, toys, baby monitors, walkie-talkies, and many other forms of detritus that modern civilization dictates one must connect to wirelessly. At this frequency, 802.11b/g can sometimes suffer from interference. Other radio technologies that use different forms of modulation don't suffer interference; Bluetooth, another 2.4 GHz technology that uses FHSS modulation, doesn't interfere with other ISM band products but can interfere (to a small degree) with 802.11b/g.

Because the 2.4 GHz band is crowded, the alternative 802.11a standard was developed in order to use the 5 GHz ISM band. Because it operates at higher frequencies, 802.11a has a higher throughput than 802.11b/g but is less effective at penetrating walls and has a lower effective range than 802.11b/g. Indoors, the range of 802.11a can be half that of 802.11b in most applications.

As it turned out, 802.11a reached the market after the 802.11b standards and therefore were used in the second wave of Wi-Fi devices that were introduced. The 802.11g standards were third, and now the 802.11n standards, which are the latest standards, are the fourth generation. Because the 802.11a standards operate at a different frequency than the 802.11b/g standards, 802.11a are unable to interoperate with 802.11b/g. When 802.11g networks detect an 802.11b device, the network speed drops down to be backwards compatible with the 802.11b standards.

Many devices are sold that include two or three of the different standards, and they go by a number of different and often proprietary names. Dual band devices were the earliest to market, and they most often included both 802.11a and 802.11b together. When 802.11g became available, products offering all three versions (a, b, and g) were most often called dual band/trimode.

The 802.11n draft standards add what is called Multiple Input Multiple Output (MIMO) to the 802.11 standards, as well as some other features. MIMO is a smart antenna technology that is described in the MIMO section later in this chapter. The 802.11n draft standards offer the ability to interoperate with 802.11b/g standards, as they are a "superset" of all of the previous standards. Although there are many n devices on the market based on the draft standards, they differ enough from one another to cause interoperability headaches for early adopters. The TGn working group of IEEE isn't expected to finalize 802.11n until December 2009. The strong recommendation given to interested parties is that if they adopt 802.11n based on the draft resolution, they only buy n devices from a single manufacturer.

Table 14.1 lists the different 802.11x standards and their characteristics.

TABLE 14.1

802.11x Characteristics

Standard	Band (GHz)	Modulation1	Throughput (Mbits/s)	Net/Gross Bit Rate (Mbps)	Range (indoor/outdoor, in meters)
802.11	2.4	IR/FHSS/DSSS	0.9	2	20/100
802.11a	5.0	OFDM	23	54	35/120
80211b	2.4	DSSS	4.3	11	38/140
802.11g	2.4	OFDM	19	54	38/140
802.11n	2.4 or 5.0	OFDM	74	600	70/250
802.11y	3.7	OFDM	23	54	50/5000

1. IR (infrared); FHSS (Frequency Hopping Spread Spectrum); DSSS (Direct-Sequence Spread Spectrum); and OSDM (Orthogonal Frequency Division Multiplexing).

802.11y

The 802.11y standards approved in September 2008 add 3.7 GHz (3650 to 3760 MHz band), high-power (20 watt maximum) radio link connections that can operate over distances of up to 5 km (3 mi.). This band overlaps with some ground station/satellite communications, and so there are some limitations on where this kind of connection can be made. In order to use 802.11y in the United States, a license must be obtained for base stations for a small fee. This license is for the base station, and not for a particular location; it can be used anywhere in the United States. 802.11y clients don't require a license, but they do require that they successfully handshake with a base station before they can transmit data. The station's license, as well as their transmissions, make it possible to identify the operators, which is important in determining which transmission might be interfering with other local transmissions.

To allow for multiple 802.11y links in the same geographical area, an enhancement was added to carrier sensing in 802.11 called the Contention Based Protocol (CBP). This protocol will establish a set of rules so that the different sessions can coexist. When contention occurs, the current proposed standard seeks to resolve it first by technical methods, and if not, to provide a dispute resolution forum to resolve any issues.

Another new feature of 802.11y is the ability of base stations to sense channels based on their current noise and available bandwidth, and to dynamically switch channels as needed. In order to maintain connections to clients, a new messaging scheme called Extended Channel Switch Announcement (ECSA) lets the access station signal the change to clients and have them switch concurrently.

Any unlicensed 802.11y device is referred to as an STA. The 802.11y protocol requires that the base station or access point not only be able to enable a client but also be able to restrict access as well. The mechanism that is used to manage the connection is called the Dependent Station Enablement (DSE).

This method of access has been referred to as the light licensing model and may be applied to other bandwidths being considered for 802.11y usage, including 4.9 GHz and 5.0 GHz. A set of other bands, referred to as the IMT-Advanced candidate bands, are at 450-862 MHz, 2300-2400 MHz, 2700-2900 MHz, 3400-4200 MHz, and 4400-5000 MHz, and are under consideration for adoption by 802.11y. It is predicted that when these devices finally become available in the consumer market, they will achieve throughputs of around 100 Mbits/s for mobile applications and 1 Gbits/s for stationary links.

These bands represent fragments that are assigned but that are often available most of the time, even in dense urban areas. The availability of bandwidth isn't uniform; it varies both by time and by geographical location. For example, in some markets, different TV channel assignments make the white spaces between channels fall in different locations. The intent is to make these bands available using different multiband switching technologies based on switching both time and location of band usage.

Modulation

The 802.11b standards, which were introduced in 1999, use the Complementary Code Keying (CCK) modulation scheme. Complementary codes are a set of sequences of the same length created so that the number of pairs of like states with a certain separation in one of the sequences is the same as the number of pairs of different states having the same separation in the other sequence. This modulation has the effect of making it easier to recognize the different states that code for symbols than the Barker codes that were used in 802.11 legacy.

The digital signal modulation used by 802.11x (with the exception of 802.11b/legacy) wireless technologies is usually a variant of Phase Shift Keying (PSK). Signals are encoded by the modulator by changing the phase of the carrier wave, with each of the phases used representing binary data. Patterns of phase changes encode for symbols (characters), which are demodulated and interpreted based on a stored signal map. When the PSK system performs a comparison to a reference set of signals, the technology is referred to as Coherent Phase Shift Keying (CPSK).

Note

Digital signal modulation can be based on Amplitude Shift Keying (ASK), Frequency Shift Keying (FSK), or Phase Shift Keying (PSK).

There are many other variations of PSK. In one type, called Differential Phase Shift Keying (DPSK), the phase of the carrier wave is varied by a certain amount or a differential instead of being changed entirely. With DPSK, it is the variation in the phase that is used to extract character information based on a stored algorithm, and a reference signal isn't used. That makes DPSK easier than CPSK as well as faster, but it also introduces more demodulation errors.

PSK modulation can be viewed using what is called a constellation diagram. In this diagram, complex numbers are represented by the real portion of the number as the x-axis (the in-phase axis) and the imaginary portion as the y-axis (the quadrature axis). The diagram is drawn in two dimensions, referred to as an Argand plane, and the mapping is referred to as an Argand diagram. This mapping allows functions that are time-varying waves to be represented by their points on a circle. The modulation scheme shown at the top of Figure 14.6 is called Binary Phase Shift Keying (BPSK), which is the simplest form of PSK available.

FIGURE 14.6

Constellation diagrams for BPSK, QPSK, and 8-PSK.

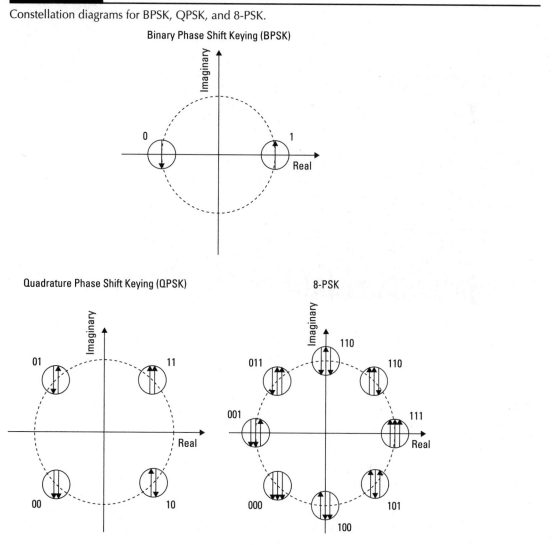

Using this modulation, the phase shifts between two states, 180 degrees out of phase with one another. For that reason, this technique is sometimes called phase reversing keying. The fact that the two states are drawn on the real axis is not significant; they could be at any point on the circle as long as their axis bisects the circle.

Of all the modulation schemes, this one provides the lowest error rate because the difference between the two states is the most extreme. However, the modulation only carries one bit of information, making this the slowest modulation. Therefore, BPSK is often replaced with faster modulation.

You can see how a progression to higher-order modulation is represented in a constellation diagram by examining the middle Argand graph in Figure 14.6. This modulation is referred to as Quadrature Phase Shift Keying (QPSK, 4-QAM, or 4-PSK), with QPSK being the most common abbreviation. In this scheme, four states are encoded, with each state representing two bits. Each adjacent symbol only differs from the next by a single bit, which is called Gray coding.

Although QPSK is shown as a single representation of four phases, mathematically, QPSK may be represented as two independent quadrature carriers, each with two phases (one phase change), modulated by BPSK. This analysis indicates that the error rate of QPSK is the same error rate you experience when you use BPSK. However, when you use QPSK, you double the data rate versus BPSK using the same bandwidth. Alternatively, you can carry more channels with this modulation, as you can have the same data rate as BPSK in half the bandwidth.

You can imagine creating a higher-order modulation scheme by doubling the states in the QPSK, which leads you to a constellation diagram containing eight states. This form of modulation is called 8-PSK, and each state encodes for three bits with Gray coding. The constellation diagram for 8-PSK is shown in the right diagram in Figure 14.6. Practically speaking, 8-PSK is the highest order that can be achieved due to high error rates. To go beyond 8-PSK, other methods such as amplitude modulation are used, with one example being Quadrature Amplitude Modulation (QAM).

QPSK forms the basis for a number of techniques that can be used for modulation. One modulation separates the two quadrature portions of QPSK so that they are separated by time, with one carrier wave being a sine wave and the other carrier wave being a cosine wave; both are 180 degrees out of phase.

Another technique, called Offset Quadrature Phase Shift Keying (OQPSK) or Staggered Quadrature Phase Shift Keying (SQPSK), offsets the timing of the odd and even bits by a bit period; thus the in-phase (real or x-axis) and the quadrature (imaginary or y-axis) never vary by more than 90 degrees at a time. OQPSK offers better performance when signals are sent through a low pass filter, which is how many transmitters are constructed. The $\pi/4$-QPSK is another offset variation, which offsets the states by rotating them by 45 degrees, or $\pi/4$.

The 802.11a wireless standards, which use 52 carriers per channel spread over the 4915-5825 GHz band, have a channel separation of 20 MHz. 802.11a have been implemented using BPSK, QPSK, 16QAM, and 64QAM modulation, and a host of encoding schemes. This results in a net bit rate (throughput) of up to 54 Mbits/s with symbol length of 3.2 μsecs.

Now that you have seen how signals are encoded onto carrier waves, let's take a look at some of the multiplexing technologies used to create the carrier waves themselves. This includes the two types of spread spectrum technologies based on frequency hopping and direct sequences, and the now more widely used orthogonal frequency division multiplexing.

Direct-Sequence Spread Spectrum

Direct-Sequence Spread Spectrum (DSSS) is the modulation that is used by 802.11b and was used by the 802.11 legacy standards. Spread spectrum refers to the manner in which a wide band of low, constant-power density is partitioned to carry multiple channels of radio signals. Spread spectrum signals require that the transmitted signal's bandwidth be much wider than the information bandwidth, and that the transmitted bandwidth can be determined independently of the information that it carries.

Note

Please refer to the related discussion in Chapter 5 on multiplexing for background information on modulation technologies.

In Figure 14.7, you see the shape of a DSSS signal, just as you would if you hooked up a spectrum analyzer to the radio receiver. The graph plots the amplitude of the radio frequency (RF) signal on the y-axis (ordinate) and frequency on the x-axis (abscissa). The top graph shows DSSS technology; while the bottom graph shows FHSS technology. Compare the graph for DSSS technology to the graph for FHSS technology, which is commonly used in cell phones and discussed in detail in the next section.

Notice that the RF signal is spread out over a bandwidth that is 20 times wider than the signal. The common range for bandwidth-to-signal ratios is 20–250:1, and signals with ratios as high as 1000 have been demonstrated. That combination of a broad spectrum and low-power signal makes spread spectrum very hard to intercept and jam — which is why the technology has been so popular in the military for so long.

Direct sequence modulates a sine wave by applying a pseudo-random noise known as a chip. Chips are overlaid onto the radio wave at high frequency and have a very short duration. The chips, which are produced by a processor known as a chipper, create a signal structure that is known by the receiver beforehand. The pseudo-noise (PN) code at the receiver is applied using the same PN sequence to reconstruct the data. The transmitter sends a number known as a seed to the receiver beforehand, which is used by the pseudo-number algorithm to calculate the PN sequence.

Without the PN sequence, the high-speed sequence of 1 and –1 values appears to an independent observer to be white noise and spreads the energy of the signal carried over a wide band. Reconstruction of the signal, known as de-spreading, takes the PN sequence and multiplies the sequence using the highly synchronized pseudo-noise signal to obtain the data. Synchronization is achieved by transmitting a data sequence that provides access to a lookup table of channel sequences. Once the transmitter and receiver are synchronized, the future data sequences serve as a check of the current location of the sequence in the table.

FIGURE 14.7

A DSSS versus an FHSS carrier wave

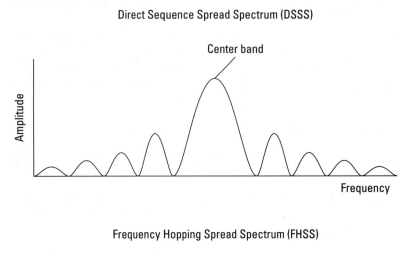

Direct Sequence Spread Spectrum (DSSS)

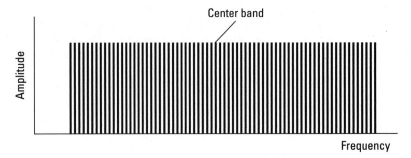

Frequency Hopping Spread Spectrum (FHSS)

A DSSS signal can be enhanced by increasing the PN sequence and using more chips per bit transmitted (improving the Signal-to-Noise ratio) within the limits of the technology employed, an effect referred to as process gain.

DSSS allows multiple channels to overlap because each signal has its own different PN sequence. This is the principle behind Code Division Multiple Access (CDMA), that multiple transmitters do not cross-correlate and the signals may be extracted independently of one another.

Spread spectrum transmission has a number of desirable features:

- Low power signals, which also helps to keep the Signal-to-Noise ratio low
- Ability to avoid other radio signals, or low narrowband interference
- Redundant transmission pathways

- Carrying capacity for multiple data streams, with each channel available to multiple users
- Security mechanism based on changing band assignments
- Low amount of fading and multipath interference

These features allow Wi-Fi to operate license-free over public radio bands. In addition to 802.11b/legacy, other devices that use DSSS are CDMA cell phones, wireless telephones (900 MHz, 2.4 GHz, and 5.8 GHz), GPS satellite (and the European Galileo equivalent), ZigBee digital radios based on the 802.15.4-2006 standards, and the automatic meter reading technology that is used by utility companies to read water, gas, and electric meters on houses.

Frequency Hopping Spread Spectrum

The Frequency Hopping Spread Spectrum (FHSS) modulation was used by 802.11 legacy in one of its modes, but it isn't used on other Wi-Fi standards. It is, however, used by other telecommunication systems, and so I briefly present it to you here. In practice, it isn't much different from DSSS. The main difference is that FHSS spreads the information by rapidly switching the carrier wave to many different frequencies using the same kind of pseudo-random number sequence for signal generation and extraction that DSSS used.

Figure 14.8 illustrates an FHSS signal shape, just as you would see it if you hooked a spectrum analyzer to a radio receiver. Notice that the shape of the wave is very different than the DSSS sinusoidal [(sin x)/x]2 wave. FHSS uses a flat, narrow signal whose bandwidth is the width of a signal versus the number of times the signal repeats. A frequency hopper can be made to be regularly spaced, as shown in Figure 14.8, or it can skip parts of the band; the data it carries can be either analog or digital.

FIGURE 14.8

An FHSS carrier wave

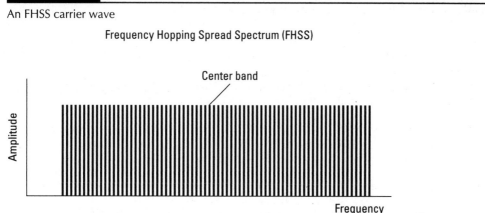

Frequency Hopping Spread Spectrum (FHSS)

FHSS transmissions are hard to detect and intercept, as the spread signal and pseudo-random nature makes it appear as if it is background noise. In order to reconstruct the signal, a receiver would need the PN sequence, which also makes it hard to intercept. FHSS (like DSSS) can be transmitted over radio bands that are carrying other types of transmissions and successfully extracted by the receiver.

Of all of the FHSS technologies in use today, the one you are most likely to encounter is Bluetooth, which uses the Adaptive Frequency Hopping (AFH) spread spectrum as its modulation. AFH uses hops over preferred frequencies, avoiding frequencies that are found to be of low quality or experiencing interference.

Orthogonal Frequency Division Multiplexing

Orthogonal Frequency Division Multiplexing (OFDM) is digital frequency division technology that is used by 802.11a/g/n/y. In this technology, multiple subcarrier waves are overlaid on top of each other with an offset so that the peak of one subcarrier overlaps with the trough of another. The use of multiple subcarriers is the multiplexing feature, while the overlap of one subcarrier is orthogonal to another. The overall carrier signal can be reduced by a Fast Fourier Transform by the transmitter and expanded by the receiver.

The easiest way to visualize how OFDM works is to consider how the signal is built up to form the carrier wave. Figure 14.9 shows a base subcarrier, which is then overlaid by five additional offset subcarriers. The top figure shows the base carrier and subcarriers, and the bottom figure shows the resultant carrier wave.

FIGURE 14.9

Combination of orthogonal subcarriers into an OFDM carrier

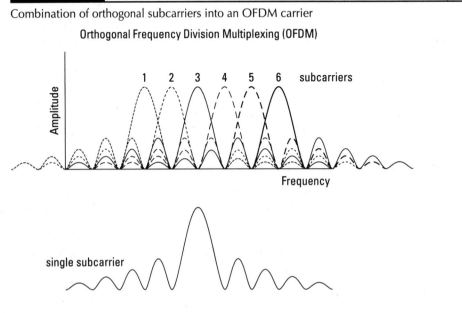

OFDM is widely used for the following reasons:

- Fast data transfer rates near the Nyquist theoretical limit, with bandwidth utilization
- Ability to suffer narrowband interference, fading, and multipath effects without loss of signal
- Ability to suffer time synchronization errors (However, OFDM is sensitive to frequency synchronization errors.)
- Efficient use of Fast Fourier Transforms for signal processing

All data transmission is degraded over distance, by resistance in wires, or for radio frequencies over wireless connection problems due to multipath or interference. *Multipath* is the term used to describe a radio signal that is sent or arrives at an antenna over two or more separate paths. This places limitations on the number of subcarriers that can be used and sometimes requires the use of a blank subcarrier called a guard band that provides additional time for signals to arrive, be buffered, and be processed before adding more data. The interference due to signal crowding is referred to as intersymbol interference (ISI), the term symbol being synonymous with an interpreted character. The guard band also helps to alleviate problems arising from imperfect orthogonality, which leads to signal degradation called intercarrier interference (ICI). Several other techniques make OFDM uniquely capable of tolerating severe interference while still being able to recover transmitted information, but ISI and ICI are two problems that OFDM suffers from.

One other disadvantage that does present a problem is that OFDM requires more power than other technologies.

Each of the subcarriers is then used to carry data, which is encoded using a modulation method such as Phase Shift Keying, quadrature amplitude modulation, or some other method. The data is therefore superimposed upon the carrier wave at a low bit rate (also called the symbol rate), and because there are a number of subcarriers, each carrying a part of the data stream, the throughput is equivalent to or higher than other forms of signaling technologies that rely on a single carrier.

OFDM is now the dominant form of multiplexing for all forms of wideband digital communication, be it wired technologies (such as ADSL, Powerline, or coaxial transmissions) or wireless technologies (such as Wi-Fi, digital radio, digital TV, and third-generation phone systems). The reason that OFDM multiplexing is so popular is that the technology allows new advances in modulation to be applied to the transmission without having to redesign the media or physical equipment.

802.11 protocol

The 802.11 protocol specifies the nature of 802.11 frames and their transport over the Physical and Media Access Control sublayer of the Data Link layer using the Carrier Sense Multiple Access with Collision Avoidance (CSMA/CA) protocol. The various 802.11x standards that were just described define the network access mechanisms and port assignments used by wireless devices to connect to Ethernet networks. Figure 14.10 illustrates the placement of the different 802.11 standards in relation to the OSI networking model.

In this model, the MAC layer handles synchronization, power management, roaming, and the MAC-MIB. The Physical layer contains the Physical Layer Convergence Protocol (PLCP) and Physical Medium Dependent (PMD) sublayers. The PLCP is the layer that handles the Carrier Sensing part of the CSMA/CA protocol. The PMD modulates and encodes the signal in the 802.11 protocol. As you can see in Figure 14.10, there are several different modulation schemes in use in the Physical layer. These include IR, CCK, FHSS, DSSS, and OFDM transmissions, which were described in the previous sections. CCK was described previously in the section on modulation.

FIGURE 14.10

The relationship of the 802.11 protocols to the OSI data model

OSI Layer 2 Data Link Layer	Logical Link Control (LLC) MAC Client 802.2					
	Medium Access Control (MAC) CSMA/CA 802.11					
OSI Layer 1 Physical Layer	Infrared (IR)	Frequency Hopping Spread Spectrum (FHSS)	Direct Sequence Spread Spectrum (DSSS)	Computer Code Keying (CCK) with DSSS	OFDM+ (BPSK/QPSK/ 16QAM/64QAM) with CCK & DSSS	OFDM+ (BPSK/QPSK/ 16QAM/64QAM)
Connection	Infrared 800 – 900 nm	2.4 GHz Radio Frequency ISM band			2.4 GHz Radio Frequency	5.0 GHz Radio Frequency
Throughput	1.0/2.0 Mbps	1.6 Mbps	1.0/2.0 Mbps	1.0/2.0/5.5/11.0 Mbps	1/2/5.5/6/9/11/12/18/ 24/36/48/54 Mbps	6/9/12/18/24/36/ 48/54 Mbps

---

Collision avoidance

There are two main systems for collision avoidance that are used on 802.11 wireless connections—Distributed Coordination Function (DCF), also called the Physical Carrier Sense Method (PCSM), and point coordination function (PCF). In DCF, the station that will transmit data listens for a quiet period and then transmits a frame. The period between frame transmissions, while short, is randomized, and with DCF the transmitting station will then send a stop and wait for an Automatic Repeat reQuest (ARQ) packet after each packet it sends. The sending station then waits for an acknowledgment (ACK) or a negative acknowledgment (NAK) reply from the receiver before sending more packets. Other stations that want to break into the conversation are limited by the fact that the wait between ARQ and ACK/NAK is much shorter than the listening period.

The second technology employed for collision avoidance is PCF. Some references refer to this technique as the virtual carrier sense method. In situations where the transmitter and receiver are separated by enough distance, the time lag between an ARQ and an ACK/NAK may be too long to avoid interruptions. Other sending stations may transmit during the delay, introducing collisions into the wireless network at the point of convergence, which usually is at the access point. This phenomenon is called the hidden node problem, because two computers on a wireless network that are separated by enough distance may appear to be hidden from one another.

Ethernet, as you may recall from Chapter 11, uses a similar version of CSMA called CSMA/CD, where instead of practicing collision avoidance, it manages collision detection. The reason for this difference is that it is difficult to detect collisions over a wireless medium, and so Wi-Fi adds additional mechanisms to avoid collisions in the first place, which unfortunately adds additional overhead and lowers throughput for wireless connections.

The potential solution to the hidden node problem is to create the equivalent of a shared managed circuit at the access point. PCF works by requiring transmitting stations to send a request to send (RTS) packet to the wireless access point. The RTS is then transmitted to other wireless nodes, and after a certain period, if the access point doesn't detect a transmission from another node, it sends a clear to send (CTS) packet to the transmitting node that sent the RTS and locks the circuit for that transmitter to use.

802.11 frame structure

The 802.11 MAC frame specification is shown in Figure 14.11. It is similar in structure to Ethernet frames, which are described in detail in Chapter 13. The frame consists of three parts: a Preamble, the PLCP Header, and the MAC PDU, which contains all of the data and the unique fields of the 802.11 protocol. When you examine the MAC PDU in detail, you find that it consists of three parts: the Header, Data, and a CRC32 checksum used to validate the frame. The Data portion is variable in length. Because the Data or payload portion of the frame originates at higher protocol levels, and CRC checksums use a standard algorithm, there's little more to say here about their use. In Figure 14.11 the dotted lines indicate that that portion of the frame or field is expanded in the bar below it.

Continuing our Fantastic Voyage into 802.11 frames, you can see that the Header field contains all of the Session layer data. It is a little unique in that regard, because it contains four address fields where an Ethernet frame would contain two address fields: Sender and Destination. An 802.11 frame not only needs to account for the sender and target for the frame but it also needs to account for the MAC of the access point through which the frame must travel. Indeed, if the network is a peer-to-peer or ad hoc network, then a fourth address field is used that specifies the initial host in the P2P network that sends the beacon frames that other clients use to connect to that P2P network. Here is a summary of the address fields:

- ADDRESS_1 corresponds to the Receiver Address (RA) or destination.
- ADDRESS_2 corresponds to the Transmitter Address (TA) or sender.
- ADDRESS_3 corresponds to the Destination Address (DA), which is the ultimate destination of the frame.
- ADDRESS_4 corresponds to the Source Address (SA), which is the MAC address of the source that originally created and sent the frame.

FIGURE 14.11

The structure of an 802.11 frame

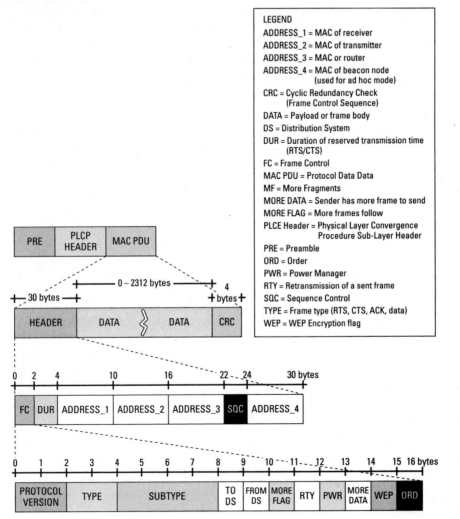

LEGEND

ADDRESS_1 = MAC of receiver
ADDRESS_2 = MAC of transmitter
ADDRESS_3 = MAC or router
ADDRESS_4 = MAC of beacon node
(used for ad hoc mode)
CRC = Cyclic Redundancy Check
(Frame Control Sequence)
DATA = Payload or frame body
DS = Distribution System
DUR = Duration of reserved transmission time
(RTS/CTS)
FC = Frame Control
MAC PDU = Protocol Data Data
MF = More Fragments
MORE DATA = Sender has more frame to send
MORE FLAG = More frames follow
PLCE Header = Physical Layer Convergence
Procedure Sub-Layer Header
PRE = Preamble
ORD = Order
PWR = Power Manager
RTY = Retransmission of a sent frame
SQC = Sequence Control
TYPE = Frame type (RTS, CTS, ACK, data)
WEP = WEP Encryption flag

The Duration field sets the amount of time that the frame is active (that is, can be forwarded before it is dropped), and a Frame Control field provides the mechanism that differentiates one form of 802.11 frame from another. In order to be able to sequence a set of frames, the Sequence Control field contains a 12-bit identifier for the Sequence number and a following 4-bit Fragment number for the frame's position in the Sequence number. A Sequence number is a counter that starts at 0 and is incremented to 4095 after which it is set back to zero. The Fragment number is incremented by one for each fragment as required, up to the limit of the field, which is 24 or 16.

The Frame Control field is the final expansion in Figure 14.11. This 16-bit field contains the following subfields:

- **Protocol Version.** This field displays the version of the 802.11 protocol used to create the frame. Any receiving STA can then determine if the frame can be properly handled based on that value.

- **Type.** The Type field contains a value that specifies whether the frame is a Control frame, Data frame, or Management frame. For example, Type 00 is a Management frame, and some of its allowed subtypes include 0100 Probe Req, 0101 Probe Resp, 1000 Beacon, and so forth.

- **Subtype.** Some frame types have an associated set of subtypes used to perform a specific operation. The Control frame subtypes include RTS, CTS, and ACK frames. A Data frame doesn't have a subtype. Management frames include the Beacon, Probe Request/Response, Association Request/Response, Reassociation Request/Response, Disassociation, Authentication, and Deauthentication.

- **To DS** and **From DS.** These two fields indicate if a frame is going to or coming from the inter-cell distribution center on a cell phone network, or to or from a router in a distributed network.

- **More Flag.** This Boolean field indicates whether there are more fragments of this particular frame being transmitted.

- **Retry (RTY).** A Boolean field that indicates that this frame has been previously sent.

- **Power Management (PWR).** A Boolean field that provides the state of the sending STA, either active or power-saving mode.

- **More Data.** A Boolean field that is used to signal a receiving STA that is in power-saving mode that more frames are on the way. APs that receive a frame with this field ON interpret it to mean that multicast or broadcast frames are being transmitted.

- **WEP.** This field indicates whether the Wireless Encryption Protocol (WEP) has been applied to the frame.

- **ORD.** The ORD field notifies the receiver that a sequence of frames with the ORD bit set to ON are to be processed in order.

Connection example

Let's consider briefly the process involved in connecting an STA (wireless client) to a wireless access point in infrastructure mode. There are three separate parts to the process: scanning for a signal, authentication, and association. During association, the STA and AP are connected using a logically equivalent named object to a network connection for a wired network. Figure 14.12 illustrates the handshake described in this section.

There are two separate types of scanning: active and passive. When actively scanning, the STA sends out Probe Req (Request) frames, and the AP then replies with a Probe Resp (Response) frame. In the passive scanning mode, the STA is monitoring the network, listening for a Beacon frame. The different frame types contain different fields in the Data or payload portion.

FIGURE 14.12

A handshake creating a connection between an STA and AP on an open system

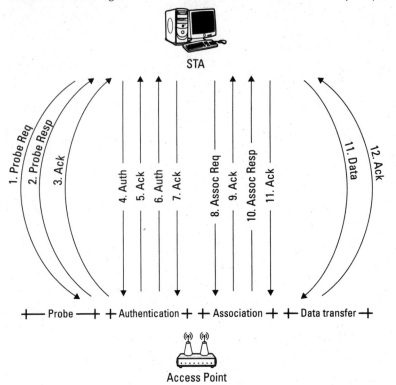

STA

1. Probe Req
2. Probe Resp
3. Ack
4. Auth
5. Ack
6. Auth
7. Ack
8. Assoc Req
9. Ack
10. Assoc Resp
11. Ack
11. Data
12. Ack

+— Probe —+ +—Authentication—+ +—Association—+ +—Data transfer—+

Access Point

The authentication portion of the handshake depends upon whether an open connection, a shared key with WEP encrypted connection, or a WPA 802.11x connection is made. The open connection is easiest; the STA sends an Authentication frame and the AP sends an Authentication frame in reply.

To create an association based on a shared key and WEP, WEP must be enabled on both endpoints of the connection. The STA sends the Authentication frame, and the AP replies with an Authentication frame with a clear text challenge. The STA then replies to the challenge by sending back an Authentication frame with the encrypted challenge response. The AP decrypts the response and compares it to the challenge text. If there is a match, an Authentication frame is generated that is marked with a successful status and sent to the STA.

Wireless Access Points and Gateways

A wireless access point (AP or WAP) is a transmitting and receiving device that is a node on a wireless network. An AP connects a wired network to a wireless one. The best way to think of an AP is that it is a wired-to-wireless bridge. An AP can also be a bridge between two wired networks when one AP connects to another AP. When you walk into a coffee shop and connect to a network, chances are that you are connecting to an AP. This type of networking is sometimes referred to as a Lilly Pad network, because wireless clients, like frogs, hop from hotspot to hotspot.

Most APs are limited to a single subnet of 255 clients, although performance limitations set a much lower practical limit for concurrent connections. You can buy an AP in 802.11a (rare), 802.11b (common), 802.11g (common), 802.11n (emerging), or combinations of two or three of these standards. Of the different combinations, 802.11b/g is the most common, 802.11a/g is less common, 802.11a/b/c is less common still, and 802.11n usually ships by itself.

Most home networks either purchase or have gateways installed at the interface of their broadband connection and the home network. Some of these gateways bridge the WAN to either a wired or wireless LAN, or both. A gateway is differentiated from an AP by the services it provides. Most gateways have DHCP and DNS servers that can be turned on, many have simple firewall functions such as Name Address Translation (NAT), and routing functions, and they often provide Universal Plug and Play (UPnP). Wireless gateways overlap with wireless routers, but are not nearly as robust in terms of their routing and firewall functionality. To designate devices that aren't pure gateways, the terms residential gateway, integrated gateway, or some other hybrid term is used.

Gateways offer the following services:

- 802.11 wireless connectivity
- Device association, setup, and configuration
- 802.3 router features and NAT traversal
- DHCP, DNS, IPv6
- Security (WEP and WPA)
- Device discovery and UPnP
- Diagnostics and utilities

In the next section, devices that extend the wireless network — repeaters and bridges — are described. Unlike gateways, which indicate network and broadcast boundaries, repeaters and bridges make the network bigger — that is, cover more area.

Repeaters and bridges

A repeater, wireless range extender, or signal booster is a device that takes the signal that it receives and retransmits it at a higher signal strength. Repeaters use the same settings as the device they are repeating, and do not add additional complexity to the wireless network. When placed near the limit of an access point's range, the repeaters add an additional area of coverage for the signal. Many APs have a special mode that allows them to be a repeater. In Figure 14.13, you can see the setting for defining a D-Link 802.11g Wireless Range Extender. A repeater may amplify the signal 50 percent or more, dependent upon the protocol, device, and antennas used.

FIGURE 14.13

Setting the repeater mode for an 802.11 access point/range extender

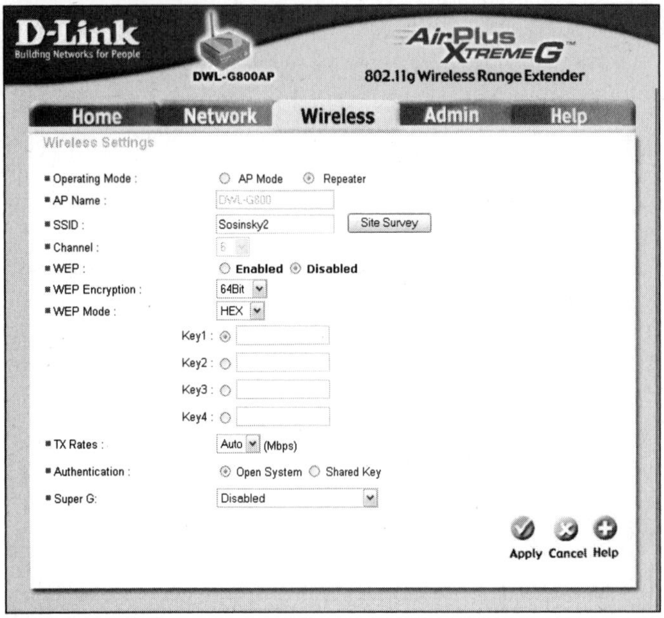

Tip

Repeaters can be finicky. When possible, use a repeater that is made by the same vendor as any AP, gateway, or router that it is repeating.

An AP can receive a signal from another AP on a different channel. When placed in repeater mode, the device needs to be set to the same channel and must also share the same SSID settings. Repeaters do reduce throughput, which limits their use on larger networks or for heavy traffic. Repeaters must both amplify a signal as well as broadcast it, which doubles the number of frames that the device transmits. However, for a home or a small office, repeaters are useful.

A good way to determine the number of wireless devices that you need is to draw a floor plan for your site with the different devices mapped out to show their coverage. This type of drawing can be valuable for determining when new devices are required, who needs to connect to which device, and many other assignments. An example of a wireless site plan is shown in Figure 14.14.

FIGURE 14.14

Using overlap profiles to make a network available throughout a floor

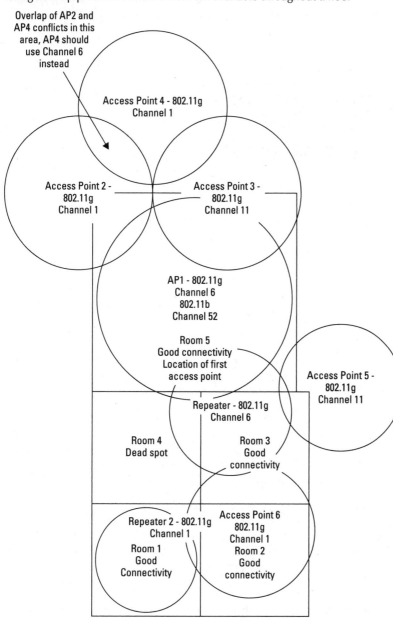

Overlap of AP2 and AP4 conflicts in this area, AP4 should use Channel 6 instead

Access Point 4 - 802.11g
Channel 1

Access Point 2 -
802.11g
Channel 1

Access Point 3 -
802.11g
Channel 11

AP1 - 802.11g
Channel 6
802.11b
Channel 52

Room 5
Good connectivity
Location of first
access point

Access Point 5 -
802.11g
Channel 11

Repeater - 802.11g
Channel 6

Room 4
Dead spot

Room 3
Good
connectivity

Repeater 2 - 802.11g
Channel 1

Access Point 6
802.11g
Channel 1

Room 1
Good
Connectivity

Room 2
Good
connectivity

Not all APs offer a bridging mode, and many that do aren't particularly efficient. Bridging tends to be better in enterprise wireless devices than those sold for the home market. It's always easier to bridge between two identical devices, and failing that, at least bridge between two devices from the same vendor using the same 802.11x protocol. To bridge two APs, do the following:

1. Open the wireless management software for AP_1 and set the device to point-to-point or wireless bridge mode.

2. Enter the MAC address for AP_2 into the bridge table.

3. Set the SSID and channel for AP_1.

4. Repeat Steps 1 to 3 for AP_2, entering the MAC address for AP_1 into that device's bridge table.

5. Position the devices and their antennas appropriately and test the connection.

You may find that vendors have different names for wireless bridging topologies: access point mode, workgroup bridge mode, point to point, redundant point to point, point to multipoint, and so on. The most common bridging topologies are:

- **Point-to-point,** a one-to-one topology.

- **Point-to-multipoint,** a one-to-many topology. Here, one access point is a root bridge and the others are non-root bridges. The root bridge is responsible for authentication and root assignment; bridge assignments should be unique and assigned the lowest bridge ID number. The root bridge should be placed in a central location to maximize throughput and coverage. In a point-to-point connection, when a root bridge isn't located the non-root bridge assumes the duties of a root bridge.

- **Redundant multipoint.** Duplicate pairs of APs are endpoints in a wireless connection, so that if one connection fails, the other can still support traffic between the two LANs.

Wireless Distribution System

You can create a bridging link between two LANs using two access points in the Wireless Distribution System (WDS) mode. APs can be a main station that is connected to a LAN, a relay station, or a remote station. The relay station is a forwarding point between two other APs. Although this system bears a topological relationship to a bridge and is sometimes referred to as repeater mode, WDS also reduces the throughput of any wireless router/client connection by half, due to the forwarding traffic at the router that is connected to the wireless client.

WDS offers two different modes:

- **Wireless Bridging between two APs,** which only supports AP-to-AP communications

- **Wireless Repeating,** where the APs communicate with one another and with a wireless client

WDS isn't a Wi-Fi standard, and if you choose to implement this system, you will have a better experience if you use products from the same vendor when doing so.

Note

Cisco's use of the acronym WDS refers to the Wireless Domain Service. This service is part of the Cisco Structured Wireless Aware Network (SWAN) that is used for roaming client services, and WLAN deployment and management.

Any wireless client that sends data to clients on a LAN through a remote AP has their frames forwarded to the relay or main AP without a change in the MAC addresses of the packets. Packets originating on the LAN are forwarded by the base AP to other members of the WDS automatically.

Each component in the WDS is assigned a different Service Set Identifier (SSI), and a table is created with each of the MAC addresses of APs in the WDS. Depending on the vendor, there may be a limit to the number of participants allowed. WDS must be configured so that all devices are on the same channel and are configured using the same security protocol (WEP or WPA) with the same keys. One problem with the current versions of WDS is that there is no mechanism for automatically changing the encryption keys during a session. This means that WDS works with WEP and with WPA-PSK, but does not support WPA2.

To set up a WDS connection, follow these steps:

1. In the network management utility, select the first two APs in your WDS system.

2. Find WDS and enable it on the first AP, entering the MAC address of the second AP into the first address box in the WDS table.

3. Select the channel of the first AP.

4. Open the management settings for the second AP, enable WDS, and enter the MAC address for the first AP in that device's WDS table.

5. Set the channel for the second AP to the same value as the first AP.

6. Continue to add APs, as required.

Caution

Care must be taken not to set up a WDS in such a way that it creates loops.

It is easy to create topological network loops with WDS, and when you do so, traffic will continue to circulate around the loop and cause network crashes. To avoid this problem, make sure that you avoid the following three scenarios:

- **Two APs with a WDS,** each connected to the same Ethernet link

- **Two APs connected by two WDS lines,** with one link being an 802.11a link and the other being an 802.11b/g link

- **Three APs connected with three links:** an 802.11b/g link, and two 802.11a links in a loop.

Figure 14.15 illustrates the three loop conditions.

FIGURE 14.15

Examples of WDS loops that can cause network crashes

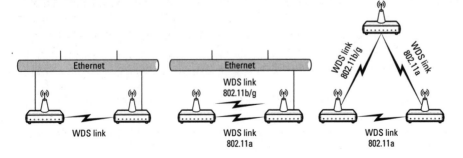

The following products are known to support WDS:

- 3COM Wireless 7760 11a/b/g PoE access point
- Alcatel Speed Touch (716 and 780)
- Apple Time Capsule, Airport Extreme, and Airport Express
- Asus WL-500g/gc/gU
- Belkin FD57230-4
- Cisco Wireless AP (Aironet)
- D-Link (DGL-4300, DWL-2100AP, DAP-1160)
- Motorola WR850G/GS
- Netgear ProSafe access point (WG102, WAG102, WG302, WAG302, and WG602v2/3)
- PLANET Wireless AP and Router (WAP-4000A, WAP-4033, WAP-4035, WAP-4036, WAP-4060PE, WRT-414, WRT-416, and WNRT-620)
- SMC EZ Connect g Wireless access point (SMCWEBT-G) SMC7988VoWBRA, SMC Barricade SMCWBR14T-G/G2
- USRobotics Professional access point (5453), MAXg (5432, 5441, 5451, 5455, 5461, 5465, and 9108), and Ndx (5454, 5464, and 9113)
- Zoom X6

These are just some of the WDS-supported devices that are available.

Wireless Routers and Gateways

As you learned in Chapter 9, routers are devices that connect two or more networks together and have some intelligence in them in the form of routing tables and algorithms for directing traffic along preferred routes. Routers are Layer 3 gateways, and function at the Network level in the OSI model.

A wireless router has the same functionality as a wired router, but adds a wireless interface so that it can function as an access point. Many small office home office (SOHO) routers have a few (four is typical) Ethernet ports, an 802.11 AP, and a parallel or USB port so that they can share a peripheral device such as a printer. The Linksys WRT54GL (802.11b/g), shown in Figure 14.16, is the classic example of a SOHO router.

FIGURE 14.16

The Linksys WRT54GL broadband router is popular because it is Linux-based, relatively inexpensive (US$60), configurable, and easily customized.

The one differentiating factor that separates an AP from a router is that an AP allows a client to browse or communicate with only one network, while a router allows a client to connect to two or more networks. Routers also examine IP packets to see what the destination is, and then route the packets based on the address. Access points do not examine the destination of packets, and forward all packets that they receive.

Consider using a router in place of an AP in the following situations:

- You have only one IP address to share. Routers provide DHCP and also DNS, as well as NAT for IP address sharing.
- You have to connect to multiple networks.

- You have a busy wireless network and require better network throughput than an AP provides.

- You require better network management, more powerful diagnostic tools, and browser-based control over a wireless network connection than most APs offer.

- You need more enhanced security, filters based on MAC addresses, IP addresses, domain names, time of day, and other features that are often offered by firewalls. Some routers support multi-session IPsec, VPN, WEP, and other security options.

Router configuration

Most wireless routers are configured by browser-based utilities. You enter the IP address for the wired portion of the router, and log into the utility with an ID and password. Although you can set most routers up manually, most are configured using some form of wizard or easy setup function. To configure a router, in most cases, you will need to provide the following pieces of information:

- The IP address and the domain server for the broadband or WAN network. In many cases, this network interface is set by DHCP by an ISP, and you set the router to accept an address automatically.

- The IP address pool for the wireless network interface. If you turn on the router's DHCP, then clients can take a dynamic address; or clients can be assigned static addresses from the same subnet.

- The assigned service set identifier (SSID) and the channel number.

- The type of security that you want to implement, and a new administrator ID and password. Although you can use the default administrator account settings, these are well known by hackers who can use them to compromise your system.

- Any filter types that you want to implement, such as MAC address filtering.

Router upgrades

There are many freeware or shareware router upgrades available. They turn a $60 router into the equivalent of a much more expensive router product with the advanced features added in software. An example of these is BrainSlayer's DD-WRT open source firmware upgrade (www.dd-wrt.com/wiki/index.php/Main_Page), which has a feature list that is too long to detail fully. Among the highlights are OpenVPN, QoS, Samba, Site Survey, WDS, MAC filtering, WPA over WDS, and others.

The Tomato router from polarcloud.com (www.polarcloud.com/tomato) is another significant upgrade to the software that many vendors include with their routers. It adds a friendly GUI, and has a number of advanced features such as a bandwidth monitor, QoS, access control, connection management (P2P), CIFS (Samba), WDS, Telnet, scripts, and wireless site survey.

The Tomato router is displayed inside a browser such as Firefox or Internet Explorer. Figure 14.17 shows the Bandwidth Usage screen inside Tomato. Tomato is particularly strong in displaying reports. You can display charts on your connection distribution based on your QoS rules.

FIGURE 14.17

Bandwidth monitoring is one of the features offered by the Tomato router software.

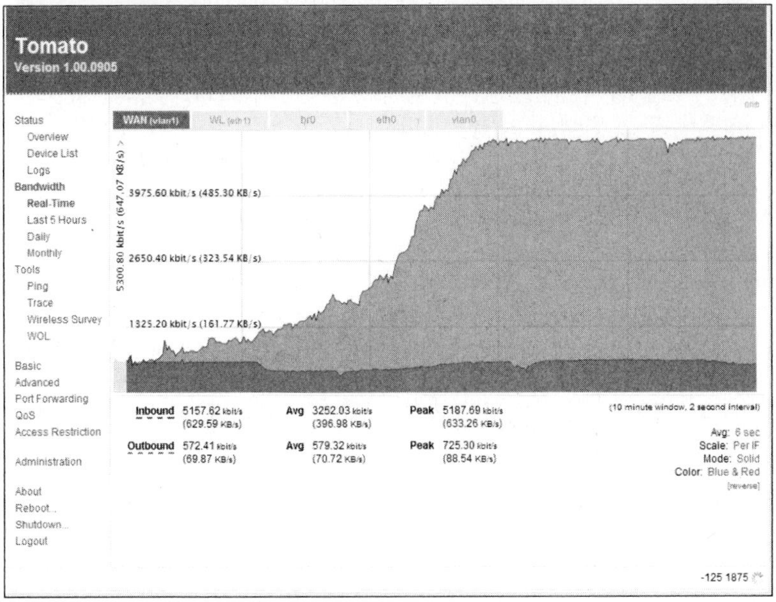

The Tomato router software is a firmware upgrade for Broadcom-based router chipset products, including:

- Linksys WRT54G v1-v4, WRT54GS v1-v4, WRT54GL v1.x, WRTSL54GS (no USB support)
- Buffalo WHR-G54S, WHR-HP-G54, WZR-G54, WBR2-G54
- Asus WL500g Premium (no USB support)
- SparkLAN WX-6615GT

In particular, this is a very popular upgrade for the Linksys WRT54GL; the "L" in the name indicates that the router uses a Linux kernel. One feature offered by Tomato is called signal boosting. The WRT54GL is set to transmit at a default power of 42 mW, but can be boosted to 251 mW as a software setting, with 70 mW considered to be a safe setting. The one setting essentially doubles the coverage of the router, which alone makes it valuable.

Taken as a whole, the Tomato router isn't quite as powerful as DD-WRT, but it is much easier to work with. Both products dramatically improve the functionality of your wireless router, provided that the model you have supports the upgrade.

OLPC XO Wireless Network

The One Laptop Per Child (OLPC; www.laptop.org) project developed as its networking technology a P2P ad hoc wireless network that is highly mobile, topology-independent, and self-healing. Each laptop can locate and find other laptops to create a network link, thus providing shared access to resources for all systems currently connected. The first model laptop, called the XO, has a number of unique features that space precludes describing here, but the wireless mesh network (WMN) that is created by XO is one of the most important features, as it enables communication on the system.

A self-configuring, self-healing mobile network is sometime referred to as a mobile wireless ad hoc mesh network, or MANET. When the wireless system involves vehicles, it may be referred to as a Vehicle Wireless Ad Hoc Network, or VANET.

The wireless mesh networking chip in the XO laptop runs software that is compliant with the IEEE 802.11s draft standards for mesh networking. It enables communications with other devices out of the box. The 802.11s standards extend the 802.11 MAC to support unicast and broadcast/multicast transmission over self-configuring multi-hop topologies. In the 802.11s mesh network architecture, each node is called a Mesh Point (MP). MPs can be standard 802.11 APs. Figure 14.18 shows the Space mesh view with discovered Wi-Fi devices.

FIGURE 14.18

The XO laptop with the Space mesh neighborhood view. Each icon on the laptop screen represents the condition of a wireless device within connection distance.

The 802.11s defines a routing protocol called the Hybrid Wireless Mesh Protocol, or HWMP, that is a mandatory component of the draft standards' compliance. HWMP is meant to be vendor-independent, allowing any device running 802.11s to participate in any MANET it finds.

The routing protocol for HWMP is based on elements of the Ad hoc On-Demand Distance Vector (AODV) routing protocol and a tree search algorithm. AODV was developed by university researchers and uses a distance-vector algorithm. AODV is currently in a draft standard and can be viewed at http://tools.ietf.org/html/rfc3561. A previous protocol called Destination-Sequence Distance Vector routing (DSDV), which AODV is based on, creates ad hoc networks using a dynamically populated lookup table of known hops; this is suitable for a network with a small number of nodes but can suffer from performance problems when a large number of paths must be calculated. AODV improves on DSDV by using an algorithm to calculate the metrics of a route, by taking into consideration both the hop count and the next hop performance information. It learns of different routes by transmitting a RouteRequest packet and waiting for a RouteReady reply.

The 802.11s standard allows for the use of a server on the network. The One Laptop Per Child server is called the OLPC XS school server. That server supports XO clients, up to 100 laptops per school server. The OLPC laptops and servers are currently the only products that you can buy with 802.11s built into them, although that will change rapidly over the next couple of years. Starting with Linux kernel version 2.2.26, the 802.11s standards will be built into the mac80211 layer of the operating system.

Antennas

Antennas play a significant role in the ability of a wireless device to transmit or receive signals. Many antennas are omni-directional, some are directional, and a few are highly directional, depending upon the nature of their construction.

Figure 14.19 shows these three different types of antenna profiles. The top profile is omni-directional, and antennas of this type tend to be spherical in design. The middle profile is directional and is directed out over two of the three Cartesian axes. Antennas that project with a directional profile are exemplified by a corner antenna. Highly directional profiles are projected down a single axis of the three Cartesian axes. Yagi antennas look like long sticks or boom microphones and have a highly directional profile. These different antenna types are shown in Figure 14.19.

Antenna characteristics

You measure the efficiency of an antenna by its gain, normally given as a rating in decibels (dB). The ratio of the output signal strength of an amplifier to the input strength of the signal is the gain. Gain is more often expressed in terms of the number of decibels that a hypothetical isotropic radiator would have in units of dBi. An isotropic radiator is one that radiates a signal equally in all directions. Antennas offer reciprocal gain (amplification both for transmission and reception). So adding a better antenna should improve the signal for both endpoints of a wireless connection.

FIGURE 14.19

Antenna directional profiles

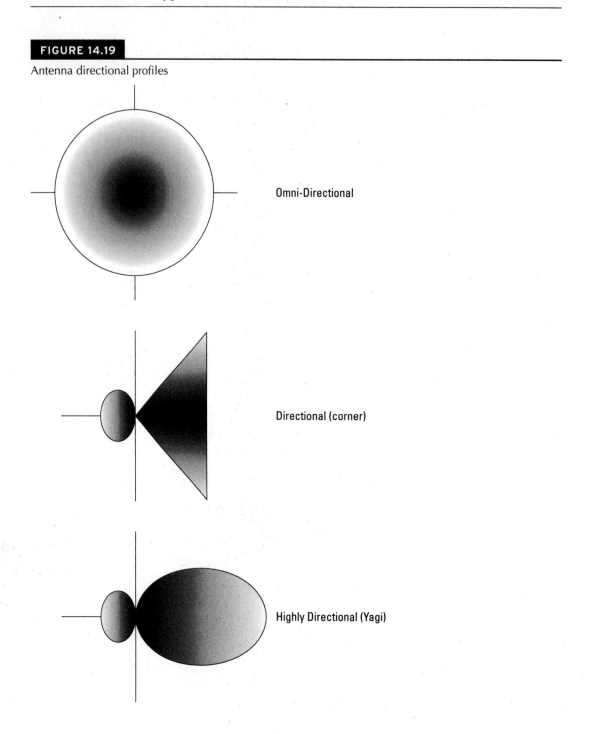

Omni-Directional

Directional (corner)

Highly Directional (Yagi)

Antennas are tuned for a specific frequency, or they are tunable. An antenna designed for an 802.11b signal won't work well for a higher-frequency 802.11g signal, although the reverse is commonly true.

Radio signals are subject to reflection effects that create interference patterns. The result is an effect called multipathing. A receptor locks onto the strongest signal, but at certain places in the path, signals interfere with one another and create dead spots. Moving a wireless antenna or changing its direction can often have a major impact on performance.

Wireless signals over air lose strength over distance, as described by the free space path loss equation. The loss varies as a square of the distance. Indoors, wireless signal loss is dependent upon the material involved. Concrete lowers a wireless signal more than wood. The amount of material is also important, and so signal strength is greater up through a ceiling than it might be traversing a wall at a highly oblique angle. Some wireless devices allow you to modify their power output, thus increasing their coverage area and the dispersion of any directional antenna attached to the device.

An omni-directional antenna radiates equally in all directions and usually takes the form of a thin rod or long, flat stick. A directional antenna is one with a wide dispersion of 80 to 120 degrees. Directional antennas are often used in room corners and radiate to all parts of the room. Directional antennas are parabolic reflectors, right-angle deflectors, and panel deflectors that concentrate the signal. Highly directional antennas use a line of perpendicular elements, a can (cylindrical enclosure), or both. The classic example of a highly directional antenna is a Yagi antenna. Some directional antennas can achieve connections in the range of 1 to 10 miles line of sight, but are very sensitive to obstructions.

The directional nature of an antenna is described by its Front-to-Back (F/B) ratio. The F/B ratio measures the center point beam strength in both directions and takes its ratio. Omni-directional antennas have F/B ratios approaching 1.0; for highly directional Yagi antennas, the ratio can be on the order of 5 or 6. Figure 14.20 shows four different types of wireless antennas— a) Hawking HAI7SIP Hi-Gain 7 dBi Omni-Directional Antenna; b) Hawking HAI8DD Hi-Gain 8 dBi Directional Dish Antenna; c) Hawking HAI15SC Hi-Gain 15 dBi Corner Antenna; d) Wade J250-915-10 900 MHz 13 dB Yagi Antenna.

An antenna's radiation pattern shows the directional nature of the signal strength. The vertical slice of the radiation pattern or elevation cut can be very different from the horizontal slice of the radiation pattern, called the azimuth. This difference is important for any WLAN that spans floors or covers an entire building. An increase in the power of the signal can narrow either the elevation plane or the azimuth plane's coverage, or both for an antenna. A radiated signal can be circular, or it can be mainly horizontal or vertical.

The orientation of an antenna is affected by its polarization. In an antenna, the magnetic and electric fields are perpendicular. With a horizontally polarized antenna, the antenna is meant to be positioned so that its electric field is parallel with the ground. For a vertically polarized antenna, the electric field should be perpendicular to the ground. Both antennas participating in a wireless connection need to have their polarization aligned.

FIGURE 14.20

Four different types of wireless antennas

Omni-Directional

a) Hawking HAI7SIP Hi-Gain 7dBi Omni-Directional Antenna

Directional

b) Hawking HAI8DD Hi-Gain 8dBi Directional Dish Antenna

Room Coverage

c) Hawking HAI15SC Hi-Gain 15dBi Corner Antenna

Highly Directional

d) Wade J250-915-10 900 MHz 13 dB Yagi

Antennas with a signal strength that is isotropic (the same in all directions) have a gain of 1 dB or 0 dB. A gain of 2 dB or 3 dB represents a doubling of the signal strength. Each additional 3 dB doubles the signal strength. You would use a higher-gain antenna to improve the transmitted signal. The limit for a wireless signal is set by law. The United States has a limit of 1000 mW, Japan's limit is 10 mW/MHz, and in Europe it is 100 mW (as measured by the Equivalent Isotropic Radiate Power, or EIRP). The gain can be different when transmitting or receiving.

An antenna's beamwidth is a measure of the angle at which a transmission drops off in each of the two principle axes. The angle is measured between the points at which the signal is half the maximum signal down the center of the beam. Narrow beamwidth antennas are more powerful and have a longer range.

Multiple-Input Multiple-Output

Multiple-Input Multiple-Output (MIMO) is a multi-antenna technology that boosts the performance of wireless transmission and reception, part of a new generation of "smart antennas" that are changing the nature of 802.11x wireless communication. MIMO itself is part of the specification of 802.11n, 802.16e WIMAX broadband mobile, and will be found in all of the next-generation 4G networks.

MIMO works by creating multiple data streams over the same band concurrently using spatial multiplexing, which has the potential to double or triple throughput. The different streams can also take different paths from the transmitter to the receiver (reflecting off of surfaces if necessary), and with proper processing, all the received signals are superposed to create an enhanced reception, which increases gain and lowers multipath interference. Figure 14.21 illustrates the superposition of two antenna signals with MIMO, plotting the Signal-to-Noise Ratio (SNR) to the frequency.

FIGURE 14.21

Combining MIMO antenna signals in a two-antenna array to enhance signal reception

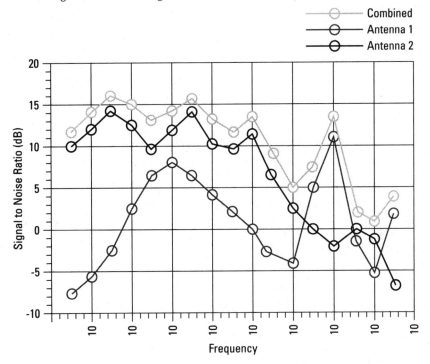

MIMO antennas offer the following benefits:

- Resistance to fading
- Larger coverage, greater capacity, and increased data throughput
- Better spectral efficiency
- Reduced power consumption
- Lower network costs

Many wireless devices sport multiple antennas and can benefit to some degree from this superposition effect. For example, when you have multiprotocol access points, such as 802.11b/g, they may come with one antenna tuned for 802.11b and another tuned for 802.11g. What separates MIMO from these other devices is that MIMO antennas have a Digital Signal Processor (DSP) that breaks the carrier wave up into a set of carriers and then transmits the RF over each antenna separately. At the receiving end, each antenna collects a signal and feeds it back into a DSP for recombination. Using MIMO results in more power being transmitted, and it can be engineered to create a more focused beam; as a result, you get both increased power gain and array gain. Figure 14.22 shows the Linksys Wireless-N PCI Adapter with MIMO technology and antennas.

FIGURE 14.22

Linksys Wireless-N PCI Adapter with MIMO technology and antennas

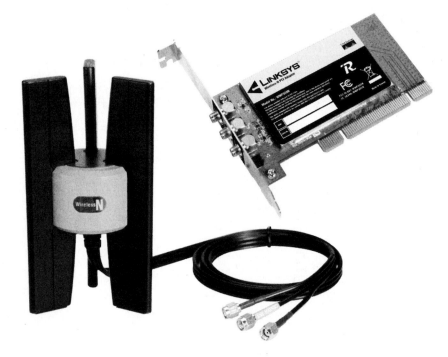

Wireless Software

Because most Wi-Fi devices are managed either in the operating system or through the software that the manufacturer bundles with the devices, the most common category of Wi-Fi software that people install are network scanners. Network scanners are already built into most desktop operating systems. When you open the Windows network connections and scan for wireless networks, the software doing the scanning is a network scanner.

The results returned in Windows XP and Vista are a pictograph with five bars representing the connection strengths: poor, fair, good, very good, and excellent. Figure 14.23 shows the Wireless Network Connection Status dialog box from Vista. While this information is useful and lets you decide which wireless network to connect to based on reception, the speed of the network, and how long the interface has been up, it's not nearly enough information to diagnose a wireless network and get a good picture on how different systems are faring. To this end, there are a number of network scanning packages that you can install that give a wide range of information that is useful. Many of these programs were developed by enthusiasts and are free or inexpensive shareware that you can try and then purchase.

FIGURE 14.23

The Wireless Network Connection Status dialog box in Microsoft Vista

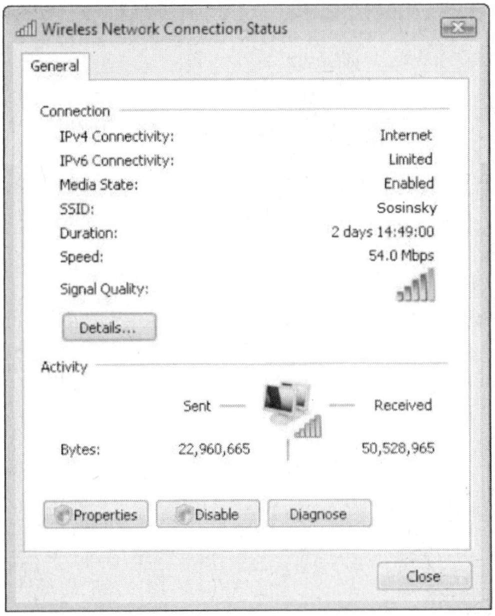

The granddaddy of network scanners is Marius Milner's Network Stumbler (http://stumbler.net), or NetStumbler, which is in version 4.0, released in 2004. This version detects 802.11a/b/g signals, provided that your Wi-Fi receiver supports them. Although this version doesn't yet work with Vista, it does work with Windows XP, 2000, and 9x. A version of NetStumbler that runs on the Windows CE operating system (handhelds and cell phones) has been released, and is called MiniStumbler.

Chances are that if you've seen a movie where the characters go wardriving, it is NetStumbler that they were using. Wardriving involves driving around town looking for a network that you can hop onto. The name comes from the 1983 film *WarGames*, where automated software would robo-dial numbers to connect to other systems.

Network scanners are useful for the following purposes:

- Checking wireless configurations
- Determining if there are unknown rogue access points
- Optimizing network connections
- Measuring the signal strength at different locations
- Finding sources of signal interference
- GPS mapping
- And, of course, wardriving for fun and profit

NetStumbler isn't an entirely passive observer. It collects network metrics by using an Active Scanning technology that transmits probe requests. This means that anyone listening can detect NetStumbler's use, particularly if there isn't a lot of competing Wi-Fi traffic in the area. Because NetStumbler relies on responses to its probe requests, it detects access points, but not standard wireless network nodes or stations.

Among the alternatives to NetStumbler are:

- **inSSIDer (www.metageek.net/products/inssider).** This is an open source program that works with the Windows Wi-Fi API to survey wireless networks. inSSIDer is offered by MetaGeek; they have several other commercial products in this area, including Wi-Spy (a spectrum analyzer), Chanalyzer, and others. Figure 14.24 shows an inSSIDer Wi-Fi network scan.
- **iStumbler (http://istumbler.net).** This is for Mac OS X, AirPort, Bluetooth, and Bonjour.
- **Kismet (http://kismetwireless.net).** This is a scanner, sniffer (it examines 802.11 frames), and intrusion-detection software package that does passive scanning. Kismet runs on both Windows and Mac OS X.
- **MacStumbler (www.macstumbler.com).** This is for the Macintosh (OS X version 10.1 or greater, an 802.11b/g scanner).

FIGURE 14.24

inSSIDer is an example of a Wi-Fi network scanner.

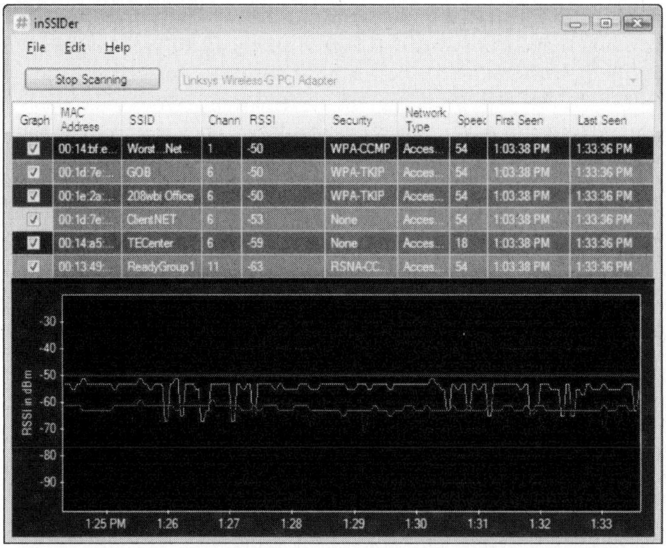

- **Microsoft Vista netsh command.** This command can be used to discover access points. The format of the command is as follows: `netsh wlan show networks mode=bssid`.

- **Vistumbler (http://vistumbler.net).** This is an AutoIT script that graphically displays the output of the `netsh` command. It is Vista-compatible.

This list is for freeware or shareware network scanners. Dedicated Wi-Fi sniffers and spectrum analyzers are also available from a variety of vendors. Some of the commercial software in this area can be high-end and rather pricey. A short list of Wi-Fi software may be found at www.tech-faq.com/wi-fi-software-tools.shtml.

Security

Part of the 802.11x protocol definition includes the methods that are used to provide port access and to authenticate connections. The LAN port used to provide network access is called the Port Access Entity (PAE). A PAE doesn't have to be a physical port; it is a logical entity that is associated with a port. PAEs can be the requestor of access (or supplicant) or the provider of access (or authenticator), or they can play both roles.

Somewhere on the wireless network is an authentication server that stores the credentials of the supplicant and responds to authenticator requests that are used to provide or deny wireless access to network services. Authentication servers can be established within an AP, or requests can be forwarded to authentication servers. A common setup sends authentication requests in the Remote Authentication Dial-In User Server (RADIUS) protocol to a RADIUS.

The authentication server can differentiate between two different port types. An uncontrolled port is a port that allows for unauthenticated communications between the authenticator (usually the wireless AP) and a wired LAN. Frames that are sent by a client are never simply passed along by the AP; an uncontrolled port requires that the frames originate on the AP. A controlled port can also be defined where data is only exchanged between wireless clients and LAN nodes through the port when the wireless client has been authorized by the 802.11x authentication server. In order to prevent contention for access to a port, the authentication server creates a unicast session key for each client. Without a session key, the wireless client's frames are dropped at the controlled port.

Wired Equivalent Privacy

Wired Equivalent Privacy (WEP) encrypts the data in 802.11 frames using a 40- or 104-bit RC4 symmetric stream algorithm that is sent over a wireless connection. The presence of encryption is indicated by the value in the WEP bit of the Field Control subfield of the Header field in an 802.11 frame. Security uses a shared key system, with each endpoint of the connection holding one of the two necessary keys. WEP defines a multicast/global key for use with multicast or broadcast sessions. A unicast session key for encryption of a point-to-point communication of unicast data that is sent between an AP and a wireless client, and for broadcast data sent from a wireless client to an AP, are also defined.

Note
WEP is considered to be relatively weak protection, as the encryption has been broken. It is better than no security, but not nearly as good as WPA. When possible, enable WPA at your APs.

The WEP encryption process works as follows:

1. The Data or payload portion of an 802.11 frame is used to create a CRC checksum (also called an Integrity Check Value, or ICV) that is used to verify the data after decryption.

2. The CRC is inserted into the frame just after the Data portion.

3. A 24-bit Initialization Vector (IV) is calculated.

4. The IV is appended to the WEP encryption key.

5. The value "IV+WEP key" is then fed to a pseudo-random number generator (PRNG) to create a key stream, which is a sequence that is the same size as the IV+WEP sequence.

6. The key stream is combined with an XOR operation with the "Data+IV" sequence to create the encrypted payload.

7. The 802.11 frame is then composed, with the IV placed before the encrypted payload.

Figure 14.25 illustrates the WEP encryption/decryption process.

FIGURE 14.25

The WEP encryption/decryption process

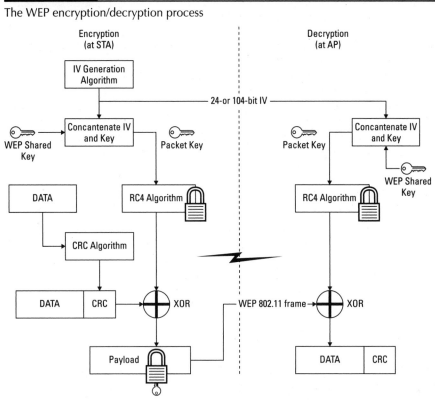

Decryption is essentially the reverse of the encryption process, and works as follows:

1. The IV is extracted from the encrypted frame and appended to the WEP encryption key. The IV is the field in front of the payload.

2. The "IV+WEP" value is input into the same PRNG that created the encrypted key stream, and the output is the same key stream that was used to create the encrypted payload.

3. The key stream is then XORed with the payload (which was the encrypted "Data+CRC"), to decrypt the combined "Data+CRC" sequence.

4. The ICV is then used to calculate the IV, and if they match, the frame is valid and the data is used.

WEP was the first of the wireless security protocols to be implemented, and it is widely used. However, the WEP protocol has some serious issues related to it. The main issue is that the WEP encryption keys must be sent securely over the wireless link. Because WEP keys are clear text, they can be sniffed. Also, WEP keys aren't changed without manual intervention. If a hacker gets access to the WEP key, then that key can be used until the sender changes the key. There is also no mechanism to manage a set of keys, and so, as the network grows, WEP key management becomes impractical.

Wi-Fi Protected Access

Wi-Fi Protected Access (WPA), and WPA2, which is the current-generation 802.11x authorization and encryption protocol, solves some of the problems of WEP by using the Temporary Key Integrity Protocol (TKIP) to generate keys. The TKIP key uses a 48-bit Initialization Vector and a 128-bit encryption key to generate a new key for every packet that is transmitted. WEP used the same key for all packets. The longer key length and varying encryption key make it impossible to gain access by simply sniffing data in transit. As with WEP, WPA provides unicast and global/multicast encryption.

With WPA, both endpoints in the association (connection) have a Pre-Shared Key (PSK), which means that the key can't be intercepted in transit; this makes WPA more secure and makes it suitable for small wireless networks. WPA ships in most modern APs after 2003, but it can be added with a firmware upgrade to older equipment from the 1999 to 2003 era. The WPA standard is maintained by the Wi-Fi Alliance, and products are submitted to their certification program for compliance, so that they can use the logo.

WPA2 is the full implementation of the mandatory requirements of the 802.11i security standard that was ratified in 2004. Any device that is WPA2-compliant must carry the Wi-Fi trademark and logo. This protocol uses the Counter Mode with Cipher Block Chaining Message Authentication Code Protocol (CCMP), which uses an Advanced Encryption Standard (AES) algorithm. Not all older devices will work with WPA2, because not all of the older routers understand both TKIP (from WPA) and AES (from WPA2). So while WPA2 is more secure, it does not offer backwards-compatibility. Figure 14.26 shows the security settings for a Netgear RangeMax router (Model WNR834B).

WPA has two levels of security defined: WPA Personal (WPA-PSK), and WPA Enterprise. WPA-PSK uses a Pre-Shared Key, which makes it convenient to use in small office home office, or SOHO, networks that don't have an 802.11x authentication server installed. To access a WPA-PSK secured network, a password is entered as either ASCII characters (8 to 63) or 64 hexadecimal digits (256 bits). With ASCII characters, a hash function combines those characters with the wireless network SSID to create a 256-bit pass-phrase string. WPA-PSK is subject to dictionary-based (lookup tables) brute force attacks, and so it's important to create strong passwords. The recommendation is for mixed password strings of 13 characters or more.

Table 14.2 lists some of the common media devices in use that offer wireless security.

FIGURE 14.26

The security settings for the Netgear WNR834B router allow it to be configured for WEP and the different forms of WPA.

NETGEAR
SMARTWIZARD | router manager
RangeMax™ NEXT Wireless Router model WNR834B

Setup Wizard | Wireless Settings

Setup
Basic Settings
Wireless Settings

Content Filtering
Logs
Block Sites
Block Services
Schedule
E-mail

Maintenance
Router Status
Attached Devices
Backup Settings
Set Password
Router Upgrade

Advanced
Wireless Settings

Wireless Network
Name (SSID):
Region: United States
Channel: 03
Mode: Up to 54Mbps

Security Options
○ None
○ WEP
● WPA-PSK (TKIP)
○ WPA2-PSK (AES)
○ WPA-PSK (TKIP) + WPA2-PSK (AES)

Security Encryption (WPA-PSK)
Passphrase: ******** (8 ~ 63 characters)
Key Update: 0 (0 no update or 30 ~ 86400 seconds)

TABLE 14.2

Wireless Security on Home Devices

Media Player	WEP	WPA-PSK	WPA2-PSK
Asus Eee PC	Yes	Yes	Yes, in hardware
iPhone	Yes	Yes	Yes
Nintendo DS	Yes	No	No
Nokia N800/N810	Yes	Yes	Yes
PlayStation 3	Yes	Yes	Yes
PlayStation Portable	Yes	Yes	No
Wii	Yes	Yes	Yes
XBox 360 Wi-Fi	Yes	Yes	No

In WPA Enterprise, a RADIUS server provides the authentication to any use requiring connection or access credentials. The AP forwards requests to the RADIUS server, which then either authenticates or denies the request based on data stored on the RADIUS server. If the RADIUS server is unable to decide the status of the request, it can request additional information from the source or a second password.

WPA is much more secure than WEP, particularly when a strong password is chosen. While AES and WPA2 are even more secure than TKIP and WPA, both are strongly preferred over WEP.

Summary

In this chapter, you learned how to create and manage wireless connections based on the IEEE 802.11 Wi-Fi standard. Wireless networks may be classified as either ad hoc or infrastructure.

Wireless networking uses radio frequencies in the 2.4 GHz or 5 GHz frequency range. Channels are created and signals are sent over carrier waves using spread spectrum transmission. Signals are encoded onto the carrier waves using modulation. The 802.11x frames are similar to Ethernet frames. Frames are sent using Carrier Sense Multiple Access with Collision Avoidance. Methods for handshaking, traffic control, and connection management were described.

Access points, gateways, and routers are the wireless devices that are used by wireless clients to connect to networks. You learned about the characteristics of these different devices. Other topics covered included wireless software, and the different forms of wireless network security methods in common use today.

In the next chapter, you learn about storage networks and how they can be integrated into data networks to improve data availability and performance.

Storage Networking

S torage networks use a collection of technologies that share storage
assets on the network. Storage I/O can represent a very large amount
of data traffic, so there is a strong incentive to isolate storage traffic on
its own dedicated network. This has led to the development of Storage Area
Networks (SANs). Hubs, switches, routers, servers, disk arrays, tape libraries, and optical jukeboxes are among the many devices that you will find on
a SAN. Storage network topologies can be direct attached, point-to-point,
arbitrated loops, and fabrics.

A model is described that categorizes the architecture of shared network
storage. This model naturally separates storage servers into block-oriented or
file-oriented solutions. The model is extended for tape devices, and it will be
shown how different network backups can be accommodated by the model,
and how devices would be configured for these different scenarios.

The concepts behind separating physical disks from logical addresses are
described. This separation allows storage to be easily virtualized. Aggregation
is used to reassemble the data stored on disk into files and information that
applications can use.

Fibre Channel is the dominant media connection technology used to create
SANs. The Fibre Channel protocol, architecture, and components are
described in this chapter. Fibre Channel networks were originally configured
using a Fibre Channel Arbitrated Loop (FC-AL) topology, but most deployments are now in the form of a Fibre Channel Switched fabric (FC-SW)
topology. The use of Fibre Channel switches and routers and their different
types of ports are described. Elements in SANs, such as individual network
interfaces and hard drives, are individually addressable, and elements can be
both grouped and isolated by the zoning techniques you learn about here.

A number of technologies are being deployed to allow storage traffic to be
sent over IP networks.

Among those that are described in this chapter are Internet Small Computer System Interface (iSCSI), Fibre Channel over IP (FCIP), and Internet Fibre Channel Protocol (iFCP).

Storage Networking

Many companies spend more than half of their technology budget on data storage. Queries to databases, backup and recovery operations, replication and mirroring, and the dozens of other important applications that require storage access lead to the situation where the bulk of network traffic is storage related. To alleviate the load placed on networks, storage traffic is often isolated on its own dedicated network, called a Storage Area Network (SAN). The term SAN may be applied to any network that isolates storage from other types of network traffic, regardless of the technology, topology, or protocols used.

Note

IBM used the acronym SAN for the term "System Area Network," but this term has fallen out of favor and is used only infrequently.

The central importance of storage networks can be summed up by this one fact: If you consider that enterprise-class storage servers, such as an EMC Symmetrix DMX-4, can hold up to 2,400 1-TB hard disks (or 2.4 petabytes of storage), then each of these systems fully loaded often costs more than the buildings that they are housed in. No wonder there's such an incentive to share these resources effectively.

Some of the devices you find on SANs include the following:

- Hubs, switches, and routers
- Storage servers and disk arrays
- Tape libraries
- Optical jukeboxes
- Virtual devices such as Logical Unit Numbers (LUNs), which are SCSI protocol identifiers for a defined storage asset

SANs are most often built using Fibre Channel switches and hubs, and linked by either optical or coaxial cable connections. The spelling "Fibre" is correct; it denotes an architecture or topology, and not the use of thin wires, as is the case with fiber optics. SANs implement a fabric architecture that allows storage assets to connect to other storage assets over multiple pathways. Fibre Channel has its own set of protocols, addressing, vocabulary, and construction apart from other networking standards that you have learned about, such as TCP/IP. Storage assets are accessed by workstations and servers on Local Area Networks (LANs) through common interface devices.

Storage networking is a very dynamic area of technology, one in which there is always something new. Storage network connections can encapsulate storage data arising on a Fibre Channel network inside TCP packets, and then send or receive that traffic across Wide Area Network (WAN) connections. Alternatively, efforts to extend locally attached storage onto the network have led to SCSI bus commands and data encapsulated over TCP/IP, making the iSCSI protocol a very valuable method for sharing storage on LANs.

In this chapter, you learn about some of the more important storage networking terms and concepts, and how to apply them to your networks.

Storage Network Types

Storage can be deployed in a number of different ways. Each type of storage offers the opportunity to share that storage asset with other networked computers.

The simplest shared network storage is created with an internal storage device, which is sometimes referred to as "captive disk." Storage that is internally connected to a host by a computer bus is referred to in the storage industry as Direct Attached Storage, or DAS. SCSI is most often used for a high-performance bus standard to captive disk.

These days, Universal Serial Bus (USB), FireWire, and external SATA (eSATA) are ubiquitous for connecting storage to desktop systems; higher-performance workstations and small servers tend to use SCSI or other higher-performance buses. In markets where storage capacity and price are more important than performance, SATA, or Serial ATA, storage is displacing SCSI at all levels of deployment, from desktops to enterprise-class storage servers. Small storage subsystems, such as external RAID arrays, are often connected to hosts using a direct point-to-point topology. Fibre Channel Point-to-Point (FC-P2P) is a single connection between two devices.

To form a network using low-level SCSI commands and data communication, that protocol must be transported over another transport protocol. The most widely used transport protocol is the Fibre Channel Protocol (FCP), which is described in detail later in this chapter. FCP is the transport of SCSI over TCP, which defines Fibre Channel networks. There are many other protocols in use that provide transport over IP networks, including:

- **ATA over Ethernet** (rarely used).
- **Fibre Channel over Ethernet (FCoE).**
- **FICON over FC.** This protocol isn't used on SANs, but is used with IBM mainframes.
- **HyperSCSI,** a version of SCSI over Ethernet.
- **iFCP and SANoIP,** which transports FCP over IP.
- **iSCSI, or SCSI over TCP/IP.** iSCSI is described later in this chapter. A version of iSCSI for RDMA (ISER) transports iSCSI over the InfiniBand (IB) protocol. IB is described in Chapter 13.

Both DAS and P2P topologies share these storage assets by creating disk or file shares within the host's operating system. The performance limits are set by the network connection (usually Ethernet), the computer bus bandwidth, and the host system's ability to process requests for storage access from other networked systems. DAS and P2P topologies are a bus architecture, and wouldn't be classified as a network.

When you have multiple Network Interface Cards (NICs) installed in a host, or dual-homed Fibre Channel NICs, you can create loop topologies. This is the architecture that IBM uses for its Token Ring networks. Dual-home Fibre Channel host bus adapters (HBAs) can create loops with up to 127 logical devices, called Fibre Channel Arbitrated Loops (FC-AL). FC-AL, once the dominant storage network topology, is now consigned to the connections in disk arrays.

The final topology in wide use in storage networks is called a switched fabric. Switched fabrics are created using either Fibre Channel or Gigabit Ethernet and offer many of the advantages of switched architecture in LANs and WANs. The main advantage is intelligent routing, but other important advantages include redundant pathways, interchangeable parts, and other factors that are described in more detail later in this chapter. Most SANs are constructed using a Fibre Channel Switched fabric (FC-SW) topology.

Figure 15.1 shows the four common storage topologies in use today.

FIGURE 15.1

The four main storage topologies

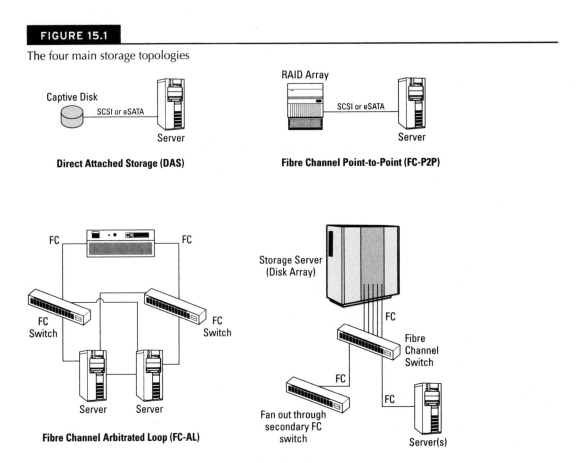

Direct Attached Storage (DAS)

Fibre Channel Point-to-Point (FC-P2P)

Fibre Channel Arbitrated Loop (FC-AL)

Fibre Channel Switched Fabrics (FC-SW)

SANs versus NAS

SANs were first developed to support particular applications such as a data warehouse with a few storage assets organized into a group. These early SANs were referred to as "SAN islands." As it became necessary to link these various islands together, Storage Area Networks were conceived as federated systems and executed. Many of the standards described in this chapter were developed in industry groups such as the Storage Networking Industry Association (SNIA, www.snia.org) and the Fibre Channel Industry Association, or FCIA (www.fibrechannel.org).

A SAN can be as simple as a switch, two or more HBAs, and the cabling necessary to connect servers and storage. Several companies, including QLogic and Hewlett-Packard, offer what is called a "SAN in a Box," a kit that includes these components and SAN management software.

One storage system that isn't found on a SAN under normal circumstances is Network Attached Storage (NAS). NAS is best classified as a file server and is normally connected to LANs using TCP/IP. NAS uses file protocols such as NFS or SMB/CIFS transported over TCP/IP for communication. By contrast, SANs use block-oriented protocols. That is a broad difference, and in the majority of cases it does separate NAS from SANs. However, some vendors have created systems that are hybrids of SAN and NAS (and in rare cases, DAS) — NAS gateway systems like the EMC Celerra for SANs exist — and so it can sometimes be hard to tell which classification the device is in. A filer or file server without the server part (the storage) is called a NAS Head, and those may well be attached to SANs, as is described a little later in this chapter.

Business Continuance Volumes

There are some applications that Storage Area Networks absolutely excel at, and for which they are invaluable. Backup and replication are the two applications that most often come to mind. Not only do SANs allow organizations to share storage assets, but they also provide the means necessary to make storage data highly fault-tolerant in a very effective way. If you have an application that is mission-critical, as many are in this 24/7 age of the Internet, you create fault tolerance by providing the means to fail over to a redundant system.

Take, for example, EMC's Business Continuance Volume (BCV) concept. A BCV is a copy of an active storage system that represents a point in time. If you want to work with the data you have, but you don't want to burden a mission-critical system, you create a BCV and then disconnect it from the primary system. The BCV is taken off-line and then connected to a different non-critical server where it can be:

- Backed up without affecting your production system or network
- Analyzed by an application such as a data warehouse analysis without impacting your primary server
- Optimized to reduce data redundancy or eliminate unnecessary data to streamline the data set
- Used as a fast secondary data system should the primary system go down, with a speed that is dependent only upon how long it takes to detach the primary storage and reattach to the BCV

BCVs can have many other uses, but the ability to remove network overhead makes the technology very attractive. EMC differentiates two different types of BCVs: a clone BCV created using mirroring and a snapshot BCV that uses a copy-on-write algorithm to propagate production changes incrementally. Snapshots are valuable in creating a historical record of file changes but are limited by the size of the storage resource that stores them.

Storage virtualization

A fundamental concept in network storage is storage virtualization, the idea that physical storage is separated from logical storage by the creation of a mapping technology. Mapping at the block level may be done through the creation of a master index, whereas in the file system or database it may be done at the index, file, or record level. Wherever the mapping is done, in hardware or in software, storage is always virtualized.

Storage virtualization abstracts identity from location; you can think of it as a form of redirection. In a block-oriented server, a set of blocks may be assigned a logical unit identifier, or LUN. Each individual block is then given an offset number that identifies that block within the LUN, and the offset is called a Logical Block Address, or LBA. The offset refers to the point in the sequence of blocks in the LUN where the block is found. The complete storage map defines a name space, which for block devices is called a virtual disk, or vdisk.

Each LUN is mounted by and presented to the storage network by the storage controller. A storage controller can be a hardware device in the Host Bus Adapter (HBA), or it can be software farther up the network stack. A Host Bus Adapter is a network interface device that connects a computer to either a network or storage device; HBAs for SCSI, Fibre Channel, and eSATA are common. HBA is less commonly applied to a USB, FireWire, IDE, and even Ethernet adapters. LUNs themselves can be the result of a mapping operation, thus allowing even more flexibility. Disk virtualization can be done in software, at the operating system level, or in hardware where a mapping table stores the necessary metadata needed to perform storage I/O redirection.

Virtualization can be a very powerful feature, enabling storage to be more centrally managed from fewer consoles. In a fully implemented, heterogeneous, virtualized shared storage network, it is possible to perform live data migrations of storage data from one server to another, all the while taking and fulfilling requests for data access from different hosts. This feature can be invaluable in terms of several issues, including the following:

- Dynamic resizing of volumes
- Network application optimization
- Replication
- Mirroring (synchronous and asynchronous)
- Point-in-time snapshots
- Disaster recovery

- Capacity management
- Performance tuning, which involves moving higher-demand data to faster storage, and improving disk utilization

Virtualization enables what is called "thin provisioning," thus allowing storage to be an on-demand asset that can be supplied in small quantities when needed. Virtualization also makes it easier to enforce an Information Lifecycle Management policy where business rules are applied to where data should reside. The downside of storage virtualization is that it is often hard to implement as a multivendor, multiplatform solution and can be hard to install and complex to manage.

Storage virtualization software is most often positioned at:

- **Hosts.** The software can be contained in the operating system as a volume manager with a kernel-level device driver, as a file system (CIFS/NFS), or though an automounter such as AUTOFS. Examples in this category are the Windows Logical Disk Manager, LVM in UNIX and Linux, Symantec VERITAS Storage Foundation (for Windows or Solaris), NetApp MultiStore/FlexVol, and FalconStor Software's IpStor NSS VA.

- **Storage devices.** The storage controller provides RAID and storage pooling, stores metadata, and migrates and replicates data. The storage controller virtualizes the HBAs in the hosts that connect to it.

- **Network services.** Specialized network servers can provide virtualization by performing what is essentially a low-level I/O redirection or routing function. These servers sit in a layer between storage and hosts at the network level, and all storage communication flows through the server. The application that runs on the server performs the mapping function. Examples of this type of technology are Coraid VS21 EtherDrive VirtualStorage, EMC Invista, LSI StorAge SVM, and FalconStor Software IPStor NSS.

- **Switches or appliances.** These devices contain software that aggregates storage as part of their redirection mechanism.

  Virtualization devices can be in-band or symmetric, in which case they are in the data path between the host and the storage device, which usually means it is part of, but at the edge of, the storage network. Because in-band appliances are in the data path, they often provide caching functionality as a performance enhancement.

  Virtualization appliances or switches can also be out-of-band or asymmetric, which means that they are not in the data path. Out-of-band appliances used to direct storage I/O in SANs are located in the hosts' Ethernet network and are typically lower-performing solutions than in-band solutions. Caching is not possible in out-of-band virtualization.

Cisco has a feature built into their Fibre Channel switches that they call Virtual Storage Area Networks, or VSANs, which are now an ANSI standard. The technology can link a set of ports on multiple switches to create a virtual fabric architecture. Different ports on a switch can be assigned to different VSANs, or multiple switches can be bound to one or more ports to define a unique VSAN. VSANs were designed to be similar to the Virtual LAN architecture that is used on Ethernet networks.

A VSAN doesn't specify the network protocol that is used; it is a network layer assignment. It is possible to create VSANs that can use the Fiber Channel Protocol (FCP), Fibre Channel over IP (FCIP), IBM's Fiber Connectivity (FICON), and the iSCSI Transport protocols, and isolate traffic in the supported Transport protocol to the VSAN. VSANs contain different management services that include zoning (described later in this chapter), device accounts, security policy definitions, and the World Wide Name, or WWN, service. One particularly nice feature of a VSAN is that you can resize a VSAN by either adding or subtracting ports from it, instead of having to actually add or remove physical switches from a Fibre Channel network.

The Shared Storage Networking Model

It is useful to have a framework within which to discuss how storage area networks are constructed, and what categories the different components, protocols, hardware, and software products fit. To this end, the Storage Networking Industry Association, or SNIA (www.snia.org), set about defining a unified theoretical model for storage networks along the lines of the seven-layer ISO/OSI or the alternative TCP/IP networking models. This model was created between 2000 and 2003 by Wayne Rickard, John Wilkes, David Black, and Harald Skadal, along with input from other SNIA members, and has become known at the SNIA Shared Storage Networking Architecture model. Figure 15.2 shows the last published version of the SNIA model.

FIGURE 15.2

The SNIA Shared Storage Networking Architecture model

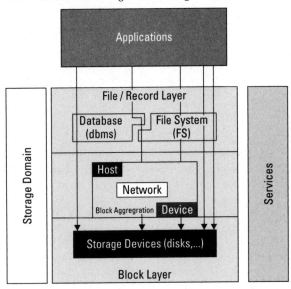

The SNIA shared storage model defines services, layers, and, most importantly, interfaces that storage devices must contain in order to be operable. For a completely functional storage request to be serviced, the request from an application must travel along one of the five different paths that are shown in Figure 15.2. You can use this model to describe how a device operates, and what type of device it must be, based upon the path it takes.

The shared tape extension

A significant portion of shared network data resides on tape-managed robotic auto-loading tape libraries (also called tape silos or tape jukeboxes), where they often serve as backups or archival storage in organizations as diverse as the Internal Revenue Service, airline reservation systems, credit card data warehouses, and other large data stores. These libraries can contain hundreds of tape heads (streamers) accessing thousands of tape cartridges that store petabytes of data. The low cost of data storage on tape offsets the slower performance that these systems offer.

Tape is a serial medium where data must be accessed sequentially. This makes random access operations slow. However, when data is streamed in sequence, the throughput of tape is high.

Tape contents are described in terms of a unit called a tape image. A single tape can hold multiple tape images that are delineated by small separator sections, which also mark the position on the tape. Just like disks, tapes must be formatted in order to be read correctly by the tape head(s). There are many ways to write data to tape; some are linear, others are linear and serpentine, many are multi-track, some are helical, and most are proprietary. All these methods share a common structural organization that is illustrated in Figure 15.3.

In Figure 15.3 tape is spooled on the roll on the right and moves left to right onto the spool on the left. As the tape passes over the tape magnetic heads, one head reads data and another tape writes data. Tape images are broken up into a sequence of tape blocks called extents, and the tape almost always writes a header and sometimes writes a trailer section as part of the formatting and record-keeping operations. Extents are separated from one another by a gap called an *Extent separator*. When a portion of the tape image must be read, the READ head reads the table of contents in the Header and then moves the tape to the position where the data begins. When data needs to be written, the new data is appended to the end of the tape; the tape moves back to the Header table of contents and adds the changes.

Tape is serial data storage. It is very slow to read data from tape because of the mechanical transport speed, although writing data can be speedy. The advantage that tape offers is that it allows for massive amounts of storage at low prices.

In the Shared Storage Model, tape systems span all levels of the model, beginning at the top in the Application layer, as shown in Figure 15.2. A common application is backup software; many industrial-strength backup programs — such as CommValut Systems Galaxy, Computer Associates ARCserve Backup, EMC Legato Networker, HP OpenView Storage Data Protector and Archive Backup System (ABS), IBM Tivoli Storage Manager (TSM), and Symantec NetBackup (formerly VERITAS NetBackup) — either support tape devices natively (mainly smaller units) or provide modules at extra cost to support enterprise-class tape systems.

FIGURE 15.3

A logical tape structure

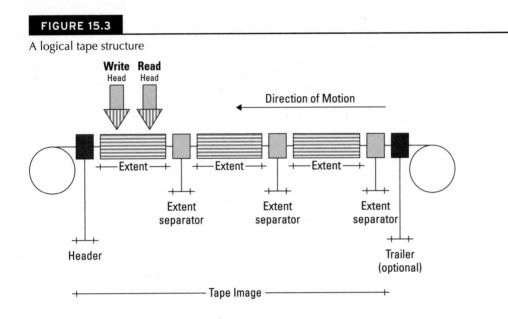

The tape format system spans the levels of the model from the application down to the host. The format operation is responsible for packing files or records into the tape extents and laying down those extents to record tape images. An open system tape solution is characterized by the tape format and all other host functions being isolated in the tape application software.

A tape is not a disk, and there isn't a direct correlation between a volume on a disk and an image on a tape. Tape is sequential, and the unit of aggregation is extents and not blocks. In the tape model, aggregation is contained in the host/network/device layers. Notice also that the model splits tape devices from tape media. This is required because tape is a removable media and would be required had this model been extended to optical jukeboxes that use removable CDs or DVDs. The split is doubly important for tape libraries because the tape heads and tape cartridge types can be mixed and matched as needed for each situation.

Different tape operation types are indicated in the tape model by arrow-headed lines in Figure 15.4. The arrow on the left in the tape section that goes through the tape format system, host, and extent aggregation corresponds to the operation of writing the file data to tape. A typical tape application that used this pathway would be the TAR command which READs data from disk. TAR is the UNIX tape archive command. That same left arrow in the tape section serves as the WRITE path for the DUMP command, which READs the files in a file system that is written to the tape. The model concentrates on the tasks that get done, rather than the devices that do them.

FIGURE 15.4

The Tape Shared Storage Model

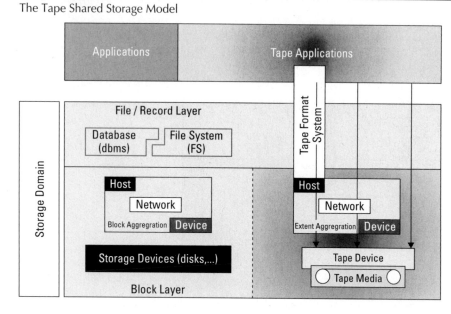

In the last scenario, the TAR command backs up files to virtual tape by first READing the data on disk and then passing the data to the backup software. The backup software then hands the data to the Tape Format system, which converts the data into tape format and passes the sequential data to the host, which then writes the virtual tape to disk.

The middle arrow that goes directly from the backup software through the network to the tape device is the WRITE to tape operation that takes as its input the DD command. DD performs a READ operation that performs a volume copy to tape.

Figure 15.5 shows these different backup scenarios.

Having now seen how network backup commands are processed to and from tape, let's take a brief look at how this architectural model uses devices. In Figure 15.6, six different tape backup technologies are shown; the explanation that follows considers these examples, starting in the upper-left corner.

The simplest example is of direct attached tape backup, where data is copied from disk to tape over a system bus. Both that example and the network attached tape backup in the top center (where the disk and tape are externalized over a network) are backups where the bus or network spans all of the layers of the tape model. The same host bus is used for commands and for data transfer from a disk array to a tape library. In both instances, aggregation is host-based using the host file system.

FIGURE 15.5

Different backup commands shown in the Shared Tape model

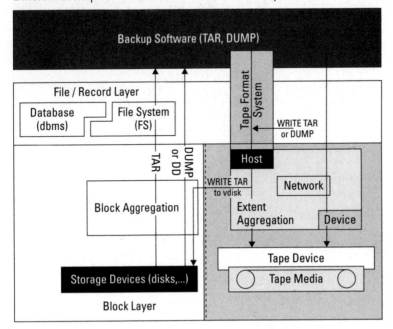

The simplest and perhaps most important backup deployment using a SAN is the one you see in the top-right corner of Figure 15.5, which is labeled Shared Tape Backup. This architecture enables what has come to be called LAN-Free Backup; commands go to the different devices from hosts, but backup traffic only flows through the storage network and not over the LAN. In this example, the tape library is shown as a single device, but many deployments of this type will partition the tape library so that multiple backups are occurring at the same time, and the backup software on different hosts is controlling different robotic tape selectors and drives.

Tape can be virtualized through the use of emulation and redirection. In the scenario shown in the lower-left example, labeled Virtual Tape Backup, a tape virtualization appliance is deployed in the data path, and from the standpoint of a host, the appliance appears as if it is a tape device. The abstraction allows a host to create a backup job and then pass that job along to the appliance for processing. The advantage of this approach over Direct Attached Tape is that the offload allows the host to work on other business. When a host is removed from the backup scenario, as is the case here, it is referred to as Server-Free Backup.

The fifth scenario is called the Tape Data Mover, shown in the lower center example in Figure 15.6. The data is stored on a disk array, but an application requires the data be moved to a captive disk. Two movement appliances are deployed, one in each of the two data paths. The arrow with a dotted line indicates that the host gives the appliance commands, at which point the movement appliance processes the remainder of the job. The first job uses the data path that takes the data in its stored location on the disk array and moves the data through the first data appliance to an interim position on tape in a tape library. The second job copies the staged data from the tape library through the second movement appliance to the intended target, which is the captive disk. The Tape Data Mover scenario shares the great benefit offered by the Shared Tape Backup scenario: it is a LAN-free backup. To that benefit is added the offload of the backup management to the movement appliances.

FIGURE 15.6

Six tape backup technologies

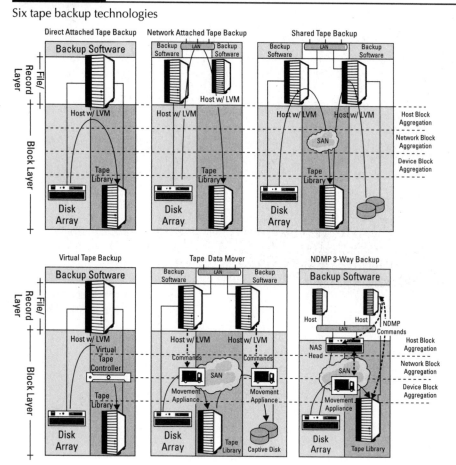

The last scenario is shown in the lower-right example in Figure 15.6 and illustrates a file server backup architecture with a data mover. The technology employed to control the backup is referred to as an NDMP 3-way backup. NDMP stands for Network Data Management Protocol, and it is a technology used by NetApp and Legato (now owned by EMC) to transport data directly to backup devices using a file server or NAS as the controller. NDMP is supported by nearly all enterprise-class backup software. The aggregation takes place in the NAS head, which receives NDMP commands from the host. The white, double-headed arrow between the movement appliance and the NAS head represents commands for working with blocks on the disk array.

The Storage Domain

In the shared storage network model, the Storage Domain is a container that organizes information in the form of files. Files are pointers to information contained on disk, organized through the use of fields, records, and metadata that provide the necessary context to understand what the data is used for and how to use it. Metadata might include the datatype, the associated application needed to view and edit the data, sequencing, and other properties that make data into useable information.

At the top of the Storage Domain, the file/record layer provides the logic necessary to package information so that it can be stored in a useful way. In many instances, the amount of data is larger than the physical units in storage that are allocated; storage is allocated into blocks on disk. The file system or database must be able to segment the information into storable pieces that can be retrieved and sequenced when required. Often file systems and databases are united into a single structure. The file system or database uses a name space or object hierarchy that permits search and retrieval operations.

Not shown in the model is an object or file cache that is used to speed up performance in the system by storing the most recently used items in memory. All storage systems use different level caches to improve performance. The use of a cache makes it absolutely mandatory that a storage system contain the logic needed to determine whether data moving from or to storage is transmitted or sequenced correctly, and if the rules that were developed to maintain data integrity were followed. These rules of logic are called system coherency, and because cache information can either be newer than or older than stored data on disk, it is essential that the coherency logic be robust.

This differentiation between information in the form of files and records, and data in the form of blocks, is an essential defining concept in the shared storage model.

Data is stored at the lowest level, the Block layer. A block contains data but has no context describing the data. Blocks are merely addressable locations on a storage device such as a hard drive, Solid State Disk (SSD), optical disk, or tape. Blocks can be written, overwritten, erased, and moved, and their order bears no relationship to anything that a person or computer program would find useful. To be able to use the data that is in blocks, there needs to be a method to aggregate the blocks. Data aggregation supplies the critical lookup table that contains the pointers that map blocks to an organizational scheme.

Aggregation

A file system or database can use information contained in blocks because they store information about which files or records correspond to which pointers in the block-oriented device, and in what order. That provides the means necessary to retrieve the information. From the standpoint of the file system or database, it is of no consequence where the physical data is stored. The system of mappings from file to pointer to storage allows the system to redirect the pointer's reference to a different block or an entirely different storage device.

This abstraction that aggregation provides is at the heart of a set of storage virtualization technologies that are critical in providing the flexibility needed to make storage networking practical. RAID, logical units and volumes, and volume manager software are all possible because of this mapping.

Not all storage operations require that data be presented in the form of usable information. In fact, the majority of operations only require that the data be handled without modification. When you back up one disk to another disk or one volume to another volume, the knowledge of which file uses which block (and vice versa) is needless overhead and is ignored. Enterprise backup and replication technologies ignore file structures and perform these operations at the block level, copying data from one location to another sector by sector, and block by block. Error-checking techniques determine whether the operations were successfully performed, but for the most part, the server or host that uses the data doesn't need to be involved in these operations. Most block-level operations are implemented by the storage systems themselves.

The bottom line is this: If you want fast data operations, you need to invest in block-oriented technologies. If you need to manage information, then you need file-oriented systems.

Device models

The Shared Storage Model shown in Figure 15.2 shows five different paths requesting data contained in storage from the Application layer. There are actually eight paths through the four different interfaces that the model creates that can be defined; the ones shown are the most useful in terms of discussing device classes that you can buy and install.

The four interfaces in the model are:

- **Application/Operating System Layer.** This layer is usually defined by an API necessary to connect the services that both layers contain.
- **Operating System/File and Record Layer.** Another API is used to tie the operating system to information.
- **File Layer/Block Layer.** This interface is where the storage network protocols are used.
- **Block Layer/Storage Device.** This interface uses low-level bus commands like SCSI to manage data.

Interfaces, regardless of what one technology or vendor calls them, are important. When you use an open standard for an API at an interface, it provides you with a measure of supplier independence that you don't have when you use one storage vendor's proprietary API.

Block-oriented storage devices typify the classic concepts embodied in a Storage Area Network model, and can occupy as many as three of the bottom layers of the model. The block layer storage device does much of the heavy lifting when it comes to storage operations. Storage devices get commands from hosts and then independently carry out those operations. Among the operations that a block-oriented server can perform are direct device-to-device block transfers used for backups, copies, and transfers; replications; mirroring; and any other application that requires storage I/O. Intelligence built into the storage servers improves performance by pre-caching contents, scrubbing disks, and performing storage maintenance.

Figure 15.7 shows how block-oriented storage servers fit into the storage networking architectural model.

FIGURE 15.7

Different conceptual block-oriented storage devices

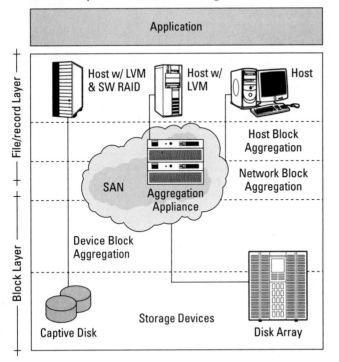

Block-oriented storage systems work well when the application passes the storage devices a command such as "copy this volume," "perform a backup," or even "make this small change to this large file." Any operation that doesn't require an understanding of how the data stored on disk relates to files or information is more efficiently handled as a block operation. If you make a small change to a database, which changes the data in one sector, a block operation only needs to change that sector. However, when a filer or file-oriented server changes the file, the whole file needs to be rewritten. There are situations where filers greatly outperform block storage servers.

File-oriented servers can be constructed in the Shared Storage model as a complete NAS file server, as a NAS head that fronts a disk array, or as a host device where the file system/database relies on an aggregation appliance to mediate storage data transactions. The three different device types, Network Attached Storage, disk arrays, and direct disk, are shown in Figure 15.8.

FIGURE 15.8

Different conceptual file-oriented storage devices (from left to right): Network Attached Storage, disk arrays, and direct disk.

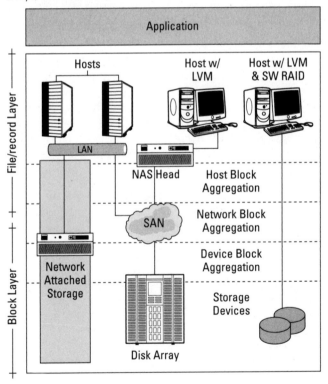

In a file-oriented storage system, there is a mapping function that relates volumes, blocks, and sectors to files or tables, records, and tuples. From the standpoint of a networked storage system, the organizational scheme of a file system, a database, or an object-oriented version of either two is irrelevant; it is the mapping function that is important. Network Attached Storage (NAS) devices such as a NetApp filer run the specialized Write Anywhere File Layout (WAFL) operating system, the Windows Storage Server 2003 R2, which runs Windows Server 2003 R2, and even a database-oriented appliance like the discontinued Oracle8i Appliance or the current Netezza Data Warehouse Appliance, work equally well as file-oriented servers. NAS spans all of the layers of the Shared Storage model, from network hosts down to captive disk.

The other types of file-oriented storage servers are created by disaggregating functionality from a NAS. If you remove the storage devices from a NAS server, what you are left with is called a NAS Head. A NAS Head has a file-oriented operating system, applications for managing volumes and RAID, and the I/O functionality necessary to send commands and receive data from a storage device. However, a NAS Head doesn't perform the basic storage operations. That function is abstracted away by a storage server connected to the same SAN that the NAS Head is connected to. From the standpoint of an application or host, a NAS Head is identical to a self-contained NAS server. NAS Heads are highly flexible appliances; they can attach to hosts via a LAN or be connected to a host with LVM (Logical Volume Manager) software directly.

The next disaggregation removes the specialized file-oriented operating system of a NAS and has the host work with storage devices directly either as captive disk or through a storage network to a disk array. In the case of a Direct Attached Storage filer, the host must be able to create logical volumes using a piece of software called a Logical Volume Manager (LVM), and possibly be able to stripe and mirror disks to create RAID arrays. The use of software RAID, either inside the operating system or through the use of third-party software such as the VERITAS Volume Manager, may not be required because many HBAs ship with hardware RAID built right onto the board. All disk arrays ship with hardware RAID, and so when a host is connected to a disk array, it only needs the LVM to perform file-oriented storage operations.

File-oriented storage servers work well when the application passes the storage devices a set of commands such as "READ these sets of files," "reindex this file system," or "take an incremental snapshot or backup of this volume." Any operation where the information isolates the storage locations and sequences of data based on files introduces efficiencies that block storage devices can't match.

The classic example of an efficient file-oriented storage application is in streaming media — the bigger the better. If the application makes a request for a single, large, streamed file, it passes a sequence of locations on disk to the storage device, which then executes the READs necessary to make the file available to the application at the host.

A block-oriented storage system wouldn't know how to process the streamed file. It would retrieve the information in one block and then request the location of the next block from the master index, which maps the file using a set of pointers, each to the next location. As the data in sequential blocks are being reassembled, there is a stream of commands for the pointers that represent the next segment that creates a significant overhead and attendant performance degradation for streaming in block devices, particularly in multiuser scenarios.

However, the smaller the files requested and the greater their number, the less the performance difference there is between the file-oriented and block-oriented storage systems. The mapping operations become comparable in complexity, with the only difference being that the mapping is done at the filer or at the storage array. The latency introduced by the network may be seen to be much smaller for passing pointers or storage locations than it is for transferring the actual files back across the storage network/LAN to the applications.

Fibre Channel Networks

Fibre Channel (FC) is a high-speed interconnect that was first deployed on supercomputers as the High Performance Parallel Interface (HPPI). HPPI has since been adapted and expanded to become FC, which has become the dominant standard for storage networking. FC is defined by a set of ANSI standards that specify not only the cabling types and connections used for the network's Physical layer, but also the Fibre Channel Protocol (FCP) as the Transport protocol. FCP is designed to encapsulate commands and data in different formats such as SCSI (the majority), ATM, and IP. Fibre Channel interconnects can be either copper or fiber optics (both single and multi-mode fiber).

Sometimes Fibre Channel networks are described in terms of class levels. Class levels describe the types of topologies and connections that are made. There are six classes of Fibre Channel networks in use:

- **Class 1** designates end-to-end connections with each frame verified. Class 1 doesn't use negotiation; each device in the point-to-point connection controls data flowing over the wire. Class 1 is not a shared storage network; it is a closed system.

- **Class 2** is a frame-switched connection that is used in shared fabric connections. Frame delivery is verified, but frame delivery need not be sequenced. The lack of sequencing means that Class 2 FC can't communicate using SCSI data, which requires sequential data flow. The iSCSI protocol provides a solution to sending SCSI over Fibre Channel, removing the need for vendors to provide a proprietary solution to this class in their switches, as some once did.

- **Class 3** offers frame switching, but without receipt acknowledgment at the switch. Frame acknowledgment is a host function in this class. Class 3 uses a buffer flow control mechanism. Class 3 FC also doesn't sequence frames, but does include a broadcast feature that can send simultaneous traffic to more than one device.

- **Class 4** provides fractional bandwidth allocation — a virtual circuit. Class 4 can share connections.

- **Class 5** proposes isochronous (same time) just-in-time service.

- **Class 6** is a multicast service that offers dedicated fabric connections.

Fibre Channel standards

Some will argue that because the standard only requires that ports be able to communicate with one another and that the interconnect be a serial bus structure, that Fibre Channel doesn't represent a true network. However, for the purposes of this book and given the number of different devices that can be attached to FC, it makes sense to treat collections of devices connected by FC as a network.

Table 15.1 lists the different Fibre Channel standards that have been introduced since the first ANSI standard in 1994. Products based on the 8 Gbits/s standard and before are compatible with one another. The newer standards of 10 Gbits/s and 20 Gbits/s are not backwards compatible. Among the manufacturers who make Fibre Channel HBAs are ATTO, Brocade, Emulex, LSI Logic, QLogic, and others. These HBAs are sometimes sold through OEM agreements and rebranded by system vendors.

Fibre Channel cables, connections, and connectors are passive devices. The signal is sent and received by a transceiver. Every connection or connector contains two transceivers, and data flows down each of the two wires or channels in opposite directions. This system eliminates problems that occur in network connections where the signal travels over the same wire. This is the case with Ethernet where you see data loss due to interference and signal contention because of two-way traffic; additional overhead is placed on the system to employ measures to combat the problem. With Fibre Channel, you have a measure of fault tolerance due to the use of a loop topology, and most Fibre Channel HBAs are dual homed for this reason.

TABLE 15.1

Fibre Channel Standards

Standard	Speed (Gbits/s)	Throughput (Mbits/s)
10GFC Parallel	12.8	Varies by connected devices
20GFC	10.5	2,000
10GFC Serial	10.5	1,000
8GFC	8.5	800
4GFC	4.25	400
2GFC	2.1	200
1GFC	1.1	100

Port designations

In Fibre Channel, a port is any logical entity that can be assigned a network address and from which, and to which, communication flows. This includes not only HBAs, but also physical and logical storage devices and hosts, switches, and hubs. Table 15.2 summarizes the different types of Fibre Channel ports in use.

TABLE 15.2

Fibre Channel Ports

Port Identifier	Name	Type	Purpose
E_port	Extender Port	Switch	Connects switches into a cascade.
EX_port	Expansion Port	Switch/Router	Connects an FC router to an FC switch. At the router, it emulates an E_port, and at the switch, it is an EX_port.
F_port	Fabric Port	Switch	Connects a fabric to a node.
FL_port	Fabric + Loop Port	Switch	Connects a switch port to both a loop and a switch.
Fx_port	Autosensing Port	Switch	Can become an F_port when connected to an N_port, or can become an FL_port when connected to an NL_port.
G_port	General Port	Switch	Can be used to emulate any other port, usually an E_port or F_port.
L_port	Loop Port	Node	Connects a node to an FC loop as an NL_port or FL_port.
N_port	Network Port	Node	Connects a node to a switch.
NL	Network + Loop Port	Node	Connects a node to both a loop and a switch.
TE_port	Trunking Expansion Port1	Switch	A Cisco VLAN standard for switch-to- switch connections that emulates an E_port.
U_port	Universal Port	Node	A term applied to any arbitrated port.

1 A trunk may also be called a Port Channel or an EISL, depending upon the vendor and device.

The Fibre Channel Protocol

The Fibre Channel Protocol uses a five-layer architecture that includes a low-level signaling layer and higher-level service layers, as shown in Figure 15.9. Layers FC-0 to FC-2 are collectively referred to as the Physical Layers and include both the media and wire protocols. Different devices can span different layers in this model. An FC hub operates at Layer FC-0 only. FC switches span the protocol from FC-0 to FC-2. An intelligent FC router spans the protocol from FC-0 all the way up to FC-4 because many FC routers also serve as SCSI routers.

FIGURE 15.9

The Fibre Channel Protocol architecture

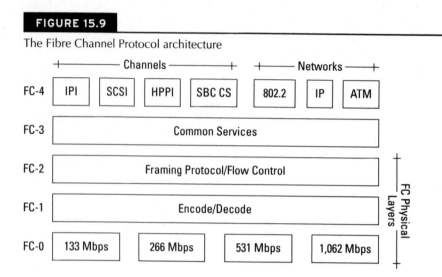

The different layers have the following purposes:

- **FC-0.** The Physical Layer (FC-0) includes the fiber cables, connectors, and the specification of electrical and optical parameters that the hardware requires. When optical fiber is used, FC-0 employs the Open Fibre Control (OFC) system to lower the power level of the laser used so that it doesn't overwhelm the FC ports in use.

- **FC-1.** The Data Link Layer (FC-1) encodes and decodes commands and data in 8-bit serial format into a 10-bit Transmission Character. The small bit sizes make it easier to send and recover a serial bit stream in case of error.

- **FC-2.** The Network Layer (FC-2) is the layer that manages data transport on an FC network. It controls the creation and management of frames, ordered sets, sequences, exchanges, and the Fibre Channel protocols. The protocols include Primitive Sequence, Fabric Login, N_Port Login, Data Transfer, and N_Port Logout.

  To manage frame traffic, FC-2 uses a flow control mechanism based on the available buffer space. Different service classes can be defined for different traffic types.

- **FC-3.** The Common Services Layer (FC-3) contains the mechanisms for managing N_port striping, allowing multiple ports to transmit data in parallel as a single information unit over multiple connections. It also supports a feature called hunt groups, where more than one port can respond to a single alias address. Hunt groups improve performance by providing access to a storage device that might be busy or blocked on another port. The third technology implemented at FC-3 is multicasting, which for FC represents the idea of sending data to more than one port at the same time. You could, for example, send data to all or any of a fabric's N_ports.

- **FC-4.** The Protocol Mapping Layer (FC-4) is an application interface layer that maps network protocols to the FC layers below FC-4. The network and bus structure supported are Small Computer System Interface (SCSI), Intelligent Peripheral Interface (IPI), High

Performance Parallel Interface (HIPPI) Framing Protocol, Internet Protocol (IP), ATM Adaptation Layer for computer data (AAL5), Link Encapsulation (FC-LE), Single Byte Command Code Set Mapping (SBCCS), and IEEE 802.2.

Fibre Channel traffic management

The Fibre Channel Protocol uses a form of traffic management based on buffer credits. Each port on the network is assigned a traffic budget. When that budget is used, data traffic is directed to the next port in the sequence. Buffer credits are defined for end-to-end flow control with N_ports, L_ports, or NL_ports serving as the endpoints. Ports acknowledge frame receipt and then an additional credit is given to the sending port, which is placed in the traffic queue. A second type of flow control, referred to as buffer-to-buffer control, manages a set of credits between two adjacent ports. Buffer-to-buffer traffic control relies on the receiving port sending a ready-to-receive signal to the sending port.

Fibre Channel Switched fabric (FC-SW) uses a different mechanism for flow control. Node and processes send their status to different ports as part of a logon ritual. As each node logs onto the FC-SW, the initiator and target ports authenticate the node logon and negotiate the connection properties, including the type of protocols used and the data transfer rates. FC-SW uses the FCP-SCSI protocol. This process logon authentication and negotiation occurs for any type of FC-SW connection, even those that use a direct attached Fibre Channel connection.

Fibre Channel flow control

Fibre Channel frames have start and end markers. The header defines the frame and contains addresses, data, error correction, and a validation data set that performs acknowledgment as well as data recovery. Frames encapsulate data in other wire protocols so that a Fibre Channel frame maps to other upper-level protocols such as SCSI, IP, HIPPI, FICON, ESCON, 802.2, and Virtual Interface Architecture (VIA). Figure 15.10 shows the structure of an FC frame.

FIGURE 15.10

Fibre Channel frames

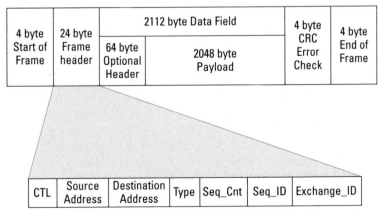

Fibre Channel Arbitrated Loops

Fibre Channel Arbitrated Loops, or FC-AL, is a topology used to connect hosts with storage devices. It was once the predominant technology used for SANs, but is now mainly used to connect the many disks in large disk arrays with host controllers. An arbitrated loop is a serial bus that can address from as few as 2 to as many as 127 logical devices or ports. The FC-AL command set is compatible with SCSI bus commands. Unlike IBM's Token Ring, an FC-AL allows multiple devices to address the bus, up to the limit of the bus's bandwidth, which is shared by all of the connected devices. As shown in Figure 15.11, FC-AL can connect to an FC switch, and through that switch, to switched fabric networks, as is indicated by the arbitrated loop on the right in Figure 15.11.

FIGURE 15.11

Fibre Channel Arbitrated Loop nodes

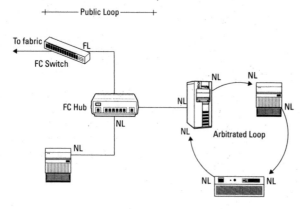

Note

While the theoretical limit of Fibre Channel is 127 devices, the practical limit is approximately 40 to 60 nodes.

The arbitration scheme used by an FC-AL is based on the SCSI bus arbitration scheme. In FC-AL, the port with the highest priority gets access to the wire to send and receive frames. SCSI uses a priority based on the bus electrical characteristics; with FC-AL, the priority is established in software as commands. This frees FC-AL to run on either copper wire or fiber optic wire.

An L_port or NL_port on an FC-AL starts communication by first issuing a ready-to-send command. As the command travels the loop, every node in turn compares its priority to the node that is requesting loop access, and then that node either takes the control command or passes the control command on. When the loop becomes available to the arbitrating port, data is exchanged and the priority changes. The next-higher priority node restarts the ready-to-send sequence and assumes command of the loop. Exchanges take place using a set of sequenced frame transfers, with frames typically in the rather small 2K range. The small size of the frame enables the communication to recover quickly from any loss because retransmission is not a lengthy process, which is essential in serial data communication.

Arbitrated loops can be constructed with either a ring or a hub (passive star). Rings are simpler to implement but have the disadvantage of failing when any device on the ring fails. Hubs still function when a device fails because each device is still on a logical ring while connected to the hub using a star topology.

FC-AL uses a subset of the different types of logical ports available. The Node Loop port (NL_port) and Fabric Loop port (FL_port) or L_ports are ports than can engage in arbitrated communication. NL_ports must be able to log onto a fabric and authenticate themselves if so connected. Name registration uses the Fabric Login (FLOGI) protocol. An NL_port would be the initiator for any communications to other nodes located on the fabric. An arbitrated loop that connects through an FL_port is considered a public loop, while an arbitrated NL_port that isn't connected to a fabric is considered to be a private loop. From the standpoint of the FC-AL protocols, a connection to a hub is not a port.

Fibre Channel Switched fabrics

A Fibre Channel Switched fabric (FC-SW) network is one in which different devices on the network are connected to one another through intermediary intelligent Fibre Channel switches. Fabric topologies have many advantages, as you will see in Chapter 17, when InfiniBand fabric and computer grid systems are described. Fabrics are scalable, fault tolerant, and flexible.

In order to implement an FC-SW, you require an FC switch, which, prior to 2003, tended to be expensive. The availability of lower-cost FC switches, as well as a drop in the per-port cost of the larger switches (called Fibre Channel Directors), have made FC-SW the dominant storage networking architecture. Brocade, Cisco, and QLogic are the best-known Fibre Channel Switch manufacturers, but there are many more. A Fibre Channel Director class switch is one that contains 128 ports or more.

Fibre Channel addressing

An FC-SW has an address space with 224 logical addresses (16,777,216). When two or more switches are used in the same network, they can be configured so that they form a mesh network. Three different addressing schemes are used in FC-SW networks: the World Wide Name (WWN), port addresses, and Arbitrated Loop Physical Addresses (AL-PAs).

A WWN, which is sometimes referred to as a WWID, is assigned by IEEE convention to both Fibre Channel and Serial Attached SCSI storage devices. WWNs serves the same function on an FC-AL network that an Ethernet MAC address does on a TCP/IP network. There are two naming conventions in use for WWNs: one, called the WWNN, is the node WWN and applies to all ports on an HBA; the second is port WWN (WWPN) and is a unique port identifier.

WWNs use a manufacturer address assigned during fabrication. The address is composed of a hexadecimal prefix 10:00 or vendor prefix 2#:##, to which is added a 3-bit vendor ID, and a 3-byte serial number. The vendor prefix is called the Organizationally Unique Identifier (OUI). In the newer WWN naming scheme, the initial half-byte is a hexadecimal 5 or 6 to which is added the 3-bit vendor ID, and a 4 1/2-byte serial number.

Examples of some of the company identifiers are 00:60:69 for Brocade; 00:1B:32 for QLogic HBAs; 00:C0:DD for QLogic FC switches; 00:60:48 for EMC Symmetrix; 00:60:16 for EMC CLARiiON, 00:A0:98 for NetApp; and 00:50:76 for IBM, among others.

Port addresses are unique 24-bit addresses that are assigned to a port. This is similar to assigning an IP address to a network controller in a TCP/IP network. Assignment of port address numbers is determined by the person or organization that configures the FC SAN.

Arbitrated Loop Physical Address (AL-PA) is used on loop topologies to define an addressable and unique address. FC loops have a small number of nodes, and thus only an 8-bit identifier with 256 addresses is needed.

Zoning

In an FC-AL storage network, you can implement a feature called zoning that segments storage assets in a manner that is similar to creating a subnet on an Ethernet network. There are four different types of zones supported by FC-AL fabrics:

- **Soft zoning.** When a soft zone is created, any host connected to the fabric will only be allowed to browse the names of the storage devices that the host has been allowed access to. Soft zoning only affects the browse function. Any host can still connect to any device if it provides the device address. So a soft zone is not a secure method for providing restricted storage access.

Note

Zoning is a feature of FC-AL networks and isn't implemented on the other types of Fibre Channel networks.

- **Hard zoning.** Hard zoning is a feature that not only restricts browsing for storage devices by name but also blocks traffic from a host to a storage device that the host doesn't have the privilege to connect to. Hard zoning is a secure method for controlling storage access and uses a frame filtering mechanism to determine the sending and receiving systems. Hard zoning is a feature of a Fibre Channel switch, and not all switches offer hard zoning.

- **Name zoning.** Every device on an FC-AL network is assigned a unique 8-byte World Wide Name (WWN). Name zoning is relatively secure, but can be spoofed.

- **Port zoning.** Zones can be created at the Fibre Channel switch port level so that ports on one switch are either allowed or denied access to ports on another switch. This feature requires switch support and usually that the two switches involved are from the same manufacturer.

The best security method uses a combination of zoning methods to secure storage network assets.

Storage over IP

There is considerable effort under way to leverage IP network infrastructure for storage networking. To some extent, IP storage networking may displace some fraction of Fibre Channel storage networks, particularly in WAN links, small LAN deployments, and lower-performance LAN applications. In this section, you learn about three different emerging storage over IP technologies:

- **iSCSI.** iSCSI uses the SCSI command set and data format to send packets over an IP network. IP essentially extends the SCSI over a much greater distance, allowing a host with DAS to appear to other nodes on the network as if it is a shared network device.

- **Fibre Channel over IP (FCIP or FC/IP).** FCIP is a tunneling protocol that encapsulates Fibre Channel frames within IP packets. FCIP is a point-to-point technology; the initiator and target encapsulate and de-encapsulate the packets to retrieve the FC frames.

- **iFCP.** iFCP adds Fibre Channel commands and data to IP packets and then sends the storage traffic as native transport over IP. It is very similar in concept to iSCSI in the sense that iFCP and iSCSI commands are wrapped by TCP for transport over IP networks. FCIP, by contrast, can only be used on Fibre Channel networks. IP packets are sent from an iFCP gateway to another iFCP gateway, and is routable; whereas FCIP is sent using a tunneling mechanism.

Storage networking and IP networking were built with two very different sets of requirements in mind. Storage networks were designed for throughput and reliable delivery. IP networks are fault tolerant, but were not designed for speed. Those differences control how any of these storage over IP protocols can be applied, as any application that is sensitive to IP networks' intrinsic latency isn't a good candidate for this storage over IP standard.

Data going from room to room may traverse one router or switch with one intervening "hop." Each hop introduces most of the latency encountered in TCP/IP networking. So a connection with one hop will probably operate satisfactorily for a high-performance connection, provided again that the bandwidth is sufficient. However, if the link must traverse a city, state, or country where the latency of multiple hops must be accommodated, then chances are that FCIP isn't going to be a satisfactory solution when connecting an OLTP database to networked storage.

You can't tell what the bandwidth of a link is without testing, and bandwidth is highly dependent on network conditions. You can, however, get some sense of the amount of latency that a small number of packets will have traveling the intended route of an FCIP connection, by simply performing a few TRACEROUTE operations at different times of the day (and week) and analyzing the latency of the different hops that are reported back. TRACEROUTE is the UNIX version of the command that is TRACERT on Windows, and TRACEPATH on Linux. Figure 15.12 shows the TRACERT command applied from my workstation out to Verizon's DNS server. The hops inside the LAN were a total of 2 ms (milliseconds), while each of the remaining hops from the Boston suburbs to New York represented a time of 372 ms, or 0.32 seconds. If the traffic is round-trip, then you need to double your estimate.

FIGURE 15.12

A TRACERT from Boston to New York with hops' latency data shown

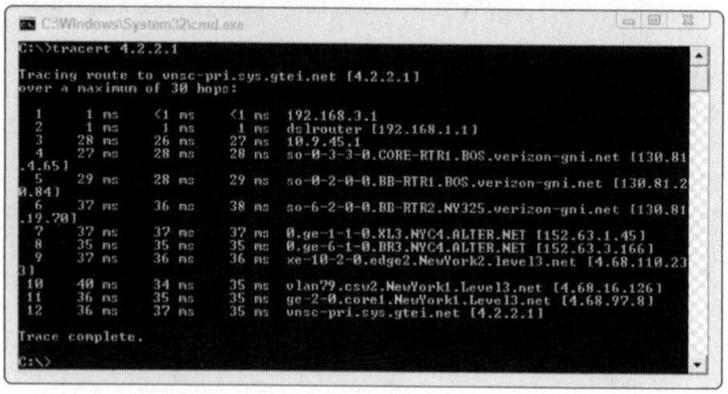

iSCSI protocol

The iSCSI protocol packages SCSI commands inside TCP packets for transport over IP networks. iSCSI is a relatively new technology that allows a host to interact with storage as if it is direct attached or point-to-point, but to present the storage to an IP network as a shared asset. iSCSI offers a number of very important advantages over SANs and Fibre Channel. Because data is sent over IP networks, it is much cheaper to deploy iSCSI as you can leverage existing networks. The distance limitation of Fibre Channel does not apply to iSCSI, making WAN links much more practical.

iSCSI is enabled either in hardware at the HBA or in software using specialized device drivers to format the packets. The use of storage over IP as the storage network makes iSCSI very attractive for use in LAN deployments, departments, workgroups, and other scenarios where the network already exists.

iSCSI clients are called initiators, commands are formatted in the SCSI Command Descriptor Block (CDB) format, and the commands are then sent to the target. iSCSI uses unique identifiers to differentiate individual initiators and targets. There are three different and separate naming conventions:

- iSCSI Qualified Name (IQN)
- Extended Unique Identifier (EUI)
- T11 Network Address Authority (NAA)

IQN is the more common of the three different formats. It takes the form iqn.yyyy-mm {reverse domain name}. An example would be iqn.2009-06.20.com.domainname:devicename.type.location.

It's important to protect iSCSI traffic, because the commands are usually sent unencrypted using text. iSCSI uses different authentication methods to establish a session between initiator and target. The simplest method uses the Challenge and Response Protocol (CHAP); more secure authentication can be enforced by using IPsec as the Network protocol. Another method used to secure iSCSI traffic is to segregate that traffic to dedicated connections enforced at the switch port level or on a VLAN. iSCSI can also be set up so that the connection requires a specific logical unit number (LUN) authorization.

An iSCSI initiator is one endpoint of a SCSI session; it sends SCSI commands to a target but does not specify the eventual location of the data or the data's LUN. An initiator on a host system is most often a device driver that emulates an iSCSI HBA. The device driver uses the host's network stack to send and receive iSCSI commands. These iSCSI device drivers can be supplied by the operating system vendor, or are made available by the HBA vendor as part of their included software.

Note

The Microsoft iSCSI page can be found at `www.microsoft.com/WindowsServer2003/technologies/storage/iscsi/default.mspx`.

Initiators are also contained in HBAs. The initiator function is embedded in firmware on the HBA, which usually adds some sort of TCP offload processing engine. iSCSI is a demanding protocol that requires a high-performance solution, and the offload function isolates much of the processing and data traffic to the HBA. iSCSI HBA is currently supported by either 10 Gigabit or Gigabit Ethernet speeds.

An iSCSI target is the endpoint of a SCSI session. It waits for commands from the initiator and responds to them. The target returns the location of the data, usually in the form of LUNs, and sends them to the initiator so that data can be requested. The iSCSI target is most often a logical disk unit of some type located on a storage system, but it can also be tape systems or optical changers. Targets can also include virtual resources such as virtual disk, virtual tape, or another virtual medium that is accessed by iSCSI software using the controllers that are internal to the devices that have virtualized components.

The software that serves as the target is a kernel-level device driver that is available in most operating systems or from the HBA vendors. Some vendors bundle iSCSI inside their disk arrays as a set of iSCSI targets that can communicate with multiple hosts.

A LUN is an addressable storage entity in a SCSI bus. It can be a single disk, a RAID set, or more often a volume that is defined from part of one of the first two physical storage assets. iSCSI treats a LUN as if it were a unique disk drive, and formats, mounts, and manages the file system on the LUN. In order to mount an iSCSI LUN, it must be formatted by an iSCSI system and its file system is then part of the iSCSI LUN definition.

iSCSI is the most popular of a number of storage networking protocols that encapsulate storage command. iFCP shares many of the characteristics of iSCSI that have been described in this section. In Figure 15.13, there are two different iSCSI topologies shown: one that uses only native iSCSI shown on the left side of Figure 15.13 and another that mixes iSCSI and Fibre Channel through an intermediate bridge that is labeled iSCSI Heterogeneous SAN on the right side of Figure 15.13.

FIGURE 15.13

A native and heterogeneous iSCSI SAN deployment

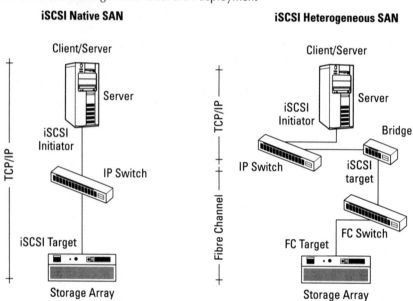

Fibre Channel over IP

Fibre Channel networks are impractical over long distances and require expensive infrastructure and specialized knowledge to implement and manage. There are vast hordes of network engineers who know TCP/IP networking and a tremendous amount of infrastructure available in that network protocol. For all of these reasons, Fibre Channel over IP, or FCIP, has an audience.

FCIP is currently used to connect "SAN islands" over WAN links. At each end of the link are FCIP gateways. From the standpoint of the network, it is irrelevant where the gateway devices are located. The major concern is whether it is possible to send the necessary traffic over the link using the bandwidth that you have available to you.

Many Fibre Channel SANs were built to provide the storage support for high-speed transactional database systems. A transactional system can sustain a wait period of a second or two to retrieve data, but longer wait periods result in serious performance degradation. The distance that an FCIP packet must travel has a fundamental impact on whether you can use FCIP in a transactional system.

There are processes that tolerate latency. Backup and replication are examples of applications where FCIP could be used. In a backup process, data is transmitted from one site to another. If there is latency, then the data throughput is simply slower. How much slower? At current speeds, data over an OC-3 IP connection takes about six times as long as over an FC SAN. Incremental backups that are sometimes called data vaults are good candidates for FCIP. A popular commercial application, called Carbonite, is a data vault. You specify a backup, and the system begins a very slow copy of all of the data. Once the data set is completely transferred (which may take days), the changes are copied with only a small delay.

Data vaulting is particularly important when the data it is protecting is valuable. Products that perform data vaulting of a live transactional system require special techniques to ensure that they capture data that the file system locks because it is in use. These programs tend to use a number of proprietary techniques to solve these types of problems. The Sarbanes-Oxley Act of 2002 in the United States included corporate record-keeping provisions that made data vaulting more popular.

Internet Fibre Channel Protocol

The Internet Fibre Channel Protocol, or iFCP, is a tunneling protocol that enables Fibre Channel data to flow from one iFCP gateway to another iFCP gateway. The protocol was designed to allow fast point-to-point connections and to link SANs over IP links. Encapsulated data inside iFCP can contain SCSI commands or data formatted in Fibre Channel over IP (FCIP) and is contained within IP packets.

Much of the network overhead for an iFCP connection is performed by TCP/IP, including routing and switching, error detection, flow controls, and recovery. Packet formation is performed at the iFCP gateway, as is frame extraction from received packets.

Storage Area Network Management

Storage Area Networks, or SANs, have hundreds if not thousands of elements that must be managed in order for the storage network to run optimally. These elements include port traffic, port assignments, disk activity, connection monitoring, host performance characteristics, and many other factors. Nearly all of the components installed on a SAN conform to industry standards, such as SNMP, so that they are discoverable and manageable. Most SAN management software is a framework that uses SNMP for command and control functions from a console (host).

The majority of these SAN management solutions are either Windows or Sun Solaris applications; many are browser-based and therefore platform independent. When Windows is used, it is common for the application to use the Windows Management Instrumentation (WMI) interface for device management.

WMI is an extension of the Web-Based Enterprise Management (WEBM) and Common Information Model (CIM) that was developed by the Distributed Management Task Force (DMTF) for standardizing instrumented components. That's a lot of acronyms, but WMI is interoperable with SNMP, and it allows Windows hosts to use the command line interface (WMIC) that Microsoft has developed for very convenient access to devices. The graphical utilities are simply front-ends for these commands.

SAN management software can be deployed in-band as an appliance or server at the edge of a SAN, or within the SAN as part of the data path. It can also be deployed as one of those devices as an out-of-band solution that is located on the data network (LAN), but that is not in the data path of storage I/O. These applications can perform discovery and mapping operations, monitor bandwidth utilization, and make changes in the environment. Examples of SAN management packages are Onaro's SANscreen (now owned by NetApp), EMC ControlCenter SAN Manager, and the IBM System Storage SAN Volume Controller (SVC). This category of software tends to be expensive but can have a very dramatic payback in terms of efficiencies.

A related area of software used in storage network management is called Storage Resource Management, or SRM, software. SRM can be deployed on networks of any type (LANs, SANs, and so on) and monitors storage assets down to the smallest level. Early SRM performed disk quota management, but with current SRM software, it is possible to determine which disks are close to full, which files are getting the most access, how many instances of a particular piece of data exist, and so forth. SRM is incredibly valuable in an enterprise and on a storage network, but its expense has kept the category relatively small. Windows Server 2008 shipped with a basic SRM application that allows you to check out this area of technology for yourself. SRM will likely become a standard module in all network operating systems sometime in the future.

Internet Storage Name Service

The Internet Storage Name Service (iSNS) is a proposed IETF standard that would unify the methods used to manage iSCSI and FCIP devices on an IP network. A number of vendors offer iSNS servers, including the OpenSolaris Project, Microsoft iSNS Server 3.0, and Linux isns for iscsi, among others. The services iSNS provides includes the following:

- Name registration
- Discovery Domain (DD)
- Login authentication
- Storage resource discovery
- State Change Notification (SCN)
- Fibre Channel and iSCSI connection management

While the Fibre Channel part of iSNS is required for any implementation, the iSCSI part is optional. The protocol creates a set of management services that emulate a Storage Area Network switched fabric. There are four parts to an iSNS network:

- **Server(s).** An iSNS server can service both iSCSI and FCIP traffic.
- **Client(s).** A client is any iSNS-aware device.
- **Database(s).** The iSNS database stores information about clients in its DD and events.
- **The iSNS Protocol (iSNSP).** The protocol is used for communication between client, servers, switches, and other targets.

Establishing an iSNS management system allows target devices to register in the DD and to be managed using logical units such as storage groups. The stored logins can be applied to sets of storage units, which allows the storage network to manage a large number of assets. Control over parts of the management structure can be delegated.

Summary

In this chapter, you learned about storage network technology and why it is so important. Some of the largest networks in use today are Storage Area Networks. Storage networks can be described in terms of their topology and the technologies that they use. One of the highlights of this chapter was a description of Fibre Channel networks. Storage network topologies can be direct attached, point-to-point, arbitrated loops, and fabrics.

The shared storage network model was presented so that you would have a vocabulary with which to describe different applications, devices, and technologies. Storage devices can be broadly categorized as either block- or file-oriented solutions. The shared storage model was extended for tape devices.

Concepts such as physical versus logical disks, storage virtualization, aggregation, and redirection make storage networks adaptable and easier to use.

In the next chapter, a number of high-performance network technologies are described.

High-Speed Interconnects

High-performance computing requires networks to function. They can be powerful systems that use high-speed networks, or distributed systems that have many members and can use low-speed networks. In this chapter, you look at both types of solutions.

Ethernet is a pervasive networking standard. The current leading-edge Ethernet systems use 10 Gigabit Ethernet (GbE). This standard is described, as well as the future forms of Ethernet that are currently under development.

Networks currently can carry more traffic than most computers can process. To make computers more efficient, a number of technologies have been introduced. TCP Offload Engines (TOEs) can remove most of the network I/O and make computers much more efficient.

Another set of technologies that are similar to TOEs are called *zero copy networks*. They create a virtual network interface that also offloads network processing. The Virtual Interface Architecture and the InfiniBand peripheral bus are examples of zero copy networks that are examined. Five of the ten most powerful computers in the world were built using this high-performance bus.

A number of different network cluster types are discussed. These include fault-tolerant systems that provide failover, load-balanced solutions that help achieve better utilization on server farms, and pervasive utility computing where distributed systems are networked together into a virtual supercomputer.

Grid or mesh computing is an important and growing area of networked computers. The largest computer projects ever built were of this kind. Examples such as Folding@home and SETI@home are considered. Grid systems are being developed to enable cloud computing, with a view toward creating computer utilities.

IN THIS CHAPTER

Different high-speed network standards

Techniques for offloading network processing

High-performance networked computers

Grid, mesh, edge, and cloud computing

High-Performance Computing

High-performance computing, or HPC, is a term used to describe systems capable of high speed or high output. The term has been applied to mainframes, supercomputers, clustered computers, and more recently, cloud, distributed, and grid computing. Most HPC systems rely on their network systems to provide the services necessary to make their architecture work.

In some cases, networks must use advanced networking hardware such as 10 Gbits/s Ethernet (and beyond), high-speed peripheral interconnects such as InfiniBand, and special function network adapters such as TOEs and the Virtual Interface Architecture. In this chapter, these technologies are discussed, as well as why they are important and where they are used currently.

You can also get high performance by using slow and unreliable connections, such as the Internet running on low-power computers or consuming a fraction of the resources of high-power computing if the scale of the project is large enough. The largest computing projects yet attempted, the ones that have performed the most compute cycles, are distributed systems that run on volunteer computers all over the world. Essentially systems of this type are massively parallel-processed supercomputers. While they aren't free for the people who pay the electric bills, they are low cost when the systems are shared for a common purpose, and they enable expensive projects to be done that otherwise wouldn't be possible.

With the emphasis on computer networking as a utility and software as a service, there is a lot of interest in computer systems that create a cloud to enable what has come to be called *pervasive computing*. That is, the availability of the network wherever you might be. The industry is moving toward this type of system both in software through operating systems and remote applications and by using virtualization technologies. That will make grid systems and distributed networks much more popular going forward.

If you are sitting in front of your PC, you might reasonably ask what does a chapter like this have to do with my network? The answer is, of course, that these technologies tend to become less expensive over time and tend to show up in next-generation hardware. It isn't unreasonable to expect to see the technologies in this chapter brought to bear on massively multicore desktop computers running parallel-processing operating systems in about five years time.

Just in case you are curious, the Top500.org project collects statistics on the most powerful computers in the world twice a year. They store the information on their site in a form that allows you to see which vendors, technologies, countries, and installations have reached specific performance levels. Top500 numbers are based on LINPACK statistics submitted by people either working for or associated with the computer systems they list. Their list was published in June 2008 to coincide with the International Supercomputer Conference, and in November when the U.S. IEEE Super Computer Conference meets. Table 16.1 shows the top ten computers in November 2008.

TABLE 16.1

Top 10 Computers

Rank	R_{max}, R_{peak}* (TFLOPS)	Code Name	Details	Vendor	Site
1	1105, 1457	Roadrunner	IBM BladeCenter QS22/LS21 122400 (Cell/Opteron)	IBM	Los Alamos Laboratory, United States, 2008
2	1059, 1381	Jaguar	Cray XT5 QC 2.3 GHz	Cray	Oak Ridge National Laboratory, United States, 2008
3	487, 609	Pleides	SGI Altrix ICE 8200EX	SGI	NASA/Ames Research Center/NAS
4	478, 596	Blue Gene/L	eServer Blue Gene Solution 212992 (Power)	IBM	Lawrence Livermore National Laboratory, United States, 2008
5	450, 557	Intrepid	Blue Gene/P Solution 163840 (Power)	IBM	Argonne National Laboratory, United States, 2008
6	433, 579	Ranger	SunBlade x6420, Opteron QC 2.3 GHz, InfiniBand	Sun	Texas Advanced Computer Center, United States, 2008
7	266, 356	Franklin	Cray XT4 Quadcore 2.1 GHz 2008	Cray	NERSC/Lawrence Berkeley Labs
8	205, 260	Jaguar	Cray XT4 30976 (Opteron)	Cray	Oak Ridge National Laboratory, United States, 2008
9	204, 284	Red Storm	Sandia/Cray Red Strom XT 3/4	Cray	NNSA/Sandia National Laboratories
10	181, 233	Dawning 5000A	Dawning 5000A, QC Opteron 1.9 GHz, Infiniband, Windows HPC	Dawning	Shanghai Computer Center

* Rmax is the highest LINPACK score, and Rpeak is the theoretical peak as measured in teraflops.

Beyond Gigabit Ethernet

Gigabit Ethernet, or GbE (also abbreviated as GigE), is the current commodity standard for Ethernet networking. That is, you can purchase GbE switches, routers, and hubs for prices that make them a practical choice for small offices and home networks. One of the most, if not the most, popular GbE cards is the Intel Pro/1000 GT. It currently sells for around $36 ($23 OEM).

Ethernet is such a pervasive standard that in this section, you'll be taking a look ahead to see what the Ethernet roadmap has in store for high-performing networks.

Ethernet standards have followed a progression where the speed increases by a factor of ten times with each new generation. So far, you have seen the following:

- 10 Mbits/s Ethernet, 10Base-T
- 100 Mbits/s Ethernet, 100Base-T
- 1 Gbits/s Ethernet, 1 GbE
- 10 Gbit/s Ethernet, 10 GbE

Note

The term Base-T refers to Ethernet running over a twisted pair of copper cables.

The 10 Gigabit Ethernet IEEE 802.3ae standard appeared in 2003 and currently is the fastest defined Ethernet standard on the market. Versions of 10 GbE have appeared for optical fiber, twisted-pair copper wire (10GBase-T), and over copper twin-ax (InfiniBand) cable. The standard defines full-duplex connections (two-way traffic) and does not support half-duplex CSMA/CD. The current market for 10 GbE technology is somewhat more than 1 million ports per year and is sold in the storage, fabric network, and virtualization markets.

You should note that there are several different 10GBase-T connection types. For optical fiber, you will find versions of 10GBase connections in R (standard Range), SR (Short Range), LR (Long Range), LRM (Long Range Multimode), ER (Extended Range), ZR, and LX4. On copper, the connection standards for 10GBase are T (802.an-2006), CX4 (802.ak), SFP+ Direct Attach, KX4, and KR. KX4 and KR are 802.3ap standards used in backplanes such as routers, switches, and blades.

10GBase-T

The 10GBase-T is the most popular connection and can be used over twisted-pair cables up to 100m in length, but it isn't the fastest of the connection types just mentioned. 10GBase-T is backwards compatible with 1GBase-T, and its ports can automatically negotiate the port speed. This standard uses RJ-45 connectors and Category 6 cabling, preferably augmented Cat6a cables. The additional partitioning in the cable helps to reduce crosstalk.

The connection modules for 10 GbE cables are called PHYs, and they connect a link layer device (a MAC) to the copper or optical fiber cable. A PHYceiver is the chip that enables a physical layer connection to a 10 GbE cable, and it comes packaged with a microcontroller in a pluggable module that fits into the backplane of a 10 GbE switch or router. PHYs exist for both LAN and WAN 10 GbE modules, but the WAN PHY, while slower, shares the same type of optics. PHYs encode and decode data for transmission and reception, and have two separate subsystems: a Physical Coding Sublayer (PCS) and a Physical Medium Dependent Layer. Other technologies that use PHY chips are USB, SATA, IrDA (sometimes), and many embedded systems.

Tip

Current information on 10 GbE products may be obtained from 10GbE.net.

You can buy 10 GbE network interface cards (NICs) from a number of vendors, including Intel, Chelsio, NetXen, Silicom, HP, Neterion, LeWiz, Tehuti Networks, and Myricom. One vendor, NetEffect, was recently purchased by Intel. NICs use PCI-X or PCI express and are connected with different types of PHY modules. The current recommendation is to buy the CX4 copper standard for 10 GbE connections less than 15m, and fiber for any distance greater than that.

Higher-Speed Gigabit Ethernet

The growing need to have faster switch and backbone connections is being driven by many factors. The use of video on sites such as YouTube, Google's only video download site, is one example of a business that has enormous bandwidth issues. The concentration of traffic onto high-speed optical backbones also makes technologies above 10 GbE attractive. To set standards for a next-generation Ethernet, a number of large companies have formed the IEEE Higher Speed Study Group (HSSG).

The current work of the study group has been to achieve a consensus among vendors on the speed of the next generation of GbE. There was contention between a set of vendors who wanted to release a 40 GbE standard that would work with the OC-768 optical backbones and support server-to-switch connections, and those who wanted to release a 100 GbE standard for switch-to-backbone connections. The result was that the study group opted to support products at both speeds.

The 802.ba standard products should appear in 2010 on either multimode fiber optic cable (for lengths greater than 100m), or on copper (less than 100m). Single-mode fiber optic cable with support of length in the 10km to 40km range but offering no multi-wavelength WDM capability will also be available. The expectation is that the 100 GbE devices that provide a switch-to-backbone capability will become available in 2011.

TCP Offloading Engines

A *TCP Offload Engine*, or TOE, is a special type of network interface that contains a dedicated TCP/IP stack and a custom ASIC dedicated and optimized for a network I/O processor. Current TOE solutions have focused on 10 Gigabit Ethernet (GbE) network interface cards, as those technologies are the most popular.

As early as 1990, Auspex created a UDP offload technology that became known as Functional Multiprocessing (FMP). Alacritech, which was formed by Larry Boucher and other Auspex engineers, became the first company to offer a TCP offloading NIC in 2001. Their current SEN2102ET 10 GbE copper wire TOE card is shown in Figure 16.1. The Microsoft Chimney Offload (previously the Partial TCP Offload Architecture) is based on technologies from Alacritech, as is Broadcom's TCP Chimney Offload Chips.

TOE is implemented in the following ways:

- **iSCSI HBAs.** These TOE HBAs are disk controllers on the computer side, and iSCSI initiators on the network side. This is a full TCP offload technology.

- **TCP Chimney Offload.** The TCP Chimney Offload technology, as it was implemented by Microsoft and Broadcom, is a partial offload system. A Chimney TOE system offloads TCP processing but allows the CPU to retain control over the connection between TCP endpoints. This addresses a major criticism of the TOE technology. TOE's detractors argue that it makes systems less secure because the system becomes unaware of the connection and the potential exists that connection can be manipulated by an outside party.

- **Parallel Stack Offload.** In a Parallel Stack Offload technology, the entire TCP/IP stack is duplicated; this is called a *Full Offload*. One stack runs on the host CPU, and the second stack runs on the TOE engine. This second TCP stack is called a *vampire trap*; it intercepts and redirects TCP traffic made by applications to the main TCP stack.

FIGURE 16.1

The 10 GbE Alacritech copper wire PCI-e 1X Ethernet TOE card. The custom ASIC is the large, black chip with the running man in the lower-right side of the card.

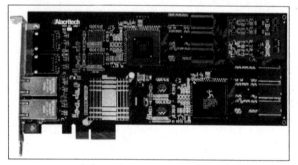

Image courtesy of Alacritech, Inc.

Cross-Ref
The TCP is described in detail in Chapter 17.

The TCP is the Transport layer (OSI Level 3) of the Internet Protocol (IP). TCP does the following things:

- Establishes and terminates the endpoints of an IP connection through handshaking
- Provides a messaging protocol
- Establishes a packet sequence
- Provides an error-checking mechanism

- Offers a sliding window congestion control
- Acknowledges packet reception

TCP does these things by adding a header to data and creating a packet. To this packet, the IP adds the addressing that defines the source system, and the address needed for the packet to make its way to the endpoint of the connection. TCP requires a significant amount of processing to manage the packets. On GbE networks, computer systems that perform a significant amount of network I/O become processor-limited. These types of systems include Web servers, terminal servers, file servers, backup servers, and many other application servers.

Note
The process of adding the header is called encapsulation, and removing it is called expansion or unpacking. Strangely, de-encapsulation isn't an English word. In networking, the terms used for establishing and breaking a logical connection over a virtual circuit are called setting up and tearing down, respectively.

If you analyze the amount of time spent by data sent by one networked application to another on a standard network without offload, the amount of time spent processing a data transfer is nearly ten times the amount of time that the data spends moving on the wire. These processor resources are stolen from the actual computing that the system is meant to be calculating. When you employ offload techniques such as TCP Offload, processor utilizations on single-core processors that were in the 85 to 95 percent range can drop to as little as 10 to 15 percent. TOE is also especially valuable in streaming multimedia applications.

TOE combines a processing function with a complete functional TCP stack. A TOE subsystem reads and writes the headers of IP packets, sends and reads the TCP messaging, and performs connection setup and teardown without the computer's CPU (or CPUs) being involved. TOE also uses forms of Direct Memory Access (DMA) to read and write to memory buffers without the CPU. Indeed, with a TOE-enabled computer, the application that is generating the request for TCP traffic only needs to have the processor send a request to the TOE systems to transfer the data, and TOE does the rest.

TOE does have one other important performance benefit. Because TOE sits on a PCI-e NIC, much of the processing and data transfer overhead is prevented from traveling over the PCI bus interface. PCI doesn't handle large numbers of small messages as well as it does large amounts of data contained in a few messages. By removing the messaging traffic from the PCI bus, the latency that PCI introduces in network traffic can be greatly reduced.

While TOE does have significant performance benefits in current networked computer technology, given the imbalance between high network versus low processor capabilities, the technology does have some disadvantages. Perhaps the most significant criticism is the one already mentioned: security. TOE takes responsibility for an essential network function away from the networked operating system. Therefore, when there are security threats, you are relying on the TOE vendor to protect your network subsystem. Because TOE removes connection information from the host, it also impacts a system's ability to manage session characteristics such as packet filtering and Quality of Service parameters.

TOE cards are expensive and aren't yet commodity items, and so they tend to be marketed as NICs for servers or they show up as chips on some Intel server motherboards. It is possible that the technology could become cheaper and more pervasive in the years to come, but at the moment TOEs are sold as proprietary systems by a limited number of vendors.

Because the Virtual Interface Architecture (VIA) uses TOE, the section on VIA later in this chapter returns to this topic.

Zero Copy Networks

A zero copy network uses a CPU offload technology to transfer information in special dedicated memory from one computer to another. This frees the CPU system resources to work on other computational tasks, making the computer more efficient. Network I/O is also improved because user-level applications can direct the kernel to transfer data without sending the data back to the application. Data is accessed using a form of direct memory access (DMA) without the need for the kernel to intervene further once the command is sent. The latency introduced by kernel/user-level context switching, which is required to cycle through different processor states when data moves from one to the other, is removed.

To enable a zero copy system, a computer must have intelligent network adapters with their own network protocol stacks. ASICs on the adapter enable it to control specialized device drivers, use file system extensions, and use DMA methods to have a Memory Management Unit copy and map data from memory to the adapter for network transfer. Most of the vendors that sell network systems of this type provide both hardware and software. However, there is growing support within networked operating systems for zero copy operations. The Linux APIs `sendfile` and `sendfile64` have zero copy support, as does Java's class libraries on UNIX and Linux through the `transferTo()` method in the `java.nio.channels.FileChannel`.

Figure 16.2 shows a schematic of zero copy file transfers versus a standard file transfer. There are two context switches for zero copy, and four for standard copy operations. In the Zero copy scenario, data is read from disk and requires a single User level command to move the data from the read buffer to the socket buffer where it can be read by the NIC. In the standard file copy, the data is read from the read buffer and then copied to the socket buffer with two User level commands. Any time you issue a User level command, you perform a context switch that changes the state of the CPU twice. A context switch interrupts the processing queue and adds significant overhead to any operation, which is why Zero copy offers a substantial benefit.

Remote Direct Memory Access (RDMA) in these systems allows application data on a sending computer to be sent to the receiving computer's memory without the use of either system's operating system. RDMA requires some special memory access programming and must populate memory with the data that is required to be transferred.

Zero copy technology shows up in very powerful distributed parallel-processing systems where the speed of the network has outpaced the computers' ability to process output.

FIGURE 16.2

Zero copy versus standard copy transfers

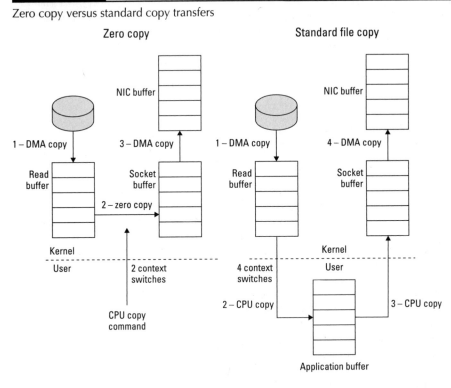

Virtual Interface Architecture

Virtual Interface Architecture, or VIA, is a high-speed cluster networking standard that was created by a consortium of companies including Intel, Microsoft, and Compaq (now part of HP) at the end of 1997. Clusters of computers were becoming popular as replacements for mainframes and super-computers of the past, and VIA was meant to help them scale more efficiently. VIA was meant to be an open interoperable standard that would replace proprietary cluster networking solutions.

VIA is used in the following:

- **InfiniBand.** A switched fabric network architecture
- **Internet Wide Area RDMA Protocol (iWARP).** An expanded version of VIA for IP networks
- **Emulex (formerly GigaLAN) cLAN**

The primary bottleneck in high-performance computer networking is the latency introduced by the excessive amount of processor utilization required to maintain all of the I/O traffic that moves from system to system. In high-performance cluster networks without some form of CPU offload

441

technique, high-speed networks consume enough processor resources to dramatically impact system performance.

Figure 16.3 shows a schematic of the virtual network interface created by VIA. The VI architecture can be described by a VI service consumer, which is an application layer function that interacts with a Vi service provider that includes a user agent overlying kernel level functions. Commands sent to the VI provider from the application are managed by a VI kernel agent, whereas data goes directly from the VI application to the virtual NIC for processing. The two agents perform tasks such as queue management and prioritization; processor intensive tasks such as addressing and packetization are performed at the VI NIC level. Notice that the data channel goes directly from the User level to the VI NIC without having to be processed by kernel level functions.

FIGURE 16.3

VIA system components

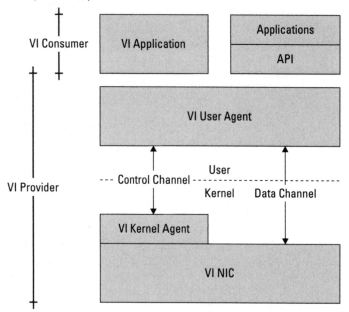

Data copies and file transfers follow what has been called the 80/80 rule:

- Eighty percent of the copy operations copy data of 256 bytes or less for control and synchronization.

- Eighty percent of the data required is contained in data of 8K or more.

These factors introduce tremendous overhead in copying operations and network file transfers. It is these kinds of problem that VIA solves.

Note

VIA networks are called System Area Networks (SANs), a usage that predates Storage Area Networks (also called SANs). To avoid confusion, this book uses the term VIA network when describing this technology. VIA is also the name of the integrated circuit manufacturer in Taiwan that makes a low-power X86 CPU that powers many laptops.

VIA is a zero copy networking protocol that bypasses the kernel mode and virtualizes the network interface. User-level applications can control and signal the network interface without CPU processing, greatly reducing processor overhead. The virtual interface is called a *provider* and the application that accesses that interface is referred to as the *consumer*. The control path is used to set up and tear down a connection. The data path sends and receives Send/Receive and Remote DMA READ/WRITE messages. VIA access is provided through the use of the Virtual Interface Provider Library (VIPL).

The Internet Wide Area RDMA Protocol, or iWARP, is an IETF standard that is another superset of VIA, one that is used on TCP/IP networks. The network interface controller for iWARP is an Ethernet TCP Offload Engine that uses the Direct Data Protocol (DDP) to initiate the zero copy operation. TCP is the transport protocol used for iWARP. iWARP uses a verb interface (like InfiniBand). Other protocols that can use iWARP are defined by the OpenFabrics Alliance for Linux, and by Winsock Direct from Microsoft.

InfiniBand

InfiniBand is derived from an industry initiative to create the next-generation replacement of the PCI bus by a couple of industry groups. The InfiniBand Trade Association (www.infinibandta.org) was formed in 1999 to create a new high-performance server peripheral and switched fabric network bus. The two original technologies were called Next Generation I/O (NGIO) and Future I/O (FIO), and when merged, they were called System I/O. InfiniBand was the result.

The InfiniBand architecture is a superset of VIA and implements connections between computer systems, high-performance storage systems, and other devices. The InfiniBand standard has been defined to grow over time and has been released in three different speeds: 1X (2 to 8 Gbits/s), 4X (8 to 32 Gbits/s), and 12X (24 Gbits/s), with the ranges defined by the use of Single, Double, and Quad Data Rate memory (SDR, DDR, and QDR).

InfiniBand doesn't implement an API that vendors can program against. Instead, the standard specifies a set of verbs and actions that must be implemented. A vendor then uses a programming language of their choice to create a control and messaging system.

An InfiniBand connection is a bidirectional link that has a 10-bit channel, 8 bits of which are data and 2 bits of which are dedicated for control signals. The faster speeds are links that are aggregated as multiples of 4 and 12 single links. A link is defined as the connection between channel adapters, which has the same role for InfiniBand that NICs have for Ethernet. A Host Channel Adapter (HCA) and a Target Channel Adapter (TCA) on a computer and a peripheral device negotiate security protocols and define QoS parameters for the connection. Channel adapter vendors include Cisco, Mellanox, and QLogic. InfiniBand switches are made by Cisco, HP, Mellanox, QLogic, and Voltaire.

InfiniBand has become the interconnect of choice for very high performance cluster computer systems. If you look at Table 16.1, you can see that five of the top ten highest-performing computers in the world are currently InfiniBand clusters.

However, InfiniBand has seen slow adoption in the industry. Some of the reluctance to adopt InfiniBand has been due to people waiting for higher-performance Ethernet standards to be developed. Fibre Channel is also hard to displace in switched fabric storage networks. Vendors are working on a Fibre Channel over InfiniBand (FCoIB) technology that they hope will make InfiniBand more popular in the Storage Area Network marketplace.

Figure 16.4 shows a hypothetical InfiniBand WAN with an emphasis on storage device connections.

FIGURE 16.4

InfiniBand can function as a high-speed and highly redundant component of a WAN.

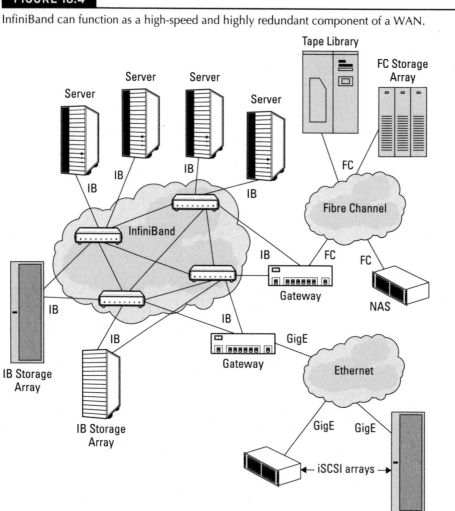

Network Clusters

Computer clusters are one area in which fast networking standards play a central if not critical role. A cluster can be created using two computers sharing a common peripheral bus. However, once you start connecting multiple computers together, separating them into server farms, or distributing them into a grid architecture, peripheral buses are replaced by networks. In the sections that follow, you look at two different types of network clusters: those that are powerful and require speedy connections and those that are just as powerful but operate with a large number of computers and use a standard network.

Network clusters are formed for the following purposes:

- **Fault tolerance.** Mission-critical applications that require zero or close to zero downtime. Table 16.2 shows different levels of fault tolerance.

- **Utilization.** Server farms that work by having a front-end system that performs load balancing where the emphasis is on server utilization.

- **Pervasive utilities.** Distributed computing where the desired result is the creation of a computer utility that can support pervasive computing applications.

TABLE 16.2

Fault Tolerance Requirements

Percent Uptime	Downtime per Year	Platform	Implementation
90 (one nine)	36 days, 12 hours, 36 minutes	Standard PC/server	No fault tolerance required
99 (two nines)	87 hours, 46 minutes	Departmental server	Restore from image
99.9 (three nines)	8 hours, 46 minutes	Highly available	Failover to a mirrored or backup server
99.95	4 hours, 23 minutes	Highly available	Failover to mirrored or backup servers
99.99 (four nines)	52 minutes, 33 seconds	Mission critical	Cluster failover to another node
99.999 (five nines)	5 minutes, 35 seconds	Fault tolerant	Entire computer duplicated for very fast failover
99.9999 (six nines)	31.5 seconds	Continuous	Stratus FT systems, and a few others

Fault tolerance in clusters is created by implementing a failover system. That failover system can be as simple as a heartbeat circuit that is constantly checking to see if one node of the cluster is still up and running. The heartbeat circuit sends out periodic messages asking if the system is and waits a certain period before retrying or issuing a command to fail over to the tem in the cluster.

The earliest Microsoft clusters were two-node clusters with a shared storage solution, as shown in Figure 16.5. The two computers were in a master-slave relationship; if one failed, then the cluster failed over in just a few seconds or so to the other system. The shared storage was a RAID solution that was highly unlikely to fail. These types of clusters can be share-something, share-nothing, or share-everything systems. Nearly all of the server hardware and network operating system vendors currently offer clustered solutions.

Failover clusters or fault-tolerant computers can be as complex as a multiply redundant computer system that is constantly updating all nodes at once. An example of a share-everything system is the Stratus FT series, which is deployed in highly mission-critical applications where failure cannot be tolerated. Their Lockstep system architecture with fully redundant systems is shown in Figure 16.6. This system is capable of *six nines* reliability (99.9999 percent) with a downtime of less than 31.5 seconds a year.

FIGURE 16.5

A simple two-node failover cluster

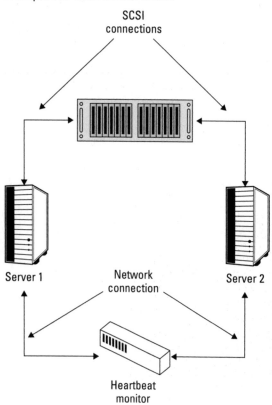

In Figure 16.6 you can see that data is written simultaneously to three separate symmetric multi-processing (SMP) systems containing N-processors/processor cores. Stratus populates these systems with proprietary chipsets: the Status North PCI (SNP) and Stratus South PCI (SSP) ASICs (Application Specific Integrated Circuits) that maintain transactional coherency as data is processed. The SNP and SSP chips are able to simultaneously communicate with the passive backplane, which is an I/O (Input/Output) interface that communicates with peripheral devices, or through network interfaces to other systems.

Networked cluster computers are among the most powerful computers ever built. The most powerful monolithic computer yet built according to Top500.org, the Roadrunner at Los Alamos Laboratory in New Mexico, was built by IBM from a BladeCenter QS22 Cluster connected by a Voltaire InfiniBand network. In June 2008, Roadrunner was reported to be the first computer to demonstrate a PFLOPS (P = peta) per second performance.

FLOPS is an acronym for Floating Point Operations Per Second and is measured using a benchmark application such as LINPACK. A hand calculator runs at about 10 FLOPS, and an Intel Quad-core QX9775 is reported to run at 51 GFLOPS. By comparison, a petaFLOPS is 1015 FLOPS, and one million GFLOPS. The highest-performing computer system in terms of FLOPS is the Folding@Home distributed computing network, which recorded 4.1 PFLOPS.

FIGURE 16.6

The Stratus Lockstep architecture has multiple redundant systems that are continuously updated.

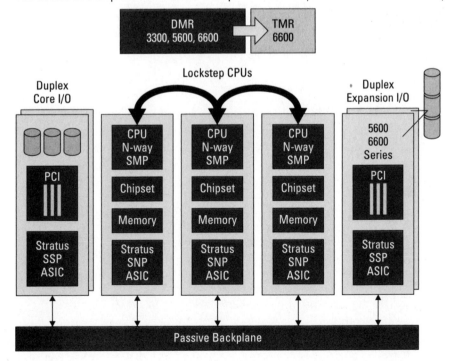

Load balancing

Server farms utilize a form of clustering called *load balancing*. Load balancing is useful when a system is I/O limited and you want to scale your servers out (more servers) rather than up (a more powerful server). Servers can be added and removed upon demand. Load-balanced clustering makes no demands upon the network speed for either the incoming or the outgoing connections, nor does it require that a load be balanced equally.

In this system, a server, router, or director switch with middleware software routes incoming IP traffic so that the work is shared across a group of servers. If a server goes offline, then it is removed from the pool and work is sent to other computers. These solutions often utilize caching to buffer incoming network traffic at peak times.

Load-balancing systems can be of the following architectural types:

- **Round robin scheduling.** A table of IP addresses are sequentially loaded.
- **Bridge load balancing.** This is done with Layer 2 devices using a virtual IP address on a LAN. Traffic to the LAN is sent to the virtual address and then forwarded to the servers that can process the request.
- **Routed load balancing.** This form of load balancing adds intelligence to the way in which servers are loaded. Typically these are Layer 3 devices, and they serve as firewalls or proxy servers spanning two subnets.

Examples of router load-balancing hardware solutions are:

- F5's BIG-IP (www.f5.com)
- Citrix NetScaler MPX (www.citrix.com/english/ps2/products/product. asp?contentID=21679)
- Coyote Point Systems Equalizer (www.coyotepoint.com)

An example of load balancing done in software is the load-balancing module that is built into Windows Server 2003 and 2008. Nearly every network server operating system that you have read about in this chapter ships with load-balancing modules. Examples of load-balancing software are:

- Balance (www.inlab.de/balance.html)
- Queue (www.gnu.org/software/gnu-queue/)
- Linux Virtual Server (www.linuxvirtualserver.org/)

Any network service is a candidate for load balancing. That includes DNS, DHCP, FTP, NNTP servers, and others. Web servers are an example of applications used in load-balanced server farm applications. Load balancers on IP networks work by listening to ports for the traffic type that is being balanced, and then forwarding the request to the backend server. Essentially they act like intelligent routers, and they are transparent to the traffic that flows through them. Figure 16.7 shows a load-balancing solution.

FIGURE 16.7

Load-balanced clusters optimize server utilization by sharing the workload to a server farm over a network.

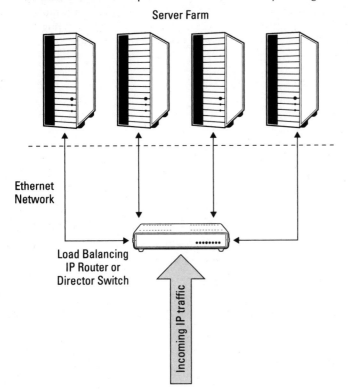

Edge computing is a form of distributed load balancing that is done to push content out to geographically distributed sites. Distributed content servers distribute content to geographically close systems on the Internet, and often those content servers are configured to be mirror sites of the original. Akamai (www.akamai.com) pioneered this category of Web service and provides their mirroring and routing servers to serve customer content. Typically edge servers don't work well with dynamic content, as coordination and replication become too difficult. Vendors typically offer QoS services and performance guarantees, and these services are mature enough that they are cost effective for businesses of all sizes. Depending upon the vendor and their network topology, edge systems can also be grid or mesh systems.

Grid systems

Grid systems are distributed systems of networked computers where the workload is shared amongst the members of the grid. In grid computing, the network can be the Internet, the connection can be slow, and the protocols can be standard Internet protocols. They are called *grid* systems because they were designed to function like a utility, providing computing power on demand. They are also called *mesh networks*. Grid computing can use a client-server model, an n-tiered model, or a peer-to-peer model, depending upon how the organized software is deployed.

Grid computing has the following advantages:

- It improves utilization rates and lessens they need to build rarely used additional capacity.
- It can create the equivalent of a supercomputer at a fraction of the price.
- It can serve the goal of interested communities.
- It could be the basis for pervasive computing where services are always on and universally available.

If enough computers are part of the grid, then even if only a fraction of these computers are working on a project at any one time, the net result can be equivalent to the largest supercomputers available today. Indeed, several grid computer systems are among the highest-performing systems in use today. Folding@home is a 4 PFLOPS system based at Stanford that is four times more powerful than the fastest supercomputer that has been created. It is used to solve protein-folding configurations.

It is a little bit of a misnomer to call a grid computer a computer; they are really virtual computer systems and their work is coordinated by a server or servers, depending upon the number of member systems. Grid systems have performed some very important work in biochemistry, economics, astronomy, and many other fields.

Many grid systems offer clients on several platforms, and their software only runs when the client computer is idle. The use of idle computer cycles is referred to as *CPU-* or *cycle-scavenging*, and other less genteel names.

SETI@home is another volunteer community of computers that is based out of the Space Sciences Laboratory at the University of California at Berkeley. SETI stands for Search for Extra Terrestrial Intelligence, and the grid aids in the search for little green men from outer space. The client software has been used on 5.2 million computers (about 300,000 active clients in over 200 countries) and runs as a screen saver (see Figure 16.8). With an aggregate of two million years of computer time, SETI@home is the largest computation project in history according to Guinness World Records. The SETI project created the Berkeley Open Infrastructure for Network Computing (BOINC), one of the largest volunteer grid systems in use.

Grid systems are the focus of a lot of industry effort as vendors evolve desktop software into applications that run on the "cloud." There's little difference between a cloud system and a grid system; both terms imply a remote service on demand. National grid systems are currently being developed and are in the prototype stage. The European Union is sponsoring a grid for physics, biology, and earth science research. A National Technology Grid is being built in the United States to test the concept of a public, on-demand computation utility.

FIGURE 16.8

The SETI@home screen saver

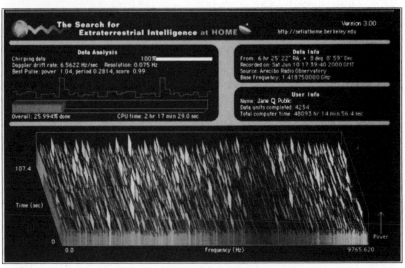

Cloud computing is being enabled by a wide variety of network operating system vendors under initiatives such as Software as a Service (SaaS), Service Oriented Architecture (SOA), the Microsoft .NET Framework, and Web 2.0 applications, among others.

Sun offers software called the Sun Grid Engine (www.sun.com/software/gridware), or SGE, which is an open source batch queuing system that is deployed on a computer cluster or computer farm. Grid deployments of these types have much in common with load-balancing solutions. The Sun Grid utility computer system was built on SGE. A commercial product called the Sun N1 Grid Engine (N1GE) is also offered by Sun, which describes this technology as Distributed Resource Management (DRM) software.

Summary

In this chapter, you learned about high-performance networked computer systems. Powerful systems tend to use high-speed networks, while distributed systems can use standard network types.

Ethernet is so widely used that any new Ethernet standard tends to be deployed widely. Currently available 10 GbE is used with high-speed servers and switches. Faster standards are currently under development.

To address processor overload, a number of network offload techniques have been developed. You looked at the TCP Offload Engine (TOE) and zero copy networks. The Virtual Interface Architecture (VIA) and the InfiniBand peripheral bus are the zero copy networks that you examined.

Networked cluster computers were described. Three types are used to provide failover, load-balanced solutions, and utility computing. Grid computing and cloud computing were briefly examined.

The next chapter begins a new section on TCP/IP networks. You also learn about the TCP transport protocol.

Part IV

TCP/IP Networking

Internet Transport Protocol

Transmission Control Protocol (TCP) and Internet Protocol (IP) are the two protocols that give rise to the acronym TCP/IP. TCP/IP is a set of protocols or agreed standards that are used to send and manage communications on a packet switched network. TCP is the technology that establishes a virtual connection between systems, manages data transmission, and ensures that the data has been reliably transferred. The data that is contained in a packet is TCP data. The mechanism used to get packets to their destination is IP. The way TCP does what it does impacts the majority of Internet communications, as well as how applications are built; it also affects network performance. IP, which is discussed in Chapter 18, is the method used to package data sent across a packet switched network and includes the methods for not only packaging data but for addressing as well.

TCP solves the problem of how to ensure reliable communications when the medium you transmit over is inherently unreliable. Packets may take different routes to get to their destination, arrive out of sequence, or be dropped entirely. TCP assembles the data by sequencing the packets, ensuring that all packets are valid, and requesting retransmission of any packet that is missing or damaged.

Devices connected over a TCP/IP network can have greatly different capabilities; for example, a PDA (personal data assistant) can be slow while a computer can be fast. TCP implements features such as flow control to vary the rate at which data is transferred and provides for multiplexing, which runs simultaneous processes to speed up performance. It can also alter the size of packets.

Not all communications require the overhead of reliable data transmission. When you send rapidly changing data such as voice or video, losing a frame doesn't dramatically impact quality. For those applications, the User Datagram Protocol, or UDP, is used. This chapter describes UDP and compares it to the TCP protocol.

Transmission Control Protocol

The Transmission Control Protocol, or TCP, is the most widely used transport protocol on computer networks today. TCP provides control mechanisms that manage the data contained in the message, ensuring that the data is sent in manageable pieces, that it arrives intact, that the data can be sequenced, and that the reassembled data is a faithful copy of the data that was sent. TCP contains a set of control commands that can vary the amount of data transferred in individual packets, as well as the rate at which packets are sent. Among the applications that rely on TCP are browsers and Web servers, e-mail programs, and file transfer programs.

TCP was developed to solve the problem of reliable communications on an inherently unreliable network. When data must be sliced into IP packets and transmitted as a set of IP requests, there needs to be a mechanism to control IP data flow. TCP allows a program to issue a single send data command and then let TCP handle the details of the data transfer.

An IP packet consists of a data chunk composed of a header section followed by the body section. Encoded in the header are the details of what the packet destination is, any preferences for the route that the packet should take, the size of the data contained in the body portion, a checksum to ensure the validity of the data, and the position in the data sequence into which this packet's data should be placed. You can think of the header and associated IP content as metadata that describes the TCP data contained in the body.

The Internet was designed to be a highly redundant mesh structure that could survive any outages to a substantial portion of the network and still be operable. When data is sent from one system to another, the system doesn't ensure that packets will travel the same route, arrive in sequence, and all arrive correctly. As a matter of fact, packets can take multiple paths to their destination, arrive out of sequence, and be lost along the way.

TCP has a control language that creates a connection between two systems, sends messages that indicate what the next required packet in the sequence is, requests retransmission of packets when required, and acknowledges when the data has been successfully reassembled. On the sending side, TCP's internal timer resends the last required packets if an acknowledgment command isn't received by a certain time. All of the additional packets sent represent an overhead that the TCP system imposes and that can dramatically lower performance.

Note

The TCP protocol was defined in RFC 793, "Transmission Control Protocol." RFC 768, "User Datagram Protocol," defines the use of UDP. An additional protocol, RFC 1122, entitled "Requirements for Internet Hosts—Communication Layers," contains details that outline the transport of both of these protocols.

TCP is designed to be a reliable means of data delivery, but it is not optimized for performance. When TCP is used, there can often be delays while packets are requested and resent, and those delays can run several seconds or more. You can get a sense for the round-trip time by performing a TRACEROUTE command to the system that is sending data. TRACEROUTE (TRACERT on Windows) is a command that sends packets to a destination and has all intermediate nodes send back messages indicating the path and time spent getting to the node to the original source.

TCP is implemented in any operating system that must run on a TCP/IP network, which today is almost any operating system that you would find on a user's desktop, as well as any connected server. Routers, gateways, and firewalls also implement TCP, as evidenced by their ability to respond to PING operations and to be inventoried and managed by SNMP (Simple Network Management Protocols) applications; also, in the case where their management console can be viewed in a browser, they support the HTTP browser protocol.

TCP is highly processor intensive, and in systems with large network I/O, such as Web servers and terminal servers, I/O can be the major performance bottleneck. There has been an effort over the last few years to develop specialized network interface adapters that contain ASICs (Application Specific Integrated Circuits) with a TCP engine built into them that takes the TCP processing load off of a system's CPU and processes it on the network interface card (NIC). These devices are called TCP Offload Engines (TOEs). Alacritech developed the first of these network adapters, and they may appear as specialized chips on motherboards in the years to come. At the moment, the technology is expensive and difficult to implement, but the results can be impressive. The addition of these cards to servers running at 80 percent or more CPU utilization can reduce this percentage to as little as single-digit utilization at the same load.

Not all data transmission requires reliability; some applications work perfectly fine when a large portion of their data arrives. Those applications work best when the data transfer rate is high. An example is streaming video. In a video application, it hardly matters if one frame of the movie drops out when there are 30 frames per second going by. However, if the data rate is high, then the movie can use a higher resolution, and that certainly matters to the viewer. Therefore, applications such as video streaming or Voice over IP (VoIP) tend to use special streaming protocols and use the User Datagram Protocol (UDP) in place of the TCP protocol. UDP is covered later in this chapter.

Packet Structure

A TCP packet consists of a header with many sections and the body of TCP data with a variable size, as determined by the current value of the receive window. Figure 17.1 shows a schematic of a TCP packet. The receive window is a negotiated value that is used to prevent a TCP memory buffer overrun at the receiving system by signaling to the sender when to send data and when to delay sending data. This form of traffic management is described in more detail later in the chapter.

FIGURE 17.1

The packet structure of a TCP packet, with all of the header sections shown

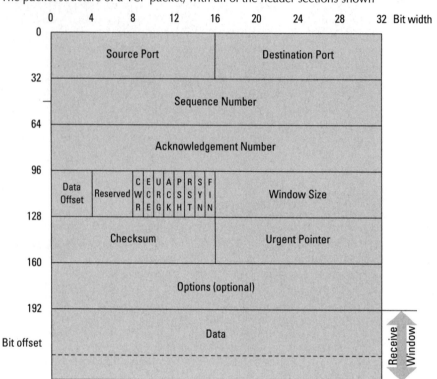

Header fields

The first four fields in the header are the Source port, Destination port, Sequence number, and Acknowledgement number. Ports are similar to a TV channel in that they represent the type of data being sent or received. A port is described as transmitting outgoing data or listening for incoming data. When data arrives at port 8080, it is recognized as data meant for a proxy server such as Microsoft Internet Security and Acceleration (ISA) Server and is sequenced and sent to that application. Port 8080 is for Alternate HTTP. If data came in on port 110, then it would be recognized as being POP3 (Post Office Protocol 3) data, and when the data is sequenced it would be sent to your mail program. Ports are described in the "Ports" section at the end of this chapter.

The Sequence number and Acknowledgement number are fields used for traffic control. If the Synchronize (SYN) flag is set to 1 (on), then the Sequence number field indicates that the number is the initial sequence number and is the start of the data. When the SYN flag is set to 0 (off), this sequence number is used to place the first byte of TCP data into the sequence that will be built.

The Acknowledgment number indicates the next byte that the receiving system needs in the current sequence that it is building when the Acknowledgement (ACK) flag is set to 1 (on). This system allows the receiver to rebuild the data in the original order starting with the first, middle, and last fragments sequentially.

Flags

The block that begins at bit offset 96 contains a number of flags that are used to determine the states of different fields and the purpose of the data. The Data Offset field at the end of the header ensures that whatever the size of the options below, the size of the TCP header is always the same; therefore, the Data Offset size is from 20 to 60 bytes. The Reserved block isn't defined and should be set to zero. What follows next is a set of eight 1-bit blocks called *Flags* or *Control bits*. Flags specify the following:

- **CWR.** Congestion Window Reduced is a flag that is set to 1 (on) when the sending system receives TCP data with the ECE flag set to 1.
- **ECE.** Echo (alternatively ECN) is set to 1 (on) when the system can perform an echo during a three-way handshake.
- **URG.** The Urgent bit is set to 1 (on) when the Urgent pointer field contains data that must be processed with priority before all other traffic.
- **ACK.** The Acknowledgement flag is set to 1 (on) when the Acknowledgement field value needs to be read.
- **PSH.** The Push flag tells TCP to send the data from this message to the Application layer immediately.
- **RST.** The Reset flag is set to 1 (on) to indicate that the connection should be reset.
- **SYN.** The Synchronize flag indicates that the Sequence number field is significant and needs to be processed.
- **FIN.** The Final flag is set to 1 (on) when there is no more data that will be sent by the sender.

Checksum field

The Checksum field contains a value that is used to determine if the entire packet has arrived correctly at its destination, and includes checks on both the header and body of the data. The value of the checksum varies, depending upon whether the packet is transmitted over an IP version 4 or an IP version 6 network, although the TCP header format is the same for both versions.

To get the checksum in IP version 4, the complement of all of the 16-bit words in the packet are found and then summed to create a 16-bit word checksum. If the packet has an odd number of octets (words), then the last octet is padded with zeros to complete the 16-bit checksum word. At the receiving end, the checksum field is padded with zeros and then the complement arithmetic is performed again.

The details of checksums aren't particularly important in the general discussion in this chapter. If you are interested in the details, they are given in RFC 793 for IP version 4 and RFC 2460 for IP version 6. However, it is worth noting that the two checksum methods used are very weak compared to methods like cyclic redundancy checks (CRCs) that are used at the application level. Indeed, most applications apply more advanced data validity checks of their own.

Control fields

As part of traffic control, the Window field specifies the size of the receive window. The size of the data block that is transferred isn't specified by TCP. It can be as small as a single byte or as large as a kilobyte, or anything in between. If a message has a size of 2048KB, then any combination of data block size that adds up to 2048KB may be used. The receiving system can set a value for the Window, based on how much room remains in the TCP memory buffer.

The Urgent pointer field is used when the Urgent (URG) flag is set to 1 (on). This field gives the offset from the sequence number for the last urgent data byte in an urgent sequence.

The Options block contains a number of different values that can be set, ranging from 0 to 8. They are as follows:

0. End of options list

1. No operation

2. Window scale

3. SACK, or Selective Acknowledgement

4. Data Offset (if required)

5. Data Offset (if required)

6. Data Offset (if required)

7. Data Offset (if required)

8. Timestamp

Data field

The final block of data is the Data field. This is the TCP data portion of the packet and contains data in the form of an Application layer protocol. Any data format that can be sent over TCP can be used in the Data field, including HTTP, FTP, POP3, SMTP, and many others; but only one type of data may be sent in a packet, and it must be sent to the port that listens for that data type.

The Data field's size isn't a set value. It can be as small as a byte and as large as the maximum window size allows. TCP has a built-in mechanism that allows the Data field's size to be set as required by conditions as part of TCP's congestion control mechanism.

Protocol Operation

TCP works by creating a connection between two systems or hosts. The connection is a virtual connection because, although the endpoints are known, the paths to the endpoints are not. An endpoint is defined by two parameters: the IP address and the port number.

To initiate a TCP transaction, a connection established by a three-way handshake is often used, as follows:

1. The sending host sends a synchronization or SYN request to the receiving host.

2. The receiving host then acknowledges the message by returning a SYN-ACK response to the sending host. An initial sequence number (ISN) for the first packet is exchanged between the two systems. That number is different with each connection.

3. The sending host then sends an ACK message to indicate that the connection has been established and that each endpoint is now an Internet socket.

Once the connection is established, data transfer can occur. A connection is defined by four parameters: the sending system's IP address, the sending port number, the receiving system's IP address, and the receiving system's port number. Because TCP supports multiplexing, a full description of the connection would include the transport protocol used to create a full-duplex description or full association:

```
(TCP, Send-IP, Send-Port, Receive-IP, Receive Port)
```

Connections can also be described in terms of their one-way relationship, which is called a half association, as follows:

```
(TCP, Send-IP, Send-Port)
```

one way, and

```
(TCP, Receive-IP, Receive Port)
```

in the opposite direction. The concept of a half association is really only valuable when different protocols are used. For example, if you click a link to download a file by FTP in your browser, your outgoing connection is HTTP and sent over port 80, while the incoming file is sent by FTP over port 21.

Active data transfer is characterized by the following actions:

1. The sending system begins to send IP packets in a size and at a rate that was negotiated in the previously described handshake.

2. The receiving system collects packets into a memory buffer and begins to reassemble them. The checksum field in each packet is used to determine whether the packet has been received correctly.

3. If a packet is missing, a retransmission is requested by the receiving system.

4. At regular intervals, the receiving system transmits an ACK command with the position of the last packet (sequence number) that was successfully assembled to the sending system. The sequence number is incremented by the number of bytes received, which is called *cumulative acknowledgment*, and the scheme is sometimes referred to as a *Positive Acknowledgement with Retransmission* (PAR) scheme. Each ACK command can set a flag that alters the rate of packet transmission, as well as the size of the data contained in each packet.

5. If the sending system doesn't receive an ACK command with instructions on which packet in the sequence it should send, then it proceeds to rebroadcast the previous set of packets.

6. When the receiving system gets the ACK message from the sending system with the current last assembled packet, the sending system continues sending additional packets from that point in the sequence.

7. When the receiving system assembles the last packet in the sequence, it performs a data check and then sends the LAST-ACK message.

TCP doesn't send an end-of-message marker with the last packet. The message is complete when the receiving computer has transmitted all of the assembled sequence into data that has been transferred to the application that consumes that data. There is no structure to the TCP data stream; TCP has no knowledge of what the data contains. It can't sequence one database record before another, or send one file before another. Any ordering or data handling is handled by the application. Therefore, it is up to the application to signal when the connection is no longer required. The lack of an application signal is the reason that connections are left in an open state when they are no longer needed.

A connection is terminated through the use of another handshake process. Each endpoint terminates the connection independently.

To terminate a connection, these steps are followed:

1. Endpoint 1 sends a FIN packet to Endpoint 2.

2. Endpoint 2 sends back an acknowledgment, or ACK, to Endpoint 1. Endpoint 1 closes its half of the connection, giving the connection a half-open status.

3. Endpoint 2 sends a FIN packet to Endpoint 1.

4. Endpoint 1 sends back an acknowledgment, or ACK, to Endpoint 2. Endpoint 2 closes its half of the connection, ending the connection entirely.

The previous summary describes a four-way handshake that employs four different transmissions. Most connection terminations employ a three-way handshake by combining step 2 and step 3 into a single FIN & ACK command.

To summarize, endpoints in an Internet socket can be in any of the following states:

1. LISTEN

2. SYN-SENT

3. SYN-RECEIVED

4. ESTABLISHED

5. FIN-WAIT-1

6. FIN-WAIT-2

7. CLOSE-WAIT

8. CLOSING

9. LAST-ACK

10. TIME-WAIT

11. CLOSED

In Figure 17.2, the different states of TCP connections are illustrated, along with the methods used for moving between the different states. Indicated are the steps for the three-way handshake that establish a connection, as well as the relationship of the Active Open and Passive Open states.

FIGURE 17.2

The state diagram for a TCP system

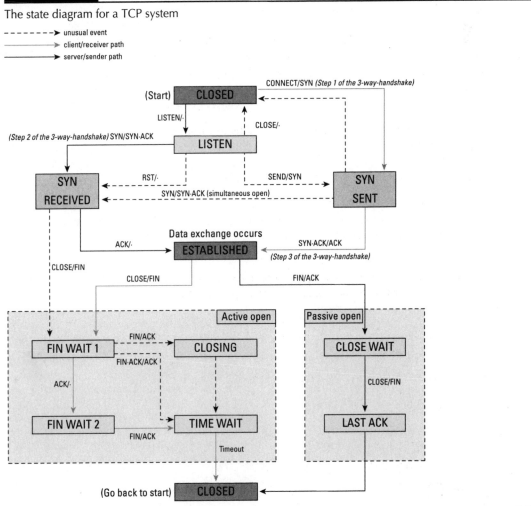

Connections

The TCP host environment for many systems installs the TCP part of the network stack into the operating system in a manner that makes it appear to programs as if TCP is just another file system. This is the case for the proprietary Winsock interface from Microsoft, as well as the BSD Sockets interface that is used on many UNIX systems such as Macintoshes. BSD is the Berkeley Software Distribution or Berkeley Unix operating system. TCP communicates through the IP module, which requires a device driver to communicate with the network.

Programs wanting to use TCP for their data transfers have the following broad classes of connection-related system calls:

- OPEN
- CLEAN
- SEND
- RECEIVE
- STATUS

The parameters passed with these program commands are the half associations that provide the address and port of the target system. Other parameters that are part of these commands are used to set the security and other factors.

Connections are therefore a response to an OPEN call to the TCP module in the sending system's network stack. That module then communicates with the receiving system's TCP module, and both of these modules use their IP modules for the transfer mechanism. When a connection is made, a return call to the application passes a handle back to the application, by which the connection may be identified. A handle is a small integer value, and that value, along with other connection parameters, is stored in a transmission control block (TCB) within the program.

Programs make two types of OPEN calls: either for an Active OPEN connection or a Passive OPEN connection. An Active OPEN command has the TCP module send a message to the receiving system that a connection is to be opened. If the receiving system returns an Active OPEN command, then the connection is made and data transfer can begin.

A Passive OPEN command puts the receiving system's TCP module into a state in which it is prepared to accept incoming packets from a sending system. A Passive OPEN command can be passed the parameter of the sending system's endpoint, in which case the TCP program is listening for those particular packets. Alternatively, the Passive OPEN command can have no endpoints, in which case the TCP module accepts any incoming communications once it receives a connection request (SYN) from any sending system. That incoming SYN request originates because of an OPEN command on the sending system.

An application that issues a Passive OPEN command places itself into a wait state. TCP then informs the application when the connection is made by passing an Active OPEN command from the sending system along to the waiting application. At that point, the Passive OPEN state on the receiving system is changed to an Active OPEN state, and data transfer begins.

Flow Control

The TCP flow control mechanism works by establishing an initial transmission rate and packet size, and then altering these parameters as needed during data transfer. The size of the packet header doesn't change, but the amount of TCP data in the body of the packet can be altered. The maximum segment size (MSS) parameter controls the size of a single segment that can be used, something that is established during the handshake, subject to the maximum transmission unit (MTU) size allowed by the network's Data Link layer.

Sliding windows

The flow control protocol used is referred to as a *sliding window* because as the packets are received and assembled, the receive window field's value can be altered by the receiver to indicate to the sender how much data it can buffer at the moment. The sending system then sends only that amount of data until the next ACK message is received, and the receive window parameter tells the sender to send that additional amount of information. Figure 17.3 illustrates how a Receive Sliding window operates.

FIGURE 17.3

A Receive Sliding window allows data to be transferred efficiently without buffer overrun.

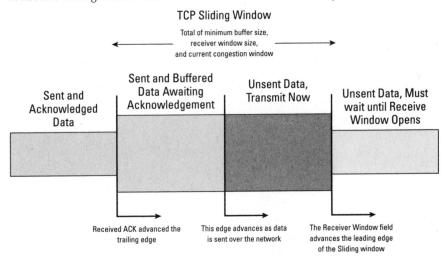

A TCP window can be from 2 to 65,535 bytes. Some systems employ a technique called *window scaling* that is negotiated in the TCP handshake. This option can increase the maximum window size up to as much as 1GB. Window scaling is reported to be problematical with many routers and firewalls, and with Vista and Linux hosts.

Congestion control

The receiver can also halt data flow. To do so, it sets the window size to zero. When the sending system detects a stop signal, it turns on a persist timer that controls the timeout for data sending. When the timer reaches its value, the sending system sends a small packet, which triggers an ACK from the receiver with a new receive window size to send. This system ensures that the data transfer doesn't permanently stop if the receiving system's next ACK message is lost.

Another method that can be used to interrupt the TCP data stream is to send additional data marked as urgent. When packets arrive with this marker, TCP stops processing data in the current stream and processes the urgent packets before returning to finish processing the original stream. Urgent packets are referred to as out-of-band (OOB) data. An example of an OOB process would be if you sent an interrupt or abort sign from the program on the sending host.

As an optimization, TCP allows the use of selective acknowledgments (SACKs). The receiver can send a SACK message at any point when a block of packets are received that can be assembled but require some previous packets in order to be a correct sequence. The SACK message has the same structure as the ACK, but provides the start and end sequence numbers that were received. For example, if bytes 0 to 2044 were received and the SACK block has the sequence numbers 4088 to 9696 for the range that was received, then the sending system would retransmit packets with the sequence numbers 2045 to 4078. SACK is optional, but widely used.

Flow control also includes mechanisms that alter the transmission rate as a function of network performance. Based on how often the sending system receives ACKs back from the receiving system, the network performance can be estimated. Longer intervals between ACKs indicate network congestion and are based on a retransmission time that estimates the round-trip time. Each TCP message contains a timestamp. TCP has a set of algorithms called slow start, congestion avoidance, fast retransmit, and fast recovery, which were developed to control the transfer rate.

Multiplexing

Multiplexing is a feature that allows a data stream to be sent using several different processes. TCP includes multiplexing as an option. When an application supports it, multiplexing can be used to speed up or optimize TCP data transfers. You see an example of multiplexing when a browser transfers a Web page using the HTTP protocol, or when a file transfer utility transfers a file over multiple connections. TCP can assemble that data from the different data streams.

Applications send their data over either a well-known port or a registered port. Apple iTunes uses port 3689 to receive data using the Digital Audio Access Protocol (DAAP). When you refresh your list of podcasts (a set of RSS feeds), multiple connections using the same port number are opened. If you have a larger video file, such as NBC's Nightly News or Meet the Press video, and no other podcasts are being downloaded, then the three streams that iTunes creates are dedicated to transferring that video file. If you have multiple podcasts to download, then those three streams are distributed between the different podcasts. Figure 17.4 illustrates multiplexing by showing three concurrent TCP streams.

FIGURE 17.4

This is an example of multiplexing three individual file streams with the same protocol and port.

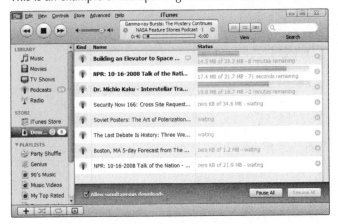

TCP doesn't know the details of which stream is associated with which podcast. It is up to iTunes to take the data and properly populate the podcast files into the correct folders so that they show up in the application. It is also up to iTunes to determine which files it wants to download and in which order. As a user, you can modify the download order by moving files up or down in the download list, pausing a download, or deleting the download entirely.

User Datagram Protocol

The User Datagram Protocol, or UDP, is an Internet Protocol that creates stateless connections between two hosts on an IP network. UDP creates a short data transfer format called a *datagram* and a connection called a *Datagram socket* between two endpoints. The virtual connection that is created uses the same concept of a port for sending data of different types between hosts. *Stateless* refers to the transfer mechanism, which doesn't attempt to ensure the validity of the data that is sent. The receiving system reconstructs data from the datagrams that arrive, without regard to whether they are in proper order or whether the sequence is complete.

Note

You sometimes see UDP referred to as the Universal Datagram Protocol, or tongue-in-cheek as the Unreliable Datagram Protocol. However, User Datagram Protocol is the formal name, as specified in RFC 768.

The fact that UDP doesn't maintain the overhead that TCP does means that UDP transfers are much faster than TCP. This makes UDP a better choice when reliable data isn't required, either because the message is short or because there is a lot of redundant or optional data being sent. Name resolution services, such as the Domain Name System (DNS) that you learn about in Chapter 19, use UDP because their messages are short and the system is a broadcast system that retransmits queries when the answers haven't yet arrived. Voice, music, and video applications use UDP because if a frame drops out of a movie or a fraction of a second of Voice over IP (VoIP) is lost, the user experience isn't degraded much. Nearly all streaming media applications use UDP as their transfer protocol on IP networks.

UDP datagrams have the very simple message format shown in Figure 17.5. The only features found in the datagram are the checksum used to determine the validity of the datagram and the ability to multiplex (or mux) datagrams, which provides for the transmission of multiple data streams for applications that support it. Both of these features are optional, as is the specification of the source port when IP version 4 is used, but a checksum is required for IP version 6.

FIGURE 17.5

The structure of a UDP datagram

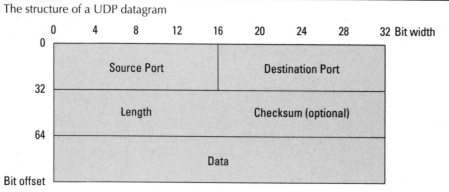

Unless a network is using a lot of media applications, UDP tends to be a minor but important component of traffic on the network. Some very important protocols use UDP, however. Not only does DNS use UDP, but the Dynamic Host Configuration Protocol (DHCP) that supplies IP addresses to clients, the Routing Information Protocol (RIP) that is used to provide dynamic routing on LANs, and the Simple Network Management Protocol (SNMP) that is used for most network management packages use UDP as well. That makes UDP a critical protocol in the Internet Protocol Suite.

In networks where there are a lot of media applications in use, UDP can crowd out TCP traffic. When TCP detects network congestion, it has mechanisms that throttle back TCP packet production to combat the congestion. This allows UDP to consume even more of the network's bandwidth, which can effectively crowd out critical traffic required by network services. TCP applications such as database access, which require the reliable data transfer of TCP to operate, can be slowed or halted until the situation is rectified. This problem has led many networks to either ban or limit the amount of streaming services that can run on the network.

Ports

Both TCP and UDP Transport Protocols use what is called a port to communicate between end-points of an Internet socket. When data packets arrive at their destination, they are examined for their source address, source port number, destination address, and destination port number. The port number is assigned by agreement to different types of data communications and maintained in a registry by the Internet Assigned Numbers Authority (IANA; www.iana.org/assignments/port-numbers).

Each computer manages its own ports independently of any other computer. A logger process, or on Linux/UNIX a super daemon process, monitors port numbers, especially the well-known ports, to determine when traffic is received.

There are three different ranges of ports:

- **Well-Known Ports.** These are ports used by common protocols and are in the range of 0 to 1023; they are administered by IANA. A selection of well-known ports is shown in Table 17.1.

- **Registered Ports.** These are ports that send or receive traffic for specific applications that are registered by vendors, industry trade groups, and other individuals and organizations. Registered ports are given the range 1024 to 49151. Registered ports are not controlled by IANA, but are listed in their registry.

- **Dynamic and/or Private Ports.** These ports are left unassigned for use. In some applications, ports are chosen randomly during a connection to improve security. These are referred to as *ephemeral ports*, and they lose their significance when the connection closes. The range for dynamic and private ports is from 49152 to 65535.

Note

Ports greater than 1023 can be assigned on the fly. Those types of ports are called transient ports, and they are specific to the particular TCP module in use.

TABLE 17.1

Common Well-Known Ports (0 to 1023)

Port	Assignment
0 - T, U	Reserved
1 - T, U	TCP Port Service Multiplexer
2 - T, U	Management Utility
3 - T, U	Compression Process
5 - T, U	Remote Job Entry
7 - T, U	Echo

continued

TABLE 17.1	(continued)
Port	**Assignment**
13 - T, U	Daytime - (RFC 867)
17 - T, U	Quote of the Day
18 - T, U	Message Send Protocol
19 - T, U	Character Generator
20 - T, U	FTP - Default Data
21 - T, U	FTP - Control command
22 - T, U	SSH Remote Login Protocol
23 - T, U	Telnet
25 - T, U	Simple Mail Transfer Protocol (SMTP)
33 - T, U	Display Support Protocol
37 - T, U	TIME Protocol
38 - T, U	Remote Access Protocol
39 - T, U	Resource Location Protocol (RLP)
41 - T, U	Graphics
42 - T, U	ARPA Host Name Server Protocol
42 - T, U	WINS (Unofficial)
43 - T, U	WHOIS Protocol
48 - T, U	Digital Audit Daemon
49 - T, U	TACACS Login Host Protocol
50 - T, U	Remote Mail Checking Protocol
53 - T, U	Domain Name System (DNS)
63 - T, U	whois++
65 - T, U	TACACS - Database Service
66 - T, U	Oracle SQL*NET
67 - T, U	Bootstrap Protocol (BOOTP) Server
68 - T, U	Bootstrap Protocol (BOOTP) Client
69 - T, U	Trivial File Transfer Protocol (TFTP)
70 - T, U	Gopher Protocol
79 - T, P	Finger Protocol
80 - T, P	Hypertext Transfer Protocol (HTTP)
82 - T, U	XFER Utility
88 - T, P	Kerberos
92 - T, U	Network Printing Protocol

Port	Assignment
105 - T, U	Mailbox Name Nameserver
107 - T, U	Remote Telnet Service Protocol
109 - T, U	Post Office Protocol 2 (POP2)
110 - T, U	Post Office Protocol 3 (POP3)
113 - T, U	Authentication Service
115 - T, U	Simple File Transfer Protocol (SFTP)
118 - T, U	SQL (Structured Query Language) Services
119 - T, P	Network News Transfer Protocol (NNTP)
123 - T, U	Network Time Protocol (NTP)
129 - T, U	Password Generator Protocol
137 - T, U	NetBIOS Name Service
138 - T, U	NetBIOS Datagram Service
139 - T, U	NetBIOS Session Service
143 - T, U	Internet Message Access Protocol (IMAP)
152 - T, U	Background File Transfer Program (BFTP)
153 - T, U	Simple Gateway Monitoring Protocol (SGMP)
156 - T, U	SQL Service
161 - T, U	Simple Network Management Protocol (SNMP)
162 - T, U	Simple Network Management Protocol Trap (SNMP TRAP)
170T	Print-srv, Network PostScript
177 - T, U	X Display Manager Control Protocol (XDMCP)
179T	Border Gateway Protocol (BGP)
194T	Internet Relay Chat (IRC)
201 - T, U	AppleTalk Routing Maintenance
213 - T, U	IPX
218 - T, U	Message Posting Protocol (MPP)
220 - T, U	Interactive Mail Access Protocol (IMAP), version 3
389 - T, U	Lightweight Directory Access Protocol (LDAP)
401 - T, U	Uninterruptible Power Supply (UPS)
427 - T, U	Service Location Protocol (SLP)
443T	Hypertext Transfer Protocol over TLS/SSL (HTTPS)
444 - T, U	Simple Network Paging Protocol (SNPP), (RFC 1568)
445T	Microsoft-DS Active Directory, Windows shares
445/UDP	Microsoft-DS SMB file sharing

continued

TABLE 17.1	*(continued)*
Port	**Assignment**
464 - T, U	Kerberos Change/Set password
500/UDP	Internet Security Association and Key Management Protocol (ISAKMP)
513T	Login
513/UDP	Who
514T	Shell
514/UDP	Syslog
515T	Line Printer Daemon
520/UDP	Routing – RIP
524 - T, U	NetWare Core Protocol (NCP)
525/UDP	Timed, Timeserver
530 - T, U	RPC
531 - T, U	AOL Instant Messenger (IRC) (Unofficial)
540T	Unix-to-Unix Copy Protocol (UUCP)
546 - T, U	DHCPv6 client
547 - T, U	DHCPv6 server
548T	Apple Filing Protocol (AFP) over TCP
554 - T, U	Real Time Streaming Protocol (RTSP)
631 - T, U	Internet Printing Protocol (IPP)
660T	Mac OS X Server Administration
666/UDP	Doom
691T	MS Exchange Routing
860T	iSCSI (RFC 3720)
953 - T, U	Domain Name System (DNS) RDNC Service
993T	Internet Message Access Protocol over SSL (IMAPS)
995T	Post Office Protocol 3 over TLS/SSL (POP3S)

Problems with TCP

TCP communications have suffered from a number of different types of attacks. In a Denial of Service (DoS) attack, the intruder can send multiple SYN packets originating from a spoofed IP address. This attack, referred to as a SYN flood, forces the receiving system (usually a server) to respond to these SYN requests and use up its resources managing bogus connections.

Another problem with TCP traffic is that the header isn't encrypted and can be read by packet sniffers that are monitoring the data. It is possible to hijack a connection by examining the sequence number and then creating a packet that has the correct sequence number in the stream. That packet doesn't need to be complex; it only needs to contain enough information to break the synchronization between systems. Once the connection is broken, the hacker has to take control of the packet routing to make their system the substitute endpoint. The incorporation of a randomly selected ISN makes it much more difficult to fall prey to connection hijacking. This form of attack is a variation of what is called the "Man-in-the-Middle" attack.

As mentioned earlier, TCP traffic can suffer when other types of broadcast traffic, such as UDP, become the majority of the network traffic. It is for that reason that TCP implements congestion control, lowering the size of the receive window to slow down transmission. At some point, TCP traffic can be brought to a standstill, a condition referred to as *congestion collapse*. There are solutions to this problem, some of which are problematical themselves.

The first solution is to limit the use of streaming media on the network. If you are in an office that uses productivity applications and don't require much multimedia content, then limiting multimedia isn't an issue. However, if your work requires the use of large amounts of streaming media, then other methods of control need to be employed. One potential solution is to employ quality of service (QoS) applications to maintain a stated level of traffic flow. Many network operating systems are beginning to implement QoS services into their core services. To get advanced QoS, many companies invest in sophisticated routers.

Another issue that crops up in high-traffic situations occurs when there is a large data stream and the receiving system starts to send back ACKs to the sender with a very small receive window. The sender then begins to send back very small packets with only a few bytes of data in them. This behavior is highly inefficient and has been given the name of silly window syndrome (SWS). To combat this behavior, newer implementations of TCP include sender-side logic, called Nagle's algorithm, which detects this condition and corrects it.

Nagle's algorithm, which is described in "Congestion Control in IP/TCP Internetworks" (RFC896), is used to address the problem of congestion caused by too many very small packets being sent at the same time. Many processes such as keystrokes from Telnet systems send data in chunks as small as 1 byte, and because all TCP headers are at least 40 bytes (20 for TCP and 20 for IPv4) the overhead in sending data of this type can be enormous. What Nagle's algorithm does is to coalesce many small outgoing messages and send them as a single unit provided that there is no response from the receiving system to messages already sent.

Nagle's algorithm is as follows:

```
IF there is new data to send
  IF the window size >= MSS AND available data is >= MSS
    SEND complete MSS segment now
  ELSE
    IF there is unconfirmed data still in the pipe
      enqueue data in the buffer until an acknowledge is received
```

```
            ELSE
               SEND data immediately
            END IF
         END IF
      END IF
```

Nagle's algorithm has one noticeable disadvantage; it leads to bad results when TCP delayed acknowledgments are used—the so-called ACK delay. Many TCP implementations do not use Nagle's algorithm or turn it off because common delay settings of 500 milliseconds (1/2 second) can lead to multiple application writes. Delays can be turned off using the TCP_NODELAY command; however, most solutions to the problem buffer commands in the application to avoid congestion due to small packet storms.

The phenomena where a receive window is sent large numbers of minute packets and is therefore starved of data to operate on is called the tinygram syndrome, and it contrasts to the silly window syndrome where the receive window is entirely filled and can't receive additional information.

Summary

This chapter described the two most important transport protocols used on TCP/IP networks: the Transmission Control Protocol (TCP) and the User Datagram Protocol (UDP). TCP is used when the data must be delivered intact with complete fidelity. UDP is used by applications that can tolerate lost data and out-of-sequence packets.

Both of these protocols create virtual connections and use the concept of ports to send data of different types from a sending system to a receiving system. Connections are made between two hosts and are independent of the path that the data takes to get there.

TCP has a number of different mechanisms to ensure that data arrives correctly. A sequencing scheme is used to reconstruct packets, and the protocol sends back acknowledgments when data arrives or when data is required. In this chapter you learned about the different flow control and congestion controls used to maintain quality.

UDP is important to streaming media applications. UDP has much less overhead than TCP and is used in situations where applications use very small broadcast messages, or in streaming applications.

In the next chapter you learn about the Internet Protocol, which controls the addressing scheme used to send packets across a TCP/IP network. In this chapter both IP version 4 and IP version 6 are described. The concepts of networks and subnets are fully disclosed.

The Internet Protocols

The Internet Protocol, or IP, is the primary protocol used to provide an end-to-end delivery of packets over a TCP/IP network. Two versions of IP exist: IPv4, which is in widespread use, and IPv6, which is being phased in. Both are described in detail in this chapter.

IP is a transport-independent protocol that works over a wide variety of networks. It was designed to be connectionless, fault tolerant, and routable. There are four different types of IPv4 routing: unicast, broadcast, directed broadcast, and multicast. IPv6 expands multicast, eliminates broadcast, and adds an anycast routing function.

The address spaces of IPv4 and IPv6 are very different. IPv4 is a 32-bit address space where addresses are usually written in a dot decimal format, ###.###.###.###. The address space can be divided into different-sized blocks by a masking technique, blocks can be subnetted, and other techniques such as NAT are used to extend the address space. Address assignment by DHCP is described in this chapter.

IPv6 is a 128-bit address space and has addresses that are usually written in a hexadecimal format, with eight blocks in the format, nnnn:nnnn:nnnn: nnnn:hhhh:hhhh:hhhh:hhhh, where n is the network ID and h is the host ID. There are different ways to express IPv6 addresses. IPv6 is autoconfigurable, and it allows for multiple addresses for each network interface. Addresses are scoped to belong to particular zones.

The reduced header size of IPv6 and the additional functionality built into the IPv6 and ICMPv6 protocols make IPv6 easier to implement on networks. A feature called Neighbor Discovery makes ad hoc networking, browsing, and router optimization particularly convenient.

IN THIS CHAPTER

How the Internet Protocol is used to send packets

How addresses are created and assigned

Different network sizes and how to create subnets

Create and use networks that have IPv6

It is believed that IPv4 will run out of available addresses by 2010 or 2011, making the adoption of IPv6 inevitable.

Internet Protocol Overview

The Internet Protocol is the Network Layer protocol responsible for maintaining the endpoints of an Internet connection. IP defines the addressing scheme used by TCP packets and the encapsulation of the data into the datagram format that is transported over an internetwork. IP is a stateful, but connectionless, protocol. That is, while the endpoints are known and can be either real or virtual, the path between the endpoints is left undefined.

Because IP makes no demands on the connection, other than that the packets arrive without error, IP traffic can flow over different types of networks and can adapt to network conditions, switching routes as needed. The IP protocol was developed to work over packet-switched internetworks running Ethernet, ATM, FDDI fiber, 802.11x wireless, and other autonomous system (AS) networks, and to survive nuclear attacks where a large percentage of the network might be rendered inoperable. There are three defined ASNs:

- **Multihomed.** The AS has two or more independent connections to the internetwork.
- **Stub.** The AS has one connection to the internetwork and one connection to another AS.
- **Transit.** The AS has two independent connections to two different autonomous systems.

The Internet, as originally conceived, was meant to connect a number of different networks into routing groups, each with a unique prefix. Each routing prefix and the hierarchical tree it defined would be managed by an Internet Service Provider or another entity that was characterized by having multiple independent connections to the internetwork and a registered Autonomous System Number (ASN) in the IANA ASN database. The Border Gateway Protocol (BGP) uses the 16-bit address space of 65,536 ASNs to route traffic to each network on the Internet. The following assignments exist for ASNs:

- **0.** This is reserved for non-routable networks or local use.
- **1–54,271.** These are assignable for network use.
- **54,272–64,511.** These are reserved for IANA and may not be routed.

IANA has assigned all but 5,000 of these addresses and so needs a larger address space for future growth. They have adopted a 32-bit address space that adds a 16-bit word to the beginning of the original address space in the form: `new.old`. In the new scheme adopted in 2007, the old assignment of 12,345 would be written as 0.12345. The expanded 32-bit namespace reserves the ASNs 1.old and 65535.65535. All other ASNs are available.

Packet switching means that IP networks are routable, using either an Interior Gateway Protocol (IGP) or an Exterior Gateway Protocol (EGP). Decisions are made at each router and potentially at any device or host on the network that determine how a packet is forwarded. In order to resolve addresses for IP traffic flowing over heterogeneous networks, IPv4 uses the Address Resolution Protocol (ARP), and IPv6 uses the Neighbor Discovery Protocol (NDP).

Note

IP routing is discussed in detail in Chapter 9.

IPv4 traffic can be unicast, broadcast, or multicast, depending upon the destination address chosen. They have the following purposes:

- **Unicast.** A unicast packet is one that carries a single destination address such as 4.2.2.1, which might be a DNS request to the Verizon.net DNS server that my network uses.

- **Multicast.** Multicast packets are duplicated at the router and sent to multiple destinations. The IPv4 address range that is reserved for multicasts is 224.0.0.0–239.255.255.255.

  The range 224.0.0.0–224.0.0.255 is reserved for multicast link-local addresses — that is, addresses that are connected by the Data Link layer protocols but are not routable. Typically, link-local addresses are those that are autoconfigurable and on the same subnet.

- **Broadcast.** Sometimes you want to broadcast a packet to every host on a network (the local subnet, actually); to do this, you would send the message to the address 255.255.255.255. Broadcasts are used for polling, requests for service, and other operations.

- **Directed Broadcast.** If you want to broadcast to a specific subnet that is different from the sending host, you would send the message to an address, ###.###.###.255.

Figure 18.1 illustrates these four forms of IPv4 routing.

FIGURE 18.1

The four types of IPv4 routing

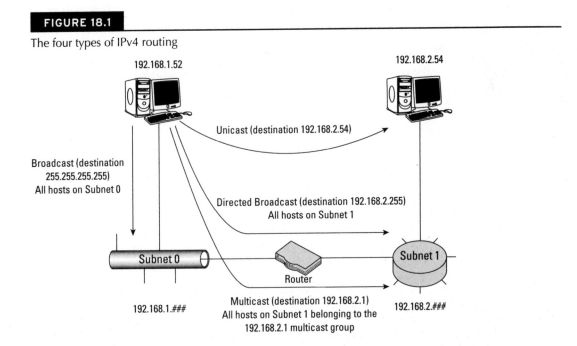

Internet Protocol Version 4

The first version of the Internet Protocol, version 4 (IPv4), is the dominant standard. It is recognized by the use of a quartet of octet addresses, ###.###.###.###, which is sometimes referred to as the dot decimal notation.

Let's consider a simple example of how IPv4 addressing works. If you PING www.nytimes.com, the address for the New York Times Digital Web site resolves to the server at 199.239.136.200. If you open up a browser such as Microsoft Internet Explorer and enter this address into the address bar, then you are taken to the New York Times Web site. You can convert IP addresses in the dot decimal format into other formats such as dotted hexadecimal, dotted octal, hexadecimal, decimal, and octal. The value for the decimal notation corresponding to nytimes.com is 3354364104, and if you enter this number into the address bar in Internet Explorer, it takes you to the New York Times Web site. Most browsers resolve the IP address in these alternate formats correctly.

Addressing

IPv4's octet addressing scheme defines a 32-bit address space. Each of the four numbers can range from 0 to 255 (28), which defines a limit of 4,294,967,296 unique addresses in the address space. When the designers of IP developed the protocol, they could never have imagined how popular the protocol would become, and so it seemed eminently reasonable that four billion addresses could never be consumed. At the time that IPv4 was specified in 1980, the population of the entire world was estimated to be 4.5 billion people, and so the IPv4 standard allowed for an IP address for every person alive at the time. In an era when refrigerators, toasters, sensors, and almost anything you can think of takes an IP address, IPv4's days are numbered (so to speak). This problem has been called IP address exhaustion. By comparison, IPv6 defines a 128-bit address space, which defines 3.4 x 1038 unique numbers.

Note

IPv4 is defined in IETF RFC 791, and in MIL-STD-1777.

To solve the problem of IPv4 address exhaustion, three different extensions to IP addressing have been introduced:

- Classless Inter-Domain Routing (CIDR)
- Variable Length Subnet Masks (VLSM)
- Subnet masking

These technologies are discussed in this chapter.

Dividing the namespace

In the early 1980s when IP was being developed, the original namespace consisted of a network ID, which was the first three numbers or octet in the address, which was followed by the host ID of three more octets, for a total of four octets. The original scheme allowed for networks with a number from 0 to 255, or 256 networks in total.

Classes

As more networks were required, the designers of IP realized that while some networks might be large, most networks would be small, with some of intermediate size. The addressing scheme was changed so that the number of octets defining the network ID could vary between one and three octets, while the number of octets assigned to host IDs would vary between three and one octets. A network that required only one octet for the network ID would allow for 224 (16,777,216) hosts; one with two octets for the network ID would allow for 216 (65,536) hosts; and small networks where three octets were used to define the network would allow for only 28 (256) hosts. This is where the notion of network classes comes from. The original assignments for Classes A through E are shown in Figure 18.2.

FIGURE 18.2

IPv4's original network class assignments

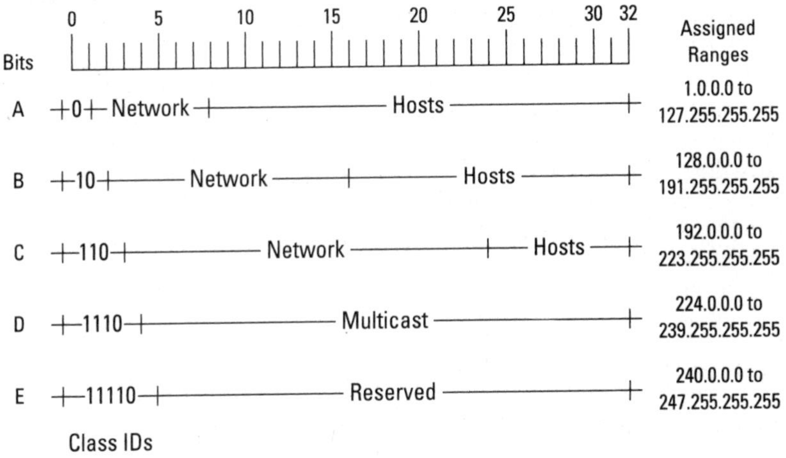

Classes were meant to allocate blocks of addresses to organizations based on their size and on the type of traffic that the network carried, either unicast or multicast. So a set of contiguous network addresses could be doled out to an organization such as AOL, while a smaller set of contiguous network addresses could be doled out to the XYZ company. These classes aren't in use today, but they often crop up in network references and books due to their historical interest. In some instances, classes are used to describe the number of addresses in a subnet that a netmask allows, as is described later in this chapter. Table 18.1 lists the different class types, as defined by RFC 791.

TABLE 18.1

Network Class Types

Class	Leading Bits	Begin	End (Routing block-CIDR)	Default Subnet Mask
Class A	0	0.0.0.0	127.255.255.255 (/8)	255.0.0.0
Class B	10	128.0.0.0	191.255.255.255 (/16)	255.255.0.0
Class C	110	192.0.0.0	223.255.255.255 (/24)	255.255.255.0
Class D (multicast)	1110	224.0.0.0	239.255.255.255 (/4)	NA
Class E (reserved)	11110	240.0.0.0	255.255.255.255 (/4)	NA

Reference: http://tools.ietf.org/html/rfc791

Classless Inter-Domain Routing

Classes became less relevant as the Internet became a public utility and the address space needed to be sliced and diced into millions of pieces. Classes eventually gave way to what is now called Classless Inter-Domain Routing (CIDR), and blocks of addresses are doled out to organizations and ISPs in all kinds of sizes. In the CIDR routing scheme published by IETF in 1993 (RFC 1518), IP addresses are assigned in a hierarchical structure that allows the addresses to be routed to the correct network, and if the address is routable, past the network portion to the correct host.

The CIDR removes the strict restriction that classes imposed, that networks be segregated based on the octet system, and in doing so, it makes it easier to route traffic on the Internet. The system creates what is called a Variable Length Subnet Mask (VLSM) and allows contiguous subnets to be aggregated into supernets. Aggregation has the effect of allowing addresses to be used more efficiently, and just as importantly, it reduces the number of router entries by hiding all of the subnets within a VLSM supernet as a single entry in the router table.

The CIDR scheme breaks the IPv4 address space into blocks that can be doled out, and represents those blocks. Each block is defined by appending a range number to an octet, in the form, ###.###.###.###/N, where N is a number from 0 to 32. (For IPv6, the range number is from 0 to 128.) The range number is in binary, and although it is appended to a dot decimal representation of the IP address, it is necessary to perform a conversion in order to establish the block size. Dot decimal is a 32-bit address space, and the numbers of N represent the excluded portion of the IP range. The larger the number, the smaller the range of addresses in the block.

To obtain the block size, you use the following formula: 232-N,, which for the value 24 would yield 28 or 256 numbers (an octet), but for 18 would yield 214 or 16,384 addresses in the block. If you specified the address 199.239.136.200/24, then that CIDR block would include all addresses from 199.239.136.0 to 199.239.137.0, a full octet of numbers. The address 199.239.136.200/28 would have a range of 199.239.136.192 to 199.239.136.207, and any address from 199.239.136.217 and above would fall outside this block assignment.

Table 18.2 lists the conversion of Classes to CIDR block prefixes. So you can see how the VSLM assignment allows for very efficient block assignments of any size.

TABLE 18.2

CIDR Block Sizes

CIDR Block Prefix	Class Equivalency	Unique Nodes
/28	1/16 Class C	16
/27	1/8 Class C	32
/26	1/4 Class C	64
/25	1/2 Class C	128
/24	Class C	256
/23	2 Class C	512
/22	4 Class C	1,024
/21	8 Class C	2,048
/20	16 Class C	4,096
/19	32 Class C	8,192
/18	64 Class C	16,384
/17	128 Class C	32,768
/16	256 Class C or 1 Class B	65,536
/15	512 Class C or 2 Class B	131,072
/14	1,024 Class C or 4 Class B	262,144
/13	2,048 Class C or 8 Class B	524,288
/12	4,098 Class C or 16 Class B	1,048,576

Block sizes smaller than /27 aren't usually assigned by an ISP. Block sizes larger than /13 are restricted to Regional Internet Registries.

With the CIDR block assignments, it is no longer necessary to store routes to individual hosts in Internet routers. Instead, using routing prefix aggregation, routes are summarized into the supernets that the blocks represent. If you had four /26 contiguous blocks, that would represent 4 x 232-26, or 256 addresses. The designation of /26 represents a 1/4 C class network. In the routing table, a single entry for the starting IP address in the form ###.###.###.###/24 would be advertised, thus consolidating all of the blocks in the range.

For a larger supernet, consider the address ###.###.0.0/16, which uses a subnet mask of 255.255.0.0. The /16 indicates that this network is equivalent to 256 contiguous C class networks or one B class network, and defines an address space with 65,536 hosts. The router entry 200.100.0.0/16 is sufficient to represent all of these hosts within a single entry. It's easy to see the flexibility and economy that this system offers. This aggregation system has collapsed the global routing tables to approximately 35,000 entries. Figure 18.3 shows a hypothetical IPv4 address aggregation scheme.

FIGURE 18.3

Aggregating IP names using the CIDR scheme

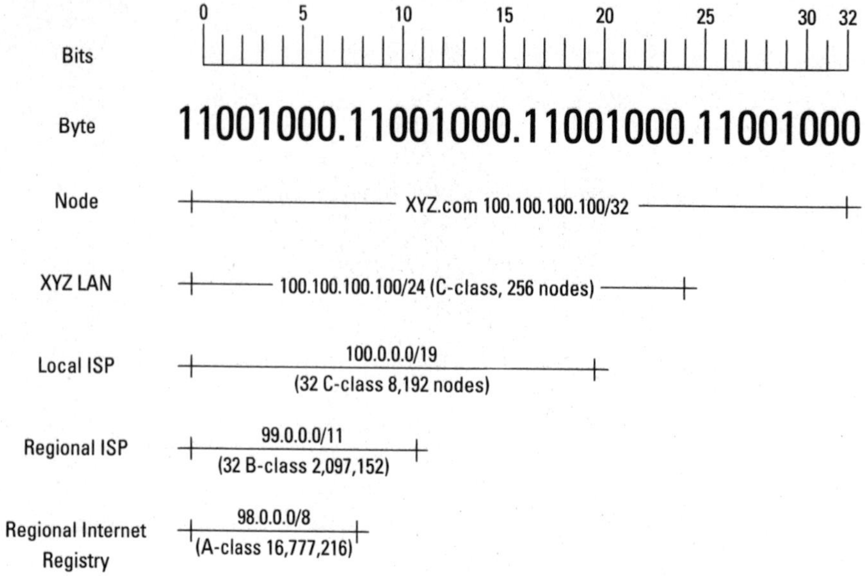

Bits	0 5 10 15 20 25 30 32	
Byte	**11001000.11001000.11001000.11001000**	
Node	XYZ.com 100.100.100.100/32	
XYZ LAN	100.100.100.100/24 (C-class, 256 nodes)	
Local ISP	100.0.0.0/19 (32 C-class 8,192 nodes)	
Regional ISP	99.0.0.0/11 (32 B-class 2,097,152)	
Regional Internet Registry	98.0.0.0/8 (A-class 16,777,216)	

Regional Internet Registries

The Internet is broken up into a set of geographical regions, each with their own large ranges, which are then further broken up into progressively smaller ranges. This hierarchy suppresses most of the entries that would exist if supernets weren't defined, and allows for very efficient routing based on both address and geography.

IP addresses are controlled by the Internet Assigned Numbers Authority (IANA), and the individual portions of the namespace hierarchy are organized into a set of regional databases or registries that segregate IP addresses on a geographical basis, as shown in Figure 18.4. Regional Internet Registries, or RIRs, are /8 or "Net-Eight" address blocks with 16,777,216 addresses, which corresponded to what was once called an A-class network. These RIRs list the IP assignments and provide a WHOIS lookup of the registry that enables the public to determine who a particular IP address is registered to. Among the services RIRs provide are:

- IPv4 and IPv6 address allocation
- WHOIS
- ASNs
- Internet Routing Registry
- Reverse DNS lookup

FIGURE 18.4

The current set of Regional Internet Registries

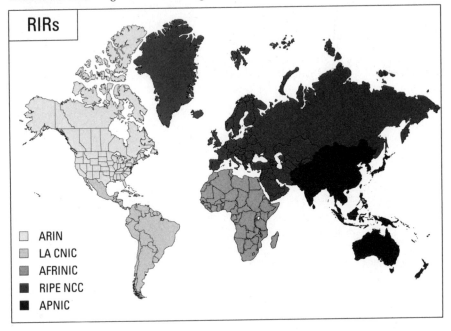

The acronyms in Figure 18.4 stand for:

- **ARIN.** American Registry for Internet Numbers (North America)
- **LA CNIC.** Latin American and Caribbean Internet Address Registry (Latin America and the Caribbean)
- **AFRINIC.** African Network Information Centre (Africa)
- **RIPE NCC.** Ripe Network Coordination Centre (Europe, the Middle East, and Central Asia)
- **APNIC.** Asia-Pacific Network Information Centre (Asia-Pacific)

Note
The IP assignments in the RIRs are separate from domain names, which are registered with the ICANN.

Reserved addresses

Not all of the addresses in the IPv4 address space are available for use; some ranges are set aside for use on private networks, while others are reserved for multicast networks. The different reserved addresses take the following forms:

- (<*NetworkID*>, 0). This is reserved for the name of the network.

- (<*NetworkID*>, -1). The -1 entry indicates that you replace all bits with 1s. This address is used to broadcast to the network.

- (-1, -1). The all 1s address is used for local network broadcast.

- (0, 0). This address indicates that the system is both the local network and the local system — essentially that it is "this host." It is encountered when a system sends a request to a BOOTP server to obtain a valid network address. It is also encountered as the entry in a router that points to the default router (also known as the default gateway).

- (0, <*HostID*>). This address refers to the host that is assigned to the host ID number on the local network.

- (127, <*all*>). This address represents the loopback adapter; all traffic is sent to the loopback adapter.

A private network, as defined in RFC 1918, is one that cannot be used on the Internet and is not routable. Any packet that comes from a device with an address in the private network ranges will be dropped by a router on the Internet.

Most LANs used in homes and offices use private IP address ranges, either for IPv4 or using the IPv6 private address ranges that have been defined. Incoming traffic to a private network must pass through a gateway or a proxy server, and requires a mechanism such as Network Address Translation (NAT) to forward incoming packets to the correct address. The use of NAT has taken some of the pressure off of moving to IPv6, but only for a while. As the IPv4 address space becomes filled, IP networking will slowly migrate to the second version of the protocol, version 6 (IPv6).

Caution

Care should be taken when two or more networks use the same private network subnet so that conflicts do not occur.

The localhost or local computer describes the loopback network interface. The loopback adapter's address range is also private. The localhost refers to an address that belongs to the host device, or more accurately, to the network interface. When packets are directed (PINGed) to the localhost, they are returned with an incoming address that is the same as the outgoing packets, just as if they traveled on a virtual network. For this reason, the localhost is referred to as the loopback adapter or a loopback device. The loopback adapter is used to test that the network interface is up and running. The most common way of testing the loopback adapter is to use the command PING 127.0.0.1. The IANA has a number of other address blocks that are reserved for private use, or kept in reserve for other purposes. Table 18.3 lists some of the reserved blocks.

TABLE 18.3

IANA Reserved Addresses

Address Block	Block Size (addresses)	Used For	RFC
0.0.0.0/8	24 (16,777,216)	Local network (used locally)	1700
10.0.0.0/8	24 (16,777,216)	Private	1918
14.0.0.8/8	24 (16,777,216)	Public (private before February 2008)	1700
127.0.0.0/8	24 (16,777,216)	Loopback	3330
128.0.0.0/16	16 (65,536)	Reserved by IANA	3330
169.254.0.0/16	16 (65,536)	Link local	3927
172.16.0.0/16	16 (65,536)	Private	1918
191.255.0.0/16	16 (65,536)	Reserved for IANA	3330
192.0.0.0/24	8 (256)	Reserved for IANA	3330
192.2.0.0/24	8 (256)	Documentation and sample code	3330
192.88.99.0/24	8 (256)	IPv6–IPv4 relay	3068
192.168.0.0/16	16 (65,536)	Private	1918
198.18.0.0/15	17 (131,072)	Network testing	2544
223.255.255.0/24	8 (256)	Reserved for IANA	3330
224.0.0.0/4	28 (268,435,456)	Multicast (D class)	3171
240.0.0.0/4	28 (268,435,456)	Reserved (E class)	1700
255.255.255.255	0 (1)	Broadcast	

Reference: www.iana.org.

In the old class network designations, the address ending in 0 was assigned as the network identifier, while the address ending in 255 was reserved for broadcasts to all of the systems on the subnet. For example, you would not assign the addresses 192.168.0.0 or 192.168.0.255 for a C class block defined by that range.

With the advent of the CIDR scheme, the situation changes and only networks that have a subnet mask between /24 (255.255.255.0) and /32 (255.255.255.255) would reserve these addresses. In a subnet defining a larger block, only the first address and the last address need to be reserved. So if you considered the block 100.100.0.0/16, the subnet mask would be 255.255.0.0, and the number of allowed addresses would be 65,536 and would define a range from 100.100.0.0 up to 100.100.255.255. In that range, 100.100.0.0 and 100.100.255.255 must be reserved, but any other numbers ending in 0 or 255 would be allowed. Examples of allowed numbers in this range would be 100.100.1.0 and 100.100.254.255.

Zero Configuration addressing

Link-local addresses are used for local networks and cannot be routed. If you are using a dynamic IP assignment from a DHCP server, then you may see an address in the range 169.254.0.0 to 169.254.255.255 when the DHCP server is unavailable and no address can be assigned. In IPv4, the link-local range 169.254.0.0/16 is assigned using a mechanism called IPv4 Link-Local or IPV4LL, which is specified in RFC 3927.

It is common to have link-local addresses assigned by automatic addressing services for local use, through a technology that is sometimes referred to as Zero Configuration Networking. Zeroconfig or Zeroconf is a service that supplies IP addresses on a network without the use of any server such as DHCP or BOOTP. Zeroconfig is responsible for the following services when it is enabled:

- Assign link-local addresses to networked devices
- Perform name resolution
- Provide a browse function
- Automatically discover network services such as printing

Microsoft's service discovery technology is called the Simple Service Discovery Protocol, and it is part of the Universal Plug and Play (UPnP) protocol. Apple's service discovery technology is called Multicast DNS/DNS-SD (mDNS). This area of technology is one that has yet to be standardized, although the IETF has proposed a standard called the Service Location Protocol (SLP), which has appeared on both Linux and Solaris. Microsoft and Apple continue to use their own technology.

You probably know these technologies by their branded names. The Apple version of the Zeroconfig is Bonjour (formerly Apple Rendezvous). The Microsoft version of this addressing scheme is called the Automatic Private IP Address (APIPA) or the Internet Protocol Automatic Configuration (IPAC) system. On Linux and BSD, the Avahi version of Bonjour can be deployed.

Recently, it has become a practice by some systems to adopt IANA reserved ranges for their internal use. For example, the Hamachi VPN service uses the 5.0.0.0/8 network range for their nodes. Because VPN is encapsulated traffic, the network addresses are hidden within routable packets; they are not exposed on the Internet and dropped. Provided that two private networks don't share the same address range, although IANA private network use is discouraged, it doesn't cause any problems.

IP datagrams

The IP header is added to the beginning of TCP data and consists of a number of standard fields that identify the source, destination, and format of the IP protocol used. Of the 13 fields, all except the optional field are required. By convention, the IP protocol writes data in big endian format. Big endian is the format used by the Sun SPARC processors, and by the Motorola processors that used to run older versions of the Macintosh. The Intel X86 architecture uses a little endian format, which means that when an IP is either sent to or received on an Intel system, the data must be converted from big endian to little endian.

In big endian notation, the most significant bit is written first, that is, bit endian numbers have the highest-order bits written first. In the IP header diagram shown in Figure 18.5, the first field for version stores the value for decimal "4", which translates to 0100 in binary. Big endian writes the value in the order of left to right.

The fields in the IP header are used for the following purposes:

- **Version.** This is the 4-bit value for the IP version number: 4 or 6.
- **Internet Header Length (IHL).** This field accounts for the use or lack of an Options field and sets the overall header length. When combined with the Fragment Offset, it allows the data portion to be reliably read.
- **Type of Service (TOS).** This field is meant to be used to specify a Quality of Service type, and has seen little use. The current use of the TOS field is to assign a Differentiated Services (DiffServe) or Explicit Congestion Notification (ECN) value that will assign IP priorities in streaming media services.

  This 8-bit field allows assignments of precedence, delays, throughput, and reliability. When streaming data is sent, throughput is emphasized and reliability is deemphasized. For file transfers, the opposite settings might be used.
- **Total Length.** This defines the size of the total datagram, up to 2^{16} bytes (65,535). The minimum value required is 576, and when a packet requires more than 2^{16} bytes, the datagrams are split into fragments.
- **Identification.** The Identification (ID) field is used to identify the fragment order of a split IP datagram.
- **Flags.** There are three 1-bit fields that are flag settings; the first always takes a zero value, and the other two indicate whether the datagram can be fragmented (Don't Fragment, or DF) as well as if there are additional fragments (More Fragments, or MF). The DF field aids in routing or suppressing fragmented packets. When data is fragmented, all of the packets have the MF field set to 1, except for the final packet.
- **Fragment Offset.** The Fragment Offset field indicates where the data in a packet fits into the original unfragmented IP datagram's sequence. In any fragmentation, the first packet takes an offset value of zero, and this field allows for 13 bits of 8-byte units, or 65,528 bytes. That allows for 8,192 fragments per datagram.
- **Time To Live.** The Time To Live (TTL) 8-bit field is a limitation that tells a host or router whether or not to continue to forward the packet. Originally this setting referred to seconds, but it has been changed to indicate the number of hops that a packet can take. Every time the packet is forwarded, the field is decremented by one, and when the field is set to zero, it is dropped by the next router. When TTL expires, the last host or router sends an ICMP message that the packet exceeded its TTL.
- **Protocol.** IP can carry a number of different protocols. This 8-bit field carries the IANA protocol assignment. Some of the more common assignments are 0, IPv6 hop-by-hop; 1, ICMP (Internet Control Message Protocol); 2, IGMP (Internet Group Management

Protocol); 6, TCP (Transmission Control Protocol); 17, UDP (User Datagram Protocol); 27, RDP (Reliable Datagram Protocol); 89, OSPF (Open Shortest Path First); 129, SMP (Simple Message Protocol); and 133, FC (Fibre Channel).

- **Header Checksum.** This 16-bit field contains a checksum that is matched at each hop in the route. When a host or router finds that the checksum doesn't match the checksum it calculates based on the header's contents, it drops the packet. The checksum is only used for the transport of the packets; TCP, UDP, and other transport and application protocols use their own checksums to determine the validity of the data once it arrives.

The checksum algorithm examines each 16-bit word in the header, a half word at a time, takes the complement, and sums all of the complements to obtain a result. That result is then complemented, and then this result is used in the checksum. To complement means that you change any 1 to 0 and vice versa.

- **Source Address.** This is the IPv4 address written in binary code.

The translation works as follows: for the address 192.168.1.1, you would have the four binary octets 11000000.10101000.00000001.00000001, which would populate this 32-bit field with the string 11000000101010000000000100000001.

Note

The address that you sniff in the Source Address field is the address of the sender. This address can be altered by Network Address Translation (NAT) to be the address of the translator device. Source addresses can also be spoofed by various methods.

- **Destination Address.** The destination address is the same type of 32-bit binary address that was entered into the Source Address field.

- **Options.** The Options field allows for additional information to be added to a packet, and was included to allow for changes and additions to the IP. This field can be left blank, or the various options can be added. Options start with a single byte that represents the option type, followed by data for that option. The Option field ends with a 0 x 00 value representing the End of Options List (EOL). An EOL is only required when the Options field doesn't complete the header because the Options field must be a multiple of four bytes. Table 18.4 lists the current options. Any option not supported by a router or host is ignored.

Alternate uses of the Options field include a set of options that set the security level, specify a complete path (Strict Source Routing) or required set of routers (Loose Source Routing), have routers add their address to the header (Record Route), and add a timestamp (Timestamp) for each router address that has been appended. These fields are deprecated; security restrictions on many modern routers drop packets that contain these older options.

- **Data.** The data portion of the datagram is the payload portion of the packet. This is data in the form indicated by the Protocol field, most often TCP or UDP data.

FIGURE 18.5

IP header structure

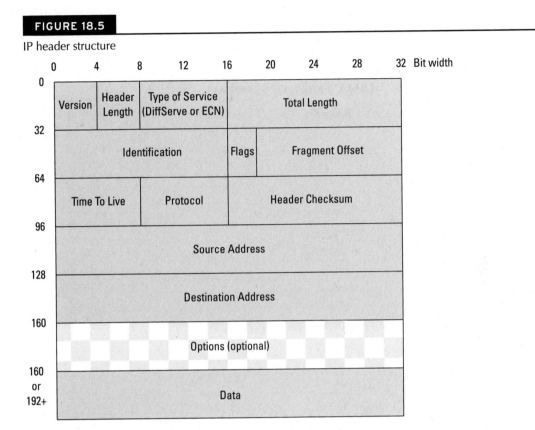

TABLE 18.4

IP Options

Field	Bits	Purpose
Copied	1	The value is 1 when the option field needs to be included in all packet fragments.
Option Class	2	The value 0 indicates a control option, the value 2 indicates debugging and measurement, and values 1 and 3 are reserved.
Option Number	5	Indicates an option.
Option Length	8	The size of the option with the length field included. This is not always used.
Option Data	Variable	Option data. This is not always used.

The Copied, Option Class, and Option Number fields can be combined into an 8-bit field called the Option Type.

Refer to Table 18.5 to view the different supported protocol types.

TABLE 18.5

IANA Protocol Numbers

Decimal	Keyword	Protocol
0	HOPOPT	IPv6 Hop-by-Hop Option
1	ICMP	Internet Control Message
2	IGMP	Internet Group Management
3	GGP	Gateway-to-Gateway
4	IP	IP in IP (encapsulation)
5	ST	Stream
6	TCP	Transmission Control
7	CBT	CBT
8	EGP	Exterior Gateway
9	IGP	Any private interior gateway
10	BBN-RCC-MON	BBN RCC Monitoring
11	NVP-II	Network Voice
12	PUP	PUP
13	ARGUS	ARGUS
14	EMCON	EMCON
15	XNET	Cross Net Debugger
16	CHAOS	Chaos
17	UDP	User Datagram
18	MUX	Multiplexing
19	DCN-MEAS	DCN Measurement Subsystems
20	HMP	Host Monitoring
21	PRM	Packet Radio Measurement
22	XNS-IDP	XEROX NS IDP
23	TRUNK-1	Trunk-1
24	TRUNK-2	Trunk-2
25	LEAF-1	Leaf-1
26	LEAF-2	Leaf-2
27	RDP	Reliable Data
28	IRTP	Internet Reliable Transaction
29	ISO-TP4	ISO Transport Protocol Class 4

Decimal	Keyword	Protocol
30	NETBLT	Bulk Data Transfer
31	MFE-NSP	MFE Network Services
32	MERIT-INP	MERIT Internodal
33	DCCP	Datagram Congestion Control
34	3PC	Third Party Connect
35	IDPR	Inter-Domain Policy Routing
36	XTP	XTP
37	DDP	Datagram Delivery
38	IDPR-CMTP	IDPR Control Message Transport Proto
39	TP++	TP++ Transport
40	IL	IL Transport
41	IPv6	IPv6
42	SDRP	Source Demand Routing
43	IPv6-Route	Routing Header for IPv6
44	IPv6-Frag	Fragment Header for IPv6
45	IDRP	Inter-Domain Routing
46	RSVP	Reservation
47	GRE	General Routing Encapsulation
48	DSR	Dynamic Source Routing
49	BNA	BNA
50	ESP	Encap Security Payload
51	AH	Authentication Header
52	I-NLSP	Integrated Net Layer Security TUBA
53	SWIPE	IP with Encryption
54	NARP	NBMA Address Resolution
55	MOBILE	IP Mobility
56	TLSP	Transport Layer Security Protocol using Kryptonet key management
57	SKIP	SKIP
58	IPv6-ICMP	ICMP for IPv6
59	IPv6-NoNxt	No Next Header for IPv6
60	IPv6-Opts	Destination Options for IPv6
61		Any host internal protocol
62	CFTP	CFTP
63		Any local network

continued

TABLE 18.5	(continued)	
Decimal	**Keyword**	**Protocol**
64	SAT-EXPAK	SATNET and Backroom EXPAK
65	KRYPTOLAN	Kryptolan
66	RVD	MIT Remote Virtual Disk
67	IPPC	Internet Pluribus Packet Core
68		Any distributed file system
69	SAT-MON	SATNET Monitoring
70	VISA	VISA
71	IPCV	Internet Packet Core Utility
72	CPNX	Computer Protocol Network Executive
73	CPHB	Computer Protocol Heart Beat
74	WSN	Wang Span Network
75	PVP	Packet Video
76	BR-SAT-MON	Backroom SATNET Monitoring
77	SUN-ND	SUN ND PROTOCOL-Temporary
78	WB-MON	WIDEBAND Monitoring
79	WB-EXPAK	WIDEBAND EXPAK
80	ISO-IP	ISO Internet
81	VMTP	VMTP
82	SECURE-VMTP	SECURE-VMTP
83	VINES	VINES
84	TTP	TTP
85	NSFNET-IGP	NSFNET-IGP
86	DGP	Dissimilar Gateway
87	TCF	TCF
88	EIGRP	EIGRP
89	OSPFIGP	OSPFIGP
90	Sprite-RPC	Sprite RPC
91	LARP	Locus Address Resolution
92	MTP	Multicast Transport
93	AX.25	AX.25 Frames
94	IPIP	IP-within-IP Encapsulation
95	MICP	Mobile Internetworking Control Pro
96	SCC-SP	Semaphore Communications Sec. Pro.
97	ETHERIP	Ethernet-within-IP Encapsulation

Decimal	Keyword	Protocol
98	ENCAP	Encapsulation Header
99		Any private encryption scheme
100	GMTP	GMTP
101	IFMP	Ipsilon Flow Management
102	PNNI	PNNI over IP
103	PIM	Protocol Independent Multicast
104	ARIS	ARIS
105	SCPS	SCPS
106	QNX	QNX
107	A/N	Active Networks
108	IPComp	IP Payload Compression
109	SNP	Sitara Networks
110	Compaq-Peer	Compaq Peer
111	IPX-in-IP	IPX in IP
112	VRRP	Virtual Router Redundancy
113	PGM	PGM Reliable Transport
114		Any 0-hop protocol
115	L2TP	Layer Two Tunneling
116	DDX	D-II Data Exchange (DDX)
117	IATP	Interactive Agent Transfer
118	STP	Schedule Transfer
119	SRP	SpectraLink Radio
120	UTI	UTI
121	SMP	Simple Message
122	SM	SM
123	PTP	Performance Transparency
124	ISIS over IPv4	
125	FIRE	
126	CRTP	Combat Radio Transport
127	CRUDP	Combat Radio User Datagram
128	SSCOPMCE	
129	IPLT	
130	SPS	Secure Packet Shield
131	PIPE	Private IP Encapsulation within IP

continued

TABLE 18.5	*(continued)*	
Decimal	**Keyword**	**Protocol**
132	SCTP	Stream Control Transmission
133	FC	Fibre Channel
134	RSVP-E2E-IGNORE	
135	Mobility Header	
136	UDPLite	
137	MPLS-in-IP	
138	manet	MANET
139	HIP	Host Identity
140-252		Unassigned
253		Use for experimentation and testing
254		Use for experimentation and testing
255	Reserved	

As IPv4 packets are transported over the network, the packet headers are verified using a CRC checksum, and if the header doesn't pass verification the packet is dropped. In most instances, nothing more happens and the source is required to send a duplicate packet when the destination sends a message the packet didn't arrive. When Quality of Service methods are in place, it is possible to use the Internet Control Message Protocol (ICMP) to signal when a packet was dropped.

Subnetting

When our favorite company XYZ gets a block of IPv4 network addresses, those network addresses are logical entities, essentially pointers to the hosts that are assigned to them. The problem with this approach is that many networks are composed of different parts that are on different physical networks, separated by geography, separated by a low-bandwidth (for example, WAN) connection, belong to more than one domain and thus have different security settings, or have some other reason why you might want to address each group separately. Just the simple act of aggregating more addresses on the same ASN results in slower routing as traffic is sorted, and in much less efficient throughput due to higher network traffic and collisions. These are all reasons why networks are subdivided.

A subdivided network is called a subnet, which is short for subnetwork, although you almost never hear the latter term in use. Subnets are created by applying a "subnet mask" to the network address space. A subnet mask is a bit mask that hides the network identification portion of a network, along with any range of host values you specify. It's a simple and elegant system for carving up a network.

Let's consider a common example that you are probably familiar with, what was once called a C-class network consisting of 256 contiguous network addresses. Most private networks set their systems up with this size of network. In a private network with the range 192.168.1.0 to 192.168.1.255, which is referred to as 192.168.1.0/24 in CIDR, a subnet mask of 255.255.255.0 is applied to hide the network identification. This mask allows any of the 256 values for the host that are possible with the last octet. Suppose that you wanted to create two separate but equal-sized subnets from this range. To do this, you would apply a subnet mask of 255.255.255.128 to your systems, and any address belonging to the range 0-127 would be in subnet 1 and any address in the range of 128-255 would be in subnet 2. You can verify this by entering the information into Subnet-Calculator.com.

Tip

The Subnet Calculator at www.subnet-calculator.com can be used to calculate subnet masks, bits, hosts, and other factors or to check your calculations. The site also offers a CIDR calculator.

The systems on each subnet are invisible to one another. However, all systems are visible from outside the network, regardless of any subnets that you define. That's why subnetting a network doesn't require that you change network interface settings or alter registrations in address databases that are outside your network.

Subnetting is a lot less mysterious than it might seem at first, if you think in terms of binary addressing. What subnet masking does is take bits that were part of the host's identification portion of the network block and mask them off so that those bits appear to be part of the network identification portion; as a result, those bits can't be changed. Figure 18.6 shows how this example looks in binary numbers. Note that the subnet mask suppresses the available range in the last octet.

FIGURE 18.6

Subnetting a /24 network into two identical subnets

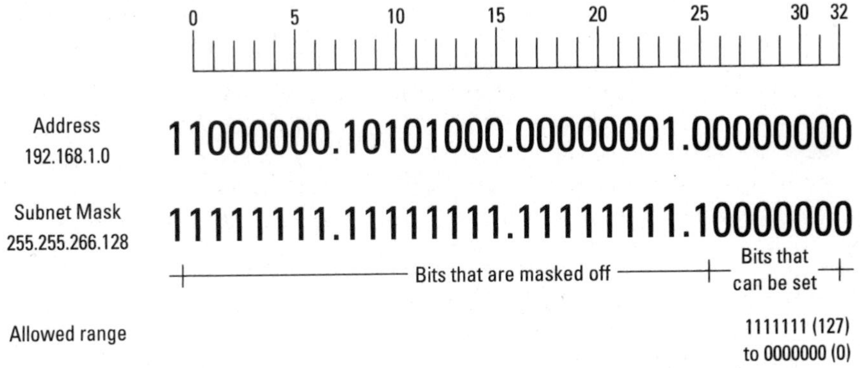

Address 192.168.1.0	11000000.10101000.00000001.00000000
Subnet Mask 255.255.266.128	11111111.11111111.11111111.10000000

├──────────── Bits that are masked off ────────────┤ Bits that can be set ┤

Allowed range

1111111 (127)
to 0000000 (0)

Should you want to carve a /24 network into more subnets, you can use the subnet mask values in Table 18.2 to do so. Every bit that is masked beyond the network identification portion of the address is referred to as the subnet identifier. In Figure 18.6, the subnet identifier is 1. Referring to Table 18.6, the network identifier for the subnet mask 255.255.255.240 would be 4.

TABLE 18.6

Subnetting a /24 Network

Last Octet in Dot Decimal	Last Octet in Binary	Unique Hosts1	Number of Possible Subnets	Effective CIDR
255	11111111	NA2	NA2	/32
254	11111110	2 (point to point)	128	/31
252	11111100	2	64	/30
248	11111000	6	32	/29
240	11110000	14	16	/28
224	11100000	30	8	/27
192	11000000	62	4	/26
128	10000000	126	2	/25
0	00000000 (no mask)	256	1 (no subnet)	

1 The unique hosts are reduced by two due to the reserved 0 and 255 values required in classful addressing. CIDR removes this restriction in almost all cases. 2 These are usually not defined at the router.

Subnets are numbered based on the length of the subnet mask and incremented based on the number of subnets you create. With no network identifier defined, the network is left unaffected and you see the Base network. In a C-class network with eight subnets defined, the subnets are labeled from 0 to 7, as shown in Figure 18.7.

When you create a subnet, you alter the routing tables to include subnet information. As packets come in, they are compared with the subnet mask to determine which subnet they reside on. Only the unmasked portion of the host's identification needs to be considered. The router then sends the packets onto the router responsible for that subnet, where the packet is then sent onto its destination.

FIGURE 18.7

The subnet numbering scheme for an 8-subnet partitions C-class network

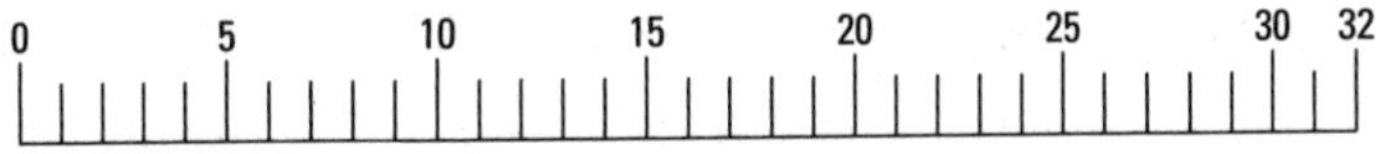

```
  0        5       10       15       20       25       30 32
  |||||||||||||||||||||||||||||||||||||||||||||
```

Base Address	
Base Address **(Subnet 0)** 192.168.1.0-31	**11000000.10101000.00000001.00000000**
Subnet 1 192.168.1.32-63	**11111111.11111111.11111111.00100000**
Subnet 2 192.168.1.64-95	**11111111.11111111.11111111.01000000**
Subnet 3 192.168.1.96-127	**11111111.11111111.11111111.01100000**
Subnet 4 192.168.1.128-159	**11111111.11111111.11111111.10000000**
Subnet 5 192.168.1.160-191	**11111111.11111111.11111111.10100000**
Subnet 6 192.168.1.191-223	**11111111.11111111.11111111.11000000**
Subnet 7 192.168.1.224-255	**11111111.11111111.11111111.11100000**

Setting an IP Address

It's important to be able to find your network interface IP configuration, and to change it when necessary. There are five main methods for setting a device's IP address:

- **Command Line Interface.** From the command line using a command such as IPCONFIG for Windows or IFCONFIG for Linux/UNIX/Solaris/Macintosh.

  The use of switches such as /ALL produce a verbose listing of addresses, and you can use other switches such as /RELEASE or /RENEW to change a dynamically assigned network address. Check your help system or MAN pages for more details.

Note
The various command line utilities rarely show IPv6 address zone information if zones are defined.

- **Graphical User Interface utility.** Typically a control panel utility found in nearly all GUI operating systems.

- **Menu or browser-based systems.** Devices such as routers, switches, and network appliances use these systems.

- **Dynamic network service such as DHCP (version 4 or 6) or BOOTP.** All network hosts and devices are capable of being a DHCP client; BOOTP clients are restricted to enabled hosts.

- **The Neighbor Discovery Protocol for IPv6.** This Link Layer protocol finds other nodes on an IPv6 link and determines the addresses of the neighbors as well as which router and routes or paths are best used to communicate with them.

An assigned IP address is stored in a number of different places. During a session, the IP address is retained in memory (RAM). In many cases, it is recorded to one or more system files, of which the HOSTS file is a prime example.

In the two sections that follow, you will learn about static IP addresses and dynamic IP addresses. A static IP address is one that you assign that remains unchanged over time. Static IP addresses are required for certain types of servers and may be used on small networks. Dynamic IP addresses are assigned by a network service and are both flexible and configurable. Dynamic IP addresses are used in networks where a pool of IP addresses must be used, in mobile devices, and in many other instances.

Static addressing

A static IP address is one that is assigned to a host or device that doesn't change with time. When you set a static address, that address stays fixed unless you physically go and change it. Some network devices require a static address to function correctly: DHCP and DNS servers, network gateways, routers, Web servers, and domain servers, to mention just a few. These systems require that devices always be able to find them at the same address whenever their services are required. For hosts and other devices that aren't required to provide services to other devices, there is no significant advantage to using static addressing.

On small networks of a dozen hosts or devices, the necessity of organizing static IP addresses so that there are no duplicate assignments or remembering which system belongs to which address is not an onerous task. There is no compelling reason not to use static IP addresses, and doing so allows you to hard-code these addresses into your HOSTS file.

On my home network, I set the following static IP addresses:

- **Host ID = 1.** This address is assigned to the network gateway.

- **Host ID = 2.** This address is assigned to the DNS server, when one is used.

- **Host ID = 3.** This address is assigned to the domain server, when one is used.

- **Host IDs = 4–20.** These addresses are used for any other device that provides a standard network service.

- **Host IDs = 21–80.** These addresses are assigned to clients.

- **Host IDs = 81–99.** I reserve these static addresses for wireless devices such as access points or routers.

- **Host IDs = 100–110.** I use these addresses for the address assignments of my TiVo's network interface.

- **Host IDs = 150–200.** These addresses form the pool of dynamic IP addresses that the DHCP server can use.

You'll notice that even though this scheme tends more often than not to assign static IP addresses to hosts, I don't religiously assign all network devices static IP addresses, nor would I want to. There are many instances when a new network device is introduced, or when a network interface loses its IP address for some reason (an operating system install, for example). In those instances, DHCP assigns an address from its pool. This scheme works for me because the network is small. If I had more than 16 to 20 network addresses to assign, I would use DHCP more extensively, and in large networks, most systems are assigned dynamic IP addresses.

To summarize, you need static IP addresses for the following systems:

- For fixed network services such as routers

- For network devices that must be accessible from outside of your network: Web servers, e-mail servers, FTP servers, and other application servers

- For some terminal service applications

- In some licensing schemes where the license is tied to a specific IP address (rare)

- For streaming services where the connection endpoints must be permanently set

Dynamic addressing

You do not need static IP addresses for clients that are requesting services, such as browsing the Internet, sending and receiving e-mail, using an Instant Messaging service, downloading or uploading files, and similar tasks. Dynamic IP addressing offers the advantage of automatically providing address configuration, which can be a very time-consuming task on a network of any significant size (greater than 50 devices). It frees the network administrator from having to remember to reset an address when a system is moved from one subnet to another.

Against these conveniences is the requirement that the dynamic address assignment service (DHCP) and the name resolutions service (DNS, for example) must be running at all times in order for the network to function correctly. However, once a dynamic address is assigned to a device, that device retains the address and only loses the assignment when the address assignment service recognizes that the device has lost its address "lease." The lease is a dynamic IP address' "Time To Live" feature.

There is a minor security benefit to be gained by using dynamic addressing. If a hacker gains access to a system on your network at a known IP address, that address will not be available to them over time if it is a dynamic address.

Dynamic Host Configuration Protocol

The Dynamic Host Configuration Protocol (DHCP) is a network broadcast service that assigns and manages dynamic IP addresses on DHCP clients. DHCP servers can be found in network switches, routers, network appliances, and on all network operating systems whether run on a server or workstation. The service is normally turned off by default so that networks don't run into the problem of having multiple conflicting DHCP servers running at the same time. DHCP also needs to be enabled on the client side in many cases.

A DHCP client sends a broadcast request when it first connects to the network or at timed intervals that are configurable. Any listening DHCP servers on the network are requested to either supply or update its Internet Protocol information. A DNS server responds to the query, validates the request, and then provides the necessary configuration parameters. Once the address is accepted, the client may initiate an ARP query to determine if the address is unique. The address process, often referred to as ROSA (for Request, Offer, Selection, and Acknowledgment), is illustrated in Figure 18.8. An assigned address is removed from the address pool, as shown by the strike-out text in the address listing at the lower left of Figure 18.8.

FIGURE 18.8

DHCP's ROSA process

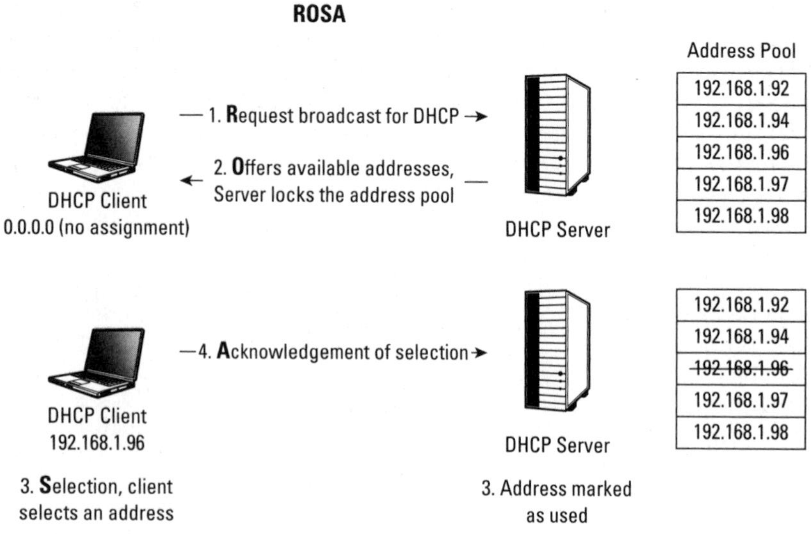

ROSA

Address Pool

192.168.1.92
192.168.1.94
192.168.1.96
192.168.1.97
192.168.1.98

— 1. **R**equest broadcast for DHCP →

← 2. **O**ffers available addresses, Server locks the address pool

DHCP Client
0.0.0.0 (no assignment)

DHCP Server

192.168.1.92
192.168.1.94
~~192.168.1.96~~
192.168.1.97
192.168.1.98

—4. **A**cknowledgement of selection→

DHCP Client
192.168.1.96

DHCP Server

3. **S**election, client
selects an address

3. Address marked
as used

DHCP configuration supplies the following pieces of information:

- IP address
- Subnet mask
- Domain name
- DNS server(s) address
- Default gateway (outbound router, proxy server, and so on)

Configuration

DHCP servers are most often set up to provide dynamic addresses. When an address is assigned from the DHCP address pool, the address has a lease during which time the address is valid. That lease can be long — 30 days is typical in enterprises — or it can be short, often on the order of 48 hours when the DHCP address is assigned by an ISP to a remote client over a broadband connection or through a Point-to-Point Protocol (PPP) dial-up or ISDN connection. Every so often, the server polls the clients for their DHCP settings, or a client queries the server to find out if its settings are still valid. If the lease has expired, the server either refreshes the address or offers a different set of addresses for the client to select from.

Different DHCP services handle these details in different ways. Large ISPs supporting many remote clients typically reassign an address for a lease that expires if the client doesn't respond to its polling. They do this because they know that the client will check its DHCP settings the next time that they connect. Although DHCP is almost always a dynamic address service, it is often possible to configure DHCP so that the address is automatically supplied to a client permanently. In some instances, the client can manually select the address from the pool, as is shown in Figure 18.8; this is uncommon, however.

Some DHCP servers support a feature called *static allocation*, where any assigned IP address records the MAC address of the client in a lookup table. Some systems do this automatically; others require that the administrator manually enter the MAC address. Static allocation is not a standard feature, and if you implement it, you need to ensure that not only does your DHCP server offer it, but that any routers on your network that the DHCP client needs also support the feature. There is a plethora of names used to describe static allocation, including the following:

- Cisco (and now Linksys, too) calls it Static DHCP.
- Older Linksys routers such as WRT54G (54GL and 54GS) wireless routers using the DD-WRT Linux firmware call it Static DHCP assignment.
- MAC/IP binding.
- Reserved IP Address (see Figure 18.9), or IP reservation.

The DHCP configuration Web page for a Netgear FVS318 router/firewall

Securing DHCP

DHCP offers no security mechanisms to protect a network against unauthorized address assignment, and requires vigilance on your part to ensure that your network doesn't have either an unauthorized DHCP server or client on the network. This is one of the reasons that you need to take care that you don't install a second DHCP server on the network inadvertently. An unauthorized DHCP server can provide a means for unauthorized clients to gain access to your network; and it is easier to have an unauthorized DHCP server on the network than you might think. DHCP is included on so many devices that it is easy to check the wrong box on a router setup wizard or move a server with an active DHCP service onto another subnet.

There is an authentication method that has been developed for DHCP (http://tools.ietf.org/html/rfc3118), and while you may find it available in your DHCP server and it is widely supported, most organizations don't adopt the Authentication for DHCP Messages option. When security is a concern, most networks adopt authentication using the IPsec protocol suite. You can also provide some security to the network by ensuring that the DNS server that provides name resolution only provides this service to systems whose network interface MAC addresses are registered as belonging to the IP address that they display, using static allocation as described in the previous section.

Cross-Ref

IPsec is described in Chapter 27.

Many firewalls and routers provide a DHCP server, as you can see in Figure 18.9. DHCP traffic is transported over UDP. If your firewall or router needs to support DHCP for incoming or outgoing traffic, you will probably need to enable this feature as well as open the following ports: Outgoing DHCP port 68 (UDP) and Incoming DHCP port 67 (UDP) at the firewall, and Outgoing DHCP port 67 (UDP) and Incoming DHCP port 68 (UDP) at the client. Incoming broadcast packets with source 0.0.0.0 and destination 255.255.255.255 must be allowed, as must outgoing packets from the DHCP server if the ROSA system is allowed to work. These are the same ports that BOOTP uses.

Bootstrap Protocol

The Bootstrap Protocol, or BOOTP, is a predecessor to the DHCP service, and is still in use today. BOOTP works similarly to and is compatible with DHCP. BOOTP is a UDP network protocol that assigns an IP address upon request during the bootstrap part of a system's startup, whereas DHCP must first load an operating system and the DHCP client before it can issue the address request. BOOTP broadcasts are sent by instructions in the Read Only Memory (ROM) of a network interface card (NIC) or from instructions in the motherboard's BIOS. The BOOTP service sends an address to the system.

BOOTP is significantly easier to use and requires little if any setup to implement. Unlike DHCP, which allows for reconfiguration once the system is running, BOOTP works only in the startup phase. It is used most often in thin clients of terminal servers where the client is a diskless workstation where the operating system is loaded as part of the boot process after the address is obtained.

Internet Control Message Protocol

The Internet Control Message Protocol (ICMP) defines the message system used to acknowledge or request actions and events related to IP data transfer. It is important for controlling traffic and congestion, signaling if a packet has arrived correctly or needs to be resent, and controlling routing. The Time To Live (TTL) parameter expiration is one event that generates an ICMP error message.

ICMP is required for the proper functioning of the IP protocol and must be correctly operating for IP communications to function. There are two versions of this protocol, one for IPv4 and another for IPv6; IPv6 is described toward the end of this chapter.

ICMP messages are generated from IP datagrams that require an ICMP action. IP encapsulates the ICMP header that contains the error, and adds the appropriate destination to the message field in the header. Because ICMP is carried over a single datagram, it doesn't require the verification features of TCP and is usually sent over UDP transport. That makes ICMP an unreliable messaging format. The message type is indicated by a field inserted into the IP header after bit 160, or later if the IP header Options field has been populated. Figure 18.10 shows the structure of an ICMP header.

FIGURE 18.10

The ICMP header structure

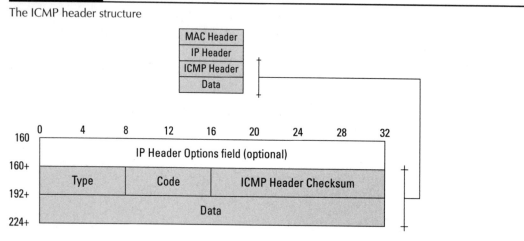

The essential fields that define the ICMP message are the type and code fields. These fields are standardized by the IANA and are described in Table 18.7.

TABLE 18.7

ICMP Types

Type	Code	Description
0 - Echo Reply	0	Echo Reply (used by PING)
1		Destination Unreachable (ICMPv6)
2		Packet too big (ICMPv6)
3 - Time Exceeded		Time exceeded (ICMPv6)
3 - Destination Unreachable	0	Destination network unreachable
	1	Destination host unreachable
	2	Destination protocol unreachable

Type	Code	Description
	3	Destination port unreachable
	4	Fragment required, Don't Fragment (DF) flag set
	5	Source route failed
	6	Destination network unknown
	7	Destination host unknown
	8	Source host isolated
	9	Network administratively prohibited
	10	Host administratively prohibited
	11	Network unreachable for Type of Service (TOS)
	12	Host unreachable for TOS
	13	Communication administratively prohibited
4 - Source Quench	0	Source quench for congestion control
4 - Parameter Problem		Parameter Problem (ICMPv6)
5 - Redirect Message	0	Redirect Datagram for the network
	1	Redirect Datagram for the host
	2	Redirect Datagram for TOS and network
	3	Redirect Datagram for TOS and host
6		Alternate Host Address
7		Reserved
8 - Echo Request	0	Echo request (used by `PING`)
9 - Router Advertisement	0	Router Advertisement
10 - Router Solicitation	0	Router discovery/solicitation/selection
11 - Time Exceeded	0	TTL expired en route
	1	Fragment reassembly time exceeded
12 - Parameter Error: Bad IP Header	0	Pointer error
	1	Missing an option
	2	Bad length (checksum error)
13 - Timestamp	0	Timestamp
14 - Timestamp Reply	0	Timestamp reply
15 - Information Request	0	Information request
16 - Information Reply	0	Information reply
17 - Address Mask Request	0	Address Mask request
18 - Address Mask Reply	0	Address Mask reply

continued

TABLE 18.7	(continued)		
Type	**Code**		**Description**
19			Reserved for security
20–29			Reserved for fault tolerance testing
30 - Traceroute	0		Information request
31			Datagram conversion error
32			Mobile host redirect
33			Where are you? (IPv6)
34			Here I am! (IPv6)
35			Mobile registration request
36			Mobile registration reply
37			Domain name request
38			Domain name reply
39			Simple Key Management for Internet Protocol (SKIP Algorithm Discovery Protocol)
40			Security failures
41			Experimental mobility protocols
42–99			Reserved
100			Private experimentation
101			Private experimentation
102–126			Reserved
127			Reserved for future ICMPv6 information messages
128			Echo request (ICMPv6)
129			Echo reply (ICMPv6)
130–199			Reserved
200			Private experimentation
201			Private experimentation
255			Reserved for future ICMPv6 information messages

Source: www.iana.org/assignments/icmp-parameters

Internet Protocol Version 6

The second version of the Internet Protocol, version 6 (IPv6), is the successor to IPv4. IPv6 was designed to provide a significantly larger address space, better granularity (self-autoconfiguration and improved routing), and improved security. For the most part, all of the Internet Protocols that work with IPv4 work with IPv6. Some Application layer protocols, such as FTP or NTPv3, that encapsulate IP network addresses fail to make the transition without being reworked due to the very different structure of IPv4 and IPv6 headers.

IPv6 solves a lot of problems that have made IPv4 networking a difficult proposition. IPv6 headers are simpler and have a native Quality of Service (QoS) mechanism, called flow labeling, built into them. The incredibly large address space means that subnets become an abstraction and not a necessity, and that Network Address Translation (NAT), which is the bane of many protocols trying to traverse a router, disappears. Just eliminating NAT removes a significant portion of network configuration errors. Voice over IP (VoIP), BitTorrent, Session Initiation Protocol (SIP), and other streaming and peer-to-peer protocols all have difficulty with NAT on IPv4 routers because they can't identify their target systems.

Routing has been greatly improved in IPv6. There are improved multicasting, anycasting, and unicasting routing mechanisms. In many instances, you don't even need routers to create LANs. Because the various subnets on an IPv6 are embedded in the network prefix, network traffic can be directed to the correct host on the correct subnet by the address alone. This ad hoc network is specific to a site and does require a router for outside traffic.

The IPv6 Neighbor Discovery (ND) Protocol can not only discover neighboring hosts and devices, but it can also discover network prefixes and the address autoconfiguration method, perform address resolution, find the next hop, detect duplicate addresses, and determine whether a neighbor is available or offline. ND consolidates these many important functions into a core networking protocol that can work in the background automatically.

Because autoconfiguration of addresses is built into IPv6, DHCP becomes largely irrelevant, although a version of DHCPv6 does exist. Autoconfiguration of IPv6 addresses is normally done by sending a query to the router. You can configure link-local addresses to be unique in IPv6, which eliminates the problem of having network collisions when two hosts on connected networks use the same IPv4 address.

In order to send IPv6 packets over an IPv4 network, it is necessary to encapsulate IPv6 packets within IPv4. This is known as tunneling, and can be set up as either an automatic system or by using predefined configured tunneling. Other tunneling methods can use UDP packets as the link layer protocol, or the ISATAP protocol to make an IPv4 network appear as if it is an IPv6 locallink. One technology, called Toredo, uses automatic tunneling over UDP to transport IPv6 packets across NAT routers. Toredo is found in Windows XP SP2 IPv6, Windows Vista, Windows Server 2003 and 2008, and Mac OS X Leopard. These technologies are meant to bridge the transition of networking from IPv4 to IPv6 and allow IPv6 to be more easily deployed in dual-stack networks.

Note

IPv5 was assigned to a streaming protocol for audio and video traffic and was unavailable for use as an IP addressing protocol.

IPv6 has turned out to be much more slowly adopted than any of its developers would have predicted due to the technologies described in the previous sections: NAT, CIDR, and subnetting in particular. However, it is only a matter of time until IPv6 becomes the dominant IP addressing protocol. IANA tracks the usage of IPv4 and has predicted that unallocated IPv4 addresses will be exhausted around May 2010 and that the Regional Internet Registries would use up their address allocations by April 2011. So if all the good reasons I've given you don't convince you that IPv6 is worth your time, then consider that at some point you will simply have no choice but to adopt it.

Addressing

IPv6 defines a 128-bit address space, which is an almost inconceivably large number. The host portion of the address is either assigned as a sequential number or derived from the network interface MAC address. The network identification and the host identification portions of the address are both 64 bits wide and are always kept separate from one another. This separation means that when you add an entry for an IPv6 network identifier into a router, it then defines the entire network. Just this one simple fact, that one network prefix routes the entire network, means that the router tables on IPv6 networks are greatly reduced compared to IPv4 networks, which leads to much better router performance. The reduced complexity of the IPv6 header is another factor in improving router performance.

In standard hexadecimal notation, a Global Unicast IPv6 address would be written as eight 4-digit groups, each separated by a colon, as follows:

```
2001:0db8:3c4d:0015:0000:0000:abcd:ef14
```

where `2001:0db8:3c4d:` is the global prefix, `0015:` is the subnet ID, and `0000:0000:abcd:ef14` is the host identifier (network interface).

There is no need to specify a subnet or the network identification of any routers along the path to that network. The addition of the network identification changes the routing for the entire set of systems on that IPv6 network.

The network classes used in IPv4 no longer apply in IPv6. A block of contiguous network addresses defining a single network can be defined by the size of the prefix. The following two addresses represent the start and end of a network range:

```
2001:0db8:3c4d:0000:0000:0000:0000:0000
2001:0db8:3c4d:ffff: ffff: ffff: ffff: ffff
```

You can use CIDR to indicate the size of the network prefix, just as you would in IPv4. In the addresses above, this would allow you to write this network block in the following form:

```
2001:0db8:3c4d::/48
```

Recall that IPv6 is a 128-bit address space, and that each of the eight blocks in the address represents 16 bits of data as written in the form of four hexadecimal characters. The three network prefix blocks indicate that the CIDR mask size is /48. This still leaves 280 or 1.21 x 1024 addresses that can be assigned. Larger CIDR values reduce the number of unique addresses that are assignable, but the size of IPv6 is so vast that even a full 64-bit network prefix still leaves 264 or 1.84 x 1019 unique addresses — over 3 billion addresses for every living person on Earth.

Subnetting doesn't disappear in IPv6 networks; however, its usefulness as anything other than a comparative metric loses its meaning. Typically a /48 network is used by large organizations allowing the 80-bit address space mentioned previously. A small network might use a /56 prefix, which allows for a 72-bit address space. A /48 network can define 65,536 (216) subnets, while a /57 network would allow for 128(27) subnets. Because autoconfiguration requires a full 60 bits in the address for assignment, you never see subnetting in IPv6 use more than the allowed 60 bits, which is not subnetted.

All IPv6 hosts must support the following features:

- Link-local addresses
- Multicast to all other nodes
- Unicast
- Anycast
- Selective multicast
- Loopback address (::1)

These various forms of routing are described in more detail later in this section.

IPv6 compressed notation

If you think that an IPv6/IPv4 address is weird, check out the full address that is used for the localhost:

```
0000:0000:0000:0000:0000:0000:0000:0001
```

It would be ugly to have to enter all of these zeros, and thankfully IPv6 doesn't require you to do so. IPv6 has a feature that is called compressed notation. With compressed notation, you can simply eliminate any block in the address that is all zeros. This compresses the localhost address down to the shortcut ::1, which is pretty handy. Similarly, you can compress the IPv6/IPv4 composite address that you saw a couple of paragraphs ago to the compressed notation ::192.168.1.52.

Compressed notation can also be applied to any blocks that have all zeros, but that are inside the address. The zero blocks do not have to be leading zeros. For example, the address

```
2001:0db8:3c4d:0015:0:0:abcd:ef14
```

may be shortened to

```
2001:0db8:3c4d:0015::abcd:ef14.
```

Compressed notation allows you to remove only one group of zeros, and with good reason. If you consider the address

```
2001:0:0:0015:0:0:0:ef14
```

compressed to

> 2001::0015::ef14

you would not be able to discern whether the address should be expanded to

> 2001:0:0:0:0: 0015:0: ef14,

or

> 2001:0:0:0: 0015:0:0: ef14,

or

> 2001:0:0: 0015:0:0:0: ef14,

or

> 2001:0: 0015:0:0:0:0: ef14.

If you understand these few principles of compressed notation, then you can see that the following addresses are all equivalent to one another:

```
2001:0db8:0000:0000:0000:0000: abcd:ef14
2001:0db8:0000:0000:0000:: abcd:ef14
2001:0db8:0:0:0:0: abcd:ef14
2001:0db8:0:0:: abcd:ef14
2001:0db8:: abcd:ef14
2001:db8:: abcd:ef14
```

which at first glance would be wildly confusing.

You may encounter compressed notation with a CIDR suffix appended to it. For example, an address such as 2001:0db8: abcd::ef14/128 indicates that the address has only one interface route. A different suffix, such as /48, indicates another router configuration for that address.

IPv6 calculators

There may be creatures somewhere who actually live in IPv6 address space. You can identify them by eight digits that they have on their two hands and feet, or some other combination that adds up to 32.

Because I have stopped growing digits some time ago, I prefer to rely on one of the many Web sites, utilities, or lookup tables that exist to support the various forms of IP-related conversions. One that I've used is called Bitcricket, and is shown in Figure 18.11. This utility can calculate subnets for IPv4/IPv6 and for CIDR routes, as well as perform conversions between dotted decimal,

decimal, hexadecimal, dotted hexadecimal, dotted binary, and binary numbers. The program is available in both Windows and Macintosh formats, and can be obtained from www.bitcricket.com/ip-subnet-calculator.html.

Figure 18.11 shows the IPv6 page of the Bitcricket utility with the different defined interfaces enumerated.

An alternative IP6 calculator utility for Linux/UNIX is IPv6calc, which can be downloaded from www.deepspace6.net/projects/ipv6calc.html.

Bitcricket may be used to do IPv4/IPv6 conversions and discovery.

Dual-stack IPv6/IPv4 addresses

The address space for IPv6 and IPv4 is not backwards compatible, and so, although you can run both protocol versions on the same computer or network, they operate independent of one another. Because most of the world is using IPv4 addresses, IPv6 would be useless if it didn't encode for an IPv4 address. To create an IPv4 address in the IPv6 address format, you would write it in the following manner:

```
0000:0000:0000:0000:0000:0000:192.168.1.52
```

Notice that the address above has only seven blocks defined by the colon delimiters and that I told you that an IPv6 address requires eight blocks. The reason that the IPv6/IPv4 address has only seven blocks is that the IPv4 block encodes for 32 bits and not the normal 16 bits for each of the IPv6 blocks. That means that the IPv4 portion of the IPv6 address is a double block.

IPv6 can use what have been generally called compatible addresses, where you mix six higher-order groups of hexadecimal digits with four groups of decimal digits in the low-order octets that IPv4 uses. Using this scheme, let's look at an address of the form

```
h:h:h:h:h:h:d.d.d.d
```

where h is a high-order byte and d is a low-order byte. This form of address allows for the following substitution:

```
::ffff:192.168.2.52
```

which in the original address is equivalent to the following notation:

```
::ffff: c0a8:0234.
```

This type of notation for a dual-stack address is not universally supported, and so you will want to check first before using it.

Address scopes and zones

An IPv6 address is defined for a particular address scope. One way to think of an address scope is that it represents the connection's endpoint limits for that network interface. A connection can span a region defined as a local link, site, or global network. If you examine IPv6 addresses on a system, you may find that there is a link-local address and a global address for the same network interface. Although a network interface must have at least one unicast IPv6 address, you can define as many IPv6 addresses to an interface as you desire.

The different address scopes that have been defined are:

- **Link-local address.** These are private network non-routable addresses and are confined to a single network or subnetwork. These addresses can be supplied by autoconfiguration technologies such as SLAAC and DHCPv6, both of which are described later in this section.

- **Unique local address.** Unique local addresses (ULAs) are private network, non-routable addresses that are guaranteed to be unique. When two network segments with these types of addresses are joined, there are no host IP address conflicts.

- **Global unicast address.** These addresses are public network addresses and are routable to other networks.

The site-local address scope defined by the original RFCs was phased out as of 2004 and is no longer in widespread use.

Any network interface connected to a particular address scope is part of a scope zone. Scope zones require that each network interface have a unique address within that zone. Addresses do not have to be unique across different zones. When you examine an IPv6 address returned from an IPCONFIG /ALL command in Windows, it takes the following form:

```
Link-local IPv6: fe80::1198:de1d:9fb3:bd11%8(Preferred)
```

The title indicates that this address is scoped to the link-local zone. The address is the string `fe80::1198:de1d:9fb3:bd11`, while the `%8` indicates the zone index number 8. The definition of a zone obviates the need for network broadcasts, and the prefix `fe80` is the local scoping. A link-local address has the same routing prefix, `fe80::/10`.

Consider the situation of a dual-homed host with two link-local addresses, the first at `fe80::a/64` and the second at `fe80::b/64`. Both of these interfaces connect to a network that has a host at `fe80::c/64`. The host at `fe80::c/64` wants to send packets to the dual-homed host at `fe80::a/64`, but because the `fe80::b/64` interface share the same link-local address, there is no way to tell which interface (`a/64` or `b/64`) that `fe80::c/64` should send the packets to. This is the problem that address scoping solves. You alter the link-local addresses to include the zone in the following manner:

```
<IPv6_Address>%<Zone_Index>
```

Different operating systems indicate the Zone Index in different ways: Microsoft Windows IPv6 uses integers such as `%1`; and Linux/UNIX use the interface name, `%eth0`.

Multicasting, which is a required field in the IPv6 header, may be used to send a packet to all of the hosts in a zone, such as the local-link `all hosts` multicast group. Multicast in IPv6 replaces broadcast that was part of IPv4. Multicasting sends packets to every network interface that is a member of the multicast group, as registered at a router; if no members are listed at that particular router, the packets are dropped. Multicasting doesn't suffer from the defect that broadcasting does, where unintended recipients receive what is called a broadcast storm.

An IPv6 host can send packets to multiple network interfaces that all have the same IPv6 anycast address. In anycast communication, any node with the destination anycast address can accept the packet, and whichever node happens to hear the packet first takes delivery. Delivery is to the nearest or best node and represents an approach toward improving reliability and failover in replicated systems. Anycast combines elements of unicast, multicast, and broadcast; probably the best way to think about anycast is that it is a shared set of unicast links.

Note

Anycasting and other IP routing technologies are discussed in detail in Chapter 9. Many DNS servers on the Internet use anycast for replication.

IPv6 anycast is supported by a specific type of address that includes a set of fields to support anycasting. To have anycast packets arrive correctly, you need to set the various network interfaces to the appropriate anycast address, and IPv6 manages the delivery of packets to those various interfaces.

Table 18.8 lists the IANA IPv6 address ranges. Many of the ranges are reserved by the IETF for future use or experimentation. Of the following ranges listed in the table, only `0000::/8`, `2000::/3`, `FC00/7`, `FE80::/10`, and `FF00::/8` are publicly available as either a loopback address or broadcast range.

TABLE 18.8

IPv6 IANA Address Ranges

Prefix	Allocation
`0000::/8`	Reserved by IETF.
	The "unspecified address," the "loopback address," and the IPv6 Addresses with Embedded IPv4 Addresses are assigned out of the `0000::/8` address block.
	`0000::/96` was previously defined as the "IPv4-compatible IPv6 address" prefix. This definition has been deprecated.
`0100::/8`	Reserved by IETF
`0200::/7`	Reserved by IETF.
	`0200::/7` was previously defined as an OSI NSAP-mapped prefix set. This definition has been deprecated.
`0400::/6`	Reserved by IETF
`0800::/5`	Reserved by IETF
`1000::/4`	Reserved by IETF
`2000::/3`	Global Unicast, addresses that are publicly routable.
	The IPv6 Unicast space encompasses the entire IPv6 address range with the exception of `FF00::/8`. IANA Unicast address assignments are currently limited to the IPv6 Unicast address range of `2000::/3`. IANA assignments from this block are registered in the IANA registry: `iana-ipv6-unicast-address-assignments`.
`2001::/32`	The address `2001:0DB8::/32` is reserved for examples and documentation, as in EXAMPLENET-WF.
`3fff:ffff::/32`	These addresses are reserved for examples and documentation.
`4000::/3`	Reserved by IETF

Prefix	Allocation
`6000::/3`	Reserved by IETF
`8000::/3`	Reserved by IETF
`A000::/3`	Reserved by IETF
`C000::/3`	Reserved by IETF
`E000::/4`	Reserved by IETF
`F000::/5`	Reserved by IETF
`F800::/6`	Reserved by IETF
`FC00::/7`	Unique Local Unicast
`FE00::/9`	Reserved by IETF
`FE80::/10`	Link-Local Unicast
`FEC0::/10`	Reserved by IETF. FEC0::/10 was previously defined as a Site-Local scoped address prefix. This definition has been deprecated.
`FF00::/8`	Multicast

Reference: www.iana.org/assignments/ipv6-address-space. The RFCs that define the IPv6 address space include 1881, 1888m 3879, 4048, 4147, 4193, 4291, and 4548.

There are two methods in use for address autoconfiguration with IPv6: the Stateless Address Autoconfiguration (SLAAC) and the DHCPv6, which is stateful. An IPv6 system initiates stateless discovery by sending an ICMPv6 router solicitation request as a multicast packet when it connects to a link-local zone. The IPv6-enabled router returns a router advertisement packet with the required configuration details. Not every IPv6 device can use this stateless mechanism to obtain an IPv6 address; routers, for example, require a stateful assignment. DHCPv6 can be used to supply IPv6 configuration information to clients that has been manually entered into the configuration table and allows the administrator to send additional information that is not discoverable by SLAAC. For the most part, autodiscovery on IPv6 networks uses SLAAC, while DHCPv6 is rarely used. When neither mechanism works correctly, the link-local address is supplied to the network interface as a default backup.

IPv6 datagrams

IPv6 datagrams are both larger and simpler than their IPv4 counterparts. The header portion of the packet is shown in Figure 18.12. Notice that IPv6 doesn't use IP header checksums to verify the validity of a transmitted packet; instead, it relies on other protocols to determine the validity. This has the effect of making IPv6 faster than IPv4.

FIGURE 18.12

IPv6 header structure

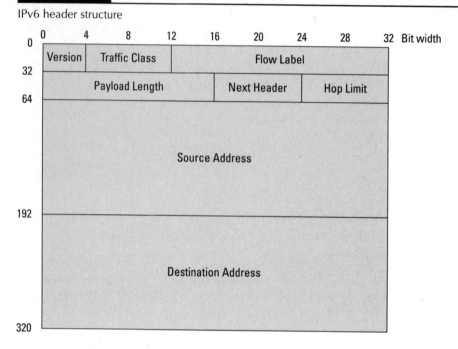

The different fields in the IPv6 header have the following purposes:

- **Version.** This is indicated by a four-bit representation of the number 6 (0110).

- **Traffic Class.** This field provides a packet priority range that is used to control packet traffic based on network conditions. Network messages indicate the amount of congestion on the network that needs to be accommodated.

- **Flow Label.** This is a QoS label that is defined for real-time services and is meant to serve the same function as the Service Type field in IPv4. This field is not in current use.

- **Payload Length.** This indicates the size of the payload in bytes. A field setting of all zeros indicates that the packet is a "Jumbogram," which is a packet that can be anywhere from 64KB up to 4GB in size. Jumbo frames require specific network hardware support and a Maximum Transmission Unit (MTU) network protocol that supports their large sizes in order to be used.

- **Next Header.** This is equivalent to the Protocol field in the IPv4 header. It can also be used to add an additional header to the packet.

- **Hop Limit.** This is the number of network hops that are allowed. This is the current replacement for the Time-To-Live parameter that is used in IPv4.

- **Source Address.** This is the IPv6 128-bit address of the source.

- **Destination Address.** This is the IPv6 128-bit address of the destination.

IPv6 Neighbor Discovery

The IPv6 Neighbor Discovery (ND) Protocol is an IPv6-only protocol that consolidates a number of important functions found in a number of IPv4 protocols, as well as adding a number of new ones. The protocol's name only provides insight into a small part of this handy technology's features. Through ND, a number of network parameters can be discovered and configured, and the IP protocol's basic functions are supported.

The Internet Protocol is a Network layer protocol in the ISO/OSI model, and the primary Internet Layer protocol of the Internet Protocol Suite. IP is responsible for datagram delivery and addressing, routing, and network interface configuration. In IPv4, the Address Resolution Protocol (ARP) provides a broadcast discovery method, and the Internet Control Message Protocol (ICMP) provides the messaging system between network hosts and devices that allows for acknowledgment, traffic control, Quality of Service, and other functions. Many of these functions are consolidated in IPv6 in ND.

As shown in Figure 18.13, ND includes router discovery and redirection, features that are part of ICMPv4. Address resolution in ND adds additional functionality to the services that the ARP provides and that IPv4 supplements. ND uses ICMPv6 messages such as Router Advertisement and Router Solicitation, Echo Request and Echo Reply, Neighbor Advertisement and Neighbor Solicitation to discover network elements. These commands and the information that they carry work with IPv6 messages such as Redirect and Router Renumbering to build optimized IPv6 routing tables.

FIGURE 18.13

The different functional components of the Network Discovery (ND) Protocol in IPv6

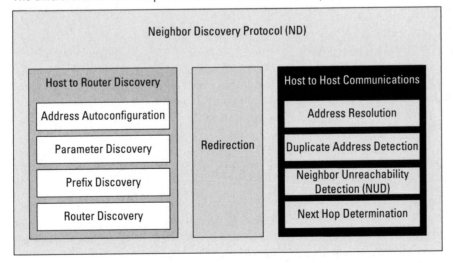

The most important functions that ND offers are the following:

- **Address resolution.** A router address query can return a valid network ID to a host at startup or when required. Multicast is used for address resolution, which is more efficient than the broadcasts that ARP uses in IPv4.

- **Autoconfiguration.** ND provides the message function that allows router configuration queries and can return network parameters.

- **Next Hop Determination.** When one host sends packets to another host, ND examines the datagram header to determine if a router is required or if the communication can be direct. When local, the communication is direct. When it is determined that the address isn't on the link-local network, ND selects the correct router that is the "next-hop." In most instances, packets use the host's local destination cache to determine where datagrams should be sent. When a next hop determination is made (which is infrequently) for a particular datagram, the destination cache is updated.

- **Redirection.** The redirect function in ND analyzes the route assigned to datagrams to determine if the best route was selected. If a better route is available, ND creates an ICMPv6 Redirect message that changes the routing for any future datagrams with a connection containing the same endpoints.

- **Router discovery and selection.** The message function in ND allows the protocol to discover which routers are on the network, and constantly updates this information. The dynamic selection of routers and available devices that the router knows about allows ND to determine which nodes are active and online and which routers are used for forwarding messages to outside the network.

- **Security.** ND runs at the Network layer and can be transported over an IPsec connection.

ICMPv6

ICMPv6 offers some additional capabilities that aren't part of ICMPv4's definition. As you can see in Table 18.7, there are additional message types that are defined for error messages (1, 2, 3, 4, 100, 101, and 127) and for informational messages (128, 129, 200, 201, and 255) that are specific to ICMPv6. Because IPv6 contains additional routing functions, ICMPv6 has some additional requirements that must be met, including the following:

- A message that was the result of a unicast routing must have a reply sent to the sending host.

- If the message is a response to a multicast group address, to an anycast address, or to a unicast address that doesn't have an assigned mode, then the source address must be a unicast address that belongs to a node.

The biggest difference between ICMPv4 and ICMPv6 is that the additional message categories were added to support the ND Protocol that is described in the previous section. Of these, the Neighbor Solicitation and Neighbor Advertisement messages provide the discovery mechanism that ND uses to populate its browse functionality. The Router Solicitation and Router Advertisement messages support the ND redirection function that allows for more intelligent routing initiated by network hosts. Redirect messages are sent as a unicast to the device that sent the datagram that initiated the redirect.

A function called Router Renumbering sends messages containing a list of router prefixes to the routers that are to be renumbered. Using the renumbering feature, a router can check the other router prefixes to see if packet prefixes match any of the renumbered routers, and if they do, it forwards the packets to that router. Router renumbering is supported by the Router Renumbering Command and by the Router Renumbering Result message. Because this mechanism allows for the mass renumbering of routers, there are mechanisms built into this feature, such as a test mode and a Sequence Number Reset message, that are meant to prevent the abuse of these router optimization functions.

Summary

In this chapter, you learned about the Internet Protocol and the central role that it plays in TCP/IP networking. IP provides the end-to-end delivery of packets but does not specify the connection or the method of transport.

IPv4 uses a 32-bit addressing scheme. You learned how addresses specify networks and interfaces, and how addresses can be manipulated to define networks and subnets. The different methods for automatic assignment of IPv4 addresses were described.

IPv6 is the more recent version of IP. It has a 128-bit address space, a simplified header, and improved routing functions. The methods used to address devices on IPv6 networks, create and work with networks, and interoperate in mixed IPv4/IPv6 dual-stack networks were described.

The next chapter describes name resolution services that translate addresses into friendly network names.

Name Resolution Services

Nameservers are a collection of networking services that translate a machine or network address into a "friendly " or readable name. When you open a Network folder on your computer and browse the network, the name service polls the systems on the network for their availability and returns their names and related information. A name service is central to the successful operation of your network. Without a functioning nameserver, your network may only display your computer's information.

There are many different name services in use. The Internet relies on the Domain Name System (DNS) protocol to translate IP addresses, such as 170.149.173.130 into nytimes.com.

While DNS is the most widely used name service, there are many other name services that are in current use. This chapter describes the simplest method, and one of the earliest, for name resolution — the HOSTS file. With the HOSTS file, your system can perform a lookup on a listing of systems that are known, even if your automated name service fails.

Windows networks use the Windows Internet Name Service (WINS) to enumerate systems using the NetBIOS protocol. This system can provide high performance on Windows networks and is commonly used.

DNS can be set up to run on a LAN and provide a name service for systems in a workgroup or, more frequently, a domain. DNS uses resource records to point to resources and describe their properties. Queries against the underlying DNS database provide a means to find network resources.

Directory services extend the idea of name servers to store information on many other aspects of network objects. Most directory services are based on Lightweight Directory Access Protocol (LDAP), which is based on the even more complex X.500 Directory Service. LDAP is the basis for the directory services used by network operating systems.

HOSTS Files

The first system that was used to perform name resolution on TCP/IP networks was the HOSTS file, and the first HOSTS file was stored on ARPAnet on a computer at Stanford Research Institute (SRI). The HOSTS file is a text file that lists the IP address in one column and the related friendly name of the host (computer system) in the second column. The system provides a lookup based on this simple database. The HOSTS file is largely of historical interest, but has some utility because it is searched in any name resolution before your DNS servers are queried. If an entry is found in the HOSTS file, then that entry is used as the definitive response for resolution.

Every computer operating system still creates a HOSTS file, and this file is checked during name resolution. Because the file must be manually maintained, most people tend to ignore it, relying on automated services such as DNS. In a network of any size, changing the entries in a HOSTS file on every computer is a daunting task. Even on a small network, if dynamic addressing is used for address assignment (as is the case for DHCP), then that severely limits the use of the HOSTS file. However, because the HOSTS file can be accessed by the local system administrator, there are still some uses for the HOSTS file that you might want to consider.

Table 19.1 lists the location of the HOSTS file in various networked operating systems.

TABLE 19.1

HOSTS Files

Operating System	Location	Notes
Linux/UNIX	/ETC/HOSTS	
Mac OS X	/PRIVATE/ETC/HOSTS	
Mac OS 9 and earlier	System Folder: Preferences	In some versions, the HOSTS file is located in the System folder
OS/2	"Bootdrive":\MPTN\ ETC\HOSTS	
Windows NT – Vista	%SystemRoot%\ SYSTEM32\DRIVERS\ ETC\HOSTS	The location of the file is controlled by the Registry key \HKEY_LOCAL_MACHINE\SYSTEM\ CurrentControlSet\Services\Tcpip\ Parameters\DataBasePath
Windows ME/98/95	%WinDir%\HOSTS	

You can view the current contents of your HOSTS file by opening the file in a text editor, terminal window, or command prompt.

In Windows, you can open and view the HOSTS file by doing the following:

1. Click Start ➪ Run, or press Windows+R.

2. Type **%SystemRoot%\SYSTEM32\DRIVERS\ETC**, and then press Enter.

3. Double-click the HOSTS file icon in Windows Explorer. The Open With dialog box appears.

4. In the Open With dialog box, select Notepad as the application, and then click OK. Figure 19.1 shows the HOSTS file in its default state.

The Windows Vista 64 HOSTS file in its default state

5. Make any changes you require to the file.

6. Click File ➪ Save As, and save the file as "HOSTS" including the quotation marks in the name. The quotation marks tell Windows to save the file without a file extension.

If you recall from Chapter 7, the addresses 127.0.0.1 and ::1 are reserved for the loopback adapter for IP version 4 and IP version 6, respectively. You add entries to the list by creating a new line, entering the address, and then adding one or more spaces followed by the system name. Here are some examples:

192.168.3.180 Maine # Carol's workstation
192.168.3.183 Duet # Allie's workstation
This is a comment, both entries above are local systems
64.233.169.104 www.Google.com
    . . .

You might initially want to add your common Web sites to your HOSTS files, and doing so will result in a small saving of time. However, the administrative overhead isn't worth the bother.

The HOSTS file is useful for blocking sites. If you want to block an outside system from getting a response from your system, you can assign that system to your loopback adapter. This technique can be applied to ad sites, spyware and malware locations, X-rated sites, and so on. For example, to block GoogleAnalytics.com, you would add the following line to your HOSTS file:

```
127.0.0.1 www.googleanalytics.com
```

The HOSTS file does not allow you to enter multiple sites by using wildcard symbols in the name or address, nor does it allow you to block individual directories. Only the top-level domain name is supported.

Alternatively, you can direct ad services such as ad.Doubleclick.net to an invalid IP address: 0.0.0.0 is a common choice, as it is the default assignment when a DHCP client fails to initialize properly and can't obtain a proper IP assignment. You can also assign the blocked site to an address that has no host on your internal network and reserve that address to always be unassigned. This type of blocking is actually a form of redirection. Redirection can be used to provide an alternative location for testing network software; however, malicious Web sites sometimes use this technique to hijack a computer.

You can imagine that a HOSTS file that blocks known bad sites would be a good idea, but that compiling the list of sites and maintaining that list would be a Herculean task. There are alternatives to this approach that you can try, and some work better than others. One approach is to download and use HOSTS files that are created by others, often communities of people who collaborate to create and maintain extensive HOSTS files.

I am not a big fan of using HOSTS files for anything other than enumerating local systems on my small network. Instead, I tend to rely on a collection of tools to block sites, including anti-virus and anti-spyware tools, and one tool in particular, SpywareBlaster from Javacool Software (see Figure 19.2), which blocks sites using blacklists. SpywareBlaster is non-resident in memory and has a low overhead when Internet Explorer or Mozilla Firefox makes a name resolution request. Within Firefox, I install the Adblock Plus extension, which also uses a blacklist to block incoming ads; I also use the NoScript extension to defeat executing scripts.

Another layer of protection is to enable the trusted zones feature found in Web browsers. I don't tend to use this feature, but it is particularly valuable on corporate networks.

SpywareBlaster employs a blacklist that you subscribe to in order to block unwanted Internet sites and content.

Address Resolution Protocol

The utility of the HOSTS file is limited by the requirement that it be manually updated. In order to automate the process of name resolution, the Address Resolution Protocol, or ARP, was developed. ARP creates a table of IP addresses and their associated physical addresses. An ARP table is dynamically maintained and then is stored in memory in an ARP cache. Dynamic entries in the ARP table are timed out, based on the ARP cache timeout setting, while static entries are maintained in the cache without timeout if the ARP cache table is operating correctly.

The ARP table consists of rows for each device that is registered:

- IP Address
- Physical Address
- IF Index (physical port or interface)
- Type of entry: 3 for dynamic; 4 for static; 2 for an invalid entry; and 1 for no assignment

ARP is encapsulated into the Data Link Layer Protocol, which means that ARP cannot be routed; it is useful for the local subnet only.

ARP requests

When the ARP cache is queried, it performs a lookup for the IP address, and when it locates a match, it returns the physical address. If no match is found, then ARP sends out a broadcast message called an ARP request to all of the devices on the network. The ARP request contains the IP address, and when the correct device detects the request, it returns a response with its physical address. The ARP table is then updated to include this information.

The ARP request and response take the following forms:

- **Hardware Type:** 1 for Ethernet; 3 for X.25; 6 for IEEE 802.X; 18 for Fibre Channel; and so on.

- **Protocol Type:** 2048 for Internet Protocol (IP); 2053 for X.25 Level 3; 32823 for AppleTalk; and so on.

- **Hardware Address Length/Protocol Address Length:** Ethernet has a hardware value of 4 bytes; IP also has a protocol length of 4 bytes.

- **Operation Code:** The Operation Code, or Opcode, is 1 for an ARP request and 2 for an ARP reply.

- **Sender Hardware Address**

- **Sender IP Address**

- **Recipient Hardware Address**

- **Recipient IP Address**

Only the node in the network with the correct Recipient IP address can reply to an ARP request. When that node receives the request, it sequentially reads the information in the request to determine if it can reply using the hardware and protocols in the request and then sends a reply. Only the ARP cache tables that have an entry for the sender IP are updated by the new information from the reply. If an entry for this node already exists, then it is updated.

Reverse Address Resolution Protocol

There are instances when a device doesn't have an IP address and can't create an ARP request or reply to one. This happens on a thin client device connecting to a terminal server where the processing is done on the server; when the client boots up, there is no assigned IP address. It can also happen when a system loses its DHCP lease. For these systems, the only address that the system has is the MAC address (or physical address) or the network interface card (NIC). To solve this problem, the Reverse Address Resolution Protocol (RARP) was developed.

A RARP request originates from a RARP client and broadcasts the physical address of the client to the RARP server. RARP requests and RARP replies have the same format that you saw for ARP. The difference between them is how the values in the different fields are entered.

Although RARP can be configured so that the reply must come from a RARP server with a particular IP address, most of the time the system accepts an answer from the first reply from any RARP server that can respond. The RARP reply is not a broadcast but is sent directly to the RARP client.

There are usually multiple RARP servers on a network because if the RARP server fails, RARP clients that start up will continue to broadcast RARP requests until a reply is received. If there are enough RARP clients sending out broadcasts, it can negatively impact network availability, a situation referred to as a *RARP storm*. A RARP failure renders a client inoperable as that client cannot start up.

RARP servers store a lookup table of IP addresses for specific nodes on the network. Each record in the table is keyed by a unique identifier specific to the RARP client. It is that unique identifier that must be sent to the RARP server to generate the RARP reply. Because a thin client cannot store an identifier (they can't be counted on to have storage), the protocol reads some other hardware-specific parameter.

Viewing the ARP cache

Most versions of TCP/IP use the ARP command. This allows you to view the ARP cache from your workstation in Linux, UNIX, Macintosh, and any recent version of Windows. The ARP command takes several switches or parameters that modify its output, and so you want to be sure that you check the help system to determine the correct version of the command to use.

You can view the entire contents of the ARP cache using the -a (All) switch in most implementations. You can specify the IP address of a system's ARP cache, which allows you to view the contents of the ARP server. Because the records contain hardware identification, ARP is a valuable tool for resolving duplicate IP addresses. Otherwise, ARP tends to be rarely used now. Figure 19.3 shows the results of an ARP request for the local system cache on a Windows system. The output lists the different network interfaces, both physical and virtual, because, as you learned in Chapter 7, a network interface behaves as logically as if it is a separate network device.

FIGURE 19.3

A reply to an ARP -a command discloses the local ARP cache.

Network Basic Input/Output System

NetBIOS is a Session layer (Layer 5) service for PCs that exposes a network application programming interface (API) that allows older applications to communicate with one another over a local area network (LAN). The acronym stands for Network Basic Input/Output System. NetBIOS was an early PC protocol, developed by a company called Sytek for the IBM PC and introduced in 1983. It became an industry standard for personal computers, even though it was originally limited to enumerating only 80 systems.

Until Microsoft fully adopted DNS name resolution, NetBIOS was the primary method for name resolution on Windows networks. NetBIOS is required by many legacy applications on Windows networks and is also required when the NetBEUI protocol is in use. NetBEUI is an extended version of NetBIOS that allows the use of frames. Note that NetBIOS/NetBEUI is a non-routable protocol that is best used on a LAN, and NetBEUI is a newer and higher-performance version of this standard.

NetBIOS traffic is carried in a transport protocol such as TCP/IP (NetBIOS over TCP or NBT, IPX/SPX [Novell Netware's legacy native format], or IEEE 802.2 [NBF]; all of these are Layer 2 Data Layer protocols). The 802.2 protocol defines Logical Link Control (LLC) software.

NetBIOS names can be different from the names assigned to a system in TCP/IP; they are limited to 15 characters and can't include spaces or the following characters:

    | ; " * ? / \

When you install Windows, the name that you enter for the system is a NetBIOS name. That name can be reassigned in the Computer Properties Computer Name tab. In most instances, the hostname used by DNS is created by prefixing the NetBIOS name to the Primary DNS Suffix. Thus, if the NetBIOS name is MyComputer and the Primary DNS Suffix is MyCompany.com, then the hostname used by DNS would be MyComputer.MyCompany.com.

NetBIOS name resolution is being deprecated in favor of DNS name resolution; Microsoft will not support NetBIOS name resolution on IP version 6 networks.

NetBIOS names are resolved through the use of broadcasts, which works well on small networks, or using a WINS Server, which provides NetBIOS name resolution on larger networks. WINS is described more fully in the next section. Depending upon how you configure the system, resolution can be B (broadcast only), P (peer or WINS only), M (mixed type, broadcast, then WINS), or H (hybrid, WINS, then broadcast).

The NetBIOS service does three things: it registers and resolves names, manages a Session service that is used during a connection, and sends datagrams (packets sent on a non-reliable network) that don't require a named connection.

Windows also uses a lookup file for NetBIOS name resolution that operates similarly to the HOSTS file that you saw in the previous section, called the LMHOSTS file. In Vista, this file is found at C:\WINDOWS\SYSTEM32\DRIVERS\ETC and the file takes a .sam file extension. It can be opened with the Notepad text editor, and is shown in Figure 19.4.

FIGURE 19.4

The LMHOSTS file provides a lookup for NetBIOS, and takes precedence over a WINS Server lookup.

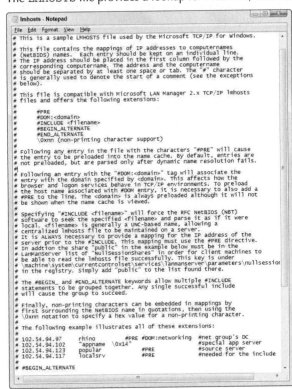

Windows Internet Name Service

Windows Internet Name Service, or WINS, is a Microsoft server technology for NetBIOS name resolution. WINS translates network addresses into NetBIOS names, just as DNS translates TCP/IP addresses into fully qualified domain names (FQDN). DNS is described in detail in the next section.

WINS is implemented as a database on a Windows server with a management interface. When a WINS client starts up, it sends a name registration request to the WINS server, and the name and associated address are registered as a record in the database. If another client needs to communicate with that first client, it sends a WINS query with the name of the first client to the server, which then responds to the request by sending the first client's IP address.

In large networks, WINS servers lower the amount of overhead in NetBIOS name resolution by providing a more efficient mechanism than broadcast queries. WINS is usually employed in large organizations as multiple servers and includes a replication service for propagating changes.

The Windows Computer Browser Service that populates the Network folder in Windows can use WINS to compose browse lists, and while NetBIOS is not routable, sending the browse lists can be routable.

WINS and DNS name resolution services can operate concurrently on the same network without conflicting with one another. Both store names in individual namespaces; DNS uses a hierarchical structure while WINS uses a flat structure. The WINS service is unaffected by the use of dynamic addressing in DNS using the DHCP service. WINS is important for networks that still contain Windows 2000, XP, or Windows Server 2003 clients. On networks that use both NetBIOS names and domain names, it is required that WINS and DNS services be available.

Domain Name System

The Domain Name System, or DNS, is the system used to translate IP addresses into FQDN or friendly names. It is the one service used on the Internet and is now used on nearly all TCP/IP LANs. DNS also stores information about mail servers, and eventually the system could be expanded to include all manner of information, such as radio-frequency identification (RFID) tags.

DNS is the result of a set of RFCs that resulted in the development of the first DNS implementation in 1983. The most widely used version of DNS software in use today on the Internet is the one that was written for UNIX that appeared in 1984 from the University of California at Berkeley, and has been reworked and expanded over the years. This version of DNS software, named the Berkeley Internet Name Domain, or BIND, is now open source software that has been heavily tested and refined. BIND appeared on Microsoft Windows with the release of Windows NT. BIND is maintained by the Internet Systems Consortium (www.isc.org/products/BIND/).

DNS works by storing a record in a database on a nameserver that is responsible for the translation of a particular domain. The top-level nameservers on the Internet are the root servers for the domains, .com, .net, .gov, .edu, .us, .uk, .ch, and so forth, which are now administered by ICANN. These top-level nameservers distribute their content through replication to secondary DNS servers in different parts of the world in order to improve performance and fault tolerance in the DNS system.

Note

Top-level domains (TLDs) are managed by ICANN, the non-profit Internet Corporation for Assigned Names and Numbers (www.icann.org) located in Marina del Rey, California.

You are probably familiar with basic domain name structure. The top-level domain (.com) is separated from the second-level domain (mydomain) by a dot, as in mydomain.com, which is sometimes referred to as an octet. Domains become further divided up based on the services they provide, so that www.mydomain.com would be one subdomain and ftp.mydomain.com would be another. It's important to note that mydomain.com and www.mydomain.com are not equivalent representations and that the latter is a subset of the former, but both of these addresses can be a hostname. The DNS specification allows for up to 127 sublevels, and up to 63 different octets.

DNS requests

When you initiate a DNS request for a Web page from a particular Web site, the request doesn't go to either the primary or secondary nameserver for that domain. Instead, the request proceeds level by level, attempting to satisfy the request from the nearest possible DNS source. The request goes to your local system to see if the name is located in your DNS cache, and if so, it returns the result. The local DNS cache doesn't normally store many records. Not all operating systems turn on a local DNS cache, and so you may need to install a package on a Linux distribution to enable this feature.

In Windows, you can see the contents of your local cache with the following command: IPCONFIG /DISPLAYDNS. Figure 19.5 shows an example of the output from a Windows Vista 64 system. The output of this command lists the name of the record in the domain, record types, time to live (TTL), and the address of the record in the final line. If you want to empty the contents of the local cache, then you can use the IPCONFIG /FLUSHDNS command.

FIGURE 19.5

To view the current contents of your local DNS cache in Windows, use the IPCONFIG /DISPLAYDNS command.

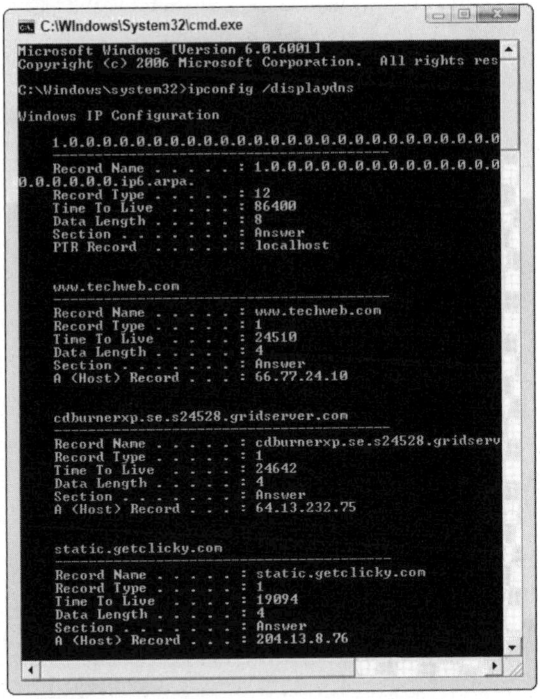

The local DNS cache doesn't store many records (depending upon how you configure it), and so if the record you need isn't in the cache or has run out of time to live, then the request is passed on to your local DNS server. If you are using DNS on a large network, and local DNS lookup is required, then your network is probably running its own DNS service. If you have a small network and use DNS for Internet name resolution, then the request is forwarded to the DNS servers that you have configured in your network interface's TCP/IP Properties dialog box, or the ones that are automatically assigned for you if you designated that option.

Many firewalls and Internet appliances come with DNS servers, and so using that as the primary DNS server for your connection is usually faster than waiting for a response from a DNS on the Internet. Most people assume that DNS requires that they enter the address for the DNS server for their Internet service provider (ISP) into their TCP/IP properties. However, that is not the case. You can use any highly available DNS server for this purpose.

Assuming your DNS request can't be satisfied by your local cache or by a DNS service on your LAN, the request is forwarded to a DNS server outside of your LAN. It arrives at the DNS server that you specified outside your LAN, or if you didn't specify one, at the DNS server of your ISP. That DNS server attempts to fetch the record relating the name you want the address of from its cache. If it doesn't find the record, it then queries the authoritative nameserver for the domain you are requesting. Eventually, the request may end up at a root nameserver, but that is very rare. The replication feature of DNS populates the vast majority of the addresses out to secondary servers. If you've ever wondered why changing an ISP for your domain takes 24 to 36 hours to take effect, this replication process is the reason.

DNS is a client-server architecture, and the client software is called a *resolver*. When a client issues a DNS query, it can be one of two types: either a recursive query or a non-recursive query. In a recursive query, the more commonly issued of the two types, the DNS server must return an answer within the time period allowed by the Time to Live parameter, even if the answer is a DNS error. In a non-recursive query, the DNS server can provide a partial answer or an error. The resolver may be configured to use either type of query, but it will iteratively move up the DNS domain structure until it can complete the entire DNS name.

Consider a request for an address for a hostname such as www.mydomain.com. The DNS query is made and sent to the root nameserver. The root nameserver doesn't contain the record, and so a response is sent to a software module called a DNS recurser with an address for the next nameserver in the chain. The recurser sends the request to the second nameserver at a lower level, which either has the record or sends a response back to the DNS recurser with the next nameserver in the sequence. The process continues iteratively until the IP address is returned.

When a successful query returns a result, the resource record (RR) for that response is stored in the cache, and the number of records retained is a function of both the cache size and the records' time to live. Not all queries are forward looking; that is, the query starts with an FQDN and the result returns an IP address. Some DNS queries are reverse queries; they try to match an IP address to an FQDN. Reverse queries are supported by third-party software.

In practice, the root nameservers and many of the upper-level DNS servers are cached at various places and almost never service DNS requests directly.

DNS is not without its defects. One problem that you can encounter when you register a DNS record that points to a nameserver and when you query that nameserver is that it points back to the original nameserver. This creates a circular dependency that cannot be resolved, and so nameservers are provided with a record that points to the previous nameserver in the chain so that circular dependencies can be broken.

DNS topology

DNS is a hierarchical namespace, which means that it is an inverted tree structure similar to a drive's file system. The top-level node in the namespace is occupied by the authoritative nameserver or the primary or root nameserver. That nameserver contains what are called *resource records*, which link that nameserver to other nameservers that contain the resource records of other nameservers as the tree fans out.

Each subsequent branch in the tree is organized into what are called *zones of authority*, with all connected nodes (DNS servers) referring to the top of that branch as their authoritative nameserver. In the domain MyCompany.com, a zone might be composed of a server at www. MyCompany.com, which is given responsibility for the zone beneath it. In DNS parlance, the domain is indicated by a record referred to as the *Start of Authority*, or SOA, and that record is then associated with the domain controller.

If the primary DNS server in the subdomain is MyDNSServer, then its address is MyDNSServer. MyCompany.com. Because the authority has been delegated to www.MyCompany.com, that DNS server becomes the primary DNS server for the zone MyCompany.com, the owner of the server is root@MyDNSServer.MyCompany.com, and the address shown in the SOA record is root. MyDNSServer.MyCompany.com.

Figure 19.6 shows a representation of the DNS namespace.

In Figure 19.6 the top zone exists as the root DNS server. That server might be the root .COM, . GOV, .EDU or some other root server. As the tree subdivides, DNS delegates the authority to respond to DNS queries to a DNS zone server, and that server services all DNS requests for that zone and if necessary for the zones beneath it. Each level DNS zone server delegates the DNS authority to the subzones beneath it so that authority is passed from the top-level DNS server to servers at levels below. The goal of the DNS hierarchy is to push DNS requests down to the lowest possible level of the tree.

FIGURE 19.6

A representation of the DNS namespace

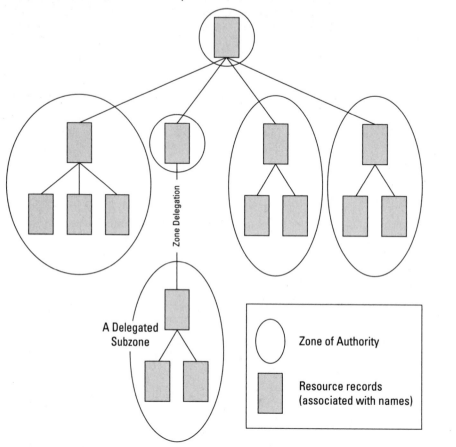

Zone Delegation

A Delegated
Subzone

Zone of Authority

Resource records
(associated with names)

Resource records

DNS is implemented as a database system that can be managed either through a set of commands in the command-line interface (CLI) or through the use of a graphical user interface (GUI) management utility. The system allows for secondary DNS servers, as well as replication schemes.

In Windows Server 2008, for example, DNS is a role that you can install on the server. For security reasons, Windows does not allow DNS to be installed on a domain controller (although it can be run on a Read-only Domain Controller [RODC]), but the DNS role can coexist with many other server roles. In a large domain, DNS activity is one of the more demanding roles that a server can engage in. It's common to dedicate a server to DNS alone.

With DNS installed, Windows Server 2008 adds the DNS Manager to the list of utilities available from the Administrative Tools folder. The DNS Manager (like other Administrative Tools) is an MMC snap-in that opens in the Microsoft Management Console, which is a framework application that supports different queries to underlying databases. Figure 19.7 shows a sample domain in the DNS Manager. Notice that there are several different record types populating the Forward Lookup Zones node that is exposed in the figure.

FIGURE 19.7

The Windows Server 2008 DNS Manager

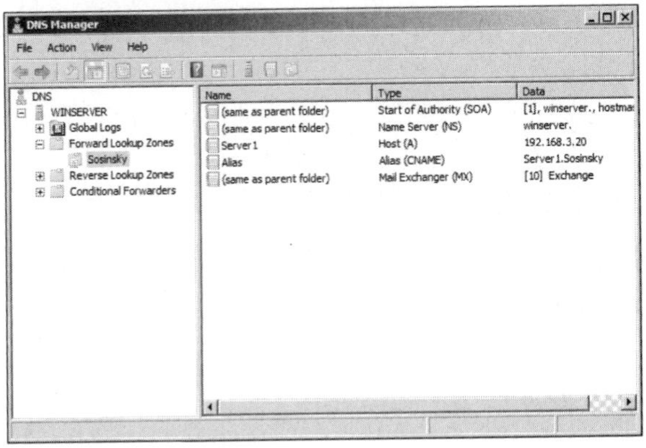

Figure 19.7 contains several common record types, with the exception of Pointer (PTR) records. that DNS uses to resolve queries. They include the following:

- **Start of Authority (SOA) record.** The SOA indicates which server is responsible for this particular zone.

- **Name Server (NS) record.** The NS record used by DNS displays the address of the nameserver for the domain. There must be one entry for any domain, and because nearly all domains employ multiple domain servers for failover and fault tolerance, it is more common to have two or more NS entries for redundancy.

- **Address (A) record.** An A record or host address should represent the bulk of the records in a DNS database for a network of any size. The A record provides the mapping of a hostname to an IP address.

- **Canonical Name (CNAME) records.** A CNAME record is an alias hostname. The alias points to the hostname indicated in the first field of the record. For the record shown in the figure, the CNAME record is the fourth record and the hostname is AliasName. CNAME records are sometimes used when you want to hide the real name of a system from a client.

- **Mail Exchange (MX) record.** An MX resource record is used to point to a mail server on the network.

- **Pointer (PTR) records.** PTR records (not shown in Figure 19.7) are used to map an IP address to the associated hostname. The reason you might want to establish PTR records is to support reverse lookups. For this reason, reverse lookups are sometimes called PTR queries. When you use PTR records, it is important to make sure that they are up to date and contain the same information for hosts that the Address or A records do.

This list details the most common DNS resource records in use for name resolution of hosts. However, as was mentioned earlier, DNS records can be created for a variety of resources. The Resource Record Type dialog box, shown in Figure 19.8, lists the different types of resource records that Windows Server 2008 currently supports. Refer to Table 19.2 for the listing of descriptions contained in the Resource Record Type dialog box.

FIGURE 19.8

The Resource Record Type dialog box

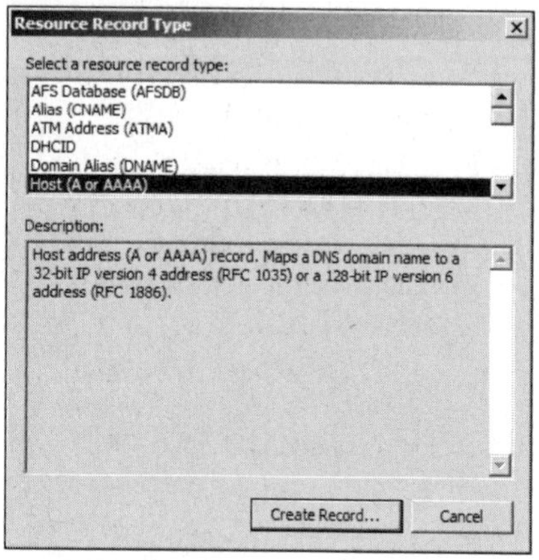

TABLE 19.2

Resource Record Types

Resource Record Type	Description
AFS Database (AFSDB)	Andrew File System Database (AFSDB) server record. Indicates the location of either of the following standard server subtypes: an AFS volume location (cell database) server or a Distributed Computing Environment (DCE) authenticated nameserver. Also supports other user-defined server subtypes that use the AFSDB resource record format. (RFC 1183)

Resource Record Type	Description
Alias (CNAME)	Alias record. Indicates an alternate or alias DNS domain name for a name already specified in other resource record types used in this zone. The record is also known as the canonical name (CNAME) record type. (RFC 1035)
ATM Address (ATMA)	ATM Address (ATMA) record. Maps a DNS domain name to an ATM address.
Host Address (A or AAAA)	Maps a DNS domain name to a 32-bit IP version 4 address (RFC 1035) or a 128-bit IP version 6 address. (RFC 1886)
Host Information (HINFO)	Host Information (HINFO) record. Indicates RFC 1700 reserved character string values for CPU and operating system types for mapping to specific DNS hostnames. This information is used by application protocols, such as FTP, that can use special procedures when communicating between computers of the same CPU and OS type. (RFC 1035)
Integrated Services Digital Network (ISDN)	Maps a DNS domain name to an ISDN telephone number. ISDN telephone numbers used with this record meet CCITT E.163/E.164 international telephone numbering standards. (RFC 1183)
Mail Exchanger (MX)	Provides message routing to a specified mail exchange host that is acting as a mail exchanger for a specified DNS domain name. MX records use a 16-bit integer to indicate host priority in message routing where multiple mail exchange hosts are specified. For each mail exchange host specified in this record type, a corresponding host address (A) type record is needed. (RFC 1035)
Mail Group (MG)	Adds domain mailboxes, each specified by a mailbox (MB) record in the current zone, as members of a domain mailing group that is identified by name in this record. (RFC 1035)
Mailbox (MB)	Maps a specified domain mailbox name to a host that hosts this mailbox. (RFC 1035)
Mailbox Information (MINFO)	Specifies a domain mailbox name to contact. This contact maintains a mail list or mailbox specified in this record. Also specifies a mailbox for receiving error messages related to the mailing list or mailbox specified in this record. (RFC 1035)
Next (NXT)	NXT resource records indicate the nonexistence of a name in a zone by creating a chain of all of the literal owner names in that zone. They also indicate what resource record types are present for an existing name.
Pointer (PTR)	Points to a location in the domain name space. PTR records are typically used in special domains to perform reverse lookups of address-to-name mappings. Each record provides simple data that points to some other location in the domain name space (usually a forward lookup zone). Where PTR records are used, no additional section processing is implied or caused by their presence. (RFC 1035)
Public Key (KEY)	Public key (KEY) record. Stores a public key that is related to a DNS domain name. This public key can be of a zone, a user, or a host or other end entity. A KEY resource record is authenticated by a SIG resource record. A zone level key must sign KEYs.

continued

TABLE 19.2	(continued)
Resource Record Type	**Description**
Rename Mailbox (MR)	Specifies the domain mailbox name for a responsible person and maps this name to a domain name for which text (TXT) resource records exist. Where RP records are used in DNS queries, subsequent queries can be needed to retrieve the text (TXT) record information mapped using the RP record type. (RFC 1183)
Responsible Person (RP)	Responsible Person (RP) record. Specifies the domain mailbox name for a responsible person and maps this name to a domain name for which text (TXT) resource records exist. Where RP records are used in DNS queries, subsequent queries may be needed to retrieve the text (TXT) record information mapped using the RP record type. (RFC 1183)
Route Through (RT)	Route Through (RT) record. Provides an intermediate-route-through binding for internal hosts that do not have their own direct wide area network (WAN) address. This record uses the same data format as the MX record type to indicate two required fields: a 16-bit integer that represents preference for each intermediate route and the DNS domain name for the route-through host as it appears elsewhere in an A, X25, or ISDN record for the zone. (RFC 1183)
Service Location (SRV)	Service Location (SRV) record. Allows administrators to use several servers for a single DNS domain, to easily move a TCP/IP service from one host to another host with administration, and to designate some service provider hosts as primary servers for a service and other hosts as backups. DNS clients that use an SRV-type query ask for a specific TCP/IP service and protocol mapped to a specific DNS domain, and receive the names of any available servers. (RFC 2052)
Signature (SIG)	Cryptographic signature (SIG) record. Authenticates a resource record set of a particular type, class, and name, and binds it to a time interval and the signer's DNS domain name. This authentication and binding is done using cryptographic techniques and the signer's private key. The signer is frequently the owner of the zone from which the resource record originated.
Text (TXT)	Text (TXT) record. Holds a string of characters that serves as descriptive text to be associated with a specific DNS domain name. The semantics of the actual descriptive text used as data with this record type depends on the DNS domain where these records are located. (RFC 1035)
Well-Known Services (WKS)	Well-Known Services (WKS) record. Describes the well-known TCP/IP services supported by a particular protocol on a particular IP address. WKS records provide TCP and UDP availability information for TCP/IP servers. If a server supports both TCP and UDP for a well-known service or if the server has multiple IP addresses that support a service, then multiple WKS records are used. (RFC 1035)
X.25	X.25 (X25) record. Maps a DNS domain name to a public switched data network (PSDN) address, such as X.121 addresses, which are typically used to identify each point of service located on a public X.25 network. (RFC 1183)

Source: Microsoft Corporation, Windows Server 2008 Record Resource Types dialog box.

Name Resolution versus Directory Services

Directory services are products that for the most part conform to the X.500 LDAP standard. Examples of directory services are Windows Active Directory, the Network Information Service used by Solaris and other UNIX/Linux implementations, Novell's excellent eDirectory, among others. The primary function of a directory service is to securely contain identification and properties for network objects. Network objects include systems, hostnames, and asset information; but they also include objects such as user and group accounts, operating system-specific domain organizational structures, application-specific data, and almost anything else that the operating system vendor and third-party vendors who extend these directories want to include in them. Directory services are extensible, and more importantly, they are secured and protected. Although name resolution is one of the main features of a directory service, it isn't the only feature and it isn't really the primary feature of these systems.

Name resolution services have a more limited role. They are focused on a mapping function and they have a severely limited ability to be extended. You can see the effect of this difference on the development of DNS. While DNS is the means used for system identification on the Internet and is nearly universally used for system identification on intranets and LANs, DNS isn't used for many of the record types that you saw in the previous section. The use of directory services suppresses the use of DNS in networked operating systems for other purposes.

Summary

In this chapter, the need to map or translate friendly names to network addresses, and vice versa, was explained. Over the years, many systems have been developed to address this need.

The first system was the HOSTS file, which, although it still exists, sees very limited use. The ARP protocol was another early attempt and is still in use. The NetBIOS protocol provides a mechanism to allow Windows computers to be enumerated on a LAN. NetBIOS servers are called WINS servers, and most large Windows networks install WINS as a naming service because of its performance advantages.

The Domain Name System, or DNS, is the name resolution service that associates IP addresses with friendly names for the Internet. In this chapter, you learned how DNS networks are constructed and how queries for name resolution are conducted against the service. DNS can also be used on LANs, and DNS is valuable for providing a unified name resolution service that can be used on TCP/IP networks.

This chapter also described the difference between name resolution services, which are essentially mapping or translation services, and directory services. Directory services are secured databases that store all kinds of information on network objects and are extensible. Modern directory services are primarily based on the X.500 LDAP protocol.

In the next chapter, you learn about the different classes of Network Operating Systems (NOS), their common characteristics and features, as well as the factors that differentiate them.

Part V

Applications and Services

Network Operating Systems

A network operating system, or NOS, is one that is optimized to provide network services. The development of network operating systems has driven the development of computer networks, and vice versa. Both are intimately related.

Each NOS must provide operating system support for hardware, run protocols and services, and provide those services or applications for client systems. Beyond these basic services, an NOS may offer administration and management utilities, naming and directory services, file and print services, Web services, backup, security, and network routing, as well as serve as the operating system upon which network applications can be installed and run.

An NOS that has a broad range of capabilities is typically referred to as a *platform*. Examples of platforms are UNIX, Linux, and Microsoft Windows. Some NOSs are optimized for special purposes; an example of this kind of NOS is Cisco's IOS operating system that runs on its routers and switches.

In this chapter, different NOSs are described, and several of the more commonly found and popular NOSs are described in some detail, particularly those that are deployed on server hardware and in the client/server or n-tiered architectural model.

UNIX is the prototype NOS and has had the greatest impact on all of the other NOSs that have come after it. A brief history of UNIX and its design goals is presented in this chapter. Important features of UNIX networking, such as the POSIX, SUS, sockets, and STREAMS, are described.

The family of UNIX-like operating systems described as Linux is also considered in detail, as is the Sun Microsystems Solaris operating system. Also described is Novell NetWare and its contribution to NOS development, including Novell's latest version called the Open Enterprise Server (OES).

The last NOS to be considered is Microsoft Windows Server. Each of these three NOSs is a leader in some aspect of server deployment. In this chapter, you learn about some of their strengths and weaknesses.

What Is a Network Operating System

A network operating system (NOS) is an operating system that is optimized to provide network services to other systems on a network. Nearly every commercial computer operating system built over the last 50 years has had some networking component.

True distributed network operating systems became necessary with the introduction of the first generation of personal clients. Early examples of network operating systems included products like Artisoft's LANtastic (now at version 8.0; http://pcmicro.com/lantastic/), which was described as a peer-to-peer NOS. LANtastic could network MS-DOS, Novell NetWare, and OS/2 clients, providing shared access to applications, files, printers, and optical drives. LANtastic was a very successful product prior to the introduction of Windows 95, but as operating system vendors began to focus on networks of personal computers, the functionality in native PC operating systems eclipsed the need for products like LANtastic.

In the early computer networking market, Novell's NetWare was the market leader on PC hardware, and was the first commercially successful NOS. Novell based NetWare on the Xerox Network Services stack, emphasizing the concept of file sharing. The first version of NetWare appeared in 1983, and achieved early market success based on IBM's validation of the product in 1984 at the time that IBM introduced the IBM PC. Early versions of NetWare ran on MS-DOS systems as Terminate and Stay Resident (TSR) programs, and could map network volumes to local drive letters. NetWare exhibited the full range of a true NOS; it could restrict access based on a user login, and be a print server. The Apple Macintosh, also released in 1984, had its own built-in networking capability, AppleTalk, which Apple continued to develop up until the dominance of TCP/IP networks.

By the time Novell released NetWare version 4 in 1995, the company was a major force in the personal computer industry. Microsoft's release of first Windows for Workgroups in 1993 and then Windows 95 did little to dent Novell's influence. It was only with the release of Windows NT that Microsoft was able to catch up.

Novell's IPX network protocol was widely used, but IPX has been deprecated in favor of TCP/IP. In fact, if you can point to one factor that shook out the computer NOS market and separated the current products from the early NOS, it was the rise of the Internet.

Protocols and services

Today, an NOS can have a broad set of capabilities. Every NOS must perform the following three functions:

- Provide operating system support for the hardware that it runs on

- Run different network protocols and services such as addressing

- Run server applications that client systems — or for peer-to-peer networks, other peers — can access

An NOS may also provide some of the following network services:

- Network administration and management.

- Names and other directory services.

- Shared file and print, Web services, backup, or replication services.

- Security services, access control, and logins. A network operating system may function as a "Triple A" server, offering authentication, authorization, and accounting.

- Traffic routing on the networks and the control of access to ports.

- Participation in high availability options such as fail-over, clustering, or run on fault tolerant (FT) or highly redundant systems.

- Scalability features such as load balancing or support systems with large processor counts (either Symmetric Multiprocessor [SMP] or Non-Uniform Memory Access [NUMA]).

General versus Special-Purpose NOS

Some NOS, such as Microsoft Windows, Novell NetWare, Sun Solaris, various flavors of Linux, and so forth, either come with nearly all of the aforementioned protocols and services in the box or have readily available add-on components that enable them. Therefore, operating systems of this type are referred to as *platforms* or, less frequently, as general-purpose NOS. Not all NOS need to be so broadly defined.

An example of a specialized NOS is Cisco Systems' IOS (which originally stood for Internetwork Operating System). IOS runs on nearly all of Cisco's routers and switches using a proprietary operating system. By contrast, Juniper Networks' JUNOS software, which the company describes as a router operating system, runs atop an implementation of FreeBSD. Special-purpose operating systems become valuable when a market category becomes large enough that the functions the category requires need to be emphasized and optimized. So, while early Internet routers often were built on various forms of Linux and the SunOS, Cisco was able to turn out even more capable routers at lower costs by creating a specialized NOS, and created an extremely successful company by doing so.

The development of general-purpose NOS has followed a somewhat different path. For the most part, platform NOSs are deployed on server hardware or as virtual machines. The tendency over the last decade has been to develop NOSs of this type as unified projects so that both the server and the client operating systems are derived from the same code base. Microsoft started this type of development effort with Windows 2000, and Windows 2003/XP and Windows 2008/Vista have followed in this mold.

Many server operating systems are now essentially the same core system as their desktop clients. The differentiation between the two arises when additional features are added, some features turned off, and other features are limited in some way. For example, Microsoft imposes a ten-connection limit for clients accessing a Web server on a Windows workstation. If you want to explore this topic in some detail, you can read about how to convert Windows Server 2003 into a Windows XP workstation at www.msfn.org/win2k3/. The process adds DirectX, Themes, System Restore, Java, and a number of other services back into Windows Server 2003.

Several server distributions of Linux follow this same pattern, but this isn't a universal pattern. Sun, for example, makes no distinction between Solaris as a server or a desktop operating system.

The network operating systems in common use are shown in Table 20.1.

TABLE 20.1

Common Platform Network Operating Systems

NOS Name	Owner	Current Version	Runs On	
AIX	IBM	6.1	64-bit RISC systems	www-03.ibm.com/ systems/power/ software/aix/ index.html
BSD	FreeBSD Project, NetBSD, OpenBSD	7.1 4.0.1 4.4	Alpha, ARM, x86, IA64, MIPS, PPC, SPARC64, SunOS4, and Xbox	www.freebsd.org/ www.netbsd.org/ www.openbsd.org/
Digital Unix (TruUnix)	Hewlett-Packard (through acquisition)	5.1B-5	Alpha (ends 2012)	www.hp.com
HP-UX	Hewlett-Packard	UNIX System V Release 4	IA64, PA-RISC (ends 2012)	www.hp.com
IOS	Cisco Systems	12.4	Cisco routers and switches	www.cisco.com/ web/psa/products/ index.html?c= 268438303

NOS Name	Owner	Current Version	Runs On	
IRIX	Silicon Graphics	6.5.23	SGI systems, PowerPC processors	www.sgi.com/products/software/irix/
Mac OS X	Apple Computer	10.5	x86, PowerPC, and ARM v6	www.apple.com/macosx/
NetWare (superseded by OES)	Novell	6.5 SP7 (equivalent to OES 2)	x86	www.novell.com
Open Enterprise Server	Novell	OES 2 SP1	x86	www.novell.com/products/open enterpriseserver/
OpenVMS	Hewlett-Packard (through acquisition)	8.0 Itanium, 8.2 (maintenance)	Alpha, VAX, IA64 (Itanium)	www.hp.com
Red Hat Linux	Red Hat	5	x86, IA64	www.redhat.com/products/
SCO OpenServer 6	The SCO Group	6.0.0 MP3	x86	www.sco.com/products/openserver6/
Solaris	Sun Microsystems	10	SPARC, x86, IA64	sun.com/solaris/
Ubuntu	Canonical	8.10	x86, IA64	www.ubuntu.com
Windows	Microsoft	2008	x86, IA64	www.microsoft.com/windows
z/OS (formerly MVS)	IBM	1.10	IBM zSeries (MVS ran on System 360/390 mainframes)	www-03.ibm.com/systems/z/os/zos/index.html

NOS Systems and Software

In the previous sections, you've seen some of the general features of an NOS. There are literally hundreds of different types of NOS available on the market today; however, space precludes a complete description of all of the individual NOSs on the market. In the sections that follow, the most popular NOSs in use today are described in more detail, in particular:

- UNIX
- Linux
- Solaris
- Novell NetWare and Open Enterprise Server
- Windows Server

UNIX

UNIX is characterized as a multi-tasking, multi-user, time-sharing NOS. It was designed around a kernel that could be more easily ported to other machine architectures (processor families) than previous operating systems, and separated user functions from kernel operations. The guiding philosophy, now sometimes referred to as the "UNIX philosophy," was to make the NOS and its components both modular and reusable.

UNIX was developed at Bell Labs for AT&T in the late 1960s and for which Dennis Ritchie developed the C programming language in 1972. Originally available under license from AT&T, the UNIX trademark is now owned by The Open Group, and the name UNIX or Unix is used by operating systems that are compliant with the Single UNIX Specification (SUS) that is described in more detail later in this chapter. Examples of UNIX operating systems include AIX, HP-UX, Solaris, and other systems that are based on UNIX System V, or alternatively, the last AT&T release, called Seventh Edition UNIX, Version 7 Unix, or simply V7 Unix. Caldera Systems acquired the rights to V7 Unix and released it into the public domain in 2002. UNIX is considered to be the enterprise NOS standard against which other enterprise NOSs are compared.

Note

Is it UNIX or Unix? You see both variants of the name in common use. UNIX in all caps is a trademark of The Open Group, and the official name given to any version of Unix that is SUS compliant and licensed. As a general class of operating system, the mixed-case version of Unix is perfectly acceptable to my way of thinking.

Other operating systems derived from UNIX concepts, but not SUS compliant, are considered "UNIX-like" — the various distributions of Linux being a good example. The impact of UNIX on NOSs that came after it cannot be underestimated — that impact has been profound. You can get an idea of just how many NOSs are either UNIX or related to UNIX by examining the Levenez UNIX family tree (`www.levenez.com/unix`) shown in Figure 20.1.

UNIX became a standard because AT&T distributed UNIX and the C programming language widely. The availability of UNIX for government and military applications, as well as a very liberal policy for distribution of UNIX to universities, led UNIX to be ported to more system types than any other operating system. UNIX became known as an "open system," although initially the license fees for commercial ventures ensured that it was not open. Versions of the UNIX operating system were developed at universities, particularly at the University of California at Berkeley (where BSD UNIX was developed) and at the Carnegie-Mellon Institute in Pittsburgh (which developed the MACH kernel). As these open versions became the leading-edge versions of UNIX, they greatly influenced AT&T's decision to make UNIX more widely available.

FIGURE 20.1

The UNIX family tree

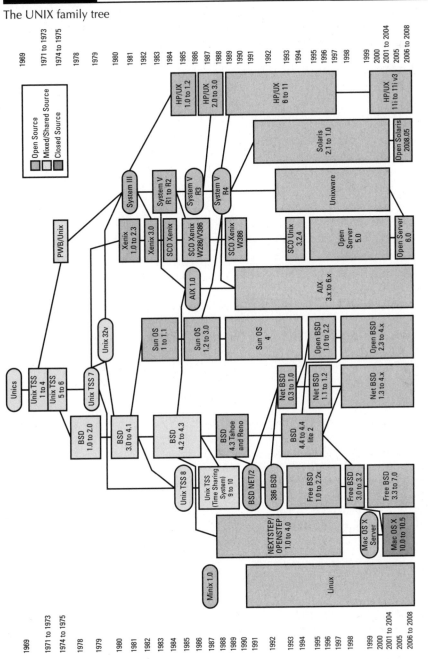

POSIX

The UNIX interface and standardization around the C language eventually led to a set of design guidelines and APIs that became an NOS model architecture. POSIX (www.pasc.org/) or Portable Operating System Interface is an Application Programming Interface (API) defined by the IEEE 1003 and ISO/IEC9945 standard. The X in POSIX arises from the IEEE-IX version of the standard. POSIX makes NOSs interoperable and therefore has been nearly universally adopted. Figure 20.2 shows some of the standard components in a POSIX reference architecture.

Familiar features of modern NOSs — including the hierarchical file system, stored plain text, the command line interpreter, inter-application or inter-process communications (IPC), concepts of shared memory, messaging and queues, semaphores, sockets, and others — were UNIX inventions, although they were not part of the original AT&T UNIX; they were added to later versions as it became necessary to support asynchronous I/O. The reliance on a system of storage, based on chunks of storage (bytes) rather than on a database record structure, also became an NOS standard.

FIGURE 20.2

The POSIX reference architecture

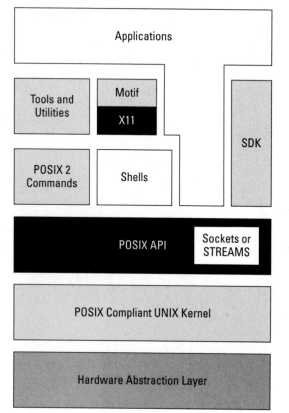

Perhaps the most important development from the standpoint of network services is that UNIX moved these services and the protocols that they required out of the operating system kernel, thus allowing developers to more readily adapt the operating system to rapidly changing networking advances. The adaptability of UNIX's networking is as responsible for its long-lasting impact as was the portability of the kernel.

STREAMS and sockets

STREAMS and sockets are the two methods that UNIX uses to instantiate a network interface, and so they play a central role in establishing network services.

A socket is an endpoint for a network connection. When the socket allows for bidirectional IP data flow, it is referred to as an *Internet socket*; when a socket uses other types of protocols, it is referred to as a *network socket*, or more simply, a socket. Internet sockets have certain properties such as the protocol in use; an assigned IP address, port, or service number; and (once the connection is made) the remote IP address and port. These characteristics give sockets a unique identity.

Network operating systems use the concept of a socket as the interface between an application process and the network stack, allowing data to flow between the two. Sockets are an interface between a system and network I/O. The development of socket-based architecture has played an important role in the evolution of modern NOSs, and has made it easier to develop consistent network driver models and have different NOSs interoperate with one another.

You can list the available sockets in UNIX and UNIX-like systems (such as Linux) by issuing the command `netstat -an`. An alternative switch, `netstat -b`, lists sockets that have been established by different applications. Figure 20.3 shows a partial output of the `netstat -an` command on Windows Vista.

Perhaps the best known of all of the network socket architectures is the Berkeley Sockets API that was originally introduced with BSD UNIX v 4.2. That API was an AT&T copyright until UC Berkeley released a version of UNIX in 1989 that was open for public adoption with license. Today, Berkeley Sockets is considered to be a standard model for network socket design.

STREAMS is an alternative to Berkeley Sockets. STREAMS appeared first in UNIX System V. STREAMS is the network architecture used in UNIX System V for I/O to allow device or special file systems to communicate through a device driver to peripheral devices using standard I/O system calls. STREAMS is modular in construction and allows drivers (which are modules) to be chained together into a STREAM. STREAMS requires more overhead than Sockets does, and in all of the operating systems that continue to use STREAMS, a Sockets API is also included. STREAMS was a required component in the original Single UNIX Specification, but in the current SUS v3, STREAMS is an optional component.

FIGURE 20.3

The `netstat -an` command allows you to view the status of network interfaces and sockets.

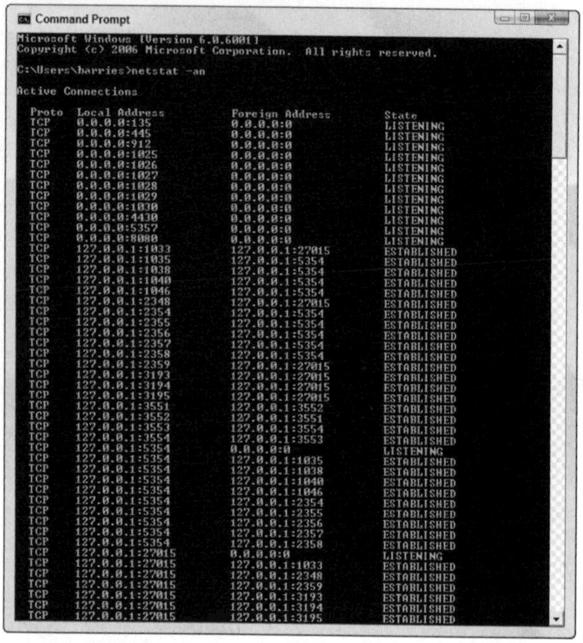

Single UNIX specification

When most people think of UNIX, they tend to think of the many different versions of UNIX that are based on AT&T's venerable network operating system. The following network operating systems are all UNIX variants:

- IBM AIX 5L V5.2

- HP-UX 11i v3

- Mac OS X Server 10.5 (Leopard)

- SCO UnixWare 7.1.3 and SCO OpenServer 5

- Sun Solaris 10

- DEC Tru64 UNIX V5.1A (now owned and supported by Hewlett-Packard)

- IBM z/OS 1.9

These variants are currently certified as complying with the Single UNIX Specification (SUS). Linux and various versions of BSD UNIX are considered to be "UNIX-like" operating systems and are non-conforming to the SUS standard.

Note

To learn more about SUS, you can read the SUS FAQ at http://opengroup.org/austin/papers/single_unix_faq. html.

The Single UNIX Specification is the result of an effort to standardize UNIX that was begun in the 1980s by the IEEE and the Open Group. Those efforts resulted in the POSIX.1 (from the acronym Portable Operating System Interface for unIX) standard that influenced the development of many NOSs in the 1980s and 1990s to set UNIX standards, which became known as the "UNIX wars" and led some of the leading UNIX vendors to form the Common Open Software Environment (COSE). COSE's most important achievement was the creation of the Common Desktop Environment (CDE), which blends the X11 environment with the OSF Motif user interface and toolkit.

From all of the aforementioned activity, the Austin Common Standards Revision Group (www. opengroup.org/austin/), or more simply the Austin Group, arose. SUS publishes a set of user and software interfaces that standardize programming for the POSIX shell, as well as a number of operating system utilities and services including file, terminal, and network services. All of the UNIX operating systems listed in the bulleted list are SUS compliant.

Linux

Linux is a UNIX-like operating system that uses the open source Linux kernel. It appears that Linux may be the most widely deployed Internet server currently in use, at least from the statistics that can be determined from Internet usage studies. Netcraft (www.netcraft.com/), an organization that tracks Web servers in current use on the Internet, reports that the various versions of Linux ran on half the Web servers, FreeBSD ran on 30 percent, and Windows Servers accounted for the remaining 20 percent. Other studies based on hardware sales that seek to measure the overall server market show Linux to have a market share around 15 percent.

Linux's penetration as a desktop operating system is much more limited, although the Ubuntu distribution appears to have captured a few percent of the desktop market. Linux has become popular in the emerging "netbook" market, appearing in systems such as the ASUS Eee and Acer Aspire One.

Versions of Linux run on systems from small, embedded devices up to supercomputers. Among the supported platforms are x86, SPARC, IA64, PowerPC, Motorola 68000, and IBM s390. Linux has broad support from the major computer equipment vendors: Dell, IBM, Hewlett-Packard, Sun Microsystems, and Nokia all sell systems that run the Linux operating system and support the open source development effort. Linux also represents nearly 88 percent of the most powerful supercomputer systems listed on the Top 500 Supercomputer Sites (www.top500.org/stats/list/32/ osfam), a statistic that surprises most people who first encounter it.

A number of major Internet sites are built using fleets of Linux systems, including four of the largest: Amazon, eBay, Google, and Yahoo!. A number of countries have made Linux their standard operating system for their government, including, most notably, some of the BRICK countries — Brazil, Russia, India, and China — as well as both Germany and France.

Distributions

There are currently perhaps 100 active distributions of Linux based on the Debian, Gentoo, RPM, or Slackware-based distribution. Among the best known of the Linux distributions are Linspire and Ubuntu (which are Debian-based versions), and Caldera Linux, Red Hat Linux, and SUSE Linux (which are based on RPM). The classes of Linux are organized around the following features:

- Debian Linux, which uses the .deb package format and ships with a broad range of software that desktop systems tend to prefer

- Gentoo Linux, which uses the Portage package system and is usually highly optimized for performance on smaller, less capable devices

- Fedora Core, which uses the RPM file format

- Red Hat Enterprise Linux, another version that uses the RPM file format and is optimized for the server market

Note

Wikipedia maintains a long list of Linux distributions with links on a jump page at http://en.wikipedia.org/wiki/ List_of_Linux_distributions

The first version of the Linux kernel was released by its developer Linus Torvalds in 1991. The current version of the kernel as of February 20, 2009 is version 2.6.28.8. Most of the additional utilities and libraries arose out of the GNU open source operating system, which was begun in 1983 by Richard Stallman and the Free Software Foundation at the Massachusetts Institute of Technology's Media Labs.

The GNU project is also responsible for the GNU General Public License (GPL), now at version 3.0 (www.gnu.org/licenses/gpl-3.0.txt), under which Linux is distributed. The term *copyleft* is sometimes applied to the GNU license. Copyleft requires that a program or other artistic work (such as Linux) be distributed free of charge, and that all modified and extended versions of the work also be distributed freely. Companies such as Red Hat and Novell that distribute commercial enterprise-class versions of Linux charge for their distributions, which does not conform to the GNU GPL. Those companies are charging for support, as well as their modifications. To conform to the GPL standards, companies selling commercial versions of Linux support open source versions of Linux that do conform.

LAMP

Linux tends to be deployed on commodity hardware and achieves large scale through horizontal scale out. Many Linux servers install what has come to be known as the LAMP software bundle. LAMP refers to the following components:

- Linux, as the operating system

- Apache, as the Web server

- MySQL, as the database server

- P, as one of the programming or scripting languages, PHP, Perl, or Python

Linux was designed using many of the design principles of UNIX that were described in the previous section. The Linux kernel is monolithic and contains process and memory management, drivers and I/O modules, device files, sockets, and the file system. Other functionality, such as the command interpreters (shells), utilities, and graphical user interfaces (GUIs), consists of user space functions. Linux is designed to comply with POSIX standards, and most distributions adopt many of the principles of SUS that you learned about in the previous section. An effort to standardize Linux is under way, known as the Linux Standard Base, which is described in the next section.

A wide variety of GUIs are available for Linux distributions, but most of these are based on the X Window System and the Motif interface guidelines. The most popular GUIs are KDE, GNOME, and Xfce, and many distributions allow you to install more than one GUI if you want. Higher-performance network servers tend to run without a GUI, relying on a Command Line Interface (CLI) and running in what is called "headless" mode — that is, without an attached monitor, keyboard, or mouse. Control of a headless server is performed over the network, often from a terminal session (graphical terminal emulator) or command prompt. Most UNIX distributions support headless mode because it provides a little more overhead for running processes. Microsoft Windows Server added a headless mode in version 2008.

Linux Standard Base

The Linux Standard Base (LSB) is a project managed by the Linux Foundation (www.linux foundation.org/) to standardize features of Linux so that different distributions will be more compatible with one another. As with SUS, described previously, LSB has a compliance certification. LSB specifies standard libraries, commands, utilities, file system components, print subsystem features, POSIX, and X Windows System extensions. LSB also specifies the nature of the RPM package format used to install Linux software. The last released version of LSB is version 3.2, released in 2008, that is submitted as ISO/IEC 23360.

Solaris

Sun Microsystems's Solaris operating system is the most commonly deployed UNIX network operating system in use today. Solaris was introduced in 1992 to replace the SunOS operating system, and to introduce an advanced network stack to support TCP/IP networking. Solaris exists in two versions: a version that runs on Sun's SPARC-based hardware systems and an x86 version that runs on the Intel standard architecture. Solaris has been positioned by Sun as one of the premier network operating systems for large enterprises, and as a preferred platform for storage network management.

The most recent version of Solaris is version 10 (SunOS 5.10). The operating system can be downloaded in either of its two architectures (SPARC x86 or IA64) from its Web site at http://sun.com/solaris/ and is free for testing and non-commercial uses. The Solaris installation allows for installation on either a server or workstation. You can install core network services alone, user services, developer services, or the entire package containing the complete network management and policy management utilities.

Although the original versions of Solaris were based on a proprietary code base, Sun has been transitioning Solaris to an industry-standard, open source model. The current version of Solaris now has the majority of its code base published as the open source version of Solaris, called OpenSolaris. Sun's commercial version of Solaris is certified as conforming to the Single UNIX Specification described in the previous section.

The original network stack for Solaris 1.x was based on a version of BSD. To improve Solaris' performance, Sun migrated the network stack in Solaris 2.x to the AT&T SVR4 architecture. Various versions of 2.x continued the transition toward the STREAMS network stack that has become the basis for networking functionality in UNIX System V. STREAMS is noted for both its modular nature and its message-passing capabilities between those modules. When you create a connection in the STREAMS architecture, there is a significant overhead, but for the long session times associated with protocols such as FTP or NFS, this overhead was not a problem.

However, as Sun moved its hardware base to more powerful multiprocessor systems, the fact that STREAM cannot easily be optimized for multiprocessor processing became a major issue. As packets are processed in a STREAM architecture, multithreading with more than one processor results in considerable context switching (kernel/user mode flips) that cannot be programmed away. By the late 1990s, Sun servers and workstations became a favorite platform both for routing and as application servers running Web server software. Internet protocols, particularly HTTP, are short-lived connections where the STREAM architecture is at a distinct disadvantage. Sun set about re-architecting its network stack with its development of Solaris 10.

Note
Solaris 2.0 to 2.6 corresponds to the SunOS version 5.0 to 5.6. Sun started numbering Solaris as whole integers starting with Solaris 7 (SunOS 5.7), with the latest version being Solaris 10 (SunOS 5.10), originally released on January 31, 2005. Solaris is the successor to the SunOS, but Sun has maintained the numbering scheme for both names.

The Solaris 10 operating system's network stack was rebuilt using what was called the "FireEngine" architecture, which merged all of the protocol layers into a single STREAM module with full multi-threading. This approach allows for a CPU synchronization that in turn allows for serial network queue abstractions ("squeue") and binds the squeue to a single processor. Solaris 10 replaces a message-passing architecture with one that uses a BSD function call-type interface.

Solaris 10 supports the NFS 4.0 file system and is architected to support network throughputs of up to 10 Gbits/s. Using a feature called Solaris Zones, multiple instances of the operating system can be run on the same hardware as virtual machines. Using the Grid Container technology, a Sun server can create a disk partition for individual users that gives those users the appearance that they are running their own operating system, essentially turning a Sun server into a terminal server.

Solaris can also attach to the ZFS (originally codenamed the Zettabyte File System), which has some unique enterprise features. ZFS supports very large volume sizes, comes with high storage capacities, and integrates both file system and volume management. In addition to built-in snapshots and cloning, ZFS introduced a data replication scheme called RAID-Z, with the entire technology taken as a whole having some very unique self-healing capabilities. Sun released ZFS into the public domain as open source software as part of the OpenSolaris project (www.opensolaris. org/os/community/zfs/).

Solaris ships with a utility called DTrace (Dynamic Tracing), which diagnoses network application performance and determines where existing bottlenecks are occurring. This information can be fed to the fault manager for remediation and optimization and/or reported to system administrators who can then run scripts on their servers to correct the network or system behavior. DTrace was the first of the OpenSolaris components to be open sourced as part of the OpenSolaris project. OpenSolaris (http://opensolaris.com/) is an open source version of the Solaris operating system.

Novell NetWare and Open Enterprise Server

Novell's NetWare has had an important position in the area of NOS development. For nearly a decade, NetWare was the preeminent NOS for PCs, and particularly for file and print services and heterogeneous networks containing many different types of clients. As Microsoft Windows Server and particularly Linux servers became more popular, NetWare as an NOS platform became less popular. Novell focused its development on network management tools such as ZenWorks, enterprise-class directory services such as eDirectory, and other products that continue to represent the state of the art in these various fields.

As a consequence of these market factors, Novell still retains leadership in these areas, but after continuing to develop NetWare through version 6.5 (first released in August 2003), the company has moved both its desktop and server offerings to Linux distributions. Netware 6.5 was superseded by the Open Enterprise Server (OES), which, at version 2 SP1, has the identical NetWare kernel. OES 1 appeared in March 2005, and OES 2 was released in October 2007.

OES is a 64-bit NOS that can be run as a virtual machine inside a Xen hypervisor atop the SUSE Linux Enterprise Server (SLES) 10. Both Xen and SUSE were Novell acquisitions. SUSE Linux is also available as openSUSE, now at version 11.1 (www.opensuse.org) for users, and SUSE Linux Enterprise, an open source server version. SUSE Linux Enterprise Desktop (www.novell.com/products/desktop/) is Novell's commercial desktop client for OES.

OES 2 is an NOS that can run on top of either a NetWare or Linux kernel. Novell has OES positioned as an enterprise solution for file, print, directory, and Web applications. When run atop the NetWare kernel, the product is referred to as OES-NetWare and can add NetWare Loadable Modules (NLMs) to add a variety of applications, most prominently Apache, eDirectory, GroupWise, iPrint, NSS, OpenSSH, Tomcat, and others. An NLM is an execution module or add-in that extends the NetWare kernel.

Windows Server

Windows Server is noted as the general-purpose server that has the strongest and broadest network application support of all of the NOS that have been discussed. Microsoft's unique advantage is that Windows controls nearly 90 percent of the worldwide desktop computer market, which makes a number of valuable features such as automated deployments, a strong NOS policy engine, and other features possible.

Microsoft also sells an extensive set of server applications under the banner of Microsoft Servers. Examples of Microsoft Server products include Biz Talk Server, Commerce Server, Exchange Server, Internet Information Server (bundled with Windows Server), ISA Server, SQL Server, Windows Storage Server (as a separate Windows edition), and others. The various versions of Windows Server itself range from Windows Home Server to Windows Small Business Server all the way up to Windows Datacenter Edition. Of all of the applications on the previous list, Microsoft Exchange has achieved a dominant position in the enterprise mail market, and SQL Server is the best-selling commercial enterprise-class database server.

Microsoft's server technology began first as a codevelopment project with IBM of the OS/2 operating system. Microsoft abandoned OS/2 and initiated the Windows NT project led by David Cutler, with the first 32-bit commercial version appearing in July 1993, and was numbered as version 3.1 to bring it into harmony with Microsoft's current desktop client. Subsequent versions of the server OS have been branded Windows Server 2000, Windows Server 2003, and Windows Server 2008.

The original design goal of NT was to create an operating system that was highly portable and could run on many different processor types. The NT hybrid kernel was isolated from machine architecture by a Hardware Abstraction Layer (HAL), and the kernel mode is separated from the user mode. Of the original architectures that included x86 (IA32), PowerPC, MIPS R3000/4000, DEC Alpha, and IA64 (Itanium and AMD64), only the x86 and IA64 versions survive. The user mode supports a number of different system APIs, including Win32, OS/2, and POSIX. The original network stack was based on the OS/2 LAN Manager, which would eventually be redesigned based on BSD UNIX. The NTFS file system is native to Windows Server and has been continually developed throughout the lifetime of the operating system. Microsoft Windows is known for very strong driver support through the Windows Driver Foundation (also known as Model), for industry-leading device support in terms of breadth, and for strong adherence to the practice of making their operating system software as backwards-compatible as possible.

Each new version of the Windows Server operating system tends to introduce a small number of major new NOS subsystems, and a long list of new features. Windows Server 2000 was notable for the introduction of the Active Directory, which was refined with Windows Server 2003. Windows Server 2003 had major improvements in the policy engine, in reliability, and in system management. Windows Server 2008 is noted for its support for a number of Web-based technologies that support distributed applications based on the .NET Framework, for new graphics routines, and for its Hyper-V virtualization technologies.

Windows Server 2008 also saw a complete redesign of the Windows TCP/IP network stack, the architecture of which is shown in Figure 20.4. NDIS is shown at the bottom and is the Windows device driver layer.

Microsoft's latest versions at the time of printing were Windows Server 2008 R2 and Vista R2 client. Windows 7, expected to be released in late 2009 or early 2010, is an optimized version of VistaWindows Server and runs on the x86 and IA64 (Itanium) systems.

FIGURE 20.4

The next-generation TCP/IP network stack that was introduced in Windows Server 2008/Vista

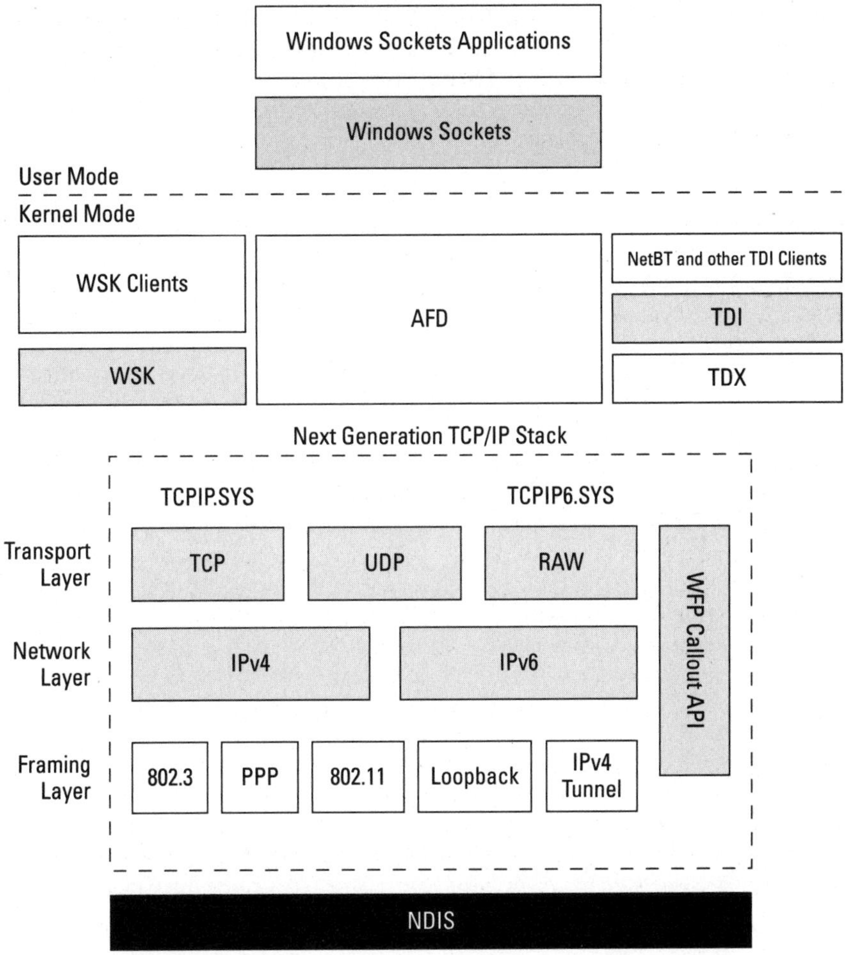

Summary

A network operating system, or NOS, provides network services to clients. It is important to understand NOS in order to understand how computer networking developed.

Every NOS must support the hardware it runs on, run protocols and services, and provide those services or applications for client systems. An NOS may offer a number of other services as well. When an NOS has broad capabilities, it is called a *platform*. UNIX, Linux, Solaris, NetWare, and Microsoft Windows Server are some of the platform NOSs that you learned about in this chapter.

In the next chapter, you learn about one of the essential NOS services, directory services. A directory service stores information about network objects for use in a variety of contexts.

Domains and Directory Services

D irectory services play a central role in the current network operating systems' client-server architecture. They provide a name service, store information about objects on the network, and allow this information to be propagated to other servers and applications. There are many directory services in use today, and modern networks use them heavily.

The smallest fundamental unit in a directory service is the domain. A domain is a collection of systems that share the same security database. Domains can be of various types and contain elements such as organizational units, user and machine accounts, and other objects that can be addressed using a unique Distinguished Name.

Most modern directory services are based on the X.500 standard. The LDAP version of X.500 was created for TCP/IP networks and is used for most of the products that are available today. The different directory services and their characteristics will be described. Among the features presented are policy engines, replication and synchronization, single sign-on, namespaces, identity management, and role-based access control.

Microsoft Active Directory (AD) is the best known and most widely used directory service. AD was built to store objects of various kinds, and includes aspects of security properties. The different classes of objects stored in AD are described, as is the way that domains are deployed and relate to one another.

Directory Services and Domains

Large computer networks create a problem for the designers of network operating systems working in the client-server model. How do you account for and manage a large number of systems, users, peripherals, and other items that run on the network? The solution boils down to storing this information in a database somewhere on the network so that the information can be accessed quickly and reliably. The software that manages this information is referred to as a *directory service*, and the fundamental unit used to store a network's information is called a *domain*. Usually a domain is associated with its own security database.

Network architects realized that they could store information about services and applications that ran on the networks, who could access those applications and how they could do so, and many other properties besides. They also realized that this information could serve as the key in a mechanism that authenticates and authorizes access, and that the system could be infinitely extensible. That meant that these databases could serve additional needs going forward that couldn't be anticipated during the initial design.

You've already seen an example of a directory service in previous chapters. The Domain Name Service is a directory service.

Cross-Ref

DNS is covered in Chapter 19.

The networked databases that were developed came to be known as directories, and they serve a function that is similar to a dictionary. The name harkens back to the idea of a phone book listing; the word *directory* was applied to many large database projects in the 1970s. Because this directory was designed to provide a network service, the term that eventually stuck was directory services. The standardization of directory services under a few industry models led to a proliferation of directory services for all of the network operating systems, and has been applied to large enterprise applications that manage data stores of all kinds.

Because the information contained in these central network databases would be clearly sensitive, they would have to be highly secure, and that security needed to be intimately related to and managed by this central information store. Some of these directory services incorporated network security in a single entity, while others worked with external security systems.

A directory service may be built using any type of database system: flat file, relational, hierarchical, peer-to-peer, and so on. The most popular directory services are the ones that are semi-relational, hierarchical, highly saleable, and that store object data. Scalability is important because you want to be able to preserve all of your information as your network grows and changes.

While directory services are similar to relational databases, there are some significant differences. Directory information is read from a lot more than they are written to; therefore, mechanisms like transaction rollbacks aren't as necessary, nor are they as well implemented as they are in Relational

Database Management Systems (RDBMS). Directory services also don't have the same requirements for performance or for normalization (optimization) that relational databases do. You'll find that many directory services create redundant data sets in multiple locations if that helps to improve performance. A relational database can be tightly designed because it is built to serve a specific function. A directory service may be called on to store a variety of diverse data that are related in random ways, and thus requires a less structured schema.

Banyan VINES

The area of directory services owes much to the development of Banyan VINES in the early 1980s. VINES was an acronym for the **V**irtual **I**ntegrated **NE**twork **S**ervice, and was a computer network operating system that was based on UNIX. For its network stack, VINES used the Xerox Network Services (XNS) protocol suite, which was popular at the time, and ran a variant called the VINES Internetwork Protocol (VIP). VINES networks were packet based, used automatic client addressing, and had a routing protocol and an Internet control protocol. Upper-level application protocols included standard file and print services. None of the technologies are particularly noteworthy; what made VINES unique was their upper-level name service, called StreetTalk.

Note
XNS was a packet-based LAN protocol suite that was used in the 1980s and 1990s as the basis for Novell NetWare, 3COM, and others. TCP/IP networking has entirely replaced the XNS networking technology.

StreetTalk was one of the early directory services. It created a namespace for the entire internetwork based on a distributed replicated database, and allowed different networks to share resources. In StreetTalk, an address was formed from a hierarchical naming scheme that reproduced an object hierarchy in the form, `object@group@organization`. An object could be a network or printer share, or it could be a user account. At the time, VINES clients were MS-DOS and Windows 3.x systems. There were no domains in a VINES network.

For nearly a decade from 1985 onward, VINES was the product of choice when you wanted to install an operating system with a directory service embedded in it. It achieved market success with a number of large deployments. Eventually, Novell introduced Novell Directory Services and Microsoft introduced the Active Directory, both of which helped to displace VINES in the marketplace. Jim Allchin, the chief architect at Banyan VINES, joined Microsoft in the mid-1990s and was important in the development of the Active Directory. Banyan grew increasingly obsolete and abandoned their brand in 1999.

Domain types

Every information system is organized around a basic unit. In databases that unit is a record, in file systems the unit is a file, and in a directory service the basic unit is a domain. A network domain describes a group of systems and associated resources that are organized by a directory service and share a common security database or security model.

There are many different schemes that are used to organize domain types. Among the more commonly encountered are the following, or some combination of any of these:

- A central master domain with a domain tree, hub, or star as shown in the single master case
- A multiple master domain structure
- Resource domains
- Remote domains where the links represented by either a trust relationship and/or replication are WAN connections
- Application-specific domains

Figure 21.1 illustrates these different domain types.

FIGURE 21.1

Different domain topologies

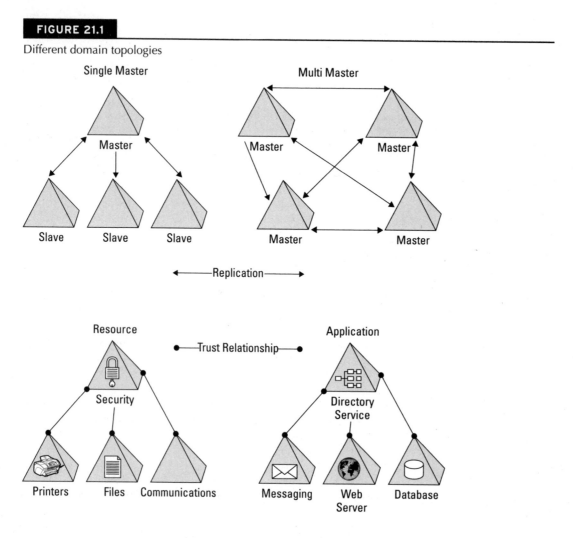

Interoperability

Migrating an established directory for a large network to another directory is one of the more painful tasks an organization's IT staff can be called on to perform. The task is much more difficult than moving data from one enterprise database to another one for two reasons: most databases either come with import/export functions or have third-party tools readily available, and directories are burdened with security functions and proprietary structures that make them difficult to crack and difficult to move data out of.

A heterogeneous directory service stores information about systems with different operating systems, a feature that would be valuable for any number of reasons. How well alien systems are represented in a directory service is a function of how hard the directory system vendor wants to work to make that happen. For some directory services, heterogeneity isn't necessarily a benefit, and homogeneity is preferable.

It isn't uncommon to have many directory services all operating on different servers throughout the network. You might see a directory service for each of the major network operating systems; some may be associated with Web servers such as APACHE, while others might be part of an enterprise mail application, such as Microsoft Exchange or Lotus Notes.

In very large organizations, there might be as many as 50 different directory services in use, and that introduces a significant amount of overhead into managing all of this information scattered about the network. To this end, directory services often try to connect to as many of these different systems as possible and exchange information with them. Any system that tries to consolidate information in this manner is often referred to as a federated service. An example of a federated database system is SAP's Enterprise Resource Planning (ERP) technology suite, which is a master database of databases.

Domain Servers

The computer system that runs the directory service is referred to as the network's domain server, or alternatively, a domain controller. For security reasons, nearly all directory services store their data and related security information on the same domain server.

In small networks, domain servers can look after a few different services beyond the directory service. An example of this type of system is the Microsoft Small Business Server (SBS). Early versions of SBS were a directory server, a DHCP/DNS server, an Exchange Server, an IIS Web Server, a Microsoft Internet Security and Acceleration (ISA) server, and perhaps a SQL Server. All of these applications are there in the SBS "box," and if the server is powerful enough, then with a maximum of 50 allowed connections, this server could perform reasonably well. The later version of SBS allows for up to 100 connections, with just a little more power required. Many installations of SBS install only a subset of these available applications.

Security experts will tell you that the fewer extraneous applications and services that a directory server runs, the safer it is. In larger networks of hundreds and thousands of users and connections, domain servers become heavily loaded with requests. In order to manage requests, different directory server systems create either duplicate peer domain servers and replicate data between them, or a class of backup domain servers. These different approaches have advantages and disadvantages with respect to system failures and preserving data coherency.

Depending upon the nature of the domain and directory service and the tasks that are being performed, a domain can have as many as one domain server for two or three systems. Some home server appliances based on Linux are marketed for this size of network. For larger networks, domain servers can service anywhere from 50 to 500 systems before they are taxed. The other servers in the domain that aren't domain servers are called resource servers and application servers; they may also be named based on the task that the server performs: file and print, backup, security, or whatever scheme the directory server enforces.

Directory Services

Directory services store metadata, or data about data. In an object database that stores network data, metadata provide the context that allows the system to determine how the data set is organized. The directory schema defines a set of object classes, to which are assigned a set of required and optional attributes. When possible, most directory services use the object classes, attributes, and ID numbers that are registered by the Internet Assigned Numbers Authority, or IANA, as standards. Every object that is a secured resource is attached to an Access Control List (ACL) that determines who can use the object.

Metadata provides the relational context that offers what is essentially a map to system resources. Many information systems have this characteristic, a separation of data from context.

A schema overlays the data in a database to provide the template used in the construction of records and files; an XML schema file serves the same function for XML data, allowing a structured document to be recreated. Because directory services are databases, it shouldn't be too surprising that they use a schema as their architectural blueprint. A directory service is an abstraction layer that separates the physical reality of clients, servers, and resources from the logical assignments with a mapping function based on a namespace assignment.

You need a directory service when your network requires the following:

- Centralized management of network services
- A defined security policy with granular privileges and rights
- The ability to delegate responsibility for different resources to different individuals
- The ability to scale your network to support more users than a peer-to-peer model supports
- The ability to support a variety of clients and operating systems
- The ability to audit network events

Directory services are not all sweetness and light; they have a downside as well. They add additional cost and complexity to a network and require that domain services always be available for the network to function properly. These additional requirements limit the use of domains on small home and office networks of fewer than 20 connected systems in most instances.

Synchronization and replication

Directory services are among the most active network services that are in use. For fault tolerance and improved performance, directory services are replicated on different servers and in different locations. Once these services have been replicated, there is a need to propagate the changes occurring on the different locations through some sort of replication scheme. Replication is a process by which data is transferred to another system, and updated frequently. An important point to note about replication is that it doesn't maintain a record of the state of the system, just its current form. The methods used by directory services to synchronize and replicate data are the same mechanisms that are used by other distributed enterprise applications such as database systems, and they vary from product to product.

Replication can be a single execution unit that is propagated from one system to many systems, or it can be an ongoing process during which changes are propagated as a set of transactions over time. Replication can require that the same change be made at every copy, something that is called active replication. Active replication works with a small number of systems with reasonable network connections, but removes many of the benefits of replication when the number of copies grows or they are on a WAN. The alternative is to make changes at one directory server and then transmit the changes between all of the other directory servers; that is referred to as passive replication. Nearly all schemes used by directory services use a passive replication scheme.

If a single copy is designated as the master copy, the replication topology is a master/slave system. This is the method used with the early versions of Microsoft Active Directory with its system of Primary Domain Controller and Backup Domain Controllers. The advantage of a master/slave system is that it is simpler to create and doesn't require some method for controlling concurrent changes to the same record. When you move to a multi-master topology, you gain performance and the added fault tolerance of not being dependant on a single master; however, this is gained at the expense of having to manage concurrency, perhaps by employing a distributed lock management service or some other form of data conflict resolution. Microsoft moved Active Directory to a multi-master system with Windows Server 2003.

Multi-master replication can suffer from inconsistencies introduced into the system by network latency because it is an asynchronous process. This type of replication doesn't always conform to the rules of providing ACID transaction, as most database management systems require. ACID stands for Atomicity, Consistency, Isolation, and Durability, and it is a method of determining whether a database transaction has the necessary properties to be processed with guaranteed certainty of being correct. For these reasons, AD doesn't use a pure multi-master replication scheme.

AD uses an update pattern that updates all directory servers, but requires a time interval to complete the update. The system for AD replication has been described as a Floating Single Master Operations system or alternatively, an Operations Masters system, and it is flexible enough to scale to a large number of domains and accommodate links of varying bandwidths.

Single sign on

In an environment where there are multiple security apparatuses, each validating a user's access to different resources, it can be quite troublesome if logon requests keep popping up. This problem has been referred to as password fatigue. You encounter the problem of password fatigue when you browse the Internet and are forced to log into one Web site after another. There are solutions to the problem of logging into a Web site. You can use a Firefox extension like BugMeNot and assume another alias (effective, but not nice), or you can use a product like RoboForm to store all of your passwords and automate your logon. However, neither of these approaches provides a universal response to the problem of password fatigue.

Directory services in large networks are constantly interacting with different directory services, domains, applications, and resources. In an effort to solve the problem of recurring logons, some directory services offer what has come to be called a single sign on (SSO) capability, or in an enterprise, an enterprise single sign on (E-SSO). The user signs on once in their domain and their credentials are stored and passed to other security objects in a form that those objects can accept. So if you entered your network operating system credentials, those credentials would be accepted by your enterprise mail program or another application.

The best of these systems require a combination of authentication that includes at least two of the following three "Somethings":

- Something that you know (your ID and password)
- Something that you have (a Smart Card)
- Something that you are (your fingerprint, your eyeballs, or your smile)

Note

Some of the security mechanisms used by SSO systems are described in Chapter 27.

SSO isn't an easy technology to implement because authentication methods for different systems can use very different technologies. They are also criticized because an SSO system removes the ability of different systems to individually challenge a request, thus lowering the overall security of the network. Only a few directory services offer this feature, often as a very expensive add-on module. For most directory services, you need to turn to third-party programs to implement this feature, such as Citrix Password Manager.

Namespaces

A directory service defines a namespace for all of the objects it contains. You've already seen the use of a namespace with the Domain Naming Service (DNS) that the Internet uses to address locations on the Internet. To be effective, a namespace must create a unique designation that should be the logical composite of the various branches of the tree. For DNS, this is called the Uniform Resource Identifier (URI).

Many organizations adopt a naming scheme for their domains that parallels how DNS would label the directory structure of a Web site. There are some good reasons to do this, foremost of which is that it enables the domain structure to be exposed to the Internet at some later date with no significant name changes. However, there is a distinct difference between how you would name a private network and how you have to name a network that is connected to the Internet, as you can see in Figure 21.2.

With a directory (like Active Directory, for example) the Directory Namespace can include the .com suffix. The name is built up from the composite of the individual nodes of the tree. The path to a node in DNS is obtained from the folder hierarchy, as follows: `www.XYZ.com/ABC/GHI`.

Note

Should you choose to use a public DNS namespace such as .COM, .GOV, or .EDU on a private network, you need to ensure that the internal and external domain names don't collide. The public DNS server should be configured to forward address requests to the internal DNS server of the private network.

FIGURE 21.2

A public versus private network and associated namespaces

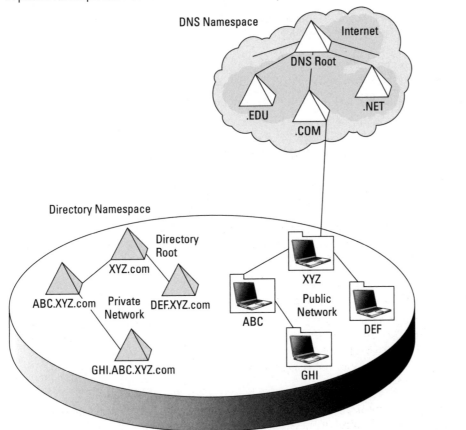

Policy engines

When you store network object information in a database, it is possible to create a set of rules that determine how objects are used. These rules are stored separately from the security engine that a network operating system uses, although some policy rules overlap.

A policy would define some feature of network behavior, including the following:

- Client desktop configuration
- Update or patch frequency
- Audit behavior
- Password complexity
- Logon and logoff actions

A group policy engine is the mechanism used to enforce a set of operational rules that you define for a network. They serve the same functions as business rules saved as stored procedures with a relational database system.

The best-known policy engine is Group Policies from Microsoft. Group Policies are stored in Active Directory. There are many other instances of policy engines associated with network operating systems. The Sun Solaris Resource Manager (SRM) offers policy management for setting resource limits. Within the SRM, you can set the number of allowed processes, connected users, number of logons, and other policies. Through scripting, SRM can set new policies upon execution. Every network operating system implements some form of policy management.

Once you start to look at third-party policy engines, you find that there are a vast number of choices available. Space precludes a fuller discussion of this topic, but one product of note is the Novell ZENworks suite of applications. These products offer many of the capabilities of policy engines and work well in a heterogeneous network environment. Figure 21.3 shows the installer page for ZENworks, which gives you an idea of the capabilities of this product.

Let's use Microsoft Active Directory as an example of what is possible for a policy engine to implement. In Figure 21.4, you can see how various Group Policies can be defined to control who has access to which resources, how responsibilities can be delegated, and what policies apply to which systems. This system of policy management began with Windows 2000 and applies to all systems (client and server) that have been released since then. With every subsequent release of a new operating system, additional policies are added to the Windows Group Policy Engine. Windows Server 2008 shipped with nearly 2,400 policy settings.

FIGURE 21.3

The ZENworks suite offers a number of policy enforcement capabilities.

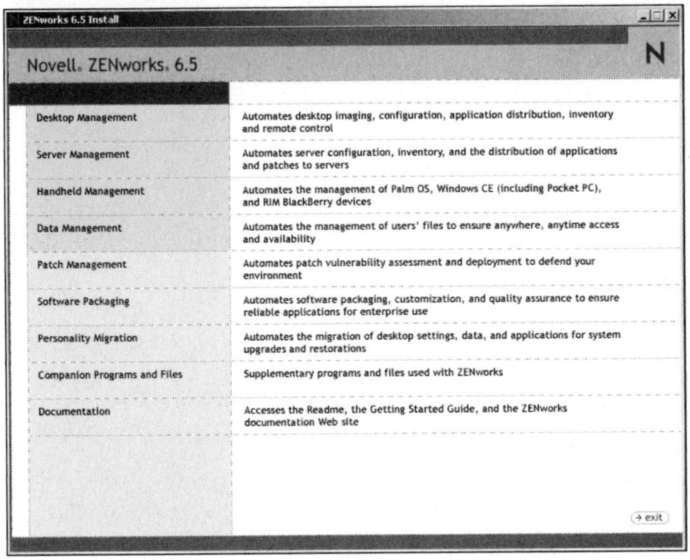

The central domain is subdivided into two different trees under Organizational Unit 11 (OU_11) and OU_12. The Domain Admin has delegated responsibility to control the network from OU_111 down to another Admin, print operations from OU_112 to the Print Operator, and OU_12 down to the OU Admin. Because the OU_12 Admin has full control, they have delegated the administration for OU_121 to an administrator with even narrower responsibilities. Delegation is performed as part of the security engine, which may or may not be part of the policy engine. For Windows Active Directory, the storage of security policies is in a separate database, but the control over these features is exposed in the central management console of the server, along with policy features, as well as throughout the other elements of the Windows GUI.

Active Directory lets you set a general policy that you can apply to a domain, and using a system of Administrative Templates, modify those policies. Policies in Windows can be changed using a utility called the Group Policy Object Editor, a snap-in for the Microsoft Management Console. Policy objects are also exposed in the Group Policy Management Console. The policies that you set in Active Directory (see Figure 21.5) apply to Windows systems; you can use a product like Centrify DirectControl (www.centrify.com/directcontrol/overview.asp) to extend policy management to UNIX, Linux, and Mac clients in a Windows network.

FIGURE 21.4

Different forms of group policy and delegations

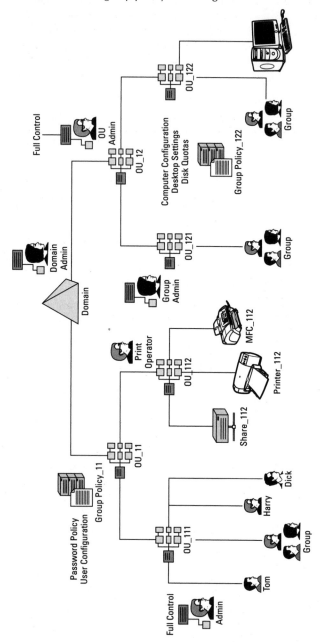

At any point in the network, you can apply a group policy that alters the behavior of network nodes at that level or below. Group Policy Objects may be targeted at sites, domains, and Organizational Units (OUs), and are applied in that order of precedence; the group policy of the OU would be the last applied. In Figure 21.4, two local policies are defined: Group Policy_11 where user and password policies are set for systems at OU_11 and below; and Group Policy_122 where a set of machine policies are applied to systems in OU_122 and below. Local group policies take precedence over general group policies according to a set of rules that Microsoft defines but are scoped to individual servers or systems.

FIGURE 21.5

Group Policy precedence in Active Directory

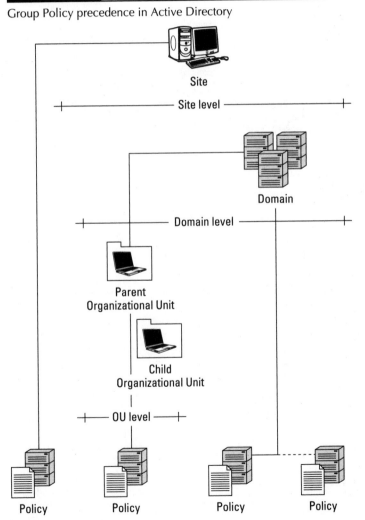

The ability to record different events into logs is an important set of policies that are referred to as auditing. Many directory services include the ability to create and store audit policies on a per-object basis. Auditing is applied in a granular fashion and can be logged for directory or resource access, replication events, and any service changes. Auditing can generate a very large volume of data, so as a general rule, audit functions are usually turned off by default in order to maintain the highest performance. However, auditing can provide the information necessary to diagnose system errors, provide metrics to improve performance, and determine how the security system reacted to an event. In Windows Server 2008, you can turn auditing on for four different categories of directory service events: access, changes, replication, and detailed replication.

Role-Based Access Control

Many network operating systems implement different classes of users that may be referred to as roles and implement a form of access that is called Role-Based Access Control (RBAC). These roles are often organized in a hierarchy with an order of precedence. Roles impart rights and impose constraints on what may be done when an action is taken. Among the systems that use RBAC are Microsoft Active Directory, Sun Solaris, SELinux, SAP R/3, Oracle, and FreeBSD.

In Windows, you find "built-in user groups," and include categories such as Administrator, Domain Admins, Domain Users, Power Users, Guests, and Print Operators. Related machine groups are defined, including Domain Controllers, Domain Computers, and Replicator. Of course, you can also create your own.

Sun Solaris RBAC appeared in version 8 and was greatly expanded by version 10. It provides a number of similar roles: All, Primary Administrator, System Administrator, Operator, Basic Solaris User, and so forth. RBAC roles have an access list that creates a profile describing what the role is capable of. In Solaris, you can work with RBAC from the command line, or using the Solaris Management Console (SMC). The SMC is shown in Figure 21.6. In it, you can attach user accounts to roles, and manage the different roles that Solaris offers.

RBACs are policy neutral; they are applied to objects, regardless of a policy in place that might contradict the role. They are meant to simulate job function and are defined in order to speed up the management of delegation assignments. With a role may come a set of permissions that allow actions such as add a user, or print to this printer. Unlike Access Control Lists, which are associated with a particular system or network object, the permissions associated with an RBAC are attached to the operation that the role allows. This is a higher-level function, more often associated with an application.

FIGURE 21.6

The Solaris Management Console provides access to RBAC features in the Solaris operating system.

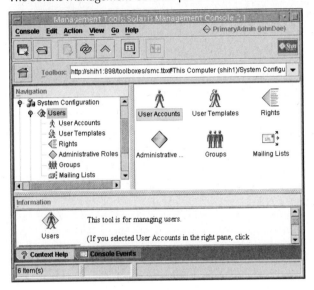

Identity management

Directory services store information on users, their accounts, and a number of related properties. As such, directory services are intimately related to the concept of identities and can store information managed by identity services and servers. Identity spans both user management and security functions and can be implemented as a service of either function or its own independent service.

In large organizations, the identity of users on the network may be stored in many different places. Identity services can help to synchronize the different information sources so that the data they contain is the same. This includes the synchronization of passwords and access rules, the ability to provision new users, and the ability to remove users who have left the organization so that network security isn't compromised.

Just like SSO described earlier, an Identity and Access (IDA) server needs to function across different network systems in order to be useful. For an IDA server, it may be necessary to:

- Manage certificates and smart cards and connect to the various certificate services.
- Provide a federated service among different directory services that are on the network to mediate identities between them. The most important directory services you might want to work with include Microsoft Active Directory, Sun Directory Server, Novell eDirectory, and IBM Tivoli Directory Server.

- Work with e-mail and messaging services' identities, and if necessary, synchronize with them. Lotus Notes and Microsoft Exchange are two examples of servers that store identities that often interact with identities in directory services.

- Manage network database identities so that a user can't log on without a valid identity. Oracle, IBM DB2, and Microsoft SQL Server are examples of database management systems that can store their own user accounts.

- Work with enterprise applications such as SAP, telephony applications, and others.

Microsoft refers to this concept of identity services as Identity Lifecycle Management and adds this capability into the Microsoft Identity Information Server (MIIS). MIIS provides a repository that gives a unified view of directory data contained in an organization. With MIIS, you could perform directory consolidation, account provisioning, synchronization, and password management.

X.500 and LDAP

The telecommunications industry created a standard to allow their different directories to interoperate with one another; this standard has come to be called the X.500 Directory Access Protocol (DAP). This protocol is applicable for any kind of network. The DAP standard could store information on objects from any of the seven layers of the ISO/OSI model. In X.500, a client can query a server in the directory service using DAP for its communication. The Directory System Agent (DSA) or database that stores the information then returns a response. DSAs are hierarchical and are connected to one another using the Directory Information Tree (DIT). The Directory User Agent (DUA) is a program like WHOIS, FINGER, or a GUI command that accesses a DSA.

Note

Lightweight Directory Access Protocol (LDAP) and DAP compliance is performed by The Open Group (www. opengroup.org). For more information about X.500, go to X.500Standard.com. Compliance is a determination of a product's interoperability with directory service standards.

The four different X.500 protocols are used in a complete X.500 scheme:

- **Directory Access Protocol (DAP).** DAP (X.511) defines a list of operations that a client using the full OSI model must support. These include Add, Bind, Compare, Delete, List, Modify, ModifyRDN, Read, and Search. Because there are so few networks that use the full OSI model, DAP never saw widespread use. However, a variety of LDAP directory services, such as Novell eDirectory, adopted this command set.

- **Directory Information Shadowing Protocol (DISP).** X.500 defines two different mechanisms for replicating directory information: caching and shadowing. Shadowing is a negotiated mechanism for replicating the stored information securely, and DISP is the protocol used for the exchange and for updates. Caching stores information in a repository for later use by other users. Caching is considered to be less reliable and secure because it can store information from privileged sources that less privileged users may be able to access.

- **Directory Operational Bindings Management Protocol (DOP).** This protocol is used to establish the agreement for data replication.

- **Directory System Protocol (DSP).** The DSP allows a Directory System Agent to talk to another Directory System Agent or to a Directory User Agent. The protocol provides access to information without having to know where the information is located.

When computer network architects began to create directory services, they only needed to apply the X.500 to TCP/IP networks and thus could narrow the definition of X.500 to only that protocol. The resulting standard was called the Lightweight Directory Access Protocol (LDAP), although the term "lightweight" is really a misnomer. LDAP is complex but is a narrower version of X.500.

Network Information Service

The Network Information Service (NIS) is an RPC-based client-server directory system that stores user and system names for a computer network in a database. NIS also defines a set of processes used to manage and access the dictory service. With NIS, an administrator can define an NIS domain that shares a common set of configuration files. Adding those configuration files to new systems or modifying them may be done remotely and relatively easily.

NIS is widely used on UNIX networks and was originally developed by Sun Microsystems. Originally called the Yellow Pages, a trademark dispute with British Telecom led to the service being renamed NIS. However, NIS command line commands all begin with the yp prefix. For example, ypbind enables an NIS client through RPC to access the NIS server. The command ypserv initiates the NIS process on the NIS server, while rpc.yppasswdd initiates the daemon that NIS clients use to change their passwords without having to log onto the master NIS domain server.

Note
A tutorial on configuring NFS may be found at: http://www.freebsd.org/doc/en/books/handbook/network-nis.html

In NIS there are three types of systems:

- **NIS master server.** These servers can contain the files for one or more NIS domains.

- **NIS slave server.** These servers contain replicated copies of the NIS database and are used to provide both redundancy and load balancing to clients. Clients attach to the NIS server that they get the first response from.

- **NIS client.** Systems that use the NIS service for security information.

NIS stores its information in text-based tables on an NIS server. These database files are referred to as NIS maps and are stored in the VAR/YP directory. NIS maps are generated on the NIS master using configuration files found in the /ETC directory, although the MASTER.PASSWD file is not generated in this manner to keep it hidden. The User list is found in the /ETC/PASSWD directory; other files such as master, group, and hosts store other NIS information in different locations. Data in NIS may be encrypted using DES, although this method isn't as secure as more modern directory services based on LDAP offer. NIS requires that you remove system account information from the NIS accounts list before initializing the NIS map.

LDAP servers

Today, nearly all modern computer network directory services are based on LDAP, which provides a measure of interoperability (albeit a small measure) to different vendors' implementations of this standard. Two notable exceptions are the Domain Naming System (DNS) and the Network Information System (NIS), which were both developed prior to the standardization of X.500 and LDAP.

Following are just a few of the many directory services based on LDAP:

- **Microsoft Active Directory** (www.microsoft.com/windowsserver2008/en/us/active-directory.aspx)
- **Novell eDirectory** (once NetWare Directory Services, or NDS; www.novell.com/products/edirectory)
- **Fedora Directory Server** (directory.fedoraproject.org)
- **OpenDS** (https://opends.dev.java.net)
- **Sun Java System Directory Server** (www.sun.com/dsee)
- **IBM Tivoli Directory Server** (www-306.ibm.com/software/tivoli/products/directory-server)
- **Apple Open Directory** (for Apple OS X Server; www.apple.com/server/macosx/open_directory.html)
- **ApacheDS** (directory.apache.org)

LDAP Data Interchange Format

The LDAP Data Interchange Format (LDIF) is a text-based interchange format that allows different LDAP servers to send and receive LDAP records. Each record contains the data associated with an object and can be retrieved for directory requests or for updates. LDIF is maintained as an IETF standard and was last modified in 2000 as a proposed standard. OpenLDAP, Netscape, Mozilla, and Microsoft all have tools for importing and exporting information in this format. There are also tools such as JXplorer, which allow you to open and edit LDIF data.

Note

To read the current RFC for LDIF, go to http://tools.ietf.org/html/rfc2849.

LDIF records take the following form:

```
DN: CN=Administrator,OU=departmentname,DC=servername,DC=com
objectClass: domain admin
CN: Administrator
```

where DN is the Distinguished Name, CN is the Conical Name, OU is the Organizational Unit, and DC is the Domain Component. An LDIF file contains one or more entries of this type, and may list multiple single-valued attributes. Commands such as ADD, REPLACE, DELETE, and so forth are embedded into the records in the following manner.

```
DN: CN=Barrie Sosinsky,OU=Writing,DC=Sample,DC=com
changetype: modify
replace: Location
Location: Room B23
-
DN: CN=Elysian Fields,OU=Evangelism,DC=Sample,DC=com
changetype: modify
add: Location
Location: Room 666
-
and so on...
```

The single hyphen line is required to separate records.

Novell eDirectory

Novell eDirectory is an object-oriented hierarchical database that supports users and groups, roles, systems, applications, and services with global and local properties. Global and local indicate scoping (of a policy, for example) to a domain or an individual server. The database may be partitioned and uses multi-master replication. Novell eDirectory is the main competitor to Microsoft Active Directory, which is covered later in this chapter. It is also the current version of what was once NetWare Directory Services (NDS) and is currently deployed on some of the largest networks using directory services. NDS predated AD and is an X.500-based directory service.

eDirectory has a very wide range of interoperability and includes Windows, Linux, NetWare, Solaris, HP-UX, and IBM AIX clients and servers; it is reported to be deployed on as many as 80 percent of the Fortune 1000 companies.

Among the protocols that directory services use to communicate with network objects are:

- **LDAP.** The Lightweight Directory Access Protocol allows directory services to be queried over TCP/IP, as described earlier in this chapter.
- **SOAP.** The Simple Object Access Protocol is used to exchange structured XML information on the Web.
- **JDBC.** The Java Database Connectivity protocol is a method for querying databases in the Java environment.
- **ODBC.** The Open Database Connectivity protocol is an API used to create SQL database queries on Windows.

  ODBC and JDBC are similar technologies on two different platforms.
- **DSML.** The Directory Service Markup Language reproduces a directory service using XML.
- **JNDI.** The Java Naming and Directory Interface is a Java API that Java clients can use to query a directory service.
- **ADSI.** The Active Directory Service Interface allows clients to query Active Directory.

Distinguished Names

LDAP directories all share a set of defined objects and a common addressing method that creates a Distinguished Name (DN) for the object. Common features of an LDAP directory are:

- **Directory tree.** The tree is hierarchical with directory objects as the nodes.

- **Nodes.** Nodes are named container objects or entities that are associated with a set of properties or attributes. LDAP allows objects to be extensible; that is, additional properties can be defined.

- **Attributes.** An attribute is a property, and its name is referred to as the type or description. An attribute can be single- or multi-valued.

- **Entries.** An entry is the unique instance of an object type. The object can be assigned a Distinguished Name, and by comparison to its parent node, a Relative Distinguished Node (RDN) may be assigned.

The DN is important because it allows the system to find and retrieve information. DNs provide a means to know how an object relates to many other objects. Essentially, they are a way of providing one-to-many relationships that aren't supported directly in directory services.

Microsoft Active Directory would use a DN in the following form:

```
/DC=<DomainName>/O=<OrganizationName>/OU=<DepartmentName>/
   CN=<ServerName>
```

where DC is the Domain Component, O is the Organization, OU is the Organizational Unit, and CN is the Common Name. All of the range of possible objects within this addressing scheme defines what is called the namespace. A namespace defines the range of possible objects that your directory collects, and not any and all objects that could exist.

Because a directory service is dynamic, you can move an object from one place to another, and when you do so, the DN for the object changes. When you move Server_1's machine account from Domain_1 to Domain_2, the DN for the server changes accordingly. To ensure that an object such as this computer is easily identifiable, LDAP assigned a unique ID to a system when the operating system is installed called a Universal Global Unique Identifier (UUID).

In Microsoft Active Directory, the UUID is called the Microsoft Globally Unique Identifier (GUID) and is a number assigned to the computer when you install the Windows operating system on it. The name is chosen from a namespace containing 2122 possible numbers, or 5.3×1036. That is significantly larger than the calculated number of stars in the universe, which has been estimated to be 7×1022.

Microsoft Active Directory

The most widely used network directory service today is Microsoft Active Directory (AD). It first appeared in Windows Server 2000 and has been upgraded with every version of Windows Server that has been released. Depending upon how you judge these things, AD is currently in its third major release.

In AD, a domain is a collection of systems that are grouped together using the Microsoft Security Account Manager database. It is a logical grouping based on a security model that applies to member systems within the same LAN, member systems located across a WAN, remote systems that intermittently log into the domain, and any other member system that can be defined and that the domain server can connect to. Any system that belongs to the domain is called a domain member, and a server is called a domain server. Any other server may be referred to as a member server, or less frequently, an application server or a resource server.

AD establishes a broad class of objects that can be managed. Users and groups are objects in the directory, and the collections of these properties, rights, and privileges are called their User and Group accounts. Computers are also objects organized by accounts, which, in this case, is called a Machine account. Figure 21.7 shows the different objects organized by AD. Table 21.1 lists the main objects stored in the Active Directory.

FIGURE 21.7

Objects in the Active Directory

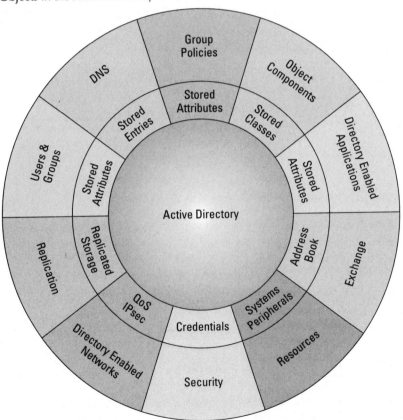

TABLE 21.1

Sample Objects Stored in the Active Directory

Object Name	Description
Users	A security object type, a person
Groups	A security object type, a group of user accounts
Computers	A security object type, specific workstations or servers
Distribution Groups	Application-specific objects
Domain	Active Directory core collection object
Organizational Unit	Active Directory collection object
Contact	Administrator for a specific object
Connection	A path, usually defined for replication between two systems
Shared folder	Path to a file system and access to files contained within
Printer	Shared printer object
Site	A container object usually defined for a geographical location
Site link	A connection object between sites
Site settings	Objects stored related to a site
Subnet	A group of network addresses that are local to one another
Subnet container	A container object storing subnet objects
Trusted domain	Pass through authentication security object

AD uses an LDAP version based on the X.500 naming scheme. The Distinguished Name (DN) in AD takes the form:

$$/DC=<OrganizationName>/OU=<DepartmentName>/CN=<ServerName>$$

where DC is the domain object class, OU is the organization unit, and CN is the conical name. Every object in AD is given a GUID, which is a unique 128-bit identifier that cannot be changed. Some objects in AD have a User Principle Name (UPN) and take the form *UserName@ DomainName*. AD supports names in the form of UNC, URL, and LDAP URL.

AD begins with the creation of a root domain, a process that can be accomplished either through the use of the Add a Domain Wizard in Windows Server 2008, or with the DCPROMO command. Additional domains can be created in a hierarchy beneath the root in a domain tree. These sub-domains are considered to be children, grandchildren, and other more distant relatives of the root. Any domain that you create in an AD topology that is private doesn't need to have its name registered with ICANN for use on the Internet.

Organization units are created to separate functions, groups, or departments, or for geographical locations. An alternative designation called a site is defined when the physical characteristic of a portion of the network changes, examples of which might be a remote office or a subnet.

A collection of domains can be associated together into a forest, with each domain having its own security database. In order to allow users and systems in different domains to communicate with one another over the network, you must establish a trust relationship. Domain controllers in a forest contain information about other domains in the forest through replication. Figure 21.8 shows the relationship of domains in a forest. A *transitive trust relationship*, as shown in Figure 21.8, is one where if an automatic trust relationship exists between domain A and B and between B and C, then a trust relationship exists between A and C. In an Active Directory forest, this is expressed in terms of an automatic trust relationship between parent, child, and root domains.

FIGURE 21.8

The relationship of forests to domains and organizational units

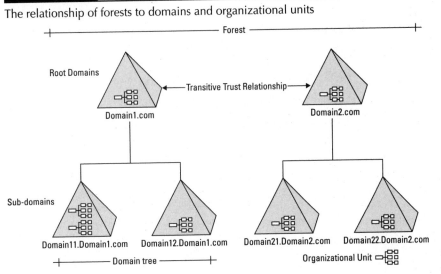

The AD database stores information about a forest in three separate contexts or partitions:

- **Configuration.** The Configuration partition stores the physical structure of a forest.
- **Domain.** The Domain partition stores the topology and configuration of a forest.
- **Schema.** The Schema partition stores all of the objects and their attributes.

Microsoft has been slicing and dicing AD for the various edition of Windows. In Windows Server 2003, AD could be configured in the Active Directory Application Mode (ADAM). ADAM allows Microsoft to deploy an application such as SQL Server or Exchange on a network as a stand-alone application with a functional directory service, and without having to create a domain server on the same server running the application. ADAM added SSL and LDAP ports to these application servers, and includes its own events in the application log.

Windows Server 2008 saw the various identity and access services segmented into a set of AD role services, shown in Figure 21.9, including certificate, rights management rights, federated, and domain services. ADAM was renamed as the Active Directory Lightweight Directory Services (LDS).

Windows Server 2008 Active Directory role services

Active Directory
Certificate Services
(AD CD)

Active Directory Right
Management Services
(AD RMS)

Active Directory
Federated Services
(AD FS)

Active Directory Domain Services (AD DS)
or
Active Directory Lightweight Directory Services (LDS)

Replication

Domain controllers are very active network services. Because they are considered mission critical, domain controllers are either backed up or replicated. The first version of Active Directory that appeared in Windows Server 2000 created a Primary Domain Controller (PDC) as a master, and replicated the data to one or more Backup Domain Controllers (BDCs). When the PDC went offline or needed maintenance, you could use DCPROMO to promote a BDC to a PDC. The system of promotion and demotion was unwieldy.

Starting with Windows Server 2003 and refined in Windows Sever 2008, Microsoft moved to a multi-master system of replicated Domain Controllers (DCs), eliminating PDCs/BDCs, to few peoples' disappointment. Now, any server that isn't a DC is a member server. The replication process replicates all of the data from the Configuration partition and the Schema partition to all DCs. The third partition, the Domain partition, is only replicated to DCs in the same domain.

Domain replication for a newly created DC can lead to significant network traffic, and is impractical for low-bandwidth WAN links. To allow for remote deployment of new DCs, Microsoft has created what they call a Read Only Domain Controller, or RODC. An RODC is a domain controller that hosts a read only version of the Active Directory database. Features of an RODC include unidirectional replication, limited credential caching, read only DNS, filter attribute set of configuration, and optimized WAN characteristics.

Summary

In this chapter, you learned what a directory service is and why it is important. Directory services provide much of the information that a network needs to be intelligent.

Directory services create a namespace and organize a network into domains and other smaller units. A domain is a collection of systems that share the same security database.

Most directory services are based on LDAP, which is a variant of the X.500 DAP standard. You learned about some of the features that directory services enable, including policy engines, replication and synchronization, single sign on, namespaces, identity management, and Role-Based Access Control. Microsoft Active Directory was presented in some detail.

In the next chapter, you learn about network file services and how they are deployed and used.

File Services and Caching

N etwork file access is one of the most important services that a net-work can provide. It represents a large share of the network traffic that you are likely to have. For this reason, a number of approaches are used to improve the response of networks to file requests, to secure con-tent, and to make sure that content is protected.

Any networked operating system can be configured to serve files to clients. Usually these systems are not optimized for file services. A class of storage servers called Network Attached Storage (NAS) is an optimized file server that you can use on your network. NAS often behaves as if it is a network appliance, and can be used by many different types of clients. The difference between a NAS and a storage area network (SAN) is that NAS transfers files, while SANs and storage arrays do block transfers.

To efficiently send a file across a network, there are a number of file services in use. The most prominent of these protocols is the Network File System (NFS) and Common Internet File System/Server Message Block (CIFS/SMB) protocol. NFS is common on Linux and UNIX, while CIFS/SMB is used on most network operating systems. Samba is an example of a CIFS/SMB server, and in this chapter a copy of Samba is installed on Ubuntu.

File service protocols provide a number of important services. They authen-ticate clients' access to network shares, maintain access lists, provide a net-work browsing function, and manage access to files by providing for file and record locking. Some of these protocols offer network printing.

Another approach to distributing file content across a network is to create a distributed file system (DFS). In this technology, you create copies of your content in various places and then have the DFS server's namespace point clients to the location of the file that is closest to them. DFS is available in Windows servers, and as third-party solutions.

Network Attached Storage

Network Attached Storage, or NAS, consists of file servers that provide file access to network clients. NAS devices range in size from small Snap Servers that aren't much larger than an external hard drive up to wardrobe-sized servers with multi-terabyte capacities like the EMC Celerra NSX server. Network Appliance Inc., now called NetApp Inc., refer to their systems as *filers*.

Many NAS systems are literally appliances, particularly the small ones. You plug the NAS into an electric socket, connect an Ethernet cable, and turn them on — they do all the rest. The NAS operating system advertises for a DHCP and DNS server, is assigned an IP address lease, and then appears on the network automatically. At that point you configure file shares, add users and groups, set access rights, and perform other functions associated with file servers. Most NAS systems are built to be promiscuous: they come with several different networking protocols built into them so that they can share files with different operating systems.

Most NAS systems implement browser-based management utilities, although the larger servers and enterprise-class devices come with a variety of powerful programs for backup, replication, and many other file-oriented features. Most NAS devices are designed to be headless — that is, they don't require a monitor — and some do not include keyboard, video, and mouse (KVM) functionality.

The development of file servers predates the introduction of NAS. Novell Netware and Sun Microsystems servers appeared in 1983 and 1984, and using the NCP and NFS protocols, they could make network shares available to clients. However, these were general-purpose servers configured as file servers, but not optimized. Another significant development was the introduction of LAN Manager by Microsoft and 3Com, which led to the development of NetBIOS over TCP and could be used by Windows clients. In 1985, the 3Com 3Server and 3+Share software appeared; it allowed system vendors to create dedicated file servers. It was clear by the 1990s that this was a significant product category.

Storage industry insiders consider Auspex Systems, founded in 1987 by Larry Boucher, to be the pioneer of the NAS category. Many of the engineers and managers from that company went on to create other companies such as NetApp, and Boucher himself became one of the founders of Adaptec. With the introduction of the NetApp filer in 1995 — more formally known as the NetApp Fabric Attached Storage (FAS) server that supported the UNIX NFS and Windows CIFS protocols — the category for dedicated and proprietary NAS servers was established. Today you will find NAS systems offered by a very wide range of vendors.

In the sections that follow, the features of networked file servers are considered, as is the difference between NAS and SAN network storage. NAS is very useful for caching content on a network and delivering that content to distributed systems, a topic which follows.

Features

A NAS filer requires four things:

- An optimized network I/O function
- An optimized disk I/O function
- A powerful file system
- A lot of disk storage, preferably in a protected form such as a Redundant Array of Inexpensive Disks (RAID)

Most of the additional functionality in general-purpose network operating systems can be stripped away in order to improve the performance in these areas. Indeed, NAS devices typically have very stripped-down operating systems that are surprisingly lightweight. NAS devices can be powered by small, embedded application-specific integrated circuits (ASICs), and some can fit on floppy disks or small USB keys.

You can build a NAS system with just about any operating system, but the majority of devices sold today are based on Linux distributions. A number of open source NAS distributions are available, the best known of which is probably FreeNAS. FreeNAS is a version of BSD (Berkeley Software Distribution) with reduced functionality that is less than 32MB in size. You can configure FreeNAS to run on a Live CD, which is a boot disk with all required operating system functionality. Other free NAS distributions include NASLite and Sun Open Storage.

Figure 22.1 shows the FreeNAS home page where you configure your NAS device. The range of features that you see in FreeNAS is common to NAS devices as a category.

FIGURE 22.1

The FreeNAS home page

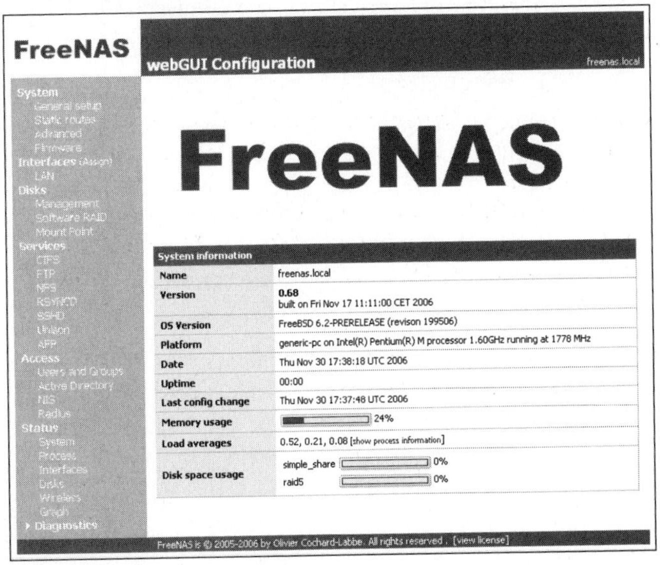

NAS devices typically support:

- A wide range of services and protocols so that they connect to clients in a heterogeneous network
- Software/hardware Redundant Array of Inexpensive Disks (RAID); RAID 0, 1, 0+1, and 5 are common
- Advanced disk utilities such as disk formatting and partitioning tools
- Active Directory integration, as well as Network Information Service (NIS) integration into UNIX/Linux directories
- System management tools, usually browser-based
- Network interface management, and protocols for accessing shared storage such as iSCSI

Microsoft has a very good NAS operating system, Windows Storage Server 2003 R2, which has appeared on a number of OEM (Original Equipment Manufacturers) systems such as HP's (Hewlett-Packard's) NAS.

Nearly all of the major computer OEMs have NAS systems in their portfolios. For Dell, their line is called the PowerVault series. HP's home NAS devices are the Media Vault service, their mid-level models are in the ProLiant Storage Server, and several NAS models are in their StorageWorks lines. HP has a large storage portfolio because they acquired Compaq, and Compaq had acquired Digital Equipment Corporation, both of which had large storage divisions. Sun Microsystems is another large vendor in the NAS area, and they have a line of Sun StorageTek NAS systems. Examples of small home NAS devices are the Snap Server, Kuro Box, TeraStation, and LinkStation.

NAS versus SAN

There is some confusion regarding the difference between NAS devices and Storage Area Network (SAN) storage servers. The two categories of devices are illustrated by considering two enterprise-class storage devices from the same vendor, EMC: the Celerra, which is a NAS server, and the Symmetrix servers, which are enterprise-class storage arrays. The difference between the two is in how data is transferred to a client.

A NAS device is a storage server with an operating system and a file system. When a client views a file on a NAS device, it does so by viewing the NAS file system. The selected file is transferred as a file to the client upon demand. By contrast, a storage array has nearly the same components as a NAS, but when you view a file stored on a storage array, you are viewing the file in your operating system's own file system. When you request a file or directory from a storage array, a mapping table maps that request to a set of blocks on a particular set of disks. It is those blocks that are transferred to you system, which is then responsible for managing the file or files contained within them.

The difference is subtle from a user's perspective: they see a file in a directory in a file system, and it is transparent to them where that file might be. However, from a system architecture standpoint, the difference between a NAS and a SAN storage array is fundamental. There are some high-performance NAS devices, but because they have the overhead of managing files, their performance is slower than storage arrays where the only overhead is direct disk access. Storage arrays are particularly good at applications such as backup and restoring, but offer no advantages when the operation is file-based. For example, when the application being accessed over the network is file-based, such as a large, streamed video file, a NAS filer is a superior solution. Table 22.1 details some of the important differences between a NAS and a SAN.

TABLE 22.1

NAS versus SAN

Feature	NAS	SAN
Network Types	TCP/IP, FDDI, ATM	Fibre Channel
Wire Protocols	TCP/IP, NFS, CIFS, HTTP	Encapsulated SCSI
Device Types	Any connected LAN system that can use the wire protocols.	A server with SCSI Fibre Channel that connects to a separate SAN network.
Data Transferred	Files and file metadata, security, user identity, and file locks. Files are identified by their position on disk.	Block data is transferred based on the block number of the disk.
Connected clients	Any network client that can connect through a wire protocol.	File sharing is through the file system of the connected operating system.
File system	Managed by the NAS.	Managed by the connected server OS.
Backups/Mirrors	Usually snapshots or images that are file-based, often capturing incremental changes.	Block-by-block copy, volumes are duplicated as direct copies.

Figure 22.2 shows a conceptual diagram of a NAS attached to a network of computers. Notice that the SAN is actually an internetwork of two different network types: Ethernet and Fibre Channel. The storage arrays are attached to the Fibre Channel network, which is referred to as the *in-band* network, while the Ethernet network connected to hosts is called the *out-of-band* network.

This separation between NAS and SANs is historically accurate and currently the rule, but future protocols may allow for Fibre Channel protocols to travel over IP networks and will blur this distinction, and products are being developed that blur the difference between NAS and SAN. Two examples of this new trend are the LeftHand Networks embedded virtual storage system and the open source Openfiler operating system, which provide both file and block-level access to storage.

Network file caching

One application of file servers is to push content out to different locations on the network. This is done in many ways. One approach is to use mirrors, replicating the entire content at different locations. This approach places a large burden on networks and can be impractical when an entire mirror must be replicated. In scenarios such as these, companies pre-build file servers and then ship them to the location where they will be deployed.

FIGURE 22.2

A NAS versus SAN topology

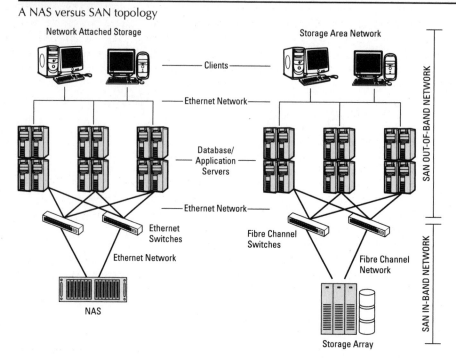

Another approach deploys NAS devices with special software that turns those filers into large, intelligent network file caches. The file cache is populated from client file requests, and so only the data that is requested is pushed out to the cache. Some of these systems set up distributed networks of caches with replication schemes. The fact that a subset of the data is cached makes this a much more efficient solution.

Many companies offer network-caching solutions. For information about Cisco's technology, go to www.cisco.com/en/US/docs/internetworking/technology/handbook/Net_caching.html. NetApp developed a line of network file-caching servers, but has sold this business to Blue Coat Systems, Inc. (www.bluecoat.com), which sells these systems under the ProxySG name.

File-caching solutions play a prominent role on the Internet. One company that specializes in this technology is Akamai (www.akamai.com). Capacity on their edge-caching network is sold as a set of solutions to various industries as Web site and Web application accelerators, for media delivery and streamed content, and for electronic software delivery. *Edge caching* is a term used to describe the distribution of content from a Web server to file caching servers that are geographically closer to the clients that use that content. Edge caching is usually sold as a service, so that if you go to a site such as XYZ.com that uses a caching solution, your request is redirected to the closed file caching server in the system.

File Service Protocols

There are several different file service protocols that are examined in this chapter, notably Network File System (NFS), Andrew File System (AFS), and Server Message Block/Common Internet File System (SMB/CIFS). The purpose of these file service protocols is to provide clients remote access to storage: these protocols make files and directories located remotely appear as if the storage were local on the client's system.

The benefits of using file services for remote file access are:

- Storage can be consolidated and protected
- The need for storage on client systems is diminished
- A user's home directory can be maintained on a file share and be made available from anywhere on the network
- Storage devices such as optical drives can be shared over the network with attendant economies

File service protocols are Applications layer protocols, but these protocols rely on Presentation layer software to manage data transfer, and remote procedure calls to access remote system data, as described in the next section.

Network File System

The Network File System, or NFS, is a protocol that is popular on UNIX and Linux, and that gives a computer access to networked file shares. It serves the same purpose as CIFS/SMB. It was developed by Sun Microsystems in 1983, and was subsequently taken over by the Internet Engineering Task Force (IETF), which was responsible for Version 4, the last released version. Sun's WebNFS software, which allows NFS file shares to be viewed and managed within a browser, has also recently been open sourced.

NFS was heavily influenced by the Andrew File System (AFS), as was the distributed file system (DFS) that is described later in this chapter. AFS is a distributed file system that contains a Kerberos security system for authentication and access control lists (ACL) for directories. AFS was developed at Carnegie Mellon University, and is named after Andrew Carnegie and Andrew Mellon. Versions of AFS are Transarc (from IBM), OpenAFS, and Aria.

NFS is considered to be a mature file transfer protocol, and is supported by nearly all networked server operating systems, although it isn't used as widely as CIFS/SMB or the NetWare Core Protocol (NCP). There is NFS support on Microsoft Windows, Novell Network, Mac OS, and the IBM AS/400 line.

NFS is implemented in Layer 7, the Application layer, as a set of routines for managing files over the network, called the NFS Procedures and Operations functions. The entire NFS protocol actually spans Layers 5 to 7, because NFS has a language set called the External Data Representation (XDR) language, which is used to define data types that can be exchanged with the network. XDR is best thought of as Presentation layer software, and is an interchange format.

Note

NFS versions 1 and 2 used UDP instead of TCP, which tended to make the system unreliable, especially across subnetworks and on internetworks. Version 3 and later use TCP and are more reliable.

The last module at the session level is the remote procedure call, or RPC, service. RPC is a component of all file services. It is these three subprotocols together that comprise the NFS system. RPC was developed as part of NFS, but has become a standard that is used for system interoperation throughout the computer industry in client-server applications (like the .NET Framework) that run over TCP/IP. RPC is the portion of the NFS module that is responsible for passing messages back and forth, and for maintaining the connection state.

NFS must be configured on both the server where the file share is and on the client. Many NAS systems come with NFS installed and allow you to simply designate a new share as an NFS share. In Windows Server 2008, the Add a Share Wizard presents you with a step that selects either NFS or NTFS access (or both) of the share as a check box selection; subsequent steps allow you to set up user and group permissions. On the client side, in Windows it is necessary to bind the NFS protocol to the network interface to provide client access.

The installation of NFS on Ubuntu Linux requires that you set up users and groups, and install NFS on the server:

1. Set up user and group permissions.
2. Install the NFS Server.
3. Create the server shares, and then export them to clients.
4. Install NFS on the client.
5. Mount the remote folder on the client, either manually or automatically at startup.
6. Test your client's NFS share access.

For more details on the exact steps, go to the Ubuntu SettingUpNFSHowTo page at https://help.ubuntu.com/community/SettingUpNFSHowTo. Another general procedure for FreeBSD may be found at www.freebsd.org/doc/en/books/handbook/network-nfs.html.

Server Message Block/Common Internet File System

The Server Message Block (SMB) is an Application layer protocol (less frequently a Presentation layer protocol) that is used to share files, printers, serial ports, and other network resources. Resources can also include access to network application programming interfaces, or APIs, named pipes (or connections), and other virtual objects. SMB uses a variety of Transport layer protocols.

SMB uses a client/server request/response mechanism to create connections between resources on one host with another host. An SMB client requests a resource such as file access from an SMB server, and SMB creates an opportunistic lock on the resource for its use.

SMB was developed by IBM for the IBM PC in 1985, and Microsoft and other companies added to it as it became a public standard. SMB is native to all versions of Windows, from Windows NT onward, OS/2, and Linux, and it was the protocol used by the LAN Manager software. There is support for SMB for nearly all networked operating systems.

SMB commands are sent using NetBIOS over TCP/IP (what Microsoft refers to as NBT) to create stateless connections between hosts. Commands include session control packets that create the connection to a network resource; file access packets that can access file shares: open, read, and write files; and depending upon the security in place, create files and directories; and a set of general message packets. The general message category includes packets that have commands that send data to printers, query for resource status, and manipulate named pipe, MailSlots, and other virtual connections. SMB has two security modes — share level and user level — both of which are described more fully later in this chapter.

Microsoft, SCO Group, and some other vendors created the Common Internet File System (CIFS), an extended version of SMB. There are many different dialects of SMB, and CIFS is considered to be one of them.

The Microsoft version of the SMB/CIFS protocol provides the following services:

- Protocol negotiation between various SMB dialects
- Opportunistic locks on network resources
- File and record locking
- Notification of file and directory modification
- Authentication and authorization for file, directory, and share access
- Extended file attribute support
- Unicode support
- Network printing
- Network browsing or services announcement

SMB/CIFS is one of the two important file transfer systems in use today; NFS is the other one. As an example of a CIFS server, the next sections take a look at the Samba file server.

Samba

Samba is the most widely used file sharing software, and it is the basis for a wide range of products. You install the Samba application on the operating system of your choice, and Samba file shares can be viewed over a network by a wide variety of clients and hosts. Samba (www.samba. org) is open source software; it takes its name from the Server Message Block (SMB) protocol, which is the same protocol that the Windows network file system uses. Samba is one of the best examples of a CIFS/SMB file server.

A Samba server can join a Windows domain as a file and print server, and even be installed on a Domain Controller, to provide file services to a domain. Samba's native CIFS/SMB file transfer protocol is the Windows native file transfer protocol; Common Internet File System (CIFS) is an extended version of SMB used by Windows and OS/2. As a Windows application, Samba supports Windows domain services. It can log into the Active Directory and be a domain member compatible with all of the Windows security protocols.

When a Windows client connects to a Samba share, it can do so using the NetBIOS over TCP (NBT) protocol. The Samba host appears to be just like any other Windows system in the Network folder. Samba also supports the Microsoft Remote Procedure Call (MSRPC), which makes Samba compatible with Web-enabled applications that are built with the .NET Framework. You can install the Samba Web Administration Tool, or SWAT, which is included with Samba distributions, to manage a Samba server from a remote browser.

Indeed, it is hard to find an operating system that you can't run a version of Samba on. Samba version 3 runs not only on Windows, but also on a variety of Linux and UNIX systems. There are versions for Sun Solaris, Netware, IBM OS/2, IBM AIX, IBM System 390, OpenVMS, Amigo OS, and Mac OS X clients. Many versions of Linux include Samba in their distribution, install the software as part of their base installations, or have a version readily available for download. SMB is universally used, but to use CIFS on some versions of Linux or UNIX, you may need to install third-party software that supports it. You can install the smbclient utility that is part of the Samba suite to allow UNIX clients to connect to Samba shares, send and receive files, and work with printer shares.

If you install Samba on a Windows system, then the SMB file share behaves as if it is a local hard drive, even if it is running on a remote system. If you install Samba on a UNIX system and join that system to a Windows domain, then the shares you create from UNIX directories appear in the Windows network as if they were standard Windows folders. In order for UNIX shares to appear on Windows, you must mount the shares first. You can use smbclient for this purpose.

When you install Samba on Linux systems, those systems format their Samba partitions with the SMB file system (smbfs). smbfs is derived from the Samba code base, but smbfs is not maintained by Samba.org, although you will find it on Samba's Linux distributions. Linux can mount an SMB share that uses smbfs directly into a Linux directory. When you browse the SMB file share, it looks just like any other local Linux directory and gives you full access rights.

Samba security

The Samba suite of programs implements all four aspects of CIFS services that you learned about in the previous section. The SMB Daemon (smbd) is responsible for the file and print functions, as well as the authentication and authorization required by either share mode or user mode. The difference between the two modes is that in share mode, a single password provides access to any authorized share user. In user mode, each user has their own user account and must supply their username and password to gain access to the share. User accounts are created and managed by the Samba System Administrator. Samba can also be placed into Active Directory (AD) security or server mode, bringing the number of security modes available in version 3 to four.

When Samba is on a Windows domain, it takes its authentication from Windows domain services or from the AD. Samba version 2 was the first version to provide Windows domain compatibility.

By Samba version 3, a Samba server is able to function as a complete Domain Controller — albeit not the latest and greatest version, but at least highly compatible with current Windows networks. Samba domain servers can use the tbdsam password backend as their authentication system, but this limits their use as stand-alone PDCs to small networks. For larger networks, an LDAP authentication backend, such as OpenLDAP, must be used. As I mentioned earlier, you can also install Samba directly on a Windows Server PDC.

To summarize, Samba can be placed into any one of the following four security modes:

- **User mode.** Access to Samba is through a user account and password.
- **Share mode.** Access is on a per-share basis by user account and password.
- **Active Directory Security.** All authentication is passed through to the Windows domain controller.
- **Server mode.** This is a deprecated feature of previous versions of Samba. In this mode, the client system logs into the Samba server as if the server is in user mode.

Samba name resolution and browse lists

The second major application is the nmdb program, which supports name resolution and browsing. Name resolution and browsing can be either a broadcast technology that involves a request/response mechanism, or a point-to-point client/server system. In the first instance, the sender builds a network resource list, while in the second instance, the server passes a previously built list of resources from a server to a client. Microsoft Windows Internet Name Service (WINS), which is a version of the NetBIOS Name Server (NBNS) used on other operating systems, builds a small database of available systems when a WINS client is detected. When name resolution is required, a query is made to the WINS server database, which takes the friendly name and then returns the IP address. The NetBIOS name service client, or nmblookup, that is included with Samba distributions can be used to locate NetBIOS names, resolve their IP addresses, and download those systems' browse lists.

NBNS servers can build browse lists across subnets, and unlike DNS, the browse list is dynamic. Access to an NBNS browse list isn't protected on a system-by-system basis, and so if you can obtain access to a particular network, then you can browse all of the resources in that network.

Compare NBNS' behavior to DNS, where records are added more or less permanently to the database and for which the common query is to resolve a name from an IP address. Reverse DNS queries exist, of course, but DNS suffers from problems related to frequent enough updates that would validate a particular system's availability or existence. With an NBNS server like Samba, the browse list is dynamic, and the systems have been or are currently registered and online; however, being a looser system than DNS, there are instances where conflicts arise.

NBNS also manages a browse list of network resources, including file shares and printer shares, by electing a Local Browse Manager (LBM) that maintains the list of NetBIOS names. When a client opens the Network folder, the browse list is obtained from the LMB (Local Master Browser) and that list is used to populate the folder.

Windows domains create a Domain Master Browser (DMB), which participates in creating a browse list with any other domain that that has a trust relationship with the first domain. If there is an LMB on the network, then the LMB will synchronize its browse list with the DMB. Each server in the domain, such as a Samba server, will eventually obtain the browse list through replication. However, the replication process can be slow, depending upon the type of network connection and the number of hosts.

Samba on Ubuntu

Samba can be installed on a Ubuntu system as a file and print server, or it can be accessed as a client when the smbmf file system is installed.

To install Samba as a server:

1. Open a terminal window and type the command **sudo aptitude install samba**.

2. Provide your root access password, and then press Enter. Samba is installed on your system. Figure 22.3 shows the results.

FIGURE 22.3

Installing Samba on Ubuntu Linux

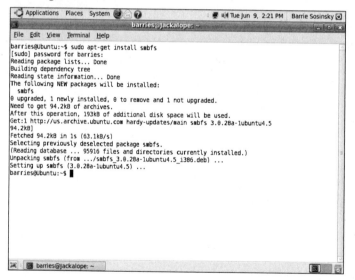

You do not need to install Samba on Ubuntu to access a Samba share over the network. Ubuntu is configured to connect to a Samba server using its native SMBCLIENT utility. This utility offers a command line function similar to FTP in that you can navigate the Samba share using commands such as CD, LS, GET, and PUT.

If you want to create a file system that Samba can use on your Ubuntu client, then you need to install the SMBFS software, as follows:

1. Open a terminal window and type the command **sudo aptitude install smbfs**.

2. Provide your root access password, and then press Enter.

As installed, Samba creates publicly accessible shares. That means in Ubuntu they are browsable from the Network Places folder and that a password is not required. If you need security for Samba shares, then you need to enable this feature in the Samba smb.conf file.

To turn security on and create users:

1. View and edit the smb.conf file by typing the following command in the Terminal window: **sudo gedit /etc/samba/smb.conf**. You can use another text editor instead of gedit for this purpose, if desired.

2. Change the line ; security = user to the following two lines:

   security = user

   username map = /etc/samba/smbusers

   Samba will check the smbusers file to retrieve the user accounts. Figure 22.4 shows the smb.conf file with the changes from Step 2.

FIGURE 22.4

The smb.conf file with user security enabled

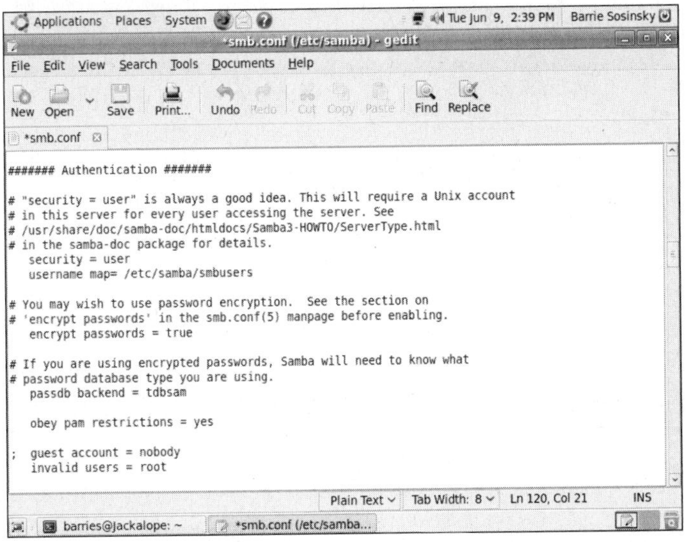

3. Save your changes to smb.conf; then close your text editor.

At this point, you have Samba installed and user security turned on. To access the Samba share, a Samba user must be created and added to the smbusers file, as follows:

1. Open the Terminal window and create a new user with the smbpasswd program by typing the following command: **sudo smbpasswd -a <username>**.

    Alternatively, you can open the Ubuntu Users and Groups administration utility and add the new user in the GUI.

2. Open the smbusers file with the following command: **sudo gedit /etc/samba/smbusers**.

3. Add the line **<ubuntuusername> = <samba username>**; then save and close the file.

4. In the Terminal window, type the following command: **sudo gedit /etc/samba/smb.conf**.

5. To create Samba user home directories (shares), change the text to add the following lines to the Share Definitions section:

    ```
    [homes]

    comment = Home Directories

    browseable = yes

    writeable = yes
    ```

    The smb.conf file should appear similar to the one you see in Figure 22.5.

The smb.conf file with home shares for users enabled

6. Save the file and close your text editor.

At this point, you should be able to browse the user share you just created on Ubuntu from your Windows system. The path to the share would be \\<*hostname*>\<*username*>.

Distributed File System

The distributed file system, or DFS, is a client-server architecture that can turn SMB file shares located across a network on many systems into a distributed file system. A client generally has access to only part of the entire file system. When a client requests access to a share in the DFS, the DFS server can direct the user to that share in a manner that makes the share appear as if it is a local resource.

DFS is particularly useful in large, geographically dispersed networks because copies of network shares can be deployed across the network to improve performance and reduce internetwork traffic. Nodes are typically distributed on a per-LAN basis. Clients can then be directed to the nearest copy of the data. Distributed file systems are extremely valuable in branch office environments, not only because of the performance advantages they offer, but also because, should any of the other nodes of the DFS become unavailable, the local node will still continue to operate without suffering any loss of content.

Figure 22.6 illustrates the use of DFS on an internetwork.

Note
The concept of a distributed data store shares some of the characteristics of a DFS, but is a different technology. A distributed data store creates group storage on a collection of peer-to-peer network nodes. User data is then copied between peers.

Microsoft has long been a supporter of DFS (its version is sometimes referred to as Dfs). Versions of DFS can run on any version of Windows Server, NT, and later. A DFS root can be hosted on a Windows NT 4.0 and Windows 2000 Server, as well as on a Samba Server. Later versions of Windows Server, 2003, and 2008 Enterprise and Datacenter servers can support multiple DFS roots on the same server. When DFS is part of a domain, its information is stored in the Active Directory and hosted on a domain controller. Microsoft DFS includes a replication and synchronization feature that propagates changes between DFS servers using the Microsoft File Replication Service (FRS).

The key to understanding DFS is the namespace that the DFS server maintains. That namespace maps to physical folders located in one or more locations. DFS namespaces map a list of folders to a list of target folders specified by their uniform naming convention (UNC) path. Targets are given a priority that determines which folders are replicated in what order. Should a client not be able to contact a folder in the namespace, it is possible to create a failback folder on another server. DFS doesn't require that you create a mapped namespace, but the feature makes DFS a much more powerful system.

FIGURE 22.6

The DFS system directs a user to a local copy of replicated data.

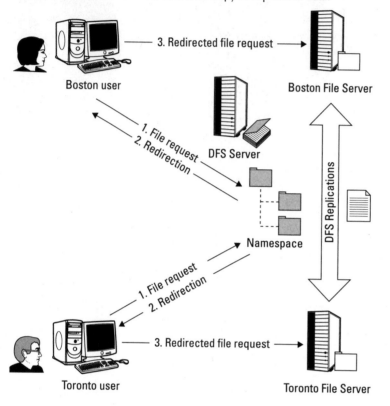

Figure 22.7 shows you a namespace mapping, along with its hierarchy.

Each object in the namespace is specified by a UNC path. Replication can take up a lot of bandwidth, and so you want to pay particular attention to the replication performance over low-bandwidth connections. For this reason, companies sometimes pre-stage a new DFS server when they are at the end of a low-bandwidth connection, such as a branch office. It's also valuable to create replication groups so that most replication traffic communicates over high-bandwidth connections.

You can choose to have DFS exist as stand-alone roots or as domain-based DFS roots. In the former case, the DFS file system can only be accessed on the system that it is installed on; stand-alone DFS does not participate in the replication and synchronization scheme that domain-based DFS servers do.

FIGURE 22.7

Namespace mapping and hierarchy

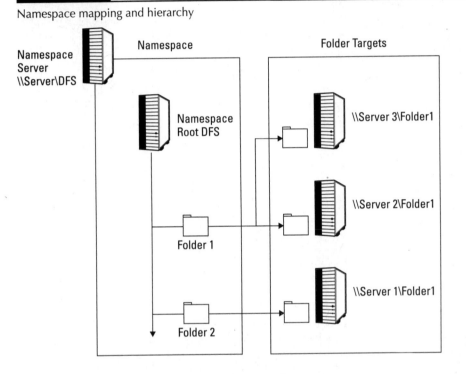

There have been many distributed file systems created over the years. CIFS/SMB, which was described earlier, is the most widely used distributed file system. Among the other more prominent examples of this technology are:

- Andrew File System (AFS)
- Apple Filing Protocol (AFP)
- DCE Distributed File System (DCE/DFS)
- Netware Core Protocol (NCP)
- Network File System (NFS)
- Coda
- InterMezzo

Note

There have been a large number of distributed file systems released over the years. Some of the higher-performance systems are distributed parallel file systems that stripe data across servers in a cluster or array. Some of these systems are built to also be fault tolerant. A discussion of these systems is outside the scope of this chapter. For more information on distributed file systems, disk file systems, memory file systems, record-oriented (database) file systems, shared disk file systems, peer-to-peer file systems, and other miscellaneous file systems, go to the Wikipedia List of File Systems page, found at http://en.wikipedia.org/wiki/List_of_file_systems.

Unfortunately, DFS isn't used as much as it should be, but it is definitely technology that is worth exploring if you have a large enough network to justify its deployment.

Summary

In this chapter, various technologies for making files available over a network were described. Although general-purpose file servers are deployed, a specially optimized file server, called a Network Attached Storage server, is an even more elegant solution.

Different file services are used to create network shares and make their content available to clients. NFS is a common protocol for UNIX clients, but SMB/CIFS is even more commonly used. SMB is the native protocol of Samba, an open source file server. In this chapter, you learned about what Samba can do, and how to install it on Ubuntu Linux.

Another technology for distributing file contents across a network is DFS. The distributed file system allows you to deploy copies of file systems across a network, and then use a DFS server to direct users to the nearest available copy of the data.

In the next chapter, Web services are described. This chapter explains what a Web server is, the HTTP protocol, and other related services.

Web Services

I n this chapter, I introduce the basis for creating and developing Web services. As more applications begin to migrate to the Internet, Web services will become increasingly important.

The Hypertext Transfer Protocol (HTTP) is the Application layer protocol that browsers use to transfer information. HTTP uses plain-text requests from a user agent or client to the server to request a resource, and the server responds with the appropriate resource in the appropriate format, provided that the request is valid. A set of status codes is defined to aid in negotiation and execution. In this chapter, you learn how HTTP messages are composed and executed.

HTTP can transfer information using HTML or XHTML, which, when processed by a browser, describes how to create and format a Web page. Web pages can contain either static or dynamic content. Some of the different ways in which dynamic content is controlled across a network are considered — server-side and client-side scripting, and CGI in particular.

A Web service is a mediated client-server application. An example of how a Web service can be implemented using SOAP as the communication or messaging protocol between service requestor and service provider will be presented. In a Web service, transactions are mediated by a service broker that runs on a third system. The purpose of the service broker is to make services discoverable and to list the capabilities of a service, as well as to pass information between the client and server.

A Service Oriented Architecture (SOA) is a framework that can be used to build distributed applications. The goal of an SOA is to allow a client to create and manage applications using services running on other systems.

A number of technologies and standards have been applied to creating SOAs and are presented to you in this chapter.

The Hypertext Transfer Protocol

The Hypertext Transfer Protocol (HTTP) is the native Application layer protocol used by Web servers and client Web browsers to transfer information between each other. HTTP uses a request/response mechanism, the request being composed of ASCII text containing one or more action verbs, and the response formulated as text formatted in a manner similar to the use of MIME in e-mail. MIME or Multipurpose Internet Mail Extensions is a text formatting standard that allows e-mail sent over the Internet to use characters in addition to ASCII, attach files to e-mails, divide messages into sections, and have headers that contain non-ASCII characters. Virtually all e-mail currently sent over the Internet is in MIME sent over SMTP.

HTTP is a stateless protocol; the information necessary to act on requests and responses is contained within the messages themselves. This frees the client and the server from the overhead of storing and managing user information. However, because HTTP is stateless, if a Web site needs to manage user data to customize a user's experience, it is forced to use other methods. The commonly used methods are writing and modifying cookies, authenticated logins for sessions, and server-side sessions.

HTTP is a standard of the IETF (Internet Engineering Task Force), and the latest version of the standard is HTTP 1.1, as defined in RFC 2616 (tools.ietf.org/html/rfc2616); its development was overseen by the World Wide Web Consortium (www.w3.org), which is responsible for the development of the Internet protocol suite (including HTTP). Although HTTP is almost always used on a TCP/IP network, the protocol's specification does not require TCP as a transport, only that the data that arrives be validated for its integrity.

In a typical HTTP exchange, a client or user agent sends a request out of outgoing port 80 to a destination server on the internetwork, which is listening on incoming port 80. The destination is formatted in the familiar Uniform Resource Locator (URL) format:

```
http://URL
```

Examples of this format include http://www.w3.org/2002/03/tutorials and http://192.168.1.1/ index, both of which are pointers to a particular resource. In the former case, the URL points to a folder called *tutorials*, while in the latter case, the URL points to a file called index.html. The reason that the latter private network address doesn't need an HTML extension on the filename is that browsers automatically assume that it is an HTML file. The resource is uniquely identified because the server must have a unique entry in the TCP/IP namespace, and because the resource must also be uniquely identified in the file system of the server. When you press the Enter key or click the Refresh button in a browser, you are requesting that the server return the resource, which is then displayed in the browser.

Note

The term Uniform Resource Name (URN) is a related concept where a resource is identified by its location in a namespace — for example, a book's Dewey Decimal number in a library catalog. URLs and URNs are both resource identifiers and belong to a general category of identification systems called Uniform Resource Identifiers (URIs).

HTTP requests

An HTTP request consists of the following parts:

1. **Header.** The header lines can contain a request for information or establish a condition. Header lines are optional, but in HTTP 1, the Host header is required.

    Examples would be: Accept: text/plain, Host: www.whitehouse.gov, or Range: bytes=200-500. The first line sets the content type to plain text, the second line gives the domain name of the server or virtual host, and the third line requests only a range of the resource's data that is being requested.

2. **Request line.** A request line contains a method (see below) or verb and the resource upon which the action is processed.

    For example, GET www.hulu.com would return the default page (often index.html) for that domain, unless the Web site has dropped a cookie on your system that returns a different page.

3. **Empty line(s),** defined as a Carriage Return (CR) followed by a Line Feed (LF), are required to separate the header and the request line from any other parts.

    In ASCII, the CR symbol is the 13th character (015 octal, 0D hex), and the LR or newline character is the 10th character (012 octal, 0A hex) of the lower 127-character ASCII set. You enter these characters in most editors using the Enter key for CR and the Shift+Enter keystroke for LR.

4. **Body (optional)** is the information returned by the server. If you requested a Web page, the HTML portion of the reply is sent back to your browser as the body part.

However, an HTTP message can be as simple as a one-line command, such as:

GET <*URL*>

Figure 23.1 shows the HTTP request GET www.google.com as displayed by the Live HTTP Headers extension of Mozilla Firefox. The GET command is followed by the optional fields, and the server responds with a 304 Not Modified status message. The first of the needed Web resources (the Google logo) then begins to be transferred. Another tool that is recommended for viewing HTTP requests is Fiddler, a browser independent tool that you can find at www.fiddler2.com/fiddler2/.

Notice the line Keep-Alive with a value of 300 seconds. This parameter was added in HTTP 1.1 in order to maintain persistent connections. In prior versions of HTTP, a connection closed when the request was satisfied. Because HTTP 1.1 can rely on a persistent connection, it can transfer information using the chunked transfer encoding method. Normally, data sent as an HTTP response is sent in one block with its length indicated in the Content-Length header field. However, with chunked transfer, encoding the data can be broken up and set into compressed pieces. Chunking allows the compression to be done on the fly instead of before transfer, which speeds up the process.

The second improvement that Keep-Alive allows is called HTTP pipelining. In HTTP pipelining, several HTTP requests are sent through a single socket without requiring a response from the server. Pipelining can result in significant improvements in the time it takes for your browser to display a Web page, particularly over low-bandwidth connections.

Other methods and verbs that HTTP 1.1 uses are shown in Table 23.1. The HTTP standard prescribes that some methods such as GETs request information without changing the server's contents or states. Methods of this type are deemed safe. However, there is no mechanism that enforces this requirement. An automated retrieval system such as a Web crawler or robot can therefore index a site using successive GETs without expecting any changes to be made. A safe request will still be logged, cached, and can alter a Web page's counter.

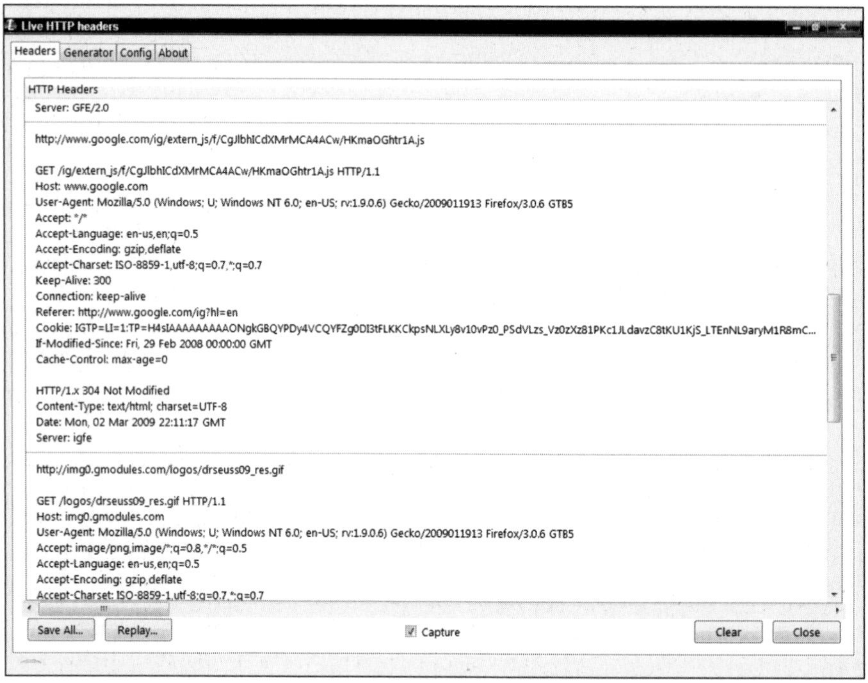

FIGURE 23.1

The request for the Google home page showing HTTP message composition in the Live HTTP Headers extension of Firefox

Some methods act on a resource once, no matter how many times you send the request. DELETE can only delete a resource once; any subsequent DELETEs will not find the resource on the server and will be ignored. A method such as DELETE, which works only once no matter how many times you request it, is called idempotent. An example of a method that is not idempotent is the POST method. On a Web form, the Submit button is usually a trigger for a POST request. That's why many Web forms ask you not to press the Submit button more than once for the transaction. Again, although HTTP 1.1 prescribes that a method be idempotent or not, there is no enforcement mechanism that ensures that this behavior is followed by a particular Web server.

TABLE 23.1

HTTP Methods or Verbs

Method	Action	Safe	Idempotent
CONNECT	Creates a tunnel using an established network connection. CONNECT is most often used to send encrypted data over secure transport (for example, HTTPS).	No	No
DELETE	Deletes the specified resource.	No	Yes
GET	Requests a resource. This is used by the Refresh button of a browser.	Yes	No
HEAD	Requests a resource, but without requiring a body section in the reply. This is used for retrieving metadata.	Yes	No
OPTIONS	Requests that the server return a list of methods that the server supports for the resource that is specified.	Yes	No
POST	Sends data to a resource for further action. This is used in the Submit button of a browser where the page has data to be acted on: forms, password validation, and so on.	No	No (mostly)
PUT	Uploads a resource.	No	Yes
TRACE	Requires an echo response for a request. TRACE allows the action of any intermediaries to be examined.	Yes	No

HTTP status codes

A response to an HTTP request returns the resource requested. However, if there is a problem, the Web server will return a one-line status code, along with explanatory text, to the client (user agent), which interprets the response and either displays it in the browser or acts upon it. The classic "404 – Not Found" error message is displayed when a server cannot respond to the request for some reason. Each browser can display different messages, but the explanations for each status code, shown in Table 23.2, are the HTTP 1.1 recommendations.

TABLE 23.2

HTTP Status Codes

Class	Status Code	Description	Notes
1xx		Informational	A provisional response that is a status line and optional headers terminated by an empty line. This only applies to HTTP 1.1.
	100	Continue	The client should continue with the request.
	101	Switching Protocols	The server will act on the client request for a change in the application protocol as indicated in the Upgrade message header field.
2xx		Successful	The request was received, understood, and accepted by the server.
	200	OK	The request succeeded.
	201	Created	The request has been fulfilled and the new resource has been created.
	202	Accepted	The request has been accepted, but the processing is not complete.
	203	Non-Authoritative Information	The data returned by the server in the header is not the definitive information from the origin server, but is obtained from a local or third-party copy. The information may be either a subset or superset of the original version.
	204	No Content	The server has fulfilled the request, but does not need to return a resource. Additional metadata may be returned by the server if the request is altered.
	205	Reset Content	The server has fulfilled the request and the client should refresh the document view.
	206	Partial Content	The server has fulfilled part of the GET request for the resource. The request must have a Range header field, and may include an If-Range header field if the request is conditional.
3xx		Redirection	Further action needs to be taken by the client to fulfill the request.
	300	Multiple Choices	The requested resource corresponds to a set of possible replies requiring that the client specify their choice.
	301	Moved Permanently	The requested resource has been moved to a different URI and any future references should use the returned URIs.

Class	Status Code	Description	Notes
	302	Found	The requested resource resides temporarily under a different URI.
	303	See Other	The response to the request can be found under a different URI and should be retrieved using a GET method for that resource.
	304	Not Modified	If the client has performed a conditional GET request and access is allowed, but the document has not been modified, the server should respond with this status code.
	305	Use Proxy	The requested resource must be accessed through a proxy indicated in the URI contained in the Location field.
	306	Unused	This status code is no longer used, but the number is held in reserve.
	307	Temporary Redirect	The requested resource resides temporarily at a different URI.
4xx		Client Error	A client error is detected by the server. Clients are directed to display the error to the user.
	400	Bad Request	The request could not be processed because the syntax is malformed.
	401	Unauthorized	The request requires user authentication. The response must contain a WWW-Authenticate header field with a challenge applicable for the requested response.
	402	Payment Required	This code is reserved for future use.
	403	Forbidden	The server understood the request but will not honor it. Authorization will not help and the request should not be repeated.
	404	Not Found	The server cannot find a matching URI for the request. The condition may be permanent or temporary.
	405	Method Not Allowed	The method in the request is not allowed for the type of resource that is indicated in the URI. The server response must indicate in an Allow header which methods are valid for the requested resource.
	406	Not Acceptable	The resource identified by the request is not capable of a response that has appropriate content characteristics, as specified by the request Content –Type header field.
	407	Proxy Authentication Required	The client must first authenticate itself with the proxy. The proxy must return a Proxy-Authenticate header field with the appropriate challenge for the proxy to obtain access to the requested resource. This is similar to the 401 message.
	408	Request Timeout	The client did not produce a request within the time that the server dedicated to servicing the request. The request should be repeated if necessary.

continued

TABLE 23.2 *(continued)*

Class	Status Code	Description	Notes
	409	Conflict	The request cannot be completed due to a conflict relating to the current state of the resource. For example, the resource may be locked. The response body should identify the source of the conflict.
	410	Gone	The requested resource is no longer available at the server and cannot be located.
	411	Length Required	The server refuses to accept the request without a Content-Length header field defining the length of the message body to be returned.
	412	Preconditioned Failed	The Preconditioned in the request header field evaluates to false at the server.
	413	Request Entity Too Large	The server denies the request because the request would result in an unacceptably long response.
	414	URI Too Long	The server is refusing service because the URI is longer than the server is willing to interpret.
	415	Unsupported Media Type	The server is refusing the request because the format of the requested resource does not conform to the requested method.
	416	Requested Range Not Satisfied	This response indicates that the request contains a range in the Range header field that is not valid for the current resource.
	417	Expectation Failed	The expectation in the Expect header could not be met.
5xx		Server Error	The server detects an error that is interfering with a response.
	500	Internal Server Error	The server encountered an unexpected error.
	501	Not Implemented	The server does not have the necessary capabilities to process the request. This can also indicate that the server does not recognize the request.
	502	Bad Gateway	The server as a gateway or proxy gets an invalid response from an upstream server needed to process the request.
	503	Service Unavailable	The server is temporarily unable to process the request. Most often, this error occurs due to a loading problem or when the server is down for maintenance.
	504	Gateway Timeout	The server as a gateway or proxy did not receive a response from an upstream server in the time allotted.
	505	HTTP Version Not Supported	The server does not support the HTTP protocol version required.

Source: www.w3.org/Protocols/rfc2616/rfc2616-sec10.html.

HTTP has been enhanced in order to create secure connections. The first of these methods appeared in early versions of HTTP and is the HTTPS protocol that is described in more detail in the following section. When you request a resource using `https://` the browser encrypts the message using SSL/TLS. In HTTP 1.1, an Upgrade header was added to the HTTP protocol. In a typical exchange between client and server, the client requests an encrypted resource:

    GET /encrypted-area HTTP 1.1

    Host: www.domain.ext

to which the server would reply:

    HTTP/1.1 426 Upgrade Required (status message)

    Upgrade: TLS/1.0, HTTP/1.1 (these are the required protocols)

    Connection: Upgrade

The response from the server indicates a client error relating to the use of legacy HTTP (1.0 and earlier).

Static versus dynamic pages

HTTP provides the Application level control that allows Web resources to be transferred from a Web server to a browser. These resources are described using the HTML, XHTML, or a related markup language, and from the content, a Web page is built by the browser. When a Web page is built using a set of stored files from the server, it is referred to as a static Web page.

When the Web page is built based on variable criteria and the page is constructed individually for a client, it is referred to as a dynamic Web page. Often dynamic Web pages are displaying information stored in a database. Web pages can be constructed and modified by scripts, either client-side or server-side. JavaScript is an example of client-side code and is an executable file bearing a `.js` extension. The advantage of client-side code is that it distributes the computing load, making it easier for Web services to scale. The downside, as you well know, is that executing code on client systems is a potent vector for security threats.

Server-side scripts impact a Web server's performance and often require that supporting software be installed on the server. Some scripting capabilities are almost always available on Web servers, with Common Gateway Interface (CGI) being a prime example. The tendency these days is to run Web servers as spare as possible in order to lower their attack surface, which means that it is not a given anymore that Web servers support the dynamic methods of your choice. When a CGI script is called, data in the form of environmental variables are passed to the CGI script. After the script runs, the results are returned by the script as standard HTTP headers and a MIME type, and forwarded to the requesting client (user agent).

The problem with server-side scripts in general, and with CGI in particular, is that for every request, an executable program must be loaded into system memory to process data. This approach is one that doesn't scale well. Alternatives to CGI have been developed that extend different Web servers so that the script runs in the Web server itself and does not have to be instantiated. Different Web servers use different add-ons or extensions — Apache modules, Netscape NSAPI, and IIS ISAPI — and these APIs are published and available for public use. Other versions of CGI, notably FastCGI and Simple Common Gateway Interface (SCGI), have been developed to enable CGI applications to run multiple scripts at once and thus eliminate the need to instantiate these scripts more times than necessary.

Web Services

A classic Web service has the elements shown in Figure 23.2: both a service provider (server) and service requester (client), as well as a service broker. Information is sent between the service requester and the service provider in a form that allows the requestor to use the service to obtain a result. As shown in Figure 23.2 the message passing protocol is SOAP, and the data is formatted in the WSDL or Web Services Description Language.

FIGURE 23.2

A Web service application implemented with SOAP

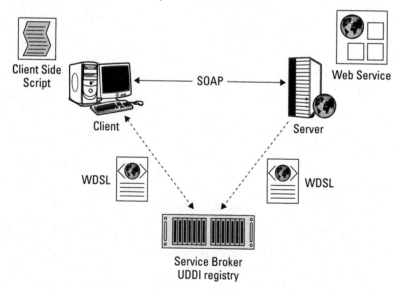

Many implementations of Web services use the SOAP Application layer protocol for their message to pass between requester and service provider. SOAP, which originally stood for Simple Object Access Protocol (but now stands for SOAP) formats data in XML and uses Remote Procedure Calls (RPCs) as its inter-application communication (IAC) mechanism. SOAP is now a W3C recommendation, currently at version 1.2.

SOAP messages can be transported using HTTP, HTTPS, and SMTP. It is an open industry standard. The fact that SOAP uses XML is both an advantage and a disadvantage. XML makes the messages both readable and editable with tools as simple as a text editor. The use of XML results in slower speeds than a binary data representation in situations of high Web service loading.

Other IAC standards — such as CORBA (www.omg.org/technology/documents/formal/components.htm), General Inter-ORB Protocol (GIOP; www.omg.org/spec/CORBA/3.1), ZeroC's Internet Communications Engine (ICE; http://zeroc.com/ice.html), and Microsoft's Distributed Component Object Model (DCOM; http://msdn.microsoft.com/library/cc201989.aspx) — are message-passing methods for distributed application development, but they use binary data for their message format. Binary XML is under development at a number of companies and may eventually be standardized and adopted.

The important characteristics in SOAP or any other IAC message-passing protocol is that it:

- Allow for transport on existing networks and be firewall friendly
- Be platform and language independent
- Run over HTTP, and preferably other protocols
- Be extensible for use by different vendors

Web services are not a classic client-server architecture. They use a service broker to mediate interaction between requestor and provider. In a Web service, information about the different services available on the server is sent in a special version of XML called Web Services Description Language (WSDL) to the service broker, where that data is then passed to the client. GoToMyPC is an example of a Web service, and its architectural diagram, shown in Chapter 32, is an example of this type of construction.

The service broker, while not required by SOAP, makes it easier to generate the client-side code that different service architectures, such as Java and .NET, require. Many service brokers use the Universal Description, Discovery, and Integration (UDDI) XML registry standard. UDDI is an open standard of OASIS (the Organization for the Advancement of Structured Information Standards; www.oasis-open.org/home/index.php), as are the WDSL markup format and many others. UDDI was meant to be a core Web service standard implemented in the form that you see in Figure 23.2, and formed the basis for storing what are referred to as white pages, yellow pages, and green pages. White pages store user ID and associated data; yellow pages store categories used in different industries to classify different systems; and green pages store technical information about services used by businesses.

The Web Services Interoperability Organization (WS-I) is an industry group that promotes interoperability between different Web services. Its work involves testing and recommending interoperability guidelines. WS-I publishes three specifications: WS-Security based on SOAP, WS-Reliability based on an OASIS standard, and WS-Transactions.

An alternative set of specifications called the Web Services Resource Framework (WSRF) is published by OASIS for use by Web services. WSRF defines different methods for maintaining session data during a distributed transaction. When a client communicates with the Web service, the message contains a resource identifier within the request. This information may be encapsulated within the WS-Addressing header as a URI, as XML data, or with a description of a particular target resource. The WSRF operations standardize READ and WRITE methods (actually GET/SET) that can work with the resource's state without the client having to be aware of the details of the individual Web service.

The overall OASIS Web service standard that is used to manage and monitor services is called Web Services Distributed Management (WSDM). WSDM plays the same role in Web service management that SNMP does in network management. Vendors use WSDM to create applications that display current status, provide Web management services, and can diagnose and repair systems remotely.

While RPC provides an architecture based on WSDL message passing, a different model called Representational State Transfer (REST) is applied to distributed architectures where standard methods for HTTP are used. A RESTful Web service can still use WSDL to convey a SOAP message over an HTTP request/reply, but it can be implemented by other methods without using SOAP.

Service Oriented Architectures

A Service Oriented Architecture (SOA) is a framework for building distributed networked applications from a set of interoperable services. SOA abstracts the service requestor from the different locations of the service providers. Indeed, a well-implemented SOA abstracts the service from the service provider. A service requestor seeking a particular service is required only to know the input to the service and to be able to use the SOA messaging format to communicate with the service. If the service provider is upgraded, or moved, or even replaced, but the architecture is maintained, then the service will continue to supply the result that is needed. This makes components in an SOA highly modular, and portable to different NOS and languages, and the whole system very flexible. Many services that are provided over the Internet are built using an SOA.

Note
Many people confuse SOA with SOAP, although they refer to entirely different technologies. SOA is an architecture, while SOAP is a messaging protocol.

In an SOA, the client or service requestor is typically a lightweight "application," and can often be running inside a browser interface. The word "application" is in quotes because the client is essentially orchestrating services running on one or more networked systems, and so the application is a name given to the particular set of services that the service requester is using at the moment. Figure 23.3 shows a conceptual diagram of an SOA. The Orchestration layer is used to describe a layer containing large capable software modules that can act in concert with other orchestration modules to perform a variety of tasks.

FIGURE 23.3

A conceptual diagram of a Service Oriented Architecture

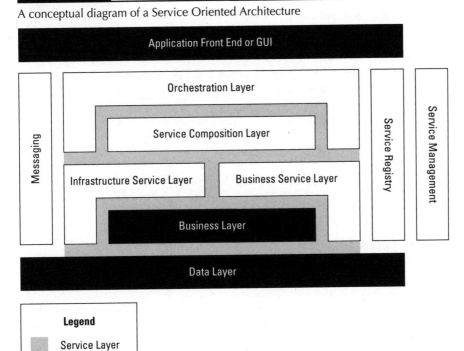

The modularity of SOA components and the independent nature of each service provider lends SOA to development in object-oriented languages such as C#, C++, C, Java, and others. Unlike many of the objects that are supported in these programming languages, SOA provider modules are very large objects combined to create executable programs. Many different technologies are used to create SOAs, including SOAP, RPC, DCOM, CORBA, REST, Jini, and Microsoft Windows Communication Foundation (WCF).

There is an industry effort under way to devise what is called a Service Component Architecture (SCA), which will provide a set of standards that different languages can all use to communicate with service providers, abstracting the language from the invoked service calls to the service providers. In the SCA, data may be represented as a set of Service Data Objects (SDOs). The transition of SCA from an industry working group to a standard is being overseen by the OASIS Open Composite Services Architecture (CSA) project (www.oasis-opencsa.org/).

Some of the important SOA frameworks, including the Microsoft .NET Framework and Java EE (Enterprise Edition), not only specify how to communicate between service requestor and service provider but also provide isolation of the service module from the operating system and other applications running on the server that they are on. Different service providers are independent of one another in an SOA. These features have allowed many legacy applications to act as service providers, which preserves the tremendous resources that have often gone into developing them.

As you can imagine, a fully implemented SOA can grow to be quite large with many components. To the user viewing a management GUI (in their browser perhaps), they might see a set of controls, data display, and other features, but each individual item or group of items could be running on individual service providers and take the form of a .NET Control or an Enterprise Java Bean (EJB). In order to understand complex environments and to be able to determine the impact of different changes as well as troubleshoot the system, a system map must be constructed that shows the different relationships. The situation is similar to modeling a database using a Computer Aided Software Engineering (CASE) tool such as ERWin, which uses entity relationship diagrams to normalize a database. The tools used to model SOAs are based on what is called the Software Oriented Modeling Framework (SOMF).

Note

Wikipedia has an introduction to service-oriented modeling that you can read at http://en.wikipedia.org/wiki/ Service-oriented_modeling. For a more detailed treatise on SOMF, you can read Service-Oriented Modeling (SOA): Service Analysis, Design, and Architecture, by Michael Bell (Wiley Publishing, Inc., 2008).

SOA is a highly attractive technology to many companies because it allows them to port their applications into services and charge for these services on an ongoing basis. In the past, if a user owned an office suite and an upgrade was created for some particular component or set of components, the vendor needed to either patch the software or provide a new version of the software for each of the users. In this new architecture, if the software is changed or upgraded, it can be upgraded at the servers without requiring all of that additional overhead and infrastructure to provide the benefits to user and vendor.

Summary

In this chapter, you learned how Web browsers communicate with a Web server to obtain resources over a network. The Hypertext Transfer Protocol (HTTP) is the Application layer protocol that browsers use to transfer information. HTTP uses a request/response mechanism to send commands, requests, and responses between the browser and server.

A Web service is a mediated client-server application. Web services can be implemented with SOAP or another messaging protocol to transfer information between a service requester and service provider. Web services are mediated by a service broker, which makes services discoverable.

You also learned about Service Oriented Architectures (SOAs) in this chapter. An SOA is a framework used to build distributed applications. SOAs have been used to create a number of well-known Web-based applications, and they serve as the future method by which applications can be delivered as services on demand.

In the next chapter, you learn about the mail protocols used on the Internet.

Mail Protocols

This chapter discusses the various technologies required to send e-mail over the Internet. Three important IP protocols form the core of these services: the Simple Mail Transfer Protocol (SMTP), Post Office Protocol (POP3), and Internet Message Access Protocol (IMAP). Together they form a system that is used to send mail from one e-mail client to another through two intervening e-mail application servers. The mechanism for polled e-mail is described.

E-mail messages consist of a header and a body. Different fields in the header are used for addresses. The SMTP protocol is used to format e-mail messages. This application protocol adds an envelope that is used by the SMTP server for routing. The Multipurpose Internet Mail Extensions, or MIME (which is an extension to SMTP), is used to segment and format e-mail messages as well as to include rich media content. The method by which MIME encodes non-ASCII or binary data is described.

A variety of e-mail clients are described. E-mail clients can support either POP3 or IMAP and offer a range of features that make getting e-mail from an incoming mail server more convenient and more secure. Other e-mail clients exist in the form of Web mail and terminal or telnet clients.

POP3 is used by clients to get e-mail from a POP3 server where the e-mail is eventually deleted at the server and retained by the client. IMAP is used by clients for server-based e-mail, where the data is stored at the server and can be stored on the client as well. IMAP is better suited for enterprise clients and for multi-user e-mail client access.

E-mail over the Internet is a client-server technology. The servers or Mail Transfer Agents (MTAs) provide router and transport functions. Some are messaging platforms. E-mail clients are the client applications. There are a very large number of e-mail clients, but they tend to offer a common set of features.

The Three Main Protocols

E-mail is one of the oldest computer network services that exist. It existed before the Internet was developed and was adapted for its use. On the Internet, the core mail protocols —SMTP, POP3, and IMAP — are prevalent and comprise a significant percentage of all messages travelling on the Internet.

Note

E-mail is defined by a set of IETF standards. The format of messages is described in RFCs 822, 1123, and 2822. RFC 822 replaced RFC 733. MIME e-mail formatting, described later in this chapter, is a draft standard contained in RFCs 2045 to 2049. For SMTP, refer to RFCs 2821 and 2822. Mail routing and DNS are contained in RFC 974.

Polled e-mail

The general sequence of sending an e-mail (see Figure 24.1) is as follows:

1. The sender's e-mail client or Mail User Agent (MUA) sends the encoded message in SMTP format to the outgoing SMTP server, which is referred to as the Mail Transfer Agent (MTA) using a Mail Submission Agent (MSA).

2. The SMTP server parses the recipient e-mail address (in the SMTP header), looking for the @ symbol to obtain the domain name, and then contacts that domain's DNS server to obtain the Mail eXchange record.

   The DNS Server returns the MX record to the SMTP server with the location of the POP3 (or IMAP) server that is listed for the domain.

3. The SMTP message is sent by a Mail Delivery Agent (MDA) over the Internet to the POP3 (or IMAP) server.

4. The POP3 (or IMAP) server sends the encoded SMTP message to the recipient's e-mail reader or client (their MUA) where the e-mail is decoded and placed into the recipient's mailbox.

   When an IMAP server, such as Microsoft Exchange or Lotus Notes, sends and receives e-mails, it uses a proprietary format for the e-mail and relies on a translation from standard protocols using either a mail gateway or some other service. If mail is requested by the recipient using a Web mail service, then the MUA involved in the final transfer is the Web browser.

Mail routing and its relationship to DNS is an important part of the mechanism for polled Internet mail. Every domain name server is required to contain a Mail eXchange (MX) record that defines where mail to that domain must be sent. An MX record can point to a specific server or host, or it can use a wild card to define an MX record that points to the default of a domain. Without this information, mail would be undeliverable.

FIGURE 24.1

A general e-mail transfer process

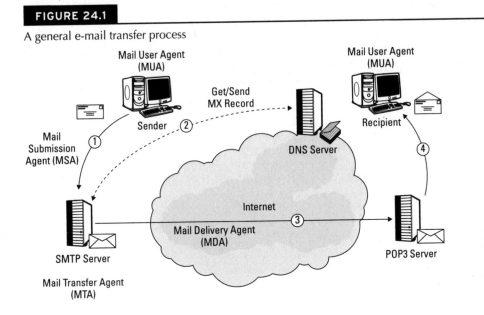

While POP3 and IMAP clients and servers use different mechanisms to transfer mail, most current e-mail servers and clients support both types of mail transfer protocols. If you open the configuration settings for an e-mail client such as Microsoft Outlook or the open source Mozilla Thunderbird client, both allow you to use either format.

The common port numbers used for these various services are shown in Table 24.1.

TABLE 24.1

Common E-mail Port Numbers

Protocol	Purpose	Both Plain Text and Encrypted	Plain Text Only	Encrypted Only
HTTP	Web mail		80	443
IMAP4	Inbound	143		993
MSA	outbound	587		
POP3	inbound	110		995
SMTP	outbound	25		465 (non-standard)

Push e-mail

Some e-mail systems are always on and provide a push service. As soon as the message arrives at the server, it is sent out to the phone without the phone having to poll the server for delivery. Push e-mail is different than e-mail clients that have a feature that checks for mail at regular periods, which is still a polling service.

Push e-mail is found in smart phones like the Research in Motion (RIM) Blackberry. Other examples include Google's new Android mobile operating system, Palm Treos, Windows Mobile (5.0 and later), the Apple iPhone, Sony Ericsson Smartphones, and others.

RIM uses a proprietary protocol; but the IDLE command of Push-IMAP and the SyncML protocols are both solutions. As long as the phone has its GPRS (roaming signal) on, the device can be located by their wireless service and the mail can be routed to their phone. Windows Mobile's push system is branded as Direct Push Technology and works with Microsoft Exchange to Pocket Outlook clients.

Push e-mail systems often employ a notification feature such as the "You've Got Mail!" alert that AOL uses. On UNIX, the `biff` program is used to send an alert to a terminal that performs the same function when mail arrives.

Another e-mail service that was developed in the 1980s and 1990s was the X.400 mail system. X.400 systems are an ITU-TS standard that is an alternative to the SMTP protocol run over TCP/IP networks according to RFC 1006. This messaging system did not achieve marketing success in the United States, but is used to some extent in Canada, and more frequently in Europe, Asia, and in South America, particularly for vendors transmitting Electronic Data Interaction, or EDI, messaging. Derivative standards exist for both the military and aviation industries. X.400's use is dwarfed by the e-mail Internet standards.

SMTP works with addresses in the form:

```
friendly.name@server.domain.ext
```

whereas an X.400 address takes the form:

```
C=no;ADMD= ;PRMD=mynetwork;O=domain;OU=server;S=Name;G=Friendly
```

Message Parts

E-mail messages are separated into two or more parts. At a minimum, there is a header and a body, and there is always a blank line separating one from the other. Most people would refer to the message as the body, but for a mail server, the message is the entire data object, header included.

Each header is broken up into several fields, some of which are required and others that are optional. The required fields are:

```
From: <sender e-mail>
To: <recipient e-mail>
Subject: <content description>
Date: <creation date>
```

Note

To view a list of header fields, go to www.iana.org/assignments/message-headers/perm-headers.html.

It is important to note that the header fields for `Reply-To:` and `From:` don't necessarily correspond to the sender or recipient's e-mail address. The address used for routing is obtained from the SMTP header, and unless the e-mail contains a digital signature that verifies the sender, any e-mail address can be used in the `From:` field.

Address fields can include mailing lists and aliases. A mailing list is a named object that is a delimited list of e-mail addresses, whereas an alias is a substitute name for one or more e-mail addresses. The technical difference between the two is that when an alias is applied to the envelope containing the message, it leaves the envelope intact. When the envelope sender is changed so that it is the owner of the list, this signifies that the address is a mailing list. The distinction is subtle, but important. Should the message not get to its destination, the owner is much more likely to care and act on a notification than the sender is.

Optional fields include:

`Cc:` Carbon copy to these e-mail addresses

`Bcc:` Blind carbon copy to these e-mail addresses

`Reply-To:` Reply to e-mail address

`Content-Type:` Display instructions, usually in MIME

`In-Reply-To:` The unique Message-ID that this message replies to

`Reference:` The unique Message-ID of both the current message and the one being replied to

A Blind Carbon Copy lists recipients who will get the e-mail, but whose names and addresses won't appear on the e-mail the recipient gets. Reply-To addresses do not have to be the same as the sender, nor must they be a single address. All of these fields can support mailing lists. MIME is described later in this chapter.

The body of a message consists of text in 7-bit ASCII. This includes all letter characters, and the "/" and "+" symbols. To use additional character sets and the upper characters of 8-bit ASCII, those additional characters must be converted into a representation in 7-bit ASCII. The process is called content encoding, or unencoding for the extraction of the original information. Several different encoding schemes are used, but the most widely used method is the one that MIME uses, called Base64. (The Base64 method is described later.) When 8-bit ASCII appears with only 7-bit ASCII characters, it is referred to as *8-bit clean*.

Many e-mail clients support not only plain text but HTML as well. HTML is plain text with embedded tags, but the formatting of HTML requires that the e-mail client have a rendering engine. The use of HTML in e-mail presents the same set of problems that HTML in browsers does; often e-mail clients render with the same browser engines your operating system uses. Links in e-mails and executable content can initiate malware or problematic actions.

Simple Mail Transfer Protocol

The Simple Mail Transfer Protocol, or SMTP, is the protocol used to send electronic mail between servers on an IP network, including the Internet. Most e-mail clients send their mail to an SMTP server as SMTP, although they use either the Post Office Protocol (POP) or the Internet Mail Access Protocol (IMAP) to receive mail. (POP and IMAP are covered in the sections that follow.) The best-known SMTP mail servers are UNIX sendmail (which was the first one), Windows Microsoft Exchange, Lotus Notes, Novell GroupWise and NetMail, Sun Java System Messaging, Postfix, qmail, and over 40 others.

An e-mail message is sent from a client to the SMTP server in the following way:

1. The message is composed by the client and the Send button is clicked.
2. The e-mail client connects to the outgoing SMTP server stored in its configuration settings through port 25.

Note
When an SMTP server sends mail to a relay SMTP server, the outgoing port is meant by the current standard to be set by a system administrator to port 587. An older SMTP port setting of 465 for secure SMTP is now deprecated.

3. The SMTP server parses the `sendto:` address into name and domain parts.
4. If the message is in the same domain as the sender, the message is passed to the POP3 server for delivery and the message is sent.
5. If the message is to a different domain, the SMTP server sends the message to a delivery agent.
6. The SMTP contacts a DNS server to obtain the Mail eXchange (MX) address of the SMTP server listed for the recipient's domain.
7. The outgoing SMTP server then sends the message through port 25 to the recipient's SMTP server where it is transferred into the POP3 or IMAP server.

   Some systems are set up with a smart host to transfer mail from the outgoing SMTP server over port 587 to an intermediate or relaying SMTP server, which then forwards it on. Any relay server that uses port 25 and forwards all traffic is referred to as an open relay server and may be blocked at their ISP. Many ISPs do not allow relay mail servers and only transfer mail on port 25.

8. The recipient's e-mail program, which is sometimes referred to as the Mail User Agent (MUA), or the intermediate SMTP server, which is sometimes called a Mail Transport Agent (MTA), sends the check mail request to initiate the mail transfer.

Not all messages can be delivered immediately, and so SMTP queues messages for a period of time and then retries periodically to resend the message. Many SMTP programs use the sendmail program as their delivery agent, and refer to the queue as a sendmail queue. The details on how long an SMTP server will try to send mail, how often it tries to resend a message in the queue, how often you are sent a message that the mail has not reached its destination, and if the mail is returned to the sender are configurable on the server.

An SMTP Envelope is the information that contains the addresses of the sender and recipient. The sender is required in case the mail is undeliverable, as it provides a means of notification. The SMTP Body is the combined header and body of the message, although the term SMTP Body is rarely used.

SMTP uses a very simple command set that is readable in the English language. Messages such as HELO for hello, MAIL FROM: for the sender's address, and so on are passed back and forth during an SMTP session. When an SMTP server responds to these commands, it does so using a set of numbers as responses. Common responses include: 220, ready; 221, closing the connection; 250, completed; 354, OK, transmit; 450, mailbox busy; 451, abort due to error; 452, aborted due to out of disk space error; 500, syntax error; 550, mailbox unavailable or does not exist; 552, aborted due to storage quota violation; and 554, transaction failed.

The Extended Simple Mail Transfer Protocol (ESMTP) is an extension of SMTP that can send multimedia files as e-mail messages. ESMTP begins when a client sends the EHLO or Extended HELLO command to initiate a connection, and an SMTP server would respond with an appropriate reply indicating a successful connection, a failure, or some other condition. A number of ESMTP commands support rich data transfer, including SIZE, BDAT, CHUNKING, DSN, ETRN, among others. ESMTP supports a pipelining feature where multiple commands can be sent at the same time.

SMTP has no built-in security mechanism. When a more secure version of SMTP is required, the SMTP-AUTH extension of the protocol can be used to force a user to log into the mail server before mail may be sent. The SMTP-AUTH extension allows a user access to the mail server, but provides no other checks on the validity or purpose of the e-mail that is sent. SMTP-AUTH can allow mail to be relayed, but requires that the relay server trust the sending SMTP server. For that reason, it is rare to find SMTP-AUTH used on the Internet.

Multipurpose Internet Mail Extensions

SMTP manages messages in the form of text files, which POP3 and IMAP clients can download. Many messages contain additional content that isn't text; therefore, there needs to be a mechanism by which content can be included in text. The mechanism that is used by nearly everyone is the Multipurpose Internet Mail Extensions, or MIME. Figure 24.2 shows the message hierarchy and how MIME segments messages.

MIME formats text sent in messages using the metaphor of an envelope. In the formatting hierarchy Root represents all of the messages that are sent to anywhere by anybody. The message advertises certain Properties, namely the Domain it came from and the Content-Type that describes the Domain information. The rounded rectangles in the figure represent either information or metadata. Regular rectangles represent formatting or organizational structure. The Transport Headers contain the routing information contained in the header, fields such as From:, To:, Reply-To:, Re:, BCC:, and so forth.

The main part of the hierarchy is the MIME branch which formats the body of the message into parts. Each part contains content, a description of the content, and the MIME version used to format the part. Parts further subdivide into Subparts, with each Subpart containing the same data and metadata formatting. The Preamble and Epilogue parts can be added to explain what the different parts are for, but are an optional feature. At some point you get to the final (lowest) level part to which you can attach Data, shown as BLOB in the figure. A BLOB or Binary Large Object is a file of any size or structure that can be appended to the message. BLOB is a container object field and can contain word processor documents, picture files, PDF files, or whatever you attach to the message.

As defined by RFCs 822 and 2822, e-mail messages are plain 7-bit ASCII text. Any language that uses upper-level ASCII (8-bit) is not accommodated by the e-mail standard. If there are any files such as pictures, documents, or formatting information that might separate one part of an e-mail from another, those are also not part of the e-mail standard. MIME adds the ability to address all of these shortcomings by adding plain text commands to e-mail messages that specify these additional capabilities.

MIME is responsible for:

- **Showing non-ASCII text (symbols).** SMTP uses the 7-bit ASCII character set. MIME extends that to the full 8-bit set that supports symbols used in other languages, such as é, á, â, æ, ç, ó, ý, and many others.
- **Specifying attachments such as pictures and documents.**
- **Separating a message into different parts.**
- **Symbols in message headers.**
- **Encoding and decoding non-ASCII e-mail content.**

A sample MIME header might start out looking similar to the following:

```
MIME-Version: 1.0
Content-Type: text/plain; charset=us-ascii
Content-Transfer-Encoding: 7bit
Content-Description: This is my example MIME message
Content-ID: <part0090829@servername.domain>
Content-Location: http://servername.domain/filename.txt
Content-Disposition: inline
This is the body of the message.
```

FIGURE 24.2

The Message and MIME hierarchy

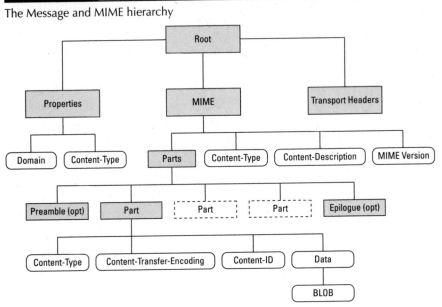

Base64 encoding

When you compose an e-mail in an e-mail client, MIME commands are added to the message which instruct the receiving e-mail client how to display the message. If your message is simple 7-bit ASCII text and nothing else, then MIME reports the content as plain text and the message is left as is. If there are attachments that accompany the message or if there is HTML content in the body portion of the message, then each part is given a MIME command that tells the client what content to expect and how to handle that part.

The encoding/decoding process deconstructs content on the sending end and restores it on the receiving end. Base64 encoding works by taking a file's data and separating it into 8-bit bytes in units 3 bytes long. These 24 sequential bits, now grouped into 3 sequential bytes, are assigned to four 6-bit characters. The 6-bit character set includes the 26 uppercase (A-Z) and 26 lowercase (a-z) ASCII letters, the 10 numbers (0-9), and the "+" and "/" symbols. The numbering sequence follows the order in the previous sentence from 0 to 63. Base64 refers to the fact that the character set is 26 or 64 characters in size. Figure 24.3 shows a representation of the encoding process.

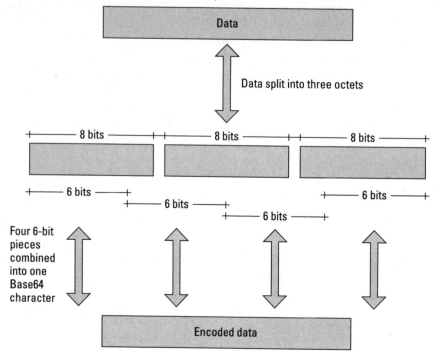

FIGURE 24.3

Encoding can take non-ASCII data and represent it in an ASCII form for e-mail transmission.

Let's consider an example of how this conversion works. Suppose that the three bytes are the numbers 124, 250, and 039 in that sequence. The bit stream that represents those three numbers is:

```
01111100
11111010
00100111
```

Encoding breaks this stream up into the following four 6-bit numbers:

```
011111
001111
101000
100111
```

The conversion of the four 6-bit binary number gives:

```
31
15
40
39
```

which is then translated into 7-bit ASCII as the following sequence:

f
P
o
n

Base64 encoding isn't the only method used to encode binary data in SMTP messages. Other techniques used are 7-bit and quoted-printable for normal SMTP, and 8-bit and binary when 8BITMIME is used as an SMTP extension. While Base64 is a common encoding scheme, Base32 and Base16 encoding schemes are also used. The difference between the three is that Base32 and Base16 (hexadecimal) use smaller character sets to encode the characters in messages. For hexadecimal encoding the symbols 0-9 are combined with the letters A-F (or f) to provide two character combinations such as A0, F2, and so forth.

MIME rendering

Any MIME message announces its presence by inserting the following line in the header:

MIME-Version: 1.0

If the content is simply ASCII text and no more, then you see the following line:

Content-Type: text/plain

A type can consist of a Content-Type as well as subtypes. To indicate that there is other content, MIME specifies different parts. An attachment is indicated using the `multipart/mixed` message, and the type of attachment is indicated by a header message `Content-Disposition:` along with the filename and extension. A Content-Disposition header can indicate which program can use the enclosed content. An example might be:

```
Content-Disposition: attachment; filename="filename.jpg"
```

A `Content-Disposition` line allows the sender to embed a plain text description of the purpose of the MIME message.

MIME also applies to other Internet protocols. Many HTTP requests are accompanied by data that is described by MIME and displayed in your browser. If an e-mail client can render HTML, then the message `multipart/alternative` instructs the client to either read the `text/plain` or the `text/html` section, depending upon whether or not the client is rendering HTML. This is usually a setting that you can control in the e-mail client. Other content types are also indicated by content-type instructions, including `image/jpg`, `audio/mp3`, or `video/mp4`. An application document can be attached with the content-type `application/msexcel`. A complete list of MIME media types may be found on the IANA (Internet Assigned Numbers Authority) at http://www.iana.org/assignments/media-types/.

The method used by MIME to encode the upper ASCII character set (8-bit ASCII) is similar to what you've already seen for Base64 encoding. The upper ASCII character is transformed into a string of ASCII characters of the following format:

```
=?charset?encoding?encoded text?=
```

Any Internet Assigned Numbers Authority (IANA) character set may be used; the encoding used is Q-encoding (quoted-printable) or B-encoding (Base64), followed by the character string that is being translated. There are some minor differences between the two encodings, but they work similarly. Thus you might see a header line such as:

```
Subject: =?iso-8859-1?Q?=New Tax Tables Listed in A2?=
```

which becomes `Subject: New Tax Tables Listed in ¢`.

MIME uses what is called a `Content-ID` header to create a unique identifier for the message part of a multi-part message. An example of a `Content-ID` would be something like:

```
Content-ID: <11.3.23957.2098389882@servername.domain.ext>
```

The only requirement is that this be a unique identifier, and so convention has it that it is separated into the hostname on the right of the @ sign, and some unique number scheme. Usually a timestamp is incorporated into the left part of the `Content-ID` string. A very similar unique header called `Message-ID` is used to identify the entire message.

Uuencoding is an alternate method for encoding non-ASCII characters into ASCII characters, which was used mainly in UNIX mail programs. The name *uuencoding* comes from the term UNIX-to-UNIX encoding. This method is an alternative to MIME. Uuencode is the UNIX program that is responsible for the encoding operation, and uudecode is the program that decodes the encoded information. MIME has largely replaced uuencoding, with Base64 used as the encoding technique.

Post Office Protocol

The Post Office Protocol, or POP, is one of the two common e-mail protocols used by client applications to retrieve mail from servers on IP networks. POP has gone through several versions, with POP3 being the most recent version. The Post Office Protocol is essentially a text file server. Messages are text that is appended to an e-mail address file.

The procedure that follows outlines a POP3 mail request:

1. A POP3 client initiates a check mail request and creates a connection to the POP3 server over port 110.

2. The POP3 server requests a name and password as authentication, which the client provides.

3. The e-mail account is given access to its message text file, and the client passes the last message received number to the server.

4. All messages numbered higher than the last received message are sent to the client, where they are appended to the end of that account's e-mail.

5. The POP3 server closes the connection and deletes the e-mail that it just sent from the account's text file on the POP3 server.

Step 5 defines a very important potential difference between the POP3 mail protocol and the IMAP protocol that is described in the next section. IMAP is server-based e-mail. When messages are sent to an IMAP client, they are retained on the server so that they may be accessed by another IMAP session at a later time or from a different location. When using a POP3 client, there is a setting in the client software that allows you to either delete all delivered mail from the server, or leave it on the server. Most people use the default setting of deleting the e-mail after it is received.

When a POP3 client elects to leave the mail on the server, it needs to be able to recognize new messages when it next connects. Should another POP3 client come along and download messages and then have the POP3 server delete them, the numbers attached to the messages that come in afterwards will no longer match what the original POP3 client expects. To solve this problem, POP3 uses a 32-bit Unique IDentification Listing (UIDL) number to identify messages. When the original POP3 client views the UIDL for a message, it can now map those messages to the current message ID. IMAP clients use a similar system, but their UIDLs are assigned as sequential numbers so that the IMAP client can retrieve the next number in the sequence.

POP3 servers use a very simple command and retrieval language. It isn't necessary to use a POP3 client to retrieve e-mail. If you have a telnet client, you can connect to the POP3 server over port 110 and send the POP3 server the session commands required to retrieve your mail. After login and sending the RETR command, the POP3 server sends your messages to the telnet client for you to read.

POP3 allows clients to log into a POP3 server using plain text or unencrypted text. A variety of authentication methods are added to POP3 to protect user logins. The most common method is called Authenticated POP (APOP), which employs an MD5 hash function to encrypt login. Many POP3 clients support APOP.

Web mail clients

Web mail is a Web client that runs inside a browser. A number of e-mail clients offer a browser version, most prominently Microsoft Outlook Web Access. A variety of Web mail services exist, many of which are Internet based; they include Hotmail (now owned by Microsoft), AOL mail, Yahoo! Mail, and Gmail (Google), among others.

Web mail providers run the mail servers that store and send a user's mail and to which any browser can connect. The client software is embedded on the server and can provide nearly all of the functions that a stand-alone client application can; and the browser renders the user interface (UI) on the client. Google's Gmail uses an interface developed in JavaScript. Many of these services are free to use at some basic level, which is usually tied to the amount of storage that they allow on their servers. When you pay for the service, your storage is increased.

The success of Web mail has led enterprise mail servers to offer this capability. There are also several open source Web client applications that you can use to connect to mail servers. Most Web mail clients are written to access either IMAP or SMTP servers. However, there are a number of Web mail clients that can connect to both POP3 and IMAP servers.

Perhaps the best-known example of one of these Web mail sites is Mail2Web.com, which is owned by SoftCom Technology Consulting Inc., in Toronto. Mail2Web's service offers many of the features of a pure e-mail client within a browser. With Mail2Web, you only need to specify the e-mail account and login, and the service connects and retrieves your mail; you don't need a Mail2Web account to use the free service.

Internet Message Access Protocol

The Internet Message Access Protocol, or IMAP, is a server-based mail program. Unlike POP3, which was described in the previous section, IMAP creates an e-mail data store on the server that you can access from an IMAP client. Microsoft Exchange and the Outlook client are the classic examples of an IMAP server and client. IMAP has some very powerful advantages over POP3, particularly for business applications. With IMAP there is a permanent record of e-mail, and your e-mail can follow you anywhere you can connect to it.

IMAP supports both online or connected sessions, and offline or disconnected sessions. To provide for situations where a system is disconnected from an IP network, most IMAP clients store their e-mail locally and synchronize the data when they connect to the IMAP server. Any changes you make locally are sent to the server the next time you connect, and any changes on the server that you might have made from another IMAP client are sent from the server to your current IMAP client.

If you have a desktop and a laptop, IMAP provides a way to have e-mail appear on both systems and an automated mechanism by which you can synchronize your work. You can synchronize POP3 e-mail between systems, but this is done manually and isn't part of the POP3 system, which makes synchronizing harder and more subject to errors.

IMAP uses a system of simple messages, just like SMTP and POP3 do, and communicates them over port 143.

Mail Servers

A mail server or Mail Transfer Agent (MTA) is an application server dedicated to mail transport. Sometimes these systems are referred to as a mail router or mail transport agent, and very infrequently as an Internet mailer, but they mean the same thing as the commonly used MTA. There are a large number of different MTAs deployed throughout the world, and because they usually don't respond to automated queries to identify themselves, the market share of the servers is a little unclear. Some studies seem to indicate that the largest number of MTAs are shared by Microsoft Exchange on the Windows platform, and sendmail, qmail, and Exim on the Linux and UNIX platforms. Other studies indicate a much broader distribution among many more products.

Mail servers are not simply a transport application, although some are configured that way. Most mail servers manage message stores, which is a rich data object database containing messages and all of the other content that is carried along with modern e-mail. The messaging portion of the application can be very feature rich and include filtering, smart routing, identity management, security, and many other features. A key feature is the establishment of user accounts and the maintenance of mailboxes. In some systems, a mailbox can be a single file, and in others, it can be a directory of files where incoming messages are stored.

Products like Microsoft Exchange and IBM Lotus Domino are servers backed by the enterprise-class databases SQL Server and DB2, respectively. Domino was originally developed as the Lotus Notes message server, integrated into a groupware collaboration platform, and can function as an application server and/or a Web server. Microsoft Exchange was developed as a messaging platform to which collaboration was added. The most popular mail server in use is sendmail, which is an open source program that replaced an older program called delivermail. Estimates are that around 30 percent of all mail servers run sendmail.

Sendmail is configurable from the command line. One way to expose sendmail is to use the Web-based GUI called Webmin, shown in Figure 24.4. Webmin (www.webmin.com) is open source software that can expose operating system services for OpenSolaris, Linux, and other flavors of UNIX. Sendmail is only one of the applications that it works with. Others include the Apache HTTP Server, MySQL, and PHP. Each of the Webmin modules loads the appropriate configuration file, essentially creating a plug-in architecture.

FIGURE 24.4

Sendmail configuration exposed in the browser GUI managed by Webmin

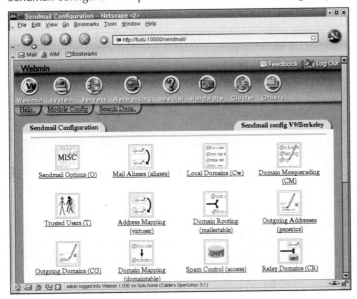

Setting Up a Mail Client

An e-mail client or Mail User Agent (MUA) is a program that can compose and send messages as well as retrieve and display them. In a client-server architecture, the e-mail client is the client portion and the mail server is the server portion. Other programs that can perform these functions are also referred to as e-mail programs, whether they run inside a browser such as Web mail or at a command prompt inside a telnet session.

Mail clients do not run as a service unless they are automatically started as a system preference. Most mail clients are configurable as either an SMTP/POP3 or IMAP client. This allows clients to download e-mail from nearly all of the Internet mail servers. Some e-mail clients such as Eudora have been largely single user, while others such as Microsoft Outlook are designed to be multiuser. The organizational structure of mailboxes is separated by accounts. So while Outlook uses a single mailbox file (PST), Eudora separates mailboxes (MBX) into different files.

To set up a mail client, you need to provide the following pieces of information:

- The account if you are using a multi-account client
- A display name or "real name"
- A valid e-mail address
- The incoming server address, either a POP3 or IMAP server
- The username used to log into the server
- The outgoing SMTP server

A typical settings dialog box is shown in Figure 24.5, taken from Eudora 2.6. Eudora 2.7 was Qualcomm's last commercial version. Eudora is in the process of being converted to an open source client that will be called Penelope, and will adopt some of the features of perhaps the best-known open source e-mail client, Mozilla's Thunderbird.

Microsoft's mail clients include Outlook Express (XP and before), Outlook (all versions), and Windows Mail (Vista). These products place a user into setup with a wizard in which you create the e-mail account before entering the settings. Windows Mail supports not only POP3 and IMAP but also HTML servers.

Note

For an extensive list of e-mail clients, their current versions, protocol support, and features, go to http://en. wikipedia.org/wiki/Comparison_of_e-mail_clients.

A list of the best-known e-mail clients would include the following programs: @mail, Eudora, Gnus, Novell GroupWise, IBM Lotus Notes, Kerio WebMail, Apple Mail, Microsoft Entourage (for the Macintosh), Microsoft Office Outlook, Outlook Express, Pine, Mozilla Mail & Newsgroups, Mozilla Thunderbird, Netscape Messenger, Novell Evolution, Opera Mail, SeaMonkey Mail & Newsgroups, and Squirrelmail.

FIGURE 24.5

FIGURE 24.5

E-mail client settings

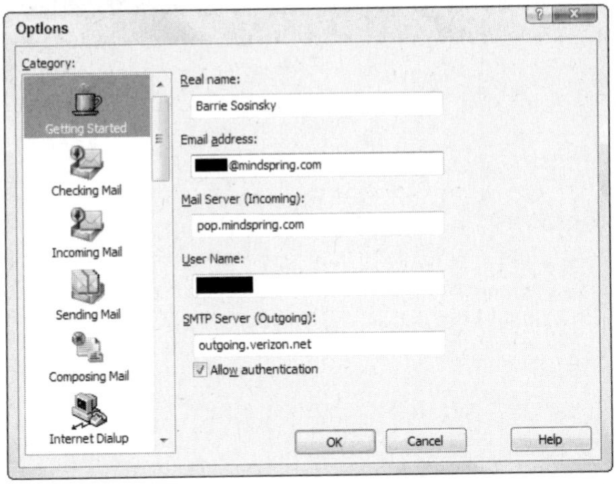

Some of the more valuable features that you can find in e-mail clients include the following:

- **Encrypted database.** This secures the database file from inspection by outside parties.

- **Indexed searches.** An e-mail client that indexes the content in its database allows for very fast searches. Some of these programs index an IMAP data store as well as a local database.

- **HTML e-mail rendering.** This feature makes an e-mail look like a browser page. The same risks apply to working with embedded content in this type of display that exist for a browser page.

- **Image blocking.** This is the ability to display a placeholder in place of the downloaded image file. This is valuable for reducing load time and can help reduce unintended click-throughs.

- **Junk mail filtering.** Filtering in general is quite valuable. This redirects e-mail by criteria that you select to be placed into the mailbox of your choice. The junk e-mail filter is a proactive mechanism that evaluates mail based on a set of criteria and places the mail into the Junk folder. The best junk filters use a Bayesian filter that learns what you consider junk and adds similar e-mails to the junk list. Eudora's filtering mechanism is shown in Figure 24.6.

- **Phishing blocker.** This tool prevents sites from displaying links that take users to sites where their information is hijacked. Usually phishing filters work off of blacklists.

- **Message templates.** Templates are documents that you can use as models for your e-mails.

FIGURE 24.6

Eudora's filter creation dialog box

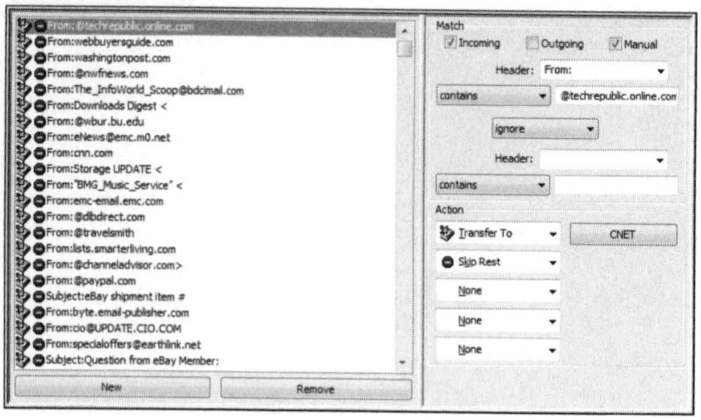

- **Encryption.** Many e-mail clients support encryption inline or through open standards such as Pretty Good Privacy (PGP) or OpenPGP or through the use of Secure MIME (S/MIME).

- **Scripting.** The ability to program actions in VBScript, JavaScript, Python, Java, PHP scripts, and others allows advanced users to add additional automation to the e-mail client. Automatic automation can do things such as add a signature, perform a search and replace, modify an address list, and so forth.

Summary

Internet e-mail is one of the most important network services that the IP protocol offers to users. It relies on three important protocols that were described in this chapter: the Simple Mail Transfer Protocol, Post Office Protocol, and Internet Message Access Protocol. The method that is used to send mail from one e-mail client to another through these services was described.

E-mail messages have a specific form and are formatted using MIME when sent using SMTP. This chapter examined how MIME works, and how data is encoded for transfer.

A variety of e-mail servers and clients were examined and surveyed.

In the next chapter, I describe the use of streaming media, sound, video, and other rich media. Streaming services allow for real-time transfer of data that requires large file sizes. The special techniques used for these services are explored.

Streaming Media

S treaming media is a network technology that sends content to a user that can be played as it arrives. Streaming is associated with a special server called a *streaming server*. A related technology called *progressive download* can use Web servers to distribute media files.

Streaming content makes heavy use of network resources. A network architecture needs to be established to create the content, stage it to servers, and route the content to clients. All streaming solutions use a set of protocols to help package, control, and manage media traffic. The four IETF standard protocols — the Real-Time Streaming Protocol, the Real-Time Control Protocol, the Real-Time Transfer Protocol, and the SMIL markup language — are described in this chapter. The difference between unicasting and multicasting is described, and delineates different media delivery systems.

To prepare content for streaming or progressive downloads, media files need to be encoded. The process takes raw files and then compresses, segments, and packages them appropriately. Encoding can create content that has either constant or variable bit rates, as well as create a package of streams in multiple bit rates.

There are four main streaming media platforms in use today: Windows Media Services, RealNetworks Helix Server, Apple QuickTime Streaming Server, and Adobe Flash Media Streaming Server. All of these servers have their own formats, but with the exception of Flash, they work with a variety of other formats.

Adobe Flash is animation software that is served as content on Web pages. Flash can contain a variety of rich media content. Flash has a nearly universal penetration on the Web and is responsible for much of the inline media player content. Microsoft has an alternative technology called Silverlight that offers many of the same capabilities but is based on the Windows Presentation Foundation and the .NET Framework.

How Streaming Works

Streaming media is the real-time delivery of content, one piece at a time, and it is pervasive and transformational technology. When you play a video from Google's YouTube.com or a TV episode from ABC.com, you are viewing video streamed over the Web. Streaming includes listening to audio on Internet radio stations such as Last.FM in media players like iTunes (see Figure 25.1), and viewing class lectures that you might download from the University of California at Berkeley or MIT. Long-distance learning is a revolution in education, and the technology described in this chapter makes it all possible.

FIGURE 25.1

Internet radio played within Apple iTunes is streamed content, unlike podcasts.

Streaming versus progressive downloads

Streaming is used to transfer content over a network so that it can be played back in parts as it arrives. Streaming refers to the manner in which the content is transported and arrives as a stream of packets. Even the verb "to stream" has entered the vernacular to describe the process. To be a little more precise, streaming occurs when media is sent from a streaming server to a client and played by a player from the memory buffer it is stored in. As you play streamed content, the player discards the content after it is played; that is, streamed content never exists as a complete file that you can save to your disk and play at a later time. This is valuable from the viewpoint of the content creator or provider as it preserves the copyrights of these parties by making it hard to duplicate the material.

Note

There are methods for using third-party tools to save streamed content such as FLV files, which are described later in this chapter.

Try as they might, there is no way that Digital Rights Management (DRM) software can protect content from those who want to copy it. At some point, the content must be displayed as output to an analog device: a speaker or a screen. If the person copying the content is willing to live with a certain loss of quality, the content can be rerecorded with a camera, microphone, or input to a second computer. This is as true of streamed content as it is of any other replay method. The problem is called the "analog hole." It is possible to tag content in ways that make the copies obvious upon closer scrutiny, but it is impossible to prevent the creation of a copy that will look to the average consumer as if it were an original.

In contrast, progressive download takes content on a Web server and delivers it to a client where it may be played as it downloads or when the download is completed. Typically, RealNetworks and Windows Media use streaming content, while QuickTime and Flash players use progressive downloads. Most players can use content supplied by both kinds of delivery methods. Figure 25.2 shows a schematic that represents the different components of streaming and progressive download using the Real-Time Streaming Protocol (RTSP) for network control of steaming media. RTSP use a messaging system called Real-Time Control Protocol (RTCP) and breaks apart files into Real Control Packets (RCP). RTSP is an Internet Engineering Task Force (IETF) standard (RFC 2326) that is described in detail later in this chapter.

In Figure 25.2, captured content is transferred to an encoding station where the media file is transformed. Encoding translates the video file into a particular format that is convenient to send. An example of an encoding format is the popular H.264. The encoded file can be sent to a Web server (shown in Figure 25.2) and transferred to a client by a unicast (1:1) transfer over the Web. This type of file transfer can be controlled by a client system (lower right) called RTCP (Real-Time Control Protocol) that is used by the client to control the flow of packets sent to it.

An alternative pathway is shown at the top of Figure 25.2. The encoded file is sent to a streaming media server where the file is packetized as an RCP data stream. The pieces of the video file are sent to a multicast router where it can be sent to multiple client systems at the same time. Multicasting can also be controlled by RTCP flow control messages. Clients decode the media file to return it to its native format for replay.

FIGURE 25.2

The different components of streaming and progressive download

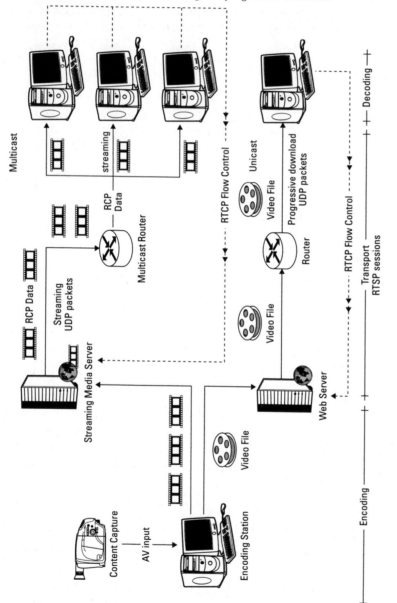

Most consumers can barely tell the difference between streaming and progressive download because they both supply playable content. Indeed, progressive downloads are sometimes referred to as pseudo-streaming, or in Apple QuickTime as fast-start streaming. The main difference between the two is found in the behavior of the fast forward, rewind, and navigation controls, and in the fact that progressive download stores a copy of the file to disk. Progressive downloads can only be played in the order from beginning to end, although you can move backwards and forwards in the part of the file that has already been downloaded and buffered. Streamed content can be played out of order, provided that the part of the content you want to view has already been downloaded.

You may encounter the terms HTTP streaming or Web server streaming; both simply represent another version of progressive downloading because they create a copy of the media file in a local cache that can be copied if the user understands the system being used. One difference, though, between progressive downloads and HTTP streaming is that the use of HTTP over port 80 makes it much easier to penetrate firewalls than other streaming transport methods.

Events can be streamed in real time or supplied as video on demand (VOD). When events are in near real time over an IP network, they are sometimes referred to as "Live-Live" or more frequently as Webcasts. On-demand implies that the media has been prerecorded and stored, and suggests but does not require that the content has also been edited or altered in some way.

Table 25.1 summarizes the two technologies of streaming versus progressive download.

TABLE 25.1

Streaming versus Progressive Download

Feature	Progressive Download	Streaming
Staging	Web server	Streaming server
Best for	Stored content replay	Video on demand (VOD), Live
Bandwidth	Insensitive to network conditions Retransmits lost packets	Sensitive to network conditions Lost packets are dropped in playback
Firewalls	Firewall friendly	Requires opening a special port most of the time
Player control	Must play in sequence	Can skip ahead if content is in buffer
Copies	Copy left on drive	No copy retained
Content protection	No	Yes
Casting	Unicast only	Broadcasts and multicasts supported

The ability to sequence a group of files can be scripted in some products like Adobe Flash. Special files that specify sequences, called Synchronized Markup Integration Language (SMIL) files, also allow you to coordinate replays. (SMIL files are discussed later in this chapter.) One of the techniques people use with streamed content is called a pre-roll or gateway file. A pre-roll/gateway file can be used to advertise content, inform the viewer about the stream that they are about to view (in case they might want to bail out), and for many other purposes.

Unicasting versus multicasting

Streaming is a point-to-point technology. A server defines one endpoint of the connection providing content and a client player or browser defines the other endpoint. When a media server maps a single stream between the two endpoints, it is called *unicasting*. You can think of unicasting as being equivalent to a private message. Unicasting is *narrowcasting*; the sender can customize the message for the audience with unique control over the message, but at an attendant cost. When a content provider uses multiple streams to broadcast a message to multiple consumers, the technology is called *multicasting*. Multicasting allows the sender to create one consistent message that has an economy of scale.

Note

RSS feeds would not be considered a streamed media application, as the entire file must be delivered to be used. RSS is a subscription service based on specifications contained in either XML or RSS text files.

Table 25.2 lists some of the important differences between unicast and multicast streaming.

TABLE 25.2

Unicasting versus Multicasting

Feature	Unicasting	Multicasting
Best used for	On demand	Live or scheduled
Bandwidth requirements	Large capacity for multiple streams	Small capacity for one stream
CPU requirements	Heavy CPU load to manage individual streams	Low CPU load to manage one stream
Client playback	Players can have individual control over playback	Players get the same content and have the same capability and timing
Infrastructure requirements	Bandwidth that scales	Multicast router(s)
Message control	High	Low

Streaming plays an important role in many enterprise deployment technologies. Products like Altiris Software Virtualization Solution (SVS), the Citrix XenApp application streaming server, and Microsoft SoftGrid (along with their Zero Touch technology) are examples of technology that relies on streamed content from distributed deployment servers. All these systems allow developers to deploy software and content in a multicast topology.

In the case of SoftGrid, applications are delivered in a way that allows them to begin operating on client systems before the entire application has been streamed to the client, a form of application virtualization. An application is prepared by the SoftGrid Sequencer, which deconstructs the application by determining its system settings, which DLLs or INI files it uses, and other parts, and then sending the parts required for startup in the first part of the stream. Because the client requests the application first, the technology is a pull technology. Figure 25.3 shows the SoftGrid implementation using the Microsoft System Center Virtual Application Server.

FIGURE 25.3

SoftGrid application streaming

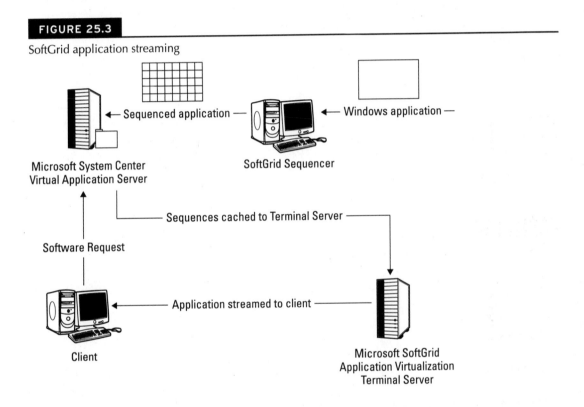

In streaming systems such as Citrix XenApp, Altiris SVS, and related deployment technologies, the systems use a push technology. When the system becomes available, it is inventoried by an agent or some other method and the software is then deployed as needed. While these systems all operate on IP networks, as a general rule, they do not use the open standards for media streaming that are described in this chapter. They tend to use XML files for coordination, response, or answer files, and proprietary methods for sending their streams down the wire.

Streaming Protocols

Streaming media content involves the delivery and control of files that have been segmented for smoother delivery. On IP networks, the IETF has a number of standard protocols used to stream content. In the sections that follow, the four most important of these standards are described. These include RTSP, RTP, RTCP, and the SMIL markup language.

These protocols control the delivery of content, network factors such as Quality of Service and congestion control, and other variables. These streaming protocols work over TCP/IP networks. Most of the time, they use UDP (User Datagram Protocol) for their transport, but in some instances TCP (Transport Control Protocol) is used.

Real-Time Streaming Protocol

The Real-Time Streaming Protocol (RTSP) is an Application layer protocol that is used to control how a media player can control a stream from a media server. It is based on IETF RFC 2326. RTSP is configured to use the well-known port 554. RTSP keeps track of the state of the session using a session ID. Any messages sent from client to server and vice versa reference this ID.

The best way to think about RTSP is that it provides a command set to a player that can issue navigation commands such as play and pause to a streaming media server. RTSP plays no role in how streaming content is segmented, encoded, or transported. Other protocols serve those functions and work hand in hand with RTSP. One common transport protocol for streaming media used with RTSP is the Real-Time Transport Protocol (RTP) that is described in the next section.

The more important RTSP commands include:

- PLAY. The PLAY message tells the player to play a stream. PLAYs can be queued and can specify a starting point in the stream. A PLAY issued for a PAUSEd stream will restart. Multiple PLAYs in a URL cause the player to play all of the media streams that the requests specify.

- PAUSE. The PAUSE message stops a media stream from playing. A PLAY command resumes playback from the point of the pause.

- SETUP. The SETUP message creates a stream connection and must be given before the stream can play. SETUP contains the URL and transport protocol, as well as the port used to receive RTP audio or video, and other RTCP transport metadata.

- TEARDOWN. The TEARDOWN message terminates the session. It ends all media stream transmission and releases all session data from the server buffer.

- DESCRIBE. The DESCRIBE message includes an RTSP URL (rtsp://...) and the streaming media file type that can be replayed.

- RECORD. A RECORD message specifies sending a stream to a server for storage.

The following streaming media servers use RTSP: Apple QuickTime Streaming Server, Darwin Streaming Server (open source QuickTime Streaming Server), Alcatel-Lucent pvServer (a.k.a. PacketVideo Streaming Server), RealNetworks Helix DNA Server, Live555 (open source), VideoLAN, Windows Media Services, and Maui X-Stream VX30.

Real-Time Transport Protocol

The Real-Time Transport Protocol, or RTP, is a method for sending packets containing rich media over the Internet. The IETF standard is described in RFCs 1889 and 3550. RTP is usually combined with RTSP (as described in the previous section), and this is the same pair of protocols used to transport VoIP as described briefly in the next chapter. RTP is used in both unicast and multicast applications. Compressed RTP (CRTP), as defined in RFC 2509, and Enhanced RTP (ERTP) are also used.

Note

RealNetworks has a version of RTP called Real Data Transport (RDT), which works with the RealNetworks RTSP server.

RTP transport on IP networks can occur with either TCP or UDP. TCP is used when a guaranteed delivery is required, while UDP is used when a certain amount of data loss can be tolerated. RTP transport of streaming media uses UDP and can be assigned to any even port in the dynamic range of 16384 to 32767. By convention, the next-higher odd port is assigned to RTSP messaging.

The use of dynamic ports often causes difficulty when trying to penetrate firewalls. To work around this problem, you can employ a STUN server to provide a mechanism for traversing firewalls. STUN stands for Simple Traversal of User Datagram Protocol through Network Address Translators. STUN works by using servers on both sides of the firewall to listen for open ports. If it is unable to penetrate the firewall from the outside, it can issue a request to a system on the inside to request the packets from the outside.

Cross-ref

STUN is described in more detail in Chapter 26.

RTP does the following things:

- Identifies content.
- Uses a sequence identification at the packet level, called a Protocol Data Unit (PDU).
- Manages streams using a Contributing Source ID (CSRC) to match a stream to one or more sources. The ability to manage separate streams allows video and audio to be handled individually, which can be helpful in a variety of circumstances.
- Time synchronization using a Synchronization Source ID (SSRC).
- Packet delivery checking. The RTSP protocol is used to monitor Quality of Service parameters.

Protocol Data Units, or PDUs, are ID numbers assigned to the following features: for OSI Layer 1, a PDU is assigned to a bit; for Layer 2, it is assigned to the frame; for Layer 3, it is assigned to the packet; for Layer 4, it is assigned to the segment; and for Layers 5 to 7, it is assigned to data. A related concept called the Service Data Unit, or SDU, is assigned to the data that one system sends another at the Layer 1 level below. For a PDU of *n*, the SDU would be *n-1*.

In Figure 25.4, the structure of an RTP packet is shown. The packet contains a number of flags in the header (the expanded portion of the packet) to indicate the extension type, the packet ID, source, and payload type. The different fields in the RTP packet header are as follows:

- **Version.** The current version of the protocol (version2).
- **Padding.** A single bit flag that indicates that there are extra bytes at the end of the packet.
- **Extension header.** An options 32-bit word that contains both the specific profile identifier and the length of the extension.
- **CSRC.** The contributing source ID lists the sources of the stream when that stream is coming from two or more sources.
- **Payload Type.** A 7-bit field that contains the format of the payload.
- **Sequence Number.** This 16-bit field is the sequence number for each of the RTP data packets. The receiving system uses the sequence number to order playback.
- **Extension.** This 1-bit flap indicates that there is an application-specific Extension header between the header and payload data.
- **CSRC Count.** This 4-bit field indicates the number of CSRC identifiers that are appended after the fixed header.
- **Marker.** A 1-bit flag used by an application to indicate that the data is important in some way to the application.
- **Timestamp.** A 32-bit field that is used to synchronize playback on the receiver.
- **SSRC.** The synchronization source identifier is a means of uniquely determining the source of the stream.

The Secure Real-Time Transport Protocol (SRTP) is a variation of the RTP protocol that defines a method for encrypting, authenticating, and error checking RTP data for both unicast and multicast streams. It is used with Secure RTCP, a version of RTCP that applies these safeguards to the messages that are used to control SRTP traffic. Message authentication is required in SRTP, but all of the other features in SRTP are optional and up to applications to implement on an individual basis. These protocols can be used in VoIP as well as streaming media applications.

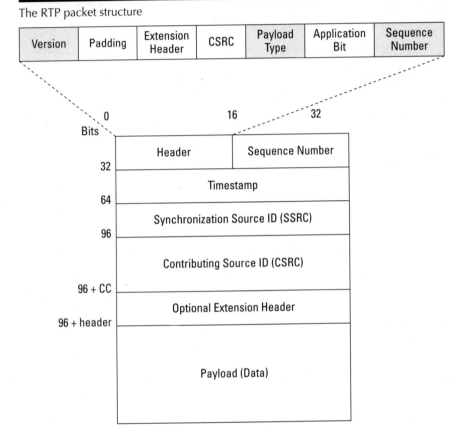

FIGURE 25.4

The RTP packet structure

Real-Time Control Protocol

The last of the real-time streaming protocols in common use is the Real-Time Control Protocol (RTCP), as defined in RFC 1889. This Session layer protocol is a messaging system that provides feedback on the performance of RTP data flow. As such, RTCP is a means of enforcing Quality of Service (QoS) functionality. RTCP monitors the arrival of bytes and packets, the amount of packets, network delays, and other statistics. Applications that are RTCP-enabled can take these statistics and alter their behavior to change the performance of the stream in order to match the QoS desired.

RTCP packets are small message packets. The following types of packets are transmitted:

- **Sender Reports.** Data is transmitted that includes the quantity of data sent and received, along with the timestamps needed to synchronize RTP packets.

- **Receiver Reports.** This message goes to clients that don't send RTP packets. It contains QoS statistics.

- **Application Specific.** This message type can be used by applications to define messages for their use.

- **Source Description.** This message type identifies the stream source and provides details on the owner of the source system.

- **Goodbye.** This message is sent when the source is shutting down a stream.

At the moment, RTCP isn't easily applied to large video broadcast systems such as IPTV (Internet Protocol-based Television). The large amount of collected data leads to long delays in sending RTCP statistics and long delays in the receiver analyzing the data.

Synchronized Markup Integration Language

The Synchronized Markup Integration Language, or SMIL (pronounced 'smile'), is an open standard that defines a markup language based on XML to support coordinated media playback. SMIL serves as input to RTSP transport, just as HTML content serves as input to HTTP transport. SMIL takes encoded files and specifies a sequence for their playback. There are SMIL editors you can use to create the files. In order to play back a SMIL sequence, a player must be SMIL-compliant. Two examples of SMIL editors are Adobe GoLive and SMOX Editor/SMOX Pad.

A SMIL file (.SMIL or .SMI file extension) is a metafile that instructs a client on how to handle a selected stream. It defines a number of session-level characteristics for a connection. SMIL can negotiate which bit rate file is streamed when multiple bit rates have been stored. Another tag can point to localized content, picking a language based on system settings, or using a different video clip or soundtrack for different users based on other criteria. SMIL can be attached to buttons, which allow the format to direct content based on a user's interaction, which could enable playlists or jukebox features. Because SMIL is a set of instructions that is external to the content it controls, it is possible to use SMIL to alter the sequence of content playback, change the entry points of playback within a specific clip, or point to any number of different streaming media or Web servers.

Note

Microsoft Synchronized Accessible Media Interchange, or SAMI, markup language files have an .SMI extension. This technology is used to place captions in PC media playback.

If you open a SMIL file in a text editor, you will find that it is similar to any other HTML file. A SMIL file must start and end with the `<SMIL>...</SMIL>` tags. There is a `<HEAD>` section that includes metadata and presentation layout information, a `<BODY>` section containing timing data and media elements, and both `<PAR>` and `<SEQ>` sections (for parallel and sequential) that are used to specify the media content by referencing their URLs. SMIL can also be tagged so that a media object is associated with a certain level of available bandwidth.

Encoding

Most media files are recorded in high-quality formats that are called raw files, which are impractical to stream across most WAN connections such as the Internet. To prepare file formats more suitable for streaming, the raw files are usually cropped to a smaller picture size, the frame rate of the video and/or the bit rate of the audio are reduced in speed and quality, and the file is then encoded, which usually involves a significant amount of compression.

Note

The input of a file to a streaming server is called ingest.

Encoding is a process by which a file is altered by an algorithm that compresses the file; unencoding is the process by which the encoded file is extracted. The software that performs the encoding is called a codec (literally, code/decode software); codecs can also be implemented in hardware in ASICs on audio/video capture boards. It is also possible to transcode an encoded file from one format to another. Encoding/decoding is often quite processor intensive and can take a long time to perform.

Table 25.3 compares single versus multiple bit rate encoding.

Although most encoding techniques use a constant bit rate input and output for their content, one technique that is helpful in terms of improving transmission over lower-bandwidth connections is to use what is called Multiple Bit Rate, or MBR, encoding. In MBR, multiple streams are encoded at different bit rates and then combined into a single file. A client that supports MBR will negotiate with the server the best bit stream based on available bandwidth. Should that bandwidth change during transmission, the client can request that a different-quality bit rate be sent.

TABLE 25.3

Single versus Multiple Bit Rate Encoding

Feature	Unicasting	Multicasting
Staging	On either a streaming or Web server	On a streaming server with software that supports it
Size	One file	Many files
Bandwidth	May pause or stop when network is congested	Slight pauses as a different bit rate stream fills the buffer
Frame sizes	Selected based on bandwidth	Frame sizes are the same for every bit rate
Audio	Selected based on bandwidth	Audio settings must be the same for every bit rate
Web integration	Must have individual controls or links for different streams	One control or link for all streams

This intelligent or adaptive streaming goes by different names in the different streaming technologies. RealMedia calls this technology SureStream, Microsoft uses the term Intelligent Streaming for Windows Media, and Apple refers to these different bit rates as alternative data rate movies. Apple stores the different bit rates as individual files in a folder on the Macintosh.

In Figure 25.5 the Windows Media Encoder 9 is shown encoding a movie file into streaming content. Microsoft makes versions of this encoder available on the their Web site for use on Windows Media Player. The Media Encoder can capture live content for playback or streaming, convert a file to video, broadcast live events, and capture screen sessions. It can output multichannel audio, interlaced video, and Multiple Bit Rate (MBR) content, insert Digital Rights Management (DRM) information, and Constant Bit Rate (CBR) and Variable Bit Rate (VBR) encoding.

FIGURE 25.5

Windows Media Encoder 9 converts audio and video files and input into streaming content.

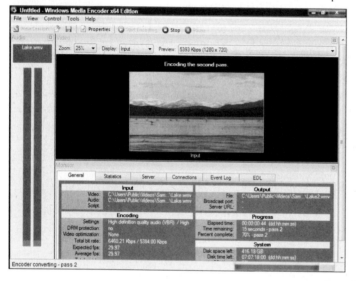

CBR encoding is best used in streaming sessions. The bit rate is set to be a constant rate within a small variance allowed by the buffer size. The quality of CBR-encoded content varies over time because the amount of compression you apply is constant. Some frames are more complex and compress more poorly than the simpler frames. Because the variation of the delivery of one stream versus another stream varies, users find that the playback of CBR streams is inconsistent from session to session. Lower bit rate streams dramatically reduce the quality of playback.

VBR encoding is used when the content will be either progressively downloaded or played locally. This type of encoding can better accommodate content that varies in complexity, and results in smaller file sizes than a CBR recording, often as little as 50 percent of the size.

Here is a list of the most commonly used encoders:

- **Barix Instreamer.** This all-in-one hardware solution is an appliance that takes analog and digital audio and converts it into MP3 streams. The Instreamer can send the streams to the streaming server, such as an Icecast or SHOUTcast server, where the content can be served to networked devices. Information on this device can be obtained from `www.barix.com`.

- **EdCast.** This program creates SHOUTcast and Icecast streams, as well as MP3, Ogg, and aacPlus files. The program or its plug-in for Winamp can be obtained at `www.oddsock.org/tools/edcast`. EdCast was previously available as Oddcast.

- **Nicecast.** Nicecast is used to create streaming audio content. It is available for Mac OS X at the Rogue Amoeba Web site at `www.rogueamoeba.com/nicecast`.

- **QuickTime Broadcaster.** The Apple live encoding solution creates MPEG-4 or H.264 video, or the 3GP mobile version of the MPEG-4 Part 14 container format on the Macintosh. It is available from the Broadcaster site at `www.apple.com/quicktime/broadcaster`, as is the QuickTime Streaming Server.

- **RealProducer.** RealProducer is RealMedia's encoder and creates the RealAudio and RealVideo formats. It can create live and downloadable content that is used on the RealNetworks Helix Server. You can download the free version and the professional version of the encoder from `www.realnetworks.com/products/producer/index.html`.

- **SAM.** This DSP plug-in for Winamp encodes audio into MP3, Ogg, and Windows Media files. To download the SAM plug-in, go to `www.spacialaudio.com/products/winamp`.

- **Windows Media Encoder.** As described earlier, you can download this program from `www.microsoft.com/windows/windowsmedia/forpros/encoder/default.mspx`.

- **Wirecast.** The Wirecast encoder is available for both Mac and PC and creates files compatible with the QuickTime Streaming architecture to be played back on either the QuickTime Streaming Server or on the Darwin server. Wirecast is available from `www.flip4mac.com/wirecast.htm`.

Streaming Servers

Streaming servers are available from a number of vendors and support a variety of streaming technologies. Most of these servers run on a single platform and offer a single streaming solution. Some are cross platform and a few are also cross technology. The most widely used streaming media servers include the following:

- **Windows Media Services.** This server is an installable service on Windows Server 2008; a prior version ran on Windows Server 2003. The 2008 edition serves up content that plays on Windows Media Player. Additional features are Fast Start, Fast Cache (caching and proxy services), Fast Recover and Fast Reconnect, authentication, multicast and unicast streaming, and broadcasting. To learn more about this server, go to `www.microsoft.com/windows/windowsmedia/forpros/server/server.aspx`.

- **Helix Server.** Currently in version 12, the Helix Server is a multi-format cross-platform streaming server from RealNetworks. It supports RealAudio and RealVideo, Windows Media, QuickTime, MPEG-4, 3GPP (H.263/H.264), and MP3, and can run on Windows Server 2003, Red Hat Linux Enterprise Level, and Solaris (on SPARC). Information on Helix may be found at `www.realnetworks.com/products/media_delivery.html`.

  RealNetworks sells the Helix Proxy server to provide caching, proxy, and gateway services for Helix content.

- **Apple QuickTime Streaming Server (QTSS).** The Apple streaming server runs on Mac OS X server, and along with the sequencer QTSS Publisher, it delivers QuickTime content over RTP/RTSP protocols. QuickTime can deliver H.264, MPEG-4, 3GPP, MP3, and AAC content, as well as MP3 files using the Icecast protocols. Version 6 integrates into Open Directory services. The QTSS home page is found at `www.apple.com/quicktime/streamingserver`.

- **Adobe Flash Media Streaming Server 3 (FMSS).** FMSS serves Flash content encoded in H.264 video or HE-ACC audio, and sent either as a stream or progressive download. To learn more about Flash Media Streaming Server, go to `www.adobe.com/products/flashmediastreaming`.

- **Wowza Media Server Pro.** This server is a much cheaper alternative to the Adobe Flash Streaming Server, and streams Flash content created by non-Flash RTSP/RTP encoders. To learn more about Wowza, go to `www.wowzamedia.com/products.html`.

- **Darwin Streaming Server.** Darwin is the Apple open source version of QTSS. It uses the same code base as QTSS, but runs on platforms other than the Macintosh, including Linux, Windows, and Solaris. Darwin's home page is located at `http://dss.macosforge.org`.

- **Icecast Streaming Media Server.** The Icecast server is an open source project that streams audio to listeners. It is very popular software for serving Internet radio content. The project publishes their libshout library to access Icecast servers, and Ices, which is a content management program that can post audio to the Icecast server. Icecast streams are compatible with SHOUTcast, another popular platform for streaming audio content. Icecast is found at `www.icecast.org/index.php`.

  Icecast is an open source streaming multimedia server solution from the Xiph.Org foundation. It uses Vorbis encoded content streamed over HTTP, or alternatively MP3 encoded content streamed over the SHOUTcast protocol. To download the software, go to `www.icecast.org`.

- **Nullsoft SHOUTcast.** This audio server is used for many of the Internet radio stations that are currently deployed. The home page is located at `www.shoutcast.com/download`.

- **SHOUTcast.** The SHOUTcast streaming media server is used to create digital audio files in either MP3 or HE-AAC format. Icecast is an open systems version of this software. SHOUTcast is available for both Mac and PC and is freeware. You can download this software from the developer, Nullsoft, at `www.shoutcast.com`.

- **Anysoft Agility.** This server is a complete video production and streaming server solution that works with a broad variety of content. It tends to be used by large media companies and includes features such as accounting, reporting, and production. The Agility home page is found at www.anystream.com/agility.aspx.

- **Unreal Media Server.** Unreal is a proprietary server that runs on Windows. It streams Windows Media and QuickTime-compatible content to browsers that have a Streaming Media Player application, ActiveX, or a Mozilla plug-in. The server is free for 15 connections, and can be obtained from www.umediaserver.net.

It can be difficult to run some of these servers, and so many of them are made available by a variety of vendors in the form of hosted services.

One of the key calculations that you need to make when considering server solutions is the amount of bandwidth that is required to support your client load. Minimum bandwidth requirements for individual connections are listed in Table 25.4, and must be *multiplied by the number of clients* that are directly supported. To support a client load beyond any single connection, solutions such as remote caches, proxy servers, and points of presence are established as part of a streaming solution.

TABLE 25.4

Server Bandwidth Requirements (Minimum)

Stream Type	Rate	Quality	Minimum Connection
Speech	800 bps	Minimum for speech	Dial up
Speech	8 Kbits/s	Telephone	Dial up
Video	16 Kbits/s	Videophone	Dial up
Audio	32 Kbits/s	AM radio (Medium Wave, or MW)	Dial up
Audio	96 Kbits/s	FM radio	DSL/ISDN
Audio	128 – 160 Kbits/s	Standard listening	DSL/ISDN
Video	128 – 384 Kbits/s	Videoconferencing	DSL/Cable modem
Audio	192 Kbits/s	Digital audio broadcast	DSL/Cable modem
Audio	320 Kbits/s	CD	DSL/Cable modem
Audio	500 Kbps – 1 Mbits/s	Lossless audio (FLAC, for example)	DSL/Cable modem
Video	1.25 Mbits/s	VCD (Video CD)	DSL/Cable modem
Audio	1.41 Mbits/s	PCM sound for Compact Disk Digital Audio	DSL/Cable modem
Video	5 Mbits/s	DVD	T1
Video	15 Mbits/s	HDTV	T2
Video	54 Mbits/s	Blu-ray	T2

In the sections that follow, I describe several of the different players and formats used for streaming media. You may be very familiar with some of these streaming file formats, such as Adobe's Flash files, which YouTube.com uses. This area of technology is very dynamic, with new products being introduced often. Microsoft's Silverlight is an example of a new streaming multimedia format that is being introduced to the market.

Streaming file formats

Streaming media files use one or more extensions for the files that each player can play, and one or more file extensions for the metafiles that are referenced in a link on a Web page that initiates the stream. If the content file is referenced in an HTML `<a href>` tag, then that file is downloaded and not streamed when the link is selected. To initiate a stream, a metafile is used as the link reference. Metafiles are usually text files (XML or SMIL, for example) that describe the media player to use, initiate the stream, and then point the stream to the player on the client system.

Tip

To search for detailed information on various file formats, go to http://Filext.com.

Sometimes the metafile and the streamed media file use the same extension, as in the case of the QuickTime .MOV extension. More often, they are different. RealMedia uses the .RM file extension for its streamed content, and the .RPM or .RAM extension for its metafile extensions. Windows Media uses .ASF and .WMV for content, and .ASX, .WAX, and .WVX for metafiles.

The reason that the Apple MOV files don't require a metafile is that the instructions for streaming are encoded into the MOV file in a hint track. Those instructions point directly to the streaming server. Sometimes this system doesn't work properly when the default player isn't QuickTime. This is more often the case on Windows systems than on the Macintosh. To address browser redirection when an RTSP link (URL) is selected, Apple uses a Reference Movie file, to which Apple also assigns the .MOV file extension. The Reference Movie is also used when the QuickTime version of MBR or alternate bit rates are used. The hints in the Reference MOV file support the negotiation required by the variable bit rate scheme from Apple.

When QuickTime is calling for a live feed to be streamed, there is no MOV file to work from. In that case, Apple uses a Session Description Protocol (SDP) file as its text metafile format to direct the player to the broadcasting server.

Players

QuickTime, Windows Media Player, and RealMedia are available as both stand-alone players and as browser plug-ins. Because these three players work with files created to work on three different and non-interoperable streaming media architectures, content providers are forced to either support these three or make compromises.

The four most popular streaming media players are:

- **Adobe Flash.** The Flash player is currently at version 10.0x. It plays Flash Video Files (.FLV extension). Adobe Flash uses an applet that installs into a browser and that decodes and plays FLV files. You can find it at `http://get.adobe.com/flashplayer`.

- **Apple QuickTime.** The QuickTime player is at version 7.5.5 and can be downloaded either alone or with iTunes. The standard player is free; Apple sells an in-place upgrade to its Pro version, which can perform file transcoding and conversions. QuickTime is the preferred format on the Macintosh. QuickTime plays Movie (MOV) files, or less frequently, QT or QTI files. It can be obtained from `www.apple.com/quicktime/download`.

- **Microsoft Windows Media player.** Currently at version 11, this player ships with Microsoft Windows and plays Windows Media Audio (WMA), Windows Media Video (WMV), and Advanced Streaming Format (ASF) files. Windows Media Player's home page is at `www.microsoft.com/windows/windowsmedia/default.mspx`.

- **RealPlayer.** Currently at version 11.0, RealPlayer is the RealNetworks cross-platform player for MP3, MPEG-4, QuickTime, and Windows Media files. It is also the player of choice for the proprietary RM files that RealMedia produces. There are versions of RealPlayer for Windows, Mac OS X, Linux, UNIX, Windows Mobile, and the Symbian OS. You can obtain RealPlayer from its Web page at `www.real.com/player`.

  RealNetworks released the Helix engine as an open source project for developers of media creation solutions. The Helix DNA client is a playback engine, and the Helix Player is the media player based on the client that runs on Linux, Solaris, FreeBSD, and Symbian. The Helix Producer can be used to add content to the Helix DNA Server for streaming content. The Helix Web site is found at `https://helix-client.helixcommunity.org`.

Among the many other media players available, the best known are the following: BearShare, FLV-Media Player, Musicmatch Jukebox, Napster, PowerDVD, VLC Media Player, WinDVD, xine, Yahoo! Music Jukebox, and Zinf.

Tip

Wikipedia maintains an extensive page listing of media players at http://en.wikipedia.org/wiki/Media_player_application_software.

All of these different technologies ensure that most Web sites providing streaming media do so in two or more formats and often in different data rates and screen sizes in order to accommodate the different player applications and connection bandwidths.

Flash

Adobe Flash is animation software for serving content in Web pages. It, along with Adobe Shockwave, has nearly universal penetration in Web-based video playback. Flash was developed by FutureWave and acquired by first Macromedia and then Adobe. The name Flash is a contraction of the words Future and Splash, a takeoff on the FutureWave name. Flash Video is both the file format and the technology for delivery of streamed video content from a Web page. Perhaps the best-known Web site using Flash Video is YouTube.com.

Shown in Figure 25.6 is the adorable spider that appeared as a Flash Video on the Science Friday Web site. Flash Video plays inside the Flash Player, which is a plug-in that is embedded inside Web pages. The current version of the player is 10.0x, and can be downloaded from `http://get.adobe.com/flashplayer`. Other players that play Flash Video include VLC media player (Mac, PC, Linux), FLV Player, QuickTime (requires the Perian video plug-in), RealPlayer, Windows Media Player, MPlayer, and xine and totem on Linux. Microsoft DirectShow is required for Media Player and Media Center Flash playback.

FIGURE 25.6

Flash Video is ubiquitous on the Web for streamed video content; nearly all players look similar to this one in FLV Media Player.

http://www.sciencefriday.com/videos/watch/10175

The Flash Video file format is FLV and supports Sorenson Spark H.263, H.264, MPEG-4 ASP, and On2 Technologies TrueMotion VP6 video codecs, as well as HE-ACC audio content. It is also possible to embed Flash Video into Shockwave Flash (SWF) files. Flash Video files themselves are defined by an open container format, but the encoding is done by a proprietary codec inside the Adobe Flash authoring program, called Adobe Flex, and other Adobe products. An FLV stream contains one video and one audio stream.

Among the file formats that Flash uses are the following:

- **F4A.** An audio format for the Flash Player with the audio/mp4 MIME type.
- **F4B.** An audio book format for the Flash Player with the audio/mp4 MIME type.
- **F4P.** The protected video format for the Flash Player with a video/mp4 MIME type.
- **F4V.** The video format for the Flash Player with a video/mp4 MIME type.

Flash Video is noted for being very compact. Flash Video can be delivered as FLV files, embedded in SWF files, sent from a Web server as a progressive download over HTTP, and streamed from the Web server to clients. For progressive download and streaming, Adobe uses the proprietary Real-Time Messaging Protocol (RTMP). The Real-Time Media Flow Protocol (RTMFP) is the technology that Adobe uses to communicate between Flash Players and the application server over the Adobe AIR framework and can be used to distribute Flash Video content. RTMP server software includes the Adobe Flash Media Server, the Wowza Media Server, and the WebORB Integration Server for .NET, Java, and ColdFusion.

As previously mentioned, streaming media doesn't leave a permanent copy of the file on your system. That means that any FLV file that you might want to view at a later time won't be available to you unless you take some extra steps to capture it. There are three methods that you can use to save FLV files: use some special-purpose Web sites that capture the video and send it to you, use a browser extension or plug-in, or purchase a commercial program that offers this functionality.

Sites that offer the ability to save online video include KeepVid (`www.keepvid.com`), or for YouTube, the YouTube Downloader site (`http://video.qooqle.jp`). The Firefox extension, called Video Downloader, can also save streamed FLV files. To save video captured off your screen, you can use programs like Snagit (from TechSmith) or Snapz Pro X 2 (from Ambrosia Software).

Silverlight

Microsoft Silverlight is a programming environment for delivering rich content to browsers with the Silverlight plug-in. Silverlight offers many of the same capabilities of Adobe Flash and Shockwave, along with animation and vector graphics. It leverages the .NET Framework and development tools and is part of the Windows Presentation Framework. Plug-ins for Silverlight exist on Windows, Mac OS X, Linux (as Moonlight), Windows Mobile 6, and Symbian.

Silverlight 2.0 includes the Media Stream Source API that allows developers to create media streams with a variable streaming technology that Microsoft calls "adaptive streaming." This technology allows the player to select a bit rate that is allocated based on the available bandwidth and CPU capacity. The API is extensible, requiring only that the streams be in a Silverlight runtime in a decodable format, such as MP3 or WMA. Media Stream Source was the technology used to run the NBC Beijing Olympics Web site.

Windows Live offers the Silverlight Streaming Service as a hosting solution for Silverlight applications. The service provides Silverlight content to Windows and Macintosh clients, and can provide the content to Microsoft Expression Web sites. Silverlight content can be created in the Microsoft Expression Encoder that is part of Expression Studio 2 and other third-party tools. Silverlight Streaming by Windows Live also integrates with the Microsoft adCenter platform. You can find more information about this streaming service at http://streaming.live.com.

Summary

In this chapter, you learned about streaming media solutions and progressive downloading. Streaming content makes heavy use of network resources. The network architecture needed was described.

Streaming solutions use a special set of protocols. The Real-Time Streaming Protocol, the Real-Time Control Protocol, the Real-Time Transfer Protocol, and the SMIL markup language were described in this chapter.

The encoding process can create content that has either constant or variable bit rates, as well as create a package of streams in multiple bit rates.

The four main streaming media platforms — Windows Media Services, RealNetworks Helix Server, Apple QuickTime Streaming Server, and Adobe Flash Media Streaming Server — were described. Flash and Silverlight streaming were also briefly considered.

In the next chapter, a related streaming technology for telephone is considered. Voice over IP is revolutionizing the telecommunications industry.

Telephony and VoIP

Telephony is the marriage of computers and telephones, enabled by two different types of networks. Telephony covers a broad range of multimedia applications, including voice, video, business, and pleasure. It is always an area of great innovation and is supported natively in network operating systems by application programming interfaces, or APIs.

You can create a network of telephones using a Private Branch Exchange (PBX) System as a management server. PBXs can network with public switched telephone network (PSTN) telephones over phone lines or with IP-enabled phones over Ethernet. Two PBX server systems are considered in detail: the open source Asterisk system and Cisco Unified Communications Manager.

Voice over Internet Protocol, or VoIP, is a rapidly developing area of technology. VoIP can be implemented in software as a softphone, using IP phones, or by adapting an existing telephone using an Analog Telephone Adapter (ATA) to connect it to an IP network. This chapter discusses the properties of IP phones.

VoIP uses a special set of protocols to send and manage communications that are described in detail in this chapter. Session protocols include Session Initiation Protocol (SIP) and Skinny Call Control Protocol (SCCP), and packets are often in Real-Time Transport Protocol (RTP) format. The problems with firewalls and NAT (Network Address Translation) traversal are described, as well as how Simple Traversal of User Datagram Protocol (STUN) solves them in some instances.

Computer Telephony Integration, or CTI, is a set of application rules that allow VARs (Value Added Resellers) and developers to create custom telephone applications. These applications draw on telephony APIs to help call centers and businesses of all types, and to power intelligent telephone systems. CTI's capabilities are briefly described.

IN THIS CHAPTER

Telephone service and protocols

PBX telephone systems

VoIP

Computer telephony integration

Video telephony in action

Dick Tracy had one, and so can you. Video telephony is on telephones, wireless phones, and Webcams, and in IM (Instant Messaging) systems. Some of the applications are described at the end of this chapter.

Telephony

Telephony is a set of services that allow computers to transmit analog sound across a network as digital data. Telephony involves an audio-to-digital conversion on the input end and a digital-to-audio conversion on the output end. In some instances, telephony services transmit discrete communications, usually in the form of audio files over standard packet-switched networks. In other instances, telephony transmits audio as it is being created and streams the result to the recipient: one example, VoIP, is described later in this chapter.

Telephony applications on networked computer systems span the following categories:

- Voice calls over a circuit-switched telephone network
- PBX simulation systems with advanced call-handling features
- Conferencing over IP networks
- Voice response systems
- VoIP calls
- Collaboration systems, shared whiteboards, and remote desktop systems
- Automated calling technologies

The software for creating and managing digital telephony has been included in most operating systems with various levels of sophistication. The field of CTI 45 now enables computers to integrate peripheral devices that send and receive networked voice and data. To support these technologies, many operating systems ship with APIs to support these features. The Windows telephony API is referred to as Microsoft Telephony API (TAPI), Sun Microsystems, Inc., has a Java Telephony API (JTAPI), and the Macintosh and Linux operating systems have similar APIs.

Telephony has had a historical role in the development of computer networks, especially in the areas of switching and routing. Many large networks have been built specifically for telephone systems in an effort to replace the manual telephone exchange with an automated system. The result of this automation was the creation of PSTN. The computer software that enables an automated telephone exchange was referred to as a *Stored Program Control* exchange, but this term is historical and is no longer used.

Prior to the commoditization of computers, telephone services were sent as analog signals over circuit-switched networks, which today is referred to as *plain old telephone service* (POTS). As data transmission became important and the volume of data traffic increased, telephone networks began upgrading their lines to provide digital services using Integrated Services Digital Network (ISDN) and Digital Subscriber Line (DSL) technologies. As phone lines morphed into digital communication networks, copper wire was replaced by light-conducting glass fiber.

Private Branch Exchange Systems

A private branch exchange (PBX) system is a telephone network that is generally installed in a medium to large office. The PSTN connects to the PBX, supplying one or more telephone lines for incoming and outgoing calls. Incoming calls for an entire company can come into a PBX and be routed appropriately. Each telephone connected to the network is referred to as an *extension*.

Office telephone systems come in the following varieties:

- **Key system.** When the extensions have a set of buttons that users press to manually choose the outgoing line, they are referred to as key systems.

- **Centrex.** Centrex is a service that is offered by the telephone company where switching and the software to control the system are located at an end office or another central office. It is similar to a PBX. A Centrex system places telephone extensions on individuals' desks, which allows both internal and external calls.

- **PBX.** These systems can be either private or circuit switched, and often connect using POTS.

- **PABX.** Private automatic branch exchanges automatically select an available outgoing line.

- **ISDN PBX.** This type of PBX connects to an ISDN line.

- **IP PBX or IPBX.** With the implementation of digital networks, most PBXs now offer VoIP on this type of PBX.

These systems emulate the function of a telephone exchange: they establish, maintain, and disconnect connections. Most of them also provide usage information. The range of calling features of PBXs can be quite large, and they can add the following unique features to a standard home telephone line: auto attendant, automated directory services, call distribution, conference calls, custom greetings and welcome messages, music or radio on hold, paging, roaming extensions, voice mail, and voice message broadcasting. In the sections that follow, three different PBX systems are described: the open source Asterisk server, Cisco's Unified Communications Manager, and Microsoft's Response Point.

Asterisk

Digium's Asterisk (www.asterisk.org) open source PBX software is one solution to create an IP or hybrid PBX system from a modestly powered computer. It is one of the more popular VoIP server applications and is widely used. Asterisk can run on various versions of UNIX, such as OpenBSD, FreeBSD, and NetBSD, as well as on Mac OS X, Sun Solaris, and Microsoft Windows. (The version that runs on Windows is called AsteriskWin32.) The hardware necessary to connect an Asterisk server to PSTN, T1, E1, and other networks is sold by Digium and a number of other vendors.

After installing Asterisk, the application must be configured to either be a VoIP system or a PBX. Setup involves altering a set of configuration files; a PBX requires a dial plan for each device. Figure 26.1 shows the calling rules for an outgoing call. These calling rules ensure that the telephone numbers called conform to a particular numeric pattern, how the call is routed, and what to do if the call fails to go through the primary routing.

FIGURE 26.1

The Asterisk GUI provides PBX management in a Web interface. Shown here is the Edit Calling Rule dialog box for outgoing calls.

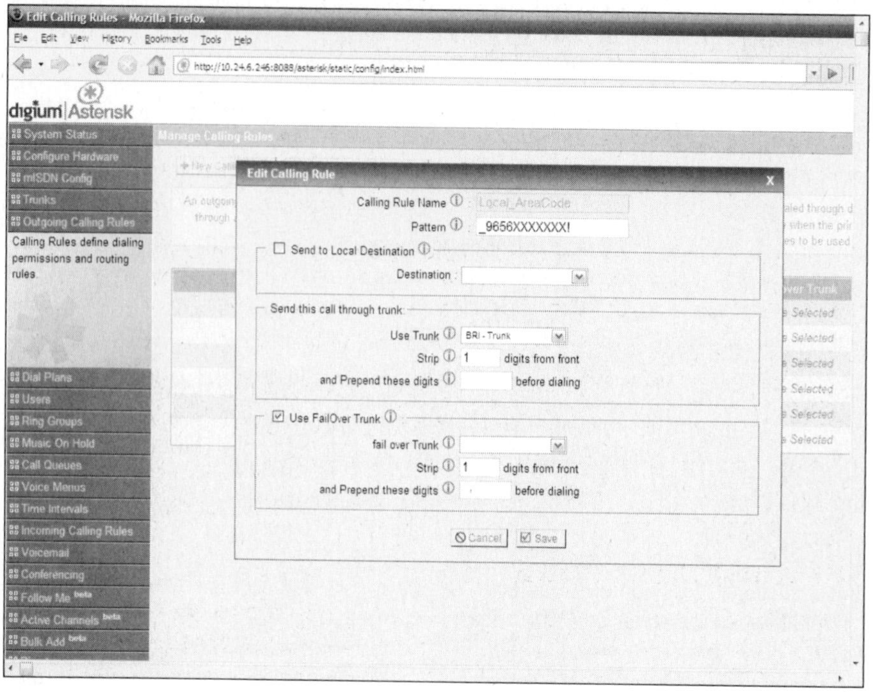

Asterisk has a programming language where extensions can be matched to contexts (scenarios) and actions can be assigned based on the logic you provide. The Asterisk Gateway Interface provides an API that can be accessed by Perl, Java, C, or PHP programs.

Applications that come with Asterisk are:

- `app_dial`. This program executes the rules for device-to-device connections.
- `app_meeting`. This program creates and manages conference calls.
- `app_voicemail`. This program stores and plays back voice messages.

There are a number of GUI interfaces that you can install to manage Asterisk. Digium offers asterisk-gui 2.0, and FreePBX is another. A distribution from trixbox called Asterisk@Home combines an installation of Asterisk and FreePBX together.

Cisco Unified Communications Manager

Cisco Unified Communications Manager (CUCM) is PBX software that manages a variety of telephony products and the components that support them. The product is better known by its older name Cisco CallManager (CCM). Cisco CallManager is installed on a Cisco Media Convergence Server (MCS) or another approved platform. MCS can be clustered with a Publisher server being supported by eight subscriber servers.

CUCM's main function is to determine the nature of a dialed phone number and then communicate with the gateway to coordinate sending or receiving calls from the public phone or private IP network.

CUCM uses the Skinny Call Control Protocol (SCCP) for signal control of telephony hardware, as well as the Media Gateway Control Protocol or Session Initiation Protocol (SIP) to communicate with network gateways, bridges, and other components. With CUCM you can also support VoIP phone calls and H.323 sessions. These protocols are described in more detail later in this chapter.

The latest release of CUCM was version 7.0 released in September 2008. Cisco has a Windows version of CUCM as well as selling an appliance. System 7 unifies the version number of the various components that make up the Communication Manager suite, including consolidating the underlying data store on IBM Informix.

Microsoft Response Point

Microsoft Response Point (www.microsoft.com/responsepoint/default.aspx) is voice-activated PBX software for offices with up to 50 telephones. A system of 10 phones would have optimal performance on a 100Base-T LAN. Service Pack 1 of the Response Point software supports both analog and VoIP telephones. IP calls use Session Initiation Protocol (SIP). Among the features of Response Point are integration with e-mail systems, and easy setup and management through a graphical user interface, as shown in Figure 26.2. The voice recognition is based on the Speech Server engine, and is powerful, easy to work with, and doesn't require training. Training is where the user gives the system voice samples so that the system can better understand the particular user's commands and speech patterns.

Response Point is built to be an open system that interoperates with hardware from a number of vendors. The software is built to run on a version of Microsoft Embedded XP software, which is supplied in the form of small appliance-sized devices from various hardware partners. When you plug the appliance into the network and turn it on, a setup wizard launches that prompts you to plug in the phones and assign them to users or locations. Configuration takes about 15 minutes to perform, which is unique in this area of hardware and software.

FIGURE 26.2

The Administrative console in Microsoft Response Point

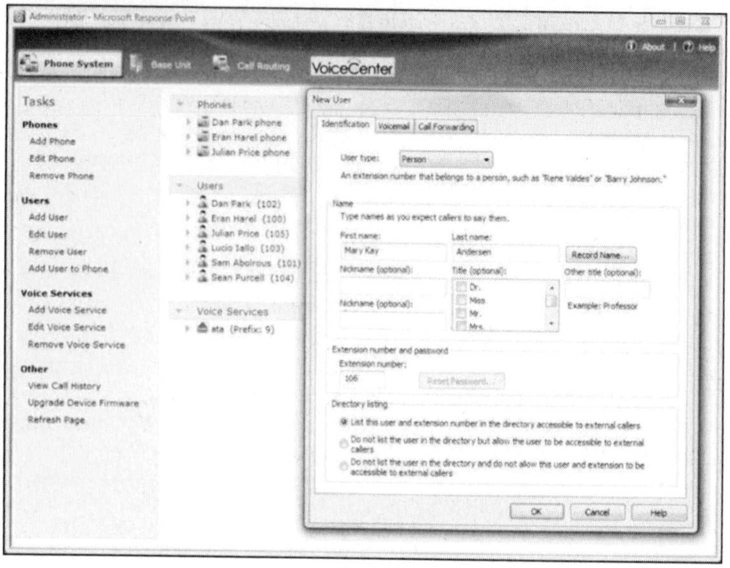

An early model Syspine, from Quanta, connects to up to eight POTS lines, and is strictly an analog configuration. The OEM (Original Equipment Manufacturer) and their VAR partners supply the PBX server hardware with the management features, and phone handsets that connect to clients complete a working Response Point system. The server must run either XP or Vista, and any client that wants full telephony support also requires that operating system.

Microsoft has kept the requirements for Response Point to a minimum, and does not require that you run a domain server, Exchange, SharePoint, or the Office Communications Server to make this system work. The Response Point server can run the required networking services for clients, such as DHCP. There aren't many hooks (special connections) to Microsoft software in the first edition: no integration into Small Business Server, import of contact databases from Outlook, or use of Active Directory if your network is running a domain server. Response Point is a new product in its first version and will evolve over time.

Voice over Internet Protocol

Voice over Internet Protocol, or VoIP, is the name given to a protocol for sending voice transmission over packet-switched networks. VoIP uses a data network, typically the Internet, to serve as the transmission medium for voice data transfer.

There is no requirement that both parties use VoIP during a connection, only that the IP-connected party has a direct connection to the data network. When telephone calls are placed from users who are connected to a PSTN to a VoIP phone, the sending party must use Direct Inward Dialing (DID) to connect to the VoIP network through a VoIP gateway using an assigned access number. Calls originating on the VoIP network are sent to the PSTN party through the DID number or numbers that were assigned to the PSTN party. In Europe, this system is called Direct Dial-In (DDI).

VoIP relies on a Digital Audio Conversion (DAC) to convert voice or sound into a digital audio file. As with other sound file formats like MP3, VoIP applies compression techniques to create a small file size, and that file is packetized by TCP and sent over IP networks. VoIP files can be very efficiently compressed, and so depending upon the quality level you select, a call lasting an hour might be no more than 20MB in size — no more than a podcast of that duration.

VoIP services are implemented in one of the following ways:

- As a software-only solution, as is the case with Skype, shown in Figure 26.3.

FIGURE 26.3

Skype's main window, shown here, supports IM chats and telephony, and is often used by 12 million users concurrently.

Courtesy of the Skype image library.

- Connecting a phone to an Internet connection through an analog telephone adapter (ATA), as is the case with Vonage (www.vonage.com), AT&T CallVantage (www.corp.att.com/voip), and Verizon VoiceWing (https://www22.verizon.com/ForYourHome/VOIP/VOIPHome.aspx).

- Connecting through a cable modem, usually as part of a TV/phone/Internet package, as with Comcast (www.comcast.com).

- Using a VoIP PBX system connected to a TCP/IP network. A VoIP-connected PBX usually requires a high-speed Internet connection such as a T1 or Fiber-Optic Service (FIOS), a LAN, phones with IP connectors (or both items as separate parts), and the PBX server. Refer to the previous section for more details.

The primary motivation for using a VoIP system has historically been the greatly reduced charges imposed for long-distance connections. The primary drawback has been that VoIP consolidates your telephone and Internet into one line, and so if your Internet connection is broken, you lose both methods of communication. Early implementations of VoIP suffered from voice quality problems, but the current technology delivers voice quality that is as good as, and often better than, telephone lines. Table 26.1 summarizes some of the advantages and disadvantages of VoIP.

TABLE 26.1

Advantages and Disadvantages of VoIP

Feature	Advantage	Disadvantage
Area Code Independence	Your phone number can be in any area code, and it is transparent to an outside caller.	
Computer Integration	When you connect a computer to an ATA, additional features such as voice mail and e-mail integration are possible.	Faxes can be hard to incorporate.
Cost	Long-distance service is inexpensive for a VoIP-to-VoIP call.	There are additional costs for DID calls.
Features	VoIP has an extensive feature set: call waiting, call forwarding, caller ID, and voice mail; three-way and conference calling are also usually included.	Calls to emergency services such as 911 aren't supported. Because VoIP isn't tied to a specific location, you can't be traced.
Interoperability		Calls through firewalls and NATs can be problematic. Doesn't work with old-style pulse phones.
Quality	Usually as good as, or better than, PSTN phone lines.	A poor or low-speed Internet connection results in poor telephone quality. Congestion can lead to jitters.
Mobility	An ATA can be used anywhere you can connect to the Internet and have electricity.	Mobile telephones aren't supported, and so you still need a cell phone.
Security	Through the use of protocols such as the Secure Real-Time Transport Protocol (SRTP), you can create a secure connection.	

Several of Cisco's switches, including the 2950, 2955, and 3550, allow their ports to be configured for VoIP traffic, a feature that they call voice Virtual Local Area Network, or voice VLAN. The traffic employs 802.1P priority tagged frames that support a class of service (CoS) (which is a form of Quality of Service) for voice and data traffic.

Analog telephone adapters

An analog telephone adapter (ATA) connects an analog telephone to a digital telephone system such as a VoIP network, essentially turning a PSTN phone into an IP phone. These devices are typically quite small and come with an Ethernet RJ45 port and a telephone RJ11 port when used for a single phone. All ATAs require a power source.

Note
A long list of currently available ATAs can be found on the VoIP-Info.org site at www.voip-info.org/wiki-Analog+Telephone+Adapters.

Larger ATAs support multiple phone connections and take an RJ14 (two-line), RJ25 (three-line), or RJ45 (four-line) jack for enterprise applications. They use a Foreign eXchange Station (FXS) port to connect the adapter to a LAN. ATAs that perform analog-to-digital conversions, or ADC, allow phones to connect directly to a VoIP server and are sometimes referred to as *VoIP gateways*. ATAs use protocols such as H.323, SIP, Media Gateway Control Protocol (MGCP), and Inter-Asterisk eXchange Protocol (IAX) and contain a codec or set of codecs to encode and decode voice communications. These protocols are described later in the chapter. ATAs are Plug-and-Play devices that don't require any configuration or computer software to connect to a VoIP server. When these devices are connected to a laptop or computer, they are managed by softphone programs.

ATAs usually come in one of two types: those that are simple connections between a phone and an IP network and devices that are keyed to a specific VoIP provider and service and that can't be used with any other system.

The Linksys SPA3102 is an example of an ATA device that can connect phones to an IP network. The SPA3102 allows a user to place a local call from a mobile or landline phone to the SPA-3102 where the caller's credentials are authenticated and the phone is connected to the Internet. If an SPA3102 is located on the receiving end of a call, then VoIP calls can be answered or routed to any PSTN phone or mobile phone.

This $70 device is shown in Figure 26.4. It comes with one RJ11 connector (POTS) FXS port, one PSTN FXO port that connects to either a PBX or Telco device, and two 100Base-T RJ45 Ethernet connections that can be connected to a LAN and a broadband connection or an ISP's router. The software that comes with this ATA can configure the FXS and FXO lines independently. This ATA is installed by an end user and configured by their ISP remotely for their particular VoIP service. It supports IP Centrex systems.

FIGURE 26.4

The Linksys SPA3102 ATA

Courtesy of Linksys image library.

Internet Protocol phones

VoIP phones can be implemented as either hardware or software (as a softphone). They have features that allow them to connect to an IP network and communicate using protocols that efficiently send voice communication as data. Some VoIP providers use proprietary standards, or come with several standard protocols, such as the Session Initiation Protocol (SIP) or the Skinny Call Control Protocol (SCCP). As mentioned earlier, you can turn a regular phone into an IP phone by adding an analog telephone adapter that provides the missing functionality.

IP phones require the following features:

- Enabling hardware (for a physical phone)

- Software to either emulate (softphone) or manage an IP phone

- A protocol stack, such as SIP, SCCP, H.323, and Skype

- DNS client

- DHCP client (sometimes)

- Real-Time Transport Protocol (RTP) support

- Tunneling protocols such as the Simple Traversal of User Datagram Protocol through Network Address Translators (STUN) to traverse firewalls and gateways

Figure 26.5 shows the D-Link DPH-140S Express Ethernet Business IP Phone. This phone comes with an Ethernet connection, speakerphone, transfer, voice mail, and an address book.

FIGURE 26.5

The D-Link DPH-140S Express Ethernet Business IP Phone

Courtesy of the D-Link press library.

VoIP protocols

As mentioned in the previous section, IP phones require a special set of protocols to create and manage connections. Usually these protocols are bundled together as a protocol stack so that the IP phone can be used on different networks and connect to different types of devices and management software. In the sections that follow, a number of the more widely used VoIP protocols are described, including:

- Session Initiation Protocol (SIP)
- Skinny Call Control Protocol (SCCP)
- Real-Time Transfer Protocol (RTP)
- Session Traversal Utilities for NAT (STUN)
- H.323
- Inter-Asterisk eXchange Protocol (IAX)
- Media Gateway Control Protocol (MGCP)

The Session Initiation Protocol, or SIP, is commonly used for voice and video communication over the Internet. It is also used for streaming multimedia, and shows up in instant messaging (IM) and even in video games. SIP supports two-party point-to-point or unicast sessions, as well as multi-stream, multiparty, and multicast sessions. The Transport layer protocol is usually as follows: TCP for point to point; UDP for VoIP, games, and applications; or Stream Control Transmission Protocol (SCTP) for streaming applications. SIP manages port assignments, addressing, and other connection functions for the data stream. Conceptually, SIP is a Session layer protocol in the ISO/OSI model, but would be an Application layer protocol in the TCP/IP model where Layers 5 to 7 are consolidated.

Skinny Call Control Protocol

The Skinny Call Control Protocol, or SCCP, is the Session layer protocol used by Cisco to connect "skinny" clients through Cisco switches to one another. Skinny Calls include the following: Cisco's line of wired and wireless IP phones (the 7900 series); the Cisco IP Communicator softphone; and the Cisco Unity voicemail server. Cisco's line of IP phones uses various protocols for communication.

All of these devices can be managed by the Cisco Unified Communications Manager (CUCM) call processing software, also called the Cisco CallManager (CCM). (Cisco Systems is very big on acronyms that start with C.) CallManager is essentially a messaging server that provides transaction management for a variety of media protocols such as SIP, ISDN, H.323 video, and the Media Gateway Control Protocol (MGCP).

Real-Time Transport Protocol and Real-Time Transfer Control

The Real-Time Transport Protocol (RTP) is a standard packet format for multimedia content sent over IP networks as either TCP or UDP data. It can be used for either unicast or multicast data. RTCP is used to manage the RTP data, as well as to provide QoS monitoring.

RTP doesn't specify which ports are to be used, but it does require that RTP be assigned an even port, and that the Real-Time Transfer Control (RTCP) protocol be assigned the next highest available odd port. The pair of ports for RTP and RTCP are assigned in the Dynamic Port range of 16384 to 32767. RTP data can be real time and interactive; RTP packets require a Session protocol like SIP or H.323 for VoIP.

Session Traversal Utilities for NAT

It can be difficult for telephony applications to successfully negotiate with network firewalls and gateways where network address translation, or NAT, operates. NATs manage application access to specific ports, and clients' access to different applications for both inbound and outbound traffic. NAT implementations can be somewhat different on different devices, and they tend to break different IP applications by denying that application access to Internet resources or allowing communications from outside the router to reach the application server. RTP, which was described in the previous section, is particularly vulnerable to NAT traversal problems due to its dynamic port assignments.

The Simple Traversal of User Datagram Protocol through Network Address Translators (STUN) protocol provides a solution to this problem. STUN is used as a service (server) on the public side of a WAN connection (such as the Internet) to obtain the appropriate public IP address and port number required for UDP to transit the device. It works by sending a series of STUN messages through the STUN listening port number 3478 to a STUN client on a LAN. The client obtains the appropriate port information and returns it to the STUN server.

The problem with some STUN clients is that they aren't able to use the transport information (IP address and port) from their location on the network. Also, not all NATs support STUN, although many do. STUN doesn't work with symmetric or bidirectional NATs that are used in enterprise-class networks. An alternative protocol called Traversal Using Relay NAT (TURN) is under development for that class of device.

Another NAT traversal mechanism under development is called Interactive Connectivity Establishment (ICE). It is specifically meant to connect VoIP clients using SIP to clients within a network.

The H.323 Protocol

The H.323 protocol of the ITU-T (International Telephone Union Telecommunication Sector) is a suite of audio-visual session transport, signaling, control, and bandwidth management standards for both point-to-point sessions as well as conferencing. H.323 is mostly used by voice and videoconferencing applications, particular real-time applications deployed over the Internet. H.323 is also used on the public telephone network, 3G mobile networks, over ISDN, and in many other places. Microsoft's NetMeeting videoconferencing software was based on the H.323 protocol.

An H.323 application relies on defined network components for its session. The most important of these elements are terminals, multiple control units (MCUs), gateways, border elements, and gate-keepers which perform name resolution. A path is defined between these different elements, which are called endpoints in H.323 applications. The minimum path definition is between two terminals.

Inter-Asterisk eXchange Protocol

The Inter-Asterisk eXchange Protocol (IAX) is used by the open source Asterisk PBX system described earlier in this chapter. In its second version, IAX2 became a published protocol allowing many vendors to interoperate with VoIP products that are based on Asterisk. IAX2 can provide trunking where many clients share the same set of channels, and channel multiplexing over a single link.

IAX2 transports VoIP data over UDP, and is usually assigned to port 4569 on routers. The data stream is controlled by a set of commands and parameters that can provide the necessary control for multiplexing the VoIP signals and controlling the flow of traffic. IAX2 is both firewall- and NAT-friendly because signaling and data both use the same transit method. This compares with some of the other protocols described in this section, including SIP, H.323, and MGCP. Those methods rely on RTP communication for session control, which is an out-of-band method. By out-of-band it is meant that the RTP communication is using a different channel.

Media Gateway Control Protocol

The Media Gateway Control Protocol (MGCP) describes an architecture that can be used to control gateway devices on an IP or on the public telephone networks. The protocol describes a set of sig-nal and control commands that are used to control VoIP traffic, and is often used by both H.323 and SIP traffic. MGCP is the internal protocol used by a Media Gateway Controller (MGC) and the Media Gateway (MG). The Media Gateway Controller is the device that performs call handling making the connection between the IP signaling device. MGCP uses a Call Agent and a Media Gateway to convert VoIP signals traversing different circuits.

MGCP became popular in VoIP applications because it does not perform encoding, nor does it transport VoIP traffic. These features are deferred to the other protocols mentioned in the previous paragraph. MGCP provides the switching mechanism and the signal and path management func-tions used by various media gateways.

Computer Telephony Integration

Computer telephony integration (CTI) is the use of computers to manage the set of services used in call centers. A CTI system can route calls to the correct person, pop up a window with the calling person's phone number, name, and history, and perform any additional actions that are required.

CTI requires specialized software, often leveraging the telephony APIs that are in networked operating systems, as well as the necessary hardware to connect the computer to the different telephone assets. CTI can be deployed on a single computer, making it appear as if that one system is a call center, or it can be client/server software that runs an actual call center.

CTI has a very broad set of capabilities that are highly dependent on the software, hardware, and, of course, the developer. A few of the more commonly encountered features are:

- Authentication
- Call queue management
- Call routing or automated call distribution
- Caller ID, also called Automatic Number Identification (ANI)
- Customer assistance
- Robocalls (call campaigns) integrated with predictive dialing
- Telemarketing
- Video conferencing
- Voice recognition and interactive voice response (IVR)

These services are supported by Microsoft's Window Telephony Application Programming Interface (TAPI) and related programming interfaces such as AT&T/Lucent/Novell's Telephone Service Application Programming Interface (TSAPI) to link those applications to hardware more easily.

Telcordia (formerly Bell Communications Research) developed the Advanced Intelligent Network (AIN or IN) telephone architecture to make CTI extensible without having to rely on built-in capabilities in switches and routers. The International Telecommunications Union (ITU) used the model of AIN to develop a version that they call Capability Set 1 (CS-1). AIN works at the switch or Service Switching Point (SSP) and forwards phone calls to the logic located at the Service Control Point (SCP). The logic analyzes the numbers entered in dialing and matches them to the service that the caller requires. In some cases the logic might return information to the caller; in other cases the call is passed off to another device or Intelligent Peripheral (IP) that is attached to another SSP where the calls are processed further. These terms are defined as part of the AIN model.

One service provided by AIN is called Local Number Portability. When you switch carriers, but retain your phone number, a call is routed at a switch to your new phone service for handling.

The Computer Supported Telephony Applications (CSTA) is an integration standard of the European Computer Manufacturer's Association (ECMA) that has been ratified as a standard by the ITU.

Video Telephony

Video telephony enables two users to talk with one another while looking at a synchronized video stream. A video telephone, or videophone if you will, was demonstrated by AT&T in their pavilion at the 1964 New York World's Fair and at Expo 67 in Montreal. Dubbed the Picturephone, it was introduced by AT&T in 1971 for the consumer market; it sold very poorly and was discontinued in 1974. It wasn't clear at the time if the price was too high or if people didn't want to be seen while talking on a phone. A more recent introduction of H.324 video using LG-Nortel videophones in Mexico in 2006 doesn't seem to be gaining traction.

One of the more popular video conferencing solutions is Skype, a VoIP application that can also support instant messaging, video transmission, and file transfer. VoIP was written by the same team of developers who did the Kazaa peer-to-peer network, and Skype became equally as popular. Skype became very popular because it offered many services such as international calling for free from computer to computer. Additional services can be purchased that allow phones to call over Skype. Skype was purchased by eBay, but is currently being spun off as a separate company. Shown in Figure 26.6 is a video conference in Skype.

FIGURE 26.6

A videoconference inside a Skype window; the small picture shows the sender.

Courtesy of the Skype press library.

Mobile VoIP

Mobile VoIP is an area of active development that enabled video telephony on a wireless network. The particular technology used is a function of the network, and its speed.

One approach is to use a SIP phone client to communicate with the network using RTP packets for the voice channel. This is the most widespread method used. Another approach is to create gateway software to send data to a SIP server where SIP and RTP can be converted into wireless network protocols.

Some GSM (Global System for Mobile Communications) phones use a technology called Unlicensed Mobile Access (UMA) Generic Access Network (GAN) for VoIP transport on the GSM backbone. UMA is a brand name, and 3GPP GAN is the technology. GAN networks transmit SIP over IP networks.

High-speed EVDO rev. A (Evolution-Data Optimized), HSDA (High-Speed Downlink Packet Access), Wi-Fi, and WiMAX (Worldwide Interoperability for Microwave Access) are fast enough that they are capable of transmitting video messages. As a general rule, Wi-Fi networks are cheaper to use than EVDO or HSDPA, but the latter two networks offer broader coverage and better audio.

Video telephony is becoming widely available on cell phones that operate on 3G (Universal Mobile Telecommunications System, or UMTS) GSM networks. According to Wireless Intelligence, in Q2, there were over 130 million cell phones capable of video telephony sold. GSM is available worldwide in 59 countries. No data is available that measures the usage of this feature, but its availability seems to be growing rapidly and the video capture feature is being widely used, something any YouTube devotee can attest to.

Video telecommunications is a boon to people who are deaf or have speech difficulties. In the United States, the Federal Communications Commission (FCC) regulates a program with cell phone providers called the Video Relay Service that sets up videophone sessions for sign language interpretation to communicate.

Webcams

Business applications for videoconferencing and telephony seem to have broader acceptance and could become much more important as business travel becomes more expensive. A number of manufacturers sell systems for videoconferencing or integrate it into telecommunication suites. Cisco's Unified Communications Manager is one example, but there are many others. The speakerphone vendor Polycom supports the addition of video to their system.

There have also been a number of laptops introduced that have cameras built into them; examples include models of the Apple Macintosh, Sony Vaio, Dell XPS, and the Asus Eee notebook. The cameras are usually placed at the top of the laptop screen and support video services for VoIP.

They are essentially Webcams. You find video conferencing support in programs as varied as AOL Instant Messenger (AIM), Skype, Windows Live Messenger, Yahoo Messenger, iChat, Camfrog, and others; the capability is widespread.

Webcams also are widely used as security devices for surveillance. Some of these cameras plug into computers through phone line connections, and others can be connected to Ethernet networks. A class of these Webcams are appliances; they have Web servers built into them whose output can be viewed in a browser. Axis, Panasonic, and others sell these cameras, sometimes under the name *network camera*.

Webcams have sprouted up everywhere, and many have been made publicly available. There are Webcams that survey the scene at Old Faithful Geyser in Yellowstone National Park (see Figure 26.7), in Times Square in New York City, and worldwide.

FIGURE 26.7

The National Park Service's streaming Webcam at Old Faithful in Yellowstone National Park.

Some of these Webcams are set up to send static pictures, usually once every minute or so; however, the newer models stream real-time video. Figure 26.7 shows a newer streaming Webcam, although the older still-image Webcam is still available on the National Park Service site.

Several sites on the Internet catalog and link to these cameras; the best known of them is Earthcam.com. It's a great diversion when you get the urge to travel but don't have the budget, or when you want to check out the conditions in a place you are going to.

Summary

In this chapter, the subjects of computer telephony and VoIP applications were introduced. Telephony is the use of telephones with computers either on phone or Ethernet networks, or both.

Operating systems enable telephony with native APIs that application vendors can build on. Computers can connect and manage phones and form the basis for PBX systems. Telephony applications built using application frameworks form the basis for CTI. Very sophisticated telephone systems are built with CTI technology.

Applications that combine voice and video were also described. These include videophones, Webcams, and video conferencing software.

The next part begins a set of chapters on network security. It covers some of the security protocols, such as HTTPS and SSL. You learn how they work, where they are used, and what networked services they protect.

Part VI

Network Security

Security Protocols and Services

N etwork security is best achieved by a set of layered and overlapping technologies. In this chapter, you learn about the different points of attack that can be used to compromise networked systems and gain access to them and the data that they contain. Network vulnerabilities can be scanned for, and some standard tools such as the National Vulnerability Database and related resources are described.

This chapter presents a checklist of the most important steps you can take to secure a network.

Two adaptive network security technologies are presented. One is called Location Awareness, and it can be used to detect the status of a network connection and its state and adjust system policies appropriately. Another technology called Network Access Protection can proactively quarantine systems that don't conform to a system health policy.

Sending traffic over the Internet involves insecure connections. You will learn about three different Internet security protocols in this chapter: IPsec, Transport Layer Security/Secure Socket Layer, and HTTPS. These technologies either encrypt data or create secure connections through tunneling and other methods.

Different methods used to encrypt network traffic are considered in this chapter. Various forms of encryption are used in cryptography, and the use of symmetric and asymmetric key algorithms is considered. These ciphers can be used to authenticate and validate data, as well as prevent the data from being compromised. As an example of these types of technologies, the Kerberos security system is described.

Network Security Overview

Your network is under attack by increasingly sophisticated and constantly evolving means. Today's news always seems to include the latest virus, Trojan, or worm; your mail contains a letter from your bank telling you that your credit card information has been hacked. If your network seems flaky or some system is acting up, you are excused for feeling paranoid. Keeping your network secure is a little like the cartoon *Spy vs. Spy*. These are uncertain times we live in, but you can discourage attackers by hardening your network, thus directing them away from your network and toward softer targets.

There is no single method for protecting a network. Any security system can be cracked or compromised, if not from the outside then certainly from the inside. The best way to secure a network is to have different layers of security so that an attacker must compromise two or more systems in order to gain access. Changing security parameters such as passwords regularly and securely partitioning different portions of a network are two other methods that are invaluable. In this chapter, you learn about some of the technologies used to secure networked systems and the traffic that flows over a network.

Network vulnerabilities

Network vulnerability is a weakness that can be exploited to gain access to that system. There are any number of ways that a system can be compromised: through poor password selection, viruses or Trojans, software bugs, an executable or script running inside the system, or through code injection. When a vulnerability becomes known and is used by others to attack similar systems, it is referred to as an exploit. Exploits travel as quickly as viruses do.

All software contains bugs or routines that can be compromised. The patches that companies offer on a regular basis, such as Microsoft Update, are meant to remove these vulnerabilities once they are discovered. When patches are released, they are analyzed for the flaws that they are meant to fix by people interested in attacking systems. An attack based on that flaw is then rushed out, and is very effective because it takes a while for systems to be updated. Attacks of this type are referred to as Zero Day exploits. Believe it or not, there are companies that provide a subscription service that informs their clients how to use Zero Day exploits to attack systems, and other companies that provide this information to clients so that they can protect themselves. Spy versus spy.

The best-practice recommendation for managing Zero Day exploits is to update and patch all systems as soon as patches become available. Many system administrators cringe at this suggestion as a best practice because patches can introduce their own problems. Patches can fix some problems while creating other problems. Automatically updating production systems introduces an element of uncertainty that wouldn't be there if the system's software were static.

One method used to uncover network vulnerabilities is to probe a network with a risk analysis tool, which is sometimes called a vulnerability scanner. Vulnerability scanners work by scanning a network for all assigned IP addresses, determining which ports are open, and building a list of applications and operating systems that are running on the various systems. Scanners of this type are port scanners, network scanners, and Web site scanners, as well as dedicated tools contained in management frameworks. Once the initial survey is complete, the scanner may either build a map of the network or create a report. If the scanner uses SNMP, WMI, or another management protocol, it can query systems and applications to determine not only what they are, but also their version numbers and patch levels. Vulnerability ratings can be assigned that provide administrators with check lists for actions that they need to perform in order to secure their network further.

An industry standard for measuring the severity of computer system vulnerability is called the Common Vulnerability Scoring System (CVSS). This metric is based on a set of measurements, and includes base or intrinsic vulnerability, perceived threats over time or temporal metrics, and deployment or environmental metrics. For more information on how this scoring system is structured, you can go to the CVSS FIRST (Forum of Incident Response and Security Teams) Web site at www.first.org/cvss/. The CVSS Special Interest Group, or SIG, develops this standard, which is currently at version 2. The metrics can be entered into an online calculator provided by the National Vulnerability Database in the CVSS scoring section to obtain the specific ratings (see the following section).

Several of these tools are publicly available; one example is Microsoft's Baseline Security Analyzer (MBSA; http://technet.microsoft.com/en-us/security/cc184924.aspx), version 2.1 being the latest one released. The MBSA uses the Microsoft Update infrastructure and a local agent to determine if a Windows system is secure and up to date. According to Microsoft, this Web-based service performs a vulnerability assessment on some three million systems a week. MBSA can not only scan systems such as Vista/Server 2008 but can also scan Windows CE and Embedded, Microsoft SQL Server, and Microsoft Internet Information Server. An MBSA sample report is shown in Figure 27.1.

FIGURE 27.1

A sample vulnerability report created by the Microsoft Baseline Security Analyzer

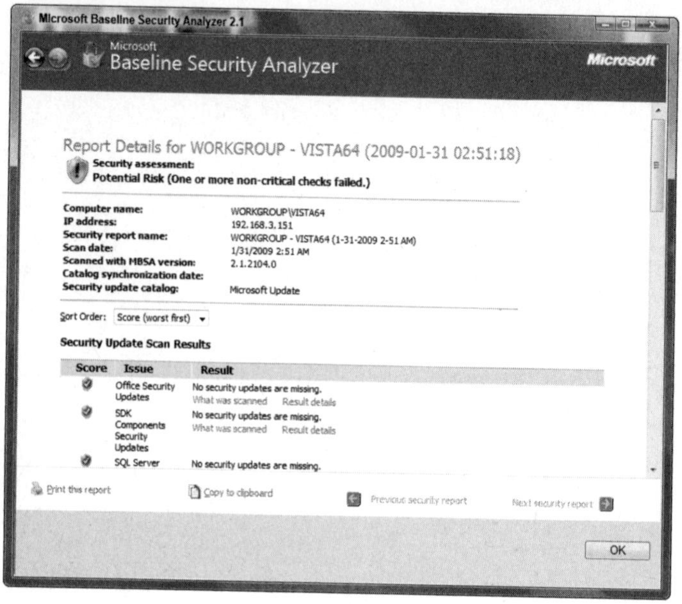

Information used to determine network vulnerability is maintained by a number of companies and organizations, including:

- Common Vulnerabilities and Exposures (CVE; `http://cve.mitre.com`)
- Computer Emergency Response Team (CERT; `www.cert.org`) at Carnegie Mellon University
- Microsoft Security Response Center (`www.microsoft.com/technet/archive/community/columns/security/essays/vulnrbl.mspx`)
- Open Source Vulnerability Database (OSVDB; `www.osvdb.org`)
- Open Web Application Security Project (`www.owasp.org/index.php/Category:Vulnerability`)
- SANS Institute (`www.sans.org`)
- Secunia vulnerability archive (`http://secunia.com`)
- SecurityFocus vulnerability archive (`www.securityfocus.com/bid`)
- Secwatch vulnerability archive (`http://secwatch.org`)
- VUPEN security vulnerability archive (`www.vupen.com/english/security-advisories/`)

Vulnerability scanning or network reconnaissance is also used by attackers attempting to gain entry to a network and is a feature of some worms.

The National Vulnerability Database

The entry for Common Vulnerabilities and Exposures, or CVE, at the start of the bullet list in the previous section refers to a dictionary of security threats that is maintained by the MITRE Corporation for the National Cyber Security Division of the United States Department of Homeland Security. CVE uses a system of identifiers that uniquely identify known security risks. These risk factors are sometimes referred to as CVE Identifiers, names, numbers, ID, or simply CVEs and are listed in the database when identified by outside parties as a candidate risk factor. Candidate risk factors are given Candidate Numbers (or CANs), and promoted to CVEs once they are reviewed and authenticated.

MITRE Corporation's function in maintaining the database is to run the editorial board, be the Candidate Numbering Authority, and make the information available to the public. The CVE database is available to the public to use for free and lists threats known internationally, along with a description of the threat's exposure and severity. From the standpoint of the CVE, a vulnerability is a software error that provides access to a system or network. An error in applying software correctly or leaving a system open is not considered a vulnerability and is not listed in the database. For example, your network operating system may allow strong passwords to be set but you do not require passwords or enforce strong passwords; that would not be considered a vulnerability. (Short passwords are subject to dictionary and brute force attacks.)

Vulnerabilities occur when:

- The attacker can execute a command as if they were a different user
- The attacker can access data that they aren't privileged to see
- The attacker can spoof another identity
- The attacker can create a situation where service is denied to others

You can perform a CVE search on the National Vulnerability Database (NVD), as found at http://nvd.nist.gov/. Figure 27.2 shows the Web page for an NVD search. The database currently lists 34,977 known vulnerabilities and can be downloaded for offline use. The data in this database supports the U.S. Information Security Program (ISAP) and serves as the content repository for the Security Content Automation Protocol used to monitor network security and provide threat assessments.

The NVD uses a structured naming system for different types of information technology systems, software, and other packages that is similar to the syntax used in Uniform Resource Identifiers (URIs) that are used on the Internet. This naming system is called the Common Product Enumeration, or CPE, Product Dictionary, and it is maintained as part of the database in XML format, which is available for download. The CPE XML file can be downloaded at `http://static.nvd.nist.gov/feeds/xml/cpe/dictionary/official-cpe-dictionary_v2.1.xml`.

FIGURE 27.2

The National Vulnerability Database lists known network security threats and provides related information about their severity and potential fixes.

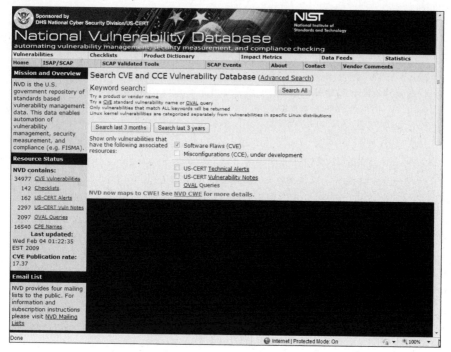

Points of Attack

Most often, network security is breached from the outside in. Typical attacks involve attacks on software or hardware vulnerabilities. However, exploits that are able to get inside the network are often most effective because they can operate stealthily.

The most common points of attack are:

- **Outside: System availability.** Systems can be overloaded by a spoof ICMP broadcast that results in a flood of ECHO replies to the system being attacked, called a smurf attack.

- **Outside: Denial of Service (DoS).** An attack where a service is overwhelmed by requests is referred to as a Denial of Service (DoS) attack. A DoS attack against domain name servers (DNS) is a common example of a DoS attack; when it is successful, it has the effect of making other system addresses on the Internet or intranet irresolvable and therefore makes those systems unavailable.

Distributed Denial of Service (DDoS) attacks refer to attacks by a large number of compromised systems that are zombies and can turned into a botnet, literally a robot network.

- **Outside/Inside: Authentication.** In a spoof, the attacker assumes the identity of another user.

- **Data in transit:** Traffic intercepted in transit, modified, and then sent on to its destination is called a man-in-the-middle attack. Data can also be subjected to eavesdropping.

- **Inside: Worms, Trojans, and other backdoor exploits** provide an attacker with a method for controlling systems inside the network and can create zombie computers. Backdoor exploits can be an executable program or algorithm that is able to evade network authentication, perform actions, and remain undetected.

  Rootkits are a form of backdoor exploit where the program is able to hide as a low-level driver or kernel module and therefore escape detection. Rootkits do not show up in file systems and may appear in process lists as a normal system process.

- **Direct internal access.** Attacks can take the form of media such as optical disks, USB keys, portable drives, and other media.

Microsoft uses a threat assessment model that they call the STRIDE approach (`http://msdn.microsoft.com/en-us/magazine/cc163519.aspx`) in developing their software. STRIDE stands for the following:

- **S**poofed identity (authentication). This lets an attacker impersonate another user. Users and systems must be authenticated; authentication can be through passwords, digital certificates, and other methods.

- **T**ampering of data (integrity). Attackers alter data. Methods used to maintain integrity include performing error-checking routines on data.

- **R**epudiation (non-repudiation). Individuals deny responsibility for their actions.

- **I**nformation disclosed (confidentiality). Attackers gain access to sensitive information. Networks restrict access to data using security access lists, domains, directory services, and other features of network operating systems to only the people who should have access.

- **D**enial of Service (availability). DoS attacks can make an essential service unavailable. Users and systems must be reliably linked to events that they initiate. Event logs may be maintained that provide audit trails, user and system credentials can be added to data, and secure communication channels can be established for transfer of data. Backup systems for important systems should exist and provide failover.

- **E**levation of privilege (authorization). A user or system wants to acquire more rights than they are enabled to have. Resources must be available when needed. Systems for managing resource access must be secure, and users must be given the lowest level of access that is suitable for their work.

Principles of secure network design

Security measures should focus on three separate levels:

- **Risk assessment and prevention.** Among the most effective technologies for risk prevention are user access control, cryptography, and firewalls. Firewalls are described in detail in Chapter 28.

- **Threat detection.** Threat detection systems include virus and spyware scanners, intrusion detection systems (IDS), event auditing, and heuristic analysis of event logs.

- **Response.** Responses to intrusion and compromise can involve system or subnet quarantine, restoring to known good backups, remediation, and protection upgrades.

Tip
Given the complexity of modern systems, a compromised system can never be repaired with 100 percent confidence that the system has been returned to perfect health. Hackers or crackers have become increasingly sophisticated in the methods that they use to infect or control systems, and may embed components as replacements for fundamental system components. Therefore, it is strongly recommended that you maintain multiple system images that you can use to return a system to a former state. For mission-critical systems, consider mirrors, Business Continuity Volumes (BCVs), and other forms of hot backup.

From the standpoint of expense and difficulty, each of the three levels of security is typically one order of magnitude more expensive than the level above it. That is, threat detection can cost 10 times what prevention measures might cost, and response can cost 100 times prevention measures as a rule of thumb. Think about how much installing virus and spyware scanning software or a firewall costs compared to the amount of time and expense it takes to remediate multiple systems that are compromised.

One of the important principles of secure network design is to minimize what is called the "attack surface" of a system or network. The attack surface is the exposed profile of a system that is available for view to a user or an attacker. The profile of an attack surface includes any of the following:

- Protocols running on the network or system

- Network interfaces that can respond to queries or messages

- Open ports

- Services running on an accessible system

- User input fields

With fewer avenues by which an attacker can penetrate a system, the security risks are lowered. However, once an attacker does gain entry to a system, a low attack surface doesn't limit the amount of damage that can be done.

Microsoft Internet Security and Acceleration (ISA) Server is an example of the concept of "secure by default." ISA Server is a content-caching gateway and proxy server and was developed from Microsoft's original Proxy Server. When you install ISA Server, all ports are closed, no protocols are active, and there are no defined entries into your network. You initialize ISA Server by opening the ports you want to allow traffic in and out on, and mapping traffic on HTTP port 80 to ISA's port 8080, and some additional ports for HTTPS, FTP, IMAP, or whatever service you want to allow. The next steps define which systems can send data, and which systems you will allow data to be received from. You define a set of rules, and those rules are applied in an order that imposes a hierarchy or precedence. It can be time-consuming to create the network security policy, but it does impose the smallest possible attack surface that ISA Server can be used for.

Here are the 14 Commandments of Network Security Practices:

1. **Use a firewall.** Always operate behind a firewall. Choose a hardware firewall in preference to a software firewall, and ensure that the firewall provides both physical and protocol isolation. A system attached to the Internet without a firewall can be compromised in minutes.

2. **Enforce strong passwords.** Always change any default password; use passwords that are at least eight characters long and combine upper- and lowercase alphabetic, numeric, symbol characters in strings that are not encountered in a dictionary.

3. **Install virus and spyware scanning software,** particularly at the gateways of your network.

4. **Have a robust system backup policy.** Keep system images for all systems.

5. **Patch your software.** Always apply patches as soon as they become available, but have backups available in case problems arise. Pay particular attention to any public network-facing software. It is particularly important to patch Web server and Web browser software, for example.

6. **Segment your network into subnets.** This provides physical isolation by IP addresses.

7. **Encrypt any sensitive data and use secure protocols for data transfer.** Don't send any data in plain text that you wouldn't allow to be published in the *New York Times*.

8. **Beware of downloadable content, hyperlinks, and unsolicited e-mail.** Turn off script execution as a default.

9. **Lower your attack surface.** Close all unnecessary ports, and turn off all unused network protocols.

10. **Beware of network shares and providing full access to shared resources.** Shares offer a potent mechanism for viruses, worms, Trojans, and other malicious software to propagate through a network. Use a strong network operating system access list control policy.

11. **Beware of mobile systems and mobile media.** Isolate traveling laptops until they are verified safe, and ensure that sensitive systems lock out media such as USB keys.

12. **Secure means secure.** Ensure that you have secure connections when using forms or HTTPS connections. Verify connections by checking the security certificates of sites. Close your browser when a secure session is completed; don't simply close a browser tab.

13. **Be a policy wonk.** Make good use of your network operating system's security policies.

    Security polices in Windows Server 2008 can lock resources by users and groups, deny software or device driver installation, prohibit the use of different device classes, lock down desktops and browsers, control access to e-mail attachments, prevent DVD burning, perform network quarantine, set user account protection actions, and perform other services. Perhaps 40 percent of the 2,400 policy settings in Windows Server 2008 are security related. Other network operating systems and add-on policy engine products, such as Novell ZenWare, offer security policy settings.

14. Be kind to your mother, to children and small animals, and to any network administrators that you encounter; and pay your taxes.

If you do all of these things on the list above, your network will be a hard target and you will be blessed.

Location Awareness and Network Access Protection

There are so many different ways in which a network can be attacked that what you really need to combat a portfolio of threats is an adaptive network strategy. Microsoft has developed a couple of these strategies and shipped them with Windows Server 2008 and Vista. The first technology is called Network Location Awareness (NLA), and it refers to the ability of a Windows server to detect system, connection, and session states and adjust the policies applied to a client appropriately.

In many instances, network clients either use a PING or send an ICMP packet to determine if a network resource can be connected to. When a laptop connects to a Windows domain using PING, PING is the mechanism that the domain would use to ascertain the state of the client. So if PING fails, the domain will not be able to apply its Group Policy. ICMP is often turned off at firewalls, so that mechanism is also unavailable for client connection modification. To solve these problems, NLA is established and client information is exchanged using a VPN connection. Every time the VPN connection refreshes, the Group Policy for both users and machines also refreshes.

With Network Location Awareness, it is possible to make the following changes in client states:

- Options can be automatically set during a Pre-Execution Environment (PXE).

- A client's group policy is updated automatically when the client connects to the domain. Other events, such as connecting a mobile device, establishment of a VPN session, a client's arousal from hibernation or standby, or the promotion of a system isolated in quarantine to the production network, all fire a Group Policy refresh.

- Clients are configured based on the resources that are detected. When a network interface card isn't detected, the driver software for that card isn't loaded automatically. Suppression of unnecessary driver downloads provides shorter boot cycles.

- The bandwidth to a client can be made part of the policy that is applied when the client connects to the domain.

There is a second approach to network protection called Network Access Protection (NAP), and it is also a resource management approach based on defined policies. NAP evaluates the condition of enabled clients (Vista) when they attempt to log into a domain. Before the client is authenticated and provided with a network connection, they are evaluated to determine if any of the following policies are violated:

- The client's firewall is turned on.

- The client's anti-virus and anti-spyware software is running, their signatures are up-to-date, and a scan has been performed recently.

- All Microsoft patches have been applied.

- Other policies specific to your particular network are violated.

Failure to meet the requirements results in a system being quarantined until remediation can be done to the system to bring it up to full compliance. NAP provides the additional measures required to ensure that network security isn't compromised from within, and represents a new direction that many network operating systems will adopt to make networks more secure. These types of systems can be modified as system policies to adapt them to specific network configurations and needs. Figure 27.3 shows a diagram of a NAP system implemented with Windows Server 2008.

In a fully configured NAP service, the NAP policy engine is supported by Health Requirement and Trusted Health Registration Authority servers. Supporting the identification and authentication of clients are Directory servers and a Certificate server. When a NAP client fails to meet the health policy requirement, it is logged into a separate subnet where it is managed by a Remediation server that addresses the client's deficiencies. Figure 27.3 shows a graphical depiction of an Internet and wireless client login with a NAP system.

FIGURE 27.3

Network Access Policy separates healthy clients from suspect clients onto different networks.

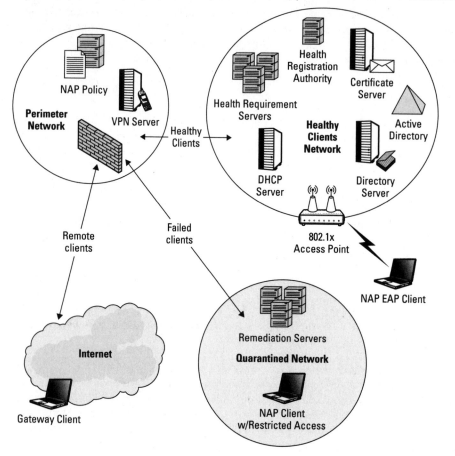

Internet Security Protocols

The Internet is an inherently insecure environment. In most instances, any traffic you send over the Internet can be intercepted and cached. To ensure that data can be sent confidentially over the Internet, several different communications protocols were developed that you can use to protect your data. In the sections that follow, you will learn about three different protocols: IPsec, Transport Layer Security (formerly Secure Sockets Layer), and HTTPS.

IPsec is a method for encrypting IP traffic and validating the integrity of the data once it arrives; the required use of IPsec is one of the main reasons that IPv6 is inherently more secure than IPv4. TLS and SSL are methods for encrypting data and sending the data over the Transport layer. HTTPS is an encryption technology combined with a secure connection, which creates a tunnel from client to server. These three methods make it possible for banks to operate over the Web, governments and the military to communicate, and all of the other conveniences you take for granted in modern internetworking to be accomplished.

IPsec

Internet Protocol Security (IPsec) is a method for encrypting and validating traffic sent over TCP/IP networks and is an open standard covered in IETF RFC 2401 (www.ietf.org/rfc/rfc2401.txt). The suite of protocols includes a cryptographic key-based mechanism for establishing the unique identity of connection endpoints. To use IPsec, both of the nodes must be running the IPsec protocol locally. IPsec can be sent as either unicast or multicast, and when sent multicast, all destination nodes share the same security information.

IPsec has two modes of operation:

- Transport mode
- Tunnel mode

Note

The spelling of IPsec with a lowercase s is recommended by the IETF. You will often see IPsec written IPSec, but this book follows the IETF's guideline.

In Transport mode, the IP packet's header is left in clear text and the data or payload is encrypted. Transport mode is used to send messages between nodes. In Tunnel model, the entire IPsec packet is encrypted and encapsulated inside an IP packet. Whereas IPsec Transport mode requires that endpoints and all connection points (routers and switches) in a data path support IPsec, Tunnel mode only requires the endpoints to be running the IPsec protocol. Tunnel mode traffic can pass through any host that supports IP traffic and is often used in Virtual Private Network (VPN) communication. Figure 27.4 shows the two datagrams in use — IPsec Transport (top datagram) and Tunnel mode (bottom datagram) where the Encapsulating Security Protocol is used to create the packet.

It is also possible to use IPsec with only one connection point supporting the protocol; then IPsec is encrypted and encapsulated at the border (or other outbound) router, and is decrypted and extracted at the border router for the destination system. When you configure IPsec this way, the traffic is visible to each of the hosts on the two networks but secure when it leaves the subnetwork that the sending system is located on.

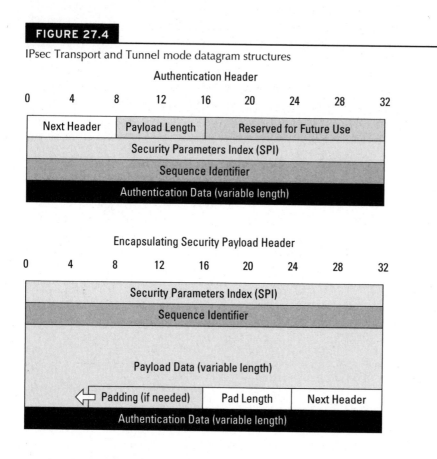

FIGURE 27.4

IPsec Transport and Tunnel mode datagram structures

IPsec is a Network level (Level 3) protocol in the OSI model and an Internet Layer protocol in the TCP/IP model. The most important protocols in the IPsec protocol suite include the following three protocols:

- **Authentication Header (AH).** AH provides the mechanism for guaranteeing the authenticity of packets delivered over stateless connections. The AH uses a hashing algorithm and a shared key to create an Integrity Check Value (ICV). ICVs serve the same function as a CRC data check. The destination decrypts the data, runs the same algorithm, and determines if the ICV that it computes is the same as the one in the datagram, which establishes the authenticity of the sender.

- **Encapsulating Security Payload (ESP).** ESP encrypts the payload data used in IPsec communication providing the means to authenticate and protect the contents of either IP v4 or IP v6 data. ESP can be used in either an encryption-only or an authentication-only mode but is usually used with both features turned on. ESP does not protect the IP header. The bottom datagram in Figure 27.4 shows an ESP packet in Tunnel mode.

In Tunnel mode the complete IP packet is encapsulated and a new header and trailer are added for transport. The packet is entirely protected in Tunnel mode. ESP header data is layered on top of the IP protocol and uses the well-known port number 50. ESP authentication data is contained in a field that uses an Integrity Check Value (ICV) to verify that the contents of the encrypted packet are correctly transported.

- **Internet Key Exchange (IKE) v1 and v2.** The IKE protocol provides a handshaking mechanism between the two connection endpoints, determines what security protocols are available and which will be used, and then creates the encryption and authentication keys that are sent to the destination system so that the packet may be identified and decrypted. IKE is described in IETF RFC 2409 (`http://tools.ietf.org/html/rfc2409`).

    IKE uses the Internet Security Association and Key Management Protocol (ISCAMP) to exchange data and negotiate the SA (Security Association). ISCAMP is a framework that can support different methods for key exchange. The two common key exchange protocols are OAKLEY, which is used for the basis of most of the technology of IKE key exchanges, and SKEME, from which IKE borrows some features such as its public key encryption technology.

Figure 27.5 shows the structure of both the AH and ESP headers in Transport mode and Tunnel mode. The Payload or Data field is of variable length.

FIGURE 27.5

The structure of IPsec Authentication and Encapsulated Security Payload headers

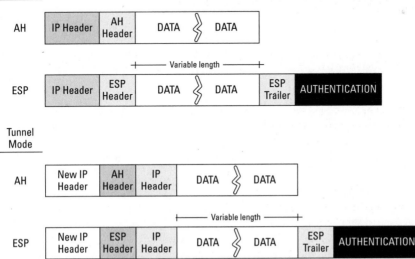

ESP encrypts the data in an IPsec datagram using one of the following three cryptographic algorithms: AES-CBC, HMAC-SHA1, or TripleDES-CBC. The endpoints in an IPsec session each have a shared key, which the destination system uses to decrypt the data. ESP can be used alone or with the AH protocol. Figure 27.5 showed the different components of an IPsec packet that are encrypted by ESP: the ESP Header, ESP Trailer, and ESP Data. The ESP Header shown in Figure 27.6 has an SPI parameter with its Security Association data, and the Sequence Number used to resequence packets upon arrival. The Trailer contains Padding, Pad Length, and Next Header information. An optional feature in ESP can authenticate the data field by using an algorithm to create an ICV that can be compared using the shared key.

The placement of the components of IPsec in a datagram ensures that the data is followed by any needed padding in the trailer to conform to a standard block size that some algorithms require in order to process the data. If authentication is used, the ESP Authentication Data trailer is part of the encrypted data because it would be stripped away if it were in a header field. It must also come after the data in order to be available after encryption is performed.

Because IPsec operates at the same level as the IP protocol itself, it is application independent and can be used to securely send packets originating from any application. This is not true of other secure protocols such as SSL, which operate at higher levels and require applications to include support for them.

IPsec negotiates the method used to transfer datagrams in this format between endpoints. Two endpoints with a negotiated security policy are in a Security Association. A security policy specifies which packets are secured and whether they use AH or ESP. The algorithm(s) used for encryption and those used for authentication are selected from a list and shared, as are the keys necessary to decrypt the data for both processes. Policies are stored locally in each device's Security Policy Database (SPD), and security associations are stored in each device's Security Association Database (SAD). When an IPsec datagram arrives at a device for processing, the device looks up the Security Parameter Index in the SPD and then applies the association that is stored for that SPI in the SAD.

Whereas IPsec is an optional component of IPv4 communication, it is a compulsory part of and integral to IPv6. Therefore, if you aren't using IPsec now, rest assured that sometime in the future you will be.

Transport Layer Security

Transport Layer Security (TLS) is a set of cryptographic protocols that is used to encrypt data over TCP/IP networks at the Transport layer. This developing standard is specified by IETF RFC 5246 (http://tools.ietf.org/html/rfc5246). TLS is a superset of the widely known Secure Socket Layer (SSL) developed by Netscape, and used for many years. SSL 3.0 was the first Web protocol chosen by the credit card companies for secure e-Commerce transactions.

TLS both encrypts and authenticates data sent from an application on one server to an unauthenticated client so that the communication is delivered securely. It is most widely used to allow Web servers to communicate with clients such as browsers, but it can be applied to all kinds of application traffic over TCP/IP.

Note

TLS can run into problems when used with virtual servers due to the fact that virtual servers must share the same certificate on a host. In a situation where X.509 is used as the authentication, you may need to either add a wildcard certificate or reissue the certificate when a new virtual server is used.

In its simplest form, TLS uses an authenticated server and an unauthenticated client. If you have a Public Key Infrastructure (PKI) installed, TLS can be configured so that both ends of the TLS connection can be mutually authenticated. TLS uses three steps:

1. **Negotiated protocol support.** The client sends its list of supported ciphers and hash function to a TLS server, which selects the strongest ones for use. This portion is called the TLS handshake, and it can be a full but simple handshake without authentication or a client-authenticated TLS handshake.

2. **Key exchange and single or mutual system authentication.** The server returns to the client a digital certificate, which includes the server name and its trusted Certificate Authority (CA) credential. The client may verify this information with the CA server.

3. **Symmetric encryption and message authentication.** The client encrypts a random number with the server's public key and sends that session key to the server where it can be decrypted using the server's private key. Both the server and the client then have the random number seed that they can use to feed to the different algorithms selected to generate the appropriate keys.

TLS supports a number of different cryptographic algorithms for both key creation and exchange and authentication algorithms. When two endpoints perform negotiation, they choose a key exchange algorithm, and an authentication algorithm. Message authentication involves the use of message authentication codes (MACs) that are created using cryptographic hash functions with HMAC. By contrast, SSL used a pseudorandom function to create its MACs. Taken as a whole, TLS negotiation selects from what is called a cipher suite.

In order for applications to use TLS, they must have built-in support for TLS. While TLS is used mainly for HTTP traffic over TCP transport, it has also been used to secure SMTP, FTP, NNTP, and XMPP traffic. OpenVPN (`http://openvpn.net/`) uses TLS to create a VPN connection between two endpoints. With OpenVPN, any network protocol may be used, and the program makes it appear that the destination system is local to the source. One other area where TLS is being widely used is in Voice over IP traffic where Session Initiation Protocol (SIP) signaling is encrypted and authenticated.

For many applications that lack TLS support, there are third-party products that encapsulate TLS traffic and transport it from one endpoint to another. One program called stunnel (`http://stunnel.mirt.net/`) is a free, open source multiplatform TLS/SSL tunneling application that serves as a wrapper for TLS data and can use PKI to create a secure connection.

HTTPS

The Hypertext Transfer Protocol Secure (HTTPS) combines the Hypertext Transfer Protocol (HTTP) with either the Transport Layer Security (TLS) or Secure Sockets Layer (SSL) protocol that was described in the previous section. An authenticated Web server uses HTTPS to create a secured connection to a browser client. When you connect with HTTPS, you enter the prefix https:// into the URL in place of the standard http:// address. HTTPS traffic uses port 443 by default, unless otherwise specified.

Note

The appearance of a lock icon in your browser indicating an SSL/TLS encrypted connection is not a guaranteed measure of security. A browser can be hijacked and still show a lock icon. Always check that the certificate matches what you expect to see and be wary.

Figure 27.6 shows a secured connection to a local bank in the Mozilla Firefox 3.0 browser. Note that the certificate organization's icon appears to the right of the URL, and that you can click the icon to open a dialog box with more detail. Microsoft Internet Explorer 8.0 duplicates this function by placing an icon to the right of the address bar, and will go so far as to color the address bar green when a verified HTTPS connection has been made.

FIGURE 27.6

The secure indicator icon in Mozilla Firefox 3.0 offers information about a site's certificate.

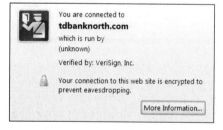

More information is provided by all browsers with detailed information about the certificate itself. Foxfire 3.0's Certificate Viewer dialog box is shown in Figure 27.7. Whenever you are on a secure connection and have any doubts about its authenticity, you should open the Certificate details in your browser to check that all of the information fields are populated by reasonable data. Whereas it may be possible to create or spoof a secure connection, it is extremely unlikely that anyone can spoof the fields in the certificate dialog box, as those fields are populated by a third party — the Certificate Authority server.

FIGURE 27.7

A digital certificate detail dialog box from Mozilla Firefox 3.0

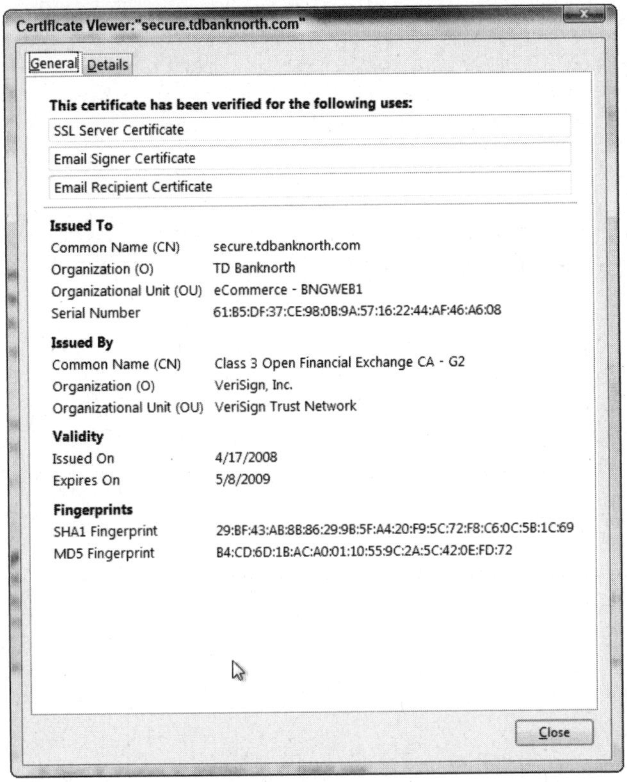

The certificates used by Web servers use a public key certificate that is created in software and submitted to a Certificate Authority (CA) for validation. This certificate is digitally signed by the CA, which means that it provides the necessary public key to anyone interested in validating communication from the Web server that the information contained in the certificate is valid. In order for a Web browser to be able to verify a certificate, it must have the signing certificate of the CA, and because a CA's function would be useless without that, most of the major CAs are found in all major browsers.

It is possible for organizations and individuals to have their own CAs, but those CAs are only useful for encrypting the traffic so that others cannot view the data. Personal or organizational CAs will not authenticate the sender. However, if an organization sends data from their server to their browsers, then the organization's CA will establish the veracity of the sender in that instance. In addition to server certificates, organizations can also create client certificates and load them into individuals' browsers. Client certificates can verify user information to the server without a login being required, and allow the server to verify this information whenever it connects to the client. These are very useful features, indeed.

Encryption and Cryptography

Cryptography is the study of methods for hiding information, and is studied as both an area of computer science and advanced mathematics. There are many methods for cryptographically securing information, including using passwords, biometrics, or devices for access to information, encrypting data with algorithms and/or with the use of keys, and a myriad of other ways.

Encryption refers to the process by which information is transformed into data so that it loses its context. Decryption is the reverse process by which the data is transformed back into information that can be read and understood. Taken together, the two algorithms that both encrypt and decrypt are called a cipher. Some ciphers require the use of a key, which is information that is used to modify the action of the cipher. Keys are generally kept secret, except when a set of keys is required by the cipher. In those instances, the sender and recipient may share a public key, but do not exchange the private or secret key(s) necessary to complete the cipher. To be truly secret, a key must be variable (that is, generated freshly with each use); otherwise, it loses its ability to protect the cipher from outsiders. All of these communications, the cipher, keys, and encrypted data are subject to authentication methods that validate that the information arrived correctly and is from whom it says it is from.

Modern-day ciphers are extremely good and difficult to crack. The three best-known cryptographic algorithms used on computers are:

- **Data Encryption Standard (DES),** designed at IBM and selected by the National Bureau of Standards as the official Federal Information Processing Standard (FIPS) for the United States government in 1976. DES uses a symmetric key algorithm and a 56-bit key. Although DES is now considered to be insecure, variations of DES such as Triple DES and the Advanced Encryption Standard (AES) are in wide use.

- **Diffie-Hellman Key Agreement Algorithm** uses a shared secret key to encrypt communication sent over insecure networks with a symmetric key cipher. The D-H algorithm was first published in 1976 by Whitfield Diffie and Martin Hellman, and was based on work using public key distribution by Ralph Merkle in the United Kingdom that was kept secret until 1997. You may sometimes (rarely) encounter this cipher under the name Diffie-Hellman-Merkle for that reason. Diffie is now the Chief Security Officer at Sun Microsystems.

- **RSA Public Key Cryptographic Algorithm** was based on work by Ron Rivast, Adi Shamir, and Leonard Adleman at MIT, published in 1977 and patented in 1983. RSA algorithms involve key generation, encryption, and decryption using both a public and private key. The public key is used to encrypt data that can only be decrypted with the private key and vice versa.

These cryptographic technologies are described in more detail in the next section. Cryptography and encryption technologies are complex fields of study that could occupy the entire content of this book. In the sections that follow, you are presented with an overview on how these technologies are most commonly applied to securing computer networks.

Brute force and ignorance

You can never prove that a cipher is unbreakable, and theoretically all ciphers are breakable, provided sufficient resources can be provided to test them, with one notable exception. That exception is a system where a one-time pad is used as the key and that pad uses verifiably random number generation. Claude Shannon proved that a one-time pad is unbreakable, provided that the pad is fully random, applied once, and has a length greater than or equal to the data being encrypted.

No modern encryption methods conform to a perfect cipher; that ideal system is too computationally demanding. However, when the potential number of variations in a data set becomes large enough, the ability of any system to break a cipher becomes practically impossible. The following example illustrates this.

A password is a key that unlocks access to a security account. If I told you that a system used a two-letter password, all lowercase, then you could manually enter each of the 676 combinations from the universe of 262 possible passwords into the computer, and in about an hour, give or take, discover the correct combination. For upper- and lowercase combinations, the universe is 2,704 in size (522), so that would take four times as long. This approach to guessing passwords is referred to as the brute force approach. A lock with four wheels, each offering numbers 0 to 9, provides a universe of 0 to 9,999 (or 10,000) possibilities, which could take the better part of a day to crack by hand.

Note

You'll find two-letter combinations at www.en.wikipedia.org/wiki/List_of_all_two-letter_ combinations and three-letter combinations, or Three-Letter Acronyms (TLAs), spread out over 14 Web pages at the same site.

The speed of computers makes brute force attacks even more powerful. Modern desktop computers are quite powerful — they are the mainframes of the past sitting right there on your desk. A brute force attack by a modern PC can find a password of six letters in a few hours, or a six-character password containing upper- and lowercase letters, numbers, and punctuation in a few days. An eight-character password of the complete ASCII character set might take a month or two to crack. It is pretty amazing to watch a demonstration of how powerful an attack can be just using brute force methods.

As a rule of thumb, most people trying to crack their way into a network aren't going to be willing to spend any more than a day or two at it, unless they know that the contents of the target are worth the effort.

Note

Many security systems come with a feature called a lockout that locks the account after a specified number of failed logon attempts. This feature is designed to defeat brute force or dictionary-based attacks.

Most brute force attacks combine random guesses with a prebuilt dictionary containing most of the short letter combinations (say, up to three or four places long), as well as all of the common names and words in one or more languages. By using a dictionary-based attack, it is possible to cycle through several million common possibilities in a couple of hours, and this approach is usually more effective than simple brute force approaches because few people use truly random passwords. You can see why complex random passwords offer so much more protection than just letters, and how the amount of work to crack a password goes up exponentially with each additional place.

Tip

There are a number of random password generators that you can find available on the Web. Some of these tools generate random passwords on the Web page itself, while others are applications that you can download or buy. The best random password generators use numbers derived from phenomena such as temperature fluctuations of a microprocessor or something similar to obtain randomness. If you use a random password generator, be sure to store your passwords in a safe place where you can refer back to them.

There are limits to brute force. The Electronic Freedom Foundation built a system called the DES Cracker in 1998 for $250,000 containing 1,800 custom chips and demonstrated that they could crack 56-bit DES in a few days. Today, systems that can perform this feat can be built for under $10,000. As you increase the size of any key, the task grows exponentially. Current technologies, such as AES, Triple DES, Twofish, Serpent, and other standards, start at key sizes of 128 bits and can be set as high as 192 or 256 bits in length.

You can use physics to argue that a 128-bit symmetric key can't be broken. The von Neumann-Landauer equation sets a value for the lowest amount of energy that you would have to consume to do a bit flip. With a universe of 2128 values ($3.40 \times e38$) and a computer operating at room temperature, this would consume 30 gigawatts of energy (1018 joules) for a year in order to perform 2128 − 1 bit operations, and this value doesn't even begin to estimate how much power it would take to test the validity of the key. The amount of time required to perform bit flips at the rate of 1018 bit flips per second would be 1013 years, or roughly the age of the universe. This assumes that the key is randomly generated.

Some day, we may have quantum computers that can operate at much higher speeds and near zero degrees absolute, and the fundamental assumptions of this argument may no longer apply. But to paraphrase Aragorn from *The Return of the King*, "Today is not this day."

Symmetric key algorithms

The first of the key-based cryptographic algorithms that were available for use were of a type called symmetric key algorithms. The most commonly used symmetric key algorithms use a block cipher, stream cipher, or a hash function. A brief description of these ciphers follows.

Block ciphers

With a block cipher, the algorithm operates on a block of text using a key that translates the output into a block of encrypted text of the same size. When the size of the message is greater than the block used, the algorithm uses the block and key to encrypt the next block-sized set of characters. The process repeats until all clear text characters are encrypted. Block ciphers can iteratively repeat the block encryption, or it can alter the algorithm used for every block that is encrypted.

The Data Encryption Standard (DES) and the Advanced Encryption Standard (AES) are block cipher algorithms. Although DES isn't used for highly secure communications, the standard remains very popular due to the high speed with which it can encrypt and decrypt data. Chances are that the e-mail cipher your e-mail client uses is DES-based, as are many ATM machine communications, as well as encrypted secure connections such as remote desktops.

Stream ciphers

A stream cipher works by generating a long key as a stream, one character after another. The creation of the key is based on a process that can't be predicted in advance, such as the generation of random passwords based on thermal variation that was described in the previous section. The longer the key, the more secure the stream cipher is.

Stream ciphers make no demand on a real-time generation of a key; indeed, you can create and store a set of stream cipher keys and use them one at a time as needed. The most well-known use of a stream cipher in this manner is called a "one-time pad." In a one-time pad, each message is encrypted using a unique key, and once used, the key is discarded — just as you would tear the top page of a pad of paper off after you used it. The key feature of a stream cipher is that each key is random and unique.

The best-known stream cipher is the RC4 standard. RC4 was developed by Ron Rivest of RSA Security and released and trademarked in 1987, but the algorithm was a trade secret until 1994. The RC comes from either "Rivest Cipher" or "Ron's Code," and variants of RC such as RC2, RC5, and RC6 have been released. In 1994, the RC4 cipher was disclosed and is now in the public domain. The RC4 algorithm is used as the encryption standard for the WPA and WEP wireless security protocols that are described in Chapter 14, and for Transport Layer Security (described earlier in this chapter).

RC4 creates a pseudorandom keystream from one of the 256 possible byte combinations and two 8-bit index pointers applying a Key Scheduling Algorithm (KSA) to create a key between 40 and 256 bits in length. This keystream is then used to encrypt clear text by applying an XOR (Exclusive OR) operation bit for bit. As RC4 works its way through the clear text, a pseudorandom generation algorithm (PRGA) increments the index values to modify the keystream. XOR takes two operands and performs a logical disjunction so that the result is one or the other values but not both. A truth table like the one shown in Table 27.1 shows this operation graphically. The decryption simply repeats the process, returning the cipher text to clear text.

TABLE 27.1

An XOR Operation Truth Table

X	Y	Result
0	0	0
0	1	1
1	0	1
1	1	0

RC4 isn't airtight, although it is difficult to crack. For example, the 104-bit RC4 standard used in 128-bit WEP wireless encryption can be cracked by a tool called AIRCRACK-PTW in less than a minute.

Hash functions

The last of the common key-based cryptographic algorithms is based on hash functions. A hash function takes a message of any size and applies a short, fixed-length hash to that message, returning a shorter length (than the original input) hash value. A hash function is a mathematical function that converts a string of any size into a smaller string integer that represents the original data. You can think of a hash function as returning an index value, and that value is the hash value, alternatively referred to as a digest, hash code, hash sum, or simply a hash. A hash value can be made public without concern that the input's original data may be exposed.

Hash functions are one-way functions. Their values can be computed, but the value offers no information or method for restoring the original data. That is because the hash value is a reduced data set and does not contain sufficient information to return the original method. A hash function that is shown to be beyond the range of computation to find another input that would yield the same hash value is described as being a weakly collision-free hash function. A hash function that can be proved to uniquely describe a hash value for each unique input is referred to as a strongly collision-free hash function. Figure 27.8 shows how a hash function is applied to a message to create a hash value starting with the message block on the left and moving to message blocks on the right, each block providing input to the hash that is obtained in the lower-right corner of the figure.

Hash functions are used in error-checking algorithms, checksums, fingerprints, and other technologies. You could use hash functions to search for duplicated records in databases, search for identical genomes in database sequences, and in a myriad of other applications.

When a cryptographic hash function is applied to data such as an e-mail message, it creates a hash that is in essence a digital signature. The receiver of the message can take the encrypted data, apply the hash value, and determine if the encrypted data is identical to what was sent. Just changing one character in an encrypted message of any length will result in a completely different hash value and a mismatch when the comparison is run. Therefore hash function cryptography is a fundamental tool in data validation methodologies as it creates what are essentially digital signatures. True digital signatures require asymmetric encryption that is a private/public key pair.

FIGURE 27.8

The use of a hash function to create a hash value

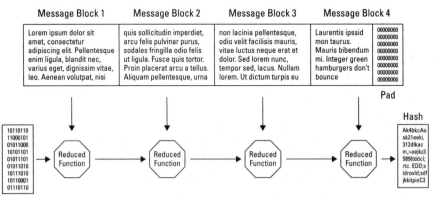

The best known of the cryptographic hash functions is the MD4 function (now cracked and deprecated), which has been replaced by the more secure MD5 function. MD4 stands for the Message Digest algorithm developed by Ronald Rivest at MIT in 1990. MD4 uses a 128-bit digest length hash to generate the digital signature. MD4 is used to create the password checks in Windows NT, Widows XP/Server 2003, and Windows Vista/Server 2008. Many of the current generation of hash functions, including MD5, the National Security Agency's (NSA's) Secure Hash Algorithm (SHA), and RACE Integrity Primitive Evaluation Message Digest (RIPEMD), are based on the MD4 technology.

A technology related to hash functions is the cryptographic Message Authentication Code (MAC) methodology. MAC uses an algorithm and a secret key to operate on input to output a MAC or tag that represents the input value. Because a secret key is involved, not only can the data be authenticated by the tag, but the data can also be verified. MAC doesn't require that the data being evaluated be encrypted when sent, but another secret key technology called Message Integrity Code (MIC) does. When a MIC is applied to a message, you will always get the same tag returned if the same algorithm is used. With MAC, the same message returns the same tag only if the same secret key is used. Because this technology is a symmetric key encryption, MAC cannot be used as a digital signature; that is, MAC doesn't prove that the sender of the document can be uniquely identified.

With a MAC, the secret key is generated by an oracle machine, which for our purposes may be considered a black box that has a Turing machine interface. You ask the oracle machine a question and it provides an answer. For MAC, the question is what secret key do you get for a specific message. The only way that an attacker can compromise a MAC is to have not only the message, but also access to the oracle machine that generates the message. Simple access to the oracle machine will not provide the key without submitting the message.

Asymmetric or public key algorithms

The second broad class of cryptographic key-based technologies is called asymmetric or public key algorithms. These algorithms use a public key to encrypt data and a private or secret key to decrypt and/or verify a hash of the message or the message itself. The Diffie-Hellman-Merkel and RSA algorithms that were mentioned briefly at the beginning of this topic are two asymmetric key algorithm technologies. Other algorithms in this category include Cramer-Shoup cryptosystems, ElGamal encryption, and Elliptic Curve algorithms.

You run across asymmetric key encryption with digital signature technologies, as the two keys provide a means for the public key to sign the encryption with one algorithm and the private key to verify the signature with the second. Keys can be generated as two interrelated pairs at the same time, but it is computationally impossible to calculate one key from another. The two-key combination also means that the content can be uniquely identified as having originated at one particular computer. The development of public key cryptography is considered to be one of the most important inventions in computer science of the last 50 years.

Underlying these public key algorithms are key generation technologies based on solving very hard computational problems. The three methods used are an integer factorization where a large number is created by multiplying a large number of smaller integers. RSA uses integer factorization, and it has been shown that a 200-digit number required nearly 1.5 years of work roughly equivalent to 50 years of computer time to solve. D-H-M uses a technology based on a discrete logarithm calculation where a logarithm is determined to be the solution to an equation $gx = h$, where g and h are members of a finite cyclic group. The third algorithm looks to compute solutions to elliptic curves based on the formula $y2 = x3 + ax + b$. These three problems are very difficult to compute using current computer technologies.

Digital signatures are used in all of the important public key infrastructure technologies such as SSL/TSL, VPNs, Kerberos, and others. The two most widely used public key algorithms are the Rivest-Shamir-Adleman (RSA) algorithm and the Digital Signature Algorithm (DSA).

Kerberos

The Kerberos protocol is a network authentication system that relies on a symmetric key infrastructure and a trusted third-party system to establish the identity of communicating parties and to ensure that the data has been delivered without interference or interception. Kerberos was created to allow data to be sent over insecure connections (the Internet, for example) while ensuring that the data hasn't been snooped or retransmitted as part of a man-in-the-middle or a replay attack. Kerberos has been extended in several ways since it was developed at MIT to include asymmetric key algorithmic authentication. Figure 27.9 shows the current implementation of Microsoft's Kerberos mechanism as it shipped in Windows Server 2008/Vista.

The Microsoft Server 2008 Kerberos infrastructure and mechanism is shown here.

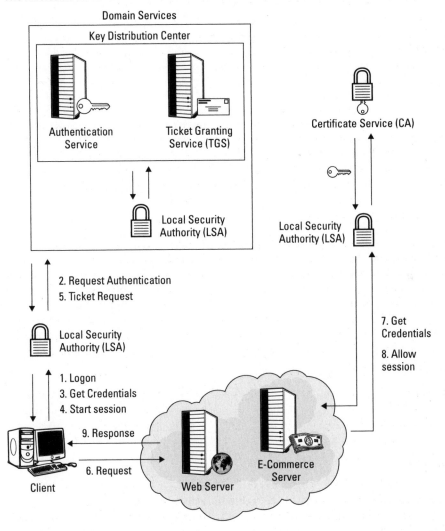

The Kerberos mechanism for authentication shown in Figure 27.9 works as follows:

1. The client logs into the network and the logon information is sent to the Local Security Authority (LSA).

2. The LSA passes the request onto the Authentication Service with a Request for Authentication and authentication is granted from the LSA to the client.

3. A request is made to Get Credentials from the LSA, and the LSA sends the appropriate credentials to the Client.

4. The Client begins it session.

5. A Ticket Request for a particular application, session, or operation is made from the Client to the LSA and passed along to the Ticket Granting Service (TGS). The ticket created at the TGS is returned to the client.

6. A Request is made to a Web server for secure information from an E-Commerce system.

7. That Web server may make a request to an E-Commerce Server which then sends a Get Credentials command to an LSA which passes the request to a Certificate Service (CA).

8. The CA sends the Credentials to the LSA which will then issue an Allow Session command.

9. The Web server sends the information requested by the Client.

The name Kerberos comes from the three-headed dog (Cerberus in Latin) that guarded Hades. It was developed as part of the Project Athena efforts at MIT and first appeared as version 4 in 1988. A later version, number 5, appeared in 1993 and was published by the IETF as RFC 1510. The MIT Kerberos standard is freely available for use, and many of the major players on the Internet, Sun Microsystems, Microsoft, Google, Apple, and others, formed the Kerberos Consortium to continue the development of this standard at MIT. Kerberos is used by many of the network operating systems that you have read about in this book, including Sun Solaris, BSD UNIX, Windows networks (from 2000 on), Mac OS X, Red Hat Linux (v.4 and later), and many others.

Note
To get information about any of the IETF's RFC you can get their description from links obtained from the IETF's RFC search page at www.ietf.org/rfc.html.

The original Kerberos used DES encryption, which led the United States government to place a ban on the export of the technology to other countries under the munitions export ban legislation, which was upheld until 2000. Windows Server 2000 was the first major network operating system to ship worldwide with Kerberos containing DES-56, and Microsoft has since begun to use RC4 as its Kerberos cipher. Other versions of Kerberos have been developed outside the United States that don't use DES. Among the best-known implementations are eBones and Heimdal.

Kerberos uses two communication protocols developed by Roger Needham and Michael Schroeder. The Symmetric Key Protocol uses a symmetric encryption algorithm to establish a session key between the endpoints of a connection. The Public Key Protocol used in Kerberos establishes the mutual authentication between the endpoints. The trusted third party in Kerberos is called a key distribution center (KDC) and is separated into two separate services: the Authentication Server (AS) and a Ticket Granting Server (TGS).

Tickets are distributed to enable a client to identify itself in a session. The KDC has a set of secret keys that it saves in a data store for each network node. The secret key is known only to the node and the KDC and to no one else. When a connection is being established, the KDC generates the session key that is used to validate the connection endpoints.

While a Kerberos mechanism involves at least eight different messages between client, TGS, and Server Service, these messages allow each node in the system to both identify itself and validate the message coming from another node. The success of each operation

1. Client logon
2. Client authentication
3. Client service authorization
4. Client service request

depends on both of the two messages exchanging tickets or session keys to match up. No message contains both pieces of information. Kerberos imposes overhead on the network, but the system is secure. However, Kerberos is not without its problems. For one, the TGS is a single point of failure and must be made fault tolerant.

Also, because Kerberos depends on the timestamps placed into the messages at each step, all systems must be in synchronization using a service such as the Network Time Protocol or the Windows Time Service (WTS). Kerberos can tolerate a certain amount of time asynchronicity, usually about ten minutes. Great time disparity leads the tickets to become invalid. These factors can be adjusted as part of domain policies and in the Kerberos settings.

The last concern is that because the Authentication Server stores all of the secret keys, if someone gains access to that server, all of the network's security can be compromised. At an individual level, a compromised client system can be made to disclose a user's password. Still, Kerberos is currently the state of the art as a network authentication and identification service and is illustrative of many of the principles that you have seen described in this chapter.

Summary

In this chapter, you learned about different aspects of network security. You saw how there are many different places where a network can be attacked, and many different methods that can be used by an attacker. The key to securing a network is to use a multilayer, overlapping, and multipronged defense. In this chapter, you saw some commonsense rules that you can apply to make your network safer.

Three Internet security protocols were described in this chapter: IPsec, TLS/SSL, and HTTPS. Encryption technologies offer protection against data compromise. This chapter considered different key-based encryption technologies and showed how they work. The Kerberos system was also described in this chapter.

Chapter 28 covers the topic of firewalls and network gateways in detail. A firewall is a primary tool for protecting a network, so the information in the next chapter extends what you have learned in this chapter.

Firewalls, Gateways, and Proxy Servers

In this chapter you learn about several different kinds of network services that are used to secure networks: firewalls, gateways, and proxy servers. These services can be implemented in software or in hardware. The use of these services helps protect a network, making it much harder for outsiders to gain unauthorized entry to private networks.

Firewalls evaluate traffic and decide which traffic to forward and which traffic to drop or return. The criteria for deciding which action to take is called a filter, and filters can be based on information in packet headers such as source address, protocol used, and many other factors. Advanced firewalls can look into packets at the Application layer performing Deep Packet Inspection. The placement of firewalls at different points in the network for different purposes is explored.

These devices perform Network Address Translation (NAT), which is explained in detail in this chapter. NAT takes a request from clients on the public network and forwards them to systems inside on a private network. This feature allows private network systems to maintain their anonymity while allowing the network to route otherwise unroutable traffic.

Gateways are systems that serve as the interface between two different networks. Gateways are Application layer (Level 7) devices. There are Security Gateways that are sold for these purposes. A proxy server is a cross between a gateway and a firewall. Proxy servers serve as the surrogate for systems on a private network, fielding all requests and serving all replies. Many proxy servers perform caching; others configured as reverse proxy servers can perform many of the functions of the applications and network services that they front.

Firewalls

In a building, a firewall is a partition that is made of fireproof material that can isolate and protect one side from fire on the other. On a network, a firewall is a set of security routines that isolate and protect systems from malicious activity by erecting a protective barrier. This protection can take the form of separating the networks using different hardware devices (physical network interfaces) using a multihomed device; this type of mechanism is referred to as physical isolation. Alternatively the firewall can speak to an outside network using one network protocol and to the inside network using another protocol; this type of mechanism is referred to as protocol isolation. The nature of modern computing is such that it is very imprudent to have a system connected to the Internet without the use of some sort of firewall.

Firewalls can be relatively simple, or they can be very complex. Firewalls can be implemented in software, or as software installed on dedicated hardware servers and appliances. A firewall can be run on top of an operating system such as Linux, UNIX, or Windows; or it can be a "black box," a self-contained unit that runs its own proprietary operating system. Firewalls can be categorized into the following groups:

- Personal firewalls such as the Windows firewall, ZoneAlarm, and others
- Router firewalls
- Hardware firewalls, either low end or high end
- Proxy firewalls
- Server firewalls

Most often, firewalls have features that span more than one of these categories. When comparing one firewall to another, three factors come into focus: features, performance (as measured by throughput), and price. Firewalls are one network device for which there are no standardized performance benchmarks, and manufacturers, knowing that their customers use their firewalls in many different ways, are loathe to quote a performance metric to potential buyers.

Firewall features

Whatever the nature of a firewall's deployment, firewalls function by applying a set of rules to the traffic that flows through them. The firewall then either forwards the traffic on or drops the packets. A firewall can be a Network layer (Level 2) filter or an Application layer (Level 7) filter, or any level between Levels 2 and 7 in the OSI model.

Here are some features to look for when evaluating firewall products:

- **Packet filtering.** Packet filtering reads the fields of IP packet headers and uses rules to allow traffic into the system. Packet filtering can also be applied to outbound traffic.

- **Network interface input filters.** These filters block traffic based on the source IP address or range, port numbers, and protocols used.

- **Network Address Translation (NAT).** NAT is a conversion system that takes incoming traffic from one subnet and changes the addressing to forward it onto systems on another subnet. NAT uses a lookup table to make the translation and is capable of working with non-routable private networks. Private networks are non-routable in the sense that traffic cannot be directed from outside the network to a specific system inside the network; routing within the private network is fully enabled. NAT isn't strictly a firewall feature — it is more commonly associated with routers and proxy servers — but it does provide technology that conceals the IP address of internal systems, which is a valuable function.

- **Stateful inspection.** A stateful inspection examines any outgoing packets and logs the destinations into a state table. When traffic is sent back from the system outside the firewall, the state table is used to determine if the packets should be forwarded on. As a general rule, stateful filters require more overhead and are slower than static packet filters.

- **Circuit inspection.** In a Circuit-level filter, sessions are managed instead of simply referencing packets or a connection in a state table. Sessions require a request from a system inside the firewall and can support applications that create multiple connections. Protocols with multiple connections include HTTP browser sessions, FTP transfers, and streaming media transfers.

  Circuit-level inspection makes it difficult for IP spoofing, Denial of Service (DoS), and network reconnaissance attacks to succeed, while the related stateful inspection filters tend to be less effective against DoS attacks.

- **Proxy firewalls.** A proxy firewall serves as a go-between with the client outside of the firewall and a system or server on the inside. There is no direct connection through the firewall. Proxy firewalls create two distinct connections, one on each side of the firewall. The outside client only communicates with the proxy, which, from the standpoint of the client, is their connection endpoint. Proxy servers can add efficiencies by caching commonly or recently used data, can validate the protocols that are passed through the firewall, and can be managed so that requests are forwarded based on the user IDs and/or group memberships.

  Of all of the aforementioned features on this list, a proxy firewall requires the most resources and is the slowest filter. However, proxy firewalls can protect networks against DoS, IP spoofing, and network reconnaissance, as well as viruses, Trojans, and worms. Proxy firewalls offer only limited Application-level protection.

- **Application filtering.** Application layer filtering is a deep packet inspection technology. It is both the most complex and slowest performing of the firewall filters in this list. This filter examines packets for the data they contain and can modify those packets as necessary.

These features and filters are discussed in more detail individually in the sections that follow.

Personal firewalls

Personal firewalls are designed to protect a single computer, or less frequently, a SOHO network that is sharing a single connection. Examples of personal firewalls include CA Personal Firewall, Comodo Firewall Pro, IPFilter, ipfirewall, Kaspersky Internet Security, Lavasoft Personal Firewall, Norton 360, Outpost Firewall Pro, PC Tools Firewall Plus, Sunbelt Personal Firewall, Sygate Personal Firewall, Trend Micro Internet Security, and ZoneAlarm, with ZoneAlarm being the best known of the group.

Note

A chart of personal firewalls may be found at http://en.wikipedia.org/wiki/Comparison_of_firewalls.

Many operating systems now ship with personal firewalls. An example of a built-in firewall is Microsoft Windows Firewall, which began shipping with Windows XP SP1. The simple addition of this firewall had a major impact on making Windows systems much less vulnerable to outside attacks; it is a basic firewall, but it is effective. Figure 28.1 shows Windows Firewall from Vista SP1, which, as it turns out, was a major upgrade from the original XP firewall. Vista Firewall can filter by IP source and destination address, source and destination TCP/IP ports, for inbound traffic (ingress), for outbound traffic (egress), and by user ID. The only basic feature missing from Vista Firewall that is included in nearly all of the products just mentioned is the ability to filter by the source or destination MAC address. XP's firewall, by comparison, lacks the ability to filter by destination IP address, source port (and to some extent destination port), and by user ID, and to set a filter for outbound traffic. To my way of thinking, it is worth replacing XP with another firewall, but using the firewall that ships with Vista.

FIGURE 28.1

The Windows Vista Firewall application can specify open traversal of the firewall by port, protocol, or, as you see here, by application.

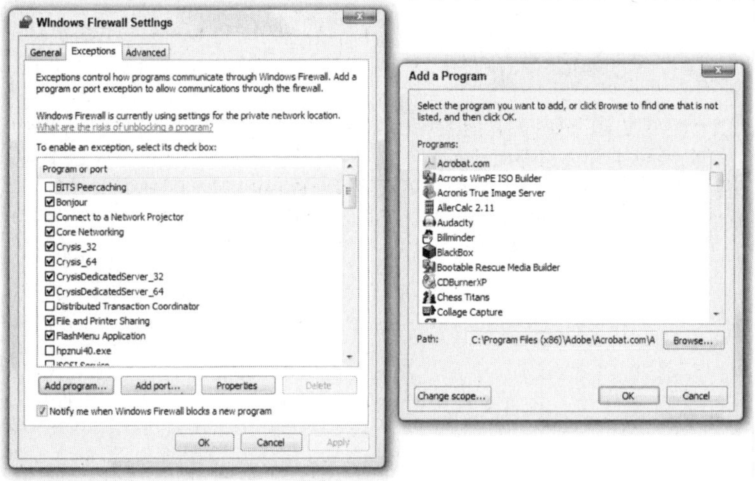

I am not a great fan of personal firewalls, although I recognize their utility. Many firewalls greatly impact a system's performance — particularly a lightly powered system like a laptop. Some firewalls, such as ZoneAlarm, constantly interrupt your work with status pop-ups and with dialog boxes seeking permission for some action that they want to take. When selecting a personal firewall, these are important factors that you want to pay particular attention to. A personal firewall should be both inexpensive (many are free) and easy to configure. Also, personal firewalls are meant to operate on their own. Running two or more firewalls at the same time should be unnecessary and is undesirable.

Router firewalls

Many routers ship with firewall features in them. Inexpensive routers tend to support address and port blocking, and provide some version of NAT for hiding internal private network addresses from view. A low-end router is often sold as a connection to the Internet. Your ISP may install one on your home network as part of their cable or DSL connection. These routers are very much like an appliance, and they only take a few settings. It is important that a low-end router functioning as a firewall come from the manufacturer with settings that effectively block unwarranted Internet traffic; usually changing the administrator account ID and password should be all that is required to get started. Additional configuration can be done to these systems as needed.

The NETGEAR FVS318 ProSafe VPN Firewall is an example of a low-end router/firewall. It is based on technology developed by SonicWALL (www.sonicwall.com), one of the better-known companies in the firewall hardware field. The FVS318 is configurable within a browser. Figure 28.2 shows the Services settings page, which is where ports are enabled. Other features found on this basic router include NAT, port assignments, blocking by domains and IP addresses, assignment of static routing, Stateful Packet Inspection (SPI), and other features.

Router/firewalls tend to be priced based on the number of concurrent users that are allowed to connect, and often are extensible. SonicWALL's systems can have anti-virus scanning added, be updated automatically over the Internet, add different types of Application-level filters with deep packet analysis, and more. A high-end router with firewall features approaches the functionality of a dedicated firewall but generally has a lower price and a lower throughput than a hardware firewall.

Router/firewalls are a very convenient choice and can allow both functions to be managed as one entity. They can be quite low in cost (the current version of the FVS318 costs $130), with very capable systems available in the $500 to $2,000 range. As a rule, low-end routers have limited functionality, tend to provide only basic controls, require a lot of configuration to be effective, and have limited throughput, particularly when they are logging events.

FIGURE 28.2

The Service settings page of a NETGEAR FVS318 router/firewall lets you enable ports and applications.

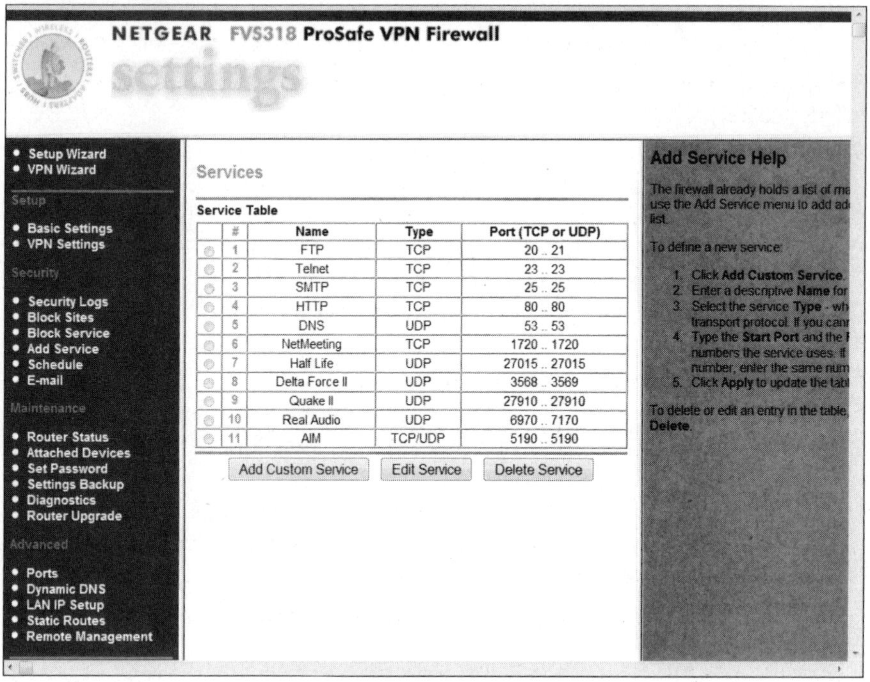

Hardware firewalls

Hardware firewalls are devices that are dedicated to firewall functions and typically have limited routing capabilities. At the low end of this category are appliance devices that are essentially Plug and Play, and aimed at the SOHO (Small Office or Home Office market segment) or small business market. In many cases, these devices are using the same software that more expensive models in a vendor's line use, and with additional payment, those features can be unlocked.

You'll find that the cheapest devices in this category have static packet filtering, NAT, address and port filtering, remote filtering, and can support from 10 to a few thousand concurrent users, with 50 users being a more common lower limit. As appliances, these devices are typically inexpensive and simple to operate. They offer low performance and poor upgradeability. Combination router/firewalls tend to be more popular than low-end dedicated firewall hardware because they offer more functionality for about the same price.

High-end dedicated firewalls are an entirely different beast altogether. These devices are meant to be impenetrable, high-performance, highly available systems, and are meant for either enterprise-class networks or for network service providers. Fault tolerance is built into many of these products through the use of a hot backup or failover system.

The highest-performing hardware firewalls often come with some advanced features to improve performance. When evaluating these types of devices, look for the following features as differentiators:

- **Multiple gigabit Ethernet interfaces, or high-speed fiber connections.** Higher I/O speeds translate to faster throughput.

- **Robust data caching.** Advanced caching can greatly improve performance, but requires dedicated disk resources.

- **Proxy and Reverse Web Proxy services.** A proxy service is a service that acts on behalf of another service or application as if it is the server providing the services. A Web proxy is a Web server that takes requests from inside the network and either processes the request (from its cache, for example) or directs it to the appropriate Web server outside the network. Reverse Web proxy servers take requests from outside the network (the Internet, perhaps) and either processes the request or redirects it to a Web server inside the network.

- **IPSec encryption/decryption off-loading to dedicated subsystems.** IPSec encryption is used for VPN traffic and for publishing an internal network service to public networks or the Internet. IPSec is a particularly slow process on most firewalls, and so acceleration improves firewall performance.

- **SSL offloading.** SSL encryption is processor intensive. An SSL accelerator can lower the processor utilization of firewalls that are front ends to Web sites, and having a firewall be the endpoint of an SSL connection can improve Web site performance significantly.

- **Modularity and the ability to scale.** Modularity means that you can add additional subsystems as you need them.

Features that differentiate higher-end hardware firewalls from other devices include the ability to block ICMP messages, Application-layer filtering support, improved logging and alerts, upgradeability, strong vendor support, and, of course, a high price. A high-end dedicated hardware firewall can support from 5,000 to 500,000 concurrent sessions. The greater capabilities of this type of hardware means that an organization has to have trained support staff or outside services manage these devices.

Server firewalls

While high-end hardware firewalls tend to run on proprietary hardware using a proprietary operating system, many vendors have chosen to implement firewalls on standard server operating systems as open solutions. The advantages of this approach are that the operation of the server is better known to support staff (so that they require less training and support), the hardware can be right-sized for the task, and a wider range of solutions may be available. Implementation of the firewall on a standard network operating system also means that any framework or management application that you use for your other server systems can be applied to this type of firewall, which is a great convenience. This category of firewall is noted for superior caching capabilities.

Functionally, there may be little difference between a high-end server firewall and a high-end hardware firewall. However, a server firewall is often easier to integrate, more scalable, and can be clustered or load balanced for greater availability than dedicated devices are. The main drawback to using server hardware in this type of application is that hardware firewalls are generally better optimized for their purpose, and so server firewalls may need higher-end hardware to perform at the same level. Also, with a well-known operating system, server firewalls are more susceptible to attack than a dedicated hardware firewall.

Security gateways

A gateway is an Application layer (Level 7) device that acts as the interface between two networks. Gateways can be implemented as hardware devices or appliances, or as software. The term gateway is somewhat generic, and generally implies that some sort of protocol conversion is occurring. At the Application layer, a gateway may translate one file type for another; at the Presentation layer, that conversion might substitute one type of encryption for another, or some other function. Gateways can perform Transport level translations, or at the Network layer, from IP to AppleTalk. The fact is that gateways are a generic term for a device that can operate at any of the OSI levels. The result is that you will often see gateways described as "mail gateways," "Web gateways," and even "security gateways."

In order for a gateway to function between two networks, it often must be able to function as a router, providing address mapping, and as a switch for building the circuit that the data must follow through the device. It is common to have a gateway serve the role of a proxy server and a firewall. Therefore, if you see the term security gateway, be aware that this might refer to a device that fits into one of the categories of firewalls that you've already seen. For the term gateway to have any real meaning, in my opinion, the emphasis has to be placed on that system's ability to perform translations at the Application level.

Network zones

Firewalls separate areas of a network into zones of different trust levels, as shown in the example of a three-tiered enterprise-class network in Figure 28.3. This network is divided into the following zones and networks:

- **The Internet.** The Internet is a zone of no trust. All packets coming in from the Internet are suspect until they are examined.

- **Border network.** The border network consists of a router that is discoverable by someone on the Internet. Routers are dual/multihomed, and this particular router has an outbound interface with the Wiley.com IP address and an inbound interface with the first of a set of private network addresses. Border networks end at the outgoing interface of the Perimeter firewall (192.168.1.2).

  A border router performs address translation and the two interfaces provide a physical isolation of one network from another. This is also true of other routers and firewalls in this example. With every change in network membership, particularly when private networks are involved, the amount of effort involved in being able to traverse the firewall without challenge goes up exponentially.

FIGURE 28.3

Different types of firewalls and their relative placements

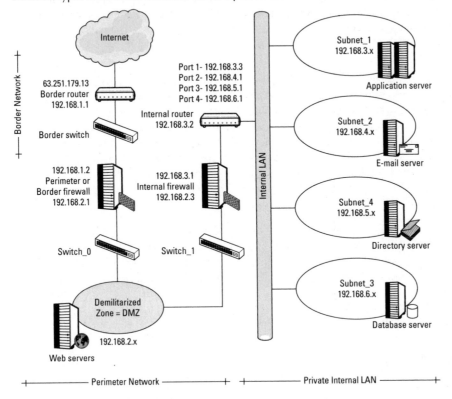

So long as your internal systems are not compromised, it becomes nearly impossible to break through multiple firewalls. In a situation where a system on Subnet_1 is compromised, that system may learn about other Subnet_1 systems and the port on the Internal router that Subnet_1 connects to (192.168.3.3), but because routers provide port isolation (another form of physical isolation), that system should not be able to learn about other subnets provided that the directory service isn't compromised.

- **Border firewall.** The Border firewall, also known as the Perimeter firewall, exists to create the Demilitarized Zone (DMZ). As a general rule, the only traffic that should pass through the Border firewall is HTTP on port 80, HTTPS on port 443, and as limited a number of additional open ports as is possible. If you have an FTP server in the DMZ, then port 20 (for data), and possibly port 21 (for control commands) should be opened. Any other ports required to support the services found on the DMZ should also be opened.

- **Demilitarized Zone (DMZ) or Perimeter network.** The DMZ is an area of intermediate trust, and is often used for Internet-facing Web servers, e-mail relays, and FTP servers. The systems on the DMZ should only contain public information. Traffic entering the DMZ is allowed some freedom of action — they can run scripts on a Web server, for example — but most actions are still restricted. The DMZ extends from the incoming interface of the Perimeter firewall (192.168.2.1) to the outgoing interface of the Internal firewall (192.168.2.3). An isolated DMZ located on an intranet is called a screened network.

  The DMZ is a good place to restrict clients outside of the network that fail to pass tests that measure the system's health. If you have a network with a network access policy (NAP) server, that system might test mobile clients to see if their anti-virus programs are up to date and have scanned their system within a certain time period. Microsoft's NAP server tests systems to see if they are sufficiently updated, among other things. A failed system would be given access to the DMZ (or some similarly restricted subnet) where its deficiencies can be addressed before allowing the client access to the Internal LAN.

- **Internal firewall/proxy server.** The Internal firewall provides yet another network address translation leading to a different private subnet. Traffic from the DMZ to the Internal network is subject to a different set of rules, less restrictive than the Perimeter firewall used, and then passed onto the internal router. Some firewalls provide Application-level services. Firewalls performing these services analyze the types of packets and routes that traffic to the appropriate application server — firewalls of this type are playing the role of a proxy server.

- **Internal LAN/Private network.** The Internal LAN consists of systems that are trusted and are subject to the least number of restrictions of any subnet on the system.

The example shown in Figure 28.3 is complex so that you can see a range of firewall placements, and has many more components than a SOHO network would have. In a common setup, the Internet connection goes to a router (in the form of a cable modem or DSL modem, for example); that router connects to a firewall, which then connects directly to systems on the network either directly or through a switch. If the firewall has three or more interfaces, you could configure the network so that the router, LAN, and a screened subnet (DMZ) are each attached to different network interfaces on the firewall. Perhaps the most common SOHO setup has a cable modem connection to the Internet where the cable modem performs the function of a hub, switch, or Wi-Fi access point and lacks a router/firewall function.

Stateless filters

The classic example of stateless firewalls is of those using packet filtering. Packet filtering is in nearly every firewall product, and was the first of the major technologies to be included in these types of products. In packet filters, packets are inspected and if the information contained in the packet matches an exclusion rule, the packet is dropped. Information that can be obtained from the packet consists of header fields that include destination and source address, protocol used, data type, and for TCP/UDP, the port number used for access or port filtering.

Packet filtering is a Network layer firewall technology. This type of filtering is considered to be "stateless," as it is the packet itself without regard for its context that is the determinant in matching the filter rule. The lack of context in applying a rule set means that stateless filters are unable to protect a network from traffic that spoofs the system into believing that it is from an approved source, of an approved data type, or some other violation when the data is really something else.

In rare cases, a firewall may be configured to return an acknowledgment that the packet was filtered, but in most cases, preserving the anonymity of the firewall is considered to be an important security feature.

Stateful filters

Stateful firewalls analyze the connection used by each packet and uses that connection to determine if this is a new session and if it can allow the connection; one that is currently in use; or one that is unknown and must be denied. This type of filter is commonly referred to as a circuit filter. Because the firewall maintains a table of connections (routes) in a state table (or state list) for its different sessions, this type of firewall uses a "stateful" filter approach. A stateful filter is classified as a dynamic packet filtering technology, as it is session- or connection-based and changes based on interaction with clients outside the firewall.

A stateful filter uses stateful packet inspection (SPI) to manage network connections. An example of this sort of rule would be "Allow traffic from Subnet_1" or "Do not allow traffic from the domain XYZ.com." Stateful firewalls are Network layer technologies, just like stateless packet filtering.

Stateful filters solve a common security problem relating to arbitrary port usage. If an application such as FTP creates a connection to an arbitrary port above the range for well-known ports, a stateless firewall would not be able to determine if the traffic was legitimate and would drop the packet. However, a stateful firewall would have registered the FTP's connection in its connection table and associates the port number with the specific session, allowing subsequent packets to be passed through to the protected network.

The connection table contains attributes of each connection — source and destination IP addresses, port number(s) — and as packets traverse the system, it registers the sequence number. The entry in the connection table only exists for the period of the session and is deleted when the session ends.

A stateful connection enforces rules based on a current connection. Figure 28.4 shows a mechanism for handling out-of-sequence and out-of-range packets. Consider the simple example of a stateful filter where a session is under way, as shown in Figure 28.4. The last packet to pass through the firewall had a packet number of 53, and so the next packet should be 54. The IP header contains information that establishes the length of the data being sent, which for this example corresponds to a data stream 80 packets long, provided that the packet sizes are uniform.

Packet 54 is passed through the firewall automatically, but packet 60 requires a decision. In a strict firewall session, a packet with a sequence number of 60 arriving out of sequence might be cached, or more likely it would be rejected until packets 55 to 59 pass through the firewall. The condition of Packet 60 is uncertain which is why a question mark is shown in the lower-right sequence. To verify the status of Packet 60 an ACK might be sent to the sending system, asking that Packet 60 be retransmitted. A comparison can be done to establish that the new packet number 60 matches the first packet number 60. Any packet that has a packet number above 80 is automatically dropped, with the assumption that the data in it is invalid. Different stateful firewalls would have different rules for how to handle out-of-sequence packets, contention when two copies with the same sequence number arrive at roughly the same time, and other issues that arise.

FIGURE 28.4

The mechanism used by a firewall's stateful filter

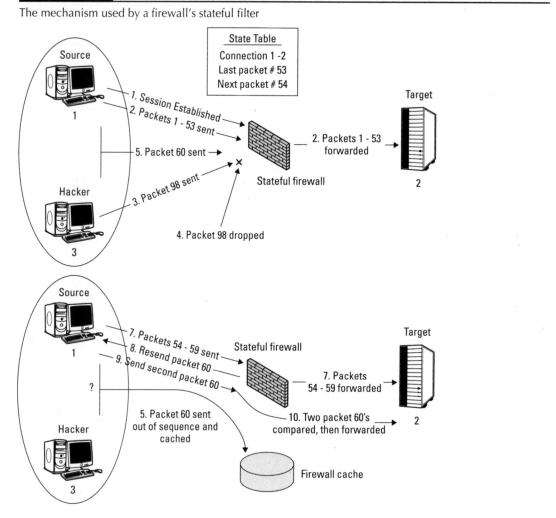

There is overhead involved in setting up the connection and in the registration of the information. When TCP is the Transport protocol, the connection requires a successful negotiation in the form of a three-way handshake. When a system wants to create a connection, it sends a packet with the SYN bit set to ON. If the firewall examines the packet and finds that it comes from an approved source, the firewall sends a packet back with both the SYN and ACK bits set to ON. The connection is ESTABLISHED when the sending system sends back a second packet with the ACK bit set to ON.

Once a connection is established, packets conforming to the established session are allowed through the firewall. A logon request initiates a session, and subsequent packets with the correct session parameters will be allowed. Another client system that attempts a logon at the same time will have packets with header fields that do not have the necessary session parameters, and therefore those packets will be blocked from transit and dropped.

The reliance on a negotiated connection and the handshaking that is involved in setting up a connection make stateful firewall susceptible to Denial of Service (DoS) attacks. A DoS attack begins with multiple systems sending out large numbers of SYN packets requesting connections, called a SYN flood. The target starts to create the connections, eventually overflowing its connection state table, at which point no other connections can be made. DoS attacks are often implemented with zombie networks, large numbers of computers that have been infected silently by worms or Trojans.

Once the TCP connection is established, the transfer of data becomes efficient. Any packet that conforms to the connection parameters is passed through after a relatively simple read of header information. Stateful firewalls do not typically filter outgoing traffic from the destination system in the trusted zone to the system outside the firewall, the assumption being that the system inside the firewall is secure. Connections, once established, exist until a certain period of time passes without any traffic being detected, after which the connection is closed and the connection information is discarded. If an application wants to maintain the connection, it can broadcast a keepalive packet, or respond to a firewall's request for the application's connection state. Connections can be ended by request and do not always need to be timed out.

Cross-Ref

The structure of IP packets is discussed in Chapter 18. Chapter 17 describes TCP handshaking in some detail.

A connectionless Transport protocol such as UDP is handled differently by a stateful firewall than a connection state protocol such as TCP is. When a UDP SYN request appears, the connection goes to the ESTABLISHED state and the packets are passed through the firewall. The connection is maintained until a timeout period without data received is observed, at which point the connection is terminated. There is no mechanism for closing a UDP connection other than a timeout.

Once a stateful firewall establishes a connection, filtering incoming packets requires that the packets' header fields be read and checked against the connection state table. This turns out to be a low overhead process and is performed efficiently.

Application filters

Application filtering filters traffic based on the application or protocols that were used to create or transmit the packet. Application filtering, which is sometimes called proxy-based filtering, is also able to determine if the traffic parameters do not match the well-known port assignment for that application type. Based on what it finds, the application filter can block, redirect, or modify packets as necessary. Application filters tend to be found on the more expensive and powerful firewalls, as they are the most sophisticated as well as the slowest filters in use.

An application filter extends the idea of a stateful filter to block traffic based on what protocol the packet is using, as well as how the protocol is being used. In a stateful filter, the firewall might have a rule that states "Allow all traffic through port 80," which is the well-known port for HTTP traffic. Many applications transport their data over HTTP in order to be compatible with browser-based interfaces. An application filter would then add the following rule: "Block HTTP traffic that contains VoIP data." Because an application filter can look inside the packets and determine what application is being used, it can apply this rule, whereas stateful and stateless filters cannot. An application filter may be considered an extension of a stateful filter.

An application firewall that examines traffic carried by the HTTP protocol and other related protocols such as HTTPS, SOAP, XML-RPC, or any other Web service for its content, is called a Deep Packet Inspection Firewall. Deep packet inspection can identify non-conforming content by comparing the data contained within the packet to a database of attack signatures, or by determining if the behavior of the Web traffic doesn't conform to normal application behavior.

Application filters are particularly useful because they can be dynamic and react intelligently to conditions. Consider the situation where an application filter monitors traffic coming into port 53, which is the well-known port for DNS. During a DNS DoS attack, requests for DNS assignments overwhelm the system and the firewall closes port 53 in response. If the firewall were a stateful firewall, it would simply close port 53. However, an application filter could determine if an internal system is requesting a DNS service from an outside system and dynamically open port 53 to let that request pass out of the firewall. Once the application filter passes the DNS request, it logs the request's state conditions into a state table. Now when DNS data is returned from an outside system in response to the internal DNS request, the application filter reads the data, recognizes that it is a valid response based on session data, opens port 53 for that incoming DNS data, and sends the response to the requesting system inside the network. It's easy to see how valuable it can be to have this feature. Even while under attack, your network would still allow the address resolution your network systems need for browsing and a myriad of other services to proceed.

Application filters tend to be added onto firewalls capable of processing them as needed. You may start out with a basic set of application filters such as a DNS filter, and then add or purchase filters for virus detection, content screening, lexical analysis, or site analysis.

Note

Lexical analysis is the method used to convert a string of characters such as source code into a sequence of tokens, a token being a categorized block of text or lexeme such as a keyword, identifier, literal, or punctuation. During lexical analysis, lexemes are categorized by function, which provides their context or meaning. The process of categorization is called tokenization. Lexemes are sent to a parser where the sequence of tokens is analyzed according to the rules of grammar of the particular programming language that created them.

Keep in mind that Application-level firewalls typically support clear text analysis but aren't able to filter encrypted traffic. If you had a Web site with an online store that used SSL encryption, the protocol commands would be hidden in the encrypted data. Firewalls with Application-level filtering tend to handle encrypted communications in different ways. Among the approaches used are terminating the SSL packets at the firewall, decrypting and re-encrypting the packets on the firewall before sending them onto the Web server, or simply passing the SSL packets through the firewall to an internal server for further handling.

Deny by default

A standard principle used by any highly secure technology is to have the device initialize to a *deny by default* state. Many firewalls, proxy servers, and other security systems come completely locked down out of the box. This can be something of a shock to anyone who hasn't encountered this situation before. When confronted with a completely blocked system, the administrator is advised to turn features on one at a time as needed. The following sequence of rules is typical:

- **Deny all traffic unless a rule specifically allows it.** This is the *deny by default* condition.

- **Block all incoming packets with internal addresses and all outgoing packets with external addresses.** These packets are typically either from attackers or errors.

- **Configure DNS traffic appropriately for both UDP- and TCP-based DNS queries.** Without address resolution, most other functions on a network won't work.

- **Enable HTTP and perhaps HTTPS traffic by opening port 80, and route this traffic appropriately.** If a proxy is used for this traffic, you'll want to configure it as a connection endpoint. For example, Microsoft ISA Server can be a Web proxy, and requires that HTTP traffic be routed over port 8080. The well-known port for HTTPS is assigned to port 443, so redirection of HTTPS traffic to either port 80 or 8080 is meant to provide a simplification for network administrators for internal traffic.

- **If you are using mail servers, enable SMTP and/or POP3 by opening their ports.**

- **If your network allows it, open the FTP ports 20 for data and 21 for control.**

- **Respond to pleas for help by individually turning on ports or routes as you learn about network functions that require access.**

These rules are applied starting at the bottom of the list and working their way up. That is, the rules have an order or precedence in which they are applied. In Microsoft ISA Server, different firewall scenarios are offered and a basic set of rules are generated from the network security template. Figure 28.5 shows one of these scenarios in ISA Server 2006.

FIGURE 28.5

An ISA Server's firewall rules when configured as a Three-Leg Perimeter firewall

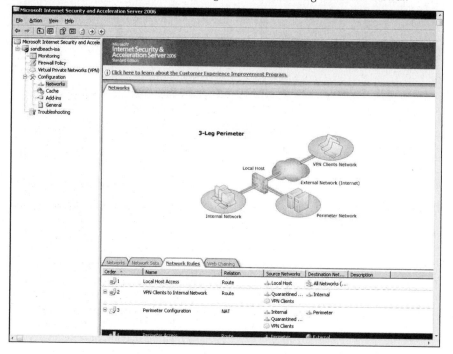

The point of this exercise is to keep your network as locked down as it can be while still allowing all necessary functions to be operable. With luck, you will be able to save your rules and export them to other devices of the same types.

Network Address Translation

Network Address Translation (NAT) is a fundamental routing mechanism that allows the network addresses of datagrams or packets to be substituted based on entries in a mapping table. What makes NAT particularly valuable and a subject in a chapter on firewalls and gateways instead of routers is that NAT is able to route traffic to private network addresses, which are otherwise unroutable. Essentially, NAT expands a single, assigned static IP address into a network of addresses. Without NAT, IPv4 would have long ago run out of available IP addresses.

When a device applies NAT to an incoming packet, it rewrites the destination address in the packet header. The entire range of devices on the private network is hidden from outside view, with only the single address of the external network interface of the routing device exposed. NAT is a general function that can map any one address to other addresses, not necessarily private IP range addresses. Outgoing packets are subject to the reverse mapping; NAT rewrites the source address of the packets (which were private IP addresses) and replaces it with the IP address of the router's external network interface that is routable.

Examples of NAT software may be found in:

- Cisco's Internetwork Operating System (IOS)
- Microsoft Windows Internet Connection Sharing (ICS) feature
- IPFilter (http://coombs.anu.edu.au/~avalon), an open source package available in many UNIX implementations such as FreeBSD, NetBSD, and Solaris 10
- Packet Filter (PF), a NAT filter included with OpenBSD, and available on many other operating systems
- Netfilter, also known as iptables and included in some Linux distributions
- WinGate (www.wingate.com), an Integrated Gateway Management system for Windows
- Microsoft Internet Security and Acceleration Server, a proxy and caching server installable on Windows Server 2003 or 2008

When you set up NAT, you can hardwire the mappings in the map table to create what is known as static NAT. The basic form of NAT rewrites the destination of incoming packets and the source of outgoing packets during NAT traversal. The more advanced form of NAT alters the IP addresses as well as the source port and destination port assignments needed for port forwarding routed traffic. This form of NAT is referred to as Port Address Translation (PAT), Network Address Port Translation (NAPT), or by Cisco as NAT overloading. All versions of NAT require that packets have their CRC (Checksum) recalculated and the CRC fields of the packets' headers rewritten during each traversal.

Note

In rare instances, packets do not have assigned port numbers; they appear on varying ports. This is true for the Internet Control Message Protocol (ICMP, which PING relies on), the Real-Time Control Protocol (RTCP), and the Real-Time Protocol (RTP), for example. RTP comes in on an even UDP port number, and any corresponding RTCP packets will then appear at the next higher odd port number. The RTP and RTCP protocols are described in detail in Chapter 25, as is their method for NAT traversal called the Session Traversal Utilities for NATs (STUN) protocol.

While the effect of a NAT traversal is easy to understand, the manner in which NAT operates within the routing device is not that easily explained. There are several different ways to map ports to systems, addresses to ports, and addresses to addresses. Let's take a look at some of the common mapping schemes that were defined as part of the original STUN protocol. Figure 28.6 shows four common NAT mapping schemes — One-to-one or Full Cone NAT, Address Restricted Cone NAT, Port Restricted Cone NAT, and Symmetric NAT. Below each diagram is the mapping table that the router/switch uses to create the virtual circuits over which data flows. Mapping entries may not always be unique, and so one hopes that the algorithm a device uses to map with at least picks an optimum traversal route.

The routes illustrating each of these different mappings appear in bold type in the map table, and to simplify the conversation, ports are shown in the half-duplex mode. The shapes you see in Figure 28.6 illustrate four different systems that are involved in the communications:

- Client system, labeled 1, with two ports labeled S1 (Source 1) and D1 (Destination 1). In the case of Symmetric NAT, Client 1 contains two source ports, S1 and S4.
- NAT traversal device. In the center of each diagram, the NAT device has an internal and external side, both of which are labeled. Ports on the NAT are E1 and E2 (External 1 and 2), and I1 and I2 (Internal 1 and 2). Symmetric NAT has additional internal ports.
- Internal System labeled 2, with two ports labeled S2 and D2.
- Internal System labeled 3, with two ports labeled S3 and D3.

The first mapping shown in the upper-left corner of Figure 28.6 is a one-to-one correlation of an internal port to an external port, called Full Cone NAT. In this scheme, ports E1-I1 and E2-I2 are each hardwired together. Traffic can flow from any client to any internal system or from any internal system to any client using either or both of these two routes. This type of NAT is simple and doesn't require much logic to implement. It tends to be used on lower-cost switches.

In the upper-right corner of Figure 28.6, a scheme called Address Restricted Cone NAT is shown. Here the mapping from an internal system to an external system is based on the IP addresses of the two systems. NAT traversal begins when an internal system (shown as 2 here) negotiates a connection with an external client. Communication proceeds by mapping the addresses S2 to D1 and S1 to D2 with a unique route. Shown in the figure, the routes cross in the NAT, but they could also have been drawn as E1-I1 and E2-I2, as only the address mapping matters. When System 3 tries to communicate through either of the internal ports to Client 1, the NAT device recognizes that the address isn't mapped to a current session and blocks traffic in or out of the ports shown. For System 3 to communicate, it would have to establish a connection through another set of ports.

In the Symmetric NAT scenario shown in the lower-right corner of Figure 28.6, all requests from an internal IP address and port combination to an external destination IP address and port combination are mapped to the same external IP address and port combination. When the same system sends traffic to two separate IP addresses, traffic is split so that each destination travels on a separate path. In the figure, Client 1 is sending data to two different IP addresses and as a result, each system IP/port address pair is unique. Communication from an external system requires that an internal system negotiate the connection first.

The final example, Port Restricted Cone NAT, shown in the lower-left corner, is similar to Address Restricted NAT but instead of blocking an IP address, the NAT restricts access to a port or ports. In this one example, port I1 is forced to operate in full-duplex mode to allow Client 1 to communicate with System 2, as port I2 is blocked.

Most vendors choose to combine different aspects of this mapping in their devices. For example, a common implementation chooses to combine Symmetric NAT with static port mapping, depending upon which direction the traffic originated from and is directed to.

FIGURE 28.6

Four different NAT traversal mapping schemes

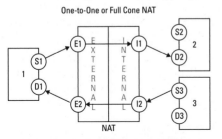

One-to-One or Full Cone NAT

Source	Destination	Internal Port	External Port
S1	D2	I1	E1
S1	D3	I2	E2
S2	D1	I2	E2
S3	D1	I2	E2

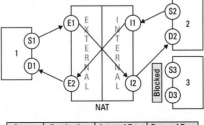

Address Restricted Cone NAT

Source	Destination	Internal Port	External Port
S1	D2	E1	I2
S1	D3	Blocked	Blocked
S2	D1	I1	E2
S3	D1	Blocked	Blocked

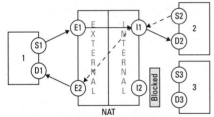

Port Restricted Cone NAT

Source	Destination	Internal Port	External Port
S1	D2	I1	E1
S1	D3	Blocked	E1
S2	D1	I1	E2
S3	D1	Blocked	E2

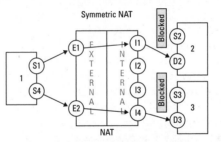

Symmetric NAT

Source	Destination	Internal Port	External Port
S1	D2	E1	I1
S1	D3	E2	I3
S2	Any	Blocked	Blocked
S3	Any	Blocked	Blocked
S4	D2	E1	I2
S4	D3	E2	I4

Another scheme maps ports Ex to Ix, where x in both instances is the same number, and then directs traffic from any other internal systems to the same host to a randomly selected port. When a system of this type is examined, it would appear to be a Symmetric NAT when multiple ports are used to connect to the same host, and an Address Restricted Cone NAT at times when there is only one connection from internal systems to an external system.

Additional NAT techniques must be used to handle IP control packets such as ICMP, and to work around instances where the NAT translator cannot correctly parse TCP or UDP data. In those instances, NAT must recompute both the TCP/UDP header and a new CRC field. NAT can often have trouble parsing encryption, IPsec being one example. The lack of a standard technique to work with transport protocols is a major reason why the developers of IPv6 chose to stay well clear of NAT.

You may also encounter some vendor-specific NAT implementations. Destination NAT (DNAT) is a technique where the destination of a packet is changed when it is outgoing, and then changed back after the destination system replies. DNAT allows an internal service to be published at a public IP address, even though the data originates on a private network.

Many times, SNAT refers to the term Source NAT, but not always. Some large vendors use the term differently. The acronym SNAT is used by Microsoft as part of their Internet Security and Acceleration (ISA) Server to mean Secure NAT. To Cisco, SNAT stands for Stateful NAT. The IETF calls SNAT Software Network Address Translation, and the technology refers to the address translation required to connect IPv6 and IPv4 networks together.

With so many variations on a theme, it's no wonder that the original name for the STUN protocol — Simple Traversal of User Datagram Protocol through Network Address Translators — had to be changed to Session Traversal Utilities for NAT; it is anything but simple.

NAT is not a transparent process, and there are several different application and protocol types that break when they try to send data across a NAT translator. The most problems arise with applications that rely on different data streams to send data and to control a session, FTP and SIP being the most prominent examples. SIP is the control protocol for Voice over IP. It is for this reason that technologies such as STUN or Internet Connectivity Establishment (ICE) were developed to aid in NAT traversal. Other potential solutions to NAT traversal problems involve the use of automatic device discovery technologies such as Universal Plug and Play (UPnP) and Bonjour (NAT-PMP), when enabled by the NAT translator. Bonjour couples network address translation with the port mapping protocol.

Proxy Servers

A proxy server is a computer or application that serves as an intermediary between a client and a network service. Client requests received at the proxy server are forwarded to the service, and the results are sent back to the proxy where they are forwarded to the client. The proxy service performs a redirection function, does none of the processing of the requests, and is the only system that the client or the service sees during this transaction. In this form, a proxy server may be called a gateway, or less often, a tunneling proxy.

Because the term *gateway* tends to be more appealing from a marketing standpoint than the term *proxy server*, you rarely encounter a proxy server that passes all requests and replies through the system unchanged. Proxy servers usually have additional actions associated with them. To my mind, a proxy server is a cross between a firewall and a gateway. A proxy server can communicate in HTTP to a Web server or to a client's browser, as well as communicate in SMTP to a mail server or FTP to an FTP server; this is so that applications behind the proxy server do not need to understand protocols other than the ones that they were designed to understand. Proxy servers are implemented as hardware or as software; they can be stand-alone servers, or they can be software (a proxy service) running on the same computer that has the application that the proxy server fronts for. Figure 28.7 shows the essential element of a proxy service as a high-level protocol translator and as a surrogate for Web access for clients.

FIGURE 28.7

The essential functionality of a proxy server, a cross between a firewall and a gateway

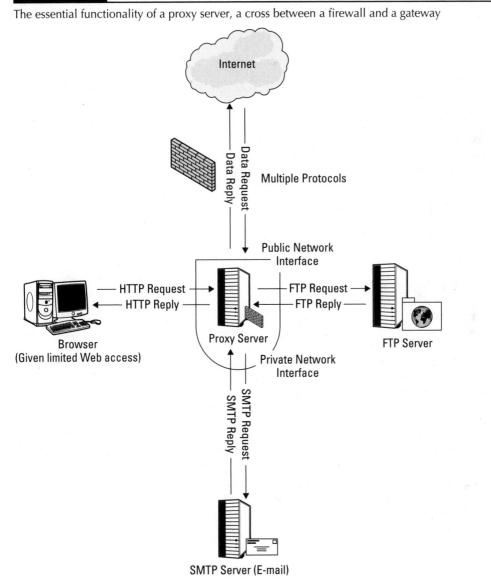

Here are some of the better-known proxy servers:

- Apache HTTP Server (http://httpd.apache.org)
- Blue Coat SGOS (www.bluecoat.com)
- I2P (www.i2p2.de)
- Microsoft ISA Server (www.microsoft.com/forefront/edgesecurity/isa server/en/us/default.aspx)
- Novell BorderManager (www.novell.com/products/bordermanager)
- Privoxy (www.privoxy.org)
- Squid (www.squid-cache.org)
- Sun Java System Web Proxy Server (www.sun.com/software/products/web_proxy)
- Tinyproxy (www.banu.com/tinyproxy)
- Tor (www.torproject.org). Tor is discussed in detail in Chapter 9.
- Varnish (http://varnish.projects.linpro.no)
- WinGate (www.wingate.com)
- yProxy (www.yproxy.com)
- Zeus Web Server (www.zeus.com)
- Ziproxy (http://ziproxy.sourceforge.net)

Proxy servers often have many of the features of a firewall. Some proxy servers can filter traffic based on content, domains, URLs, MIMEs, keywords, or on the basis of URL patterns and content attributes. Others can use whitelists to pass traffic through the proxy server or blacklists to deny access. Proxy servers are not effective when examining encrypted traffic and will pass encrypted traffic through without being able to apply content filtering to it.

Because many actions that proxy servers take are important events and may need to be analyzed at some point, nearly any proxy server will log information about its decisions into a log file, which is almost always in a standard database or spreadsheet format such as CSV. One important set of security filters that proxy servers should be able to apply is access to proxy services based on the user's security credentials; this may require a user login.

One common enhancement is to add a disk cache to the proxy server and the logic necessary to know when a request has already been served. A caching proxy will then return the matching results from the cache instead of passing the request again onto the service. Caching is always a feature associated with any proxy server that is handling Web traffic, and in those instances, the proxy may be referred to as a *Web proxy*. Nearly all Web proxy servers serve to mask the true identity of a user connecting from one network to another (most often the Internet), and as such, they can be considered either an open proxy or an anonymous proxy.

There are many instances where network services do not want to forward traffic from an open proxy server, with e-mail and IRC traffic being two instances. Some systems test for the presence of an open proxy, while others consult known lists of open proxy systems and deny transit of their data through the system.

Transparent proxy servers and honeypots

Because a proxy server can hide the identity of users on one network from another network, it is possible to use proxy servers as a means to examine traffic that flows between two endpoints, which can be done for many purposes. When this is done for nefarious purposes, the proxy may be referred to as a hostile proxy; when it is done to intercept traffic and impose a set of policies, the proxy may be referred to as an intercepting proxy. An intercepting proxy has the functionality of a gateway and may be transparent to the user. Cisco uses the term *transparent proxy* to define a router Web Cache Control Protocol that is used to determine which routes to send traffic on based on the cache content, another form of redirection.

Another use of proxy servers is to create security traps called *honeypots*. A honeypot is used to lure unauthorized users of a network to that system, where their actions can be monitored and their identity can be discovered. Honeypots that appear to be open proxy systems are sometimes referred to as a *sugarcane*. A honeypot should not contain any data of value, nor should it be a production system. Because the idea is to allow an intrusion, it is important that the honeypot be carefully isolated from any other systems of value. Special programs, called victim hosts, are sometimes used to create seemingly important information. Victim hosts can be decoys that are meant to distract intruders; they can also be structured to provide detailed information about the nature of any attack.

Reverse proxy servers

In all of the instances mentioned so far, the proxy server fronts a service. However, there is one form of proxy server, called a reverse proxy, where the service passes data directly to the proxy server instead. The most common example of a reverse proxy is when you have Web servers sending data to a local proxy server for additional processing.

The reverse proxy server may perform Secure Socket Layer (SSL) encryption/decryption for the Web servers using an SSL accelerator or offload module, and by doing so for multiple Web servers, the reverse proxy server can allow the Web servers to use the same SSL Server Certificate used by the reverse proxy server. A reverse proxy server may offer faster compression, and the ability to publish the service to another network, which is called Extranet Publishing. Caching content is almost always a feature of a reverse proxy server.

Figure 28.8 shows how a reverse Web proxy is deployed.

FIGURE 28.8

A reverse Web proxy appears to be the Web server or servers themselves.

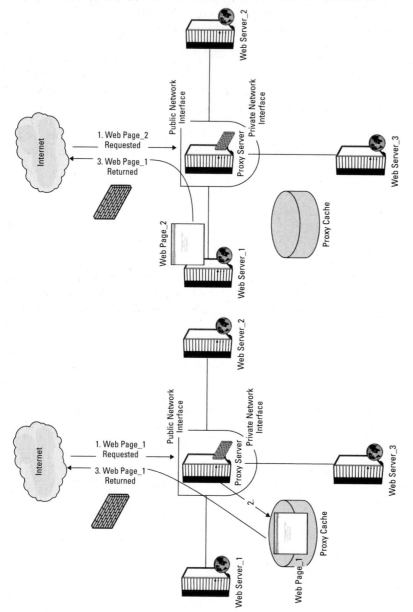

On the left side of Figure 28.8, a request is made by a client outside the network for a static page called Web Page_1 from a Web server within. The request goes to the proxy server. As a first step, the proxy server, knowing that this is a static page, checks its cache, finds Web Page_1, and serves it up from the cache to the client. It has performed the service of the Web server. In the second scenario, the client asks for Web Page_2. After checking its cache and not finding that page, because dynamic pages should never be cached, the reverse proxy server sends a request to one or more of the Web servers to provide Web Page_2. Web Server_1 either finds the page (static content) or creates the page (dynamic content) and then sends it to the proxy server for forwarding to the client. Again, as far as the client is concerned, the proxy server is the Web server. A reverse proxy server plays the role of the application or service it fronts.

The benefits of this approach are that the cache accelerates performance, the proxy server can load balance between the three Web servers, and if one Web server needs content from another Web server, the proxy server can fetch it. As a result, the proxy server makes the Web servers much more efficient.

Summary

Firewalls offer advanced protection against a number of network hazards. They increase protection of a network, making it much harder for outsiders to gain unauthorized entry to private networks. Firewalls use filters to decide how to handle incoming and outgoing traffic. Advanced firewalls can use Deep Packet Inspection to understand the content of packets. Firewalls are placed at different points in the network for different purposes.

Network Address Translation takes requests from clients on the public network and forwards them to systems inside a private network. This feature allows private network systems to maintain their anonymity.

Gateways are systems that serve as the interface between two different networks. A proxy server is a cross between a gateway and a firewall. Proxy servers serve as the surrogate for systems on a private network.

In the next chapter, you learn about Virtual Private Networks, which allow you to create secure communication channels between computers, regardless of where those computers are located.

Virtual Private Networks

Virtual Private Networks, or VPNs, are a fundamental building block for creating secure links and for enabling secure internetworking. To create VPNs, you need to create a connection, usually one over a public provider network such as the Public Switched Telephone Network (PSTN) or the Internet.

VPNs use a whole host of Data Link and Session layer protocols — Levels 2 and 3 in the OSI model. Some of these protocols are used to secure the data, usually by a process of encryption using cryptography. Other protocols encapsulate data to provide the necessary mechanism to support the VPN connection. Still other protocols are used to transport data over a VPN.

When the payload portion of a packet is encrypted and encapsulated, that data is sent using VPN transport. When the entire packet, both the payload and header, is encrypted and then encapsulated, the data is sent using VPN tunneling. VPN tunneling is most often either remote access or site to site.

VPNs are a combination of hardware and software. VPNs require a routing function to establish a connection and the software necessary to provide the data translation and packaging mechanisms. The various devices used on VPN systems — routers, gateway/concentrators, network access servers, and others — are described in this chapter.

A variety of VPN software packages, such as OpenVPN, LogMeIn Hamachi, and tinc, are mentioned. The procedure to create a VPN link between Vista and Windows Server 2008 is also described.

Tunneling and encryption protocols are covered in detail, as is the encapsulation process. Encryption on IP networks often uses the IPsec protocol suite. A common protocol for encapsulation is the Generic Routine Encapsulation protocol. The various point-to-point protocols used to enable remote access VPN — PPTP, L2TP, and L2F — are also described.

IN THIS CHAPTER

VPN and where it is used

VPN types and topologies

VPN devices and software

VPN encryption, encapsulation, and transport protocols

VPN Technologies

In a highly connected world, there is a need for people and organizations to communicate securely with one another. Local Area Networks (LANs) are secured by methods such as Challenge Handshake Authentication System (CHAP), but these methods are less secure when a network is shared or when Wide Area Network (WAN) links are used. Remote users of a network provide yet another set of issues. The cost of maintaining leased lines for WAN links is cost prohibitive for organizations, as well as being impractical for the average user.

A solution to this problem is the use of Virtual Private Networks, or VPNs, to create secure links over a connection defined by a virtual circuit. A VPN is a private data network that connects over public networks with tunneling and security protocols.

VPN types

Historically, VPNs developed first over private leased telephone lines, and then over public networks. The first type of VPNs were called *trusted VPNs* and relied on the privacy of the leased line for its security. Because trusted VPNs can transit a number of devices en route, the VPN clients are depending upon the VPN service provider to maintain security.

Trusted VPNs use the following Data Link Layer 2 or Session Link Layer 3 technologies:

- **ATM Layer 2 virtual circuits.**
- **Frame relay Layer 2 virtual circuits.**
- **Multiprotocol Label Switching (MPLS) Layer 2 frame transport.**
- **The Draft Martini transport uses ATM, Frame Relay, Ethernet, Ethernet VLAN, PPP, High Data Link Control (HDLC), or any other point-to-point transport over MPLS.** Draft Martini is sometimes called Any Transport over MPLS (AToM). Draft Martini is a Layer 2 protocol.
- **MPLS routing controlled by the Layer 3 Border Gateway Protocol (BGP) used on the Internet.**

The Internet made security even more problematic. Trusted VPN technology could not be counted on to protect the data en route from snooping. To make VPN more secure, encryption was applied and removed at the endpoints of the VPN prior to transiting the Internet. The endpoints were often edge routers or other devices. VPNs of this type are called *secure VPNs*.

Secure VPNs use the following encryption protocols:

- **IPsec encryption using either tunnel or transport.**
- **L2TP over IPsec for remote access client/server VPNs.**
- **IEEE.802.1Q tunneling (Q in Q).** This tunneling protocol can tunnel data in the Ethernet 802.1Q frame format on a shared backbone by adding an additional Q tag to the beginning of the header.

- **MPLS LSP.** A Label Switch Path (LSP) connects Label Switch Routers (LSRs) over an MPLS network.

- **Secure Sockets Layer (SSL) 3.0 or Transport Layer Security Protocol (TLS, or less commonly TLSP) with encryption.**

IPsec, L2TP, and TLS are all IETF standards. SSL is an earlier version of TLS. These are all Level 4 Transport layer protocols used on the Internet to place encrypted payloads into routable packets.

The third category of VPNs combines aspects of the first two and is called a *hybrid VPN*. On a hybrid VPN, the Internet is assumed to be a WAN and a secure VPN segment is created that spans that part of the VPN. The remaining portions on either side may or may not be secured, but at a minimum, they offer the capabilities of a trusted VPN. Vendors offering hybrid solutions provide a management console that can create and modify the VPN, providing a guaranteed Quality of Service that a VPN provider meets. Hybrid VPNs can be created on any type of secure VPN that can be carried over a trusted VPN.

VPN links

Broadly speaking, there are four different types of VPNs deployed today:

- **Internal LAN link.** This is a link from one computer to another within a LAN.

- **Intranetwork WAN links.** These are links from one LAN to another LAN on the same network.

- **Extranet WAN links.** These are links from one LAN to another LAN on different networks, often from one company to another.

- **Remote Access link.** This is a transient WAN link from a remote user or system. Remote access links are not shared.

VPN links can be created over dialup, broadband, network, and even wireless connections. Generally speaking, a VPN link can be either remote access or site to site. VPN technologies that encrypt the payload portion of their packets but not the header are referred to as *VPN transport*. VPN technologies that encrypt both the header and payload portion of the packets, and then encapsulate as datagrams within another packet, are referred to as *VPN tunnels*.

Figure 29.1 shows VPN connections over different types of WAN links, such as a leased line, standard LAN line, or Wi-Fi link, from a conceptual standpoint. The routers, switches, and other devices necessary to implement a VPN are not shown in this figure, nor are the actual VPN endpoints. VPNs can be provisioned (configured and managed) either by a customer, as shown for the tunnel between Dilbert and his home office, or by a service provider over leased lines or the Internet. When one VPN provider's service is transported over another VPN provider's service, the VPN service is called a *carrier of carriers*. The resulting service offered to the customer is a carrier's carrier VPN service.

FIGURE 29.1

Different types of VPNs

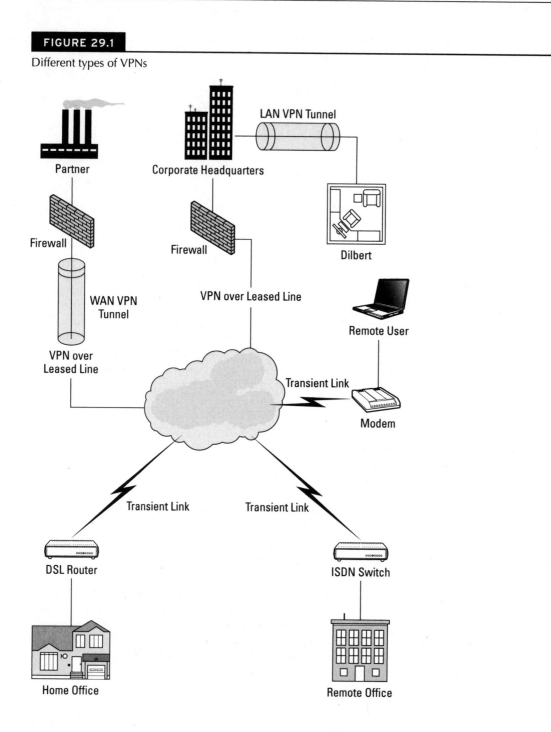

Service provider VPNs can be categorized as follows:

- IPsec VPN
- Virtual Private LAN Service (VPLS)
- Virtual Private Wire Service (VPWS)
- IP Private LAN Service (IPLS)
- Virtual Router (VR)
- BGP/MPLS

Customer VPNs are usually either of the following:

- IPsec VPN
- GRE VPN

Site-to-site topologies

VPN can be implemented in either hardware or software; often VPN solutions are a combination of the two. High-performance VPN hardware can be found in many different network devices. Devices can be categorized by where they are on a VPN and their function. The broadest range of devices is found on a site-to-site topology where two sites connect across a provider network or VPN backbone. Figure 29.2 shows site-to-site topologies, which use many of the elements described in the following list of VPN device categories:

- **Customer (C) and Provider (P) systems.** Computers, routers, or switches on the source and destination LAN are connected by a VPN link. To those systems, the resource appears to be a local resource and the VPN is invisible. A P system can't connect to customer networks or view a VPN on the customer network.

- **Customer Edge (CE) and Provider Edge (PE) systems.** An edge device connects to another edge device, creating a WAN link. The CE device can view the VPN if that VPN is located on the customer network; the PE device cannot. The PE device can view the VPN if that VPN is on the provider network; the CE device cannot.

    A customer edge router and switch can be indicated as CE-r and CE-s, respectively, and the provider versions would be indicated as PE-r and PE-s. Some VPN edge devices can be both routing and switching and take an -rs label.

- **Gateway or Concentrator.** This device can be either the endpoint for a VPN connection or the endpoints of many VPN connections, respectively. They are typically used for edge devices in place of CEs or as a remote access entry for the VPN. These kinds of devices are often given several different names, depending upon their placement and the protocol that they use. You may see any of the following: PPTP Network Server (PNS), L2TP Network Server (LNS), or L2F Home or Network Gateway.

- **Network Access Server (NAS).** These devices provide the network interface between a public network like the telephone system (Public Switched Telephone Network, or PSTN) and an IP backbone and can be a VPN tunnel endpoint.

  The function of a NAS is to authenticate a user logon request, and if it is authentic, to pass the traffic through. NAS are also used to provide these functions for VoIP services.

Note

The acronym NAS is also used for Network Attached Storage servers. Those devices are described in Chapter 22.

- **AAA ("Triple A") servers.** These VPN servers perform authentication, authorization, and accounting services.

  Authentication verifies user, group, and machine accounts. Authorization provides the rules related to resource access. Both of these functions are usually implemented as pass-through security from a domain controller or another authority. If there is no security authority, the AAA server takes over these tasks. The accounting function provides statistical data that is helpful for maintaining security, for troubleshooting, and, of course, for billing.

FIGURE 29.2

A site-to-site VPN topology

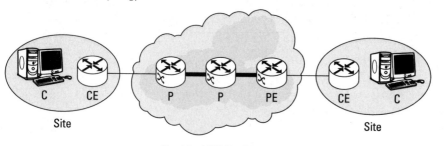

Provider VPN Backbone

Legend

C = Customer System
CE = Customer Edge System
P = Provider System
PE = Provider Edge System

VPN providers often employ an internally protected and redundant VPN backbone called a *Virtual Private LAN Service* (VPLS). This type of VPN is created by separating the Provider Edge (PE) device into one that faces the user (U-PE) and another that faces the network (N-PE). Figure 29.3 shows the internal elements of a VPLS backbone.

VPLS and the similar IP Only LAN Service (IPLS) VPNs are sometimes called Multipoint-to-Multipoint (M2M) VPNs. An example of a Point-to-Point (P2P) circuit VPN is the Virtual Private Wire Service (WPSN) VPN, Draft Martini, and L2TP v.3 emulated circuits. All of these technologies are based on Layer 2 protocols.

The Provider VPLS backbone

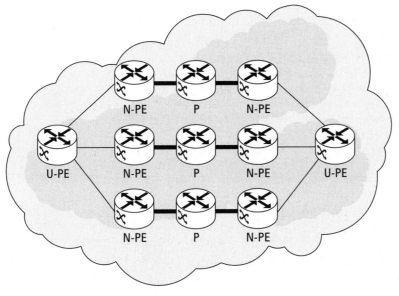

Provider VPLS Backbone

VPN hardware

The Virtual Private Network Consortium (VPNC), which helps to create interoperability standards in this area, maintains a members list at www.vpnc.org/member-list.html. You can see a list of features supported by different products that use IPsec by vendor at www.vpnc.org/vpnc-IPsec-features-chart.html. That same list compiled for SSL is maintained at www.vpnc.org/vpnc-ssl-features-chart.html.

The two companies that are most associated with hardware VPN solutions are Cisco Systems (www.cisco.com/en/US/products/hw/vpndevc/) and Juniper Networks (www.juniper.net/).

Cisco is one vendor that sells end-to-end VPN solutions for a large range of situations. The Cisco 1700 series routers have built-in VPN. These routers can also be configured as a firewall within the Cisco Internetwork Operating System (Cisco IOS) that runs on the 1700s. A higher-performance

VPN device is the Cisco Adaptive Security Appliance (ASA), which replaced their PIX Firewall and VPN 3000 Series Concentrator in 2005. The most current ASA models introduced in 2008 were the 5580 series. The 5580 comes with Cisco's Min OS 8.1 operating system, which can support SSL and IPsec VPN over six interface cards, with up to 10,000 remote users simultaneously connected by VPN.

VPN software

There are many VPN software solutions. In this section, some of the better-known products are described, with an emphasis on open source/freeware products and capabilities built into operating systems.

One of the best-known VPN packages is the OpenVPN (`http://openvpn.net/index.php/home.html`) SSL client/server software. Versions of OpenVPN are available for Linux, Windows (2.1 supports Vista), and the Macintosh. OpenVPN is configured from either the command line as a daemon or service or by using one of the Graphical User Interface front ends that you can download from `http://openvpn.net/index.php/documentation/graphical-user-interface.html`.

With OpenVPN, you can create SSL/TSL VPN connections of various types, including remote access, site-to-site, Wi-Fi, and backbone links. The enterprise versions of OpenVPN support failover and load balancing between servers, as well as providing resource access controls. VPN connections can be authenticated by this software using certificates, smart cards, and other methods. The detailed How To page at `http://openvpn.net/index.php/documentation/howto.html#install` contains instructions on how to get started with the program.

Another popular VPN product on Windows is LogMeIn Hamachi (`https://secure.logmein.com/products/hamachi/vpn.asp?lang=en`). It is notable for its ease of installation and configuration. Hamachi is a UDP VPN that uses a mediation server to establish a connection between two peer endpoints and then instantiate (bootstrap) the direct connection. Once the connection is established, the server no longer participates in the VPN.

Originally a freeware product, LogMeIn still offers a basic version for free and has a commercial Premium version. The LogMeIn Hamachi product is a VPN service that creates a virtual network of up to 256 systems with 50 connected users over the Internet.

Among the other features offered by LogMeIn Hamachi are:

- Firewall and broadband router NAT traversal
- Remote access control using Windows Remote Desktop
- Network drive access
- Peer-to-peer and group chats
- User accounts with passwords and privileges
- Relays for connections when direct connections can't be made point-to-point

- Built-in Web proxy for users connected to a Hamachi network from a public location such as a cyber café

- It can run on a Windows server as a service.

Another open source VPN program that is available on multiple platforms is tinc (www.tinc-vpn. org/). Versions of tinc support Linux, OpenBSD, NetBSD, Windows 2000/XP, Mac OS X, and Sun Solaris on both IP v.4 and IP v.6 networks. tinc makes a best effort to send traffic between tunnel endpoints by the most direct route. The program offers the ability to bridge Ethernet segments.

Microsoft Internet Security and Acceleration (ISA) Server 2006, which runs on Windows Server 2003, can be configured as a VPN endpoint. Originally released in 1997 as Microsoft Proxy Server, it became a platform for security (firewall), routing, and caching functions. ISA Server creates VPNs using either Layer 2 Tunneling Protocol (L2PT) over IPsec, or the Point-to-Point Tunneling Protocol (PPTP). Both are discussed in more detail later in this chapter.

ISA Server 2006 has a feature called Quarantine Control. When a remote client connects to the server, the client is evaluated by a number of criteria that you specify either within the Windows security model or from a RADIUS server. If the client doesn't have anti-virus software or the latest patch from Microsoft Update, for example, then the client is given only limited access until the configuration changes.

A new version of Microsoft ISA Server is to be released for Windows Server 2008 under the name Microsoft Forefront Threat Management Gateway (TMG). It is expected to also be part of the Windows Essential Business Server. The product Web site can be found at www.microsoft.com/forefront/default.mspx.

The Windows Server 2008 VPN Service

To create an incoming VPN connection on a Windows Server 2008, you need to turn the service on using the following procedure:

1. From the Control panel in the Network Connection dialog box, click File and then select the New Incoming Connection command.

2. In the Who may connect to this computer? dialog box (shown in Figure 29.4) of the Allow Connections to this Computer Wizard, select the user accounts that can connect by VPN to Windows Server 2008, and click the Next button.

3. In the How will people connect? page, disable the Through the Internet check box if the VPN is used on your LAN, or leave it enabled for a WAN connection; then click the Next button.

4. In the Networking software allows this computer to accept connections from other kinds of computers dialog box (shown in Figure 29.5), make sure that the network protocols required for a connection are installed, and that their parameters are correct for the VPN connection you want to establish; then click the Next button.

    Make sure that the IP v.4 address is the one you will provide on the client side, or install IP v.6 if required.

FIGURE 29.4

The Who may connect to this computer? dialog box

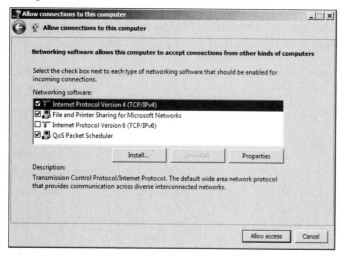

FIGURE 29.5

The Networking software allows this computer page to accept connections from other kinds of computers dialog box

5. The Wizard creates the incoming connection and posts the final dialog box that you see in Figure 29.6.

FIGURE 29.6

The people you chose can now connect to the computer dialog box

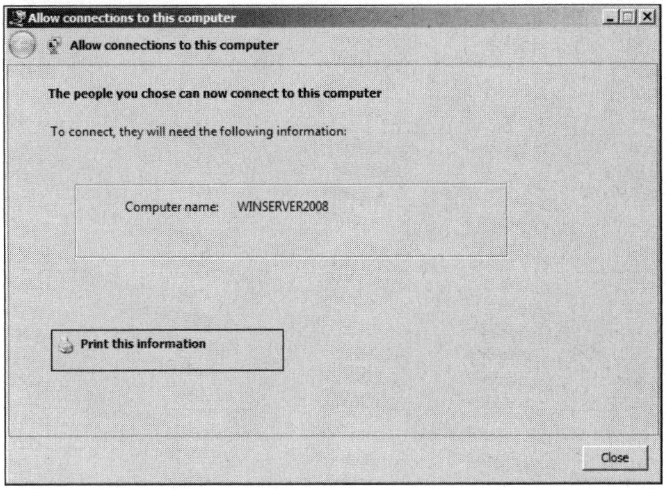

The Vista client

VPN client software is common to most operating systems. As an example, a VPN client for Windows Vista 64 is configured as follows:

1. Click Start, and then select the Network command.

2. Click the Set up a connection or network link, and in the Choose a connection option dialog box (see Figure 29.7), select Connect to a workplace; then click Next.

3. In the How do you want to connect? dialog box (see Figure 29.8), click Use my Internet connection (VPN).

FIGURE 29.7

The Choose a Connection Option or Network Wizard in Vista

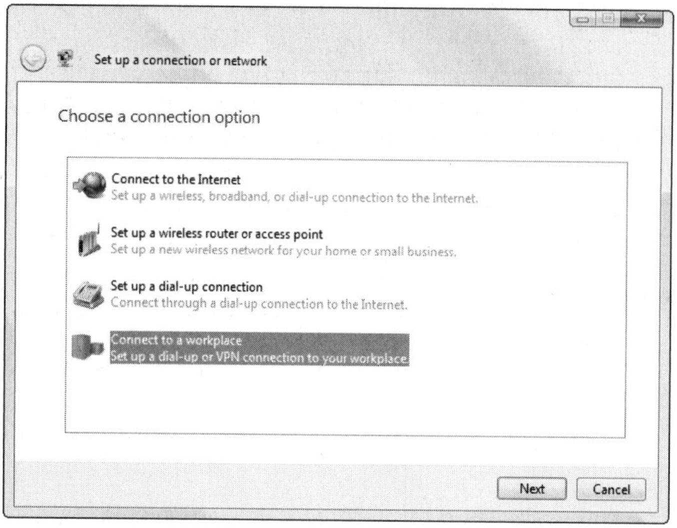

FIGURE 29.8

The How do you want to connect? dialog box

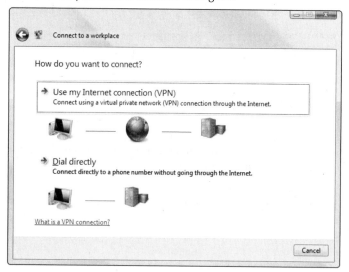

4. The Type the Internet address to connect to dialog box appears (see Figure 29.9). In the Internet address field, type the Internet address as the FQDN (Fully Qualified Domain Name), or the IP address.

5. In the Destination name field, type the name that you want to appear for the virtual network interface in your Network Connections dialog box.

6. Select the Use a smart card option, the Allow other people to use this connection option, or the Don't connect now; just set it up so I can connect later option by enabling the check box or boxes; then click the Next button.

   You can check one or more of these check boxes, and change these VPN settings later.

FIGURE 29.9

The Type the Internet address to connect to dialog box

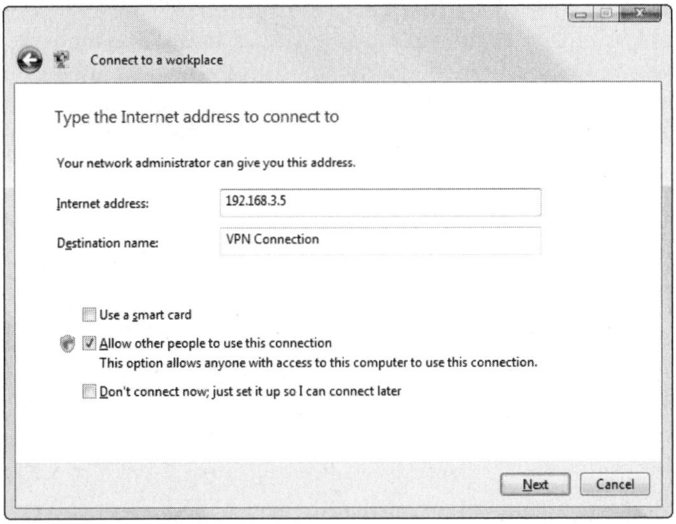

7. In the Type your user name and password dialog box, enter the details and the domain name (optional), and then click the Connect button.

   The connection is established and the VPN network interface appears in the Network connections dialog box. The server appears in your Network folder when you browse for neighbors.

Encryption

VPN traffic is encrypted and decrypted at the endpoints of the VPN connection by the software that creates the VPN. Encryption is either by public key or symmetric key encryption. Public key encryption, also known as asymmetric key encryption, works by using a private or public key to encrypt data and using the other key to decrypt the data once it arrives. The well-known Pretty Good Privacy (PGP) software uses a public key encryption system. Symmetric key encryption works by using the same secret key at each endpoint.

Cross-Ref

For more information on encryption, see Chapter 27.

The symmetric key mechanism is essentially a key exchange. A commonly used method is the Diffie-Hellman key exchange. In this mechanism, the sender and receiver create a public/private key pair. The public keys are then exchanged between sender and recipient. Each endpoint then participates in creating a shared secret offline, and that shared secret is used as the key for the symmetric algorithm.

In a VPN route that goes from a PC on LAN A to a PC on LAN B, the following segments can be encrypted:

1. PC A to Server A
2. Server A to Router A
3. Router A to Firewall A
4. Firewall A across the WAN to Firewall B
5. Firewall B to Router B
6. Router B to Server B
7. Server B to PC B

The one link that is always encrypted, regardless of which endpoints you select, is segment 4, where the data travels across a WAN and can be seen by others. Many routers function as their network's edge device in place of firewalls, and servers may or may not be in the chain. Indeed, the destination endpoint can be a server. So there is considerable variance in how one goes about setting up a VPN connection.

Tunneling

Tunneling is the name given to the process of encapsulation, routing, and the removal of encapsulation. Tunnels do not require that the data enclosed be encrypted, although it almost always is. The tunnel is a logical path, but it appears as if it is a point-to-point connection in the network. The devices that are inside the tunnel — routers, gateways, switches, or proxy servers — are invisible to the sending (source) and receiving (destination) systems.

Internet Protocol Security, or IPsec, is another method used to encrypt VPN traffic. When IPsec, GRE, PPTP, or L2TP (the carrier protocols) encrypts the data or payload of an IP packet and sends that packet to the VPN endpoint where the packet's payload is decrypted, this is called *IPsec transport*.

When IPsec or another carrier protocol encrypts the entire packet (both header and payload) and the encrypted packet is sent to the other VPN endpoint, this is referred to as a *VPN tunnel*. Tunneling works by encapsulating the encrypted packet inside another packet. The encrypted packet is referred to as the *passenger packet*. The container packet is unencrypted, and contains the addressing information. The endpoints of the tunnel are called *tunnel interfaces*, with the local side of the tunnel being the source and the remote side being the destination.

A tunnel is considered to be more secure than transport because more information is hidden from view; however, a tunnel requires more network resource overhead to operate.

The fact that a VPN tunnel uses encrypted packets means that the technology makes no demands on what kind of data the VPN carries. You can send any type of data through the tunnel, and even use addresses that are in private IP ranges and therefore non-routable. A tunnel can allow a user to send a packet type that would be disallowed at the port level and even perhaps by network security. If the sender knows that an application server has the private address 192.168.1.10, then the encrypted packets can be sent to that address, even if they come from outside the LAN. This feature makes VPN a very powerful technology.

Tunneling Protocols

Tunneling uses a variety of different protocols for transport. One set of protocols are used to encapsulate the encrypted packet, another set is used as transport by the network that carries the tunnel (TSL/SSL, for example), and a third protocol is used in the header of the encrypted protocol that contains the addressing required by the packet (a wrapper). The wrapper can use IPsec, GRE, PPTP, and L2TP for packet encapsulation. For example, on the Internet, the carrier protocol would probably be TCP/IP, and for the encrypted header, the network transport protocol or passenger protocol used might be NBT for Windows, IPX for Netware, or perhaps the Internet Protocol on almost any network.

Generic Routing Encapsulation

The Generic Routing Encapsulation, or GRE, protocol is commonly used as the encapsulation protocol for VPNs that connect one LAN to another. It is a routing protocol. GRE does not encrypt packets, but it can perform both multicasts and broadcasts. The edge router on the sending network uses GRE to package the passenger packet, and the edge router on the receiving network reads the header GRE information, extracts the passenger packet, and sends it on its way. GRE makes it appear as if remote networks connected by a tunnel are local to one another. GRE tunnels are often placed into VPN tunnels to use the encryption features VPN offers.

GRE supports physical IP addresses as well as valid logical or virtual IP addresses. For example, when you create a site-to-site VPN, you can use either the network interface address facing the client or the router's loopback interface address. A loopback interface is not the same as a NIC address. The loopback interface is a logical interface (or a set of them) on the router that is always on.

IPsec tunnels

IPsec is a suite of protocols that can be used for encapsulation of IP traffic on tunnels for remote access as well as site to site. IPsec must run not only on endpoints of the VPN but also on the firewalls in between or any other device with a routing function, in order for the packets to be routed correctly. IPsec has the additional requirement that the devices running the protocol share a key and be configured to allow this type of traffic to be forwarded.

IPsec can be used in the IPsec tunnel mode, without the use of a carrier protocol. In this mode, IPsec also provides the encapsulation that the carrier protocol would. Typically, IPsec tunnels in a site-to-site topology go from the CE device on one site to the CE device on another through the provider network. The primary reason that you would create an IPsec tunnel is that it works on routers, gateways, and other endpoints that cannot run L2TP over IPsec or PPTP VPN tunnels.

Secure Sockets Layer/Transport Layer Security

The Secure Sockets Layer (SSL) v.3 protocol creates secure connections for remote access users. The Transport Layer Security (TLS) protocol is the newer IETF standard that is derived by SSL v.3. In many ways, the two protocols are very similar.

TSL is an older protocol that was developed by Netscape. SSL's security isn't as powerful as IPsec, L2TP v.2, L2F, or even PPTP when the VPN doesn't include client software to enforce the security. Although these clientless connections are easy to create and configure, because SSL is included in all modern browsers, clientless or Web-based VPN connections are common. It is possible to strengthen SSL/TLS by adding client software that supports these protocols.

Point-to-Point tunneling protocols

VPN tunnels over remote access links use the Point-to-Point Protocol (PPP) as their carrier over IP networks.

Point-to-Point Tunneling Protocol

The Point-to-Point Tunneling Protocol (PPTP) is a Layer 2 Data Link protocol that tunnels remote access PPP data between a remote user and a NAS or gateway/concentrator. The PPTP tunnel can also be set up to include the remote access network segment.

PPTP provides either 40-bit or 128-bit encryption for a remote client connection. PPTP connections can use CHAP or EAP-TLS authentication from Microsoft. PPTP connections provide only the user authentication that PPP enables, and so this protocol should only be used when the source computer does not need to be authenticated.

The PPP packets that PPTP encapsulates are given a GRE and IP header. To encrypt PPTP on Windows, you can use the Microsoft Point-to-Point Encryption (MPPE) protocol. MPPE creates its session keys from passwords using either MS-CHAP (Challenge Handshake Authentication Protocol) or EAP (Extensible Authentication Protocol), which means that encryption is dependent upon the strength of the user's password.

Figure 29.10 shows a PPTP encapsulation packet. The encapsulation process adds an IP Header field and the protocol Header (shown here as GRE) to the front of the encrypted packet. From the standpoint of a router, the packet appears just like any other IP packet, with the PPP Frame being the packet's payload.

FIGURE 29.10

The PPTP protocol encapsulation packet format

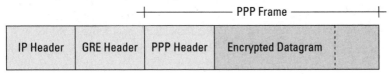

PPTP is an older format that is supported on Windows but not on many other platforms. Microsoft recommends that users adopt the L2TP protocol instead.

Layer 2 Forwarding Protocol

Layer 2 Forwarding (L2F) is a Cisco protocol that tunnels PPP or SLIP (Serial Line Interface Protocol) frames. L2F is usually deployed on a NAS and a VPN gateway. The remote connections to the NAS are tunneled through the VPN that spans these two devices and forwarded to a home VPN gateway.

Layer 2 Tunneling Protocol

The Layer 2 Tunneling Protocol (L2TP) v.3 allows a remote access user to connect a NAS to a gateway/concentrator tunnel and send PPP frames through it. The tunnel can also be extended to include the remote network segments.

Because L2TP doesn't have security, its traffic is usually secured by IPsec. Traffic can flow over ATM, Frame Relay, PPP, VLAN, or PPP over IP networks. L2TP v.3 is the latest of the three protocols and incorporates elements of both PPTP and L2F in it. L2TP encapsulates PPP frames into packets; IPsec encrypts those packets. L2TP over IPsec not only uses PPP user authentication but also requires machine authentication by either a certificate or shared key. L2TP is the PPP remote access protocol that is currently favored.

The L2TP packet is constructed by first adding the L2TP and UDP headers and the IPsec Encapsulating Security Payload trailer to the passenger packet. IPsec encrypts this data and then adds the IPsec Encapsulating Security Payload header and the IPsec Authentication trailer to the carrier packet. An IP address header is added to complete the L2TP encapsulated packet that is transmitted through the VPN tunnel. UDP is used because it is more efficient than TCP and because the use of a tunnel ensures that data will more often arrive in sequence. Figure 29.11 shows an L2TP encapsulated packet.

The L2TP protocol encapsulation packet format

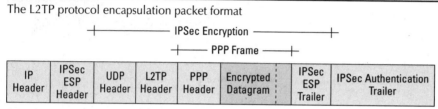

ESP = Encapsulating Security Payload

While L2TP is a strong VPN protocol in wide use, it is not without its problems. As is true with many WAN technologies, L2TP over IPsec often has problems with Network Address Translation (NAT) Traversal on older platforms. The NAT routing system works at the firewall or proxy server by changing the IP address and potentially the port number in the UDP header, leaving the encapsulated IPsec portion of the packet untouched. If this redirection isn't done correctly or can't be recognized, the packet will be dropped when it reaches its destination.

Summary

In this chapter, you learned about Virtual Private Networks, or VPNs, and how they are used to create secure links on networks, over WANs and on the Internet. Modern networking would not be possible without these important technologies. The first VPNs were created to transfer data over the telephone network. Later systems moved to leased lines, and then to the Internet.

VPN uses a number of Layer 2 and Layer 3 protocols to enable its technology. VPN links are typically either remote access or site to site. VPN data is sent using either VPN transfer or by VPN tunneling. Techniques used to secure VPN data — encryption, encapsulation, and others — were described in detail, as were a number of different types of VPNs that have been created.

The next chapter describes network management. Networks are big, complex structures that change frequently. The software and methods for managing networks and systems efficiently are important for a network of almost any size.

Part VII

Network Management and Diagnostics

Network Management

Network management tools are essential for a network of any size. The development of large networks in the telephone industry and the military started a process of standardization that has led to a number of standard network protocols used to manage modern networks. This chapter uses the ITU-T classification for management software called *FCAPS* to organize different types of management tools. FCAPS stands for Fault, Configuration, Accounting and Administration, Performance, and Security.

Fault management software detects specific events associated with errors and helps you determine what has gone wrong. Events can be viewed inside event viewers, and the different properties associated with each event allow you to identify them. Because faults can generate many duplicate events and lead to event cascades, determining faults is a challenging enterprise.

Configuration management software allows you to determine the configuration of different network devices, change that configuration, and save your modifications. The related topics of network software deployments, upgrades, patch management, and system lifecycles are described in this chapter.

The different factors involved in managing network event accounting, security, and performance monitoring are described. All of these topics involve trapping events of the right type and analyzing their behavior. Performance monitoring tools extend event logging to determine quantitative values and metrics that can be used to troubleshoot networks as well as optimize performance. The concept of counters and agents is explored as related to their use in measuring events.

A number of network management systems are sold that allow you to perform management functions. Some of these tools are framework applications, while others are proprietary solutions. Some of the leading products in this area are described.

The Importance of Network Management

Network management is an issue for networks of any size. The potential problems you can encounter increase exponentially as the number of network nodes grows. As networks grow beyond the size of a small workgroup, the cost of labor involved in managing systems greatly outpaces the cost of the automated systems described in this chapter that help you manage them. Network management software therefore has a very high return on investment (ROI) and very short payback periods that are often measured in months and not years.

Unfortunately, many networks grow quite large before their owners make the connection between the cost savings that management automation can achieve and the cost of continually adding IT staff to perform tasks more or less manually. Certainly the additional $250 to $500 that management frameworks add to the annual cost of each networked computer is a barrier to their adoption, as is the tendency of each of these products to lock customers into specific technologies. Until the true costs of working without network management software are calculated, IT staff responsible for administering the network must spend an increasing amount of their working hours troubleshooting network-related problems.

In the sections that follow, some of the more important features of network management packages are considered. FCAPS, an acronym that describes the terms: fault, configuration, accounting and administration, and security has been used to standardize management packages and is considered first. These different aspects of network management are considered sequentially.

FCAPS

Most of the standards and vocabulary in the area of network management come from the two main areas that had the earliest experience in heterogeneous networking: the telephone industry and the military.

As discussed in Chapter 13, the telephone industry was a pioneer in large switched network design and maintenance. By the 1970s, the telecommunication industry, through various working groups, set about standardizing many aspects of their technologies. Some of the impetus for this work was the breakup of Ma Bell (the AT&T network) into the Baby Bells. Eventually, the network management portion of the work was consolidated in the ITU-T group of the OSI. The ITU-T group created a network management model that is often called the ISO Telecommunications Management Network model. Like its much better known Open Systems Interconnect (ISO/OSI) seven-layer protocol model, the management network model was meant to be an open system with each area of management having its own protocol set.

The acronym FCAPS was coined to cover the major areas in the ITU-T network management standard. These initials stand for:

- Fault. Fault management includes event logging, error analysis, error remediation, and data recovery.

- Configuration. Configuration management includes asset management, inventorying, software deployment, package management, and service and network provisioning.

- Accounting and Administration. These functions include statistical reporting and integrated billing functions.

- Performance. Performance management extends event monitoring to collect network system and component metrics, as well as providing software metering functions.

- Security. Security management either installs or works with a policy engine, and can manage user and system identities either through self-contained functionality or in concert with directory services.

Although the ISO's initial concept was to create separate protocols for each of these five different areas under an umbrella that was to be called the Systems Management Overview (SMO) standard, it became clear during development that all areas could be supported by a common approach with a single protocol. From this work, the Common Management Information Protocol (CMIP) emerged as ITU-T Recommendation X.700 (www.itu.int/rec/T-REC-X.700/en). CMIP systems work with managed objects, each having a unique descriptor in a namespace, known as a Distinguished Name (DN). The concepts are very similar to the one for X.500 directory services (LDAP) that is described in detail in Chapter 21.

CMIP is a competitor to the much more widely used IETF Simple Network Management Protocol (SNMP) standard, but CMIP has many more capabilities than SNMP. CMIP includes a number of different actions in the form of verbs or commands that modify managed network elements. SNMP, in contrast, only allows you to change the state of a managed element through the use of a SET command. SET is essentially a WRITE operation to an object value. The reason that SNMP is so widely known and CMIP is not is that most networked devices on TCP/IP networks come with SNMP support. SNMP hardware benefits both from economy of scale and by being less complex; it is also cheaper to implement, making them cheaper to fabricate and deploy.

Cross-Ref
SNMP is described in detail in Chapter 4.

Systems management has had a long history within the computer industry and there are many standards that apply to managing desktops, deploying systems, and other management tasks. You've already seen some of these management protocols, such as SNMP and WEBM. Here are some other protocol standards that you might encounter:

- NETCONF (www.ietf.org/html.charters/netconf-charter.html), which, like SNMP, is an IETF standard

- Common Information Model (www.dmtf.org/standards/cim/), WS-Management (a SOAP protocol; www.dmtf.org/standards/wbem/wsman), and SMASH (Systems Management Architecture for Server Hardware; www.dmtf.org/standards/smash/), all of which are DMTF standards or initiatives. The Desktop Management Interface (DMI; www.dmtf.org/standards/dmi/) standard is another DMTF framework for PC management but has been deprecated in favor of the newer CIM standard.

- JMX (Java Managed Extensions; java.sun.com/products/JavaManagement/), which is a Java initiative for managing network objects (MBeans or Managed Beans)

There are many more protocol standards that are either industry specific or so poorly known that they are not worth mentioning here.

While FCAPS isn't nearly as well known as the seven-layer ISO/OSI networking model, FCAPS is a convenient organizational scheme for describing the different functions of network management. The sections that follow are named after the FCAPS model, after which some examples of network frameworks are considered.

Fault management

A fault is an error in hardware or software that leads to an undesired result. The goal of fault management is to identify when a fault has occurred, isolate the cause of the fault, and provide the necessary information so that you can remediate the cause of the error. Most operating systems and applications are great at producing error reports, and fault management systems are also great at capturing and displaying errors. What they are not great at is helping you determine the exact nature of what has gone wrong.

Fault management systems work by detecting specific events that are associated with error conditions or by determining a fault from a collection of events. All modern network operating systems and their desktop counterparts are event-driven; that is, the software sits in a wait state until it receives a command that it needs to act on. Some events are maintenance items, others check memory integrity, and so on. Events are typed and may be trapped selectively, with the ones of interest logged to an event log (usually a database file) and/or sent over the network in a standard Application layer protocol such as SNMP, or for some vendors, in a proprietary protocol. The isolation and understanding of events of different types is the first line of defense in any fault management routine.

In the next sections, you learn about how events can be logged, how events can trigger alarms based on conditions, and how analyzing events is your first line of defense in solving problems and optimizing your network.

Event log files

Figure 30.1 shows the Event log for a Windows Vista 64 system, with an error event in the System log highlighted. Different operating systems come with a core set of events that are very similar to one another, although different names are used. The Windows Event Viewer is representative of this class of utilities. Notice that each event has an associated set of properties, an EventID or

Reference Type, Date and Time, Source, and the name of the log file the event was recorded into. Because there are so many events, all event viewers allow you to set filters that control the particular events that are viewed. Although the Event Viewer here shows a local view, you can also use this utility to log onto a remote system and view that system's various event files.

Tip

Error IDs, their descriptions, and other properties that network operating systems and applications disclose are often described in technical notes on the Web sites of the vendors who create them. Often the best way to determine what an error means is to simply Google these terms.

FIGURE 30.1

The Windows Event Viewer

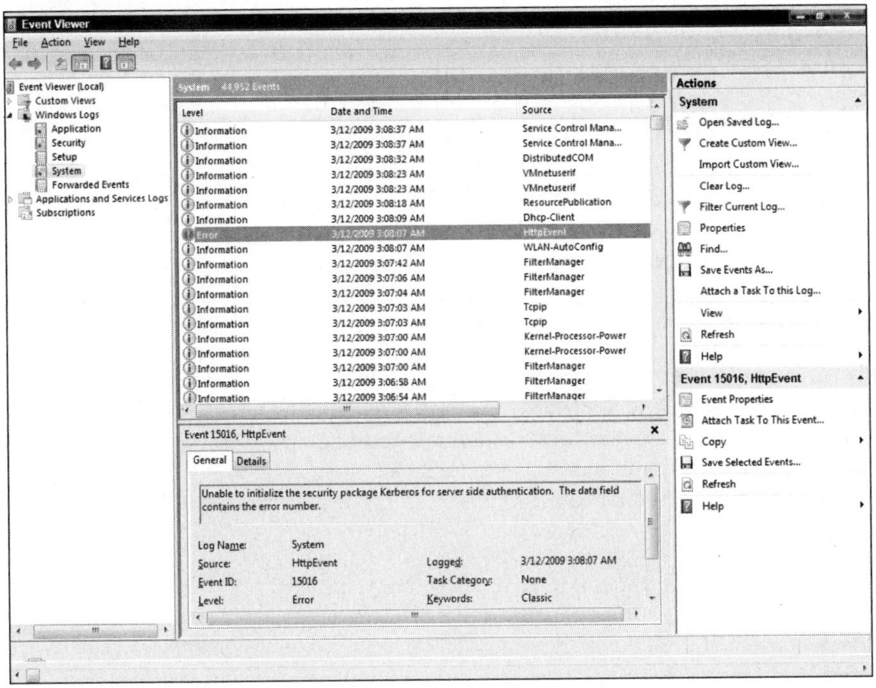

This particular Event Viewer is a Microsoft Management Console (MMC) component and can be launched either as a stand-alone utility or, as is the case with Windows Server 2008, within the Server Manager console (described later in this chapter).

Different versions of UNIX and Linux store their events into either a MESSAGES or SYSLOG file, which can then be viewed with different command line and GUI tools. In Ubuntu, by default, the System logs are found in the /VAR/LOG directory, which includes the SYSLOG, DMESG, KERN.

LOG, DAEMON.LOG, and other log files. Provided you have Monitor system log privileges, you can use the System Log Viewer in Ubuntu to open a utility that looks very similar to Figure 30.1. These log files are stored as delimited text, and so you can open a Terminal session and use a reader command such as GREP to view the contents of the individual files.

There are two types of event trapping systems: counters and agents. Counters are built into an application or operating system by its developers, while agents are lightweight executables that are installed by other programs to monitor counter values. As a general rule, counters run with higher privileges and have lower-level access to event information than agents do. However, a well-executed network management package such as Altiris will install a local agent on a system that is low level and difficult to remove. In either case, the data being captured by a counter or agent should be identical.

Counters and agents are not only used to READ/WRITE to event logs but also provide empirical data that is used to measure performance. Because event viewers are strictly viewer applications, you don't have control over counters and agents from within an event viewer application. To alter how events are monitored, or if they are even monitored at all, you need to work within performance monitoring applications, which are covered later in this chapter.

Alarms

In addition to detecting faults, fault management functions will also create alarms. An alarm is a detected error condition that may be categorized in terms of type and severity and logged to a database or sent out in some form of notification. Because error conditions are detected by the appearance of an event alarm, management systems are just another form of event viewer with filters for types of events, and some rules on how to handle events of the type being monitored.

When the device or system function automatically sends out an alarm, the system is referred to as a passive management system. When a program is polling devices listening for a "heartbeat," a response to a PING for example, that system is an active management system. Depending upon the system function and the manner in which the network management package is written, its functions can be either active or passive, or both.

Alarms may be categorized as being either analog or digital. A digital alarm is a binary system with two states: ON or OFF, 1 or 0, or TRUE or FALSE. The 1 or 0 value is what is actually stored in the alarm register, and what you see is simply a function of how you format the output. A register is simply an address in memory that can be referenced and contains a value related to some variable. In some rare instances, binary alarm management systems supply a third value, which either appears as NULL, NA (for Not Available), or simply leaves the output display blank. Many database applications handle binary fields in this manner.

An analog alarm is one that can take a range of values. An example of an analog field might be one that measures dropped frames. Analog alarms have a value property that can be any number in its range, or if no range is defined, any value at all within the limits of the number of numeric places supported by that alarm's register. You may find that the management application that you are working with allows you to set individual portions of the range in a manner similar to this:

- Low-Low: 0 – <20 percent
- Low: 20 – <35 percent
- Middle: 35 – <65 percent
- High: 65 – <80 percent
- High-High: 80 – 100 percent

Because analog values are generally more useful with performance metrics, they tend to provide rates or quantities, such as number of frames dropped per second or number of nearest neighbor routers that respond to a discovery command and are often built into performance monitoring tools.

Alarm management applications are most often put in place because they flag faults that need to be corrected. Therefore, these applications most often come with a notification feature. There are a wide variety of methods used to notify other applications about an error condition: the error may be displayed in a GUI application such as an Alarm Human Machine Interface (HMI) console, the alarm may generate an SNMP event that is sent to another application, the alarm may be placed inside an e-mail and sent using SMTP to a mail server, or the alarm may be sent as a fax (old school) or as an SMS text message (nu schl).

Event correlation

Fault management packages must be written in such a way that they can recognize when many events are all caused by the same error condition, a process referred to as event correlation. In any system where a fault or error has occurred, it is uncommon for only a single error event to be generated. For example, if an action requires access to a USB device and that connection has failed, the system may attempt to contact the device many times over the action's timeout period, generating an error event each time. It is not useful to have a fault management system report hundreds of error events when in reality there is only one error being described. Nearly all fault management packages will suppress or summarize duplicate error events so that meaningful data is presented to the user.

The engine that performs the analysis of event correlations is called the event correlator, and these systems can rise to the level of being artificial intelligence systems. The four common stages of an event correlation are:

- **Filtering,** discarding irrelevant events.
- **Aggregation,** or event de-duplication, which removes duplicates of the same event.
- **Masking,** which results in hiding events that are the result of an error and do not pertain to the actual error. Some references refer to this function as topological masking.
- **Root Cause Analysis (RCA),** which is the methodology that uses event dependencies to create an environment model that allows for the error's ultimate explanation to be exposed. A root cause analysis will result in information such as "disk XXX is full" in place of "disk WRITE to XXX fails," for example.

Many event correlation systems are bundled into help desks and work in concert with what is called a Trouble Ticket system, or alternatively, an Incident Management (IcM) system. When an error is detected, it is assigned an ID; a ticket is then entered into the database and logged. As information regarding the error is determined, it is added to the database until an explanation or fix is uncovered. These systems often have status assignments that allow organizations to use them in project development. They are as useful in network management as they are in software development projects.

More problematical is the situation where a fault gives rise to an event cascade. Returning to the errant USB device, let's assume that the device is a USB key with a file stored on it that must be used by another program. That program sends out a READ command for the file, which the operating system redirects. After multiple attempts, the file can't be accessed and the whole process begins to generate multiple distinct errors in the system's event log. The cause might be the key itself, or a damaged USB port, and the USB bus reports the error. As the error moves up the food chain, a cascade of related error events are generated. The operating system can report errors, the application can report errors, and so on. All these errors relate to the same fault, but because they all appear in an error log, it is left up to you, gentle user, to figure out the cause of the pattern.

The more sophisticated a fault management package is, the better that package is at parsing the related errors and defining the underlying fault. Even the most discriminating management package will often present the user with multiple related errors that will need to be put into context in order to determine the ultimate cause. So my advice to you, if you are ever in the position of having to evaluate one network management package over another, is to focus on how well the package handles event cascades and duplications as one of the key differentiators of performance, and how well it is able to translate that ability into ascertaining the relationship between events and causality.

Configuration management

Configuration management refers to the tasks involved in managing the configuration and identity of systems and users on a network, as well as attending to modifications that may be needed.

Tasks that fall under the banner of configuration management are:

- Setting up computers and network devices
- Installing and configuring software, known as software configuration management (SCM)
- Managing the different users and groups on a network, including their accounts and roles
- Updating and patching software and systems as required
- Provision of dedicated network connections
- Documenting the configuration of all of these network components

The goal of configuration management is to set up systems to automate repetitive tasks, reduce complexity by requiring a set of standards, and actively monitor systems for conditions. One way that you can reduce complexity to make configuration management easier is to set reference standards for the hardware and software that you allow to run on your network. A standard system that's been tested and certified forms a reference platform that may be rolled out (duplicated or cloned) and reduces much of the work involved in individual system configuration.

Most system management packages use consoles to monitor and manage networks. The next section describes some of the more common aspects of consoles. A key management task is to manage network system lifecycles, which is the topic covered after the discussion on consoles.

Consoles

Local configuration management is an onerous task, and so most management solutions are remote solutions, preferably performed in a centralized management console or dashboard. This dashboard feature has long been a staple of management framework applications, but is found now as a management feature in operating systems as well. As Microsoft has continued to develop their MMC technology, they've been able to consolidate most of the utilities for networked system management within a saved console on Windows Server 2008 called the Server Manager, an example of which is shown in Figure 30.2.

The structure of the Server Manager display collapses the view from dozens of tools to the hierarchical tree control in the left pane of the window, letting you manage your local and remote systems from one place. When you highlight a tool such as the Reliability Monitor, it is displayed in the central panel of the console, and although it isn't shown in this particular figure, when a tool has available options, a third panel on the right appears with the appropriate commands. Using the Server Manager, you can have several of these tools open at a time, such as the Active Directory configuration utility, the Policy tool, and others, and save the configuration for later use.

FIGURE 30.2

The Windows Server 2008 Server Manager is an MMC framework application that helps bring order to chaos.

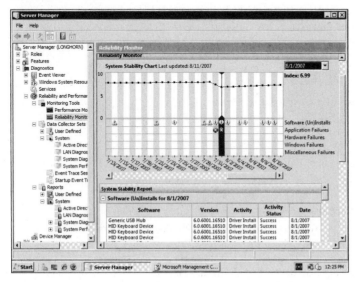

While other features in Windows Server 2008, such as PowerShell, may turn out to be more important in the long run, from an administrative point of view, no other feature will have more impact than the consolidation of utilities within the Server Manager. It isn't that this console view is unique or even that it breaks new ground, but simply that it is both comprehensive and part of the OS that will ensure its use.

A central console is an enormous time saver, and the care and quality of such a console is a desirable feature in any management tool. All of the network frameworks described later in this book provide a container application such as the MMC into which applications may be installed. Some of these management packages are closed and proprietary, but many framework vendors publish their APIs, thus allowing third parties to create modules for the framework.

Note
Microsoft publishes the interface for creating MMC snap-ins: http://msdn.microsoft.com/en-us/library/ ms692755(VS.85).aspx.

Software lifecycles and deployments

All software and hardware have lifecycles during which they are useful, and after which they are not. The goal of configuration management is to ensure that the lifecycles of network components are as long as they are practicable, and to maximize the utility of systems during their lives.

Systems — which include both hardware and software — progress through a set of six common conditions or states. The sections that follow consider these stages in order from the start of the system's life to the end. All of these stages make different requirements of configuration management software, and while each management package handles configuration differently, there are some universal themes that may be associated with each stage. Deployment technology — also referred to as electronic software distribution (ESD), desktop management, or automated software delivery — is the number one requested feature in network framework technology. If this functionality isn't in the base framework package, it is usually the first add-on module that is purchased for use.

State 1. Systems are newly acquired and current.

In State 1, the management package must add the acquired system to its inventory and be capable of monitoring the system. If the acquired system isn't purchased as a completely installed system, management software must be able to configure the system as described in State 2. In this stage, a management package must be able to install an agent and register the various properties of the system into an asset database. Among the many properties that might be stored for view are:

- An asset ID tag or software license number
- The serial numbers and types of components associated with the system
- Specific model or product names, as well as their version numbers
- Assigned values such as system names stored in a directory service

Not all management frameworks ship with full accounting and inventory modules; in some systems, this is an add-on module that must be purchased later. However, all management frameworks require some means of identifying systems in order to be able to identify systems that are to be deployed or upgraded. Not all systems must be managed, and it may even be desirable from a cost or security standpoint to isolate non-managed systems from outside monitoring.

State 2. Systems are in inventory or to be deployed.

Configuration management software can create and store system states, either in the form of installable software packages of some type, or for complete computer systems as an installable container file that is referred to as an image file. Most people are familiar with various image files, and they come in a wide variety of forms. The best-known image files are ISO files, the name being taken from the International Organization for Standardization. ISO files are sometimes called archive files or disk images and their definition arises from the manner in which the ISO 9660 file system on CD-ROMs was organized. The 9660 file system has been replaced by the Universal Disk Format (UDF; ISO/IEC 13346 or ECMA-167), which is maintained by the Optical Storage Technology Association (OSTA) for use on all sorts of optical media.

Other image file formats include Microsoft Windows Imaging Format (WIM) files, Symantec's Ghost (from General Hardware Oriented System Transfer) GHO files, Acronis True Image Server, and many more. All of these file formats have as their properties the same general concept: they store an index that you can browse that describes the contents of the individual files/directories/drives that the image contains, and the data is stored either in its native form (and can therefore be directly copied) or as a compressed version that must be extracted to recover. Because images are containers, most utilities allow you to add additional content or remove files, thus providing for drive snapshots, custom installations based on some subset of the files contained in the image, and other features. Figure 30.3 shows an Acronis TIB file, Acronis's native True Image Backup file format.

The use of image files for system installation has had a very interesting effect on the manner in which Microsoft is now distributing its different versions of Windows. In Windows prior to Windows Server 2008/Vista, different versions of Windows would require separate builds and installation media. Starting with 2008 and going forward, Microsoft consolidated all of the files into a WIM container file, and through user selection of the version type, one build served all with great economy.

Image files are not only used by backup utilities, but they are also at the heart of all deployment utilities. In a tightly managed network, organizations acquire systems and validate configurations that they are willing to support. Those reference systems are then deployed onto the network. A reference system may include a number of feature restrictions designed to narrow the number of support issues that network IT staff must deal with, such as the following: support for only certain hardware and software; lockdown of user privileges and desktop features; and restrictions on what may be installed. Deployment typically takes place by supplying a script to the system that points to the image on a network share and provides whatever automation is required.

FIGURE 30.3

Acronis True Image TIB files are disk image container files and can be used for backup and recovery, disk cloning operations, and deployments.

Microsoft distributes a set of network deployment tools under the name of Microsoft Deployment Toolkit (www.microsoft.com/downloads/details.aspx?FamilyID=3bd8561f-77ac-4400-a0c1-fe871c461a89&displaylang=en) that is packaged as a framework solution. With this tool, you can deploy Windows Server 2003/XP and Windows Server 2008/Vista images customized with appropriate drivers, Windows update packages, and service packs, and with Microsoft Office or other applications installed. This toolkit is an excellent means for learning about deployment technologies, and many of the lessons it teaches are applicable to the other network management framework deployment packages that are available.

The deployment tools that are part of this package include the following:

- **Application Compatibility Toolkit,** which compares applications with a compatibility database.

- **Microsoft Assessment and Planning,** which compares hardware with the Hardware Compatibility List.

- **Microsoft Deployment Workbench,** a browser-like interface to all of the tools and to reference resources such as white papers on best practices.

- **Windows Automated Installation Kit (WAIK),** a set of tools for creating and deploying system images, which includes the Windows System Image Manager for managing an image library; ImageX, a command line utility for creating images; Windows Preinstallation Environment (Windows PE); and User State Migration Tool (USMT) for capturing user profile information.

- **Windows Deployment Services,** a new version of the Microsoft Remote Image Server.

Figure 30.4 shows the Windows System Image Manager tool. This tool allows you to select system images in the Windows WIM format, customize those images with drivers and installation packages, build "answer files" (which are the scripts needed to run automated Windows installations), and set the network shares that serve as the distribution shares for network installation.

FIGURE 30.4

The Windows System Image Manager tool

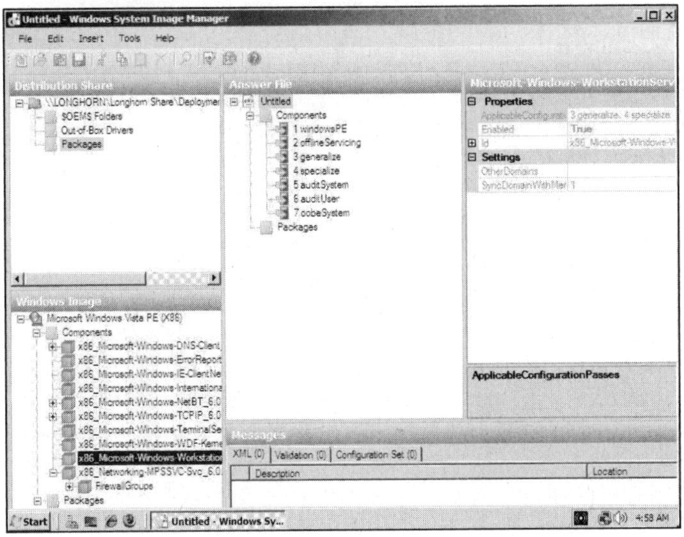

Once configured under the Microsoft Deployment Toolkit, images can be scheduled to be rolled out using either what is called a Zero Touch (automated with no user intervention or user interaction) or Lite Touch (set up manually for deployment upon request by an administrator) deployment method. The images you create can be deployed using Microsoft System Center Configuration Manager 2007, or the older version of this management framework package, Microsoft System Management Server 2003 (SMS).

With hardware support, all late-version computers support what is known as the Preboot Execution Environment, or PXE. In a system configured to boot to PXE and enabled in the BIOS to do so, a computer will boot up into a very minimal operating system and begin a discovery process for a PXE server over the network. If the system discovers the PXE server, they exchange credentials and begin a process by which the entire system image is sent over the wire from server to client. PXE is used in thin client-server applications, but it can also be used to remotely deploy a disk image to a computer system.

Tip

If your intent is to bring a system back to the same state after a user has completed their session, there are better methods to refresh a system than doing an over-the-wire restore from a system image. Consider using a tool such as Windows SteadyState (www.microsoft.com/windows/products/winfamily/sharedaccess/default.mspx) or Faronics Deep Freeze (www.faronics.com/). Doing so avoids having to service all of the traffic involved in moving gigabytes of data about the network.

Configuration management software may aid in testing and validating standard system reference images, managing image libraries, and performing remote installation of these images across a network.

State 3. Systems are aging and must be monitored.

As systems age, configuration management software not only provides the ability to allow for asset management (as described later in the chapter), but it also allows intelligent decisions to be made based on the age, utilization, license requirements, and performance of these systems. There are a large number of network monitoring packages available on the market to service this particular function. Among the important features of a monitoring package are:

- Device auto discovery (almost all monitor programs use SNMP) and mapping
- Agent deployment and distributed monitoring
- Event logging, triggers, and alerts
- Trend data, charting, reports (including Service Level Agreement, or SLA), and prediction
- Inventory
- License compliance
- Scripting and extensibility through plug-ins
- Web interface

Different packages support different sets of the features in the list above.

Note

A jump page comparing a number of different network monitoring software systems is maintained at en.wikipedia.org/wiki/Comparison_of_network_monitoring_systems. Another jump page for network monitoring tools may be found on the Stanford SLAC Web site at www.slac.stanford.edu/xorg/nmtf/nmtf-tools.html.

State 4. Systems require a patch or minor upgrade that must be applied.

While there are many different systems for applying system patches, application upgrades, or full service packs, many organizations simply allow their users or systems to automatically update themselves. However, patches, upgrades, and any software that needs to be deployed slipstream into a production system are best configured using a policy engine. With a policy engine, you can set rules that determine who gets which software and when, and you can script or automate these upgrades as network installations. In carefully managed systems, any software upgrade is tested before deployment.

State 5. Systems are obsolete and must be significantly upgraded.

The computers produced over the last few years are often significantly more powerful than the original operating system that they shipped with required. Therefore, it is certainly possible that as the system ages, updating the system contains additional value that a networked organization can capture. There are three different methods used for upgrading systems:

- **Bare Metal.** This is a fresh installation onto a system that removes all previous data.

- **In-Place Upgrade.** The system is upgraded by a new version installed over the old system. For most network operating systems and applications, in-place upgrades are supported if the version difference isn't too great. This upgrade retains user settings.

- **Side-by-Side Upgrade.** In a side-by-side upgrade, applications and settings are migrated from the old system to a system containing a newer version of the operating system. This is the most difficult upgrade to perform.

As a general rule, bare metal installations create the cleanest, most stable system but do not preserve the investment the user has in their system's configuration. In-place upgrades are a reasonable compromise that creates a workable system that may require additional work to eliminate faults. Side-by-side upgrades are the most difficult to achieve and require special software that compares applications to a database of known good, compatible versions.

In Microsoft's deployment technology, the Application Compatibility Toolkit (ACT) performs this application validation function. ACT works by deploying a set of agents on systems that will be upgraded, and collecting system information. That information is then collected and compared at a management console, which is populated with information from the online Microsoft Compatibility Exchange service. That service also provides a resource that can be used to obtain additional information about compatibility, as well as discuss online with other professionals experiences that they are having. Microsoft System Center Operations Manager (SCOM) may be used to deploy ACT agents and to manage this process.

Figure 30.5 shows how ACT works in concert with Microsoft's Compatibility Exchange operating through a network framework management console. In Figure 30.5, systems on a LAN/WAN have a set of agents deployed on them: inventory, user settings, browser, and others. Those agents report on the condition of individual systems and send the data in XML format to a Log Processing server, which stores the data in a SQL database. The data in the database is used by the Application Compatibility server to determine in concert with the Microsoft Compatibility Exchange service what steps must be taken to correct deficiencies.

FIGURE 30.5

Microsoft ACT is an agent-based network inventory system that can work with Microsoft System Center, and which is used to check application compatibilities for upgrade deployments.

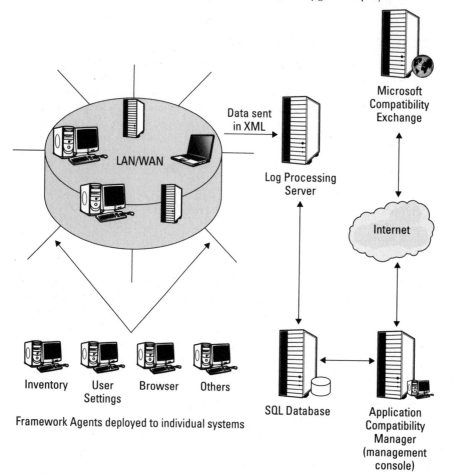

System upgrades are, like any operating system deployment, installable over a network using network management tools. However, unlike fresh installations, system upgrades often require network tools to capture, store, and restore the customization and personalization settings as well as user data from the old system to the upgraded system. These settings are a "user state," which is not only the user's profile (in Documents and Settings on a Windows system, for example) but also their data. When a system is multiuser, you need to capture multiple user states. Microsoft's deployment technology uses a command line tool called SCANSTATE to capture user states, and a complementary tool called LOADSTATE to restore state data.

State 6. Systems are obsolete and must be replaced.

The last stage is the recognition that a system is no longer useful. Systems that are at the end of life may find use in less demanding applications such as a router, a PBX, or some similar applications. Some systems may also be useful to others, while some simply need to be discarded.

Accounting and administration

The accounting function in network management tools refers to the measurement of usage data for the purposes of billing customers or departments, ensuring that services are being distributed fairly, or validating that an organization has met its Service Level Agreements (SLAs) for network services. Accounting services rely on trend data supplied by performance-monitoring tools with the additional ability to determine which users or groups are either responsible for or the beneficiary of that particular activity.

Examples of common network functions that are collected for billing purposes are:

- The amount of data flowing through a connection
- The number of particular events related to an activity such as creating a remote connection
- The amount of a particular network resource, such as a shared disk, that has been consumed
- Peak usage rates

Accounting functions are built into a number of different protocols, including RADIUS, TACACS, and Diameters, all of which are referred to as AAA services. AAA, as you will learn in Chapter 30, stands for Authentication, Authorization, and Accounting. RADIUS, for example, is a connection protocol that stands for Remote Authentication Dial-In User Service and is used by ISPs, e-mail services, network access points, Web servers, and many other network functions where security and accounting operations both need to be performed. AAA servers typically pass some functions, such as authentication, through to other network services.

Accounting is available in many network framework products, although typically this function is purchased as an add-in module and is not part of a core product that you might buy from a vendor. The exceptions to this rule are network framework products that service industries such as the ones mentioned previously.

Because many networks do not require an accounting function, the term *administration* has been used as an alternate function to satisfy the FCAPS acronym. Administrative functions would include the management of users and groups, setting access to resources, and providing access to important network functions, such as setting policies, running backup or replication, managing backups, and configuring storage, among other tasks. The different administration functions in network framework tools vary considerably, and there is some overlap in the administrative function with other areas in FCAPS, such as security and configuration.

Performance management

The goal of performance management is to establish how a network performs under standard conditions as well as providing the means needed to optimize performance. The measurement of network performance establishes a baseline against which future changes can be compared. Performance monitors extend the use of counters and agents to quantitatively measure the information that these systems provide. The data collected by performance monitors can measure a very broad set of variables that affect the network. Here are some of the more important functions of a performance monitor:

- Network traffic as a function of the protocol used
- Network loading and throughput by node or segment
- Collision rate
- Frame error rate
- Network traffic as a function of node

The key to working with performance monitors is to understand the use of counters. Counters play an essential role in operating system development. When developers "bring up" an operating system, the counters that they add to the different modules of the operating system provide the developers with immediate feedback on the impact of the changes in the programs that have been made. So in addition to trapping and recording events, some event types are measured for frequency, duration, value, or whatever parameter is most useful to understand the particular subsystem that the counter monitors. For CPUs, you will find counters such as processor utilization, processor queue length, processor time, and so forth; for disks, you will find counters such as disk accesses, amount of data transferred, queue length, and so forth. When you open a performance monitor application, and each operating system has one, the data you see is based on counters. Any application that has been performance optimized has a set of counters that were used, and so counters are found in most enterprise-class applications such as large databases.

In Figure 30.6, the Windows Performance Monitor's Add Counters dialog box is shown. Many objects whose performance is of interest, such as network interfaces, offer numerous measured parameters that their counters are able to supply. Counters you add show up as charts in the Performance Monitor.

If you have worked with a performance monitor tool, then you know that you first select the counters to observe from what is usually a long list organized by class, and then wait for the data to populate the tool. Different operating systems give their counters with different names, and expose different sets of installed counters, although the concepts being used are nearly the same. Many counters are not exposed to users because they impact system performance when they are turned on. For example, Microsoft doesn't expose some of their disk counters, and if you are interested in those particular counters, you must first know about them and then install them. Different application vendors have different policies on the use of their counters: some expose them, others don't, and unfortunately, many application vendors don't go to the trouble of optimizing their products and therefore may not have any counters to offer. To learn more about counters, you will need to do a little research on the particular product of interest.

FIGURE 30.6

To measure different aspects of system and network performance, you need to add the counters to performance monitor tools.

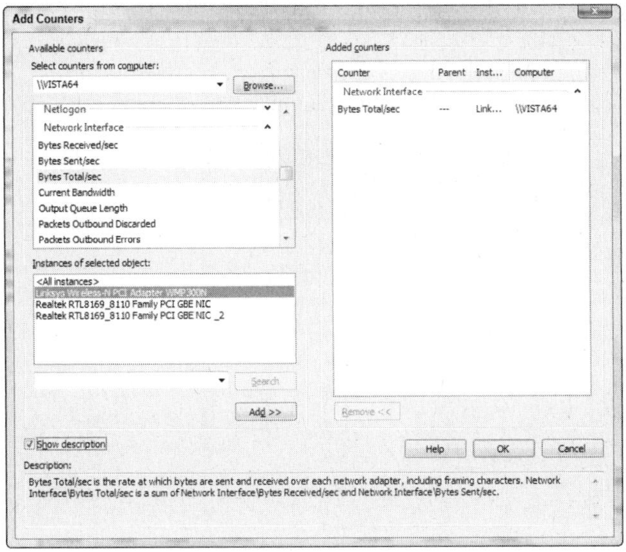

Performance studies using performance monitors can be an invaluable tool in determining network and system faults. The clearest picture is obtained by considering event types as well as event metrics. Broadly speaking, network management tools are either an event monitor or a performance monitor; a few are both. Every network operating system ships with a performance monitor. Windows performance monitor PERFMON is an MMC snap-in that can be launched as a stand-alone utility, as a component of the Task Manager (the utility you see when you press the Ctrl+Alt+Del keystroke), or as part of the Reliability and Performance Monitor, shown in Figure 30.7, that shipped with Windows Server 2008/Vista.

One particular class of network-performance monitoring tools are sniffers. These tools are known by a variety of names: packet analyzer, network analyzer, packet sniffer, Ethernet sniffer, or protocol analyzer. A packet sniffer intercepts traffic flowing over a network so that the contents may be read and analyzed, and possibly written to a log file. A packet sniffer can also decode the contents of the packet and categorize the nature of the protocols used.

Warning

Packet sniffers are the weapons of choice for many hackers. When you deploy them, you need to ensure that unauthorized personnel do not get access to these tools running on your network.

FIGURE 30.7

Windows Vista's Reliability and Performance Monitor includes the PERFMON tool, as well as fault management (reliability) tools.

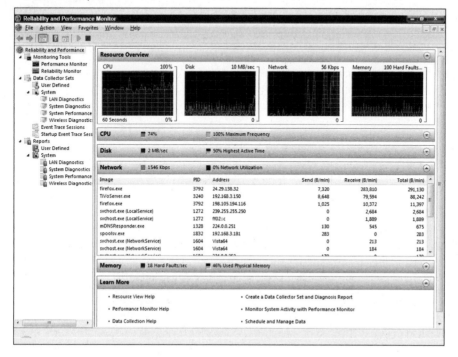

Packet sniffers can be configured so that they intercept traffic on a segment, at a switch port on a router or host, or on what is referred to as a monitor port. A monitor port takes all incoming packets to a switch and duplicates them, sending the originals onto their destination while capturing the duplicate packets for analysis. In the case of wireless networks, Wi-Fi sniffers usually capture the traffic on an individual channel. Packet sniffers are among the most widely used performance-monitoring tools available; they can be used for a range of tasks, including:

- Network fault analysis
- Detecting security breaches
- Gathering network usage statistics, creating reports, and optimizing performance
- Determining the protocols in use, and rule-based packet filtering
- Capturing sessions

There are a number of packet sniffers that you can download; most are distributed freely. Microsoft Network Monitor (NETMON; www.microsoft.com/downloads/details.aspx?familyid=f4db40af-1e08-4a21-a26b-ec2f4dc4190d&displaylang=en&tm) is perhaps the best-known sniffer used on Windows. Kismet, tcpdump, and Wireshark are available for Windows, Mac OS X, Linux, BSD, and Solaris. Sun distributes the utility SNOOP for packet sniffing on Solaris.

A high-end commercial packet sniffer is WildPackets OmniPeek (www.wildpackets.com/), a network server (hardware) and software package. OmniPeek comes with a plug-in API that allows network monitoring to be automated. OmniPeek starts at $1,200 at the time of this writing, and with plug-ins, it can remotely monitor Cisco switches and access points, Linux hosts, and other vendors' network devices. Hardware appliances of this type are sometimes referred to as network management systems (NMS).

Figure 30.8 shows a session being captured inside Microsoft Network Monitor. The frame on the left shows the different endpoints of network traffic, while the central frame on the right has the data from the actual packets. Network Monitor can run in what is called promiscuous mode, where the complete contents of a packet can be viewed.

FIGURE 30.8

Microsoft Network Monitor is a packet sniffer that you can use to evaluate traffic on your network.

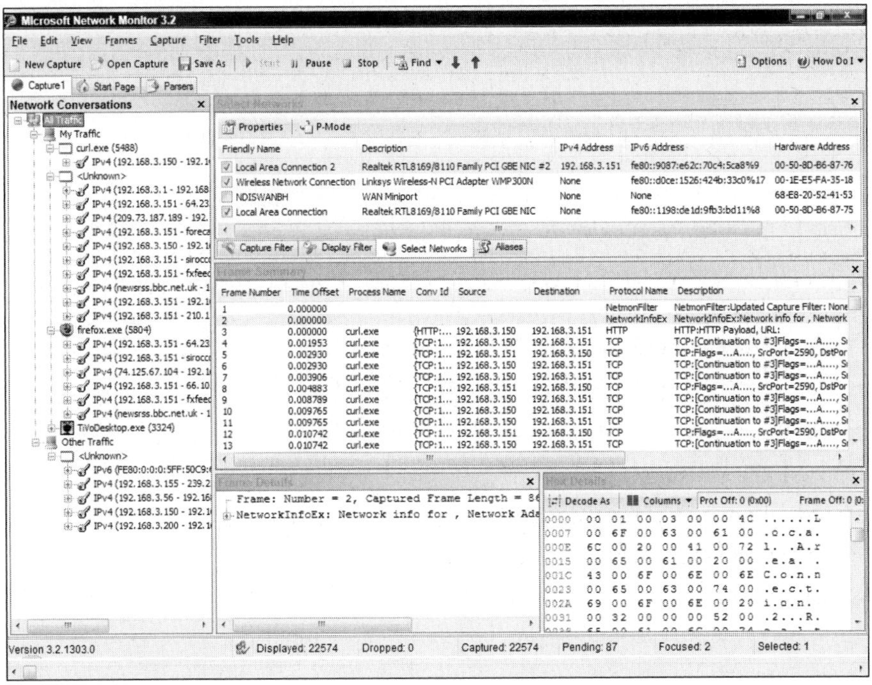

Security management

The security management function in network management tools provides the means to allow or deny access to networked resources to users and groups. Most network operating systems include security management as part of the operating system, and so for those operating systems, security management software provides a means of accessing and modifying operating system settings. This may mean that the utility provides a view of important network settings stored in directory services, access to environmental variables on systems, and other functions. For network systems that don't have directory services, the security management utility may provide the entire service.

Network security relies on two important functions: authentication of users and systems, and protection of data traveling over the network through the use of methods such as encryption. Security management software may create a key-based infrastructure, be an encyptor/decryptor, or perform other functions that allow these services to be performed. Another important category of services that security management software provides is risk assessment and risk analysis.

Network Management Software Categories

A network management framework refers to a form of system management software package that is used to integrate different categories of network utilities under a common user interface and with a common application API. The framework supplies the necessary services, such as remote agent deployment and network communications, that enable the applications to function. Some frameworks are proprietary and closed, and others are extensible and open. Most framework applications are sold in different configurations or "levels," which usually include a base or core functionality along with an a la carte menu of potential add-ons.

Pricing for these systems is highly variable and can include a base system cost, based on the number of consoles or management servers deployed, client licenses based on the number of seats, or nearly any pricing scheme that you might imagine. Because many of these installations are customized for the organization that purchases them, many network management framework vendors do not advertise pricing, and quote custom pricing on a per-job basis.

Because a framework application is designed to be customizable and therefore accommodate many different types of applications, describing the functionality of the category is similar to describing the different types of software that run under any network operating system. In some respects, a network framework is similar to a network operating system, except that a network operating system operates at all levels of the network model, whereas a network management framework is an Application layer system with elements such as remote agents and transport protocols operating at the Network layer and above.

In the list that follows, I've tried to order the different network system management functions that are typically available in the market-leading products in the order from most commonly deployed functions at the top to least commonly deployed functions at the bottom. The list has another very important characteristic that it defines: The higher up on the list a function is, the more likely it is that the function is included in the core or base network framework product. The lower down on the list a function is, the more likely it is to be purchased as an add-on module at additional cost.

The system management functions found in framework applications are:

- User and system activity monitoring
- Network resource utilization monitoring
- Asset management and inventorying
- Operating system and software deployments
- License compliance
- Backup management
- Anti-virus and anti-spyware monitoring
- Storage management
- Security management
- Directory services management

Network Frameworks

A network framework is a design specification based on published APIs (Application Programming Interfaces) that are used to create software that can be run in a similar manner or in a similar environment. With systems such as Microsoft .NET Framework or Sun's Java, the framework refers to a set of libraries, utilities, methods of programming or scripting, and other elements that are used to construct a software module. Vendors often publish the APIs for their frameworks in the hopes that developers will create applications that are useful for customers.

The Microsoft Management Console (MMC) is an example of a framework application where the goal is to provide a common interface into which modules called snap-ins may be placed so that the MMC can be configured to provide a console appropriate to the type of management or configuration that an administrator needs to do.

Table 30.1 lists some of the better-known and widely used network management packages in an approximate order in terms of their market share:

- Hewlett-Packard OpenView
- Microsoft SMS/Service Center Manager
- Novell ZENworks
- BMC Patrol
- IBM Tivoli Framework

- CA NSM (formerly Unicenter)
- Avocent LANDesk
- Symantec Altiris

Note

Hewlett-Packard's OpenView has gone through a couple of rebrandings over the last few years. The products are now part of a group of products under Hewlett-Packard Software and Services, but the names and functionality of the products remain the same.

Some of these management frameworks have a very long history to them, and support large numbers of related applications: OpenView and Tivoli are notable in this regard. Space precludes a full description of all of the tools that are available for these products, but if you want to get a sense for the range of functionality that can be managed within a network management framework, take a look at their descriptions on the Web sites noted in Table 30.1.

TABLE 30.1

Network Management Packages

Product Name	Owner	FCAPS	Platform	Reference
Altiris Management Suite	Altiris	FCAPS	Proprietary	www.symantec.com/business/theme.jsp?themeid=altiris
CA NSM (formerly Unicenter Network and Systems Management)	Computer Associates	FCAPS	Proprietary	www.ca.com/us/system-management.aspx
CiscoWorks LAN Management Solution	Cisco Systems	FCAP -	Proprietary	www.cisco.com/en/US/products/sw/cscowork/ps2425/index.html
IBM Director	IBM	FC - - -	Proprietary	www-03.ibm.com/systems/management/director/
KACE	KACE Networks	- CA - S	Proprietary, uses SNMP, WMI, and PXE	www.kace.com/
LANDesk Management Suite	LANDesk	FCAPS	Proprietary	www.landesk.com/
NetDirector	Emu Software	FC - - S	Proprietary, XML-RPC	www.netdirector.org/
Netrac	TTI Telecom	FC - P -	Proprietary	www.tti-telecom.com/

Product Name	Owner	FCAPS	Platform	Reference
OpenView	Hewlett-Packard	FCAPS	Proprietary	www.managementsoftware.hp.com/
PATROL	BMC Software	- CAP -	Proprietary	www.bmc.com
Realité	SMILabs/Digital Zone	- CA - S	Proprietary	translate.google.ru/translate?prev=_t&hl=en&ie=UTF-8&u=http%3A%2F%2Frealite.ru%2F&sl=ru&tl=en&history_state0=
Spiceworks IT Desktop	Spiceworks	F - A - -	Open source	www.spiceworks.com/
System Center Configuration Manager (formerly Systems Management Server, or SMS)	Microsoft	- CA - S	Proprietary, uses SNMP and WMI	www.microsoft.com/smserver/default.mspx
TeamQuest Performance Software	TeamQuest Corporation	- CAP -	Proprietary	www.teamquest.com/
Tivoli Framework	IBM	FCAPS	Proprietary, uses COBA, SNMP, WMI, and CIM	www-01.ibm.com/software/tivoli/
WhatsUp Gold	Ipswitch Systems	FCAPS	Proprietary	www.whatsupgold.com/
ZABBIX	ZABBIX SIA	- - AP -	Open systems, uses SNMP, ICMP, and others	www.zabbix.com/
Zenoss Core	Zenoss	FCAP -	Open system, uses SNMP, WMI, XML-RPC, and SSH	www.zenoss.com/product/advantage
ZENworks	Novell	FCAPS	Proprietary	www.zenoss.com/product/advantage
Zyrion Traverse	Zyrion	F - - P -		www.zyrion.com/

FCAPS stands for the following: F = Fault Management, C = Configuration Management, A = Accounting and Administration, P = Performance Management, and S = Security Management.

Another increasingly popular network management option is the use of a Managed Service Provider (MSP) that specializes in these types of monitoring and maintenance activities.

Summary

In this chapter, you learned about different categories of network management tools and how they are used to improve network performance and eliminate errors. This chapter used the FCAPS classification to describe network management software types. FCAPS stands for Fault, Configuration, Accounting and Administration, Performance, and Security.

Understanding events and the software that can monitor them is essential to performing network management. Events can be monitored by system counters and by agents, both of which are essentially small programs. Performance monitoring tools can be used to troubleshoot networks as well as optimize performance.

Faults can generate many duplicate events and lead to event cascades; determining faults is a challenging enterprise. Configuration management software allows you to change the configuration of different network devices, and deploy software over the network. Network deployments, upgrades, patch management, and system lifecycles were described in this chapter.

Network management systems are suites of utilities that allow you to perform various management functions. Leading framework applications and proprietary products in this area were presented.

In the next chapter, some of the tools you learned about in this chapter are applied to diagnosing different common network problems.

CHAPTER 31

Network Diagnostic Commands

This chapter focuses on the various command line tools for diagnosing network problems, determining network conditions, and modifying different network parameters. These tools allow you to sequentially test individual network components, continually narrowing down the range of potential problems until the malfunctioning part or system is located.

Command shells have been a part of computer technology since time immemorial. They remain popular with users and network administrators alike, as they allow for both powerful network command and control, as well as a lightweight environment in which testing may be done. The various command shells or command line interfaces (CLIs) used for network management are described. Many of these shells are not only single command line processors but can also run small programs or scripts. As an example of the use of the CLI in testing and isolating faults, the use of PING and IPCONFIG to test a broken Internet connection is described.

This chapter presents a collection of network-related commands for the most widely used shells in Linux, Windows, and UNIX, as well as their description and syntax. The syntax shown is a sample that varies slightly, depending upon the platform involved.

Windows NetShell's NET commands have been used since Windows NT to manage network elements. At the NETSH command line, you can manage services, change device settings, configure and attach to network resources, and gain access to Windows Management Instrumentation (WMI) objects over the network. Microsoft introduced a more powerful command line environment called PowerShell with Windows Server 2008/Vista that performs these functions and more. PowerShell is described in some detail.

Network Diagnostics

Network problems can be difficult to isolate and often require knowledge of a number of specialized tools. As network operating systems have matured and embraced a wide range of technologies, vendors have incorporated many network tools into their products. Many of these tools are command line utilities, often with powerful capabilities, while still other tools are expressed as functionality within the graphical interface of the operating system or inside a graphical utility. This chapter describes a range of network tools that you can use to diagnose problems and solve them, as well as different approaches you can use in this endeavor. Many of these tools have been presented to you in previous chapters, but in this chapter, many more new tools are described which should help give you some context of how and when to apply a specific tool.

The best approach to network diagnostic problem solving is a methodical one:

1. Document the problem requiring a solution.

2. Collect any required information regarding systems and connections involved.

3. Select the correct diagnostic tool or tools, and examine their results.

4. Continually narrow the scope of the problem.

5. Segment, isolate, and test potential faults using a process of testing, substitution, and/or swapping.

6. Confirm your hypothesis by demonstrating the removal of the fault.

Network Commands

Commands entered at the command line provide a powerful method for determining the status of a network, modifying conditions, and performing many other tasks. In the sections that follow, the various CLIs or shells found in Linux, Windows, and UNIX are briefly described and the important network-oriented commands are listed.

Command line tools

The command shell or command line interpreter is a text-based interface to a program that takes user input and translates it into commands that the operating system can act on. Different command line tools use different programming languages, and those differences, combined with differences in the way that vendors implement network operating systems, means that there is considerable variation in the syntax of network commands and the manner in which options are implemented. CLIs have been on computers since the early 1960s, and the minimal requirements of this environment, speed of command entry, and low overhead have ensured that every network operating system, or NOS, available today ships with a native CLI. Many third-party CLIs are available, and most of them are available cross-platform. Network CLI utilities form a major portion of the available command set for most systems, and this section highlights some of the more important utilities.

Note

As a general rule, working with a CLI offers a knowledgeable person more control and power over their computer environment than a GUI utility; however, it is much harder to master. I recommend that you concentrate on the purpose of the utilities and use the help within the CLI or online help to find the information you need for a specific task. Different operating systems and shells use different methods for displaying help. Among the more common methods are entering the command itself, using the / ? switch, and entering MAN <utilityname>. Googling a command usually takes you to detailed information on the command.

Command shell programs include:

- **CMD.COM.** This utility is responsible for the command prompt in Windows 7, Vista, Windows Server, Windows CE, and OS/2.

- **SH, BASH, CSH, and KSH.** These UNIX shells stand for the Bourne Shell (SH), Bourne Again Shell (BASH), C Shell (CSH), and Korn Shell (KSH). Depending upon your version of UNIX or Linux, different shells can be the default, and the system may run more than one shell. Less commonly encountered UNIX shells include the Almquist Shell (ASH) and its Debian counterpart (DASH), TENEX C Shell (TCSH), ES Shell, Easy Shell (ESH), Friendly Interactive Shell (FISH), RC Shell, Scheme Shell (SCSH), Stand-alone Shell (SASH), Windows SSH (or Secure Shell), and Z Shell (ZSH).

- **TCLSH and WISH.** These are shells used with the Tcl scripting language.

- **EFI.** The Extensible Firmware Interface (EFI) Shell runs as the BIOS replacement for modern processors.

- **Windows Script Host (WSH).** This is used on Windows to automate different Active Scripting language routines based on JScript, VBScript, PerlScript, and others (it is extensible). It is an automation technology that provides an enhanced version of batch programming capabilities. Common uses of WSH are for logon scripts, system configuration, and network management.

- **PowerShell.** This Windows scripting language is implemented as a command line shell for Windows 7, Vista, Server 2008/2003, and XP (SP2/SP3). PowerShell uses the .NET Framework to run scripts that perform administrative tasks.

- **REXX.** IBM's scripting language shell.

- **PHPsh.** A shell for the PHP language.

- **Python.** The Python interpreter can be opened in a CLI.

- **JavaScript and BeanShell.** JavaScript is an interactive interface to the JavaScript scripting language; BeanShell is a shell for Java itself. Several different versions of JavaScript exist.

Note

You can find a comparison table for command shells at http://en.wikipedia.org/wiki/Comparison_of_computer_shells.

There are many more CLI shells, but the previous list compiles the ones with the most extensive networking capabilities.

The following utilities are part of the TCP/IP command suite: ARP, FINGER, FTP, HOSTNAME, IPCONFIG/IFCONFIG, LPQ, LPR, NBTSTAT, NETSTAT, NSLOOKUP, PING, RCP, REXEC, ROUTE, RSH, TFTP, and TRACERT. They have been covered in detail in previous chapters.

Cross-Ref
Many of the TCP and IP commands are covered in Chapters 17 and 18, respectively.

Let's consider one set of commonly encountered problems for which the command line utilities are particularly convenient and powerful: a browser that does not connect to the Internet. To fix a broken Internet connection, you might do the following:

1. Open a second browser and verify that the first browser isn't the reason that Internet data can't be browsed.

2. Open a command prompt and enter **PING WWW.YAHOO.COM**.

   A successful PING indicates that you have a working Internet connection and that you can resolve DNS names to IP addresses. The problem is probably related to the browser in question. Yahoo was selected as an example because it is a site that is almost always available, and one that hasn't turned its PING response off. Any other similar site will do.

3. At the command prompt, enter **PING 69.147.76.15** (This is the IP Address for www. yahoo.com).

   A successful PING indicates that you have a working Internet connection, but that you couldn't resolve external DNS queries. To fix this problem, you would check your DNS references, and if you were running a DNS server, you would check the DNS server.

4. At the command prompt, enter **PING** *<Gateway IP address>*.

   The Gateway address to use is the one entered into the network interface used for the Internet connection. If the PING isn't successful, you should check the conditions of the gateway (or firewall) as well as any cables leading to the gateway.

5. At the command prompt, enter **PING** *<Network Node Name>*.

   The node can be any network system or router that allows you to trace the route back from the gateway to your host. The command PING *<Network Node Address>* can also be used to check systems and DNS settings. If you have eliminated any connection errors leading up to your system, then the last set of settings to check is the local host itself.

6. At the command prompt, enter IPCONFIG (on Windows or Macintosh) or IFCONFIG (on UNIX or Linux).

   If the address settings are incorrect, then change them; if there is no assigned dynamic IP address, refresh your DHCP settings or check the status of your DHCP server. Use IPCONFIG/RELEASE and IPCONFIG/RENEW for this purpose. (Different platforms use slightly different switches.)

PING always returns one of these responses:

- **Normal response.** The host is alive within the Time-to-Live parameter (usually 1 to 10 hops).
- **Destination does not respond.** No answer was returned.
- **Unknown host.** The host is unknown and cannot be reached.
- **Destination unreachable.** The target is known but the default gateway cannot reach the target.
- **Network or host unreachable.** There is no entry in the route table for the host or network.

Steps 1 to 6 illustrate the practice of continually narrowing the scope of your troubleshooting and thus are theoretically considered best practice. In the real world, however, a problem with the local host is a more likely event than other steps on the list, and so I tend to try an IPCONFIG/IFCONFIG early in the process. Figure 31.1 shows a sequence similar to the one described.

FIGURE 31.1

A sample session attempting to diagnose a network connection for browser connectivity

Let's assume that you performed all of the steps above and that your network interface is up, all of your intermediate nodes respond to PINGs, and you can resolve DNS queries to get a named Internet site to respond to a PING. All parts of your Internet connection are functioning, but your

browser still doesn't operate correctly, and information isn't displaying correctly. The next steps that you need to take check for other aspects of connectivity. Examine the response times to see if they are reasonable. Usually, long response times are associated with a certain number of "did not respond" responses. You may want to use the TRACEROUTE command to check the path used to destination sites, as well as the performance of each hop on the route.

The next step in checking connectivity is to determine if the particular protocol you are using can be sent and received. A PING traverses the same port that your browser's HTTP traffic does, the well-known port 80, or if your firewall supports it, a port that maps to port 80. Microsoft ISA Server, for example, uses port 8080 for HTTP traffic by default. You should check your firewall settings — both your network firewall and any local firewall — to determine that HTTP traffic is allowed, and, more importantly, that this particular browser is an approved application to use the HTTP port.

In Table 31.1, various CLI networking commands for Linux (L), Windows (W), and UNIX (U) are highlighted. Although syntax for these commands is listed in Table 31.1, the syntax varies depending upon which shell you are using, and in the case of Windows, which particular version of that operating system you are using. The syntax shown for Windows is based on CMD.COM for Windows XP. You should check your current platform's documentation to obtain the correct syntax and to get an explanation of the various options and switches.

TABLE 31.1

Command Line Commands for Networking

Command	Platform	Description	Syntax
AC	L/U	Print user connect time statistics.	AC [**-d** | --daily-totals] [**-y** | --print-year] [**-p** | --individual-totals] [people] [**-f** | --file filename] [**-a** | --all-days] [--complain] [**--reboots**] [**--supplants**] [**--timewarps**] [**--compatibility**] [**--tw-leniency num**] [**--tw-suspicious num**] [**-z** | --print-zeros] [**--debug**] [**-V** | --version] [**-h** | --help]
ARP	L/U/W	Displays and modifies entries in the Address Resolution Protocol (ARP) cache, which contains one or more tables that are used to store IP addresses and their resolved Ethernet or Token Ring physical addresses. There is a separate table for each Ethernet or Token Ring network adapter installed on your computer.	ARP [-**a** [InetAddr] [-**N** IfaceAddr]] [-**g** [InetAddr] [-**N** IfaceAddr]] [-**d** InetAddr [IfaceAddr]] [-**s** InetAddr EtherAddr [IfaceAddr]]

Command	Platform	Description	Syntax
ATMADM	W	Monitors connections and addresses that are registered by the ATM Call Manager on an asynchronous transfer mode (ATM) network. You can use atmadm to display statistics for incoming and outgoing calls on ATM adapters. Used without parameters, atmadm displays statistics for monitoring the status of active ATM connections.	ATMADM [/c] [/a] [/s]
BASH	L/U	Starts the BASH Shell.	BASH [options]
CHDIR (CD)	L/W/U	Displays the name of the current directory or changes the current folder. Used with only a drive letter (for example, CHDIR C:), chdir displays the names of the current drive and folder. Used without parameters, chdir displays the current drive and directory.	CHDIR [[/d] [Drive:][Path] [..]] [[/d] [Drive:][Path] [..]] CD [[/d] [Drive:][Path] [..]] [[/d] [Drive:][Path] [..]]
CHKDSK	W	Creates and displays a status report for the disk. The CHKDSK command also lists and corrects errors on the disk. The CHKDSK command with the parameters listed below is only available when you are using the Recovery Console. The CHKDSK command with different parameters is available from the command prompt.	CHKDSK [drive:] [/p] [/r]
CMSTP	W	Installs or removes a Connection Manager service profile. Used without optional parameters, CMSTP installs a service profile with default settings appropriate to the operating system and to the user's permissions.	ServiceProfileFileName.**exe** **/q:a /c:"cmstp.exe** ServiceProfileFileName.**inf** [/nf] **[/ni]** **[/ns]** **[/s]** **[/su]** **[/u]"** **cmstp.exe** [/nf] [/ni] [/ns] [/s] **[/su]** [/u] "[Drive:][Path] ServiceProfileFileName.**inf"**
COMP	W	Compares the contents of two files or sets of files byte by byte. COMP can compare files on the same drive or on different drives, and in the same directory or in different directories. When COMP compares the files, it displays their locations and filenames. Used without parameters, COMP prompts you to enter the files to compare.	COMP [data1] [data2] [/d] [/a] [/l] [/n=number] [/c]

continued

TABLE 31.1   *(continued)*

Command	Platform	Description	Syntax
COMPACT	W	Displays and alters the compression of files or directories on NTFS partitions. Used without parameters, COMPACT displays the compression state of the current directory.	COMPACT [{/**c** | /**u**}] [/**s**[:*dir*]] [/**a**] [/**i**] [/**f**] [/**q**] [*FileName*[...]]
COMPRESS	L/U	Compresses a file and adds the .z extension.	COMPRESS [-**c**][-**f**][-**v**] *file-names*
COPY (CP)	L/W/U	Copies one or more files from one location to another.	COPY [/**d**] [/**v**] [/**n**] [{/**y** | /-**y**}] [/**z**] [{/**a** | /**b**}] *Source* [{/**a** | /**b**}] [+ *Source* [{/**a** | /**b**}] [+ ...]] [*Destination* [{/**a** | /**b**}]]
CRONTAB	L/U	Creates and lists files that run on a schedule.	CRONTAB [-**e**] [-**l**] [-**r**] [*filename*]
CSH	L/U	Starts the C Shell.	CSH [-**b**] [-**c**] [-**e**] [-**f**] [-**i**] [-**n**] [-**s**] [-**t**] [-**v**] [-**V**] [-**x**] [-**X**] [*scriptname*]]
DHCLIENT	L/U	The Dynamic Host Configuration Protocol Client automatically assigns IP addressing to a DHCP client	DHCLIENT [-**p** *port*] [-**d**] [-**e** *VAR=value*] [-**q**] [-**1**] [-**r**] [-**lf** *lease-file*] [-**pf** *pid-file*] [-**cf** *config-file*] [-**sf** *script-file*] [-**e** *ENVVAR=value*] [-**s** *server*] [-**g** *relay*] [-**n**] [-**nw**] [-**w**] [*if0* [...*ifN*]]
DIG	L/U	The DNS lookup utility automatically converts friendly names to IP addresses.	DIG [@*server*] [-**b** *address*] [-**c** *class*] [-**f** *filename*] [-**k** *file-name*] [-**p** *port#*] [-**t** *type*] [-**x** *addr*] [-**y** *name:key*] [-**4**] [-**6**] [**name**] [**type**] [**class**] [**queryopt**...]
DIRCMP	L/W/U	Compares files in two directories and indicates whether they are identical or not.	DIRCMP [-**d**] [-**s**] [-**w** *n*] *directoryone directorytwo*
DISKCOPY	W	Copies the contents of the floppy disk in the source drive to a formatted or unformatted floppy disk in the destination drive. Used without parameters, DISKCOPY uses the current drive for the source disk and the destination disk.	DISKCOPY [*drive1*: [*drive2*:]] [/**v**]

Command	Platform	Description	Syntax
EXPAND	L/W/U	Expands one or more compressed files. This command is used to retrieve compressed files from distribution disks.	EXPAND [-r] *Source* [*Destination*] EXPAND **-d** *source.cab* [**-f:***files*] EXPAND *source.cab* **-f:***files Destination*
FINGER	L/W/U	Displays information about a user or users on a specified remote computer (typically a computer running UNIX) that is running the Finger service or daemon. The remote computer specifies the format and output of the user information display. Used without parameters, FINGER displays help.	FINGER [**-l**] [*User*] [*@host*] [...]
FTP	L/W/U	Transfers files to and from a computer running a File Transfer Protocol (FTP) service such as Internet Information Services. FTP can be used interactively or in batch mode by processing ASCII text files.	FTP [**-v**] [**-d**] [**-i**] [**-n**] [**-g**] [**-s:***FileName*] [**-a**] [**-w:***WindowSize*] [**-A**] [*Host*]
GETFACL	L/U	Shows file attributes.	GETFACL [**-a**] [**-d**] *file*
GETMAC	W	Returns the Media Access Control (MAC) address and list of network protocols associated with each address for all network cards in each computer, either locally or across a network.	GETMAC[**.exe**] [**/s** *Computer* [**/u** *Domain\User* [**/p** *Password*]]] [**/fo** {**TABLE**|**LIST**|**CSV**}] [**/nh**] [**/v**]
GPRESULT	W	Displays Group Policy settings and Resultant Set of Policy (RSOP) for a user or a computer.	GPRESULT [**/s** *Computer* [**/u** *Domain\User* /**p** *Password*]] [**/user** *TargetUserName*] [**/scope** {**user** | **computer**}] [**/v**] [**/z**]
HOST	L/U	The DNS lookup utility converts friendly names to IP addresses.	HOST [**-a***CdlnrTwv*] [**-c** *class*] [**-N** *ndots*] [**-R** *number*] [**-t** *type*] [**-W** *wait*] [**-4**] [**-6**] {*name*} [**-***]
HOSTNAME	L/W/U	Displays the host name portion of the full computer name of the computer.	HOSTNAME
IPCONFIG	W	Displays all current TCP/IP network configuration values and refreshes Dynamic Host Configuration Protocol (DHCP) and Domain Name System (DNS) settings. Used without parameters, IPCONFIG displays the IP address, subnet mask, and default gateway for all adapters.	IPCONFIG [**/all**] [**/renew** [*Adapter*]] [**/release** [*Adapter*]] [**/flushdns**] [**/displaydns**] [**/registerdns**] [**/showclassid** *Adapter*] [**/setclassid** *Adapter* [*ClassID*]]

continued

TABLE 31.1 *(continued)*

Command	Platform	Description	Syntax
IFCONFIG	L/U	An identical command to IPCONFIG on Windows with platform-specific parameters.	IFCONFIG [-L] [-m] **interface** [*create*] [*address_family*] [**address**[*/prefixlength*] [*dest_address*]] [*parameters*]
			IFCONFIG **interface** *destroy*
			IFCONFIG **-a** [**-L**] [**-d**] [**-m**] [**-u**] [*address_family*]
			IFCONFIG **-l** [**-d**] [**-u**] [*address_family*]
			IFCONFIG [**-L**] [**-d**] [**-m**] [**-u**] [**-C**]
IFUP / IFDOWN	L/U	Closes or opens a network interface.	IFUP [**-nv**] [**--no-act**] [**--verbose**] [**-i FILE**|*--interfaces=FILE*] [**--allow CLASS**] **-a**|**IFACE**...
			IFDOWN [**-nv**] [**--no-act**] [**--verbose**] [**-i FILE**|*--interfaces=FILE*] [**--allow CLASS**] **-a**|*IFACE*...
IPSECCMD	W	Configures Internet Protocol Security (IPSec) policies in a directory service or in a local or remote registry. IPSECCMD is a command line alternative to the IP Security Policies Microsoft Management Console (MMC) snap-in. IPSECCMD has three modes: dynamic mode, static mode, and query mode.	To add a rule: IPSECCMD [\\ *ComputerName*] **-f** *FilterList* [**-n** *NegotiationPolicyList*] [**-t** *TunnelAddr*] [**-a** *AuthMethodList*] [**-1s** *SecurityMethodList*] [**-1k** *MainModeRekeySettings*] [**-1p**] [**-1f** *MMFilterList*] [**-1e** *SoftSAExpirationTime*] [**-soft**] [**-confirm**] [{**-dialup**	**-lan**}] To delete all dynamic policies: IPSECCMD **-u**
IPXROUTE	W	Displays and modifies information about the routing tables used by the IPX protocol. Used without parameters, IPXROUTE displays the default settings for packets that are sent to unknown, broadcast, and multicast addresses.	IPXROUTE **servers** [*/type=x*] IPXROUTE **ripout** *network* IPXROUTE **resolve** {**guid**	**name**} {*guid*	*AdapterName*} IPXROUTE **board**= *n* [**def**] [**gbr**] [**mbr**] [**remove**=*xxxxxxxxxxx*] IPXROUTE **config**

Command	Platform	Description	Syntax
IRFTP	W	Sends files over an infrared link. Used without parameters or used with **/s**, IRFTP opens the Wireless Link dialog box, where you can select the files that you want to send without using the command line.	IRFTP [*Drive*:\] [[*Path*] *FileName*] [/**h**] IRFTP /**s**
KSH	L/U	Starts the Korn Shell.	KSH [-**a**] [-**b**] [-**C**] [-**e**] [-**f**] [-**h**] [-**i**] [-**k**] [-**m**] [-**n**] [-**o**] [-**p**] [-**s**] [-**t**] [-**u**] [-**v**] [-**x**] [+ **o** *option*] [+**A** *name*] [*arg*]
LODCTR	W	Registers new Performance counter names and Explain text for a service or device driver, and saves and restores counter settings and Explain text.	LODCTR [*ComputerName*] *FileName* [/**s**:*FileName*] [/**r**:*FileName*]
LOGMAN	W	Manages and schedules performance counter and event trace log collections on local and remote systems.	LOGMAN [**create** {*counter* | *trace*} *collection_name*] [**start** *collection_name*] [**stop** *collection_name*] [**delete** *collection_name*] [**query** {*collection_name*|**providers**}] [**update** *collection_name*]
LPQ	L/U/W	Displays the status of a print queue on a computer running Line Printer Daemon (LPD). Used without parameters, LPQ displays command line help for the LPQ command.	LPQ –**S** *ServerName* -**P** *PrinterName* [-**l**]
LPR	L/U/W	Sends a file to a computer running Line Printer Daemon (LPD) in preparation for printing. Used without parameters, LPR displays command line help for the LPR command.	LPR [-**S** *ServerID*] -**P** *PrinterName* [-**C** *BannerContent*] [-**J** *JobName*] [{-**o** | -**o l**}] [-**d**] [-**x**] *FileName*
MII-TOOL	L/U	A utility that views or sets the network interface Media Independent Interface (MII) unit. Fast 433333 Ethernet adapters use this function to negotiate link parameters.	MII-TOOL [-**v**, --*verbose*] [-**V**, --*version*] [-**R**, --*reset*] [-**r**, --*restart*] [-**w**, --*watch*] [-**l**, --*log*] [-**A**, --*advertise=media*,...] [-**F**, --*force=media*] [*interface* ...]
MKDIR	L/W/U	Creates a directory or subdirectory.	MKDIR [*Drive*:]*Path* MD [*Drive*:]*Path*

continued

TABLE 31.1 *(continued)*

Command	Platform	Description	Syntax
MOUNT / UMOUNT	L//U	Mounts or unmounts file systems and remote system resources.	MOUNT [**-p** | **-v**]
			MOUNT [**-F** *FSType*] [*generic_ options*] [**-o** *specific_options*] [**-O**] **special** | *mount_point*
			MOUNT [**-F** *FSType*] [*generic_ options*] [**-o** *specific_options*] [**-O**] **special mount_point**
			MOUNT **-a** [**-F** *FSType*] [**-V**] [*current_options*] [**-o** *specific_ options*] [*mount_point ...*]
			UMOUNT [-V] [-o specific_ options] special |mount_point
			UMOUNT -a [-V] [-o specific_ options] [mount_point...]
MOUNTVOL	W	Creates, deletes, or lists a volume mount point. MOUNTVOL is a way to link volumes without requiring a drive letter.	MOUNTVOL [*Drive:*]*Path VolumeName*
			MOUNTVOL [*Drive:*]*Path* **/d**
			MOUNTVOL [*Drive:*]*Path* **/L**
			MOUNTVOL *Drive:* **/s**
MOVE (MV)	L/W/U	Moves one or more files from one directory to the specified directory.	MOVE [{**/y** | **/-y**}] [*source*] [*target*]
			mv [**-f**] [**-i**] [*source*] [*target*]
NBTSTAT	W	Displays NetBIOS over TCP/IP (NetBT) protocol statistics, NetBIOS name tables for both the local computer and remote computers, and the NetBIOS name cache. NBTSTAT allows a refresh of the NetBIOS name cache and the names registered with Windows Internet Name Service (WINS). Used without parameters, NBTSTAT displays help.	NBTSTAT [**-a** *RemoteName*] [**-A** *IPAddress*] [**-c**] [**-n**] [**-r**] [**-R**] [**-RR**] [**-s**] [**-S**] [*Interval*]
NETSTAT	L/W/U	Displays active TCP connections, ports on which the computer is listening, Ethernet statistics, the IP routing table, IPv4 statistics (for the IP, ICMP, TCP, and UDP protocols), and IPv6 statistics (for the IPv6, ICMPv6, TCP over IPv6, and UDP over IPv6 protocols). Used without parameters, NETSTAT displays active TCP connections.	NETSTAT [**-a**] [**-e**] [**-n**] [**-o**] [**-p** *Protocol*] [**-r**] [**-s**] [*Interval*]

Command	Platform	Description	Syntax
NSLOOKUP	L/W/U	Displays information that you can use to diagnose Domain Name System (DNS) infrastructure. Before using this tool, you should be familiar with how DNS works. The NSLOOKUP command line tool is available only if you have installed the TCP/IP protocol.	NSLOOKUP [-SubCommand ...] [{ComputerToFind| [-Server]}] Subcommands: EXIT, FINGER, HELP, LS, LSERVER, ROOT, SERVER, SET, SET ALL, SET CLASS, SET D2, SET DEBUG, SET DEFNAME, SET DOMAIN, SET IGNORE, SET PORT, SET QUERYTYPE, SET RECURSIVE, SET RETRY, SET ROOT, SET SEARCH, SET SRCHLIST, SET TIMEOUT, SET TYPE, SET VC, and VIEW
PATHPING	W	Provides information about network latency and network loss at intermediate hops between a source and destination. PATHPING sends multiple Echo Request messages to each router between a source and destination over a period of time, and then computes results based on the packets returned from each router. Because PATHPING displays the degree of packet loss at any given router or link, you can determine which routers or subnets might be having network problems. PATHPING performs the equivalent of the TRACERT command by identifying which routers are on the path. It then sends pings periodically to all of the routers over a specified time period and computes statistics based on the number returned from each.	PATHPING [-n] [-h MaximumHops] [-g HostList] [-p Period] [-q NumQueries [-w Timeout] [-T] [-R] [TargetName]
PERFMON	W	Allows you to open a Windows Performance console.	PERFMON.exe [file_name] [/HTMLFILE:converted_file settings_file]
PING	L/W/U	Verifies IP-level connectivity to another TCP/IP computer by sending Internet Control Message Protocol (ICMP) Echo Request messages. The receipt of corresponding Echo Reply messages is displayed, along with round-trip times. PING is the primary TCP/IP command used to troubleshoot connectivity, reachability, and name resolution.	PING [-t] [-a] [-n Count] [-l Size] [-f] [-i TTL] [-v TOS] [-r Count] [-s Count] [{-j HostList | -k HostList}] [-w Timeout] [TargetName]

continued

TABLE 31.1	(continued)		
Command	**Platform**	**Description**	**Syntax**
PRINT	W	Sends a text file to a printer.	PRINT [**/d:**Printer] [Drive:] [Path] FileName [...]
RASDIAL	W	You can automate the connection process for any Microsoft client by using a simple batch file and the RASDIAL command. The RASDIAL command starts a network connection by using a specified entry.	RASDIAL connectionname [username [password | *]] [/ domain:domain] [/ phone:phonenumber] [/ callback:callbacknumber] [/ phonebook:phonebookpath] [/ prefixsuffix] The RASDIAL command disconnects a network connection by using the following syntax: RASDIAL [connectionname] / disconnect
RCP	L/U/W	Copies files between a Windows XP computer and a system running RSHD, the remote shell service (daemon). Windows XP and Windows 2000 do not provide RSHD service.	RCP [{**-a** | **-b**}] [**-h**] [**-r**] [host] [.user:] [Source] [Host][.User:] [Path\Destination]
RELOG	W	Extracts performance counters from performance counter logs into other formats, such as text-TSV (for tab-delimited text), text-CSV (for comma-delimited text), binary-BIN, or SQL.	RELOG [FileName [filename ...]] [**-a**] [**-c** Path [path ...]] [**-cf** FileName] [**-f** {**bin** | **csv** | **tsv** | **SQL**}] [**-t** value] [**-o** {output file | DSN!counter_log}] [**-b** M/d/yyyy [[hh:]mm:]ss] [**-e** M/d/yyyy [[hh:]mm:]ss] [**-config** FileName] [**-q**]
RENAME (REN)	W	Changes the name of a file or a set of files.	RENAME [Drive:][Path] filename1 filename2 REN [Drive:][Path] filename1 filename2
REMSH (rsh)	L/U/W	The remote shell command allows you to run a command on a different system.	REMSH [options] [**-l** username] hostname [#port] command
REPLACE	W	Replaces files in the destination directory with files in the source directory that have the same name. You can also use REPLACE to add unique filenames to the destination directory.	REPLACE [drive1:][path1] FileName [drive2:][path2] [**/a**] [**/p**] [**/r**] [**/w**] REPLACE [drive1:][path1] FileName [drive2:][path2] [**/p**] [**/r**] [**/s**] [**/w**] [**/u**]

Command	Platform	Description	Syntax
REXEC	L/U/W	Runs commands on remote computers running the REXEC service (daemon). The REXEC command authenticates the username on the remote computer before executing the specified command. Windows XP and Windows 2000 do not provide the REXEC service.	REXEC [*Host*] [**-l** *UserName*] [**-n**] [*Command*]
RMDIR (RD)	L/U/W	Removes (or deletes) a directory.	RMDIR [*Drive:*]*Path* [**/s**] [**/q**] RD [*Drive:*]*Path* [**/s**] [**/q**]
ROUTE	W	Displays and modifies the entries in the local IP routing table.	ROUTE [**-f**] [**-p**] [*Command* [*Destination*] [**mask** *Netmask*] [*Gateway*] [**metric** *Metric*]] [**if** *Interface*]]
RSH	W	Runs commands on remote computers running the RSH service or daemon. Windows XP and Windows 2000 do not provide an RSH service.	RSH [*Host*] [**-l** *UserName*] [**-n**] [*Command*]
SH	L/U	Runs jobs through the Bourne Shell.	SH [**-a**] [**-c**] [**-C**] [**-e**] [**-E**] [**-f**] [**-h**] [**-i**] [**-l**] [**-k**] [**-m**] [**-n**] [**-p**] [**-r**] [**-s**] [**-t**] [**-T**] [**-u**] [**-v**] [**-x**] [*argument*]
SHUTDOWN	L/U/W	Allows you to shut down or restart a local or remote computer. Used without parameters, SHUTDOWN will logoff the current user.	SHUTDOWN [{**-l** | **-s** | **-r** | **-a**}] [**-f**] [**-m** [*ComputerName*]] [**-t** *xx*] [**-c** "*message*"] [**-d**[**u**] [**p**]:*xx:yy*]
SUBST	W	Associates a path with a drive letter. Used without parameters, SUBST displays the names of the virtual drives that your system knows about.	SUBST [*drive1*: [*drive2:*]*Path*] SUBST *drive1* : **/d**
TASKKILL	W	Ends one or more tasks or processes on a local (default) or remote system. Processes can be killed by process ID or image name.	TASKKILL [**/s** *Computer*] [**/u** *Domain\User* [**/p** *Password*]]] [**/fi** *FilterName*] [**/pid** *ProcessID*]|[**/im** *ImageName*] [**/f**] [**/t**]
TASKLIST	W	Displays a list of applications and services with their Process ID (PID) for all tasks running on either a local or a remote computer.	TASKLIST [**.exe**] [**/s** *computer*] [**/u** *domain\user* [**/p** *password*]] [**/fo** {**TABLE** | **LIST** | **CSV**}] [**/nh**] [**/fi** *FilterName* [**/fi** *FilterName2* [...]]] [**/m** [*ModuleName*] | **/svc** | **/v**]

continued

TABLE 31.1 *(continued)*			
Command	**Platform**	**Description**	**Syntax**
TCMSETUP	W	Sets up or disables the TAPI client.	TCMSETUP [**/q**] [**/x**] **/c** *Server1* [*Server2...*]
			TCMSETUP [**/q**] **/c /d**
TELNET	L/W/U	The TELNET commands allow you to communicate with a remote computer that is using the Telnet protocol. You can run TELNET without parameters in order to enter the Telnet context, indicated by the TELNET prompt (TELNET >). From the TELNET prompt, use the following commands to manage a computer running Telnet Client: CLOSE, DISPLAY, ENTER, OPEN, QUIT, SET, STATIS. UNSET, and ?/HELP with their appropriate parameters.	TELNET [*RemoteServer*] Telnet Sessions are discussed later in this chapter.
TFTP	L/U/W	Transfers files to and from a remote computer, typically a computer running UNIX, that is running the Trivial File Transfer Protocol (TFTP) service or daemon.	TFTP [**-i**] [**Host**] [{**get** | **put**}] [*Source*] [*Destination*]
TRACERPT	W	Processes event trace logs or real-time data from instrumented event trace providers and allows you to generate trace analysis reports and CSV (comma-delimited) files for the events generated.	TRACERPT [*FileName* [*filename ...*]] [**-o** [*FileName*]] [**-report** [*FileName*]] [**-rt** *session_name* [*session_name ...*]] [**-summary** [*FileName*]] [**-config** [*FileName*]
TRACERT	W	Determines the path taken to a destination by sending Internet Control Message Protocol (ICMP) Echo Request messages to the destination with incrementally increasing Time-to-Live (TTL) field values. The path displayed is the list of near-side router interfaces of the routers in the path between a source host and a destination. The near-side interface is the interface of the router that is closest to the sending host in the path.	TRACERT [**-d**] [**-h** *MaximumHops*] [**-j** *HostList*] [**-w** *Timeout*] [*TargetName*]
TRACEROUTE	L/U	An identical command to TRACERT on Windows with platform-specific parameters.	TRACEROUTE [**-d**] [**-F**] [**-I**] [**-n**] [**-v**] [**-x**] [**-f** *first_ttl*] [**-g** *gateway* [**-g** *gateway*] | **-r**] [**-i** *iface*] [**-m** *max_ttl*] [**-p** *port*] [**-q** *nqueries*] [**-s** *src_addr*] [**-t** *tos*] [**-w** *waittime*] **host** [*packetlen*]

Command	Platform	Description	Syntax
TREE	W	Graphically displays the directory structure of a path or of the disk in a drive.	TREE [*Drive:*] [*Path*] [/**f**] [/**a**]
TYPEPERF	W	Writes performance counter data to the command window, or to a supported log file format. To stop TYPEPERF, press Ctrl+C.	TYPEPERF [*Path* [*path* ...]] [-**cf** *FileName*] [-**f** {*csv*|*tsv*|*bin*}] [-**si** *interval*] [-**o** *FileName*] [-**q** [*object*]] [-**qx** [*object*]] [-**sc** *samples*] [-**config** *FileName*] [-**s** *computer_name*]
UNLODCTR	W	Removes Performance counter names and Explain text for a service or device driver from the system registry.	UNLODCTR [\\ *ComputerName*] *DriverName*
W32TM	W	A tool used to diagnose problems occurring with Windows Time.	W32TM {/**config** [/**computer**: *ComputerName*] [[/**update**] [/**manualpeerlist**:*ListOf ComputerNames*]] [/**syncfrom flags**:*ListOfFlags*]]|/**monitor** |/**ntte**|/**ntpte**|/**register**|/**resync** [{:*ComputerName*] [/**nowait**]| [/**rediscover**}]|/**tz**|/**unregister**}
W	L/U	Shows the current users and tasks.	W [-**husfVo**] [*user*]
WHOIS	L/W/U	Displays the Internet username directory service.	WHOIS [-**h** *host*] *identifier*
XINIT	L/U	Starts the X window system. The STARTX script is used as the interface for XINIT	X [*options*]
XCOPY	W	Copies files and directories, including subdirectories.	XCOPY *Source* [*Destination*] [/**w**] [/**p**] [/**c**] [/**v**] [/**q**] [/**f**] [/**l**] [/**g**] [/**d**[:*mm-dd-yyyy*]] [/**u**] [/**i**] [/**s** [/**e**]] [/**t**] [/**k**] [/**r**] [/**h**] [{/**a**|/**m**}] [/**n**] [/**o**] [/**x**] [/**exclude**:*file1*[+[*file2*]] [+[*file3*]] [{/**y**|/-**y**}] [/**z**]

Source: http://technet.microsoft.com/en-us/library/bb490864.aspx.

Legend: W = Windows, Italic text indicates variable data, bold text indicates required text that must be entered, items inside brackets ([]) are optional, and those between braces ({}) are a set of choices from which only one may be used. For more details about the individual elements of these commands, refer to the source shown above.

IPCONFIG and its Linux/UNIX equivalent IFCONFIG may be the most useful TCP/IP commands in your arsenal. In addition to displaying the state of a network interface, IPCONFIG also allows you to change a static IP address, as well as release and renew any dynamic IP address.

Network Shells

Network shells are command line interfaces that support network management tools, particularly for remote administration. Consoles that are network shells exist on all platforms and are supported by local processes installed either by the operating system or by management software. A network shell has the following two requirements:

- An agent, daemon, or process must exist on the remote system that can accept a command, usually in the form of a remote process call (RPC) command.

- A client utility or shell is required that can format and send a command to the remote process.

Network shells for Windows include the NetShell environment that ships with all versions of Windows, as well as PowerShell, an administration command/scripting environment that shipped with Windows Server 2008/Vista. PowerShell is meant to replace NetShell and other Windows CLI scripting tools. The sections that follow briefly look at some of these environments.

The Windows NetShell

Windows NT introduced a command line tool for network administrators called NetShell. Using the NetShell CLI, you can carry out batch commands and scripts, or enter single commands from a central console that modifies the settings and actions of remote systems. The NetShell API, which is part of the Microsoft Windows Software Development Kit (SDK), allows developers to create helper DLLs (Dynamic Link Libraries) that implement the various NetShell commands in their programs.

A NetShell command operates in a particular context, which is scoped for a certain area of networking capabilities. For example, NetShell commands operating through a helper DLL can link to a dynamic library that controls a certain networking function and modify that function. The example usually cited is modification of the Dynamic Host Configuration Protocol (DHCP) where NetShell commands are directed to the `DHCPCSVC.DLL` dynamic link library that releases, renews, or refreshes dynamic addresses.

When NetShell loads, it proceeds to read the Windows Registry to obtain a list of helper DLLs, many of which ship with Windows and to which additional extensions can be added. Microsoft publishes the list of helpers in their various Resource Kits.

The main benefit that the NetShell commands offer to the average Windows user or administrator is that you can enter the NetShell Shell environment and enter commands at that command line. To enter the NetShell root context, you would do the following:

1. In Windows, enter **CMD** in the Start menu Run dialog box, and then press Enter.

2. At the `C:\` prompt, enter **NETSH** and press Enter.

   You see the `NETSH>` prompt appear, indicating that you are in the NetShell root context. The `EXIT` and `BYE` commands allow you to leave the NetShell environment.

There are so many uses of the NET Commands that the entire chapter could be used to illustrate their versatility. You can simulate most of the functions of Windows Explorer from within the NetShell, as the following examples demonstrate. Figure 31.2 shows a Command Prompt session in Vista where you enter the NetShell and display the various commands that NetShell's root context offers. Other contexts available are ADVFIREWALL, BRIDGE, DHCPCLIENT, FIREWALL, HTTP, INTERFACE, IPSEC, LAN, NAP, NETIO, P2P, RAS, RPC, WINHTTP, and WLAN. If you had opened this session on a Windows Server, you would see NetShell contexts associated with server functions. Table 31.2 lists some of the more common NETSH commands.

TABLE 31.2

NetShell Commands

Command	Context	Description
..	Global	Moves up one level
? or HELP	Global	Displays command-specific help.
AAAA	Global	Enter the AAAA context.
AAAA ADD/DELETE/ SET/SHOW ACCTSERVER	RAS	Configures or displays RADIUS accounting servers.
AAAA ADD/DELETE/ SET/SHOW AUTHSERVER	RAS	Configures or displays RADIUS authentication servers.
AAAA SET/SHOW ACCOUNTING	RAS	Configures or displays the accounting provider.
AAAA SET/SHOW AUTHENTICATION	RAS	Configures or displays the authentication provider.
ADD ALIAS	Global	Adds an alias to a command.
ADD HELPER	Global	Adds a Netsh helper DLL.
ADD/DELETE/SHOW AUTHTYPE	RAS	Configures or displays the permitted authentication types.
ADD/DELETE/SHOW AUTHTYPE	RAS	Configures or displays the permitted authentication types.
ADD/DELETE/SHOW CLIENT	RAS	Configures or displays currently connected remote access clients.
ADD/DELETE/SHOW CLIENT	RAS	Configures or displays currently connected remote access clients.
ADD/DELETE/SHOW LINK	RAS	Configures or displays the configuration of software compression and link control protocol (LCP) extensions.
ADD/DELETE/SHOW MULTILINK	RAS	Configures or displays Multilink and Bandwidth Allocation Protocol (BAP) settings.

continued

TABLE 31.2 *(continued)*

Command	Context	Description
`ADD/DELETE/SHOW REGISTEREDSERVER`	RAS	Configures or displays whether the specified remote access server computer is a member of the RAS and IAS Servers security group in the Active Directory directory service of the specified domain.
`ADD/DELETE/SHOW REGISTEREDSERVER`	RAS	Configures or displays whether the specified remote access server computer is a member of the RAS and IAS Servers security group in the Active Directory directory service of the specified domain.
`APPLETALK SET ACCESS`	RAS	Configures whether AppleTalk traffic from remote access clients is forwarded to the networks to which the remote access server is connected.
`APPLETALK SET NEGOTIATION`	RAS	Configures whether AppleTalk is negotiated for remote access connections.
`APPLETALK SHOW CONFIG`	RAS	Displays AppleTalk remote access configuration.
`CMD`	Global	Opens a command window.
`COMMIT`	Global	Commits changes made in offline mode.
`DELETE ALIAS`	Global	Deletes an alias from a command.
`DELETE HELPER`	Global	Removes a `NETSH` helper DLL.
`DHCP`	Global	Enters the `DHCP` context.
`DUMP`	Global	Writes configuration to a text file.
`EXEC`	Global	Executes a script file which contains `NETSH` commands.
`FLUSH`	Global	Discards changes in offline mode.
`INTERFACE`	Global	Enter the `INTERFACE` context.
`INTERFACE IP`	Global	Enter the `INTERFACE IP` context.
`INTERFACE IPV6`	Global	Enter the `INTERFACE IPV6` context.
`INTERFACE PORTPROXY`	Global	Enter the interface `PORTPROXY` context.
`INTERNET PROTOCOL SECURITY`	Global	Enter the `IPSEC` context.
`IP ADD/DELETE RANGE`	RAS	Adds or removes a range of addresses from the static IP address pool.
`IP ADD/DELETE/SET/ SHOW FILTER`	Routing	Adds, deletes, configures, or displays IP packet filters on a specified interface.
`IP ADD/DELETE/SET/ SHOW INTERFACE`	Routing	Adds, deletes, configures, or displays general IP routing settings on a specified interface.
`IP ADD/DELETE/ SET/SHOW PERSISTENTROUTE`	Routing	Adds, deletes, configures, or displays persistent routes.

Command	Context	Description
IP ADD/DELETE/SET/ SHOW PREFERENCE FORPROTOCOL	Routing	Adds, deletes, configures, or displays the preference level for a routing protocol.
IP ADD/DELETE/SET/ SHOW RTMROUTE	Routing	Adds, deletes, configures, or displays a non-persistent Route Table Manager route.
IP ADD/DELETE/SET/ SHOW SCOPE	Routing	Adds, deletes, or displays a multicast scope.
IP ADD/DELETE/SHOW BOUNDARY	Routing	Adds, deletes, or displays multicast boundary settings on a specified interface.
IP AUTODHCP ADD/ DELETE EXCLUSION	Routing	Adds or deletes an exclusion from the DHCP allocator range of addresses.
IP AUTODHCP SET/ SHOW GLOBAL	Routing	Configures or displays global DHCP allocator parameters.
IP AUTODHCP SET/ SHOW INTERFACE	Routing	Configures or displays DHCP allocator settings for a specified interface.
IP DELETE POOL	RAS	Deletes the static IP address pool.
IP DNSPROXY SET/ SHOW GLOBAL	Routing	Configures or displays global DNS proxy parameters.
IP DNSPROXY SET/ SHOW INTERFACE	Routing	Configures or displays DNS proxy parameters for a specified interface.
IP IGMP ADD/DELETE/ SET/SHOW INTERFACE	Routing	Adds, deletes, configures, or displays IGMP on the specified interface.
IP IGMP SET/SHOW GLOBAL	Routing	Configures or displays IGMP global settings.
IP IGMP SHOW GROUPTABLE	Routing	Displays the IGMP host groups table.
IP IGMP SHOW IFSTATS	Routing	Displays the IGMP statistics for each interface.
IP IGMP SHOW IFTABLE	Routing	Displays the IGMP host groups for each interface.
IP IGMP SHOW PROXYGROUPTABLE	Routing	Displays the IGMP group table for the IGMP proxy interface.
IP IGMP SHOW RASGROUPTABLE	Routing	Displays the group table for internal interface used by the remote access server.
IP NAT ADD/DELETE ADDRESSMAPPING	Routing	Adds or deletes a NAT address mapping.
IP NAT ADD/DELETE ADDRESSRANGE	Routing	Adds or deletes an address range to the NAT interface public address pool.
IP NAT ADD/DELETE PORTMAPPING	Routing	Adds or deletes a NAT port mapping.

continued

TABLE 31.2 (continued)

Command	Context	Description
IP NAT ADD/DELETE/ SET/SHOW INTERFACE	Routing	Adds, deletes, configures, or displays network address translation (NAT) settings for a specified interface.
IP NAT SET/SHOW GLOBAL	Routing	Configures or displays global network address translation (NAT) settings.
IP OSPF ADD/DELETE/ SET/SHOW AREA	Routing	Adds, removes, configures, or displays an OSPF area.
IP OSPF ADD/DELETE/ SET/SHOW INTERFACE	Routing	Adds, removes, configures, or displays OSPF on a specified interface.
IP OSPF ADD/DELETE/ SET/SHOW VIRTIF	Routing	Adds, removes, configures, or displays an OSPF virtual interface.
IP OSPF ADD/DELETE/ SHOW NEIGHBOR	Routing	Adds, removes, configures, or displays an OSPF neighbor.
IP OSPF ADD/DELETE/ SHOW PROTOFILTER	Routing	Adds, removes, configures, or displays routing information sources for OSPF external routes.
IP OSPF ADD/DELETE/ SHOW ROUTEFILTER	Routing	Adds, removes, configures, or displays route filtering for OSPF external routes.
IP OSPF SET/SHOW GLOBAL	Routing	Configures or displays global OSPF settings. This feature is not available on the Itanium-based versions of the Windows operating systems. This content is not available in this preliminary release.
IP OSPF SHOW AREASTATS	Routing	Displays OSPF area statistics.
IP OSPF SHOW LSDB	Routing	Displays the OSPF link state database.
IP OSPF SHOW VIRTIFSTATS	Routing	Displays OSPF virtual link statistics.
IP RELAY ADD/DELETE DHCPSERVER	Routing	Adds or removes a DHCP server IP address to the list of DHCP server addresses.
IP RELAY ADD/ DELETE/SET INTERFACE	Routing	Adds, removes, or configures DHCP Relay Agent settings on a specified interface.
IP RELAY SET GLOBAL	Routing	Configures DHCP Relay Agent global settings.
IP RELAY SHOW IFBINDING	Routing	Displays IP address bindings for interfaces.
IP RELAY SHOW IFCONFIG	Routing	Displays DHCP Relay Agent configuration for each interface.
IP RELAY SHOW IFSTATS	Routing	Displays DHCP statistics for each interface.

Command	Context	Description
IP SET ACCESS	RAS	Configures whether IP traffic from remote access clients is forwarded to the networks to which the remote access server is connected.
IP SET ADDRASSIGN	RAS	Configures the method by which the remote access server assigns IP addresses to incoming connections.
IP SET ADDRREQ	RAS	Configures whether remote access clients or demand-dial routers can request their own IP addresses.
IP SET NEGOTIATION	RAS	Configures whether IP is negotiated for remote access connections.
IP SET/SHOW LOGLEVEL	Routing	Configures or displays the global IP logging level.
IP SHOW BOUNDARYSTATS	Routing	Displays IP multicast boundaries.
IP SHOW CONFIG	RAS	Displays IP remote access configuration.
IP SHOW HELPER	Routing	Displays all Netsh utility subcontexts of IP.
IP SHOW MFE	Routing	Displays multicast forwarding entries.
IP SHOW MFESTATS	Routing	Displays multicast forwarding entry statistics.
IP SHOW PROTOCOL	Routing	Displays all running IP routing protocols.
IP SHOW RTMDESTINATIONS	Routing	Displays destinations in the Route Table Manager routing table.
IP SHOW RTMROUTES	Routing	Displays routes in the Route Table Manager routing table.
NETWORK BRIDGE	Global	Enter the BRIDGE context.
NETWORK DIAGNOSTICS (DIAG)	Global	Enter the DIAG context.
OFFLINE	Global	Sets the mode to offline.
ONLINE	Global	Sets the mode to online.
POPD	Global	Pops a context from the stack. The stack is a stored buffer of recent commands.
PUSHD	Global	Pushes the current context on the stack.
QUIT OR BYE OR EXIT	Global	Exits NETSH.
RAS SET/SHOW AUTHMODE	RAS	Configures or displays whether and when dial-in connections are authenticated.
REMOTE ACCESS	Global	Enter the RAS context.
ROUTING	Global	Enter the ROUTING context.
RPC HELPER	Global	Enter the RPC context.
SET AUDIT-LOGGING	Global	Turns logging on or off.

continued

TABLE 31.2 *(continued)*

Command	Context	Description
SET LOGLEVEL	Global	Sets level of logging information.
SET MACHINE	Global	Sets the system to which NetShell commands are applied.
SET MODE	Global	Sets the mode to online or offline.
SET/SHOW AUTHMODE	RAS	Configures or displays whether and when dial-in connections are authenticated.
SET/SHOW CREDENTIALS	Interface	Configures or displays the user name, password, and domain name on a demand-dial interface.
SET/SHOW INTERFACE	Interface	Enables, disables, connects, disconnects, and displays the configuration of demand-dial interfaces.
SET/SHOW TRACING	RAS	Configures or displays tracing settings.
SET/SHOW USER	RAS	Configures or displays remote access settings for user accounts.
SHOW ACTIVESERVERS	RAS	Displays current servers running Routing and Remote Access on your network.
SHOW ACTIVESERVERS	RAS	Displays current servers running Routing and Remote Access on your network.
SHOW ALIAS	Global	Displays all defined aliases.
SHOW AUDIT-LOGGING	Global	Displays audit logging settings.
SHOW HELPER	Global	Displays the NETSH helper DLLs.
SHOW LOGLEVEL	Global	Displays the level of logging information.
SHOW MACHINE	Global	Displays the system to which NetShell commands are applied.
SHOW MODE	Global	Displays the current mode.
SHOW NETDLLS	Global	Displays version of the NETSH helper DLLs.
SHOW VERSION	Global	Displays the version of Windows and NETSH utility.
WINS	Global	Enters the WINS context.

Source: Microsoft Technet (technet.mircrosoft.com/en-us/library).

A very common use of NetShell is to start and stop network services. The command has the following syntax:

```
NET [START/STOP/PAUSE/CONTINUE] <ServiceName>
```

These commands duplicate the action of going into the Windows Services console and clicking the Start, Stop, Pause, and Continue buttons. If you have a service that you think might have hung up and may be malfunctioning, you can use the following sequence to restart that service.

```
NETSH>NET STOP DHCP
NETSH>NET START DHCP
```

FIGURE 31.2

A display of commands available in the root context of NetShell

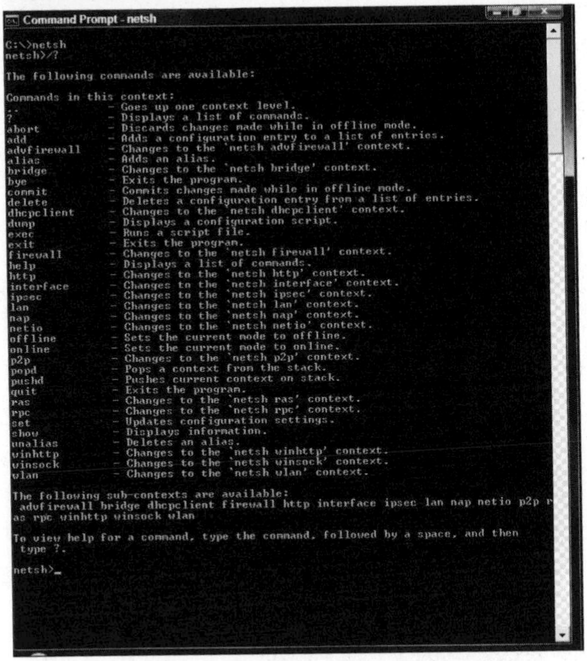

NetShell allows for the following major classes of commands:

- NET, to manage network resources
- MODE, to configure a system device
- SC, to allow for service control
- PsService, to provide a means to view and control services
- WMIC Service, to allow a user to access WMI control over services

Telnet sessions

Telnet stands for the Telecommunications Network protocol, one of the earliest of the Internet's standard protocols. With a Telnet client, you can use a CLI to perform commands on a remote system. Because of its long history, Telnet is supported natively on all network operating systems, and there are many third-party Telnet clients available. While Telnet has some limited popularity on UNIX systems, particularly with old timers, most modern courses on network administration tend to teach other methods for light-footprint, character-based command session systems.

Telnet is an 8-bit text transfer protocol where commands are carried as 7-bit ASCII with a single character of the upper ASCII character set referred to as a "Telnet character." TCP port number 23 is the well-known Telnet port. Although early versions of Telnet were not standardized, versions after 1973 tended to conform to what is called the "New Telnet" standard, which extends IETF RFC 15. The extensions used mean that Telnet is slightly different from one NOS to another.

While Telnet is convenient, easy to learn, and easy to use, the general consensus is that Telnet is insecure and that it should be deprecated. The reasons for this are evident:

- Telnet sessions send and receive clear text, not encrypted data, and are therefore subject to interception.

- Telnet daemons (processes) have been hacked into several times and have not been sufficiently strengthened.

- Telnet sessions do not provide a means to determine that the endpoints of a connection are authentic; the user simply provides a login that can be intercepted.

There have been sporadic attempts to add security to the Telnet protocol, but for the most part, SSH clients have turned out to be adequate for remote command line sessions and have replaced these clients. You may still encounter Telnet's use on mainframe and legacy systems, as an entry into routers and switches, and in some other specialized situations. The open source PuTTY (www.chiark.greenend.org.uk/~sgtatham/putty/) utility is a combination Telnet/SSH client that you can use for Windows and UNIX, and as an XTERM terminal emulator.

Starting with Windows Vista, Microsoft stopped installing the Telnet client as part of their standard installation; however, you can add the Vista Telnet client back into Vista as an add-on system component. You can find a listing of the various Telnet commands at http://technet.microsoft.com/en-us/library/bb491013.aspx.

PowerShell

PowerShell is the latest expression of the command line interface introduced in Windows Server 2008/Vista (also available for Windows Server 2003/XP) for administration of systems. PowerShell unites a CLI with a standardized command language composed of over 60 verbs, and with the capability to run scripts. PowerShell was designed to be backwardly compatible with many older Microsoft technologies, as well as other common CLIs from other platforms. PowerShell commands can act on thousands of Windows, Office, .NET Framework objects, and the WMI objects, among others. PowerShell commands can act on both local and remote systems, registries, the Active Directory, and services. The intent at Microsoft is to rewrite the command consoles of their enterprise applications, with PowerShell as the underlying command structure. The latest version of Exchange was the first application to ship with a management console of this type.

Among the various features that you can control with PowerShell are:

- Local and remote system management
- System services, processes, and the Registry

- ActiveX Data Objects (ADOs), Component Object Model (COM) objects, and .NET Framework objects
- Active Directory Service Interface (ADSI) objects
- Windows Management Instrumentation (WMI) objects
- Terminal Server configuration and management
- Internet Information Services 7.0 configuration and management
- XML-based data or HTML files
- Scripts written in various scripting languages, or deployed with the Windows Scripting Host

Windows PowerShell is both a Windows shell and command interpreter environment with a built-in scripting language. The PowerShell runtime engine contains its own command parser as well as automation for binding command parameters. PowerShell 1.0 initially shipped with 129 built-in command utilities called CMDLETs (pronounced "command-lets") that can operate on objects, some of which can be used to format and display command results with the PowerShell CLI.

Note

PowerShell's Web site is located at www.microsoft.com/powershell, along with information about the download of this command environment. Version 1.0 runs on Windows XP/Server 2003/Vista/Server 2008/7 and is available for x86, x86-64, and IA-64 (Itanium) systems. Version 2.0 is available in preview form and will be released soon after this book has shipped. Later versions of these operating systems have PowerShell as an optional Windows add-on in the standard operating system distribution.

To start PowerShell from the command prompt:

1. Click Start, click Run, and then enter **CMD** in the Run dialog box, or press the Windows logo+R keystroke.
2. Press the Enter key to open a command prompt.
3. Change directories to the one that contains the PowerShell program by entering **%SystemRoot%\System32\WindowsPowerShell\v1.0** and then pressing the Enter key.
4. Enter **PowerShell.exe -NoProfile** to start PowerShell without a profile file that is used to modify the program.

Alternatively, you can start PowerShell from the Start menu command, as follows: click Start, click All Programs, click Windows PowerShell 1.0, and then click Windows PowerShell to start the program.

When PowerShell runs, it loads the console and snap-ins (collections of CMDLETs and providers), and then profile files are processed. You can think of a profile as a script that customizes the PowerShell environment, adding aliases, changing the console configuration, and adding special functions. Profiles can apply to an administrator, all users, a single user, or a group of users. PowerShell has a feature called the "Execution Policy" that limits users from running scripts without certain safeguards.

PowerShell uses a collection of CMDLETs or providers that are snap-ins of related functionality. Each snap-in runs in its own namespace. For example, the Core snap-in's namespace is Microsoft. PowerShell.Core. Core CMDLETs alter the way the PowerShell engine operates. Other snap-ins are Host, Management, Security, and Utility snap-ins. To see which snap-ins are part of your installation, enter the following command:

GET-PSSNAPIN.

To determine which CMDLETs are in a snap-in, you can use the following command:

GET-COMMAND -COMMANDTYPE CMDLET | WHERE-OBJECT {$_.PSSNAPIN -MATCH "<snapin_name>"}

Or, to see which providers are included, use this command:

GET-PSPROVIDER | FORMAT-TABLE NAME, PSSNAPIN

Table 31.3 lists some of the important PowerShell CMDLETs.

TABLE 31.3

PowerShell 1.0 CMDLETS

Name	Definition	Description
ADD-CONTENT (AC)	ADD-CONTENT [-Path] <String[]> [-Value] <Object[...	Add content to an item
ADD-HISTORY	ADD-HISTORY [[-InputObject] <PSObject[]>] [-Pass...	Add entries to the session history.
ADD-MEMBER	ADD-MEMBER [-MemberType] <PSMemberTypes> [-Name]...	Add a member to a particular PowerShell object.
ADD-PSSNAPIN	ADD-PSSNAPIN [-Name] <String[]> [-PassThru] [-Ve...	Add a snap-in to the console.
CLEAR-CONTENT (CLC)	CLEAR-CONTENT [-Path] <String[]> [-Filter <Strin...	Remove the content from an item or specific location.
CLEAR-HOST (CLEAR/ CLS)	Clear-Host or CLS	Clears the display.
CLEAR-ITEM (CLI)	CLEAR-ITEM [-Path] <String[]> [-Force] [-Filter ...	Remove the content from a variable or alias.
CLEAR-ITEMPROPERTY (CLP)	CLEAR-ITEMPROPERTY [-Path] <String[]> [-Name] <S...	Remove a property from an item.

Name	Definition	Description
CLEAR-VARIABLE (CLV)	CLEAR-VARIABLE [-Name] <String[]> [-Include <Str...	Clear a variable value.
COMPARE-OBJECT	COMPARE-OBJECT [-ReferenceObject] <PSObject[]> [...	Compare objects to one another.
CONVERTFROM-SECURESTRING	CONVERTFROM-SECURESTRING [-SecureString] <Secure...	Convert a secure string to an encrypted standard sting.
CONVERT-PATH (CVPA)	CONVERT-PATH [-Path] <String[]> [-Verbose] [-Deb...	Convert a PS path to a provider path.
CONVERTTO-HTML	CONVERTTO-HTML [[-Property] <Object[]>] [-InputO...	Convert the input into an HTML table
CONVERTTO-SECURESTRING	CONVERTTO-SECURESTRING [-String] <String> [[-Sec...	Convert an encrypted standard string into a secure string.
COPY-ITEM (COPY/CP/ CPI))	COPY-ITEM [-Path] <String[]> [[-Destination] <St...	Copy an item from the location in the namespace.
COPY-ITEMPROPERTY (CPP)	COPY-ITEMPROPERTY [[-path] | [-literalPath]] string[] [[-destination] string[]]...	Copy a property along with its value.
DO	[:Loop_label] DO { command_block } while (condition)	Continue a loop while a condition is true.
COPY-ITEMPROPERTY	COPY-ITEMPROPERTY [-Path] <String[]> [-Destinati...	
EXIT		Quit PowerShell or exit a script.
EXPORT-ALIAS	EXPORT-ALIAS [-Path] <String> [[-Name] <String[]...	Export an alias list to a file.

continued

TABLE 31.3 *(continued)*

Name	Definition	Description
EXPORT-CLIXML	EXPORT-CLIXML [-Path] <String> [-Depth <Int32>] ...	Create a CLIXML listing of PowerShell objects.
EXPORT-CONSOLE	EXPORT-CONSOLE [[-Path] <String>] [-Force] [-NoC...	Export the console configuration to a file.
EXPORT-CSV (EPCSV)	EXPORT-CSV [-Path] <String> -InputObject <PSObje...	Export to Comma Delimited Values (a spreadsheet format).
FOR	FOR (init; condition; repeat) {command_block}	Loop through items that match a condition.
FOREACH (FOREACH)	FOREACH (item in collection) {ScriptBlock}	Loop for each value in the pipeline.
FOREACH-OBJECT	FOREACH-OBJECT [-Process] <ScriptBlock[]> [-Inpu...	Loop for each object in the PowerShell pipeline.
FORMAT-CUSTOM (FC)	FORMAT-CUSTOM [[-Property] <Object[]>] [-Depth <...	Create a custom format for output in a view.
FORMAT-LIST (FL)	FORMAT-LIST [[-Property] <Object[]>] [-GroupBy <...	Format the output of a view as a list of properties.
FORMAT-TABLE (FT)	FORMAT-TABLE [[-Property] <Object[]>] [-AutoSize...	Format the output as a table.
FORMAT-WIDE (FW)	FORMAT-WIDE [[-Property] <Object>] [-AutoSize] [...	Format the output as a table listing a single property.
GET-ACL	GET-ACL [[-Path] <String[]>] [-Audit] [-Filter <...	Get the permissions for a file or registry key.
GET-ALIAS (GAL)	GET-ALIAS [[-Name] <String[]>] [-Exclude <String...	Return the alias name for a Cmdlet.
GET-AUTHENTICODE SIGNATURE	GET-AUTHENTICODESIGNATURE [-FilePath] <String[]>...	Get the signature object of a file.
GET-CHILDITEM (DIR/ LS/GCI)	GET-CHILDITEM [[-Path] <String[]>] [[-Filter] <S...	Get the contents of a folder or registry key that pertains to a child item.
GET-COMMAND (GCM)	GET-COMMAND [[-ArgumentList] <Object[]>] [-Verb ...	Return command description.
GET-CONTENT (CAT/ TYPE/GC)	GET-CONTENT [-Path] <String[]> [-ReadCount <Int6...	Get the content from an item or specific location.

Name	Definition	Description
GET-CREDENTIAL	GET-CREDENTIAL [-Credential] <PSCredential> [-Ve...	Get a security credential (username/password).
GET-CULTURE	GET-CULTURE [-Verbose] [-Debug] [-ErrorAction <A...	Get the regional information of the system.
GET-DATE	GET-DATE [[-Date] <DateTime>] [-Year <Int32>] [-...	Get the current date and time.
GET-EVENTLOG	GET-EVENTLOG [-LogName] <String> [-Newest <Int32...	Get the eventlog data.
GET-EXECUTIONPOLICY	GET-EXECUTIONPOLICY [-Verbose] [-Debug] [-ErrorA...	Get the execution policy for the shell.
GET-HELP (HELP)	GET-HELP [[-Name] <String>] [-Category <String[]...	Open the help file.
GET-HISTORY (HISTORY/H/GHY)	GET-HISTORY [[-Id] <Int64[]>] [[-Count] <Int32>]...	Get a listing of the sessions command history.
GET-HOST	GET-HOST [-Verbose] [-Debug] [-ErrorAction <Acti...	Get the host (system) information.
GET-ITEM (GI)	GET-ITEM [-Path] <String[]> [-Filter <String>] [...	Get a file or registry object, or another namespace object.
GET-ITEMPROPERTY (GP)	GET-ITEMPROPERTY [-Path] <String[]> [[-Name] <St...	Retrieves the properties of an object.
GET-LOCATION (PWD/GL)	GET-LOCATION [-PSProvider <String[]>] [-PSDrive ...	Get and display the current location.
GET-MEMBER (GM)	GET-MEMBER [[-Name] <String[]>] [-InputObject <P...	List the properties of an object.
GET-PFXCERTIFICATE	GET-PFXCERTIFICATE [-FilePath] <String[]> [-Verb...	Get pf certificate information.
GET-PROCESS (PS/GPS)	GET-PROCESS [[-Name] <String[]>] [-Verbose] [-De...	Get a list of running processes on a machine.

continued

TABLE 31.3 (continued)

Name	Definition	Description
GET-PSDRIVE (GDR)	GET-PSDRIVE [[-Name] <String[]>] [-Scope <String...	Get the DriveInfo for a defined PSDrive.
GET-PSPROVIDER	GET-PSPROVIDER [[-PSProvider] <String[]>] [-Verb...	Ge information about the specified provider.
GET-PSSNAPIN	GET-PSSNAPIN [[-Name] <String[]>] [-Registered] ...	List the PowerShell snap-ins in use on the computer.
GET-SERVICE (GSV)	GET-SERVICE [[-Name] <String[]>] [-Include <Stri...	Get a list of services.
GET-TRACESOURCE	GET-TRACESOURCE [[-Name] <String[]>] [-Verbose] ...	Get components that are instrumented for tracing.
GET-UICULTURE	GET-UICULTURE [-Verbose] [-Debug] [-ErrorAction ...	Get the ui culture information.
GET-UNIQUE (GU)	GET-UNIQUE [-InputObject <PSObject>] [-AsString]...	Get the unique items in a collection.
GET-VARIABLE (GV)	GET-VARIABLE [[-Name] <String[]>] [-ValueOnly] [...	Get a PowerShell variable.
GET-WMIOBJECT (GWMI)	GET-WMIOBJECT [-Class] <String> [[-Property] <St...	
GROUP-OBJECT (GROUP)	GROUP-OBJECT [[-Property] <Object[]>] [-NoElemen...	Group objects that contain the same value for a shared property.
IF	If (condition) {commands_ to_execute} [elseif (condition2) {commands_to_ execute}] else {commands_ to_execute} ...	Perform a command based on the state of a condition.
IMPORT-ALIAS (IPAL)	IMPORT-ALIAS [-Path] <String> [-Scope <String>] ...	Import an alias from a file.
IMPORT-CLIXML	IMPORT-CLIXML [-Path] <String[]> [-Verbose] [-De...	Import a CLIXML file and use it to rebuild the PS object.
IMPORT-CSV (IPCSV)	IMPORT-CSV [-Path] <String[]> [-Verbose] [-Debug...	Get the values from a CSV file and send objects to the pipeline.

Name	Definition	Description
INVOKE-EXPRESSION	INVOKE-EXPRESSION [-Command] <String> [-Verbose]...	Run a PowerShell expression.
INVOKE-HISTORY (R/IHY)	INVOKE-HISTORY [[-Id] <String>] [-Verbose] [-Deb...	Invoke a previously run Cmdlet from history.
INVOKE-ITEM (II)	INVOKE-ITEM [-Path] <String[]> [-Filter <String>...	Invoke an executable file or open a file.
JOIN-PATH	JOIN-PATH [-Path] <String[]> [-ChildPath] <Strin...	Combine a path and child-path.
MEASURE-COMMAND	MEASURE-COMMAND [-Expression] <ScriptBlock> [-In...	Measure the running time of a Cmdlet.
MEASURE-OBJECT	MEASURE-OBJECT [[-Property] <String[]>] [-InputO...	Measure the properties of an object.
MOVE-ITEM (MOVE/ MV/MI)	MOVE-ITEM [-Path] <String[]> [[-Destination] <St...	Move an item to a new location.
MOVE-ITEMPROPERTY (MP)	MOVE-ITEMPROPERTY [-Path] <String[]> [-Destinati...	Move a property from one location to another.
NEW-ALIAS (NAL)	NEW-ALIAS [-Name] <String> [-Value] <String> [-D...	Create an alias.
NEW-ITEM (NI)	NEW-ITEM [-Path] <String[]> [-ItemType <String>]...	Create a new item in a namespace.
NEW-ITEMPROPERTY	NEW-ITEMPROPERTY [-Path] <String[]> [-Name] <Str...	Set a new property of an item at a location.
NEW-OBJECT	NEW-OBJECT [-TypeName] <String> [[-ArgumentList]...	Create a new .NET object.
NEW-PSDRIVE (MOUNT/ NDR)	NEW-PSDRIVE [-Name] <String> [-PSProvider] <Stri...	Create a new PSDrive.
NEW-SERVICE	NEW-SERVICE [-Name] <String> [-BinaryPathName] <...	Create a new service.
NEW-TIMESPAN	NEW-TIMESPAN [[-Start] <DateTime>] [[-End] <Date...	Create a timespan object.

continued

TABLE 31.3 *(continued)*

Name	Definition	Description
NEW-VARIABLE (NV)	NEW-VARIABLE [-Name] <String> [[-Value] <Object>...	Create a new variable.
OUT-DEFAULT	OUT-DEFAULT [-InputObject <PSObject>] [-Verbose]...	Send output to default.
OUT-FILE	OUT-FILE [-FilePath] <String> [[-Encoding] <Stri...	Send command output to a file.
OUT-HOST (OH)	OUT-HOST [-Paging] [-InputObject <PSObject>] [-V...	Send the pipelined output to the host.
OUT-NULL	OUT-NULL [-InputObject <PSObject>] [-Verbose] [-...	Send output to null.
OUT-PRINTER (LP)	OUT-PRINTER [[-Name] <String>] [-InputObject <PS...	Send the output to a printer.
OUT-STRING	OUT-STRING [-Stream] [-Width <Int32>] [-InputObj...	Send objects to the host as strings.
POP-LOCATION (POPD)	POP-LOCATION [-PassThru] [-StackName <String>] [...	Set the current location from the stack.
POWERSHELL	PS	Launch a PowerShell session.
PUSH-LOCATION (PUSHD)	PUSH-LOCATION [[-Path] <String>] [-PassThru] [-S...	Push the current location onto the stack.
QUEST AD CMDLETS		Read/Write to the Active Directory.
READ-HOST	READ-HOST [[-Prompt] <Object>] [-AsSecureString]...	Read a line of input from the host console.
REMOVE-ITEM (RM/DEL/ ERASE/RDRI/RMDIR)	REMOVE-ITEM [-Path] <String[]> [-Filter <String>...	Remove an item.
REMOVE-ITEMPROPERTY (RP)	REMOVE-ITEMPROPERTY [-Path] <String[]> [-Name] <...	Delete the property and its value from an item.
REMOVE-PSDRIVE (RDR)	REMOVE-PSDRIVE [-Name] <String[]> [-PSProvider <...	Delete a defined PSDrive.

Name	Definition	Description
REMOVE-PSSNAPIN	REMOVE-PSSNAPIN [-Name] <String[]> [-PassThru] [...	Remove a PowerShell shap-in from this computer.
REMOVE-VARIABLE (RV)	REMOVE-VARIABLE [-Name] <String[]> [-Include <St...	Remove a variable.
RENAME-ITEM (REN/ RNI)	RENAME-ITEM [-Path] <String> [-NewName] <String>...	Remove an item.
RENAME-ITEMPROPERTY (RNP)	RENAME-ITEMPROPERTY [-Path] <String> [-Name] <St...	Rename the property of an item.
RESOLVE-PATH (RVPA)	RESOLVE-PATH [-Path] <String[]> [-Credential <PS...	Resolves the wildcards in a path.
RESTART-SERVICE	RESTART-SERVICE [-Name] <String[]> [-Force] [-Pa...	Stop and restart a service.
RESUME-SERVICE	RESUME-SERVICE [-Name] <String[]> [-PassThru] [-...	Resume a suspended service.
RUN/CALL (&)	& [Cmdlet]	Run a command (the call operator).
SELECT-OBJECT (SELECT)	SELECT-OBJECT [[-Property] <Object[]>] [-InputOb...	Select the properties of objects.
SELECT-STRING	SELECT-STRING [-Pattern] <String[]> -InputObject...	Search strings and files for matches to patterns.
SET-ACL	SET-ACL [-Path] <String[]> [-AclObject] <ObjectS...	Set permissions.
SET-ALIAS (SAL)	SET-ALIAS [-Name] <String> [-Value] <String> [-D...	Create or change an alias.
SET-AUTHENTICODE SIGNATURE	SET-AUTHENTICODESIGNATURE [-FilePath] <String[]>...	Put a signature into a file or .ps1 script.
SET-CONTENT (SC)	SET-CONTENT [-Path] <String[]> [-Value] <Object[...	Sets the content from an item or specific location.
SET-DATE	SET-DATE [-Date] <DateTime> [-DisplayHint <Displ...	Set the current date and time for the system.
SET-EXECUTIONPOLICY	SET-EXECUTIONPOLICY [-ExecutionPolicy] <Executio...	Modify the execution policy for the shell based on user preferences.
SET-ITEM (SI)	SET-ITEM [-Path] <String[]> [[-Value] <Object>] ...	Change the value of an item.

continued

TABLE 31.3 (continued)

Name	Definition	Description
SET-ITEMPROPERTY (SP)	SET-ITEMPROPERTY [-Path] <String[]> [-Name] <Str...	Set the value of a property.
SET-LOCATION (CD/ CHDIR/SL)	SET-LOCATION [[-Path] <String>] [-PassThru] [-Ve...	Set the current working location.
SET-PSDEBUG	SET-PSDEBUG [-Trace <Int32>] [-Step] [-Strict] [...	Trun script debugging on or off.
SET-SERVICE	SET-SERVICE [-Name] <String> [-DisplayName <Stri...	Change the start mode or properties of a service.
SET-TRACESOURCE	SET-TRACESOURCE [-Name] <String[]> [[-Option] <P...	Trace a PowerShell component.
SET-VARIABLE (SET/SV)	SET-VARIABLE [-Name] <String[]> [[-Value] <Objec...	Sets or saves a value to a variable.
SORT-OBJECT (SORT)	SORT-OBJECT [[-Property] <Object[]>] [-Descendin...	Sort objects by property value.
SPLIT-PATH	SPLIT-PATH [-Path] <String[]> [-LiteralPath <Str...	Return part of a path.
START-SERVICE (STSV)	START-SERVICE [-Name] <String[]> [-PassThru] [-I...	Start a service.
START-SLEEP (SLEEP)	START-SLEEP [-Seconds] <Int32> [-Verbose] [-Debu...	Suspend shell, script, or runspace activity.
START-TRANSCRIPT	START-TRANSCRIPT [[-Path] <String>] [-Append] [-...	Start the transcript of a command shell session.
STOP-PROCESS (KILL/ SPPS)	STOP-PROCESS [-Id] <Int32[]> [-PassThru] [-Verbo...	Stop a running process.
STOP-SERVICE (SPSV)	STOP-SERVICE [-Name] <String[]> [-Force] [-PassT...	Stop a service.
STOP-TRANSCRIPT	STOP-TRANSCRIPT [-Verbose] [-Debug] [-ErrorActio...	Stop the transcription process.
SWITCH		Multiple if statements.
SUSPEND-SERVICE	SUSPEND-SERVICE [-Name] <String[]> [-PassThru] [...	Suspend a running serivce.

Name	Definition	Description
TEE-OBJECT	TEE-OBJECT [-FilePath] \<String\> [-InputObject \<P...	Send input objects to two places.
TEST-PATH	TEST-PATH [-Path] \<String[]\> [-Filter \<String\>] ...	Return a true if the path exists, else return false.
TRACE-COMMAND	TRACE-COMMAND [-Name] \<String[]\> [-Expression] \<...	Trace a command or expression.
UPDATE-FORMATDATA	UPDATE-FORMATDATA [[-AppendPath] \<String[]\>] [-P...	Update and append format data files.
UPDATE-TYPEDATA	UPDATE-TYPEDATA [[-AppendPath] \<String[]\>] [-Pre...	Update the current extended type configuration.
WHERE-OBJECT (WHERE)	WHERE-OBJECT [-FilterScript] \<ScriptBlock\> [-Inp...	Filter objects that are passed to the pipeline.
WHILE	WHILE (condition) {command_block}	Loop when a condition is true.
WRITE-DEBUG	WRITE-DEBUG [-Message] \<String\> [-Verbose] [-Deb...	Write a debug message to the host display.
WRITE-ERROR	WRITE-ERROR [-Message] \<String\> [-Category \<Erro...	Write an object to the error pipeline.
WRITE-HOST	WRITE-HOST [[-Object] \<Object\>] [-NoNewline] [-S...	Display objects using the host user interface.
WRITE-OUTPUT (ECHO)	WRITE-OUTPUT [-InputObject] \<PSObject[]\> [-Verbo...	Write an object to the pipeline.
WRITE-PROGRESS	WRITE-PROGRESS [-Activity] \<String\> [-Status] \<S...	Display a progress bar.
WRITE-VERBOSE	WRITE-VERBOSE [-Message] \<String\> [-Verbose] [-D...	Write a sting to the host's verbose display.
WRITE-WARNING	WRITE-WARNING [-Message] \<String\> [-Verbose] [-D...	Write a warning message.
#	# \<String\>	Make a comment or leave a remark.

The ellipses in the table signify that you can add additional terms to the command identical to the one that is shown previous to the ellipses.

What you find is that nearly all providers are in the PowerShell Core, that the Certificate provider is part of the Security snap-in, and that additional providers are added by third parties to support management functions.

Many of PowerShell's commands allow for the optional use of various UNIX commands. For example, you can enter the command Get-Help, or alternatively use the alias MAN (for UNIX Manual pages) for the same command. There are numerous aliases built into the PowerShell CLI.

One of PowerShell's often used capabilities is the enumeration of services, as well as service management. You can see what services are running on a system by using the GET-SERVICE command by itself, so that START-SERVICE <*servicename*> will start a service, and STOP-SERVICE <*servicename*> will stop that service. This capability is useful to examine a remote system using the following syntax (which is available in version 2.0 and later):

GET-SERVICE –COMPUTERNAME <*systemname*>

Similarly, you can use GET-PROCESS to display all running processes on your local system, or filter the list by using the NAME <string>. As you experiment with the GET-PROCESS command, you will find that you can expose many more parameters about processes than are found in the Task Manager. PowerShell gives you much finer control over services and processes, as well as access to remote systems for which you have access privileges. Figure 31.3 shows the GET-PROCESS CMDLET in action.

FIGURE 31.3

The GET-PROCESS | MORE command lists all processes running on a system.

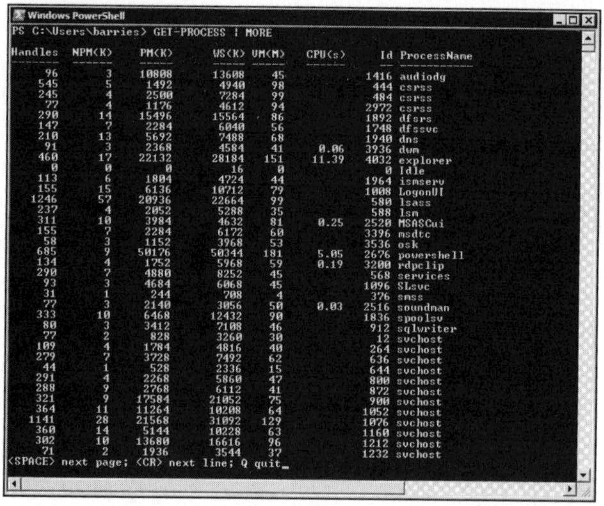

You can navigate file systems in PowerShell in much the same manner that you navigate file systems in MS-DOS using the SET-LOCATION command. PowerShell creates an abstraction called a PowerShell Drive that provides access to a data store. PowerShell allows you to map the Registry as drives, as well as the Certificate store. The Registry maps to the HKCU: and HKLM: drives, which are the Hive Key Current User and Hive Key Local Machine, respectively. The Certificate store mounts as the CERT: drive. In this regard, PowerShell is unique. You can't access the Registry in either CMD.EXE or a program such as Windows Explorer, and this PowerShell cmdlet gives an administrator powerful access to system settings both on local and remote systems.

To see a complete list of all WMI objects, you can use the following command:

GET-WMIOBJECT -LIST

PowerShell will return 200 to 300 WMI providers. If you want to get information about a specific service, you can enter it by name. When you use the command GET-WMIOBJECT WIN32_PROCESS, you may be surprised by the depth of information that WMI provides. PowerShell maintains a help topic on WMIOBJECT that you can access by entering GET-HELP WMIOBJECT. If you enter the following command:

GET-WMIOBJECT WIN32_SERVICE -COMPUTERNAME <IP ADDRESS or systemname>

PowerShell will return the services running on the system whose IP address you specify.

A PowerShell script is a text file with the .ps1 file extension. You execute a script by entering <path>\<scriptname.ps1> at the prompt. The path must be a fully qualified path, but the .ps1 extension is optional.

In PowerShell, you must set an execution policy that allows a script to run. Scripts won't run unless you validate them, and you can use a digital signature as part of that validation. To learn more about digital signing, enter the command **GET-HELP ABOUT_SIGNING**.

PowerShell supports WSH scripts, and while both offer access to COM automation objects, PowerShell has the ability to provide an interactive command session.

Going forward, anyone interested in command line management of Windows networked systems should concentrate on learning and using PowerShell instead of the older tools such as the NET commands, Windows Scripting Host (WSH), and other technologies in this area.

Summary

This chapter described command line tools for network management. Command shells or command line interpreters allow for network command and control as well as being a lightweight environment in which testing may be done. The various command shells or CLIs used for network management were described. Many of these shells are not only single command line processors but can also run small programs or scripts.

Shells used in Linux, Windows, and UNIX were described. Windows NetShell's NET commands and PowerShell were described in some detail.

In the next chapter, remote networking utilities are described.

CHAPTER 32

Remote Access

Remote access describes a system of client/server software that connects a remote client to a remote access server. In this chapter, remote access software that connects clients through the Public Switched Telephone Network is highlighted, but the trend in this area of software is toward remote clients connected using Virtual Private Network (VPN) connections over the Internet. A variety of remote access connection protocols are used, including SLIP, PPP, PPPoE, PPTP, and L2TP. Their relationship to remote access software is described.

Remote desktop software allows a client system to remotely connect to a host system so that the desktop of the host is shown on the client system; this software will be described in this chapter. Among the uses of remote desktop software are remote computing, remote system management, help desk applications, remote learning, and thin client/server applications. Remote desktop protocols are low-bandwidth connections that are optimized to send graphics data from server to client.

The different remote desktop connection protocols, such as ICA, RDP, X11, and others, are described. Among the applications described are Microsoft Remote Desktop Connection, Citrix GoToMyPC, and others.

Remote access servers not only provide a connection to a network but must also allow access to the network based on the user's credentials. One remote access server in common use is the Remote Authentication Dial-In User Service (RADIUS) system. RADIUS is an authentication, authorization, and accounting ("Triple A") server.

The nature of a RADIUS session is described, as is the range of different devices that the RADIUS service may be found on. RADIUS can be used to validate roaming clients. A future version of RADIUS called the Diameter protocol is discussed.

Remote Access

Remote access technology appears in nearly all network server operating systems, supported by applications offered by the operating system vendor or vigorously supported by the third-party market. It is used to enable remote clients to connect to the local area network securely. Typically the Remote Access Server (RAS) runs on a server, and Remote Access Client (RAC) software runs on the client as a client/server application. The client connects to the server either through a dial-up connection, or over the Internet using a standard Internet connection technology such as ADSL, ISDN, or something else over a Virtual Private Network (VPN).

Remote access server technology used to be the preferred connection technology when clients connected over dial-up connections on the telephone network. Dial-up access had a number of significant advantages: telephone lines were ubiquitous worldwide, modem technology based on digital audio conversion (DAC) technology was inexpensive and could be miniaturized, and the dial-up connection technology used was independent of any network hardware or software that a system was using.

Figure 32.1 shows some of the common scenarios for remote access technology. The four most common remote access scenarios are users connecting to a LAN through a Remote Access Server (often a RADIUS server), over the Internet from a client on another LAN (say in a branch office), from a computer in a SOHO (Small Office Home Office), or a remote client (usually a laptop) connecting through a wireless access point.

Although the cost of dial-up tended to be high and the security of a dial-up connection was low when dial-up connections were first used, as the technology matured, dial-up got cheaper and security protocols were developed that improved the connection security. The one factor of dial-up technology that can't be improved is the overall transfer speed. The bandwidth of a standard phone line connection (D0) is 56 Kbits/s, and although modems could approach this throughput with advanced compression technology, modems couldn't advance much beyond this limit. The use of multiple phone lines ganged together has served as an interim solution, but for the most part, phone line connections are being replaced by mobile network connection technologies such as Wi-Fi and DSL.

For all of these reasons, remote access server technology isn't nearly as important a topic as it used to be, although RAS is an important part of VPNs. The use of RAS over the Internet has become the most widely used form of remote access because Internet connectivity has become pervasive in most countries and regions. When connecting over the Internet to a RAS server using a VPN connection, you gain the advantage of a much higher bandwidth and much smaller incremental charges than phone lines, as well as the many authentication and encryption options that have been developed for the Internet protocol suite.

FIGURE 32.1

Remote access is most often applied to services provided for remote clients connected over the public telephone network.

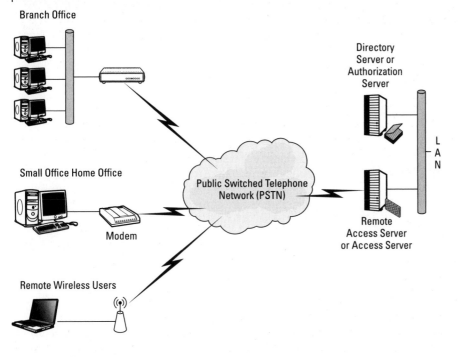

Cross-Ref

VPNs are covered in Chapter 29.

The whole point of remote access is to provide an experience for a connected user that is identical to the experience that the user might have with a direct connection to a LAN. To enable this experience, not only must the bandwidth of the connection be sufficiently high, but the user must also be authenticated and authorized on a per-resource basis, and the connection must be sufficiently protected. Modern remote access technology focuses on these three issues, as well as providing for an accounting function that service providers need.

In the sections that follow, you learn about some of the standard protocols used to make remote connections possible, the services that work with these standard protocols, and technologies that allow you to view the desktop of a remote system on your local computer.

Remote connection protocols

It is through the use of a remote access protocol that the connection between the remote user and the remote access server can be managed. The most commonly used remote access protocols today are:

- Serial Line Internet Protocol (SLIP)
- Point-to-Point Protocol (PPP)
- Point-to-Point Protocol over Ethernet (PPPoE)
- Point-to-Point Tunneling Protocol (PPTP)
- Layer 2 Tunneling Protocol (L2TP)

Cross-Ref

All of the aforementioned protocols are described in detail in Chapter 29, and all are connection protocols.

The SLIP, PPP, and PPPoE protocols are used for dial-up remote access, whereas PPTP and L2TP are used for VPN protocols when connecting remotely from one LAN to another (a WAN connection). Remote access requires more than simply a connection method. In order to authenticate and authorize a remote connection, different protocols needed to be developed. The most important authorization service in use is the Remote Authentication Dial-In Service (RADIUS), which is discussed in detail later in the chapter. The Microsoft version of RADIUS was called the Internet Authentication Service (IAS) prior to Windows Server 2003, and the Network Policy Server (NPS) from Windows 2003 on forward.

The original remote connection protocol by dial-up was SLIP; it was developed as the method for connecting green-screen terminals to mainframes, particularly to large UNIX-based systems. SLIP, which stands for Serial Line Internet Protocol, is a method for connecting to the Internet using serial ports and modem communications. SLIP is now considered to be obsolete, having been replaced by PPP, which has more advanced support for addressing and error control. SLIP continues to see limited use in situations where low-overhead communications are essential, such as in microcontroller applications, and in the BlueCore Serial Protocol used by some Bluetooth controllers.

Remote access services

A remote access service is a network service that accepts incoming connections from remote users, validates the credentials of the user, creates a secure connection, and serves as a gateway for access to network resources. Remote access servers can be implemented to accept connections in any one of the following types:

- From PPP or SLIP connections using DSL modems over WAN connections, that is, over long-distance links
- Routed traffic over an IP network
- VPN connections over an IPsec tunnel or some other secure connection type

Cross-Ref

VPN connections over an IPsec tunnel are discussed in Chapter 29.

- ATM broadband connections, or some other WAN protocol
- An asynchronous terminal connection using Telnet, TN3270, or a similar type of connection

Many remote access servers accept some combination of the aforementioned traffic, and often can translate between the different protocols that are used, when needed.

While most of the original RAS servers supported dial-in connections, today RAS is more commonly used for remote broadband services. When a remote access server is used for routing Internet traffic, it is referred to as a broadband RAS, or alternatively BRAS or BBRAS. BRAS are used to aggregate traffic from Digital Subscriber Line Access Multipliers (DSLAMs) so that the traffic can be managed and Quality of Service (QoS) can be applied. A BRAS is the endpoint of a remote client's PPP connections (either PPP over Ethernet or ATM), and adds the necessary session-level information, such as IP destinations, to packets that enable the communication to find its target. Many BRAS servers are front ends to a variety of AAA servers (Authentication, Authorization, and Accounting), the most common of which are the RADIUS servers that are described in detail later in the chapter.

Remote desktops

The term *remote desktop* is applied to software and a connection protocol that allows a remote system to display the graphical user interface of the system it is connected to inside a window on the client. While remote desktop technology is a form of remote access, it is different in both implementation and impact from the other types of remote access that this chapter has focused on. While remote access allows a client to gain access to network resources just as if the remote client were a local system, remote desktop software allows the client to control and view the server system as if the user were sitting in front of the system itself. An active remote desktop connection is referred to as a *session*, the same name given to a terminal server connection.

Remote desktop technology is used in the following applications:

- Remote computing applications
- Remote system management applications
- Help desk applications
- Remote learning applications
- Thin client/server applications

Remote desktop clients connect to systems using VPN connection protocols that are optimized for low-bandwidth transmission of keyboard and mouse input from the client, and display output from the server. These connection protocols are typically encrypted; the data that flows over these connections is highly compressed, making it possible for the client to connect to the server over low-speed connections such as phone lines with very good performance on the client. Remote desktop connection protocols are therefore a form of VPN connection protocol with emphasis on optimized graphic capabilities and remote printing and not necessarily focused on overall data throughput.

Note

For a comparison chart of remote desktop software by product name, operating system, and capabilities, go to en.wikipedia.org/wiki/Comparison_of_remote_desktop_software.

The most important remote desktop protocols in use today are:

- **Independent Computing Architecture (ICA),** the Citrix proprietary protocol that is used with Citrix WinFrame and XenApp (formerly called the Citrix MetaFrame and Presentation Servers).

- **Remote Desktop Protocol (RDP),** the Microsoft connection protocol used by its remote desktop software to connect to Windows systems. Clients using RDP are available for all modern desktop operating systems, and RDP clients can connect to systems using the Windows TS Gateway available in Windows 2008.

- **X Window System v X11,** used by many operating systems, but particularly UNIX and Linux, to connect clients to server systems.

- **NX Technology (NX),** a protocol that can be used by X Window Systems as an alternative to the X11 protocol.

- **Virtual Network Computing (VNC),** which uses the Remote Frame Buffering (RFB) protocol for remote desktop connections, is used by the RealVNC open source software.

ICA, RDP, and X11 work by using kernel-level drivers to redirect the graphic display subsystem output to the remote client. The other remote desktop connection protocols used by software such as PC Anywhere, VNC, and others use application-layer software to create and manage the VPN connection.

The Microsoft native Windows RDP server software is referred to as *Terminal Services* in Windows 2000, and *Remote Desktop Services* in Windows 2003/XP, Windows Server 2008/Vista, and Windows 7. On the Mac OS X desktop, the software is called *Remote Desktop*. Two open source RDP clients are XRDP (xrdp.sourceforge.net) and RDESKTOP (www.rdesktop.org). Figure 32.2 shows the Remote Desktop Connection client connection properties dialog box, which alters the features that you see in the remote desktop client software based on the speed of the connection you are using. You can also turn features on and off if they are of interest or if you want to improve performance.

Note

Microsoft offers a Web conferencing service called Microsoft Live Meeting (office.microsoft.com/en-us/livemeeting/default.aspx), and their enterprise conferencing server system is the Office Communications Server 2007 (office.microsoft.com/en-us/communicationsserver/default.aspx). LiveMeeting replaced the older NetMeeting product. Other important products in this area include IBM Lotus Sametime (www.ibm.com/sametime), Glance (www.glance.net), and WebEx (www.webex.com).

FIGURE 32.2

The Remote Desktop Connection client in Windows 7 and Vista allows you to adjust the features available in a remote desktop window.

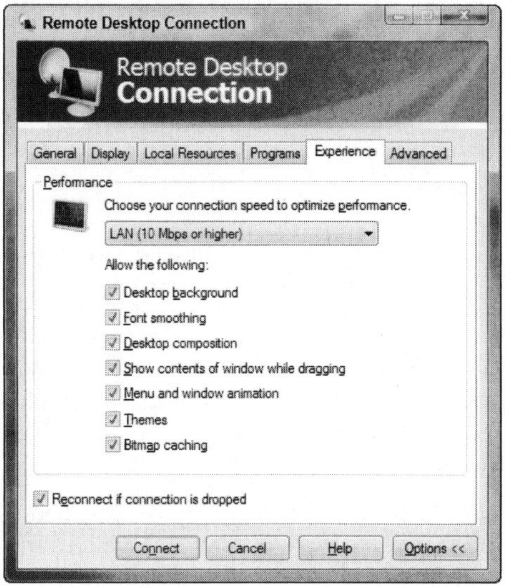

Remote desktop software is widely used in the help desk market. The two best-selling products in this area are Symantec (formerly Norton) pcAnywhere v12.5 (www.symantec.com/norton/symantec-pcanywhere) and Citrix Systems' GoToMyPC (www.gotomypc.com/). Symantec sells its product as a client/server application, while Citrix has combined the client/server software with a Web-based subscription service that transmits highly encrypted data in a manner that allows GoToMyPC clients to work through very selective firewalls.

Figure 32.3 shows GoToMyPC system architecture. GoToMyPC uses the GoToMyPC Broker to listen for session connection requests, authenticate clients, and then initiate a GoToMyPC session. Once the session is under way, the GoToMyPC Broker uses the Encrypted Polling Protocol (EPP) to ensure that the remote PC and host PC are the validated endpoints in the session that it created. This approach prevents another system from intercepting GoToMyPC traffic. Because all data flows through the GoToMyPC Communications Server where the encrypted packets are relayed, communications between the Broker and Communications Server is the additional check that maintains the validity of the host and remote systems in the remote desktop session.

GoToMyPC has been extended to include the GoToAssist conferencing feature and is sold as the GoToMeeting subscription service by Citrix Systems. This software broadcasts the desktop of a remote computer to a set of GoToMeeting clients over the Internet. The broadcasts are encrypted and password protected, and use a host-based architecture similar to that used by GoToMyPC. GoToMeeting can allow a single application to be shown, or the entire host desktop; it can also allow any of the participants to take over control of the host system, as well as record the session for later playback. A more expanded version of GoToMeeting called GoToWebinar, which allows for larger audiences, is also available.

FIGURE 32.3

The GoToMyPC system architecture uses a Web-based set of servers to authenticate sessions and to manage and relay session data.

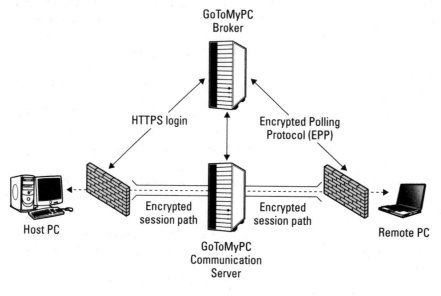

RADIUS Servers

The Remote Authentication Dial-In User Service (RADIUS) is the name of a networking protocol that allows remote users to be authenticated and connect to a LAN. RADIUS is deployed in the form of RADIUS servers, which can range from small RADIUS servers deployed on a SOHO network for a few users up to large enterprise-class RADIUS servers deployed in large telecommunication companies (TELCOS) or ISPs that service thousands of user connections, and all sizes in between. RADIUS also plays a central role in IEEE 802.11i security and works along with WEP to create a secure tunnel with Extensible Authentication Protocol (EAP) or Protected Extensible Authentication Protocol (PEAP) between remote clients and the Wi-Fi network. RADIUS is also commonly used by VoIP systems, where remote clients such as broadband phones connect to the VoIP server using a secure technology such as the Session Initiation Protocol (SIP) to the SIP registrar server.

Cross-Ref

802.11x Wi-Fi technologies are described in Chapter 14. For information about VoIP, return to Chapter 26.

RADIUS servers are essentially security gateways, and fall into a class of network services that are often referred to as AAA ("Triple A") servers. AAA servers refer to the following functions:

- **Authentication.** The RADIUS server provides a means to identify a remote user, and to enable or disable their connection. During authentication, a RADIUS server can determine whether the user's phone number is the authorized phone number, whether that user has a session in progress, as well as perform other tasks. Thus RADIUS can prevent a user with a stolen password from calling into a system from an unknown phone number.

  RADIUS servers may maintain a copy of the network user accounts, or it can be part of what is referred to as a *Pluggable Authentication Service* (PAM) architecture where authentication is passed through to a network access server or a domain server. Although storing user account information on a RADIUS server is certainly convenient from a manageability standpoint, doing so provides an attacker with all of the security information necessary to compromise the network should they gain access to the system. For this reason, it is preferred to have RADIUS pass authentication through to other servers on a session-by-session basis.

- **Authorization.** The RADIUS server determines the access rights and privileges that the user can have on the network. Authorization also determines the connection type that the RADIUS client may provide, such as PPP or Telnet.

- **Accounting.** RADIUS servers maintain detailed event logs and can organize event data to provide usage data for billing or accounting purposes. A RADIUS client sends usage information periodically to the RADIUS server during sessions, and the client can send an accounting request message to the server when logons or logoffs occur.

Note

RADIUS is an open standard as described in IETF RFC 2865 (`tools.ietf.org/html/rfc2865`). The accounting functionality in RADIUS is described in IETF RFC 2866 (`tools.ietf.org/html/rfc2866`). However, because RADIUS is extensible, different vendors implement RADIUS using their own set of attributes.

RADIUS servers are used in a wide variety of applications. You will find RADIUS as one of the services in routers; wireless access points; just behind firewalls or proxy servers in a perimeter network; as part of Web and e-mail servers; as Internet facing devices; and in VPN systems. RADIUS is the default authentication protocol for wireless networks conforming to the new 802.11i Wi-Fi standard.

Cisco uses the remote authentication protocol standard called the Terminal Access Controller Access-Control System (TACACS) in its routers and network servers. The original version of TACACS was designed for use in authenticating UNIX servers. Cisco has gone on to update and extend TACACS into a version called TACACS+ that is both a proprietary Cisco standard and incompatible with the original version of TACACS. Cisco recommends TACACS+ instead of

RADIUS, even though both protocols are often available on Cisco routers. Cisco has published the specifications for TACACS+ as an IETF RFC draft (see http://tools.ietf.org/html/draft-grant-tacacs-02/). TACACS+ is used for authentication and authorization, but not for accounting, and runs over TCP port 49 by default.

In the two sections that follow, you learn about the elements of RADIUS sessions and the way in which RADIUS allows mobile clients to roam.

RADIUS sessions

A RADIUS session has the following steps:

1. A remote user connects to a RADIUS client device using PPP or another Data Layer link protocol, and initiates a login.

2. The RADIUS client — a router, gateway, Network Access Server (NAS), or another device — creates a secure encrypted connection to the RADIUS server using a shared secret MD5-generated key encryption mechanism.

   RADIUS uses UDP port 1812 for authentication and 1813 for accounting. Older implementations of RADIUS used the unofficial ports 1645 and 1646 for these two functions, respectively. Some RADIUS implementations use both sets of ports; Microsoft uses 1812/1813 while Cisco and Juniper Networks RADIUS servers use 1645/1646.

3. A RADIUS Access Request message is then transmitted to the RADIUS server with the login information (user ID and password), system information (network address and login location) included using the Password Authentication Protocol (PAP), Challenge-Handshake Authentication Protocol (CHAP), or Extensible Authentication Protocol (EAP).

4. The RADIUS server verifies the login request either against a local database or with the authentication service running on the network.

   Authentication services can include LDAP servers (for a domain validation), Active Directory servers (on Windows networks), Kerberos servers (for a certificate validation), or SQL Server (or some other database for a database validation).

5. The validation then results in an Access Accept, Access Reject, or Access Challenged response.

   - *Access Accept* provides the user access to the resource that was requested. An Access Accept condition does not apply to all resources; each additional resource is checked as required, and the RADIUS client also verifies the original access offered on a periodic basis.

   - *Access Reject* locks the user out of the network, denying them access to the resource that was requested.

   - *Access Challenge* occurs when the system requires additional information in order to create a secure channel from the RADIUS server to the remote client that tunnels through the RADIUS client.

6. An Access Accept response results in the NAS (Network Attached Storage) providing the following services to the remote client: supply a static or dynamic IP address; assign a Time-To-Live for the session; download the client's Access Control List (ACL); and set up for L2TP, VLAN, and any QoS session parameters required.

7. Once the session is established at the RADIUS client, accounting begins with an Accounting Start message, which creates the session account record. Subsequent Interim Accounting messages populate the session account record, and an Account Stop message closes the session account record out.

Accounting information that is stored includes the following: time of session; number of packets and amount of data transferred; user and machine identification; network address; and point of attachment information. This database can then be used to generate billable information and statistical reporting, or for any other purpose.

RADIUS servers are available as open source freeware and shareware programs such as FreeRADIUS (www.freeradius.org), GNU Radius (www.gnu.org/software/radius), and OpenRADIUS (www. xs4all.nl/~evbergen/openradius/), among others; they are also available as commercial programs such as Juniper Networks' Steel Belted Radius (www.juniper.net/products_and_services/aaa_ and_802_1x/steel_belted_radius/index.html), and in some network server operating systems such as Windows Server. RADIUS was added to Windows as the IAS Server, starting with Windows Server 2000 in the Option Pack.

In Windows Server 2008, the Microsoft RADIUS server was renamed from the Internet Authentication Service (IAS) to the Network Policy Server (NPS), but the functionality remained about the same. RADIUS is now a relatively mature technology. Figure 32.4 shows how an NPS server is deployed on a Windows network. In this scheme, the NAS operates as the RADIUS client and provides the necessary network access once the authentication request to the RADIUS server is returned successfully.

FIGURE 32.4

A RADIUS server deployed on a Windows Server 2003 or later network

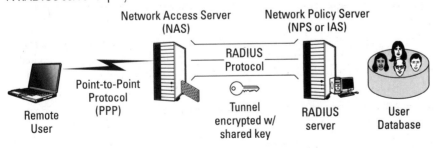

A RADIUS server can be configured to be a RADIUS client to other RADIUS servers. That is, a RADIUS server can perform the function of a proxy client, passing through authentication and accounting to other RADIUS servers. This proxy function is important when you deploy RADIUS in a perimeter network and need to ensure authenticated access to other portions of the network.

RADIUS roaming

Many RADIUS implementations require that the client be mobile and therefore must support a roaming feature. When a RADIUS client roams between networks, the client must have the AAA status moved to a different RADIUS server. Each set of RADIUS servers exists in what is called a *realm*. In order to identify a remote user connected to a RADIUS server, the server information is added using an @ sign and a postfix or by adding a backwards slash "\" and a prefix to the name of the client, or both. An example of the extended name would be domain_1.ext\userid@domain_2. ext, where two realms are indicated. A realm is simply a name given to the RADIUS server group and is not registered or tracked in any way; therefore, realm names are totally arbitrary.

Realms are stored in tables on the RADIUS servers, and any unknown realm must first be contacted or configured before a roaming client is allowed onto a network. RADIUS servers therefore play the role of a proxy server in that they forward AAA requests from roaming remote users that they can't find in their realm table to the domain server of the roaming client. The roaming table is manageable, and additional RADIUS servers can be added, modified, or stripped (removed) from the table. RADIUS doesn't specify how these management functions are implemented.

A remote client connects through a RADIUS client using a secure authenticated connection. When the client roams, security issues arise concerning how to establish a new secure connection. RADIUS solves this problem by establishing a two-layer security scheme, the details of which are dependent on the vendor implementation. With EAP, a secure tunnel is created between the authenticating RADIUS server (the inner identity) and the domain server, and an additional tunnel (the outer identity), which communicates in clear text, is used to allow proxy systems to route the packets appropriately. A roaming system can also create a secure, encrypted tunnel between RADIUS servers, thus hiding the user's security details from further view.

The Diameter protocol

RADIUS technology is getting a little old. The technology was first described by Merrit Network for NSFnet and developed by Livingston Enterprises in 1991. The replacement technology that is currently being developed is known as the Diameter protocol. Diameter replaces RADIUS's use of UDP transport with the reliable transport protocols TCP and SCTP. The name Diameter is a takeoff on the name RADIUS, as a diameter is twice the length of a radius, so the name has no other significance. As defined currently, the Diameter protocol is not backwards compatible with RADIUS, but RADIUS systems can be upgraded to Diameter.

Diameter is currently defined by the IETF RFC 3588 (`tools.ietf.org/html/rfc3588`) and includes all of the elements for an AAA server that RADIUS has. A Diameter service can be extended with vendor-specific attributes and with additional commands. As with RADIUS,

Diameter is a connection protocol and not an application. Diameter offers both Network and Transport layer security and can create secure tunnels over IPsec or TLS, over either stateful or stateless connections. There are a number of either new or improved features in Diameter that weren't in RADIUS, including:

- Dynamic peer discovery with Domain Name Service Records (DNS SRV) or Name Authority Pointer Records (NAPTR)

- Application layer acknowledgment and error messaging

- Session capability negotiation

- A client-server architecture

- Improved roaming capabilities

- A full set of AAA functions

A Diameter session between two peers begins first with the creation of a TCP or SCTP transport connection. One node acts as the initiator and the other acts as the target. The initiator sends a Capabilities-Exchange-Request (CER) to the target, which responds with a Capabilities-Exchange-Answer (CEA), leading to a negotiated TLS connection. Once the connection is established, applications can begin exchanging messages.

A TLS connection is monitored for activity. If a certain period of inactivity is detected, either peer sends a Device-Watchdog-Request (DWR) to the other peer, and that peer must return a Device-Watchdog-Answer (DWA) in exchange. Failure to exchange this information leads either peer to send a Disconnect-Peer-Request (DPR) message. If a Disconnect-Peer-Answer (DPA) isn't forthcoming, then the transport protocol is contacted and the connection is terminated.

Note
You can use the search page at www.ietf.org/rfc.html to find the RFCs mentioned in the following list, or any of IETF's other RFCs. The general form for any RFC URL is www.ietf.org/rfc/rfc####.txt, where #### is the RFC number padded with zeros to get to four digits if necessary.

Among the various Diameter-enabled applications so far defined by the IETF, you will find the following:

- Applications that are part of the 3GPP IP Multimedia Subsystem (www.3gpp.org/) for wireless connectivity

- Bootstrapping Server Function for mutual authentication of cellular network devices and servers, which is part of the 3GPP Standard (www.3gpp.org/)

- Diameter Credit-Control Application (DCCA, RFC 4006; `tools.ietf.org/html/rfc4006`)

- Diameter Extensible Authentication Protocol Application (RFC 4072; `tools.ietf.org/html/rfc4072`)

- Diameter Mobile IPv4 Application (MobileIP, RFC 4004; `http://tools.ietf.org/html/rfc4004`)

- Diameter Network Access Server Application (NASREQ, RFC 4005; `tools.ietf.org/html/rfc4005`)

- Diameter Session Initiation Protocol Application (RFC 4740)

Summary

In this chapter, different remote access technologies were described. Remote access used to be concerned primarily with low-bandwidth phone connections of clients to servers. The penetration of broadband technologies and the Internet has made VPN connections the dominant form of remote access. In this chapter, the various forms of remote access technologies were surveyed.

Remote desktop software is a related client/server technology to remote access. However, unlike remote access, where the connection is optimized for maximum data throughput and the remote client appears as a connected node on the network, remote desktop connections are optimized for graphic data transfer and low bandwidth. Different types of remote desktop software were described.

Remote access servers not only function as a point of access to a network, but they must also validate the client and selectively allow the remote client access to network resources. RADIUS servers were described as an example of what is known as a "Triple A" server, which stands for the functions authentication, authorization, and accounting.

TCP - UDP Port Assignments

Table A.1 lists many common ports in use for both the TCP and UDP protocols, under the Port column as T and U, respectively. The most widely used ports are typically found in the range 1 to 1023 and are referred to as the "well-known ports." A large range of port assignments are registered by vendors for specific applications. Over time, many of these port assignments become just as popular as well-known ports. Registered ports are found in the range 1024 to 49191. Finally, ICANN allows the remaining ports from 49152 to 65535 to be used either dynamically or for private assignments. Ports in the high range are not registered or assigned; they are for use by anyone at any time.

In many instances, TCP and UDP use the same numbers for the same protocol, but not always. Nor is a single protocol such as HTTP necessarily found on only one port assignment. There can be multiple ports assigned, and in the case of HTTP, the two common port assignments are not a contiguous range: both 80 and 8080 (for firewalls) are commonly used.

TABLE A.1

Well-Known Ports: 1 to 1023
Registered Ports: 1024 to 49191
Dynamic and Private Ports: 49152 to 65535 (unassigned)

Port	Assignment	Notes
0 - T, U	Reserved	
0 - T, U	Shirt Pocket netTunes; Shirt Pocket launchTunes	
1 - T, U	TCP Port Service Multiplexer	
2 - T, U	Management Utility	
3 - T, U	Compression Process	
5 - T, U	Remote Job Entry	
6 - T, U	Unassigned	
7 - T, U	Echo	
8 - T, U	Unassigned	
9 - T, U	Discard	
10 - T, U	Unassigned	
11 - T, U	Active Users	
12 - T, U	Unassigned	
13 - T, U	Daytime - (RFC 867)	
14 - T. P	Unassigned	
15 - T, U	Unassigned	
16 - T, U	Unassigned	
17 - T, U	Quote of the Day	
18 - T, U	Message Send Protocol	
19 - T, U	Character Generator	
20 - T, U	FTP - Default Data	
21 - T, U	FTP - Control Command	
22 - T, U	SSH Remote Login Protocol	
23 - T, U	Telnet	
24 - T, U	Any private mail system	
25 - T, U	Simple Mail Transfer Protocol (SMTP)	
26 - T, U	RSFTP	Unofficial
27 - T, U	New User System FE	
28 - T, U	Unassigned	
29 - T, U	MSG ICP	

Port	Assignment	Notes
30 - T, U	Unassigned	
31 - T, U	MSG Authentication	
32 - T, U	Unassigned	
33 - T, U	Display Support Protocol	
34 - T, U	Unassigned	
35 - T, U	Any private printer server protocol	
35 - T, U	QMS Magicolor 2 printer server protocol	Unofficial
36 - T, U	Unassigned	
37 - T, U	TIME protocol	
38 - T, U	Remote Access Protocol	
39 - T, U	Resource Location Protocol (RLP)	
40 - T, U	Unassigned	
41 - T, U	Graphics	
42 - T, U	ARPA Host Name Server Protocol	
42 - T, U	WINS	Unofficial
43 - T, U	WHOIS Protocol	
44 - T, U	MPM FLAGS Protocol	
45 - T, U	Message Processing Module	
46 - T, U	MPM (default send)	
47 - T, U	NI FTP	
48 - T, U	Digital Audit Daemon	
49 - T, U	TACACS Login Host Protocol	
50 - T, U	Remote Mail Checking Protocol	
51 - T, U	IMP Logical Address Maintenance	
52 - T, U	Xerox Network Services (XNS) Time Protocol	
53 - T, U	Domain Name System (DNS)	
54 - T, U	Xerox Network Services (XNS) Clearinghouse	
55 - T, U	ISI Graphics Language	
56 - T, U	Xerox Network Services (XNS) Authentication	
56 - T, U	Route Access Protocol (RAP)	Unofficial
57 - T	Mail Transfer Protocol (MTP)	Unofficial
57 - T, U	Any private mail system	
58 - T, U	Xerox Network Services (XNS) Mail	

continued

TABLE A.1	(continued)	
Port	**Assignment**	**Notes**
59 - T, U	Any private file service	
60 - T, U	Unassigned	
61 - T, U	NI Mail	
62 - T, U	ACA Services	
63 - T, U	whois++	
64 - T, U	Communications Integrator (CI)	
65 - T, U	TACACS - Database Service	
66 - T, U	Oracle SQL*NET	
67 - T, U	Bootstrap Protocol (BOOTP) Server	
68 - T, U	Bootstrap Protocol (BOOTP) Client	
69 - T, U	Trivial File Transfer Protocol (TFTP)	
70 - T, U	Gopher Protocol	
71 - T, U	Remote Job Service	
72 - T, U	Remote Job Service	
73 - T, U	Remote Job Service	
74 - T, U	Remote Job Service	
75 - T, U	Any private dial out service	
76 - T, U	Distributed External Object Store	
77 - T, U	Any private RJE server	
78 - T, U	Vettcp	
79 - T, P	Finger Protocol	
80 - T, P	Hypertext Transfer Protocol (HTTP)	
81 - T, P	Unassigned	
82 - T, U	XFER Utility	
83 - T, U	MIT ML Device	
84 - T, U	Common Trace Facility	
85 - T, U	MIT ML Device	
86 - T, U	Micro Focus Cobol	
87 - T, U	Any private terminal link	
88 - T, P	Kerberos	
90 - T, U	DNSIX Security Attribute Token Map	
90 - T, U	PointCast	Unofficial
91 - T, U	MIT Dover Spooler	

Port	Assignment	Notes
92 - T, U	Network Printing Protocol	
93 - T, U	Device Control Protocol	
94 - T, U	Tivoli Object Dispatcher	
95 - T, U	SUPDUP	
96 - T, U	DIXIE Protocol Specification	
97 - T, U	Swift Remote Virtual File Protocol	
98 - T, U	TAC News	
99 - T, U	Metagram Relay	
100 - T	Unauthorized use	
101 - T, U	NIC Host Name Server	
102 - T, U	ISO Transport Service Access Point (TSAP) Class 0 Protocol	
103 - T, U	Genesis Point-to-Point Trans Net	
104 - T, U	ACR-NEMA Digital Imag. & Comm. 300	
105 - T, U	Mailbox Name Nameserver	
106 - T, U	3COM-TSMUX	
106 - T, U	Insecure poppassd Protocol	Unauthorized
107 - T, U	Remote Telnet Service Protocol	
108 - T, U	SNA Gateway Access Server	
109 - T, U	Post Office Protocol 2 (POP2)	
110 - T, U	Post Office Protocol 3 (POP3)	
111 - T, U	Sun Remote Procedure Call	
112 - T, U	McIDAS Data Transmission Protocol	
113 - T, U	Authentication Service	
114 - T, U	Deprecated June 2004	
115 - T, U	Simple File Transfer Protocol (SFTP)	
116 - T, U	ANSA REX Notify	
117 - T, U	UUCP Path Service	
118 - T, U	Structured Query Language (SQL) Services	
119 - T, P	Network News Transfer Protocol (NNTP)	
120 - T, P	CFDPTKT	
121 - T, P	Encore Expedited Remote Pro.Call	
122 - T, P	SMAKYNET	
123 - T, U	Network Time Protocol (NTP)	

continued

TABLE A.1 *(continued)*

Port	Assignment	Notes
124 - T, U	ANSA REX Trader	
125 - T, U	Locus PC-Interface Net Map Ser	
126 - T, U	NxEdit	Previously assigned to Unisys Unitary Login
127 - T, U	Locus PC-Interface Conn Server	
128 - T, U	GSS X License Verification	
129 - T, U	Password Generator Protocol	
130 - T, U	Cisco FNATIVE	
131 - T, U	Cisco TNATIVE	
132 - T, U	Cisco SYSMAINT	
133 - T, U	Statistics Service	
134 - T, U	INGRES-NET Service	
135 - T, U	DCE endpoint resolution	
135 - T, U	Microsoft End Point Mapper (EPMAP), AKA DCE/RPC Locator service	Unofficial
137 - T, U	NetBIOS Name Service	
138 - T, U	NetBIOS Datagram Service	
139 - T, U	NetBIOS Session Service	
140 - T, U	EMFIS Data Service	
141 - T, U	EMFIS Control Service	
142 - T, U	Britton-Lee IDM	
143 - T, U	Internet Message Access Protocol (IMAP)	
152 - T, U	Background File Transfer Program (BFTP)	
153 - T, U	Simple Gateway Monitoring Protocol (SGMP)	
156 - T, U	SQL Service	
158 - T, U	Distributed Mail Service Protocol (DMSP)	Unofficial
161 - T, U	Simple Network Management Protocol (SNMP)	Official
162 - T, U	Simple Network Management Protocol Trap (SNMPTRAP)	Official
170 - T	Print-srv, Network PostScript	Official
177 - T, U	X Display Manager Control Protocol (XDMCP)	Official
179T	Border Gateway Protocol (BGP)	Official
194T	Internet Relay Chat (IRC)	Official
201 - T, U	AppleTalk Routing Maintenance	Official

Port	Assignment	Notes
209 - T, U	The Quick Mail Transfer Protocol	Official
213 - T, U	IPX	Official
218 - T, U	Message Posting Protocol (MPP)	Official
220 - T, U	Interactive Mail Access Protocol (IMAP) version 3	Official
259 - T, U	Efficient Short Remote Operations (ESRO)	Official
264 - T, U	Border Gateway Multicast Protocol (BGMP)	Official
311 - T	Mac OS X Server Admin (officially AppleShare IP Web administration)	Official
318 - T, U	PKIX Time Stamp Protocol (TSP)	Official
323 - T, U	Internet Message Mapping Protocol (IMMP)	Unofficial
366 - T, U	On-Demand Mail Relay (ODMR)	Official
369 - T, U	Rpc2portmap	Official
387 - T, U	AppleTalk Update-based Routing Protocol (AURP)	Official
389 - T, U	Lightweight Directory Access Protocol (LDAP)	Official
401 - T, U	Uninterruptible Power Supply (UPS)	Official
402 - T	Altiris Deployment Client	Unofficial
411 - T	Direct Connect Hub	Unofficial
412 - T	Direct Connect Client-to-Client	Unofficial
427 - T, U	Service Location Protocol (SLP)	Official
443 - T	Hypertext Transfer Protocol over TLS/SSL (HTTPS)	Official
444 - T, U	Simple Network Paging Protocol (SNPP) (RFC 1568)	Official
445T	Microsoft-DS Active Directory, Windows shares	Official
445 -U	Microsoft-DS SMB file sharing	Official
464 - T, U	Kerberos Change/Set password	Official
465T	Cisco protocol	Unofficial
465T	SMTP over SSL	Unofficial
500 - U	Internet Security Association and Key Management Protocol (ISAKMP)	Official
502 - T, U	Modbus Protocol	Unofficial
513T	Login	Official
513 - U	Who	Official
514T	Shell	Official
514 - U	Syslog	Official

continued

TABLE A.1	*(continued)*	
Port	**Assignment**	**Notes**
515 - T	Line Printer Daemon (print service)	Official
517 - U	Talk	Official
518 - U	Ntalk	Official
520T	Extended filename server (EFS)	Official
520 - U	Routing Internet Protocol (RIP)	Official
524 - T, U	NetWare Core Protocol (NCP)	Official
525 - U	Timed, Timeserver	Official
530 - T, U	RPC	Official
531 - T, U	AOL Instant Messenger, IRC	Unofficial
540T	Unix-to-Unix Copy Protocol (UUCP)	Official
542 - T, U	Commerce (Commerce Applications)	Official
543T	Kerberos login (klogin)	Official
544T	Kerberos Remote shell (kshell)	Official
546 - T, U	DHCPv6 client	Official
547 - T, U	DHCPv6 server	Official
548T	Apple Filing Protocol (AFP) over TCP	Official
550 - U	new-rwho, new-who	Official
554 - T, U	Real Time Streaming Protocol (RTSP)	Official
556T	Remotefs, RFS, rfs_server	Official
560 - U	Remote Monitor (rmonitor)	Official
561 - U	Monitor	Official
563 - T, U	NNTP protocol over TLS/SSL (NNTPS)	Official
587T	Simple Mail Transfer Protocol (message submission)	Official
591T	FileMaker 6.0 (and later) Web Sharing (HTTP Alternate, also see port 80)	Official
593 - T, U	HTTP RPC Ep Map, R	Official
631 - T, U	Internet Printing Protocol (IPP)	Official
636 - T, U	Lightweight Directory Access Protocol over TLS/SSL (LDAPS)	Official
639 - T, U	Multicast Source Discovery Protocol (MSDP)	Official
646 - T, U	Label Distribution Protocol (LDP), a routing protocol used in MPLS networks	Official
647 - T	Dynamic Host Configuration Protocol (DHCP) Failover	Official

Port	Assignment	Notes
648 - T	Registry Registrar Protocol (RRP)	Official
652 - T	Dynamic Tunnel Configuration Protocol (DTCP)	Unofficial
654 - T	Ad-hoc On-demand Distance Vector (AODV)	Official
655 - T	IEEE Media Management System (IEEE MMS)	Official
657 - T, U	IBM Remote Monitoring and Control (RMC) Protocol	Official
660 - T	Mac OS X Server administration	Official
666 - U	Doom	Official
674 - T	Application Configuration Access Protocol (ACAP)	Official
691 - T	MS Exchange Routing	Official
694 - U	Linux-HA High Availability Heartbeat	Unofficial
695 - T	IEEE Media Management System over SSL (IEEE-MMS-SSL)	Official
698 - U	Optimized Link State Routing (OLSR)	Official
700 - T	Extensible Provisioning Protocol (EPP)	Official
701 - T	Link Management Protocol (LMP)	Official
702 - T	Internet Registry Information Service (IRIS) over Blocks Extensible Exchange Protocol (BEEP)	Official
706 - T	Secure Internet Live Conferencing (SILC)	Official
712 - T	Topology Broadcast based on Reverse-Path Forwarding (TBRPF) routing protocol	Official
749 - T, U	Kerberos Administration	Official
750 - T	RFile	Official
750 - U	Loadav	Official
750 - U	Kerberos version IV (Kerberos IV)	Official
751 - T, U	Pump	Official
751 - T, U	Kerberos authentication (kerberos_master)	Unofficial
752 - T	qrh	Official
752 - U	qrh	Official
752 - U	userreg_server, Kerberos Password (kpasswd) server	Unofficial
753 - T	Reverse Routing Header (RRH)	Official
753 - U	Reverse Routing Header (RRH)	Official
753 - U	Kerberos userreg server (passwd_server)	Unofficial
754 - T	tell send	Official

continued

TABLE A.1 *(continued)*

Port	Assignment	Notes
754 - T	Kerberos v5 slave propagation (krb5_prop)	Unofficial
754 - U	tell send	Official
760 - T, U	ns	Official
783 - T	SpamAssassin spamd daemon	Unofficial
829 - T	Certificate Management Protocol (CMP)	Unofficial
860 - T	iSCSI	Official
873 - T	rsync file synchronization protocol	Official
901 - T	Samba Web Administration Tool (SWAT)	Unofficial
901T - U	VMware Virtual Infrastructure Client	Unofficial
902 - T	VMware Server Console	Unofficial
904 - T	VMware Server Alternate	Unofficial
953 - T, U	Domain Name System (DNS) RDNC Service	Official
989 - T, U	FTPS Protocol (data): FTP over TLS/SSL	Official
990 - T, U	FTPS Protocol (control): FTP over TLS/SSL	Official
992 - T, U	TELNET protocol over TLS/SSL	Official
993 - T	Internet Message Access Protocol over SSL (IMAPS)	Official
995 - T	Post Office Protocol 3 over TLS/SSL (POP3S)	Official
1025 - T	NFS-or-IIS	Unofficial
1026 - T	Microsoft DCOM services	Unofficial
1029 - T	Microsoft DCOM services	Unofficial
1058 - T, U	nim, IBM AIX Network Installation Manager (NIM)	Official
1059 - T, U	nimreg, IBM AIX Network Installation Manager (NIM)	Official
1080 - T	SOCKS proxy	Official
1085 - T, U	WebObjects	Official
1098 - T, U	RMI Activation (rmiactivation)	Official
1099 - T, U	RMI Registry (rmiregistry)	Official
1109 - T	Kerberos Post Office Protocol (KPOP)	Unofficial
1140 - T, U	AutoNOC Network Operations protocol	Official
1167 - U	Phone, conference calling	Unofficial
1194 - T, U	OpenVPN	Official
1214 - T	Kazaa	Official

Port	Assignment	Notes
1220 - T	QuickTime Streaming Server administration	Official
1223 - T, U	TrulyGlobal Protocol (TGP)	Official
1234 - U	VLC media player Default port for UDP/RTP stream	Unofficial
1270 - T, U	Microsoft System Center Operations Manager (SCOM; AKAMS MOM) agent	Official
1293 - T, U	Internet Protocol Security (IPSec)	Official
1311 - T	Dell Open Manage HTTPS	Unofficial
1352 - T	IBM Lotus Notes/Domino Remote Procedure Call (RPC) Protocol	Official
1387 - T, U	cadsi-lm, LMS International (formerly Computer Aided Design Software, Inc. [CADSI]) LM	Official
1414 - T	IBM WebSphere MQ (formerly known as MQSeries)	Official
1417 - T, U	Timbuktu Service 1 Port	Official
1418 - T, U	Timbuktu Service 2 Port	Official
1419 - T, U	Timbuktu Service 3 Port	Official
1420 - T, U	Timbuktu Service 4 Port	Official
1433 - T, U	Microsoft SQL Server database management system Server	Official
1434 - T, U	Microsoft SQL Server database management system Monitor	Official
1494 - T	Citrix XenApp Independent Computing Architecture (ICA) thin client protocol	Official
1512 - T, U	Microsoft Windows Internet Name Service (WINS)	Official
1521 - T	Oracle database default listener, in future releases official port 2483	Unofficial
1524 - T, U	ingreslock, ingres	Official
1526 - T	Oracle database common alternative for listener	Unofficial
1533 - T	IBM Sametime IM — Virtual Places Chat SQL Server	Official
1547 - T, U	Laplink	Official
1581 - U	MIL STD 2045-47001 VMF	Official
1589 - U	Cisco VLAN Query Protocol (VQP) / VMPS	Unofficial
1645 - T, U	radius, RADIUS authentication protocol (default for Cisco and Juniper Networks RADIUS servers)	Unofficial

continued

TABLE A.1	*(continued)*	
Port	**Assignment**	**Notes**
1646 - T, U	radaccT, RADIUS accounting protocol (default for Cisco and Juniper Networks RADIUS servers)	Unofficial
1677 - T, U	Novell GroupWise clients	Official
1701 - U	Layer 2 Forwarding Protocol (L2F) & Layer 2 Tunneling Protocol (L2TP)	Official
1723 - T, U	Microsoft Point-to-Point Tunneling Protocol (PPTP)	Official
1725 - U	Valve Steam Client	Unofficial
1755 - T, U	Microsoft Media Services (MMS, ms-streaming)	Official
1761 - T, U	cft-0	Official
1761 - T	Novell ZENworks Remote Control utility	Unofficial
1762–1768 - T, U	cft-1 to cft-7	Official
1812 - T, U	radius, RADIUS authentication protocol	Official
1813 - T, U	radaccT, RADIUS accounting protocol	Official
1863 - T	Microsoft Notification Protocol (MSNP)	Official
1900 - U	Microsoft SSDP for UPnP devices	Official
1935 - T	Adobe Macromedia Flash Real Time Messaging Protocol (RTMP)	Official
1975–1977 - U	Cisco TCO (Documentation)	Official
1985 - U	Cisco HSRP	Official
1994 - T, U	Cisco Serial Tunneling — Synchronous Data Link Control (STUN-SDLC) Protocol	Official
1998 - T, U	Cisco X.25 over TCP (XOT) service	Official
2000 - T, U	Cisco SCCP (Skinny)	Official
2002 - T	Secure Access Control Server (ACS) for Windows	Unofficial
2030	Oracle Services for Microsoft Transaction Server	Unofficial
2049 - U	Network File System	Official
2053 - T	knetd Kerberos de-multiplexor	Unofficial
2083 - T	Secure Radius Service (RadSec)	Official
2083 - T	CPanel default SSL	Unofficial
2086 - T	GNUnet	Official
2086 - T	WebHost Manager default	Unofficial
2087 - T	WebHost Manager default SSL	Unofficial
2105 - T, U	IBM MiniPay	Official
2105 - T, U	eklogin Kerberos encrypted remote login (rlogin)	Unofficial

Port	Assignment	Notes
2161 - T	APC Agent	Official
2181 - T, U	EForward - document transport system	Official
2190 - U	TiVoConnect Beacon	Unofficial
2219 - T, U	NetIQ NCAP Protocol	Official
2220 - T, U	NetIQ End2End	Official
2222 - T	DirectAdmin default	Unofficial
2302 - U	Halo	Unofficial
2369 - T	BMC Software CONTROL-M/Server — Configuration Agent	Unofficial
2370 - T	BMC Software CONTROL-M/Server	Unofficial
2404 - T	IEC 60870-5-104	Official
2427 - U	Cisco MGCP	Official
2447 - T, U	Ovwdb — OpenView Network Node Manager (NNM) daemon	Official
2483 - T, U	Oracle database listening (replaces port 1521)	Official
2484 - T, U	Oracle database listening for SSL client connections to the listener	Official
2598 - T	New ICA — when Session Reliability is enabled, TCP port 2598 replaces port 1494	Unofficial
2710 - T	XBT BitTorrent Tracker	Unofficial
2710 - U	XBT BitTorrent Tracker experimental UDP tracker extension	Unofficial
2735 - T, U	NetIQ Monitor Console	Official
2809 - T	IBM WebSphere Application Server (WAS) Bootstrap/rmi default	Unofficial
2948 - T, U	WAP-push Multimedia Messaging Service (MMS)	Official
2949 - T, U	WAP-pushsecure Multimedia Messaging Service (MMS)	Official
2967 - T	Symantec AntiVirus Corporate Edition	Unofficial
3025 - T	netpd.org	Unofficial
3074 - T, U	Xbox Live	Official
3260 - T, U	iSCSI target	Official
3268 - T, U	msft-gc, Microsoft Global Catalog (LDAP service)	Official
3269 - T, U	msft-gc-ssl, Microsoft Global Catalog over SSL	Official
3283 - T	Apple Remote Desktop reporting (officially Net Assistant)	Official

continued

851

TABLE A.1 *(continued)*

Port	Assignment	Notes
3306 - T, U	MySQL database system	Official
3389 - T	Microsoft Terminal Server (RDP) officially registered as Windows Based Terminal (WBT)	Unofficial
3396 - T, U	Novell NDPS Printer Agent	Official
3455 - T, U	Reservation Protocol (RSVP)	Official
3689 - T	Digital Audio Access Protocol (DAAP) for Apple iTunes and AirPort Express	Official
3702 - T, U	Web Services Dynamic Discovery (WS-Discovery), used by various components of Windows Vista	Official
3868 - T, Stream Control Transfer Protocol (SCTP)	Diameter base protocol (RFC 3588)	Official
3872 - T	Oracle Management Remote Agent	Unofficial
3899 - T	Remote Administrator	Unofficial
3900 - T	udt_os, IBM UniData UDT OS[30]	Official
4100	WatchGuard Authentication Applet—default	Unofficial
4125 - T	Microsoft Remote Web Workplace administration	Unofficial
4224 - T	Cisco Discovery Protocol (CDP)	Unofficial
4500 - U	IPsec NAT traversal	Official
4664 - T	Google Desktop Search	Unofficial
4993 - T, U	Home FTP Server Web Interface Default Port	
4899 - T, U	Radmin remote administration tool (sometimes used as a Trojan)	Official
5000 - T	UPnP—Windows network device interoperability	Unofficial
5001 - T, U	Iperf (Tool for measuring TCP and UDP bandwidth performance)	Unofficial
5001 - T	Slingbox and SlingPlayer	Unofficial
5003 - T, U	FileMaker	Official
5004 - T, U, Datagram Congestion Control Protocol (DCCP)	Real-time Transport Protocol (RTP) media data	Official
5005 - T, U, DCCP	Real-time Transport Protocol (RTP) control protocol	Official
5050 - T	Yahoo! Messenger	Unofficial
5060 - T, U	Session Initiation Protocol (SIP)	Official

Port	Assignment	Notes
5061 - T	Session Initiation Protocol (SIP) over TLS	Official
5093 - U	Statistical Package for the Social Sciences (SPSS) License Administrator	Unofficial
5104 - T	IBM Tivoli Framework NetCOOL/Impact HTTP Service	Unofficial
5190 - T	ICQ and AOL Instant Messenger	Official
5351 - T, U	NAT Port Mapping Protocol	Official
5353 - U	Multicast DNS (MDNS)	Official
5355 - T, U	Link-Local Multicast Name Resolution (LLMNR)	Official
5432 - T, U	PostgreSQL database system	Official
5445 - U	Cisco Unified Video Advantage	Unofficial
5500 - T	VNC remote desktop protocol	Unofficial
5517 - T	SETIQueue Proxy server client for SETI@Home project	Unofficial
5631 - T	pcANYWHEREdata	Official
5632 - U	pcANYWHERE-sta	Official
5800 - T	VNC remote desktop protocol—for use over HTTP	Unofficial
5814 - T, U	Hewlett-Packard Support Automation (HP OpenView Self-Healing Services)	Official
5900 - T, U	Virtual Network Computing (VNC) remote desktop protocol (used by Apple Remote Desktop and others)	Official
6000 - T	X11	Official
6001 - U	X11	Official
6005 - T	BMC Software CONTROL-M/Server	Unofficial
6346 - T, U	gnutella-svc, Gnutella (FrostWire, LimeWire, Shareaza, and so on)	Official
6347 - T, U	gnutella-rtr, Gnutella alternate	Official
6444 - T, U	Sun Grid Engine — Qmaster Service	Official
6445 - T, U	Sun Grid Engine — Execution Service	Official
6571	Windows Live FolderShare client	Unofficial
6600 - T	Music Playing Daemon (MPD)	Unofficial
6660–6664 - T	Internet Relay Chat	Unofficial
6665–6669 - T	Internet Relay Chat	Official
6679 - T	IRC SSL (Secure Internet Relay Chat)	Unofficial

continued

Port	Assignment	Notes
6697 - T	IRC SSL (Secure Internet Relay Chat)	Unofficial
6771 - U	Polycom server broadcast	Unofficial
6881–6887 - T, U	BitTorrent	Unofficial
6888 - T, U	MUSE	Official
6888 - T, U	BitTorrent	Unofficial
6889–6890 - T, U	BitTorrent	Unofficial
6891–6900 - T, U	BitTorrent	Unofficial
6891–6900 - T, U	Windows Live Messenger (File transfer)	Unofficial
6901 - T, U	Windows Live Messenger (Voice)	Unofficial
6901 - T, U	BitTorrent	Unofficial
6902–6968 - T, U	BitTorrent	Unofficial
6969 - T	BitTorrent tracker	Unofficial
6970–6999 - T, U	BitTorrent	Unofficial
7001 - T	BEA WebLogic Server's HTTP server	Unofficial
7002 - T	BEA WebLogic Server's HTTPS server	Unofficial
7005 - T, U	BMC Software CONTROL-M/Server and CONTROL-M/Agent	Unofficial
7006 - T, U	BMC Software CONTROL-M/Server and CONTROL-M/Agent	Unofficial
7010 - T	Cisco AON AMC (AON Management Console)	Unofficial
7400 - T, U	Real Time Publish Subscribe (RTPS) DDS Discovery	Official
7401 - T, U	Real Time Publish Subscribe (RTPS) DDS User-Traffic	Official
7402 - T, U	RTPS (Real Time Publish Subscribe) DDS Meta-Traffic	Official
7777 - T	iChat server file transfer proxy	Unofficial
7777 - T	Default used by Windows backdoor program tini.exe	Unofficial
8000 - T, U	Intel Remote Desktop Management Interface (iRDMI)	Official
8000–8001 - T	Internet radio streams such as SHOUTcast	Unofficial
8002 - T	Cisco Systems Unified CallManager Intercluster	Unofficial
8008 - T	HTTP Alternate	Official
8008 - T	IBM HTTP Server administration default	Unofficial

TABLE A.1 (continued)

Port	Assignment	Notes
8080 - T	HTTP alternate (http_alt) — commonly used for Web proxy and caching server, or for running a Web server as a non-root user	Official
8080 - T	Apache Tomcat	Unofficial
8081 - T	HTTP alternate, such as McAfee ePolicy Orchestrator (ePO)	Unofficial
8086 - T	Kaspersky AntiVirus Control Center	Unofficial
8087 - U	Kaspersky AntiVirus Control Center	Unofficial
8090 - T	HTTP Alternate (http_alt_alt) — used as an alternative to port 8080	Unofficial
8192 - T	Sophos Remote Management System	Unofficial
8193 - T	Sophos Remote Management System	Unofficial
8194 - T	Sophos Remote Management System	Unofficial
8200 - T	GoToMyPC	Unofficial
8220 - T	Bloomberg	Unofficial
8222	VMware Server Management User Interface (insecure Web interface)	Unofficial
8243 - T, U	HTTPS listener for Apache Synapse	Official
8280 - T, U	HTTP listener for Apache Synapse	Official
8294 - T	Bloomberg	Unofficial
8333	VMware Server Management User Interface (secure Web interface)	Unofficial
8400 - T, U	cvp, CommVault Unified Data Management	Official
8500 - T	ColdFusion Macromedia/Adobe ColdFusion default	Unofficial
8880 - U	cddbp-al - T, CD DataBase (CDDB) Protocol (CDDBP) alternate	Official
8880 - T	cddbp-al - T, CD DataBase (CDDB) Protocol (CDDBP) alternate	Official
8880 - T	WebSphere Application Server SOAP connector default	Unofficial
8888 - T	Sun AnswerBook dwhttpd server (deprecated by docs.sun.com)	Unofficial
8888 - T	GNUmp3d HTTP music streaming and Web interface	Unofficial
9000 - T	Buffalo LinkSystem Web access	Unofficial
9000 - U	UDPCast	Unofficial

continued

TABLE A.1 *(continued)*

Port	Assignment	Notes
9001	cisco-xremote router configuration	Unofficial
9001	Tor network default	Unofficial
9030 - T	Tor often used	Unofficial
9043 - T	WebSphere Application Server Administration Console secure	Unofficial
9050 - T	Tor	Unofficial
9051 - T	Tor	Unofficial
9060 - T	WebSphere Application Server Administration Console	Unofficial
9080 - U	glrpc, Groove Collaboration software GLRPC	Official
9080 - T	glrpc, Groove Collaboration software GLRPC	Official
9080 - T	WebSphere Application Server HTTP Transport (port 1) default	Unofficial
9110 - U	SSMP Message Protocol	Unofficial
9443 - T	WSO2 Web Services Application Server HTTPS transport (officially WSO2 Tungsten HTTPS)	Official
9443 - T	WebSphere Application Server HTTP Transport (port 2) default	Unofficial
9535 - T	mngsuite, LANDesk Management Suite Remote Control	Official
9535 - T	BBOS001, IBM WebSphere Application Server (WAS) High Availability Manager Communications	Unofficial
9535 - U	mngsuite, LANDesk Management Suite Remote Control	Official
9800 - T, U	WebDAV Source	Official
9800	WebCT e-learning portal	Unofficial
9898 - T	Tripwire — File Integrity Monitoring Software	Unofficial
9999 - T	Lantronix UDS-10/UDS100[43] RS-485 to Ethernet Converter TELNET control	Unofficial
10000	Webmin — Web-based Linux admin tool	Unofficial
10000	Backup Exec	Unofficial
10001 - T	Lantronix UDS-10/UDS100[44] RS-485 to Ethernet Converter default	Unofficial
10017	AIX, NeXT, HPUX — rexd daemon control	Unofficial
10113 - T, U	NetIQ Endpoint	Official

Port	Assignment	Notes
10114 - T, U	NetIQ QCheck	Official
10115 - T, U	NetIQ Endpoint	Official
10116 - T, U	NetIQ VoIP Assessor	Official
11211	memcached	Unofficial
11371	OpenPGP HTTP key server	Official
11576	IPStor Server management communication	Unofficial
12035 - U	Linden Lab viewer to sim	Unofficial
12345	NetBus — remote administration tool (often a Trojan)	Unofficial
12975 - T	LogMeln Hamachi (VPN tunnel software)	Unofficial
13000–13050 - U	Linden Lab viewer to sim	Unofficial
13720 - T, U	Symantec NetBackup — bprd	Official
13721 - T, U	Symantec NetBackup — bpdbm	Official
13724 - T, U	Symantec Network Utility — vnetd	Official
13782 - T, U	Symantec NetBackup — bpcd	Official
13783 - T, U	Symantec VOPIED Protocol	Official
13785 - T, U	Symantec NetBackup Database — nbdb	Official
13786 - T, U	Symantec nomdb	Official
14567 - U	Battlefield 1942 and mods	Unofficial
16000 - T	shroudBNC	Unofficial
16080 - T	Mac OS X Server Web (HTTP) service with performance cache	Unofficial
16384 - U	Iron Mountain Digital online backup	Unofficial
18180 - T	DART Reporting server	Unofficial
19226 - T	Panda Software AdminSecure Communication Agent	Unofficial
19638 - T	Ensim Control Panel	Unofficial
19771 - T, U	Softros LAN Messenger	Unofficial
19813 - T	4D Database Client Server Communication	Unofficial
19880 - T	Softros LAN Messenger	Unofficial
20000	Distributed Network Protocol (DNP), used in SCADA	Official
20000	Usermin, Web-based user tool	Unofficial
20014 - T	DART Reporting server	Unofficial

continued

TABLE A.1 *(continued)*

Port	Assignment	Notes
20720 - T	Symantec i3 Web GUI server	Unofficial
22347 - T, U	WibuKey, WIBU-SYSTEMS AG Software protection system	Official
22350 - T, U	CodeMeter, WIBU-SYSTEMS AG Software protection system	Official
24444	NetBeans integrated development environment	Unofficial
24800	Synergy: keyboard/mouse sharing software	Unofficial
25999 - T	Xfire	Unofficial
26000 - T, U	id Software Quake server	Official
27000 - U	(Through 27006) id Software QuakeWorld master server	Unofficial
27010	Half-Life and its mods, such as Counter-Strike	Unofficial
27015	Half-Life and its mods, such as Counter-Strike	Unofficial
27374	Sub7 default. Most script kiddies do not change from this.	Unofficial
27500 - U	(Through 27900) id Software QuakeWorld	Unofficial
27900	(Through 27901) Nintendo Wi-Fi Connection	Unofficial
28910	Nintendo Wi-Fi Connection	Unofficial
29900	(Through 29901) Nintendo Wi-Fi Connection	Unofficial
29920	Nintendo Wi-Fi Connection	Unofficial
30564 - T	Multiplicity: keyboard/mouse/clipboard sharing software	Unofficial
31337 - T	Back Orifice — remote administration tool (often a Trojan)	Unofficial
32976 - T	LogMeIn Hamachi (VPN tunnel software; also port 12975)	Unofficial
33434 - T, U	Traceroute	Official
34443	Linksys PSUS4 print server	Unofficial
37777 - T	Digital Video Recorder hardware	Unofficial
36963	Counter-Strike 2D multiplayer (2D clone of popular Counter-Strike computer game)	Unofficial
40000 - T, U	SafetyNET p Real-time Industrial Ethernet Protocol	Official
47808 - T, U	BACnet Building Automation and Control Networks	Official

Reference: www.iana.org/assignments/port-numbers. The list above is edited and is not as complete as the list of ports on this official site. Also, their list is updated on a regular basis.

Index

A

A (Address) record, 535
-a (All) switch, 527
A or AAAA (Host Address), 537
AAA ("Triple A") servers, 744, 775, 833
ABR (Available Bit Rate), 101–102
AC command, 790
Access Accept, RADIUS, 834–835
Access Challenge, RADIUS, 834
access point, 375–380
Access Reject, RADIUS, 834
accounting, 744, 761, 775, 833, 835
ACID (Atomicity, Consistency, Isolation, and Durability), 567
Acknowledgement (ACK) flag, TCP, 459
ACO (Asynchronous Connectionless Oriented), 273
acquired systems, 768–769
ACT (Application Compatibility Toolkit), 773–774
active data transfer, TCP, 461–462
Active Directory (AD), 567, 570–573, 580–584, 597
Active Directory Application Mode (ADAM), 583
active hubs, 190
active management system, 764
Active Monitor, 295
active network discovery, 79
Active OPEN command, 464
Active RED, 198
active replication, 567
active scanning mode, STA, 373
active star network, 18
active T-junctions, 174
AD (Active Directory), 567, 570–573, 580–584, 597
ad hoc networks, 5, 354–355
Ad hoc On-Demand Distance Vector (AODV) routing, 206, 385
ADAM (Active Directory Application Mode), 583
adaptability, 120

Adaptive Frequency Hopping (AFH) spread spectrum, 368
Adaptive RED, 198
Adaptive Security Appliance (ASA), 746
"adaptive streaming", 659
adaptive switching, 192–193
Add-Drop Multiplexer (ADM), 95
Address (A) record, 535
address exhaustion, IP, 478
address fields, e-mail, 625
address ranges, IPv6, 514–515
address resolution, ND, 518
Address Resolution Protocol (ARP), 70, 525–527
Address Restricted Cone NAT, 730–731
addressing, 138–141, 423–424, 497–500
ADM (Add-Drop Multiplexer), 95
administration, 761
Adobe Flash, 657–659
Adobe Flash Media Streaming Server 3 (FMSS), 654
ADSL (Asymmetric DSL), 326–327, 329, 331
ADU (Application Data Unit) frame, 312
Advanced Intelligent Network (AIN or IN) telephone architecture, 675
advertisement, network, 62–63
AFH (Adaptive Frequency Hopping) spread spectrum, 368
AFS (Andrew File System), 593
AFSDB (Andrew File System Database) server record, 536
agents, 73–74, 764
aggregation, 480–482, 765
Agility streaming server, 655
aging systems, 772
AH (Authentication Header), 696–697
AIN (Advanced Intelligent Network) telephone architecture, 675
Alacritech TOE card, 437–438
Alias record, 537
aliases, 625, 822
All Route (AR) frame, 193
AL-PA (Arbitrated Loop Physical Address), 424

Index

Index

Index

Index

Index

Index

Index

PTR (Pointer) records, 536, 537
public key algorithms, 708
public key encryption, 752
Public Key (KEY) record, 537
Public Switched Telephone Network (PSTN), 322–325
pull technology, 645
pulse modulation (PM), 179–180
Pulsed Code Modulation (PCM), 92, 332–333
Push (PSH) flag, TCP, 459
push e-mail, 624
pushes, MPLS, 347
PUT method, 609
PuTTY utility, 810
PVST (Per-VLAN Spanning Tree), 226
PXE (Preboot Execution Environment), 771–772
Python, 787

Q

Q in Q (IEEE.802.1Q tunneling), 740
Q-encoding (quoted-printable), 632
QoS (Quality of Service), 82, 97, 101–102, 117–120, 346–347, 473
QPSK (Quadrature Phase Shift Keying), 363–364
QTSS (QuickTime Streaming Server), 654
Quadrature Phase Shift Keying (QPSK), 363–364
Quagga software, 196
Quarantine Control, ISA Server, 747
QuickTime Broadcaster encoder, 653
QuickTime player, 657
QuickTime Streaming Server (QTSS), 654
quoted-printable (Q-encoding), 632

R

raceways, cable, 157–158
radiation, electromagnetic, 176–179
radiation pattern, antenna, 387
radio astronomy bands, 181–182
radio frequency communications, 95
radio frequency devices, X10 network, 307
Radio Frequency with DSSS, 359
Radio Frequency with FHSS, 359
radio links, 181–182
RADIUS (Remote Authentication Dial-In User Service) servers, 775, 832–838
Random Early Detection (RED), 198

random password generators, 704
Rapid Per-VLAN Spanning Tree (R-PVST), 226
Rapid Spanning Tree Protocol (RSTP), 222–226
RARP (Reverse Address Resolution Protocol), 526–527
RAS (Remote Access Server), 826, 828–829
RASDIAL command, 798
Rate-Adaptive DSL (RDSL), 329
raw files, 651
RBAC (Role-Based Access Control), 574–575
RBOC (Regional Bell Operating Companies), 323
RC4 standard, 705–706
RCA (Root Cause Analysis), 765
RCP command, 798
RDMA (Remote Direct Memory Access), 440
RDP (Remote Desktop Protocol), 830
RDSL (Rate-Adaptive DSL), 329
reactive strategy, 112
Read Only Domain Controller (RODC), 584
read-only memory (ROM) card, 138
real time streaming, 643
Real Time Variable Bit Rate (RT-VBR), 101–102
Realité, 783
realms, RADIUS, 836
RealNetworks Helix engine, 657
RealPlayer, 657
RealProducer encoder, 653
Real-Time Media Flow Protocol (RTMFP), 659
Real-Time Messaging Protocol (RTMP), 659
Real-Time Streaming Protocol (RTSP), 641, 646–647
Real-Time Transfer Control Protocol (RTCP), 673
Real-Time Transport Protocol (RTP), 647–650, 673
Receive mechanism, DBF, 202
Receive Sliding window, 465
Receiver Reports, RTCP, 650
Reconfigurable Optical Add-Drop Multiplexers (ROADMs), 95
RECORD command, 646
record types, DNS, 535–536
recurring logons, 568
RED (Random Early Detection), 198
Red Hat Enterprise Linux, 554
redirect function, ND, 518
redundant multipoint bridging topologies, 378
Reed's law, 14
Reference Movie files, 656
Regional Bell Operating Companies (RBOC), 323

Index

Index

Index